THE
BOOK OF MORMON

TRANSLATED BY
JOSEPH SMITH, JR.

COMPARED WITH THE ORIGINAL MANUSCRIPT AND THE KIRTLAND EDITION OF 1837, WHICH WAS CAREFULLY RE-EXAMINED AND COMPARED WITH THE ORIGINAL MANUSCRIPT BY JOSEPH SMITH AND OLIVER COWDERY

AUTHORIZED EDITION

INDEPENDENCE, MISSOURI
Published by the Board of Publication of the Reorganized Church of Jesus Christ of Latter Day Saints
1926

THE BOOK OF MORMON.

AN ACCOUNT WRITTEN BY THE HAND OF MORMON UPON PLATES TAKEN FROM THE PLATES OF NEPHI.

Wherefore, it is an abridgment of the record of the people of Nephi, and also of the Lamanites; written to the Lamanites, who are a remnant of the house of Israel; and also to Jew and Gentile; written by way of commandment, and also by the spirit of prophecy and of revelation. Written, and sealed up, and hid unto the Lord, that they might not be destroyed; to come forth by the gift and power of God unto the interpretation thereof; sealed by the hand of Moroni, and hid up unto the Lord, to come forth in due time by the way of Gentile; the interpretation thereof by the gift of God.

An abridgment taken from the Book of Ether; also, which is a record of the people of Jared; who were scattered at the time the Lord confounded the language of the people, when they were building a tower to get to heaven: which is to shew unto the remnant of the house of Israel what great things the Lord hath done for their fathers; and that they may know the covenants of the Lord, that they are not cast off for ever; and also to the convincing of the Jew and Gentile that Jesus is the Christ, the Eternal God, manifesting himself unto all nations. And now if there are faults, they are the mistakes of men; wherefore, condemn not the things of God, that ye may be found spotless at the judgment seat of Christ.

A Marvelous Work and A Wonder Edition, 2007.
Printed in the United States of America
ISBN 1-60135-710-9

THE TESTIMONY OF THREE WITNESSES.

Be it known unto all nations, kindreds, tongues, and people, unto whom this work shall come, that we, through the grace of God the Father, and our Lord Jesus Christ, have seen the plates which contain this record, which is a record of the people of Nephi, and also of the Lamanites, their brethren, and also of the people of Jared, who came from the tower of which hath been spoken; and we also know that they have been translated by the gift and power of God, for his voice hath declared it unto us; wherefore we know of a surety, that the work is true. And we also testify that we have seen the engravings which are upon the plates; and they have been shewn unto us by the power of God, and not of man. And we declare with words of soberness, that an angel of God came down from heaven, and he brought and laid before our eyes, that we beheld and saw the plates, and the engravings thereon; and we know that it is by the grace of God the Father, and our Lord Jesus Christ, that we beheld and bear record that these things are true; and it is marvelous in our eyes, nevertheless, the voice of the Lord commanded us that we should bear record of it; wherefore, to be obedient unto the commandments of God, we bear testimony of these things. And we know that if we are faithful in Christ, we shall rid our garments of the blood of all men, and be found spotless before the judgment seat of Christ, and shall dwell with him eternally in the heavens. And the honor be to the Father, and to the Son, and to the Holy Ghost, which is one God. Amen.

OLIVER COWDERY.
DAVID WHITMER.
MARTIN HARRIS.

AND ALSO THE TESTIMONY OF EIGHT WITNESSES.

Be it known unto all nations, kindreds, tongues, and people, unto whom this work shall come, that Joseph Smith, Jr., the translator of this work, has shewn unto us the plates of which hath been spoken, which have the appearance of gold; and as many of the leaves as the said Smith has translated, we did handle with our hands: and we also saw the engravings thereon, all of which has the appearance of ancient work, and of curious workmanship. And this we bear record with words of soberness, that the said Smith has shewn unto us, for we have seen and hefted, and know of a surety, that the said Smith has got the plates of which we have spoken. And we give our names unto the world, to witness unto the world that which we have seen; and we lie not, God bearing witness of it.

CHRISTIAN WHITMER.
JACOB WHITMER.
PETER WHITMER, JR.
JOHN WHITMER.
HIRAM PAGE.
JOSEPH SMITH, SEN.
HYRUM SMITH.
SAMUEL H. SMITH.

PREFACE.

At a General Conference of the Reorganized Church of Jesus Christ of Latter Day Saints, in April, 1906, the following preamble and resolution were adopted:

"Whereas, There are several editions of the Book of Mormon extant, differing in divisions of chapters and paragraphs, thereby rendering it impossible to prepare concordance and works of reference, therefore,

"Resolved, That we recommend . . . the appointment of a committee . . . to investigate and prepare a uniform plan for the divisions of chapters and verses, and, if thought advisable, to prepare or adopt a system of references."

Frederick M. Smith, Heman C. Smith, Richard S. Salyards, Francis M. Sheehy, Columbus Scott, Edmund L. Kelley, and Frederick B. Blair were appointed.

The committee appointed Frederick M. Smith, Heman C. Smith, and Richard S. Salyards as a sub-committee to do the work of reversification, etc., with instructions to use the large-type, Lamoni edition as a basis; to leave the chapters as in the original Palmyra edition.

The sub-committee completed the work of reversification, and in so doing made "all verses from the Book of Isaiah to correspond in their divisions" to the versification of the Inspired Translation of the Holy Scriptures, and indicated such matter by reference notes.

The general committee indorsed the work of the sub-committee. It concluded to broaden the scope of its work by making provision for comparison of the Lamoni edition with the Original Manuscript and the Kirtland edition. It adopted the following as instruction to the sub-committee for the completion of the work:

"Resolved, That it be the sense of this committee that in the publication of the new work we follow the corrections of the Book of Mormon so as to make the new work in accordance with the Original Manuscript and the Kirtland edition of the Book of Mormon, published by Pratt & Goodson, of 1837, that the work may be completed as corrected by Joseph Smith and Oliver Cowdery."

The sub-committee were authorized to "examine proofs and corrections" according to the foregoing resolution; to proof-read the matter as published; and to prepare a suitable index. They were also instructed to indicate by paragraph signs the divisions into paragraphs according to the Palmyra edition, and to hand over the work for publication.

The sub-committee carefully compared the Original Manuscript with the Kirtland and the large-type editions. One member of the committee read from the Manuscript, one followed the Kirtland edition, the other recorded all corrections in the large-type edition. The Manuscript is legible; there was little difficulty in reading it. They also referred to the Palmyra edition in the examination of the text. There is very little difference in the paragraphs in the Palmyra and the Kirtland editions.

The Preface to the Kirtland edition contains the following paragraph:

"Individuals acquainted with book printing, are aware of the numerous typographical errors which always occur in manuscript editions. It is only necessary to say, that the whole has been carefully reëxamined and compared with the original manuscripts, by Elder Joseph Smith, Jr., the translator of the Book of Mormon, assisted by the present printer, Brother O. Cowdery, who formerly wrote the greatest portion of the same, as dictated by Brother Smith."

The committee found errors, including omissions, in the Lamoni edition; also some matter in the Original Manuscript omitted in the Palmyra or the Kirtland edition, or in both those editions; such omissions evidently being overlooked in proof-reading.

Where differences occurred between the Manuscript and the Kirtland editior, the committee were governed by the subject-matter of the context. There were no material differences in the sense of the text of the Manuscript and of the Kirtland edition.

Numerous minor changes were made, many of which have improved the subject-matter. Among the more important corrections we note the following:

Concerning the prohibition of polygamy; book of Jacob, chapter 2:6, 7: "I *must* testify unto you concerning the wickedness of your hearts"; *must*, instead of *might*. 2:45: "Behold ye have done greater *iniquity* than the Lamanites, our brethren." *Iniquity*, singular form, specific; instead of *iniquities* in other editions. Ether 1:16: "The Palmyra and Kirtland editions both read, "thy families," referring to the brother of Jared and the commandment to migrate. The manuscript reads, "thy family"; the singular instead of the plural form of the word. The text was made to read according to the manuscript.

Samples of matter omitted in one or all early editions, included in this correct edition:

Book of Alma 4:8: "there having been a city built which was called the city of Gideon." 12:5: "even as with the power and authority." 15:55: "yea, decreeth unto them decrees which are unalterable." 16:157: "And now behold, will not this strengthen your faith? Yea, it will strengthen your faith, for ye will say, I know that this is a good seed, for behold, it sprouteth and beginneth to grow." 25:59: "yea, they would not partake of wine."

Book of Nephi 2:32: "and the land which was between the land of Zarahemla."

Samples of corrections:

1. Nephi 3:219: The Palmyra and Kirtland editions read, "whose foundation is the devil"; the Manuscript reads, "founder"; the text was made to conform to the Manuscript.

2 Nephi 12:84: *"White* and a delightsome," instead of *"pure* and a delightsome."

Mosiah 11:190: *wading*, instead of *wandering*.

Alma 3:89: *inherit,* instead of *"enter* the kingdom." 15:27: *"where* they had pitched their tents," instead of *whence.* 21:108: "armies" should march, instead of *servants*.

Book of Nephi 1:9: *"build* cities," instead of *"fill* cities."

Names corrected:

Ammeron, for *Ammaron,* wherever given. (This does not refer to *Amaron,* book of Omni.) *Jeneum,* instead of *Joneam,* Mormon 3:15. *Cumenihah,* instead of *Camenihah,* wherever given.

Mosiah 9:170: The Manuscript reads, "King Benjamin had a gift from God"; the Kirtland edition reads, "King Mosiah." The text was made to read, "King Mosiah."

The name *Mosiah* was inserted in brackets after the words *King Benjamin* in book of Ether 1:95, in harmony with the reading of the book of Mosiah 9:170.

The committee concluded that instead of providing marginal references, a concordance to the Book of Mormon should be provided.

FREDERICK M. SMITH, *Chairman.*
RICHARD S. SALYARDS, *Secretary.*

LAMONI, IOWA, July 17, 1908.

THE BOOK OF MORMON.

THE FIRST BOOK OF NEPHI.

HIS REIGN AND MINISTRY.

CHAPTER 1.

An account of Lehi and his wife Sariah, and his four sons, being called (beginning at the eldest), Laman, Lemuel, Sam, and Nephi. The Lord warns Lehi to depart out of the land of Jerusalem, because he prophesieth unto the people concerning their iniquity; and they seek to destroy his life. He taketh three days' journey into the wilderness with his family. Nephi taketh his brethren and returns to the land of Jerusalem after the record of the Jews. The account of their sufferings. They take the daughters of Ishmael to wife. They take their families and depart into the wilderness. Their sufferings and afflictions in the wilderness. The course of their travels. They come to the large waters. Nephi's brethren rebelleth against him. He confoundeth them, and buildeth a ship. They call the place Bountiful. They cross the large waters into the promised land, &c. This is according to the account of Nephi; or in other words, I, Nephi wrote this record.

1 ¶I, Nephi, having been born of goodly parents, therefore I was taught somewhat in all the learning of my father; and having seen many afflictions in the course of my days—nevertheless, having been highly favored of the Lord in all my

days; yea, having had a great knowledge of the goodness and the mysteries of God, therefore I make a record of my proceedings in my days; yea, I make a record in the language of my father, which consists of the learning of the Jews and the language of the Egyptians.

2 And I know that the record which I make is true; and I make it with mine own hand; and I make it according to my knowledge.

3 ¶For it came to pass, in the commencement of the first year of the reign of Zedekiah, king of Judah (my father Lehi having dwelt at Jerusalem in all his days); and in that same year there came many prophets, prophesying unto the people that they must repent, or the great city Jerusalem must be destroyed.

4 Wherefore it came to pass that my father Lehi, as he went forth, prayed unto the Lord, yea, even with all his heart, in behalf of his people.

5 ¶And it came to pass, as he prayed unto the Lord, there came a pillar of fire and dwelt upon a rock before him; and he saw and heard much; and because of the things which he saw and heard, he did quake and tremble exceedingly.

6 ¶And it came to pass that he returned to his own house at Jerusalem; and he cast himself upon his bed, being overcome with the Spirit and the things which he had seen;

7 And being thus overcome with the Spirit, he was carried away in a vision, even that he saw the heavens open, and he thought he saw God sitting upon his throne, surrounded with numberless concourses of angels in the attitude of singing and praising their God.

8 ¶And it came to pass that he saw one descending out of the midst of heaven, and he beheld that his luster was above that of the sun at noon-day;

9 And he also saw twelve others following him, and their brightness did exceed that of the stars in the firmament; and they came down and went forth upon the face of the earth;

10 And the first came and stood before my father, and gave unto him a book, and bade him that he should read.

11 ¶And it came to pass that as he read, he was filled with the Spirit of the Lord, and he read, saying, Wo, wo unto Jerusalem! for I have seen thine abominations;

12 Yea, and many things did my father read concerning Jerusalem—that it should be destroyed, and the inhabitants thereof, many should perish by the sword, and many should be carried away captive into Babylon.

13 ¶And it came to pass that when my father had read and saw many great and marvelous things, he did exclaim many things unto the Lord; such as, Great and marvelous are thy works, O Lord God Almighty! Thy throne is high in the heavens, and thy power, and goodness, and mercy are over all the inhabitants of the earth; and because thou art merciful, thou wilt not suffer those who come unto thee that they shall perish!

14 And after this manner was the language of my father in the praising of his God; for his soul did rejoice, and his whole heart was filled, because of the things which he had seen; yea, which the Lord had shewn unto him.

15 And now I, Nephi, do not make a full account of the things which my father hath written, for he hath written many things which he saw in visions and in dreams;

16 And he also hath written many things which he prophesied and spake unto his children, of which I shall not make a full account; but I shall make an account of my proceedings in my days.

17 Behold I make an abridgment of the record of my father, upon plates which I have made with mine own hands; wherefore after I have abridged the record of my father, then will I make an account of mine own life.

18 ¶Therefore, I would that ye should know, that after the Lord had shewn so many marvelous things unto my father Lehi, yea, concerning the destruction of Jerusalem, behold he went forth among the people, and began to prophesy and to declare unto them concerning the things which he had both seen and heard.

19 ¶And it came to pass that the Jews did mock him

because of the things which he testified of them; for he truly testified of their wickedness and their abominations;

20 And he testified that the things which he saw and heard, and also the things which he read in the book, manifested plainly of the coming of a Messiah, and also the redemption of the world.

21 ¶And when the Jews heard these things, they were angry with him; yea, even as with the prophets of old, whom they had cast out, and stoned, and slain;

22 And they also sought his life, that they might take it away.

23 But behold I, Nephi, will shew unto you that the tender mercies of the Lord are over all those whom he hath chosen, because of their faith, to make them mighty even unto the power of deliverance.

24 ¶For behold it came to pass that the Lord spake unto my father, yea, even in a dream, and said unto him, Blessed art thou Lehi, because of the things which thou hast done;

25 And because thou hast been faithful and declared unto this people the things which I commanded thee, behold they seek to take away thy life.

26 ¶And it came to pass that the Lord commanded my father, even in a dream, that he should take his family and depart into the wilderness.

27 And it came to pass that he was obedient unto the word of the Lord, wherefore he did as the Lord commanded him.

28 ¶And it came to pass that he departed into the wilderness.

29 And he left his house, and the land of his inheritance, and his gold, and his silver, and his precious things, and took nothing with him, save it were his family, and provisions, and tents, and he departed into the wilderness;

30 And he came down by the borders near the shore of the Red Sea;

31 And he traveled in the wilderness in the borders which were nearer the Red Sea;

32 And he did travel in the wilderness with his family

which consisted of my mother Sariah, and my elder brothers, who were Laman, Lemuel, and Sam.

33 ¶And it came to pass that when he had traveled three days in the wilderness, he pitched his tent in a valley by the side of a river of water.

34 And it came to pass that he built an altar of stones, and he made an offering unto the Lord, and gave thanks unto the Lord our God.

35 And it came to pass that he called the name of the river Laman, and it emptied into the Red Sea; and the valley was in the borders near the mouth thereof.

36 ¶And when my father saw that the waters of the river emptied into the fountain of the Red Sea, he spake unto Laman, saying, O that thou mightest be like unto this river, continually running into the fountain of all righteousness.

37 And he also spake unto Lemuel: O that thou mightest be like unto this valley, firm and steadfast, and immovable in keeping the commandments of the Lord.

38 Now this he spake because of the stiffneckedness of Laman and Lemuel; for behold they did murmur in many things against their father, because he was a visionary man, and had led them out of the land of Jerusalem, to leave the land of their inheritance, and their gold, and their silver, and their precious things, to perish in the wilderness.

39 And this they said he had done because of the foolish imaginations of his heart.

40 And thus Laman and Lemuel, being the eldest, did murmur against their father.

41 And they did murmur because they knew not the dealings of that God who had created them.

42 Neither did they believe that Jerusalem, that great city, could be destroyed according to the words of the prophets.

43 And they were like unto the Jews, who were at Jerusalem, who sought to take away the life of my father.

44 ¶And it came to pass that my father did speak unto them in the valley of Lemuel, with power, being filled with the Spirit, until their frames did shake before him.

45 And he did confound them, that they durst not utter against him; wherefore they did as he commanded them.

46 And my father dwelt in a tent.

47 ¶And it came to pass that I, Nephi, being exceeding young, nevertheless being large in stature, and also having great desires to know of the mysteries of God,

48 Wherefore I did cry unto the Lord; and behold he did visit me, and did soften my heart that I did believe all the words which had been spoken by my father; wherefore I did not rebel against him like unto my brothers.

49 And I spake unto Sam, making known unto him the things which the Lord had manifested unto me by his Holy Spirit.

50 ¶And it came to pass that he believed in my words;

51 But behold Laman and Lemuel would not hearken unto my words:

52 And being grieved because of the hardness of their hearts, I cried unto the Lord for them.

53 ¶And it came to pass that the Lord spake unto me, saying, Blessed art thou Nephi, because of thy faith, for thou hast sought me diligently, with lowliness of heart.

54 And inasmuch as ye shall keep my commandments, ye shall prosper, and shall be led to a land of promise; yea, even a land which I have prepared for you; yea, a land which is choice above all other lands.

55 And inasmuch as thy brethren shall rebel against thee, they shall be cut off from the presence of the Lord.

56 And inasmuch as thou shalt keep my commandments, thou shalt be made a ruler and a teacher over thy brethren.

57 For behold, in that day that they shall rebel against me, I will curse them even with a sore curse, and they shall have no power over thy seed, except they shall rebel against me also.

58 And if it so be that they rebel against me, they shall be a scourge unto thy seed, to stir them up in the ways of remembrance.

59 ¶And it came to pass that I, Nephi, returned from speaking with the Lord, to the tent of my father.

60 And it came to pass that he spake unto me, saying: Behold I have dreamed a dream, in the which the Lord hath commanded me that thou and thy brethren shall return to Jerusalem.

61 For behold, Laban hath the record of the Jews, and also a genealogy of thy forefathers, and they are engraven upon plates of brass.

62 Wherefore the Lord hath commanded me that thou and thy brothers should go unto the house of Laban, and seek the records, and bring them down hither into the wilderness.

63 And now, behold thy brothers murmur, saying it is a hard thing which I have required of them; but behold I have not required it of them; but it is a commandment of the Lord.

64 Therefore go, my son, and thou shalt be favored of the Lord, because thou hast not murmured.

65 ¶And it came to pass that I, Nephi, said unto my father, I will go and do the things which the Lord hath commanded, for I know that the Lord giveth no commandments unto the children of men, save he shall prepare a way for them that they may accomplish the thing which he commandeth them.

66 ¶And it came to pass that when my father had heard these words, he was exceeding glad, for he knew that I had been blessed of the Lord.

67 And I, Nephi, and my brethren took our journey in the wilderness with our tents, to go up to the land of Jerusalem.

68 ¶And it came to pass that when we had come up to the land of Jerusalem, I and my brethren did consult one with another; and we cast lots who of us should go in unto the house of Laban.

69 And it came to pass that the lot fell upon Laman; and Laman went in unto the house of Laban, and he talked with him as he sat in his house.

70 And he desired of Laban the records which were en-

graven upon the plates of brass, which contained the genealogy of my father.

71 ¶And behold it came to pass that Laban was angry, and thrust him out from his presence; and he would not that he should have the records.

72 Wherefore, he said unto him, Behold thou art a robber, and I will slay thee.

73 But Laman fled out of his presence, and told the things which Laban had done, unto us.

74 And we began to be exceeding sorrowful, and my brethren were about to return unto my father in the wilderness.

75 But, behold, I said unto them, that as the Lord liveth, and as we live, we will not go down unto our father in the wilderness, until we have accomplished the thing which the Lord hath commanded us.

76 Wherefore let us be faithful in keeping the commandments of the Lord;

77 Therefore let us go down to the land of our father's inheritance, for behold he left gold and silver, and all manner of riches.

78 And all this he hath done, because of the commandments of the Lord; for he knowing that Jerusalem must be destroyed, because of the wickedness of the people.

79 ¶For behold, they have rejected the words of the prophets.

80 Wherefore if my father should dwell in the land after he hath been commanded to flee out of the land, behold he would also perish.

81 Wherefore it must needs be that he flee out of the land.

82 And behold it is wisdom in God that we should obtain these records, that we may preserve unto our children the language of our fathers;

83 And also that we may preserve unto them the words which have been spoken by the mouth of all the holy prophets, which have been delivered unto them by the Spirit and power of God, since the world began, even down unto this present time.

84 ¶And it came to pass that after this manner of language did I persuade my brethren, that they might be faithful in keeping the commandments of God.

85 And it came to pass that we went down to the land of our inheritance, and we did gather together our gold, and our silver, and our precious things.

86 And after we had gathered these things together, we went up again unto the house of Laban.

87 ¶And it came to pass that we went in unto Laban, and desired him that he would give unto us the records which were engraven upon the plates of brass, for which we would give unto him our gold, and our silver, and all our precious things.

88 ¶And it came to pass that when Laban saw our property, that it was exceeding great, he did lust after it, insomuch that he thrust us out, and sent his servants to slay us, that he might obtain our property.

89 And it came to pass that we did flee before the servants of Laban, and we were obliged to leave behind our property, and it fell into the hands of Laban.

90 ¶And it came to pass that we fled into the wilderness, and the servants of Laban did not overtake us, and we hid ourselves in the cavity of a rock.

91 And it came to pass that Laman was angry with me, and also with my father, and also was Lemuel; for he hearkened unto the words of Laman.

92 Wherefore Laman and Lemuel did speak many hard words unto us, their younger brothers, and they did smite us even with a rod.

93 ¶And it came to pass as they smote us with a rod, behold an angel of the Lord came and stood before them, and he spake unto them, saying, Why do ye smite your younger brother with a rod?

94 Know ye not that the Lord hath chosen him to be a ruler over you, and this because of your iniquities?

95 Behold ye shall go up to Jerusalem again, and the Lord will deliver Laban into your hands.

96 And after the angel had spoken unto us, he departed.

97 And after the angel had departed, Laman and Lemuel again began to murmur, saying, How is it possible that the Lord will deliver Laban into our hands?

98 Behold he is a mighty man, and he can command fifty, yea, even he can slay fifty; then why not us?

99 ¶And it came to pass that I spake unto my brethren, saying, Let us go up again unto Jerusalem, and let us be faithful in keeping the commandments of the Lord; for behold he is mightier than all the earth, then why not mightier than Laban and his fifty, yea, or even than his tens of thousands.

100 Therefore let us go up; let us be strong like unto Moses; for he truly spake unto the waters of the Red Sea, and they divided hither and thither, and our fathers came through out of captivity on dry ground, and the armies of Pharaoh did follow and were drowned in the waters of the Red Sea.

101 Now behold ye know that this is true; and ye also know that an angel hath spoken unto you, wherefore can ye doubt?

102 Let us go up; the Lord is able to deliver us, even as our fathers, and to destroy Laban even as the Egyptians.

103 ¶Now when I had spoken these words, they were yet wroth, and did still continue to murmur; nevertheless they did follow me up until we came without the walls of Jerusalem.

104 And it was by night: and I caused that they should hide themselves without the walls.

105 And after they had hid themselves, I, Nephi, crept into the city, and went forth towards the house of Laban.

106 And I was led by the Spirit, not knowing beforehand the things which I should do.

107 Nevertheless I went forth, and as I came near unto the house of Laban, I beheld a man, and he had fallen to the earth before me, for he was drunken with wine.

108 And when I came to him I found that it was Laban.

109 And I beheld his sword, and I drew it forth from the sheath thereof, and the hilt thereof was of pure gold, and the workmanship thereof was exceeding fine: and I saw that the blade thereof was of the most precious steel.

110 ¶And it came to pass that I was constrained by the Spirit that I should kill Laban;

111 But I said in my heart, Never at any time have I shed the blood of man, and I shrunk and would that I might not slay him.

112 And the Spirit said unto me again, Behold the Lord hath delivered him into thy hands; yea, and I also knew that he had sought to take away mine own life; yea, and he would not hearken unto the commandments of the Lord; and he also had taken away our property.

113 ¶And it came to pass that the Spirit said unto me again, Slay him, for the Lord hath delivered him into thy hands.

114 Behold the Lord slayeth the wicked to bring forth his righteous purposes.

115 It is better that one man should perish, than that a nation should dwindle and perish in unbelief.

116 ¶And now, when I, Nephi, had heard these words, I remembered the words of the Lord which he spake unto me in the wilderness, saying, That inasmuch as thy seed shall keep my commandments, they shall prosper in the land of promise.

117 Yea, and I also thought that they could not keep the commandments of the Lord according to the law of Moses, save they should have the law.

118 And I also knew that the law was engraven upon the plates of brass.

119 And again, I knew that the Lord had delivered Laban into my hands for this cause, that I might obtain the records according to his commandments.

120 Therefore I did obey the voice of the Spirit, and took Laban by the hair of the head, and I smote off his head with his own sword.

121 ¶And after I had smitten off his head with his own sword, I took the garments of Laban and put them upon mine own body; yea, even every whit; and I did gird on his armor about my loins.

122 And after I had done this, I went forth unto the treasury of Laban.

123 And as I went forth towards the treasury of Laban, behold I saw the servant of Laban, who had the keys of the treasury.

124 And I commanded him in the voice of Laban, that he should go with me into the treasury; and he supposed me to be his master Laban, for he beheld the garments and also the sword girded about my loins.

125 And he spake unto me concerning the elders of the Jews, he knowing that his master Laban had been out by night among them.

126 And I spake unto him as if it had been Laban.

127 And I also spake unto him that I should carry the engravings which were upon the plates of brass, to my elder brethren, who were without the walls.

128 And I also bade him that he should follow me.

129 And he supposing that I spake of the brethren of the church, and that I was truly that Laban whom I had slain, wherefore he did follow me.

130 And he spake unto me many times concerning the elders of the Jews, as I went forth unto my brethren, who were without the walls.

131 ¶And it came to pass that when Laman saw me, he was exceedingly frightened, and also Lemuel and Sam.

132 And they fled from before my presence; for they supposed it was Laban, and that he had slain me, and had sought to take away their lives also.

133 ¶And it came to pass that I called after them, and they did hear me; wherefore they did cease to flee from my presence.

134 And it came to pass that when the servant of Laban

beheld my brethren, he began to tremble, and was about to flee from before me, and return to the city of Jerusalem.

135 ¶And now I, Nephi, being a man large in stature, and also having received much strength of the Lord, therefore I did seize upon the servant of Laban, and held him that he should not flee.

136 ¶And it came to pass that I spake with him, that if he would hearken unto my words, as the Lord liveth, and as I live, even so that if he would hearken unto our words, we would spare his life.

137 And I spake unto him, even with an oath, that he need not fear; that he should be a free man like unto us, if he would go down in the wilderness with us.

138 And I also spake unto him, saying, Surely the Lord hath commanded us to do this thing, and shall we not be diligent in keeping the commandments of the Lord?

139 Therefore, if thou wilt go down into the wilderness to my father, thou shalt have place with us.

140 ¶And it came to pass that Zoram did take courage at the words which I spake.

141 Now Zoram was the name of the servant; and he promised that he would go down into the wilderness unto our father.

142 And he also made an oath unto us, that he would tarry with us from that time forth.

143 Now we were desirous that he should tarry with us for this cause, that the Jews might not know concerning our flight into the wilderness, lest they should pursue us and destroy us.

144 ¶And it came to pass that when Zoram had made an oath unto us, our fears did cease concerning him.

145 And it came to pass that we took the plates of brass and the servant of Laban, and departed into the wilderness, and journeyed unto the tent of our father.

146 ¶And it came to pass that after we had come down into the wilderness unto our father, behold he was filled with joy, and also my mother Sariah was exceeding glad, for she truly

had mourned because of us; for she had supposed that we had perished in the wilderness;

147 And she also had complained against my father, telling him that he was a visionary man; saying, Behold thou hast led us forth from the land of our inheritance, and my sons are no more, and we perish in the wilderness.

148 And after this manner of language had my mother complained against my father.

149 ¶And it had come to pass that my father spake unto her, saying, I know that I am a visionary man; for if I had not seen the things of God in a vision, I should not have known the goodness of God, but had tarried at Jerusalem, and had perished with my brethren.

150 But behold I have obtained a land of promise, in the which things I do rejoice;

151 Yea, and I know that the Lord will deliver my sons out of the hands of Laban, and bring them down again unto us in the wilderness.

152 And after this manner of language did my father Lehi comfort my mother Sariah concerning us, while we journeyed in the wilderness up to the land of Jerusalem, to obtain the record of the Jews.

153 ¶And when we had returned to the tent of my father, behold their joy was full, and my mother was comforted;

154 And she spake, saying, Now I know of a surety that the Lord hath commanded my husband to flee into the wilderness;

155 Yea, and I also know of a surety that the Lord hath protected my sons, and delivered them out of the hands of Laban, and gave them power whereby they could accomplish the thing which the Lord hath commanded them.

156 And after this manner of language did she speak.

157 ¶And it came to pass that they did rejoice exceedingly, and did offer sacrifice and burnt offerings unto the Lord; and they gave thanks unto the God of Israel.

158 And after they had given thanks unto the God of Israel, my father Lehi took the records which were engraven upon

the plates of brass, and he did search them from the beginning.

159 And he beheld that they did contain the five books of Moses, which gave an account of the creation of the world;

160 And also of Adam and Eve, who were our first parents;

161 And also a record of the Jews from the beginning, even down to the commencement of the reign of Zedekiah, king of Judah;

162 And also the prophecies of the holy prophets, from the beginning, even down to the commencement of the reign of Zedekiah;

163 And also many prophecies which have been spoken by the mouth of Jeremiah.

164 ¶And it came to pass that my father Lehi also found upon the plates of brass a genealogy of his fathers;

165 Wherefore he knew that he was a descendant of Joseph; yea, even that Joseph who was the son of Jacob, who was sold into Egypt, and who was preserved by the hand of the Lord, that he might preserve his father Jacob and all his household from perishing with famine.

166 And they were also led out of captivity and out of the land of Egypt, by that same God who had preserved them.

167 And thus my father Lehi did discover the genealogy of his fathers.

168 And Laban also was a descendant of Joseph, wherefore he and his fathers had kept the records.

169 ¶And now when my father saw all these things he was filled with the Spirit, and began to prophesy concerning his seed; that these plates of brass should go forth unto all nations, kindreds, tongues and people, who were of his seed.

170 Wherefore he said that these plates of brass should never perish, neither should they be dimmed any more by time.

171 And he prophesied many things concerning his seed.

172 ¶And it came to pass that thus far I and my father had kept the commandments wherewith the Lord had commanded us.

173 And we had obtained the record which the Lord had commanded us, and searched them and found that they were desirable; yea, even of great worth unto us, insomuch that we could preserve the commandments of the Lord unto our children.

174 Wherefore it was wisdom in the Lord that we should carry them with us as we journeyed in the wilderness towards the land of promise

CHAPTER 2.

1 ¶And now I, Nephi, do not give the genealogy of my fathers in this part of my record; neither at any time shall I give it after upon these plates which I am writing; for it is given in the record which has been kept by my father; wherefore I do not write it in this work.

2 For it sufficeth me to say that we are a descendant of Joseph.

3 And it mattereth not to me that I am particular to give a full account of all the things of my father, for they can not be written upon these plates, for I desire the room that I may write of the things of God.

4 For the fullness of mine intent is that I may persuade men to come unto the God of Abraham, and the God of Isaac, and the God of Jacob, and be saved.

5 Wherefore the things which are pleasing unto the world, I do not write, but the things which are pleasing unto God and unto those who are not of the world.

6 Wherefore I shall give commandment unto my seed, that they shall not occupy these plates with things which are not of worth unto the children of men.

7 And now I would that ye might know, that after my father Lehi had made an end of prophesying concerning his seed, it came to pass that the Lord spake unto him again, saying, that it was not meet for him, Lehi, that he should take his family into the wilderness alone; but that his sons

should take daughters to wife, that they might raise up seed unto the Lord in the land of promise.

8 ¶And it came to pass that the Lord commanded him that I, Nephi, and my brethren, should again return unto the land of Jerusalem, and bring down Ishmael and his family into the wilderness.

9 ¶And it came to pass that I, Nephi, did again, with my brethren, go forth into the wilderness to go up to Jerusalem.

10 And it came to pass that we went up unto the house of Ishmael, and we did gain favor in the sight of Ishmael, insomuch that we did speak unto him the words of the Lord.

11 ¶And it came to pass that the Lord did soften the heart of Ishmael and also his household, insomuch that they took their journey with us down into the wilderness to the tent of our father.

12 And it came to pass that as we journeyed in the wilderness, behold Laman and Lemuel, and two of the daughters of Ishmael, and the two sons of Ishmael, and their families, did rebel against us; yea, against I, Nephi, and Sam, and their father Ishmael, and his wife, and his three other daughters.

13 ¶And it came to pass in the which rebellion they were desirous to return unto the land of Jerusalem.

14 And now I, Nephi, being grieved for the hardness of their hearts, therefore I spake unto them, saying, yea, even unto Laman and unto Lemuel, Behold ye are mine elder brethren; and how is it that ye are so hard in your hearts, and so blind in your minds, that ye have need that I, your younger brother, should speak unto you, yea, and set an example for you?

15 How is it that ye have not hearkened unto the word of the Lord?

16 How is it that ye have forgotten that ye have seen an angel of the Lord?

17 Yea, and how is it that ye have forgotten what great things the Lord hath done for us in delivering us out of the hands of Laban, and also that we should obtain the record?

18 Yea, and how is it that ye have forgotten that the Lord

is able to do all things according to his will, for the children of men, if it so be that they exercise faith in him; wherefore let us be faithful to him.

19 And if it so be that we are faithful to him, we shall obtain the land of promise; and ye shall know at some future period that the word of the Lord shall be fulfilled concerning the destruction of Jerusalem;

20 For all things which the Lord hath spoken concerning the destruction of Jerusalem must be fulfilled.

21 For behold, the Spirit of the Lord ceaseth soon to strive with them;

22 For behold they have rejected the prophets, and Jeremiah have they cast into prison.

23 And they have sought to take away the life of my father, insomuch that they have driven him out of the land.

24 ¶Now behold, I say unto you, that if ye will return unto Jerusalem ye shall also perish with them.

25 And now, if ye have choice, go up to the land, and remember the words which I speak unto you, that if ye go ye will also perish; for thus the Spirit of the Lord constraineth me that I should speak.

26 ¶And it came to pass that when I, Nephi, had spoken these words unto my brethren they were angry with me.

27 And it came to pass that they did lay their hands upon me—for behold, they were exceeding wroth—and they did bind me with cords, for they sought to take away my life, that they might leave me in the wilderness to be devoured by wild beasts.

28 ¶But it came to pass that I prayed unto the Lord, saying, O Lord, according to my faith which is in thee, wilt thou deliver me from the hands of my brethren;

29 Yea, even give me strength that I may burst these bands with which I am bound.

30 ¶And it came to pass that when I had said these words, behold, the bands were loosed from off my hands and feet, and I stood before my brethren, and I spake unto them again.

31 ¶And it came to pass that they were angry with me again, and sought to lay hands upon me;

32 But behold, one of the daughters of Ishmael, yea, and also her mother, and one of the sons of Ishmael, did plead with my brethren, insomuch that they did soften their hearts; and they did cease striving to take away my life.

33 ¶And it came to pass that they were sorrowful, because of their wickedness, insomuch that they did bow down before me, and did plead with me, that I would forgive them of the thing that they had done against me.

34 ¶And it came to pass that I did frankly forgive them all that they had done, and I did exhort them that they would pray unto the Lord their God for forgiveness.

35 And it came to pass that they did so.

36 And after they had done praying unto the Lord we did again travel on our journey toward the tent of our father.

37 ¶And it came to pass that we did come down unto the tent of our father.

38 And after I and my brethren, and all the house of Ishmael, had come down unto the tent of my father, they did give thanks unto the Lord their God;

39 And they did offer sacrifice and burnt offerings unto him.

40 ¶And it came to pass that we had gathered together all manner of seeds of every kind; both of grain of every kind, and also of the seeds of fruits of every kind.

41 And it came to pass that while my father tarried in the wilderness he spake unto us, saying, Behold, I have dreamed a dream; or in other words, I have seen a vision.

42 And behold, because of the thing which I have seen, I have reason to rejoice in the Lord because of Nephi, and also of Sam; for I have reason to suppose that they, and also many of their seed, will be saved.

43 But behold, Laman and Lemuel, I fear exceedingly because of you; for behold, methought I saw in my dream a dark and dreary wilderness.

44 ¶And it came to pass that I saw a man, and he was dressed in a white robe; and he came and stood before me.

45 And it came to pass that he spake unto me, and bade me follow him.

46 And it came to pass that as I followed him, I beheld myself that I was in a dark and dreary waste.

47 And after I had traveled for the space of many hours in darkness I began to pray unto the Lord, that he would have mercy on me according to the multitude of his tender mercies.

48 ¶And it came to pass after I had prayed unto the Lord, I beheld a large and spacious field.

49 And it came to pass that I beheld a tree, whose fruit was desirable to make one happy.

50 ¶And it came to pass that I did go forth and partake of the fruit thereof; and I beheld that it was most sweet above all that I ever before tasted.

51 Yea, and I beheld that the fruit thereof was white, to exceed all the whiteness that I had ever seen.

52 And as I partook of the fruit thereof, it filled my soul with exceeding great joy;

53 Wherefore I began to be desirous that my family should partake of it also; for I knew that it was desirable above all other fruit.

54 And as I cast my eyes round about, that perhaps I might discover my family also, I beheld a river of water; and it ran along, and it was near the tree of which I was partaking the fruit.

55 And I looked to behold from whence it came; and I saw the head thereof a little way off;

56 And at the head thereof I beheld your mother Sariah, and Sam, and Nephi; and they stood as if they knew not whither they should go.

57 ¶And it came to pass that I beckoned unto them; and I also did say unto them with a loud voice that they should come unto me and partake of the fruit, which was desirable above all other fruit.

58 ¶And it came to pass that they did come unto me, and partake of the fruit also.

59 And it came to pass that I was desirous that Laman and Lemuel should come and partake of the fruit also;

60 Wherefore, I cast mine eyes towards the head of the river, that perhaps I might see them.

61 ¶And it came to pass that I saw them, but they would not come unto me, and partake of the fruit.

62 And I beheld a rod of iron; and it extended along the bank of the river, and led to the tree by which I stood.

63 And I also beheld a straight and narrow path, which came along by the rod of iron, even to the tree by which I stood;

64 And it also led by the head of the fountain unto a large and spacious field, as if it had been a world;

65 And I saw numberless concourses of people, many of whom were pressing forward, that they might obtain the path which led unto the tree by which I stood.

66 ¶And it came to pass that they did come forth and commence in the path which led to the tree.

67 And it came to pass that there arose a mist of darkness; yea, even an exceeding great mist of darkness, insomuch that they who had commenced in the path did lose their way, that they wandered off and were lost.

68 ¶And it came to pass that I beheld others pressing forward, and they came forth and caught hold of the end of the rod of iron;

69 And they did press forward through the mist of darkness, clinging to the rod of iron, even until they did come forth and partake of the fruit of the tree.

70 And after they had partaken of the fruit of the tree they did cast their eyes about as if they were ashamed.

71 And I also cast my eyes round about, and beheld on the other side of the river of water a great and spacious building;

72 And it stood as it were in the air, high above the earth;

73 And it was filled with people, both old and young, both male and female;

74 And their manner of dress was exceeding fine;

75 And they were in the attitude of mocking and pointing their fingers towards those who had come at, and were partaking of the fruit.

76 And after they had tasted of the fruit they were ashamed, because of those that were scoffing at them; and they fell away into forbidden paths and were lost.

77 ¶And now I, Nephi, do not speak all the words of my father.

78 But, to be short in writing, behold, he saw other multitudes pressing forward; and they came and caught hold of the end of the rod of iron; and they did press their way forward, continually holding fast to the rod of iron, until they came forth and fell down and partook of the fruit of the tree.

79 And he also saw other multitudes feeling their way towards that great and spacious building.

80 ¶And it came to pass that many were drowned in the depths of the fountain;

81 And many were lost from his view, wandering in strange roads.

82 And great was the multitude that did enter into that strange building.

83 And after they did enter into that building they did point the finger of scorn at me, and those that were partaking of the fruit also; but we heeded them not.

84 These are the words of my father: For as many as heeded them, had fallen away.

85 And Laman and Lemuel partook not of the fruit, said my father.

86 ¶And it came to pass after my father had spoken all the words of his dream or vision, which were many, he said unto us, because of these things which he saw in a vision, he exceedingly feared for Laman and Lemuel;

87 Yea, he feared lest they should be cast off from the presence of the Lord;

88 And he did exhort them then with all the feeling of a

tender parent, that they would hearken to his words, that, perhaps the Lord would be merciful to them, and not cast them off;

89 Yea, my father did preach unto them.

90 ¶And after he had preached unto them, and also prophesied unto them of many things, he bade them to keep the commandments of the Lord;

91 And he did cease speaking unto them.

92 And all these things did my father see, and hear, and speak, as he dwelt in a tent, in the valley of Lemuel; and also a great many more things, which can not be written upon these plates.

93 And now, as I have spoken concerning these plates, behold, they are not the plates upon which I make a full account of the history of my people;

94 For the plates upon which I make a full account of my people, I have given the name of Nephi;

95 Wherefore, they are called the plates of Nephi, after mine own name; and these plates also are called the plates of Nephi.

96 ¶Nevertheless, I have received a commandment of the Lord that I should make these plates for the special purpose that there should be an account engraven of the ministry of my people.

97 Upon the other plates should be engraven an account of the reign of the kings, and the wars and contentions of my people;

98 Wherefore, these plates are for the more part of the ministry; and the other plates are for the more part of the reign of the kings, and the wars and contentions of my people.

99 Wherefore, the Lord hath commanded me to make these plates for a wise purpose in him; which purpose I know not.

100 But the Lord knoweth all things from the beginning;

101 Wherefore, he prepareth a way to accomplish all his works among the children of men; for behold he hath all power unto the fulfilling of all his words.

102 And thus it is. Amen.

CHAPTER 3.

1 ¶And now I, Nephi, proceed to give an account upon these plates, of my proceedings, and my reign and ministry; wherefore, to proceed with mine account, I must speak somewhat of the things of my father, and also of my brethren.

2 ¶For behold, it came to pass after my father had made an end of speaking the words of his dream, and also of exhorting them to all diligence, he spake unto them concerning the Jews, that after they should be destroyed, even that great city Jerusalem, and many be carried away captive into Babylon, according to the own due time of the Lord they should return again; yea, even be brought back out of captivity;

3 And after they should be brought back out of captivity they should possess again the land of their inheritance.

4 ¶Yea, even six hundred years from the time that my father left Jerusalem, a prophet would the Lord God raise up among the Jews, even a Messiah; or, in other words, a Savior of the world.

5 And he also spake concerning the prophets, how great a number had testified of these things, concerning this Messiah, of whom he had spoken, or this Redeemer of the world.

6 Wherefore, all mankind were in a lost and in a fallen state, and ever would be, save they should rely on this Redeemer.

7 ¶And he spake also concerning a prophet, who should come before the Messiah, to prepare the way of the Lord;

8 Yea, even he should go forth and cry in the wilderness, Prepare ye the way of the Lord and make his paths straight;

9 For there standeth one among you whom ye know not; and he is mightier than I, whose shoe's latchet I am not worthy to unloose.

10 And much spake my father concerning this thing.

11 ¶And my father said he should baptize in Bethabara, beyond Jordan; and he also said he should baptize with water; even that he should baptize the Messiah with water.

12 And after he had baptized the Messiah with water, he

should behold and bear record that he had baptized the Lamb of God, who should take away the sins of the world.

13 ¶And it came to pass after my father had spoken these words, he spake unto my brethren concerning the gospel which should be preached among the Jews,

14 And also concerning the dwindling of the Jews in unbelief.

15 And after they had slain the Messiah who should come, and after he had been slain, he should rise from the dead, and should make himself manifest by the Holy Ghost unto the Gentiles.

16 ¶Yea, even my father spake much concerning the Gentiles, and also concerning the house of Israel, that they should be compared like unto an olive tree, whose branches should be broken off, and should be scattered upon all the face of the earth.

17 Wherefore he said it must needs be that we should be led with one accord into the land of promise, unto the fulfilling of the word of the Lord that we should be scattered upon all the face of the earth.

18 And after the house of Israel should be scattered, they should be gathered together again;

19 Or, in fine, after the Gentiles had received the fullness of the gospel, the natural branches of the olive tree, or the remnants of the house of Israel, should be grafted in, or come to the knowledge of the true Messiah, their Lord and their Redeemer.

20 And after this manner of language did my father prophesy and speak unto my brethren;

21 And also many more things, which I do not write in this book; for I have written as many of them as were expedient for me in mine other book.

22 And all these things of which I have spoken, were done as my father dwelt in a tent in the valley of Lemuel.

23 ¶And it came to pass after I, Nephi, having heard all the words of my father concerning the things which he saw in a vision;

24 And also the things which he spake by the power of the Holy Ghost; which power he received by faith on the Son of God;

25 And the Son of God was the Messiah who should come;

26 ¶I, Nephi, was desirous also that I might see, and hear, and know of these things, by the power of the Holy Ghost, which is the gift of God unto all those who diligently seek him, as well in times of old as in the time that he should manifest himself unto the children of men:

27 For he is the same yesterday, to-day, and for ever.

28 And the way is prepared from the foundation of the world, if it so be that they repent and come unto him;

29 For he that diligently seeketh shall find;

30 And the mysteries of God shall be unfolded unto them by the power of the Holy Ghost, as well in this time as in times of old;

31 And as well in times of old as in times to come;

32 Wherefore, the course of the Lord is one eternal round.

33 Therefore remember, O man, for all thy doings thou shalt be brought into judgment.

34 Wherefore, if ye have sought to do wickedly in the days of your probation, then ye are found unclean before the judgment seat of God;

35 And no unclean thing can dwell with God; wherefore ye must be cast off for ever.

36 And the Holy Ghost giveth authority that I should speak these things and deny them not.

37 ¶For it came to pass after I had desired to know the things that my father had seen, and believing that the Lord was able to make them known unto me,

38 As I sat pondering in mine heart I was caught away in the Spirit of the Lord, yea, into an exceeding high mountain, which I never had before seen, and upon which I never had before set my foot.

39 And the Spirit said unto me, Behold, what desirest thou?

40 And I said, I desire to behold the things which my father saw.

41 And the Spirit said unto me, Believest thou that thy father saw the tree of which he hath spoken?

42 And I said, Yea, thou knowest that I believe all the words of my father.

43 ¶And when I had spoken these words, the Spirit cried with a loud voice, saying, Hosanna to the Lord, the most high God; for he is God over all the earth, yea, even above all.

44 And blessed art thou, Nephi, because thou believest in the Son of the most high God; wherefore, thou shalt behold the things which thou hast desired.

45 And behold, this thing shall be given unto thee for a sign, that after thou hast beheld the tree which bore the fruit which thy father tasted, thou shalt also behold a man descending out of heaven; and him shall ye witness; and after he have witnessed him, ye shall bear record that it is the Son of God.

46 ¶And it came to pass that the Spirit said unto me, Look! and I looked and beheld a tree; and it was like unto the tree which my father had seen; and the beauty thereof was far beyond, yea, exceeding of all beauty; and the whiteness thereof did exceed the whiteness of the driven snow.

47 ¶And it came to pass after I had seen the tree, I said unto the Spirit, I behold thou hast shewn unto me the tree which is precious above all.

48 And he said unto me, What desirest thou?

49 And I said unto him, To know the interpretation thereof:

50 For I spake unto him as a man speaketh; for I beheld that he was in the form of a man; yet, nevertheless, I knew that it was the Spirit of the Lord: and he spake unto me as a man speaketh with another.

51 ¶And it came to pass that he said unto me, Look! and I looked as if to look upon him, and I saw him not; for he had gone from before my presence.

52 ¶And it came to pass that I looked and beheld the great city of Jerusalem, and also other cities.

53 And I beheld the city of Nazareth: and in the city of Nazareth I beheld a virgin, and she was exceedingly fair and white.

54 ¶And it came to pass that I saw the heavens open; and an angel came down and stood before me; and he said unto me, Nephi, what beholdest thou?

55 And I said unto him, A virgin, most beautiful and fair above all other virgins.

56 And he said unto me, Knowest thou the condescension of God?

57 And I said unto him, I know that he loveth his children; nevertheless I do not know the meaning of all things.

58 And he said unto me, Behold, the virgin whom thou seest is the mother of the Son of God, after the manner of the flesh.

59 ¶And it came to pass that I beheld that she was carried away in the Spirit;

60 And after she had been carried away in the Spirit for the space of a time, the angel spake unto me, saying, Look!

61 And I looked and beheld the virgin again, bearing a child in her arms.

62 And the angel said unto me, Behold the Lamb of God, yea, even the Son of the Eternal Father!

63 Knowest thou the meaning of the tree which thy father saw?

64 And I answered him, saying, Yea, it is the love of God, which sheddeth itself abroad in the hearts of the children of men; wherefore it is the most desirable above all things.

65 And he spake unto me, saying, Yea, and the most joyous to the soul.

66 And after he had said these words, he said unto me, Look! And I looked, and I beheld the Son of God going forth among the children of men:

67 And I saw many fall down at his feet and worship him.

68 ¶And it came to pass that I beheld that the rod of iron,

which my father had seen, was the word of God, which led to the fountain of living waters, or to the tree of life; which waters are a representation of the love of God;

69 And I also beheld that the tree of life was a representation of the love of God.

70 And the angel said unto me again, Look and behold the condescension of God!

71 And I looked and beheld the Redeemer of the world, of whom my father had spoken;

72 And I also beheld the prophet who should prepare the way before him.

73 And the Lamb of God went forth and was baptized of him;

74 And after he was baptized, I beheld the heavens open, and the Holy Ghost come down out of heaven and abode upon him in the form of a dove.

75 And I beheld that he went forth ministering unto the people in power and great glory;

76 And the multitudes were gathered together to hear him;

77 And I beheld that they cast him out from among them.

78 And I also beheld twelve others following him.

79 ¶And it came to pass that they were carried away in the Spirit, from before my face, and I saw them not.

80 And it came to pass that the angel spake unto me again, saying, Look! And I looked, and I beheld the heavens open again,

81 And I saw angels descending upon the children of men; and they did minister unto them.

82 And he spake unto me again, saying, Look! And I looked, and I beheld the Lamb of God going forth among the children of men.

83 And I beheld multitudes of people who were sick, and who were afflicted with all manner of diseases, and with devils, and unclean spirits;

84 And the angel spake and shewed all these things unto me.

85 And they were healed by the power of the Lamb of God, and the devils and the unclean spirits were cast out.

86 ¶And it came to pass that the angel spake unto me again, saying, Look! And I looked and beheld the Lamb of God, that he was taken by the people; yea, the Son of the everlasting God was judged of the world; and I saw and bear record.

87 And I, Nephi, saw that he was lifted up upon the cross, and slain for the sins of the world.

88 And after he was slain, I saw the multitudes of the earth, that they were gathered together to fight against the apostles of the Lamb; for thus were the twelve called by the angel of the Lord.

89 And the multitude of the earth was gathered together;

90 And I beheld that they were in a large and spacious building, like unto the building which my father saw.

91 And the angel of the Lord spake unto me again, saying, Behold the world and the wisdom thereof;

92 Yea, behold, the house of Israel hath gathered together to fight against the twelve apostles of the Lamb.

93 ¶And it came to pass that I saw and bear record, that the great and spacious building was the pride of the world;

94 And it fell; and the fall thereof was exceeding great.

95 And the angel of the Lord spake unto me again, saying, Thus shall be the destruction of all nations, kindreds, tongues and people, that shall fight against the twelve apostles of the Lamb.

96 ¶And it came to pass that the angel said unto me, Look and behold thy seed, and also the seed of thy brethren!

97 And I looked and beheld the land of promise;

98 And I beheld multitudes of people, yea, even as it were in number as many as the sand of the sea.

99 ¶And it came to pass that I beheld multitudes gathered together to battle, one against the other; and I beheld wars, and rumors of wars, and great slaughters with the sword among my people.

100 ¶And it came to pass that I beheld many generations

pass away, after the manner of wars and contentions in the land;

101 And I beheld many cities, yea, even that I did not number them.

102 ¶And it came to pass that I saw a mist of darkness on the face of the land of promise;

103 And I saw lightnings, and I heard thunderings, and earthquakes, and all manner of tumultuous noises;

104 And I saw the earth and the rocks that they rent;

105 And I saw mountains tumbling into pieces;

106 And I saw the plains of the earth, that they were broken up;

107 And I saw many cities, that they were sunk;

108 And I saw many that they were burned with fire;

109 And I saw many that did tumble to the earth, because of the quaking thereof.

110 ¶And it came to pass after I saw these things, I saw the vapor of darkness, that it passed from off the face of the earth;

111 And behold, I saw multitudes who had fallen because of the great and terrible judgments of the Lord.

112 And I saw the heavens open, and the Lamb of God descending out of heaven; and he came down and shewed himself unto them.

113 And I also saw and bear record that the Holy Ghost fell upon twelve others, and they were ordained of God, and chosen.

114 ¶And the angel spake unto me, saying, Behold the twelve disciples of the Lamb, who are chosen to minister unto thy seed.

115 And he said unto me, Thou remembereth the twelve apostles of the Lamb? Behold they are they who shall judge the twelve tribes of Israel:

116 Wherefore, the twelve ministers of thy seed shall be judged of them; for ye are of the house of Israel; and these twelve ministers whom thou beholdest, shall judge thy seed.

117 And behold they are righteous for ever; for because of

their faith in the Lamb of God, their garments are made white in his blood.

118 ¶And the angel said unto me, Look! And I looked and beheld three generations pass away in righteousness, and their garments were white, even like unto the Lamb of God.

119 And the angel said unto me, These are made white in the blood of the Lamb, because of their faith in him.

120 And I, Nephi, also saw many of the fourth generation, who passed away in righteousness.

121 ¶And it came to pass that I saw the multitudes of the earth gathered together.

122 And the angel said unto me, Behold thy seed, and also the seed of thy brethren.

123 And it came to pass that I looked and beheld the people of my seed gathered together in multitudes against the seed of my brethren; and they were gathered together to battle.

124 ¶And the angel spake unto me, saying, Behold the fountain of filthy water which thy father saw; yea, even the river of which he spake; and the depths thereof are the depths of hell;

125 And the mists of darkness are the temptations of the devil, which blindeth the eyes, and hardeneth the hearts of the children of men, and leadeth them away into broad roads, that they may perish, and are lost;

126 And the large and spacious building which thy father saw is vain imaginations and the pride of the children of men.

127 And a great and a terrible gulf divideth them; yea, even the word of the justice of the eternal God, and the Messiah who is the Lamb of God, of whom the Holy Ghost beareth record, from the beginning of the world until this time, and from this time henceforth and for ever.

128 And while the angel spake these words, I beheld and saw that the seed of my brethren did contend against my seed, according to the word of the angel;

129 And because of the pride of my seed, and the tempta-

tions of the devil, I beheld that the seed of my brethren did overpower the people of my seed.

130 ¶And it came to pass that I beheld and saw the people of the seed of my brethren, that they had overcome my seed; and they went forth in multitudes upon the face of the land.

131 And I saw them gathered together in multitudes;

132 And I saw wars and rumors of wars among them; and in wars, and rumors of wars, I saw many generations pass away.

133 And the angel said unto me, Behold, these shall dwindle in unbelief.

134 ¶And it came to pass that I beheld after they had dwindled in unbelief, they became a dark and loathsome, and a filthy people, full of idleness and all manner of abominations.

135 ¶And it came to pass that the angel spake unto me, saying, Look! And I looked and beheld many nations and kingdoms.

136 And the angel said unto me, What beholdest thou?

137 And I said, I behold many nations and kingdoms.

138 And he said unto me, These are the nations and kingdoms of the Gentiles.

139 ¶And it came to pass that I saw among the nations of the Gentiles the foundation of a great church.

140 And the angel said unto me, Behold the foundation of a church, which is most abominable above all other churches, which slayeth the saints of God, yea, and tortureth them and bindeth them down, and yoketh them with a yoke of iron, and bringeth them down into captivity.

141 ¶And it came to pass that I beheld this great and abominable church; and I saw the devil that he was the foundation of it.

142 And I also saw gold and silver, and silks, and scarlets, and fine twined linen, and all manner of precious clothing; and I saw many harlots.

143 And the angel spake unto me, saying, Behold the gold, and the silver, and the silks, and the scarlets, and the fine

twined linen, and the precious clothing, and the harlots, are the desires of this great and abominable church;

144 And also for the praise of the world do they destroy the saints of God, and bring them down into captivity.

145 ¶And it came to pass that I looked and beheld many waters; and they divided the Gentiles from the seed of my brethren.

146 And it came to pass that the angel said unto me, Behold the wrath of God is upon the seed of thy brethren!

147 And I looked and beheld a man among the Gentiles, who was separated from the seed of my brethren by the many waters; and I beheld the Spirit of God, that it came down and wrought upon the man; and he went forth upon the many waters, even unto the seed of my brethren, who were in the promised land.

148 ¶And it came to pass that I beheld the Spirit of God, that it wrought upon other Gentiles; and they went forth out of captivity, upon the many waters.

149 ¶And it came to pass that I beheld many multitudes of the Gentiles upon the land of promise;

150 And I beheld the wrath of God that it was upon the seed of my brethren; and they were scattered before the Gentiles, and were smitten.

151 And I beheld the Spirit of the Lord, that it was upon the Gentiles; that they did prosper, and obtain the land for their inheritance; and I beheld that they were white, and exceeding fair and beautiful, like unto my people before they were slain.

152 ¶And it came to pass that I, Nephi, beheld that the Gentiles who had gone forth out of captivity did humble themselves before the Lord, and the power of the Lord was with them;

153 And I beheld that their mother Gentiles were gathered together upon the waters, and upon the land also, to battle against them;

154 And I beheld that the power of God was with them;

CHAP. 3.] FIRST BOOK OF NEPHI. 35

and also that the wrath of God was upon all those that were gathered together against them to battle.

155 And I, Nephi, beheld that the Gentiles that had gone out of captivity were delivered by the power of God out of the hands of all other nations.

156 ¶And it came to pass that I, Nephi, beheld that they did prosper in the land;

157 And I beheld a book, and it was carried forth among them.

158 And the angel said unto me, Knowest thou the meaning of the book?

159 And I said unto him, I know not.

160 And he said, Behold, it proceedeth out of the mouth of a Jew; and I, Nephi, beheld it;

161 And he said unto me, The book that thou beholdest is a record of the Jews, which contains the covenants of the Lord which he hath made unto the house of Israel;

162 And it also containeth many of the prophecies of the holy prophets;

163 And it is a record like unto the engravings which are upon the plates of brass, save there are not so many; nevertheless, they contain the covenants of the Lord which he hath made unto the house of Israel;

164 Wherefore, they are of great worth unto the Gentiles.

165 ¶And the angel of the Lord said unto me, Thou hast beheld that the book proceeded forth from the mouth of a Jew; and when it proceeded forth from the mouth of a Jew it contained the plainness of the gospel of the Lord, of whom the twelve apostles bear record; and they bear record according to the truth which is in the Lamb of God:

166 Wherefore, these things go forth from the Jews in purity unto the Gentiles, according to the truth which is in God:

167 And after they go forth by the hand of the twelve apostles of the Lamb, from the Jews unto the Gentiles, thou seest the foundation of a great and abominable church, which is most abominable above all other churches;

168 For behold, they have taken away from the gospel of the Lamb many parts which are plain and most precious;

169 And also many covenants of the Lord have they taken away;

170 And all this have they done that they might pervert the right ways of the Lord; that they might blind the eyes and harden the hearts of the children of men:

171 Wherefore, thou seest that after the book hath gone forth through the hands of the great and abominable church that there are many plain and precious things taken away from the book, which is the book of the Lamb of God;

172 And after these plain and precious things were taken away, it goeth forth unto all the nations of the Gentiles:

173 And after it goeth forth unto all the nations of the Gentiles, yea, even across the many waters which thou hast seen, with the Gentiles which have gone forth out of captivity;

174 Thou seest because of the many plain and precious things which have been taken out of the book, which were plain unto the understanding of the children of men, according to the plainness which is in the Lamb of God;

175 Because of these things which are taken away out of the gospel of the Lamb, an exceeding great many do stumble, yea, insomuch that Satan hath great power over them;

176 Nevertheless thou beholdest that the Gentiles who have gone forth out of captivity, and have been lifted up by the power of God above all other nations upon the face of the land, which is choice above all other lands,

177 Which is the land that the Lord God hath covenanted with thy father that his seed should have for the land of their inheritance, will not utterly destroy the mixture of thy seed, which are among thy brethren;

178 Neither will he suffer that the Gentiles shall destroy the seed of thy brethren;

179 Neither will the Lord God suffer that the Gentiles shall for ever remain in that awful state of blindness, which thou beholdest they are in because of the plain and most precious

parts of the gospel of the Lamb which have been kept back by that abominable church, whose formation thou hast seen.

180 Wherefore, saith the Lamb of God, I will be merciful unto the Gentiles, unto the visiting of the remnant of the house of Israel in great judgment.

181 ¶And it came to pass that the angel of the Lord spake unto me, saying, Behold, saith the Lamb of God, after I have visited the remnant of the house of Israel, and this remnant of whom I speak is the seed of thy father;

182 Wherefore, after I have visited them in judgment, and smitten them by the hand of the Gentiles;

183 And after the Gentiles do stumble exceedingly because of the most plain and precious parts of the gospel of the Lamb which has been kept back, by that abominable church, which is the mother of harlots, saith the Lamb, I will be merciful unto the Gentiles in that day, insomuch that I will bring forth unto them in mine own power, much of my gospel, which shall be plain and precious, saith the Lamb;

184 For behold, saith the Lamb, I will manifest myself unto thy seed, that they shall write many things which I shall minister unto them, which shall be plain and precious;

185 And after thy seed shall be destroyed and dwindle in unbelief, and also the seed of thy brethren; behold, these things shall be hid up, to come forth unto the Gentiles by the gift and power of the Lamb;

186 And in them shall be written my gospel, saith the Lamb, and my rock and my salvation;

187 And blessed are they who shall seek to bring forth my Zion at that day, for they shall have the gift and the power of the Holy Ghost;

188 And if they endure unto the end, they shall be lifted up at the last day, and shall be saved in the everlasting kingdom of the Lamb;

189 And whoso shall publish peace, yea, tidings of great joy, how beautiful upon the mountains shall they be.

190 ¶And it came to pass that I beheld the remnant of the seed of my brethren, and also the book of the Lamb of God,

which had proceeded forth from the mouth of the Jew, that it came forth from the Gentiles, unto the remnant of the seed of my brethren;

191 And after it had come forth unto them, I beheld other books which came forth by the power cf the Lamb, from the Gentiles unto them, unto the convincing of the Gentiles, and the remnant of the seed of my brethren, and also the Jews, who were scattered upon all the face of the earth, that the records of the prophets and of the twelve apostles of the Lamb are true.

192 ¶And the angel spake unto me, saying, These last records which thou hast seen among the Gentiles shall establish the truth of the first, which are of the twelve apostles of the Lamb, and shall make known the plain and precious things which have been taken away from them;

193 And shall make known to all kindreds, tongues and people, that the Lamb of God is the Son of the Eternal Father, and the Savior of the world; and that all men must come unto him or they can not be saved;

194 And they must come according to the words which shall be established by the mouth of the Lamb;

195 And the words of the Lamb shall be made known in the records of thy seed, as well as in the records of the twelve apostles of the Lamb;

196 Wherefore, they both shall be established in one;

197 For there is one God and one Shepherd over all the earth;

198 And the time cometh that he shall manifest himself unto all nations, both unto the Jews, and also unto the Gentiles;

199 And after he has manifested himself unto the Jews and also unto the Gentiles; then he shall manifest himself unto the Gentiles, and also unto the Jews,

200 And the last shall be first, and the first shall be last.

201 ¶And it shall come to pass, that if the Gentiles shall hearken unto the Lamb of God in that day that he shall manifest himself unto them in word, and also in power, in very

CHAP. 3.] FIRST BOOK OF NEPHI. 39

deed, unto the taking away of their stumbling-blocks, and harden not their hearts against the Lamb of God, they shall be numbered among the seed of thy father;

202 Yea, they shall be numbered among the house of Israel;

203 And they shall be a blessed people upon the promised land for ever;

204 They shall be no more brought down into captivity;

205 And the house of Israel shall no more be confounded;

206 And that great pit which hath been digged for them by that great and abominable church, which was founded by the devil and his children, that he might lead away the souls of men down to hell;

207 Yea, that great pit which hath been digged for the destruction of men, shall be filled by those who digged it, unto their utter destruction, saith the Lamb of God;

208 Not the destruction of the soul, save it be the casting of it into that hell which hath no end;

209 For behold, this is according to the captivity of the devil, and also according to the justice of God, upon all those who will work wickedness and abomination before him.

210 ¶And it came to pass that the angel spake unto me, Nephi, saying, Thou hast beheld that if the Gentiles repent, it shall be well with them;

211 And thou also knowest concerning the covenants of the Lord unto the house of Israel;

212 And thou also hast heard, that whoso repenteth not, must perish;

213 Therefore, wo, be unto the Gentiles, if it so be that they harden their hearts against the Lamb of God;

214 For the time cometh, saith the Lamb of God, that I will work a great and a marvelous work among the children of men;

215 A work which shall be everlasting, either on the one hand or on the other;

216 Either to the convincing of them unto peace and life eternal, or unto the deliverance of them to the hardness of their hearts and the blindness of their minds, unto their being

brought down into captivity and also unto destruction, both temporally and spiritually, according to the captivity of the devil, of which I have spoken.

217 ¶And it came to pass that when the angel had spoken these words, he said unto me, Remember thou the covenants of the Father unto the house of Israel?

218 I said unto him, Yea.

219 And it came to pass that he said unto me, Look and behold that great and abominable church, which is the mother of abominations, whose founder is the devil.

220 And he said unto me, Behold, there are save two churches only:

221 The one is the church of the Lamb of God, and the other is the church of the devil;

222 Wherefore, whoso belongeth not to the church of the Lamb of God belongeth to that great church, which is the mother of abominations;

223 And she is the whore of all the earth.

224 ¶And it came to pass that I looked and beheld the whore of all the earth, and she sat upon many waters;

225 And she had dominion over all the earth, among all nations, kindreds, tongues and people.

226 ¶And it came to pass that I beheld the church of the Lamb of God, and its numbers were few, because of the wickedness and abominations of the whore who sat upon many waters;

227 Nevertheless, I beheld that the church of the Lamb, who were the saints of God, were also upon all the face of the earth;

228 And their dominions upon the face of the earth were small, because of the wickedness of the great whore whom I saw.

229 ¶And it came to pass that I beheld that the great mother of abominations did gather together in multitudes upon the face of all the earth, among all the nations of the Gentiles, to fight against the Lamb of God.

230 ¶And it came to pass that I, Nephi, beheld the power

of the Lamb of God, that it descended upon the saints of the church of the Lamb, and upon the covenant people of the Lord, who were scattered upon all the face of the earth;

231 And they were armed with righteousness and with the power of God in great glory.

232 ¶And it came to pass that I beheld that the wrath of God was poured out upon the great and abominable church, insomuch that there were wars and rumors of wars among all the nations and kindreds of the earth,

233 And as there began to be wars and rumors of wars among all the nations which belonged to the mother of abominations, the angel spake unto me, saying,

234 Behold, the wrath of God is upon the mother of harlots;

235 And behold, thou seest all these things;

236 And when the day cometh that the wrath of God is poured out upon the mother of harlots, which is the great and abominable church of all the earth, whose foundation is the devil,

237 Then at that day, the work of the Father shall commence, in preparing the way for the fulfilling of his covenants which he hath made to his people, who are of the house of Israel.

238 ¶And it came to pass that the angel spake unto me, saying, Look! And I looked and beheld a man, and he was dressed in a white robe;

239 And the angel said unto me, Behold one of the twelve apostles of the Lamb!

240 Behold, he shall see and write the remainder of these things;

241 Yea, and also many things which have been;

242 And he shall also write concerning the end of the world;

243 Wherefore, the things which he shall write are just and true;

244 And behold, they are written in the book which thou beheld proceeding out of the mouth of the Jew;

245 And at the time they proceeded out of the mouth of the Jew, or, at the time the book proceeded out of the mouth of the Jew, the things which were written were plain and pure, and most precious and easy to the understanding of all men.

246 And behold, the things which this apostle of the Lamb shall write, are many things which thou hast seen;

247 And behold, the remainder shalt thou see;

248 But the things which thou shalt see hereafter, thou shalt not write; for the Lord God hath ordained the apostle of the Lamb of God that he should write them.

249 And also others who have been, to them hath he shown all things, and they have written them;

250 And they are sealed up to come forth in their purity according to the truth which is in the Lamb, in the own due time of the Lord, unto the house of Israel.

251 ¶And I, Nephi, heard and bear record, that the name of the apostle of the Lamb was John, according to the word of the angel.

252 And behold, I, Nephi, am forbidden that I should write the remainder of the things which I saw and heard; wherefore, the things which I have written sufficeth me;

253 And I have not written but a small part of the things which I saw.

254 And I bear record, that I saw the things which my father saw, and the angel of the Lord did make them known unto me.

255 And now I make an end of speaking concerning the things which I saw, while I was carried away in the Spirit;

256 And if all the things which I saw are not written, the things which I have written are true. And thus it is. Amen.

CHAPTER 4.

1 ¶And it came to pass that after I, Nephi, had been carried away in the Spirit, and seen all these things, I returned to the tent of my father.

2 And it came to pass that I beheld my brethren, and they were disputing one with another, concerning the things which my father had spoken unto them;

3 For he truly spake many great things unto them, which were hard to be understood, save a man should inquire of the Lord;

4 And they being hard in their hearts, therefore they did not look unto the Lord as they ought.

5 And now I, Nephi, was grieved because of the hardness of their hearts, and also because of the things which I had seen, and knew they must unavoidably come to pass because of the great wickedness of the children of men.

6 ¶And it came to pass that I was overcome because of my afflictions, for I considered that mine afflictions were great above all, because of the destructions of my people; for I had beheld their fall.

7 ¶And it came to pass that after I had received strength, I spake unto my brethren, desiring to know of them the cause of their disputations.

8 And they said, Behold, we can not understand the words which our father hath spoken concerning the natural branches of the olive tree, and also concerning the Gentiles.

9 And I said unto them, Have ye inquired of the Lord?

10 And they said unto me, We have not; for the Lord maketh no such thing known unto us.

11 Behold, I said unto them, How is it that ye do not keep the commandments of the Lord?

12 How is it that ye will perish because of the hardness of your hearts?

13 Do ye not remember the things which the Lord hath said, If ye will not harden your hearts, and ask me in faith, believing that ye shall receive, with diligence in keeping my

commandments, surely, these things shall be made known unto you?

14 ¶Behold, I say unto you, that the house of Israel was compared unto an olive tree, by the Spirit of the Lord which was in our fathers;

15 And behold, are we not broken off from the house of Israel; and are we not a branch of the house of Israel?

16 And now, the thing which our father meaneth concerning the grafting in of the natural branches through the fullness of the Gentiles, is, that in the latter days, when our seed shall have dwindled in unbelief, yea, for the space of many years and many generations, after the Messiah shall be manifested in body unto the children of men, then shall the fullness of the gospel of the Messiah come unto the Gentiles, and from the Gentiles unto the remnant of our seed;

17 And at that day shall the remnant of our seed know that they are of the house of Israel, and that they are the covenant people of the Lord;

18 And then shall they know and come to the knowledge of their forefathers, and also to the knowledge of the gospel of their Redeemer, which was ministered unto their fathers by him;

19 Wherefore, they shall come to the knowledge of their Redeemer, and the very points of his doctrine, that they may know how to come unto him and be saved.

20 And then at that day, will they not rejoice and give praise unto their everlasting God, their rock and their salvation?

21 Yea, at that day, will they not receive the strength and nourishment from the true vine?

22 Yea, will they not come unto the true fold of God?

23 Behold, I say unto you, Yea: they shall be remembered again among the house of Israel;

24 They shall be grafted in, being a natural branch of the olive tree, into the true olive tree;

25 And this is what our father meaneth;

26 And he meaneth that it will not come to pass, until after they are scattered by the Gentiles;

27 And he meaneth that it shall come by way of the Gentiles, that the Lord may shew his power unto the Gentiles, for the very cause that he shall be rejected of the Jews, or of the house of Israel:

28 Wherefore, our father hath not spoken of our seed alone, but also of all the house of Israel, pointing to the covenant which should be fulfilled in the latter days;

29 Which covenant the Lord made to our father Abraham, saying, In thy seed shall all the kindreds of the earth be blessed.

30 ¶And it came to pass that I, Nephi, spake much unto them concerning these things;

31 Yea, I spake unto them concerning the restoration of the Jews, in the latter days;

32 And I did rehearse unto them the words of Isaiah, who spake concerning the restoration of the Jews, or of the house of Israel;

33 And after they were restored, they should no more be confounded, neither should they be scattered again.

34 And it came to pass that I did speak many words unto my brethren, that they were pacified, and did humble themselves before the Lord.

35 ¶And it came to pass that they did speak unto me again, saying, What meaneth this thing which our father saw in a dream?

36 What meaneth the tree which he saw?

37 And I said unto them, It was a representation of the tree of life.

38 And they said unto me, What meaneth the rod of iron which our father saw, that led to the tree?

39 And I said unto them, that it was the word of God; and whoso would hearken unto the word of God, and would hold fast unto it, they would never perish;

40 Neither could the temptations and the fiery darts of the

adversary, overpower them unto blindness, to lead them away to destruction.

41 Wherefore, I, Nephi, did exhort them to give heed unto the word of the Lord;

42 Yea, I did exhort them with all the energies of my soul, and with all the faculty which I possessed, that they would give heed to the word of God, and remember to keep his commandments always, in all things.

43 And they said unto me, What meaneth the river of water which our father saw?

44 And I said unto them, that the water which my father saw, was filthiness;

45 And so much was his mind swallowed up in other things, that he beheld not the filthiness of the water;

46 And I said unto them, that it was an awful gulf, which separateth the wicked from the tree of life, and also from the saints of God.

47 And I said unto them, that it was a representation of that awful hell, which the angel said unto me was prepared for the wicked.

48 And I said unto them that our father also saw, that the justice of God did also divide the wicked from the righteous;

49 And the brightness thereof was like unto the brightness of a flaming fire, which ascendeth up unto God for ever and ever, and hath no end.

50 ¶And they said unto me, Doth this thing mean the torment of the body in the days of probation, or doth it mean the final state of the soul after the death of the temporal body, or doth it speak of the things which are temporal?

51 And it came to pass that I said unto them, that it was a representation of things both temporal and spiritual;

52 For the day should come that they must be judged of their works, yea, even the works which were done by the temporal body in their days of probation;

53 Wherefore, if they should die in their wickedness, they must be cast off also, as to the things which are spiritual, which are pertaining to righteousness;

54 Wherefore, they must be brought to stand before God to be judged of their works:

55 And if their works have been filthiness, they must needs be filthy:

56 And if they be filthy, it must needs be that they can not dwell in the kingdom of God:

57 If so, the kingdom of God must be filthy also.

58 But behold, I say unto you, the kingdom of God is not filthy, and there can not any unclean thing enter into the kingdom of God;

59 Wherefore, there must needs be a place of filthiness prepared for that which is filthy.

60 And there is a place prepared, yea, even that awful hell of which I have spoken, and the devil is the foundation of it:

61 Wherefore, the final state of the souls of men is to dwell in the kingdom of God, or to be cast out because of that justice of which I have spoken;

62 Wherefore, the wicked are rejected from the righteous, and also from that tree of life, whose fruit is most precious and most desirable above all other fruits:

63 Yea, and it is the greatest of all the gifts of God.

64 And thus I spake unto my brethren. Amen.

CHAPTER 5.

1 ¶And now it came to pass that after I, Nephi, had made an end of speaking to my brethren, behold, they said unto me: Thou hast declared unto us hard things, more than we are able to bear.

2 ¶And it came to pass that I said unto them, that I knew that I had spoken hard things against the wicked, according to the truth; and the righteous have I justified, and testified that they should be lifted up at the last day; wherefore, the guilty taketh the truth to be hard, for it cutteth them to the very center.

3 And now, my brethren, if ye were righteous, and were willing to hearken to the truth, and give heed unto it, that ye

might walk uprightly before God, then ye would not murmur because of the truth, and say, Thou speakest hard things against us.

4 And it came to pass that I, Nephi, did exhort my brethren, with all diligence, to keep the commandments of the Lord.

5 And it came to pass that they did humble themselves before the Lord; insomuch that I had joy and great hopes of them, that they would walk in the paths of righteousness.

6 Now, all these things were said and done, as my father dwelt in a tent in the valley which he called Lemuel.

7 ¶And it came to pass that I, Nephi, took one of the daughters of Ishmael to wife; and also, my brethren took of the daughters of Ishmael to wife; and also, Zoram took the eldest daughter of Ishmael to wife.

8 And thus my father had fulfilled all the commandments of the Lord which had been given unto him.

9 And also, I, Nephi, had been blessed of the Lord exceedingly.

10 ¶And it came to pass that the voice of the Lord spake unto my father, by night, and commanded him, that on the morrow, he should take his journey into the wilderness.

11 And it came to pass that as my father arose in the morning, and went forth to the tent door, to his great astonishment, he beheld upon the ground a round ball, of curious workmanship; and it was of fine brass.

12 And within the ball were two spindles; and the one pointed the way whither we should go into the wilderness.

13 ¶And it came to pass that we did gather together whatsoever things we should carry into the wilderness, and all the remainder of our provisions which the Lord had given unto us;

14 And we did take seed of every kind, that we might carry into the wilderness.

15 ¶And it came to pass that we did take our tents, and depart into the wilderness, across the river Laman.

16 And it came to pass that we traveled for the space of four days, nearly a south, south-east direction, and we did

pitch our tents again; and we did call the name of the place Shazer.

17 ¶And it came to pass that we did take our bows and our arrows, and go forth into the wilderness, to slay food for our families; and after we had slain food for our families, we did return again to our families in the wilderness, to the place of Shazer.

18 And we did go forth again, in the wilderness, following the same direction, keeping in the most fertile parts of the wilderness, which were in the borders near the Red Sea.

19 And it came to pass that we did travel for the space of many days, slaying food by the way, with our bows and our arrows, and our stones and our slings;

20 And we did follow the directions of the ball, which led us in the more fertile parts of the wilderness.

21 And after we had traveled for the space of many days, we did pitch our tents for the space of a time, that we might again rest ourselves and obtain food for our families.

22 ¶And it came to pass that as I, Nephi, went forth to slay food, behold, I did break my bow, which was made of fine steel; and after I did break my bow, behold, my brethren were angry with me, because of the loss of my bow, for we did obtain no food.

23 And it came to pass that we did return without food to our families.

24 And being much fatigued because of their journeying, they did suffer much for the want of food.

25 ¶And it came to pass that Laman and Lemuel, and the sons of Ishmael, did begin to murmur exceedingly, because of their sufferings and afflictions in the wilderness; and also my father began to murmur against the Lord his God; yea, and they were all exceeding sorrowful, even that they did murmur against the Lord.

26 ¶Now it came to pass that I, Nephi, having been afflicted with my brethren, because of the loss of my bow; and their bows having lost their springs, it began to be exceeding difficult, yea, insomuch that we could obtain no food.

27 And it came to pass that I, Nephi, did speak much unto my brethren, because they had hardened their hearts again, even unto complaining against the Lord their God.

28 And it came to pass that I, Nephi, did make out of wood a bow, and out of a straight stick, an arrow; wherefore, I did arm myself with a bow and an arrow, with a sling, and with stones.

29 And I said unto my father, Whither shall I go, to obtain food?

30 And it came to pass that he did inquire of the Lord, for they had humbled themselves because of my word; for I did say many things unto them in the energy of my soul.

31 ¶And it came to pass that the voice of the Lord came unto my father; and he was truly chastened because of his murmuring against the Lord, insomuch that he was brought down into the depths of sorrow.

32 And it came to pass that the voice of the Lord said unto him, Look upon the ball, and behold the things which are written!

33 And it came to pass that when my father beheld the things which were written upon the ball, he did fear and tremble exceedingly; and also my brethren, and the sons of Ishmael, and our wives.

34 ¶And it came to pass that I, Nephi, beheld the pointers which were in the ball, that they did work according to the faith, and diligence, and heed, which we did give unto them.

35 And there was also written upon them a new writing, which was plain to be read, which did give us understanding concerning the ways of the Lord; and it was written and changed from time to time, according to the faith and diligence which we gave unto it.

36 And thus we see, that by small means, the Lord can bring about great things.

37 ¶And it came to pass that I, Nephi, did go forth up into the top of the mountain, according to the directions which were given upon the ball.

38 And it came to pass that I did slay wild beasts, insomuch that I did obtain food for our families.

39 And it came to pass that I did return to our tents, bearing the beasts which I had slain;

40 And now, when they beheld that I had obtained food, how great was their joy.

41 And it came to pass that they did humble themselves before the Lord, and did give thanks unto him.

42 ¶And it came to pass that we did again take our journey, traveling nearly the same course as in the beginning;

43 And after we had traveled for the space of many days, we did pitch our tents again, that we might tarry for the space of a time.

44 ¶And it came to pass that Ishmael died, and was buried in the place which was called Nahom.

45 And it came to pass that the daughters of Ishmael did mourn exceedingly, because of the loss of their father, and because of their afflictions in the wilderness;

46 And they did murmur against my father, because he had brought them out of the land of Jerusalem, saying, Our father is dead; yea, and we have wandered much in the wilderness, and we have suffered much affliction, hunger, thirst, and fatigue; and after all these sufferings, we must perish in the wilderness with hunger.

47 And thus they did murmur against my father, and also against me; and they were desirous to return again to Jerusalem.

48 And Laman said unto Lemuel, and also unto the sons of Ishmael, Behold, let us slay our father, and also our brother Nephi, who has taken it upon him to be our ruler and our teacher, who are his elder brethren.

49 Now, he says that the Lord has talked with him, and also that angels have ministered unto him!

50 But behold, we know that he lies unto us; and he tells us these things, and he worketh many things by his cunning arts, that he may deceive our eyes, thinking, perhaps, that he may lead us away into some strange wilderness;

51 And after he has led us away, he has thought to make himself a king and a ruler over us, that he may do with us according to his will and pleasure.

52 And after this manner did my brother Laman stir up their hearts to anger.

53 ¶And it came to pass that the Lord was with us; yea, even the voice of the Lord came and did speak many words unto them, and did chasten them exceedingly;

54 And after they were chastened by the voice of the Lord, they did turn away their anger, and did repent of their sins, insomuch that the Lord did bless us again with food, that we did not perish.

55 ¶And it came to pass that we did again take our journey in the wilderness; and we did travel nearly eastward, from that time forth.

56 And we did travel and wade through much affliction in the wilderness; and our women did bear children in the wilderness.

57 And so great were the blessings of the Lord upon us, that while we did live upon raw meat in the wilderness, our women did give plenty of suck for their children, and were strong, yea, even like unto the men; and they began to bear their journeyings without murmurings.

58 And thus we see that the commandments of God must be fulfilled.

59 And if it so be that the children of men keep the commandments of God, he doth nourish them, and strengthen them, and provide means whereby they can accomplish the thing which he has commanded them;

60 Wherefore, he did provide means for us while we did sojourn in the wilderness.

61 And we did sojourn for the space of many years, yea, even eight years in the wilderness.

62 And we did come to the land which we called Bountiful, because of its much fruit, and also wild honey;

63 And all these things were prepared of the Lord, that we might not perish.

64 And we beheld the sea, which we called Irreantum, which being interpreted, is, many waters.

65 ¶And it came to pass that we did pitch our tents by the sea-shore;

66 And notwithstanding we had suffered many afflictions, and much difficulty, yea, even so much that we can not write them all, we were exceedingly rejoiced when we came to the sea-shore;

67 And we called the place Bountiful, because of its much fruit.

68 ¶And it came to pass that after I, Nephi, had been in the land of Bountiful for the space of many days, the voice of the Lord came unto me, saying, Arise, and get thee into the mountain.

69 And it came to pass that I arose and went up into the mountain, and cried unto the Lord.

70 ¶And it came to pass that the Lord spake unto me, saying, Thou shalt construct a ship, after the manner which I shall shew thee, that I may carry thy people across these waters.

71 And I said, Lord, whither shall I go, that I may find ore to molten, that I may make tools to construct the ship, after the manner which thou hast shewn unto me?

72 And it came to pass that the Lord told me whither I should go to find ore, that I might make tools.

73 ¶And it came to pass that I, Nephi, did make bellows wherewith to blow the fire, of the skins of beasts;

74 And after I had made bellows, that I might have wherewith to blow the fire, I did smite two stones together, that I might make fire;

75 For the Lord had not hitherto suffered that we should make much fire, as we journeyed in the wilderness;

76 For he said, I will make thy food become sweet, that ye cook it not;

77 And I will also be your light in the wilderness;

78 And I will prepare the way before you, if it so be that ye shall keep my commandments;

79 Wherefore, inasmuch as ye shall keep my commandments, ye shall be led toward the promised land; and ye shall know that it is by me that ye are led.

80 Yea, and the Lord said also, that after ye have arrived to the promised land, ye shall know that I, the Lord, am God;

81 And that I, the Lord, did deliver you from destruction;

82 Yea, that I did bring you out of the land of Jerusalem.

83 Wherefore, I, Nephi, did strive to keep the commandments of the Lord, and I did exhort my brethren to faithfulness and diligence.

84 ¶And it came to pass that I did make tools of the ore which I did molten out of the rock.

85 And when my brethren saw that I was about to build a ship, they began to murmur against me, saying,

86 Our brother is a fool, for he thinketh that he can build a ship;

87 Yea, and he also thinketh that he can cross these great waters.

88 And thus my brethren did complain against me, and were desirous that they might not labor, for they did not believe that I could build a ship;

89 Neither would they believe that I was instructed of the Lord.

90 ¶And now it came to pass that I, Nephi, was exceeding sorrowful, because of the hardness of their hearts;

91 And now when they saw that I began to be sorrowful, they were glad in their hearts, insomuch that they did rejoice over me, saying,

92 We knew that ye could not construct a ship, for we knew that ye were lacking in judgment; wherefore, thou canst not accomplish so great a work;

93 And thou art like unto our father, led away by the foolish imaginations of his heart;

94 Yea, he hath led us out of the land of Jerusalem; and we have wandered in the wilderness for these many years;

95 And our women have toiled, being big with child; and

they have borne children in the wilderness and suffered all things, save it were death;

96 And it would have been better that they had died, before they came out of Jerusalem, than to have suffered these afflictions.

97 Behold, these many years we have suffered in the wilderness, which time we might have enjoyed our possessions, and the land of our inheritance; yea, and we might have been happy;

98 And we know that the people who were in the land of Jerusalem, were a righteous people;

99 For they kept the statutes and the judgments of the Lord, and all his commandments according to the law of Moses; wherefore, we know that they are a righteous people;

100 And our father hath judged them, and hath led us away because we would hearken unto his word;

101 Yea, and our brother is like unto him.

102 And after this manner of language did my brethren murmur and complain against us.

103 ¶And it came to pass that I, Nephi, spake unto them, saying, Do ye believe that our fathers, who were the children of Israel, would have been led away out of the hands of the Egyptians, if they had not hearkened unto the words of the Lord?

104 Yea, do ye suppose that they would have been led out of bondage, if the Lord had not commanded Moses that he should lead them out of bondage?

105 Now ye know that the children of Israel were in bondage; and ye know that they were laden with tasks, which were grievous to be borne;

106 Wherefore, ye know that it must needs be a good thing for them, that they should be brought out of bondage.

107 Now ye know that Moses was commanded of the Lord to do that great work;

108 And ye know that by his word the waters of the Red Sea were divided hither and thither, and they passed through on dry ground.

109 But ye know that the Egyptians were drowned in the Red Sea, who were the armies of Pharaoh;

110 And ye also know that they were fed with manna in the wilderness;

111 Yea, and ye also know that Moses, by his word, according to the power of God which was in him, smote the rock, and there came forth water, that the children of Israel might quench their thirst;

112 And notwithstanding they being led, the Lord their God, their Redeemer, going before them, leading them by day and giving light unto them by night, and doing all things for them which were expedient for man to receive, they hardened their hearts, and blinded their minds, and reviled against Moses and against the true and living God.

113 ¶And it came to pass that according to his word, he did destroy them;

114 And according to his word, he did lead them;

115 And according to his word, he did do all things for them;

116 And there was not anything done, save it were by his word.

117 And after they had crossed the river Jordan, he did make them mighty, unto the driving out the children of the land, yea, unto the scattering them to destruction.

118 And now do ye suppose that the children of this land, who were in the land of promise, who were driven out by our fathers, do ye suppose that they were righteous? Behold, I say unto you, Nay.

119 Do ye suppose that our fathers would have been more choice than they, if they had been righteous?

120 I say unto you, Nay;

121 Behold, the Lord esteemeth all flesh in one.

122 He that is righteous, is favored of God.

123 But behold, this people had rejected every word of God, and they were ripe in iniquity; and the fullness of the wrath of God was upon them;

124 And the Lord did curse the land against them, and

bless it unto our fathers; yea, he did curse it against them unto their destruction;

125 And he did bless it unto our fathers, unto their obtaining power over it.

126 Behold, the Lord hath created the earth that it should be inhabited;

127 And he hath created his children, that they should possess it.

128 And he raiseth up a righteous nation; and destroyeth the nations of the wicked.

129 And he leadeth away the righteous into precious lands, and the wicked he destroyeth, and curseth the land unto them for their sakes.

130 He ruleth high in the heavens, for it is his throne, and this earth is his footstool.

131 And he loveth those who will have him to be their God.

132 Behold, he loved our fathers; and he covenanted with them, yea, even Abraham, Isaac, and Jacob: and he remembered the covenants which he had made;

133 Wherefore, he did bring them out of the land of Egypt, and he did straighten them in the wilderness with his rod, for they hardened their hearts, even as ye have; and the Lord straightened them because of their iniquity.

134 He sent fiery-flying serpents among them; and after they were bitten, he prepared a way that they might be healed;

135 And the labor which they had to perform was to look! and because of the simpleness of the way, or the easiness of it, there were many who perished.

136 And they did harden their hearts from time to time, and they did revile against Moses, and also against God;

137 Nevertheless, ye know that they were led forth by his matchless power into the land of promise.

138 And now, after all these things, the time has come that they have become wicked, yea, nearly unto ripeness;

139 And I know not but they are at this day about to be destroyed;

140 For I know that the day must surely come that they must be destroyed, save a few only who shall be led away into captivity;

141 Wherefore, the Lord commanded my father that he should depart into the wilderness;

142 And the Jews also sought to take away his life; yea, and ye also have sought to take away his life;

143 Wherefore, ye are murderers in your hearts, and ye are like unto them.

144 Ye are swift to do iniquity, but slow to remember the Lord your God.

145 Ye have seen an angel, and he spake unto you; yea, ye have heard his voice from time to time;

146 And he hath spoken unto you in a still, small voice, but ye were past feeling, that ye could not feel his words;

147 Wherefore, he has spoken unto you like unto the voice of thunder, which did cause the earth to shake as if it were to divide asunder.

148 And ye also know that by the power of his almighty word he can cause the earth that it shall pass away;

149 Yea, and ye know that by his word he can cause the rough places to be made smooth, and smooth places shall be broken up.

150 O, then, why is it that ye can be so hard in your hearts?

151 Behold, my soul is rent with anguish because of you, and my heart is pained: I fear lest ye shall be cast off for ever.

152 Behold, I am full of the Spirit of God, insomuch that my frame has no strength.

153 ¶And now it came to pass that when I had spoken these words, they were angry with me, and were desirous to throw me into the depths of the sea;

154 And as they came forth to lay their hands upon me, I spake unto them, saying, In the name of the Almighty God, I command you that ye touch me not, for I am filled with the power of God, even unto the consuming of my flesh;

155 And whoso shall lay their hands upon me, shall wither even as a dried reed; and he shall be as nought before the power of God, for God shall smite him.

156 ¶And it came to pass that I, Nephi, said unto them, that they should murmur no more against their father, neither should they withhold their labor from me, for God had commanded me that I should build a ship.

157 And I said unto them, If God had commanded me to do all things, I could do them.

158 If he should command me that I should say unto this water, Be thou earth, it should be earth; and if I should say it, it would be done.

159 And now, if the Lord has such great power, and has wrought so many miracles among the children of men, how is it that he can not instruct me that I should build a ship?

160 ¶And it came to pass that I, Nephi, said many things unto my brethren, insomuch that they were confounded, and could not contend against me;

161 Neither durst they lay their hands upon me, nor touch me with their fingers, even for the space of many days.

162 Now they durst not do this, lest they should wither before me, so powerful was the Spirit of God; and thus it had wrought upon them.

163 ¶And it came to pass that the Lord said unto me, Stretch forth thine hand again unto thy brethren, and they shall not wither before thee, but I will shock them, saith the Lord; and this will I do that they may know that I am the Lord their God.

164 ¶And it came to pass that I stretched forth my hand unto my brethren, and they did not wither before me; but the Lord did shake them, even according to the word which he had spoken.

165 And now they said, We know of a surety that the Lord is with thee, for we know that it is the power of the Lord that has shaken us.

166 And they fell down before me, and were about to

worship me, but I would not suffer them, saying, I am thy brother, yea, even thy younger brother;

167 Wherefore worship the Lord thy God, and honor thy father and thy mother, that thy days may be long in the land which the Lord thy God shall give thee.

168 ¶And it came to pass that they did worship the Lord, and did go forth with me; and we did work timbers of curious workmanship.

169 And the Lord did shew me from time to time after what manner I should work the timbers of the ship.

170 Now I, Nephi, did not work the timbers after the manner which was learned by men, neither did I build the ship after the manner of men;

171 But I did build it after the manner which the Lord had shewn unto me; wherefore, it was not after the manner of men.

172 ¶And I, Nephi, did go into the mount oft, and I did pray oft unto the Lord; wherefore, the Lord shewed unto me great things.

173 ¶And it came to pass that after I had finished the ship according to the word of the Lord, my brethren beheld that it was good, and that the workmanship thereof was exceeding fine;

174 Wherefore, they did humble themselves again before the Lord.

175 ¶And it came to pass that the voice of the Lord came unto my father, that we should arise and go down into the ship.

176 And it came to pass that on the morrow, after we had prepared all things, much fruits and meat from the wilderness, and honey in abundance, and provisions, according to that which the Lord had commanded us,

177 We did go down into the ship with all our loading and our seeds, and whatsoever thing we had brought with us, every one according to his age;

178 Wherefore, we did all go down into the ship, with our wives and our children.

CHAP. 5.] FIRST BOOK OF NEPHI. 61

179 ¶And now, my father had begat two sons in the wilderness; the eldest was called Jacob, and the younger, Joseph.

180 And it came to pass after we had all gone down into the ship, and had taken with us our provisions and things which had been commanded us,

181 We did put forth into the sea, and were driven forth before the wind, towards the promised land;

182 And after we had been driven forth before the wind for the space of many days, behold, my brethren, and the sons of Ishmael, and also their wives, began to make themselves merry, insomuch that they began to dance, and to sing, and to speak with much rudeness,

183 Yea, even that they did forget by what power they had been brought thither;

184 Yea, they were lifted up unto exceeding rudeness.

185 And I, Nephi, began to fear exceedingly, lest the Lord should be angry with us, and smite us, because of our iniquity, that we should be swallowed up in the depths of the sea;

186 Wherefore, I, Nephi, began to speak to them with much soberness;

187 But behold, they were angry with me, saying, We will not that our younger brother shall be a ruler over us.

188 ¶And it came to pass that Laman and Lemuel did take me and bind me with cords, and they did treat me with much harshness;

189 Nevertheless, the Lord did suffer it, that he might shew forth his power, unto the fulfilling of his word which he had spoken concerning the wicked.

190 ¶And it came to pass that after they had bound me, insomuch that I could not move, the compass, which had been prepared of the Lord, did cease to work;

191 Wherefore, they knew not whither they should steer the ship, insomuch, that there arose a great storm, yea, a great and terrible tempest;

192 And we were driven back upon the waters for the space of three days;

193 And they began to be frightened exceedingly, lest they should be drowned in the sea;

194 Nevertheless, they did not loose me.

195 And on the fourth day which we had been driven back, the tempest began to be exceeding sore.

196 ¶And it came to pass that we were about to be swallowed up in the depths of the sea.

197 And after we had been driven back upon the waters for the space of four days, my brethren began to see that the judgments of God were upon them, and that they must perish, save that they should repent of their iniquities;

198 Wherefore, they came unto me and loosed the bands which were upon my wrists, and behold, they had swollen exceedingly; and also mine ankles were much swollen, and great was the soreness thereof.

199 Nevertheless, I did look unto my God, and I did praise him all the day long; and I did not murmur against the Lord because of mine afflictions.

200 ¶Now, my father Lehi, had said many things unto them, and also unto the sons of Ishmael; but behold, they did breathe out much threatenings against any one that should speak for me;

201 And my parents being stricken in years, and having suffered much grief because of their children, they were brought down, yea, even upon their sick beds.

202 Because of their grief, and much sorrow, and the iniquity of my brethren, they were brought near even to be carried out of this time, to meet their God;

203 Yea, their grey hairs were about to be brought down to lie low in the dust;

204 Yea, even they were near to be cast, with sorrow, into a watery grave.

205 And Jacob and Joseph also, being young, having need of much nourishment, were grieved because of the afflictions of their mother;

206 And also my wife, with her tears and prayers, and

CHAP. 5.] FIRST BOOK OF NEPHI. 63

also my children, did not soften the hearts of my brethren, that they would loose me;

207 And there was nothing, save it were the power of God, which threatened them with destruction, could soften their hearts;

208 Wherefore, when they saw that they were about to be swallowed up in the depths of the sea, they repented of the thing which they had done, insomuch that they loosed me.

209 ¶And it came to pass after they had loosed me, behold, I took the compass, and it did work whither I desired it.

210 And it came to pass that I prayed unto the Lord; and after I had prayed, the winds did cease, and the storm did cease, and there was a great calm.

211 ¶And it came to pass that I, Nephi, did guide the ship, that we sailed again towards the promised land.

212 And it came to pass that after we had sailed for the space of many days, we did arrive to the promised land;

213 And we went forth upon the land, and did pitch our tents; and we did call it the promised land.

214 ¶And it came to pass that we did begin to till the earth, and we began to plant seeds; yea, we did put all our seeds into the earth, which we had brought from the land of Jerusalem.

215 And it came to pass that they did grow exceedingly; wherefore, we were blessed in abundance.

216 ¶And it came to pass that we did find upon the land of promise, as we journeyed in the wilderness, that there were beasts in the forests of every kind, both the cow, and the ox, and the ass, and the horse, and the goat, and the wild goat, and all manner of wild animals, which were for the use of men.

217 And we did find all manner of ore, both of gold, and of silver, and of copper.

218 ¶And it came to pass that the Lord commanded me, wherefore I did make plates of ore, that I might engraven upon them the record of my people.

219 And upon the plates which I made, I did engraven the

record of my father, and also our journeyings in the wilderness, and the prophecies of my father; and also many of mine own prophecies have I engraven upon them.

220 And I knew not at the time when I made them, that I should be commanded of the Lord to make these plates;

221 Wherefore, the record of my father, and the genealogy of his forefathers, and the more part of all our proceedings in the wilderness, are engraven upon those plates of which I have spoken;

222 Wherefore, the things which transpired before I made these plates, are, of a truth, more particularly made mention upon the first plates.

223 ¶And after I had made these plates by way of commandment, I, Nephi, received a commandment, that the ministry, and the prophecies, the more plain and precious parts of them should be written upon these plates;

224 And that the things which were written, should be kept for the instruction of my people, who should possess the land, and also for other wise purposes, which purposes are known unto the Lord;

225 Wherefore I, Nephi, did make a record upon the other plates, which gives an account, or which gives a greater account of the wars and contentions and destructions of my people.

226 And this have I done, and commanded my people what they should do, after I was gone, and that these plates should be handed down from one generation to another, or from one prophet to another, until further commandments of the Lord.

227 And an account of my making these plates shall be given hereafter;

228 And then, behold, I proceed according to that which I have spoken; and this I do, that the more sacred things may be kept for the knowledge of my people.

229 Nevertheless, I do not write anything upon plates, save it be that I think it be sacred.

230 And now, if I do err, even did they err of old.

231 Not that I would excuse myself because of other men,

CHAP. 5.] FIRST BOOK OF NEPHI. 65

but because of the weakness which is in me, according to the flesh, I would excuse myself.

232 For the things which some men esteem to be of great worth, both to the body and soul, others set at nought, and trample under their feet.

233 Yea, even the very God of Israel, do men trample under their feet;

234 I say, trample under their feet; but I would speak in other words:

235 They set him at nought, and hearken not to the voice of his counsels;

236 And behold, he cometh according to the words of the angel, in six hundred years from the time my father left Jerusalem.

237 And the world, because of their iniquity, shall judge him to be a thing of nought; wherefore, they scourge him, and he suffereth it; and they smite him, and he suffereth it.

238 Yea, they spit upon him, and he suffereth it, because of his loving kindness and his long-suffering towards the children of men.

239 And the God of our fathers, who were led out of Egypt, out of bondage, and also were preserved in the wilderness by him;

240 Yea, the God of Abraham, and of Isaac, and the God of Jacob, yieldeth himself according to the words of the angel, as a man, into the hands of wicked men, to be lifted up according to the words of Zenock,

241 And to be crucified, according to the words of Neum,

242 And to be buried in a sepulcher, according to the words of Zenos, which he spake concerning the three days of darkness,

243 Which should be a sign given of his death, unto those who should inhabit the isles of the sea;

244 More especially given unto those who are of the house of Israel.

245 For thus spake the prophet, The Lord God surely shall visit all the house of Israel at that day;

246 Some with his voice, because of their righteousness, unto their great joy and salvation;

247 And others with the thunderings and the lightnings of his power, by tempest, by fire, and by smoke, and vapor of darkness, and by the opening of the earth, and by mountains which shall be carried up;

248 And all these things must surely come, saith the prophet Zenos.

249 And the rocks of the earth must rend;

250 And because of the groanings of the earth, many of the kings of the isles of the sea shall be wrought upon by the Spirit of God, to exclaim, The God of nature suffers.

251 And as for those who are at Jerusalem, saith the prophet, shall be scourged by all people, because they crucify the God of Israel, and turn their hearts aside, rejecting signs and wonders, and power and glory of the God of Israel;

252 And because they turn their hearts aside, saith the prophet, and have despised the Holy One of Israel, they shall wander in the flesh, and perish, and become a hiss and a byword, and be hated among all nations;

253 Nevertheless, when that day cometh, saith the prophet, that they no more turn aside their hearts against the Holy One of Israel, then will he remember the covenants which he made to their fathers;

254 Yea, then will he remember the isles of the sea;

255 Yea, and all the people who are of the house of Israel, will I gather in, saith the Lord, according to the words of the prophet Zenos, from the four quarters of the earth;

256 Yea, and all the earth shall see the salvation of the Lord, saith the prophet;

257 Every nation, kindred, tongue and people, shall be blessed.

258 ¶And I, Nephi, have written these things unto my people, that perhaps I might persuade them that they would remember the Lord their Redeemer;

259 Wherefore, I speak unto all the house of Israel, if it so be that they should obtain these things.

260 For behold, I have workings in the spirit, which doth weary me, even that all my joints are weak, for those who are at Jerusalem;

261 For had not the Lord been merciful, to shew unto me concerning them, even as he had prophets of old, I should have perished also;

262 And he surely did shew unto the prophets of old, all things concerning them;

263 And also he did shew unto many concerning us;

264 Wherefore, it must needs be, that we know concerning them, for they are written upon the plates of brass.

CHAPTER 6.

1 ¶Now it came to pass that I, Nephi, did teach my brethren these things.

2 And it came to pass that I did read many things to them, which were engraven upon the plates of brass, that they might know concerning the doings of the Lord in other lands, among people of old.

3 And I did read many things unto them, which were written in the book of Moses;

4 But that I might more fully persuade them to believe in the Lord their Redeemer, I did read unto them that which was written by the prophet Isaiah;

5 For I did liken all scriptures unto us that it might be for our profit and learning.

6 Wherefore, I spake unto them, saying, Hear ye the words of the prophet, ye who are a remnant of the house of Israel, a branch who have been broken off; hear ye the words of the prophet, which were written unto all the house of Israel, and liken them unto yourselves, that ye may have hope as well as your brethren, from whom ye have been broken off.

7 For after this manner has the prophet written:

8 [1]Hearken and hear this, O house of Jacob, who are called

[1]Isaiah 48.

by the name of Israel, and are come forth out of the waters of Judah, who swear by the name of the Lord, and make mention of the God of Israel; yet they swear not in truth, nor in righteousness.

9 Nevertheless, they call themselves of the Holy city, but they do not stay themselves upon the God of Israel, who is the Lord of hosts; yea, the Lord of hosts is his name.

10 Behold, I have declared the former things from the beginning; and they went forth out of my mouth, and I shewed them; I did shew them suddenly.

11 And I did it because I knew that thou art obstinate, and thy neck was an iron sinew, and thy brow brass;

12 And I have, even from the beginning, declared to thee; before it came to pass I shewed them thee; and I shewed them for fear lest thou shouldst say, Mine idol hath done them, and my graven image, and my molten image hath commanded them.

13 Thou hast seen and heard all this; and will ye not declare them? And that I have shewed thee new things from this time, even hidden things, and thou didst not know them.

14 They are created now, and not from the beginning; even before the day when thou heardest them not, they were declared unto thee, lest thou shouldst say, Behold, I knew them.

15 Yea, and thou heardest not; yea, thou knewest not; yea, from that time thine ear was not opened; for I knew that thou wouldst deal very treacherously, and wast called a transgressor from the womb.

16 ¶Nevertheless, for my name's sake will I defer mine anger, and for my praise will I refrain from thee, that I cut thee not off.

17 For, behold, I have refined thee; I have chosen thee in the furnace of affliction.

18 For mine own sake, yea, for mine own sake, will I do this; for I will not suffer my name to be polluted, and I will not give my glory unto another.

19 ¶Hearken unto me, O Jacob, and Israel, my called; for I am he; I am the first, and I am also the last.

20 Mine hand hath also laid the foundation of the earth, and my right hand hath spanned the heavens; I call unto them, and they stand up together.

21 All ye, assemble yourselves, and hear; who among them hath declared these things unto them? The Lord hath loved him; yea, and he will fulfill his word which he hath declared by them; and he will do his pleasure on Babylon, and his arm shall come upon the Chaldeans.

22 Also, saith the Lord: I the Lord, yea, I have spoken; yea, I have called him, to declare, I have brought him, and he shall make his way prosperous.

23 ¶Come ye near unto me: I have not spoken in secret from the beginning; from the time that it was declared, have I spoken; and the Lord God, and his Spirit hath sent me.

24 And thus saith the Lord, thy Redeemer, the Holy One of Israel: I have sent him, the Lord thy God who teacheth thee to profit, who leadeth thee by the way thou shouldst go, has done it.

25 O that thou hadst hearkened to my commandment! then had thy peace been as a river, and thy righteousness as the waves of the sea;

26 Thy seed also had been as the sand; the offspring of thy bowels like the gravel thereof: his name should not have been cut off nor destroyed from before me.

27 ¶Go ye forth of Babylon, flee ye from the Chaldeans, with a voice of singing declare ye, tell this, utter to the end of the earth; say ye, The Lord hath redeemed his servant Jacob.

28 And they thirsted not; he led them through the deserts: he caused the waters to flow out of the rock for them: he clave the rock also, and the waters gushed out.

29 And notwithstanding he hath done all this, and greater also, there is no peace, saith the Lord, unto the wicked.

30 ¶And again: Hearken, O ye house of Israel, all ye that are broken off and are driven out, because of the wicked-

ness of the pastors of my people; yea, all ye that are broken off, that are scattered abroad, who are of my people, O house of Israel.

31 ²Listen O isles, unto me; and hearken, ye people, from far; the Lord hath called me from the womb; from the bowels of my mother hath he made mention of my name.

32 And he hath made my mouth like a sharp sword; in the shadow of his hand hath he hid me, and made me a polished shaft: in his quiver hath he hid me,

33 And said unto me, Thou art my servant, O Israel, in whom I will be glorified.

34 Then I said, I have labored in vain, I have spent my strength for nought, and in vain; surely, my judgment is with the Lord, and my work with my God.

35 ¶And now, saith the Lord, that formed me from the womb that I should be his servant, to bring Jacob again to him: Though Israel be not gathered, yet shall I be glorious in the eyes of the Lord, and my God shall be my strength.

36 And he said, It is a light thing that thou shouldst be my servant to raise up the tribes of Jacob, and to restore the preserved of Israel. I will also give thee for a light to the Gentiles, that thou mayest be my salvation unto the ends of the earth.

37 Thus saith the Lord, the Redeemer of Israel, his Holy One, to him whom man despiseth, to him whom the nations abhorreth, to servant of rulers, kings shall see and arise, princes also shall worship, because of the Lord that is faithful.

38 Thus saith the Lord, In an acceptable time have I heard thee, O isles of the sea, and in a day of salvation have I helped thee: and I will preserve thee, and give thee my servant for a covenant of the people, to establish the earth, to cause to inherit the desolate heritages;

39 That thou mayest say to the prisoners, Go forth; to

²Isaiah 49.

them that sit in darkness, Shew yourselves. They shall feed in the ways, and their pastures shall be in all high places.

40 They shall not hunger nor thirst, neither shall the heat nor the sun smite them; for he that hath mercy on them shall lead them, even by the springs of water shall he guide them.

41 And I will make all my mountains a way, and my highways shall be exalted.

42 And then, O house of Israel, behold, these shall come from far; and lo, these from the north and from the west; and these from the land of Sinim.

43 ¶Sing, O heavens; and be joyful, O earth; for the feet of those who are in the east shall be established; and break forth into singing, O mountains; for they shall be smitten no more: for the Lord hath comforted his people, and will have mercy upon his afflicted.

44 But behold, Zion hath said, The Lord hath forsaken me, and my Lord hath forgotten me; but he will shew that he hath not.

45 For can a woman forget her sucking child, that she should not have compassion on the son of her womb? Yea, they may forget, yet will I not forget thee, O house of Israel.

46 Behold, I have graven thee upon the palms of my hands; thy walls are continually before me.

47 Thy children shall make haste against thy destroyers; and they that made thee waste shall go forth of thee.

48 ¶Lift up thine eyes round about, and behold: all these gather themselves together, and they shall come to thee. And as I live, saith the Lord, thou shalt surely clothe thee with them all, as with an ornament, and bind them on even as a bride.

49 For thy waste and thy desolate places, and the land of thy destruction, shall even now be too narrow by reason of the inhabitants; and they that swallowed thee up, shall be far away.

50 The children whom thou shalt have, after thou hast lost the first, shall again in thine ears say, The place is too straight for me: give place to me that I may dwell.

51 Then shalt thou say in thine heart, Who hath begotten me these, seeing I have lost my children, and am desolate, a captive, and removing to and fro? and who hath brought up these? Behold, I was left alone; these, where have they been?

52 Thus saith the Lord God, Behold, I will lift up mine hand to the Gentiles, and set up my standard to the people; and they shall bring thy sons in their arms, and thy daughters shall be carried upon their shoulders.

53 And kings shall be thy nursing fathers, and their queens thy nursing mothers: they shall bow down to thee with their face towards the earth, and lick up the dust of thy feet; and thou shalt know that I am the Lord: for they shall not be ashamed that wait for me.

54 For shall the prey be taken from the mighty, or the lawful captives delivered?

55 But thus saith the Lord, Even the captives of the mighty shall be taken away, and the prey of the terrible shall be delivered: for I will contend with him that contendeth with thee, and I will save thy children.

56 And I will feed them that oppress thee with their own flesh: they shall be drunken with their own blood, as with sweet wine: and all flesh shall know that I the Lord am thy Savior and thy Redeemer, the mighty one of Jacob.

CHAPTER 7.

1 ¶And now it came to pass that after I, Nephi, had read these things which were engraven upon the plates of brass, my brethren came unto me and said unto me, What meaneth these things which ye have read?

2 Behold, are they to be understood according to the things which are spiritual, which shall come to pass according to the spirit and not the flesh?

3 And I, Nephi, said unto them, Behold, they were made manifest unto the prophet, by the voice of the Spirit:

4 For by the Spirit are all things made known unto the

prophets, which shall come upon the children of men according to the flesh.

5 Wherefore, the things of which I have read, are things pertaining to things both temporal and spiritual:

6 For it appears that the house of Israel, sooner or later, will be scattered upon all the face of the earth, and also among all nations,

7 And behold there are many who are already lost from the knowledge of those who are at Jerusalem.

8 Yea, the more part of all the tribes have been led away;

9 And they are scattered to and fro upon the isles of the sea;

10 And whither they are, none of us knoweth, save that we know that they have been led away.

11 And since they have been led away, these things have been prophesied concerning them, and also concerning all those who shall hereafter be scattered and be confounded, because of the Holy One of Israel; for against him will they harden their hearts;

12 Wherefore, they shall be scattered among all nations, and shall be hated of all men.

13 Nevertheless, after they have been nursed by the Gentiles, and the Lord has lifted up his hand upon the Gentiles and set them up for a standard, and their children have been carried in their arms, and their daughters have been carried upon their shoulders, behold, these things of which are spoken, are temporal: for thus are the covenants of the Lord with our fathers;

14 And it meaneth us in the days to come, and also all our brethren who are of the house of Israel.

15 And it meaneth that the time cometh that after all the house of Israel have been scattered and confounded, that the Lord God will raise up a mighty nation among the Gentiles, yea, even upon the face of this land;

16 And by them shall our seed be scattered.

17 And after our seed is scattered, the Lord God will pro-

ceed to do a marvelous work among the Gentiles, which shall be of great worth unto our seed;

18 Wherefore, it is likened unto their being nourished by the Gentiles, and being carried in their arms, and upon their shoulders.

19 And it shall also be of worth unto the Gentiles:

20 And not only unto the Gentiles, but unto all the house of Israel, unto the making known of the covenants of the Father of heaven unto Abraham, saying, In thy seed shall all the kindreds of the earth be blessed.

21 And I would, my brethren, that ye should know that all the kindreds of the earth can not be blessed unless he shall make bare his arm in the eyes of the nations.

22 Wherefore, the Lord God will proceed to make bare his arm in the eyes of all the nations, in bringing about his covenants and his gospel, unto those who are of the house of Israel.

23 Wherefore, he will bring them again out of captivity, and they shall be gathered together to the lands of their inheritance;

24 And they shall be brought out of obscurity, and out of darkness;

25 And they shall know that the Lord is their Savior and their Redeemer, the mighty one of Israel.

26 And the blood of that great and abominable church, which is the whore of all the earth, shall turn upon their own heads;

27 For they shall war among themselves, and the sword of their own hands shall fall upon their own heads, and they shall be drunken with their own blood.

28 And every nation which shall war against thee, O house of Israel, shall be turned one against another,

29 And they shall fall into the pit which they digged to ensnare the people of the Lord.

30 And all that fight against Zion, shall be destroyed.

31 And that great whore, who hath perverted the right ways of the Lord; yea, that great and abominable church, shall tumble to the dust, and great shall be the fall of it.

32 For behold, saith the prophet, The time cometh speedily, that Satan shall have no more power over the hearts of the children of men:

33 For the day soon cometh, that all the proud and they who do wickedly, shall be as stubble; and the day cometh that they must be burned.

34 For the time soon cometh, that the fullness of the wrath of God shall be poured out upon all the children of men:

35 For he will not suffer that the wicked shall destroy the righteous.

36 Wherefore, he will preserve the righteous by his power, even if it be so that the fullness of his wrath must come, and the righteous be preserved, even unto the destruction of their enemies by fire.

37 Wherefore, the righteous need not fear; for thus saith the prophet, They shall be saved, even if it so be as by fire.

38 Behold, my brethren, I say unto you, that these things must shortly come; yea, even blood, and fire, and vapor of smoke must come;

39 And it must needs be upon the face of this earth;

40 And it cometh unto men according to the flesh, if it so be that they will harden their hearts against the Holy One of Israel:

41 For behold, the righteous shall not perish; .

42 For the time surely must come, that all they who fight against Zion, shall be cut off.

43 And the Lord will surely prepare a way for his people, unto the fulfilling of the words of Moses, which he spake, saying:

44 A prophet shall the Lord your God raise up unto you, like unto me; him shall ye hear in all things whatsoever he shall say unto you.

45 And it shall come to pass that all those who will not hear that prophet, shall be cut off from among the people.

46 And now I, Nephi, declare unto you, that this prophet of whom Moses spake, was the Holy One of Israel;

47 Wherefore, he shall execute judgment in righteousness;

48 And the righteous need not fear, for they are those who shall not be confounded.

49 But it is the kingdom of the devil which shall be built up among the children of men, which kingdom is established among them which are in the flesh:

50 For the time speedily shall come, that all churches which are built up to get gain, and all those who are built up to get power over the flesh, and those who are built up to become popular in the eyes of the world, and those who seek the lusts of the flesh and the things of the world, and to do all manner of iniquity;

51 Yea, in fine, all those who belong to the kingdom of the devil, are they who need fear, and tremble, and quake;

52 They are those who must be brought low in the dust;

53 They are those who must be consumed as stubble:

54 And this is according to the words of the prophet.

55 And the time cometh speedily, that the righteous must be led up as calves of the stall, and the Holy One of Israel must reign in dominion, and might, and power, and great glory.

56 And he gathereth his children from the four quarters of the earth;

57 And he numbereth his sheep, and they know him;

58 And there shall be one fold and one shepherd:

59 And he shall feed his sheep, and in him they shall find pasture.

60 And because of the righteousness of his people, Satan has no power;

61 Wherefore, he can not be loosed for the space of many years;

62 For he hath no power over the hearts of the people, for they dwell in righteousness, and the Holy One of Israel reigneth.

63 And now behold, I, Nephi, say unto you, that all these things must come according to the flesh.

64 But, behold, all nations, kindreds, tongues, and people, shall dwell safely in the Holy One of Israel, if it so be that they will repent.

65 ¶And now I, Nephi, make an end; for I durst not speak further as yet, concerning these things.

66 Wherefore, my brethren, I would that ye should consider that the things which have been written upon the plates of brass, are true;

67 And they testify that a man must be obedient to the commandments of God.

68 Wherefore, ye need not suppose that I and my father are the only ones that have testified, and also taught them.

69 Wherefore, if ye shall be obedient to the commandments, and endure to the end, ye shall be saved at the last day.

70 And thus it is. Amen.

THE SECOND BOOK OF NEPHI.

CHAPTER 1.

An account of the death of Lehi. Nephi's brethren rebelleth against him. The Lord warns Nephi to depart into the wilderness. His journeyings in the wilderness, &c.

1 ¶And now it came to pass after I, Nephi, had made an end of teaching my brethren, our father, Lehi, also spake many things unto them, how great things the Lord had done for them, in bringing them out of the land of Jerusalem.

2 And he spake unto them concerning their rebellions upon the waters, and the mercies of God in sparing their lives, that they were not swallowed up in the sea.

3 And he also spake unto them concerning the land of promise which they had obtained, how merciful the Lord had been in warning us that we should flee out of the land of Jerusalem.

4 For, behold, said he, I have seen a vision, in which I know that Jerusalem is destroyed;

5 And had we remained in Jerusalem, we should also have perished.

6 But, said he, notwithstanding our afflictions, we have obtained a land of promise, a land which is choice above all other lands;

7 A land which the Lord God hath covenanted with me should be a land for the inheritance of my seed.

8 Yea, the Lord hath covenanted this land unto me, and to my children for ever;

9 And also all those who should be led out of other countries, by the hand of the Lord.

10 Wherefore, I, Lehi, prophesy according to the workings of the Spirit which is in me, that there shall none come into this land, save they shall be brought by the hand of the Lord.

11 Wherefore, this land is consecrated unto him whom he shall bring.

12 And if it so be that they shall serve him according to the commandments which he hath given, it shall be a land of liberty unto them;

13 Wherefore, they shall never be brought down into captivity: if so, it shall be because of iniquity:

14 For if iniquity shall abound, cursed shall be the land for their sakes;

15 But unto the righteous, it shall be blessed for ever.

16 And behold, it is wisdom that this land should be kept as yet from the knowledge of other nations;

17 For, behold, many nations would overrun the land, that there would be no place for an inheritance.

18 Wherefore, I, Lehi, have obtained a promise, that inasmuch as those whom the Lord God shall bring out of the land of Jerusalem shall keep his commandments, they shall prosper upon the face of this land;

19 And they shall be kept from all other nations, that they may possess this land unto themselves.

20 And if it so be that they shall keep his commandments, they shall be blessed upon the face of this land,

21 And there shall be none to molest them, nor to take away the land of their inheritance; and they shall dwell safely for ever.

CHAP. 1.] SECOND BOOK OF NEPHI. 79

22 But behold, when the time cometh that they shall dwindle in unbelief, after they have received so great blessings from the hand of the Lord; having a knowledge of the creation of the earth, and all men, knowing the great and marvelous works of the Lord from the creation of the world; having power given them to do all things by faith; having all the commandments from the beginning, and having been brought by his infinite goodness into this precious land of promise;

23 Behold, I say, If the day shall come that they will reject the Holy One of Israel, the true Messiah, their Redeemer and their God, behold, the judgments of him that is just, shall rest upon them;

24 Yea, he will bring other nations unto them, and he will give unto them power, and he will take away from them the lands of their possessions, and he will cause them to be scattered and smitten.

25 Yea, as one generation passeth to another, there shall be bloodsheds and great visitations among them;

26 Wherefore, my sons, I would that ye would remember; yea, I would that ye would hearken unto my words.

27 O that ye would awake; awake from a deep sleep, yea, even from the sleep of hell, and shake off the awful chains by which ye are bound, which are the chains which bind the children of men, that they are carried away captive down to the eternal gulf of misery and wo!

28 Awake! and rise from the dust, and hear the words of a trembling parent, whose limbs ye must soon lay down in the cold and silent grave, from whence no traveler can return; a few more days, and I go the way of all the earth.

29 But behold, the Lord hath redeemed my soul from hell: I have beheld his glory, and I am encircled about eternally in the arms of his love.

30 And I desire that ye should remember to observe the statutes and the judgments of the Lord: behold, this hath been the anxiety of my soul, from the beginning.

31 My heart hath been weighed down with sorrow from

time to time; for I have feared, lest for the hardness of your hearts, the Lord your God should come out in the fullness of his wrath upon you, that ye be cut off and destroyed for ever;

32 Or that a cursing should come upon you for the space of many generations; and ye are visited by sword, and by famine, and are hated, and are led according to the will and captivity of the devil.

33 O my sons, that these things might not come upon you, but that ye might be a choice and a favored people of the Lord!

34 But behold, his will be done: for his ways are righteousness for ever; and he hath said that, Inasmuch as ye shall keep my commandments ye shall prosper in the land; but inasmuch as ye will not keep my commandments ye shall be cut off from my presence.

35 And now that my soul might have joy in you, and that my heart might leave this world with gladness because of you; that I might not be brought down with grief and sorrow to the grave,

36 Arise from the dust, my sons, and be men, and be determined in one mind, and in one heart united in all things, that ye may not come down into captivity; that ye may not be cursed with a sore cursing;

37 And also, that ye may not incur the displeasure of a just God upon you, unto the destruction, yea, the eternal destruction of both soul and body.

38 Awake, my sons: put on the armor of righteousness.

39 Shake off the chains with which ye are bound, and come forth out of obscurity, and arise from the dust.

40 Rebel no more against your brother, whose views have been glorious, and who hath kept the commandments from the time that we left Jerusalem, and who hath been an instrument in the hands of God in bringing us forth into the land of promise;

41 For were it not for him we must have perished with hunger in the wilderness;

42 Nevertheless, ye sought to take away his life; yea, and he hath suffered much sorrow because of you.

43 And I exceedingly fear and tremble because of you, lest he shall suffer again;

44 For behold, ye have accused him that he sought power and authority over you;

45 But I know that he hath not sought for power nor authority over you; but he hath sought the glory of God, and your own eternal welfare.

46 And ye have murmured because he hath been plain unto you.

47 Ye say that he hath used sharpness; ye say that he hath been angry with you.

48 But behold, his sharpness was the sharpness of the power of the word of God, which was in him;

49 And that which ye call anger, was the truth, according to that which is in God, which he could not restrain, manifesting boldly concerning your iniquities.

50 And it must needs be that the power of God must be with him, even unto his commanding you, that ye must obey.

51 But behold, it was not him, but it was the Spirit of the Lord which was in him, which opened his mouth to utterance, that he could not shut it.

52 ¶And now my son Laman and also Lemuel and Sam, and also my sons who are the sons of Ishmael, behold, if ye will hearken unto the voice of Nephi, ye shall not perish.

53 And if ye will hearken unto him, I leave unto you a blessing, yea, even my first blessing.

54 But if ye will not hearken unto him, I take away my first blessing, yea, even my blessing, and it shall rest upon him.

55 And now, Zoram, I speak unto you: Behold, thou art the servant of Laban; nevertheless, thou hast been brought out of the land of Jerusalem, and I know that thou art a true friend unto my son Nephi, for ever.

56 Wherefore, because thou hast beeen faithful, thy seed

shall be blessed with his seed, that they dwell in prosperity long upon the face of this land;

57 And nothing, save it shall be iniquity among them, shall harm or disturb their prosperity upon the face of this land for ever.

58 Wherefore, if ye shall keep the commandments of the Lord, the Lord hath consecrated this land for the security of thy seed with the seed of my son.

59 And now, Jacob, I speak unto you: Thou art my first born in the days of my tribulation in the wilderness.

60 And behold, in thy childhood thou hast suffered afflictions and much sorrow, because of the rudeness of thy brethren.

61 Nevertheless, Jacob, my first born in the wilderness, thou knowest the greatness of God; and he shall consecrate thine afflictions for thy gain.

62 Wherefore thy soul shall be blessed, and thou shalt dwell safely with thy brother Nephi; and thy days shall be spent in the service of thy God.

63 Wherefore, I know that thou art redeemed, because of the righteousness of thy Redeemer: for thou hast beheld, that in the fullness of time, he cometh to bring salvation unto men.

64 And thou hast beheld in thy youth his glory; wherefore, thou art blessed even as they unto whom he shall minister in the flesh:

65 For the Spirit is the same, yesterday, to-day, and for ever.

66 And the way is prepared from the fall of man, and salvation is free.

67 And men are instructed sufficiently, that they know good from evil.

68 And the law is given unto men.

69 And by the law, no flesh is justified; or, by the law, men are cut off.

70 Yea, by the temporal law, they were cut off; and also

by the spiritual law they perish from that which is good, and become miserable for ever.

71 Wherefore, redemption cometh in and through the holy Messiah: for he is full of grace and truth.

72 Behold, he offereth himself a sacrifice for sin, to answer the ends of the law, unto all those who have a broken heart and a contrite spirit; and unto none else can the ends of the law be answered.

73 Wherefore, how great the importance to make these things known unto the inhabitants of the earth, that they may know that there is no flesh that can dwell in the presence of God, save it be through the merits, and mercy, and grace of the holy Messiah,

74 Who layeth down his life according to the flesh, and taketh it again by the power of the Spirit,

75 That he may bring to pass the resurrection of the dead, being the first that should rise.

76 Wherefore, he is the first fruits unto God, inasmuch as he shall make intercession for all the children of men;

77 And they that believe in him, shall be saved.

78 And because of the intercession for all, all men come unto God;

79 Wherefore, they stand in the presence of him, to be judged of him, according to the truth and holiness which is in him.

80 Wherefore, the ends of the law which the Holy One hath given, unto the inflicting of the punishment which is affixed, which punishment that is affixed is in opposition to that of the happiness which is affixed, to answer the ends of the atonement;

81 For it must needs be, that there is an opposition in all things.

82 If not so, my first born in the wilderness, righteousness could not be brought to pass; neither wickedness; neither holiness nor misery; neither good nor bad.

83 Wherefore, all things must needs be a compound in one;

84 Wherefore, if it should be one body, it must needs

remain as dead, having no life, neither death nor corruption, nor incorruption, happiness nor misery, neither sense nor insensibility.

85 Wherefore, it must needs have been created for a thing of nought;

86 Wherefore, there would have been no purpose in the end of its creation.

87 Wherefore, this thing must needs destroy the wisdom of God, and his eternal purposes; and also, the power, and the mercy, and the justice of God.

88 And if ye shall say there is no law, ye shall also say there is no sin.

89 And if ye shall say there is no sin, ye shall also say there is no righteousness.

90 And if there be no righteousness, there be no happiness.

91 And if there be no righteousness nor happiness, there be no punishment nor misery.

92 And if these things are not, there is no God.

93 And if there is no God, we are not, neither the earth, for there could have been no creation of things, neither to act nor to be acted upon; wherefore, all things must have vanished away.

94 ¶And now, my son, I speak unto you these things, for your profit and learning:

95 For there is a God, and he hath created all things, both the heavens and the earth, and all things that in them is;

96 Both things to act, and things to be acted upon;

97 And to bring about his eternal purposes in the end of man, after he had created our first parents, and the beasts of the field and the fowls of the air, and in fine, all things which are created, it must needs be that there was an opposition;

98 Even the forbidden fruit in opposition to the tree of life; the one being sweet and the other bitter;

99 Wherefore, the Lord God gave unto man, that he should act for himself.

100 Wherefore, man could not act for himself, save it should be that he was enticed by the one or the other.

101 ¶And I, Lehi, according to the things which I have read, must needs suppose that an angel of God, according to that which is written, had fallen from heaven;

102 Wherefore he became a devil, having sought that which was evil before God.

103 And because he had fallen from heaven, and had become miserable for ever, he sought also the misery of all mankind.

104 Wherefore, he said unto Eve, yea, even that old serpent, who is the devil, who is the father of all lies; wherefore he said, Partake of the forbidden fruit, and ye shall not die, but ye shall be as God, knowing good and evil.

105 And after Adam and Eve had partaken of the forbidden fruit, they were driven out of the garden of Eden, to till the earth.

106 And they have brought forth children; yea, even the family of all the earth.

107 And the days of the children of men were prolonged, according to the will of God, that they might repent while in the flesh;

108 Wherefore, their state became a state of probation, and their time was lengthened, according to the commandments which the Lord God gave unto the children of men.

109 For he gave commandment that all men must repent;

110 For he shewed unto all men that they were lost, because of the transgression of their parents.

111 And now, behold, if Adam had not transgressed, he would not have fallen; but he would have remained in the garden of Eden.

112 And all things which were created, must have remained in the same state which they were, after they were created; and they must have remained for ever, and had no end.

113 And they would have had no children; wherefore, they would have remained in a state of innocence, having no joy, for they knew no misery; doing no good, for they knew no sin.

114 But behold, all things have been done in the wisdom of him who knoweth all things.

115 Adam fell, that men might be; and men are, that they might have joy.

116 And the Messiah cometh in the fullness of time, that he may redeem the children of men from the fall.

117 And because that they are redeemed from the fall, they have become free for ever, knowing good from evil;

118 To act for themselves, and not to be acted upon, save it be by the punishment of the Lord, at the great and last day, according to the commandments which God hath given.

119 Wherefore, men are free according to the flesh; and all things are given them which are expedient unto man.

120 And they are free to choose liberty and eternal life, through the great mediation of all men, or to choose captivity and death, according to the captivity and power of the devil:

121 For he seeketh that all men might be miserable like unto himself.

122 ¶And now, my sons, I would that ye should look to the great Mediator, and hearken unto his great commandments;

123 And be faithful unto his words, and choose eternal life, according to the will of his Holy Spirit,

124 And not choose eternal death, according to the will of the flesh and the evil which is therein,

125 Which giveth the spirit of the devil power to captivate, to bring you down to hell, that he may reign over you in his own kingdom.

126 ¶I have spoken these few words unto you all, my sons, in the last days of my probation;

127 And I have chosen the good part, according to the words of the prophet.

128 And I have none other object, save it be the everlasting welfare of your souls. Amen.

CHAPTER 2.

1 ¶And now I speak unto you, Joseph, my last born.

2 Thou wast born in the wilderness of mine afflictions; yea, in the days of my greatest sorrow did thy mother bear thee.

3 And may the Lord consecrate also unto thee this land, which is a most precious land, for thine inheritance and the inheritance of thy seed with thy brethren, for thy security for ever, if it so be that ye shall keep the commandments of the Holy One of Israel.

4 And now, Joseph, my last born, whom I have brought out of the wilderness of mine afflictions, may the Lord bless thee for ever, for thy seed shall not utterly be destroyed.

5 For behold, thou art the fruit of my loins; and I am a descendant of Joseph, who was carried captive into Egypt.

6 And great were the covenants of the Lord, which he made unto Joseph; wherefore, Joseph truly saw our day.

7 And he obtained a promise of the Lord, that out of the fruit of his loins, the Lord God would raise up a righteous branch unto the house of Israel;

8 Not the Messiah, but a branch which was to be broken off; nevertheless, to be remembered in the covenants of the Lord,

9 That the Messiah should be made manifest unto them in the latter days, in the spirit of power, unto the bringing of them out of darkness unto light; yea, out of hidden darkness and out of captivity unto freedom.

10 For Joseph truly testified, saying: A seer shall the Lord my God raise up, who shall be a choice seer unto the fruit of my loins.

11 Yea, Joseph truly said, Thus saith the Lord unto me: A choice seer will I raise up out of the fruit of thy loins; and he shall be esteemed highly among the fruit of thy loins.

12 And unto him will I give commandment, that he shall do a work for the fruit of thy loins, his brethren, which shall be of great worth unto them, even to the bringing of them to the knowledge of the covenants which I have made with thy fathers.

13 And I will give unto him a commandment, that he shall do none other work save the work which I shall command him.

14 And I will make him great in mine eyes: for he shall do my work.

15 And he shall be great like unto Moses, whom I have said I would raise up unto you, to deliver my people, O house of Israel.

16 And Moses will I raise up, to deliver thy people out of the land of Egypt.

17 But a seer will I raise up out of the fruit of thy loins; and unto him will I give power to bring forth my word unto the seed of thy loins;

18 And not to the bringing forth my word only, saith the Lord, but to the convincing them of my word, which shall have already gone forth among them.

19 Wherefore, the fruit of thy loins shall write; and the fruit of the loins of Judah shall write;

20 And that which shall be written by the fruit of thy loins, and also that which shall be written by the fruit of the loins of Judah, shall grow together,

21 Unto the confounding of false doctrines, and laying down of contentions, and establishing peace among the fruit of thy loins,

22 And bringing them to the knowledge of their fathers in the latter days;

23 And also to the knowledge of my covenants, saith the Lord.

24 And out of weakness he shall be made strong, in that day when my work shall commence among all my people, unto the restoring thee, O house of Israel, saith the Lord.

25 And thus prophesied Joseph, saying: Behold, that seer will the Lord bless;

26 And they that seek to destroy him, shall be confounded:

27 For this promise, of which I have obtained of the Lord, of the fruit of thy loins, shall be fulfilled.

28 Behold, I am sure of the fulfilling of this promise.

29 And his name shall be called after me; and it shall be after the name of his father.

30 And he shall be like unto me; for the thing which the Lord shall bring forth by his hand, by the power of the Lord shall bring my people unto salvation;

31 Yea, thus prophesied Joseph, I am sure of this thing, even as I am sure of the promise of Moses: for the Lord hath said unto me, I will preserve thy seed for ever.

32 And the Lord hath said, I will raise up a Moses; and I will give power unto him in a rod;

33 And I will give judgment unto him in writing.

34 Yet I will not loose his tongue, that he shall speak much: for I will not make him mighty in speaking.

35 But I will write unto him my law, by the finger of mine own hand; and I will make a spokesman for him.

36 And the Lord said unto me also, I will raise up unto the fruit of thy loins: and I will make for him a spokesman.

37 And I, behold, I will give unto him, that he shall write the writing of the fruit of thy loins, unto the fruit of thy loins; and the spokesman of thy loins shall declare it.

38 And the words which he shall write, shall be the words which are expedient in my wisdom should go forth unto the fruit of thy loins.

39 And it shall be as if the fruit of thy loins had cried unto them from the dust; for I know their faith.

40 And they shall cry from the dust; yea, even repentance unto their brethren, even after many generations have gone by them.

41 And it shall come to pass that their cry shall go, even according to the simpleness of their words.

42 Because of their faith, their words shall proceed forth out of my mouth unto their brethren, who are the fruit of thy loins;

43 And the weakness of their words will I make strong in their faith, unto the remembering of my covenant which I made unto thy fathers.

44 ¶And now, behold, my son Joseph, after this manner did my father of old prophesy.

45 Wherefore, because of this covenant thou art blessed:

for thy seed shall not be destroyed, for they shall hearken unto the words of the book.

46 And there shall raise up one mighty among them, who shall do much good, both in word and in deed, being an instrument in the hands of God, with exceeding faith,

47 To work mighty wonders, and do that thing which is great in the sight of God, unto the bringing to pass much restoration unto the house of Israel, and unto the seed of thy brethren.

48 And now, blessed art thou, Joseph.

49 Behold, thou art little; wherefore, hearken unto the words of thy brother Nephi, and it shall be done unto thee, even according to the words which I have spoken.

50 Remember the words of thy dying father. Amen.

CHAPTER 3.

1 ¶And now I, Nephi, speak concerning the prophecies of which my father hath spoken, concerning Joseph, who was carried into Egypt:

2 For behold, he truly prophesied concerning all his seed.

3 And the prophecies which he wrote, there are not many greater.

4 And he prophesied concerning us, and our future generations;

5 And they are written upon the plates of brass.

6 Wherefore, after my father had made an end of speaking concerning the prophecies of Joseph, he called the children of Laman, his sons, and his daughters, and said unto them,

7 Behold my sons, and my daughters, who are the sons and the daughters of my first born, I would that ye should give ear unto my words:

8 For the Lord God hath said, That inasmuch as ye shall keep my commandments, ye shall prosper in the land;

9 And inasmuch as ye will not keep my commandments, ye shall be cut off from my presence.

10 But behold, my sons and my daughters, I can not go down to my grave, save I should leave a blessing upon you:

11 For behold, I know that if ye are brought up in the way ye should go, ye will not depart from it.

12 Wherefore, if ye are cursed, behold, I leave my blessing upon you, that the cursing may be taken from you, and be answered upon the heads of your parents.

13 Wherefore, because of my blessing, the Lord God will not suffer that ye shall perish; wherefore, he will be merciful unto you, and unto your seed for ever.

14 ¶And it came to pass that after my father had made an end of speaking to the sons and daughters of Laman, he caused the sons and daughters of Lemuel to be brought before him.

15 And he spake unto them, saying: Behold, my sons and my daughters, who are the sons and the daughters of my second son;

16 Behold, I leave unto you the same blessing which I left unto the sons and daughters of Laman; wherefore, thou shalt not utterly be destroyed; but in the end thy seed shall be blessed.

17 And it came to pass that when my father had made an end of speaking unto them, behold, he spake unto the sons of Ishmael, yea, and even all his household.

18 And after he had made an end of speaking unto them, he spake unto Sam, saying:

19 Blessed art thou, and thy seed: for thou shalt inherit the land, like unto thy brother Nephi.

20 And thy seed shall be numbered with his seed;

21 And thou shalt be even like unto thy brother, and thy seed like unto his seed; and thou shalt be blessed in all thy days.

22 ¶And it came to pass after my father Lehi had spoken unto all his household, according to the feelings of his heart, and the Spirit of the Lord which was in him, he waxed old.

23 And it came to pass that he died, and was buried.

24 ¶And it came to pass that not many days after his

death, Laman and Lemuel, and the sons of Ishmael, were angry with me because of the admonitions of the Lord:

25 For I, Nephi, was constrained to speak unto them, according to his word.

26 For I had spake many things unto them, and also my father, before his death;

27 Many of which sayings, are written upon mine other plates: for a more history part are written upon mine other plates.

28 And upon these, I write the things of my soul, and many of the scriptures which are engraven upon the plates of brass:

29 For my soul delighteth in the scriptures, and my heart pondereth them, and writeth them for the learning and the profit of my children.

30 Behold, my soul delighteth in the things of the Lord; and my heart pondereth continually upon the things which I have seen and heard.

31 Nevertheless, the great goodness of the Lord, in showing me his great and marvelous works, my heart exclaimeth, O wretched man that I am; yea, my heart sorroweth because of my flesh.

32 My soul grieveth because of mine iniquities.

33 I am encompassed about because of the temptations and the sins which doth so easily beset me.

34 And when I desire to rejoice, my heart groaneth because of my sins; nevertheless, I know in whom I have trusted.

35 My God hath been my support; he hath led me through mine afflictions in the wilderness; and he hath preserved me upon the waters of the great deep.

36 He hath filled me with his love, even unto the consuming of my flesh.

37 He hath confounded mine enemies, unto the causing of them to quake before me.

38 Behold, he hath heard my cry by day, and he hath given me knowledge by visions in the night time.

39 And by day have I waxed bold in mighty prayer before

him; yea, my voice have I sent up on high; and angels came down and ministered unto me.

40 And upon the wings of his Spirit hath my body been carried away upon exceeding high mountains.

41 And mine eyes have beheld great things; yea, even too great for man; therefore I was bidden that I should not write them.

42 O then, if I have seen so great things; if the Lord in his condescension unto the children of men, hath visited me in so much mercy, why should my heart weep, and my soul linger in the valley of sorrow, and my flesh waste away, and my strength slacken, because of mine afflictions?

43 And why should I yield to sin, because of my flesh?

44 Yea, why should I give way to temptations, that the evil one have place in my heart, to destroy my peace and afflict my soul?

45 Why am I angry because of mine enemy?

46 Awake, my soul! No longer droop in sin.

47 Rejoice, O my heart, and give place no more for the enemy of my soul.

48 Do not anger again, because of mine enemies.

49 Do not slacken my strength, because of mine afflictions.

50 Rejoice, O my heart, and cry unto the Lord, and say, O Lord, I will praise thee for ever; yea, my soul will rejoice in thee, my God, and the rock of my salvation.

51 O Lord, wilt thou redeem my soul?

52 Wilt thou deliver me out of the hands of mine enemies?

53 Wilt thou make me that I may shake at the appearance of sin?

54 May the gates of hell be shut continually before me, because that my heart is broken and my spirit is contrite?

55 O Lord, wilt thou not shut the gates of thy righteousness before me, that I may walk in the path of the low valley, that I may be strict in the plain road?

56 O Lord, wilt thou encircle me around in the robe of thy righteousness?

57 O Lord, wilt thou make a way for mine escape before mine enemies?

58 Wilt thou make my path straight before me?

59 Wilt thou not place a stumbling block in my way?

60 But that thou wouldst clear my way before me, and hedge not up my way, but the ways of mine enemy.

61 O Lord, I have trusted in thee, and I will trust in thee for ever.

62 I will not put my trust in the arm of flesh; for I know that cursed is he that putteth his trust in the arm of flesh.

63 Yea, cursed is he that putteth his trust in man, or maketh flesh his arm.

64 Yea, I know that God will give liberally to him that asketh.

65 Yea, my God will give me, if I ask not amiss: therefore I will lift up my voice unto thee; yea, I will cry unto thee, my God, the rock of my righteousness.

66 Behold, my voice shall for ever ascend up unto thee, my rock and mine everlasting God. Amen.

CHAPTER 4.

1 ¶Behold, it came to pass that I, Nephi, did cry much unto the Lord my God, because of the anger of my brethren.

2 But behold, their anger did increase against me; insomuch that they did seek to take away my life.

3 Yea, they did murmur against me, saying: Our younger brother thinks to rule over us; and we have had much trial because of him; wherefore, now let us slay him, that we may not be afflicted more because of his words.

4 For behold, we will not have him to be our ruler: for it belongs unto us, who are the elder brethren, to rule over this people.

5 Now I do not write upon these plates, all the words which they murmured against me.

6 But it sufficeth me to say, that they did seek to take away my life.

7 ¶And it came to pass that the Lord did warn me, that I, Nephi, should depart from them, and flee into the wilderness, and all those who would go with me.

8 Wherefore, it came to pass that I, Nephi, did take my family, and also Zoram and his family, and Sam, mine elder brother, and his family, and Jacob, and Joseph, my younger brethren, and also my sisters, and all those who would go with me.

9 And all those who would go with me, were those who believed in the warnings and the revelations of God; wherefore, they did hearken unto my words.

10 And we did take our tents and whatsoever things were possible for us, and did journey in the wilderness for the space of many days.

11 And after we had journeyed for the space of many days, we did pitch our tents.

12 And my people would that we should call the name of the place Nephi; wherefore, we did call it Nephi.

13 And all those who were with me, did take upon them to call themselves the people of Nephi.

14 And we did observe to keep the judgments, and the statutes, and the commandments of the Lord, in all things, according to the law of Moses.

15 And the Lord was with us; and we did prosper exceedingly: for we did sow seed, and we did reap again in abundance.

16 And we began to raise flocks, and herds, and animals of every kind.

17 And I, Nephi, had also brought the records which were engraven upon the plates of brass; and also the ball, or compass, which was prepared for my father, by the hand of the Lord, according to that which is written.

18 ¶And it came to pass that we began to prosper exceedingly, and to multiply in the land.

19 And I, Nephi, did take the sword of Laban, and after the manner of it did make many swords, lest by any means

the people who were now called Lamanites, should come upon us and destroy us:

20 For I knew their hatred towards me and my children, and those who were called my people.

21 And I did teach my people to build buildings, and to work in all manner of wood, and of iron, and of copper, and of brass, and of steel, and of gold, and of silver, and of precious ores, which were in great abundance.

22 And I, Nephi, did build a temple; and I did construct it after the manner of the temple of Solomon, save it were not built of so many precious things:

23 For they were not to be found upon the land;

24 Wherefore, it could not be built like unto Solomon's temple.

25 But the manner of the construction was like unto the temple of Solomon; and the workmanship thereof was exceeding fine.

26 ¶And it came to pass that I, Nephi, did cause my people to be industrious, and to labor with their hands.

27 And it came to pass that they would that I should be their king.

28 But I, Nephi, was desirous that they should have no king; nevertheless, I did for them according to that which was in my power.

29 And behold, the words of the Lord had been fulfilled unto my brethren, which he spake concerning them, that I should be their ruler and their teacher;

30 Wherefore, I had been their ruler and their teacher, according to the commandment of the Lord, until the time they sought to take away my life.

31 Wherefore, the word of the Lord was fulfilled which he spake unto me, saying: That inasmuch as they will not hearken unto thy words, they shall be cut off from the presence of the Lord.

32 And behold they were cut off from his presence.

33 And he had caused the cursing to come upon them, yea, even a sore cursing, because of their iniquity.

34 For behold, they had hardened their hearts against him, that they had become like unto a flint;

35 Wherefore, as they were white, and exceeding fair and delightsome, that they might not be enticing unto my people, the Lord God did cause a skin of blackness to come upon them.

36 And thus saith the Lord God, I will cause that they shall be loathsome unto thy people, save they shall repent of their iniquities.

37 And cursed shall be the seed of him that mixeth with their seed: for they shall be cursed even with the same cursing.

38 And the Lord spake it, and it was done.

39 And because of their cursing which was upon them, they did become an idle people, full of mischief and subtlety, and did seek in the wilderness for beasts of prey.

40 And the Lord God said unto me, They shall be a scourge unto thy seed, to stir them up in remembrance of me;

41 And inasmuch as they will not remember me, and hearken unto my words, they shall scourge them even unto destruction.

42 ¶And it came to pass that I, Nephi, did consecrate Jacob and Joseph, that they should be priests and teachers over the land of my people.

43 And it came to pass that we lived after the manner of happiness.

44 And thirty years had passed away from the time we left Jerusalem.

45 And I, Nephi, had kept the records upon my plates, which I had made of my people, thus far.

46 ¶And it came to pass that the Lord God said unto me, Make other plates; and thou shalt engraven many things upon them which are good in my sight, for the profit of thy people.

47 Wherefore, I, Nephi, to be obedient to the commandments of the Lord, went and made these plates upon which I have engraven these things.

48 And I engraved that which is pleasing unto God.

49 And if my people are pleased with the things of God, they will be pleased with mine engravings which are upon these plates.

50 And if my people desire to know the more particular part of the history of my people, they must search mine other plates.

51 And it sufficeth me to say, that forty years had passed away, and we had already had wars and contentions with our brethren.

CHAPTER 5.

1 ¶The words of Jacob, the brother of Nephi, which he spake unto the people of Nephi:

2 Behold, my beloved brethren, I, Jacob, having been called of God, and ordained after the manner of his holy order,

3 And having been consecrated by my brother, Nephi, unto whom ye look as a king or a protector, and on whom ye depend for safety,

4 Behold, ye know that I have spoken unto you exceeding many things;

5 Nevertheless, I speak unto you again; for I am desirous for the welfare of your souls.

6 Yea, mine anxiety is great for you; and ye yourselves know that it ever has been.

7 For I have exhorted you with all diligence; and I have taught you the words of my father;

8 And I have spoken unto you concerning all things which are written from the creation of the world.

9 ¶And now, behold, I would speak unto you concerning things which are, and which are to come;

10 Wherefore, I will read you the words of Isaiah.

11 And they are the words which my brother has desired that I should speak unto you.

12 And I speak them unto you for your sakes, that ye may learn and glorify the name of your God.

13 And now the words which I shall read, are they which Isaiah spake concerning all the house of Israel;

14 Wherefore, they may be likened unto you; for ye are of the house of Israel.

15 And there are many things which have been spoken by Isaiah, which may be likened unto you, because ye are of the house of Israel.

16 ¶And now, these are the words:

17 [1]Thus saith the Lord God; Behold, I will lift up mine hand to the Gentiles, and set up my standard to the people;

18 And they shall bring thy sons in their arms, and thy daughters shall be carried upon their shoulders.

19 And kings shall be thy nursing fathers, and their queens thy nursing mothers:

20 They shall bow down to thee with their faces towards the earth, and lick up the dust of thy feet;

21 And thou shalt know that I am the Lord: for they shall not be ashamed that wait for me.

22 ¶And now I, Jacob, would speak somewhat concerning these words: For behold, the Lord has shewn me that those who were at Jerusalem, from whence we came, have been slain and carried away captive;

23 Nevertheless, the Lord has shewn unto me that they should return again.

24 And he also has shewn unto me, that the Lord God, the Holy One of Israel, should manifest himself unto them in the flesh;

25 And after he should manifest himself, they should scourge him and crucify him, according to the words of the angel, who spake it unto me.

26 And after they have hardened their hearts and stiffened their necks against the Holy One of Israel, behold the judgments of the Holy One of Israel shall come upon them.

27 And the day cometh that they shall be smitten and afflicted.

28 Wherefore, after they are driven to and fro, for thus

---

[1]Isaiah 49:22.

saith the angel, many shall be afflicted in the flesh and shall not be suffered to perish, because of the prayers of the faithful, they shall be scattered, and smitten, and hated;

29 Nevertheless, the Lord will be merciful unto them, that when they shall come to the knowledge of their Redeemer, they shall be gathered together again to the lands of their inheritance.

30 ¶And blessed are the Gentiles, they of whom the prophet has written:

31 For behold, if it so be that they shall repent and fight not against Zion, and do not unite themselves to that great and abominable church, they shall be saved:

32 For the Lord God will fulfill his covenants which he has made unto his children: and for this cause the prophet has written these things.

33 Wherefore, they that fight against Zion and the covenant people of the Lord, shall lick up the dust of their feet;

34 And the people of the Lord shall not be ashamed.

35 For the people of the Lord are they who wait for him: for they still wait for the coming of the Messiah.

36 And behold, according to the words of the prophet, the Messiah will set himself again the second time, to recover them;

37 Wherefore, he will manifest himself unto them in power and great glory, unto the destruction of their enemies, when that day cometh when they shall believe in him;

38 And none will he destroy that believe in him.

39 And they that believe not in him, shall be destroyed, both by fire, and by tempest, and by earthquakes, and by bloodsheds, and by pestilence, and by famine.

40 And they shall know that the Lord is God, the Holy One of Israel:

41 [2]For shall the prey be taken from the mighty, or the lawful captive delivered?

42 But thus saith the Lord; Even the captives of the

---

[2]Isaiah 49 : 24-26.

mighty shall be taken away, and the prey of the terrible shall be delivered: for the mighty God shall deliver his covenant people.

43 For thus saith the Lord: I will contend with them that contendeth with thee, and I will feed them that oppress thee, with their own flesh;

44 And they shall be drunken with their own blood, as with sweet wine;

45 And all flesh shall know that I the Lord am thy Savior and thy Redeemer, the mighty One of Jacob.

46 [a]Yea, for thus saith the Lord: Have I put thee away, or have I cast thee off for ever?

47 For thus saith the Lord: Where is the bill of your mother's divorcement?

48 To whom have I put thee away, or to which of my creditors have I sold you?

49 Yea, to whom have I sold you?

50 Behold, for your iniquities have ye sold yourselves, and for your transgressions is your mother put away;

51 Wherefore, when I came, there was no man; when I called, yea, there was none to answer.

52 ¶O, House of Israel, is my hand shortened at all that it can not redeem, or have I no power to deliver?

53 Behold, at my rebuke, I dry up the sea, I make their rivers a wilderness and their fish to stink, because the waters are dried up; and they die because of thirst.

54 I clothe the heavens with blackness, and I make sackcloth their covering.

55 The Lord God hath given me the tongue of the learned, that I should know how to speak a word in season unto thee, O house of Israel.

56 When ye are weary, he waketh morning by morning.

57 He waketh mine ear to hear as the learned.

58 The Lord God hath appointed mine ear, and I was not rebellious, neither turned away back.

[a]Isaiah 50.

59 I gave my back to the smiter, and my cheeks to them that plucked off the hair.

60 I hid not my face from shame and spitting, for the Lord God will help me: therefore shall I not be confounded.

61 Therefore have I set my face like a flint, and I know that I shall not be ashamed; and the Lord is near, and he justifieth me.

62 Who will contend with me?

63 Let us stand together.

64 Who is mine adversary?

65 Let him come near me, and I will smite him with the strength of my mouth: for the Lord God will help me.

66 And all they who shall condemn me, behold, all they shall wax old as a garment, and the moth shall eat them up.

67 ¶Who is among you that feareth the Lord; that obeyeth the voice of his servant; that walketh in darkness, and hath no light?

68 Behold, all ye that kindle fire, that compass yourselves about with sparks, walk in the light of your fire, and in the sparks which ye have kindled.

69 This shall ye have of mine hand: Ye shall lie down in sorrow.

70 [4]Hearken unto me, ye that follow after righteousness: Look unto the rock from whence ye are hewn, and to the hole of the pit from whence ye are digged.

71 Look unto Abraham, your father, and unto Sarah, she that bare you: for I called him alone, and blessed him.

72 For the Lord shall comfort Zion: he will comfort all her waste places;

73 And he will make her wilderness like Eden, and her desert like the garden of the Lord.

74 Joy and gladness shall be found therein, thanksgiving and the voice of melody.

75 Hearken unto me, my people; and give ear unto me, O my nation:

[4]Isaiah 51.

76 For a law shall proceed from me, and I will make my judgment to rest for a light for the people.

77 My righteousness is near; my salvation is gone forth, and mine arm shall judge the people.

78 The isles shall wait upon me, and on mine arm shall they trust.

79 Lift up your eyes to the heavens, and look upon the earth beneath:

80 For the heavens shall vanish away like smoke, and the earth shall wax old like a garment; and they that dwell therein, shall die in like manner.

81 But my salvation shall be for ever; and my righteousness shall not be abolished.

82 ¶Hearken unto me, ye that know righteousness, the people in whose heart I have written my law;

83 Fear ye not the reproach of men; neither be ye afraid of their revilings;

84 For the moth shall eat them up like a garment, and the worm shall eat them like wool.

85 But my righteousness shall be for ever; and my salvation from generation to generation.

86 ¶Awake, awake! Put on strength O arm of the Lord: awake as in the ancient days.

87 Art thou not it that hath cut Rahab, and wounded the dragon?

88 Art thou not it which hath dried the sea, the waters of the great deep;

89 That hath made the depths of the sea a way for the ransomed to pass over?

90 Therefore, the redeemed of the Lord shall return, and come with singing unto Zion; and everlasting joy and holiness shall be upon their heads;

91 And they shall obtain gladness and joy: sorrow and mourning shall flee away.

92 I am he; yea, I am he that comforteth you:

93 Behold, who art thou, that thou shouldst be afraid of

man, who shall die, and of the son of man, who shall be made like unto grass;

94 And forgettest the Lord thy maker, that hath stretched forth the heavens, and laid the foundations of the earth;

95 And hast feared continually every day, because of the fury of the oppressor, as if he were ready to destroy?

96 And where is the fury of the oppressor?

97 The captive exile hasteneth, that he may be loosed, and that he should not die in the pit, nor that his bread should fail.

98 But I am the Lord thy God, whose waves roared: the Lord of hosts is my name.

99 And I have put my words in thy mouth, and have covered thee in the shadow of mine hand, that I may plant the heavens and lay the foundations of the earth, and say unto Zion, Behold, thou art my people.

100 Awake, awake, stand up, O Jerusalem, which hast drunk at the hand of the Lord the cup of his fury;

101 Thou hast drunken the dregs of the cup of trembling wrung out;

102 And none to guide her among all the sons she hath brought forth;

103 Neither that taketh her by the hand, of all the sons she hath brought up.

104 These two sons are come unto thee; who shall be sorry for thee: thy desolation and destruction, and the famine and the sword:

105 And by whom shall I comfort thee?

106 Thy sons have fainted, save these two: they lie at the head of all the streets, as a wild bull in a net: they are full of the fury of the Lord, the rebuke of thy God.

107 ¶Therefore, hear now this, thou afflicted, and drunken, and not with wine:

108 Thus saith thy Lord, The Lord and thy God pleadeth the cause of his people:

109 Behold, I have taken out of thine hand the cup of trem-

bling, the dregs of the cup of my fury; thou shalt no more drink it again.

110 But I will put it into the hand of them that afflict thee; who have said to thy soul, Bow down that we may go over:

111 And thou hast laid thy body as the ground, and as the street to them that went over.

112 ¶Awake, awake, put on thy strength, O Zion; put on thy beautiful garments, O Jerusalem, the holy city:

113 For henceforth there shall no more come into thee, the uncircumcised and the unclean.

114 Shake thyself from the dust; arise, sit down, O Jerusalem: loose thyself from the bands of thy neck, O captive daughter of Zion.

CHAPTER 6.

1 ¶And now, my beloved brethren, I have read these things that ye might know concerning the covenants of the Lord; that he has covenanted with all the house of Israel;

2 That he has spoken unto the Jews, by the mouth of his holy prophets, even from the beginning down, from generation to generation, until the time comes that they shall be restored to the true church and fold of God;

3 When they shall be gathered home to the lands of their inheritance, and shall be established in all their lands of promise.

4 ¶Behold, my beloved brethren, I speak unto you these things that ye may rejoice, and lift up your heads for ever, because of the blessings which the Lord God shall bestow upon your children.

5 For I know that ye have searched much, many of you, to know of things to come;

6 Wherefore I know that ye know that our flesh must waste away and die;

7 Nevertheless, in our bodies we shall see God.

8 Yea, I know that ye know, that in the body he shall shew himself unto those at Jerusalem, from whence we came;

9 For it is expedient that it should be among them;

10 For it behooveth the great Creator that he suffereth himself to become subject unto man in the flesh, and die for all men, that all men might become subject unto him.

11 For as death hath passed upon all men, to fulfill the merciful plan of the great Creator, there must needs be a power of resurrection,

12 And the resurrection must needs come unto man by reason of the fall;

13 And the fall came by reason of transgression;

14 And because man became fallen, they were cut off from the presence of the Lord;

15 Wherefore, it must needs be an infinite atonement;

16 Save it should be an infinite atonement, this corruption could not put on incorruption.

17 Wherefore, the first judgment which came upon man, must needs have remained to an endless duration.

18 And if so, this flesh must have laid down to rot and to crumble to its mother earth, to rise no more.

19 ¶O the wisdom of God! his mercy and grace!

20 For behold, if the flesh should rise no more, our spirits must become subject to that angel who fell from before the presence of the eternal God, and became the devil, to rise no more.

21 And our spirits must have become like unto him, and we become devils, angels to a devil, to be shut out from the presence of our God, and to remain with the father of lies, in misery, like unto himself;

22 Yea, to that being who beguiled our first parents;

23 Who transformeth himself nigh unto an angel of light, and stirreth up the children of men unto secret combinations of murder, and all manner of secret works of darkness.

24 ¶O how great the goodness of our God, who prepareth a way for our escape from the grasp of this awful monster;

25 Yea, that monster, death and hell, which I call the death of the body, and also the death of the spirit.

26 And because of the way of deliverance of our God, the

Holy One of Israel, this death, of which I have spoken, which is the temporal, shall deliver up its dead, which death is the grave.

27 And this death of which I have spoken, which is the spiritual death, shall deliver up its dead; which spiritual death is hell;

28 Wherefore, death and hell must deliver up their dead, and hell must deliver up its captive spirits,

29 And the grave must deliver up its captive bodies, and the bodies and the spirits of men will be restored, one to the other;

30 And it is by the power of the resurrection of the Holy One of Israel.

31 ¶O how great the plan of our God! For on the other hand, the paradise of God must deliver up the spirits of the righteous, and the grave deliver up the body of the righteous;

32 And the spirit and the body is restored to itself again, and all men become incorruptible, and immortal, and they are living souls, having a perfect knowledge like unto us, in the flesh;

33 Save it be that our knowledge shall be perfect;

34 Wherefore, we shall have a perfect knowledge of all our guilt, and our uncleanness, and our nakedness;

35 And the righteous shall have a perfect knowledge of their enjoyment, and their righteousness, being clothed with purity, yea, even with the robe of righteousness.

36 ¶And it shall come to pass, that when all men shall have passed from this first death unto life, insomuch as they have become immortal, they must appear before the judgment seat of the Holy One of Israel;

37 And then cometh the judgment; and then must they be judged according to the holy judgment of God.

38 And assuredly, as the Lord liveth, for the Lord God hath spoken it, and it is his eternal word, which can not pass away, that they who are righteous shall be righteous still, and they who are filthy shall be filthy still;

39 Wherefore, they who are filthy are the devil and his angels;

40 And they shall go away into everlasting fire, prepared for them; and their torment is as a lake of fire and brimstone, whose flames ascendeth up for ever and ever; and has no end.

41 ¶O the greatness and the justice of our God! For he executeth all his words, and they have gone forth out of his mouth, and his law must be fulfilled.

42 But, behold, the righteous, the saints of the Holy One of Israel, they who have believed in the Holy One of Israel; they who have endured the crosses of the world, and despised the shame of it; they shall inherit the kingdom of God, which was prepared for them from the foundation of the world: and their joy shall be full for ever.

43 ¶O the greatness of the mercy of our God, the Holy One of Israel! For he delivereth his saints from that awful monster the devil, and death, and hell, and that lake of fire and brimstone, which is endless torment.

44 ¶Oh how great the holiness of our God! For he knoweth all things, and there is not anything save he knows it.

45 And he cometh into the world that he may save all men, if they will hearken unto his voice;

46 For behold, he suffereth the pains of all men: yea, the pains of every living creature, both men, women and children, who belong to the family of Adam.

47 And he suffereth this, that the resurrection might pass upon all men, that all might stand before him at the great and judgment day.

48 And he commandeth all men that they must repent, and be baptized in his name, having perfect faith in the Holy One of Israel, or they can not be saved in the kingdom of God.

49 And if they will not repent and believe in his name, and be baptized in his name, and endure to the end, they must be damned;

50 For the Lord God, the Holy One of Israel, hath spoken it;

51 Wherefore he hath given a law; and where there is no law given there is no punishment;

52 And where there is no punishment, there is no condemnation;

53 And where there is no condemnation, the mercies of the Holy One of Israel have claim upon them, because of the atonement:

54 For they are delivered by the power of him: for the atonement satisfieth the demands of his justice upon all those who have not the law given to them, that they are delivered from that awful monster, death and hell, and the devil, and the lake of fire and brimstone, which is endless torment;

55 And they are restored to that God who gave them breath, which is the Holy One of Israel.

56 ¶But wo unto him that has the law given; yea, that has all the commandments of God, like unto us, and that transgresseth them, and that wasteth the days of his probation; for awful is his state!

57 ¶O that cunning plan of the evil one!

58 O the vainness, and the frailties, and the foolishness of men!

59 When they are learned, they think they are wise, and they hearken not unto the counsel of God, for they set it aside, supposing they know of themselves;

60 Wherefore, their wisdom is foolishness, and it profiteth them not. And they shall perish.

61 ¶But to be learned is good, if they hearken unto the counsels of God.

62 But wo unto the rich, who are rich as to the things of the world.

63 For because they are rich, they despise the poor, and they persecute the meek, and their hearts are upon their treasures: wherefore their treasure is their God.

64 And behold, their treasure shall perish with them also.

65 And wo unto the deaf, that will not hear: for they shall perish.

66 Wo unto the blind, that will not see: for they shall perish also.

67 Wo unto the uncircumcised of heart: for a knowledge of their iniquities shall smite them at the last day.

68 Wo unto the liar: for he shall be thrust down to hell.

69 Wo unto the murderer, who deliberately killeth: for he shall die.

70 Wo unto them who commit whoredoms: for they shall be thrust down to hell.

71 Yea, wo unto those that worship idols: for the devil of all devils delighteth in them.

72 And, in fine, wo unto all those who die in their sins: for they shall return to God, and behold his face, and remain in their sins.

73 ¶O, my beloved brethren, remember the awfulness in transgressing against that Holy God, and also the awfulness of yielding to the enticings of that cunning one.

74 Remember, to be carnally minded, is death, and to be spiritually minded, is life eternal.

75 ¶O, my beloved brethren, give ear to my words.

76 Remember the greatness of the Holy One of Israel.

77 Do not say that I have spoken hard things against you; for if ye do, ye will revile against the truth: for I have spoken the words of your Maker.

78 I know that the words of truth are hard against all uncleanness; but the righteous fear them not, for they love the truth, and are not shaken.

79 ¶O then, my beloved brethren, come unto the Lord, the Holy One.

80 Remember that his paths are righteousness.

81 Behold, the way for man is narrow, but it lieth in a straight course before him, and the keeper of the gate is the Holy One of Israel: and he employeth no servant there;

82 And there is none other way, save it be by the gate, for he can not be deceived; for the Lord God is his name.

83 And whoso knocketh, to him, will he open; and the wise, and the learned, and they that are rich, who are puffed up because of their learning, and their wisdom, and their riches; yea, they are they, whom he despiseth;

84 And save they shall cast these things away, and consider themselves fools before God, and come down in the depths of humility, he will not open unto them.

85 But the things of the wise and the prudent, shall be hid from them for ever; yea, that happiness which is prepared for the saints.

86 O, my beloved brethren, remember my words: Behold, I take off my garments and I shake them before you:

87 I pray the God of my salvation that he view me with his all-searching eye;

88 Wherefore, ye shall know at the last day, when all men shall be judged of their works, that the God of Israel did witness that I shook your iniquities from my soul, and that I stand with brightness before him, and am rid of your blood.

89 ¶O, my beloved brethren, turn away from your sins; shake off the chains of him that would bind you fast;

90 Come unto that God who is the rock of your salvation.

91 Prepare your souls for that glorious day, when justice shall be administered unto the righteous; even the day of judgment, that ye may not shrink with awful fear;

92 That ye may not remember your awful guilt in perfectness, and be constrained to exclaim, Holy, holy are thy judgments, O Lord God Almighty.

93 But I know my guilt; I transgressed thy law, and my transgressions are mine; and the devil hath obtained me, that I am a prey to his awful misery.

94 But behold, my brethren, is it expedient that I should awake you to an awful reality of these things?

95 Would I harrow up your souls, if your minds were pure?

96 Would I be plain unto you according to the plainness of the truth, if ye were freed from sin?

97 Behold, if ye were holy, I would speak unto you of holiness; but as ye are not holy, and ye look upon me as a

teacher, it must needs be expedient that I teach you the consequences of sin.

98 Behold, my soul abhorreth sin, and my heart delighteth in righteousness; and I will praise the holy name of my God.

99 Come, my brethren, every one that thirsteth, come ye to the waters; and he that hath no money, come buy and eat; yea, come buy wine and milk without money and without price.

100 Wherefore, do not spend money for that which is of no worth, nor your labor for that which can not satisfy.

101 Hearken diligently unto me, and remember the words which I have spoken; and come unto the Holy One of Israel,

102 And feast upon that which perisheth not, neither can be corrupted, and let your soul delight in fatness.

103 Behold, my beloved brethren, remember the words of your God; pray unto him continually by day, and give thanks unto his holy name by night.

104 Let your hearts rejoice, and behold how great the covenants of the Lord, and how great his condescensions unto the children of men;

105 And because of his greatness, and his grace and mercy, he has promised unto us that our seed shall not utterly be destroyed, according to the flesh, but that he would preserve them; and in future generations, they shall become a righteous branch unto the house of Israel.

106 ¶And now, my brethren, I would speak unto you more; but on the morrow I will declare unto you the remainder of my words. Amen.

CHAPTER 7.

1 ¶And now I, Jacob, speak unto you again, my beloved brethren, concerning this righteous branch of which I have spoken.

2 For behold, the promises which we have obtained, are promises unto us according to the flesh;

3 Wherefore, as it has been shown unto me that many of

our children shall perish in the flesh, because of unbelief, nevertheless God will be merciful unto many;

4 And our children shall be restored, that they may come to that which will give them the true knowledge of their Redeemer.

5 Wherefore, as I said unto you, it must needs be expedient that Christ (for in the last night the angel spake unto me that this should be his name) should come among the Jews, among those who are the more wicked part of the world;

6 And they shall crucify him: For thus it behooveth our God;

7 And there is none other nation on earth that would crucify their God.

8 For should the mighty miracles be wrought among other nations, they would repent, and know that he be their God;

9 But because of priestcrafts and iniquities, they at Jerusalem will stiffen their necks against him, that he be crucified.

10 Wherefore, because of their iniquities, destructions, famines, pestilence and bloodsheds, shall come upon them;

11 And they who shall not be destroyed, shall be scattered among all nations.

12 ¶But behold, thus saith the Lord God: When the day cometh that they shall believe in me, that I am Christ, then have I covenanted with their fathers that they shall be restored in the flesh, upon the earth, unto the lands of their inheritance.

13 And it shall come to pass that they shall be gathered in from their long dispersion from the isles of the sea, and from the four parts of the earth;

14 And the nations of the Gentiles shall be great in the eyes of me, saith God, in carrying them forth to the lands of their inheritance.

15 Yea, the kings of the Gentiles shall be nursing fathers unto them, and their queens shall become nursing mothers;

16 Wherefore the promises of the Lord are great unto the Gentiles, for he hath spoken it, and who can dispute?

17 But behold, this land, saith God, shall be a land of thine

inheritance; and the Gentiles shall be blessed upon the land.

18 And this land shall be a land of liberty unto the Gentiles: and there shall be no kings upon the land, who shall raise up unto the Gentiles.

19 And I will fortify this land against all other nations;

20 And he that fighteth against Zion, shall perish, saith God; for he that raiseth up a king against me, shall perish.

21 For I the Lord, the King of heaven, will be their king; and I will be a light unto them for ever, that hear my words.

22 Wherefore, for this cause, that my covenants may be fulfilled, which I have made unto the children of men, that I will do unto them while they are in the flesh, I must needs destroy the secret works of darkness, and of murders, and of abominations;

23 Wherefore, he that fighteth against Zion, both Jew and Gentile, both bond and free, both male and female, shall perish:

24 For they are they who are the whore of all the earth;

25 For they who are not for me, are against me, saith our God.

26 For I will fulfill my promises which I have made unto the children of men, that I will do unto them while they are in the flesh.

27 Wherefore, my beloved brethren, thus saith our God: I will afflict thy seed by the hand of the Gentiles;

28 Nevertheless, I will soften the hearts of the Gentiles, that they shall be like unto a father to them;

29 Wherefore, the Gentiles shall be blessed and numbered among the house of Israel.

30 Wherefore, I will consecrate this land unto thy seed, and they who shall be numbered among thy seed, for ever, for the land of their inheritance:

31 For it is a choice land, saith God unto me, above all other lands;

32 Wherefore, I will have all men that dwell thereon, that they shall worship me, saith God.

33 ¶And now, my beloved brethren, seeing that our merci-

ful God has given us so great knowledge concerning these things, let us remember him, and lay aside our sins, and not hang down our heads, for we are not cast off;

34 Nevertheless, we have been driven out of the land of our inheritance; but we have been led to a better land:

35 For the Lord has made the sea our path, and we are upon an isle of the sea.

36 But great are the promises of the Lord unto those who are upon the isles of the sea;

37 Wherefore, as it says isles, there must needs be more than this; and they are inhabited also by our brethren.

38 For behold, the Lord God has led away from time to time from the house of Israel, according to his will and pleasure.

39 And now, behold, the Lord remembereth all those who have been broken off; wherefore, he remembereth us also.

40 Therefore cheer up your hearts, and remember that ye are free to act for yourselves; to choose the way of everlasting death, or the way of eternal life.

41 Wherefore, my beloved brethren, reconcile yourselves to the will of God, and not to the will of the devil and the flesh;

42 And remember after ye are reconciled unto God, that it is only in and through the grace of God that ye are saved.

43 Wherefore, may God raise you from death, by the power of the resurrection, and also from everlasting death, by the power of the atonement,

44 That ye may be received into the eternal kingdom of God, that ye may praise him through grace divine. Amen.

CHAPTER 8.

1 ¶And now Jacob spake many more things to my people at that time; nevertheless, only these things have I caused to be written; for the things which I have written sufficeth me.

2 ¶And now I, Nephi, write more of the words of Isaiah; for my soul delighteth in his words.

3 For I will liken his words unto my people; and I will

send them forth unto all my children: for he verily saw my Redeemer, even as I have seen him.

4 And my brother Jacob also, has seen him as I have seen him; wherefore, I will send their words forth unto my children, to prove unto them that my words are true.

5 Wherefore, by the words of three, God hath said, I will establish my word.

6 Nevertheless, God sendeth more witnesses; and he proveth all his words.

7 Behold, my soul delighteth in proving unto my people the truth of the coming of Christ:

8 For, for this end hath the law of Moses been given:

9 And all things which have been given of God from the beginning of the world, unto man, are the typifying of him.

10 And also, my soul delighteth in the covenants of the Lord which he hath made to our fathers;

11 Yea, my soul delighteth in his grace, and his justice, and power, and mercy, in the great and eternal plan of deliverance from death.

12 And my soul delighteth in proving unto my people, that save Christ should come, all men must perish.

13 For if there be no Christ, there be no God; and if there be no God, we are not, for there could have been no creation.

14 But there is a God, and he is Christ; and he cometh in the fullness of his own time.

15 ¶And now I write some of the words of Isaiah, that whoso of my people shall see these words, may lift up their hearts and rejoice for all men.

16 Now, these are the words; and ye may liken them unto you, and unto all men.

17 ¶[1]The word that Isaiah, the son of Amoz, saw, concerning Judah and Jerusalem:

18 And it shall come to pass in the last days, when the mountain of the Lord's house shall be established in the top of the mountains, and shall be exalted above the hills, and all nations shall flow unto it,

---

[1]Isaiah 2

19 And many people shall go and say, Come ye, and let us go up to the mountain of the Lord, to the house of the God of Jacob; and he will teach us of his ways, and we will walk in his paths: for out of Zion shall go forth the law, and the word of the Lord from Jerusalem.

20 And he shall judge among the nations, and shall rebuke many people; and they shall beat their swords into plow shares, and their spears into pruning hooks; nation shall not lift up sword against nation, neither shall they learn war any more.

21 O house of Jacob, come ye and let us walk in the light of the Lord; yea come, for ye have all gone astray, every one to his wicked ways.

22 ¶Therefore, O Lord, thou hast forsaken thy people, the house of Jacob, because they be replenished from the east, and hearken unto soothsayers like the Philistines, and they please themselves in the children of strangers.

23 Their land also is full of silver and gold, neither is there any end of their treasures; their land is also full of horses, neither is there any end of their chariots;

24 Their land also is full of idols; they worship the work of their own hands,—that which their own fingers have made:

25 And the mean man boweth not down, and the great man humbleth himself not: therefore forgive him not.

26 ¶O ye wicked ones, enter into the rock, and hide thee in the dust, for the fear of the Lord, and the glory of his majesty shall smite thee.

27 And it shall come to pass that the lofty looks of man shall be humbled, and the haughtiness of men shall be bowed down, and the Lord alone shall be exalted in that day.

28 For the day of the Lord of hosts soon cometh upon all nations; yea, upon every one; yea, upon the proud and lofty, and upon every one who is lifted up; and he shall be brought low;

29 Yea, and the day of the Lord shall come upon all the cedars of Lebanon, for they are high and lifted up; and upon all the oaks of Bashan,

30 And upon all the high mountains, and upon all the hills, and upon all the nations which are lifted up,

31 And upon every people, and upon every high tower, and upon every fenced wall,

32 And upon all the ships of the sea, and upon all the ships of Tarshish, and upon all pleasant pictures.

33 And the loftiness of man shall be bowed down, and the haughtiness of men shall be made low; and the Lord alone shall be exalted in that day.

34 And the idols he shall utterly abolish.

35 And they shall go into the holes of the rocks, and into the caves of the earth, for the fear of the Lord shall come upon them: and the glory of his majesty shall smite them, when he ariseth to shake terribly the earth.

36 In that day a man shall cast his idols of silver, and his idols of gold, which he hath made for himself to worship, to the moles and to the bats;

37 To go into the clefts of the rocks, and into the tops of the ragged rocks, for the fear of the Lord shall come upon them, and the majesty of his glory shall smite them when he ariseth to to shake terribly the earth.

38 Cease ye from man, whose breath is in his nostrils; for wherein is he to be accounted of?

39 ¶[2]For behold, the Lord, the Lord of hosts, doth take away from Jerusalem and from Judah the stay and the staff, the whole staff of bread, and the whole stay of water,

40 The mighty man, and the man of war, the judge, and the prophet, and the prudent, and the ancient,

41 The captain of fifty, and the honorable man, and the counselor, and the cunning artificer, and the eloquent orator.

42 And I will give children unto them to be their princes, and babes shall rule over them.

43 And the people shall be oppressed, every one by another, and every one by his neighbor: the child shall behave himself proudly against the ancient, and the base against the honorable.

[2]Isaiah 3.

44 When a man shall take hold of his brother of the house of his father, and shall say, Thou hast clothing, be thou our ruler, and let not this ruin come under thy hand;

45 In that day shall he swear, saying: I will not be a healer; for in my house there is neither bread nor clothing: make me not a ruler of the people.

46 For Jerusalem is ruined, and Judah is fallen: because their tongues and their doings have been against the Lord, to provoke the eyes of his glory.

47 ¶The shew of their countenance doth witness against them, and doth declare their sin to be even as Sodom, and they can not hide it. Wo unto their souls, for they have rewarded evil unto themselves.

48 Say unto the righteous, that it is well with them; for they shall eat the fruit of their doings.

49 Wo unto the wicked! for they shall perish: for the reward of their hands shall be upon them.

50 ¶And my people, children are their oppressors, and women rule over them. O my people, they who lead thee cause thee to err, and destroy the way of thy paths.

51 The Lord standeth up to plead, and standeth to judge the people.

52 The Lord will enter into judgment with the ancients of his people, and the princes thereof: for ye have eaten up the vineyard, and the spoil of the poor in your houses.

53 What mean ye? Ye beat my people to pieces, and grind the faces of the poor, saith the Lord God of hosts.

54 ¶Moreover the Lord saith, Because the daughters of Zion are haughty, and walk with stretched forth necks and wanton eyes, walking and mincing as they go, and making a tinkling with their feet:

55 Therefore the Lord will smite with a scab the crown of the head of the daughters of Zion, and the Lord will discover their secret parts.

56 In that day the Lord will take away the bravery of their tinkling ornaments, and cauls, and round tires like the moon,

57 The chains and the bracelets, and the mufflers,

58 The bonnets, and the ornaments of the legs, and the head-bands, and the tablets, and the ear-rings,

59 The rings, and nose-jewels,

60 The changeable suits of apparel, and the mantles, and the wimples, and the crisping-pins,

61 The glasses, and the fine linen, and hoods, and the veils.

62 ¶And it shall come to pass, instead of sweet smell, there shall be stink; and instead of a girdle, a rent; and instead of well set hair, baldness; and instead of a stomacher, a girding of sackcloth; burning instead of beauty.

63 Thy men shall fall by the sword, and thy mighty in the war.

64 And her gates shall lament and mourn; and she shall be desolate, and shall sit upon the ground.

65 ¶[3]And in that day, seven women shall take hold of one man, saying, We will eat our own bread, and wear our own apparel: only let us be called by thy name, to take away our reproach.

66 In that day shall the branch of the Lord be beautiful and glorious; the fruit of the earth excellent and comely to them that are escaped of Israel.

67 ¶And it shall come to pass, them that are left in Zion, and remain in Jerusalem, shall be called holy, every one that is written among the living in Jerusalem:

68 When the Lord shall have washed away the filth of the daughters of Zion, and shall have purged the blood of Jerusalem from the midst thereof by the spirit of judgment, and by the spirit of burning.

69 And the Lord will create upon every dwelling place of Mount Zion, and upon her assemblies, a cloud and smoke by day, and the shining of a flaming fire by night: for upon all the glory of Zion shall be a defense.

70 And there shall be a tabernacle for a shadow in the daytime from the heat, and for a place of refuge, and a covert from storm and from rain.

[3]Isaiah 4.

71 ¶¹And then will I sing to my well beloved a song of my beloved touching his vineyard. My well beloved hath a vineyard in a very fruitful hill:

72 And he fenced it, and gathered out the stones thereof, and planted it with the choicest vine, and built a tower in the midst of it, and also made a wine-press therein: and he looked that it should bring forth grapes, and it brought forth wild grapes.

73 And now, O inhabitants of Jerusalem, and men of Judah, judge, I pray you, betwixt me and my vineyard.

74 What could have been done more to my vineyard, that I have not done in it? Wherefore, when I looked that it should bring forth grapes, it brought forth wild grapes.

75 And now go to; I will tell you what I will do to my vineyard: I will take away the hedge thereof, and it shall be eaten up; and I will break down the wall thereof, and it shall be trodden down:

76 And I will lay it waste; it shall not be pruned nor digged; but there shall come up briers and thorns: I will also command the clouds that they rain no rain upon it.

77 For the vineyard of the Lord of hosts is the house of Israel, and the men of Judah his pleasant plant: and he looked for judgment, and behold oppression; for righteousness, but behold a cry.

78 ¶Wo unto them that join house to house, till there can be no place, that they may be placed alone in the midst of the earth!

79 In mine ears, saith the Lord of hosts, of a truth many houses shall be desolate, and great and fair cities without inhabitant.

80 Yea, ten acres of vineyard shall yield one bath, and the seed of a homer shall yield an ephah.

81 ¶Wo unto them that rise up early in the morning, that they may follow strong drink; that continue until night, and wine inflame them!

82 And the harp, and the viol, the tabret and pipe, and

¹Isaiah 5.

wine are in their feasts; but they regard not the work of the Lord, neither consider the operation of his hands.

83 ¶Therefore, my people are gone into captivity, because they have no knowledge: and their honorable men are famished, and their multitude dried up with thirst.

84 Therefore, hell hath enlarged herself, and opened her mouth without measure: and their glory, and their multitude, and their pomp, and he that rejoiceth, shall descend into it.

85 And the mean man shall be brought down, and the mighty man shall be humbled, and the eyes of the lofty shall be humbled:

86 But the Lord of hosts shall be exalted in judgment, and God that is holy shall be sanctified in righteousness.

87 Then shall the lambs feed after their manner, and the waste places of the fat ones shall strangers eat.

88 Wo unto them that draw iniquity with cords of vanity, and sin as it were with a cart-rope;

89 That say, Let him make speed, hasten his work, that we may see it: and let the counsel of the Holy One of Israel draw nigh and come, that we may know it.

90 ¶Wo unto them that call evil good, and good evil; that put darkness for light, and light for darkness; that put bitter for sweet, and sweet for bitter!

91 Wo unto the wise in their own eyes, and prudent in their own sight!

92 Wo unto the mighty to drink wine, and men of strength to mingle strong drink:

93 Who justify the wicked for reward, and take away the righteousness of the righteous from him!

94 Therefore, as the fire devoureth the stubble, and the flame consumeth the chaff, their root shall be rottenness, and their blossoms shall go up as dust; because they have cast away the law of the Lord of hosts, and despised the word of the Holy One of Israel.

95 Therefore, is the anger of the Lord kindled against his people, and he hath stretched forth his hand against them, and hath smitten them: and the hills did tremble, and their carcasses were torn in the midst of the streets. For all this

his anger is not turned away, but his hand stretched out still.

96 ¶And he will lift up an ensign to the nations from far, and will hiss unto them from the end of the earth; and behold, they shall come with speed swiftly:

97 None shall be weary nor stumble among them; none shall slumber nor sleep; neither shall the girdle of their loins be loosed, nor the latchet of their shoes be broken:

98 Whose arrows shall be sharp, and all their bows bent, and their horses' hoofs shall be counted like flint, and their wheels like a whirlwind, their roaring like a lion.

99 They shall roar like young lions: yea, they shall roar, and lay hold of the prey, and shall carry away safe, and none shall deliver.

100 And in that day they shall roar against them like the roaring of the sea; and if they look unto the land, behold, darkness and sorrow, and the light is darkened in the heavens thereof.

CHAPTER 9.

1 ¶[1]In the year that king Uzziah died, I saw also the Lord sitting upon a throne, high and lifted up, and his train filled the temple.

2 Above it stood the seraphims; each one had six wings; with twain he covered his face, and with twain he covered his feet, and with twain he did fly.

3 And one cried unto another, and said, Holy, holy, holy, is the Lord of hosts; the whole earth is full of his glory.

4 And the posts of the door moved at the voice of him that cried, and the house was filled with smoke.

5 ¶Then said I, Wo is unto me! for I am undone; because I am a man of unclean lips, and I dwell in the midst of a people of unclean lips; for mine eyes have seen the King, the Lord of hosts.

6 Then flew one of the seraphims unto me, having a live

---

[1]Isaiah 6.

coal in his hand, which he had taken with the tongs from off the altar:

7 And he laid it upon my mouth, and said, Lo, this has touched thy lips; and thine iniquity is taken away, and thy sin purged.

8 Also I heard the voice of the Lord, saying, Whom shall I send, and who will go for us? Then I said, Here am I; send me.

9 ¶And he said, Go, and tell this people, hear ye indeed, but they understood not; and see ye indeed, but they perceived not.

10 Make the heart of this people fat, and make their ears heavy, and shut their eyes; lest they see with their eyes, and hear with their ears, and understand with their heart, and be converted, and be healed.

11 Then said I, Lord, how long? And he said, Until the cities be wasted without inhabitant, and the houses without man, and the land be utterly desolate;

12 And the Lord have removed men far away, for there shall be a great forsaking in the midst of the land.

13 ¶But yet in it there shall be a tenth, and they shall return, and shall be eaten: as a teil-tree, and as an oak whose substance is in them, when they cast their leaves: so the holy seed shall be the substance thereof.

14 ¶ªAnd it came to pass in the days of Ahaz the son of Jotham, the son of Uzziah, king of Judah, that Rezin, king of Syria, and Pekah, the son of Remaliah, king of Israel, went up towards Jerusalem to war against it, but could not prevail against it.

15 And it was told the house of David, saying, Syria is confederate with Ephraim. And his heart was moved, and the heart of his people, as the trees of the wood are moved with the wind.

16 Then said the Lord unto Isaiah, Go forth now to meet Ahaz, thou, and Shear-jashub thy son, at the end of the conduit of the upper pool in the highway of the fuller's field;

ªIsaiah 7.

17 And say unto him, Take heed, and be quiet; fear not, neither be faint-hearted for the two tails of these smoking fire-brands, for the fierce anger of Rezin with Syria, and the son of Remaliah.

18 Because Syria, Ephraim, and the son of Remaliah, have taken evil counsel against thee, saying,

19 Let us go up against Judah, and vex it, and let us make a breach therein for us, and set a king in the midst of it, yea, the son of Tabeal:

20 Thus saith the Lord God, it shall not stand, neither shall it come to pass.

21 For the head of Syria, is Damascus; and the head of Damascus, Rezin: and within threescore and five years shall Ephraim be broken, that it be not a people.

22 And the head of Ephraim is Samaria, and the head of Samaria is Remaliah's son. If ye will not believe, surely ye shall not be established.

23 ¶Moreover, the Lord spake again unto Ahaz, saying,

24 Ask thee a sign of the Lord thy God; ask it either in the depths, or in the heights above.

25 But Ahaz said, I will not ask, neither will I tempt the Lord.

26 And he said: Hear ye now, O house of David; is it a small thing for you to weary men, but will ye weary my God also?

27 Therefore the Lord himself shall give you a sign: Behold, a virgin shall conceive, and shall bear a son, and shall call his name Immanuel.

28 Butter and honey shall he eat, that he may know to refuse the evil, and to choose the good.

29 For before the child shall know to refuse the evil and choose the good, the land that thou abhorrest shall be forsaken of both her kings.

30 ¶The Lord shall bring upon thee, and upon thy people, and upon thy father's house, days that have not come, from the day that Ephraim departed from Judah, the king of Assyria.

31 And it shall come to pass in that day, that the Lord

shall hiss for the fly that is in the uttermost part of Egypt, and for the bee that is in the land of Assyria.

32 And they shall come, and shall rest all of them in the desolate valleys, and in the holes of the rocks, and upon all thorns, and upon all bushes.

33 In the same day shall the Lord shave with a razor that is hired, by them beyond the river, by the king of Assyria, the head, and the hair of the feet, and it shall also consume the beard.

34 And it shall come to pass in that day, a man shall nourish a young cow, and two sheep;

35 And it shall come to pass, for the abundance of milk they shall give, he shall eat butter; for butter and honey shall every one eat that is left in the land.

36 And it shall come to pass in that day, every place shall be, where there were a thousand vines at a thousand silverlings, which shall be for briers and thorns.

37 With arrows and with bows shall men come thither; because all the land shall become briers and thorns.

38 And all hills that shall be digged with the mattock, there shall not come thither the fear of briers and thorns; but it shall be for the sending forth of oxen, and the treading of lesser cattle.

39 ¶[3]Moreover, the word of the Lord said unto me, Take thee a great roll, and write in it with a man's pen concerning Mahershalal-hash-baz.

40 And I took unto me faithful witnesses to record, Uriah the priest, and Zechariah the son of Jeberechiah.

41 And I went unto the prophetess; and she conceived and bare a son. Then said the Lord to me, Call his name Mahershalal-hash-baz.

42 For behold, the child shall not have knowledge to cry, My father, and my mother, before the riches of Damascus and the spoil of Samaria shall be taken away before the king of Assyria.

43 ¶The Lord spake also unto me again, saying,

---

[3]Isaiah 8.

44 Forasmuch as this people refuseth the waters of Shiloah that go softly and rejoice in Rezin and Remaliah's son;

45 Now therefore, behold, the Lord bringeth up upon them the waters of the river, strong and many, even the king of Assyria, and all his glory: and he shall come up over all his channels, and go over all his banks:

46 And he shall pass through Judah; and he shall overflow and go over, he shall reach even to the neck; and the stretching out of his wings shall fill the breadth of thy land, O Immanuel.

47 ¶Associate yourselves, O ye people, and ye shall be broken in pieces; and give ear all ye of far countries: gird yourselves, and ye shall be broken in pieces; gird yourselves, and ye shall be broken in pieces.

48 Take counsel together and it shall come to nought; speak the word, and it shall not stand: for God is with us.

49 ¶For the Lord spake thus to me with a strong hand, and instructed me that I should not walk in the way of this people, saying,

50 Say ye not, a confederacy, to all to whom this people shall say, a confederacy; neither fear ye their fear, nor be afraid.

51 Sanctify the Lord of hosts himself, and let him be your fear, and let him be your dread.

52 And he shall be for a sanctuary; but for a stone of stumbling and for a rock of offense to both the houses of Israel, for a gin and a snare to the inhabitants of Jerusalem.

53 And many among them shall stumble, and fall, and be broken, and be snared, and be taken.

54 Bind up the testimony, seal the law among my disciples.

55 And I will wait upon the Lord, that hideth his face from the house of Jacob, and I will look for him.

56 Behold, I and the children whom the Lord hath given me are for signs and for wonders in Israel from the Lord of hosts, which dwelleth in mount Zion.

57 ¶And when they shall say unto you, Seek unto them that have familiar spirits, and unto wizards that peep, and

mutter: should not a people seek unto their God? for the living to hear from the dead?

58 To the law and to the testimony: and if they speak not according to this word, it is because there is no light in them.

59 And they shall pass through it hardly bestead and hungry; and it shall come to pass, that when they shall be hungry, they shall fret themselves, and curse their king and their God, and look upward.

60 And they shall look unto the earth; and behold trouble, and darkness, dimness of anguish, and shall be driven to darkness.

61 ¶⁴Nevertheless the dimness shall not be such as was in her vexation, when at the first he lightly afflicted the land of Zebulun, and the land of Naphtali, and afterward did more grievously afflict by the way of the Red Sea beyond Jordan in Galilee of the nations.

62 The people that walked in darkness have seen a great light: they that dwell in the land of the shadow of death, upon them hath the light shined.

63 Thou hast multiplied the nation, and increased the joy: they joy before thee according to the joy in harvest, and as men rejoice when they divide the spoil.

64 For thou hast broken the yoke of his burden, and the staff of his shoulder, the rod of his oppressor.

65 For every battle of the warrior with confused noise, and garments rolled in blood; but this shall be with burning and fuel of fire.

66 For unto us a child is born, unto us a son is given: and the government shall be upon his shoulder: and his name shall be called Wonderful, Counselor, The mighty God, The everlasting Father, The Prince of Peace.

67 Of the increase of government and peace there is no end, upon the throne of David, and upon his kingdom, to order it, and to establish it with judgment and with justice from

⁴Isaiah 9.

henceforth even for ever. The zeal of the Lord of hosts will perform this.

68 ¶The Lord sent his word unto Jacob and it hath lighted upon Israel.

69 And all the people shall know, even Ephraim and the inhabitants of Samaria, that say in the pride and stoutness of heart,

70 The bricks are fallen down, but we will build with hewn stones: the sycamores are cut down, but we will change them into cedars.

71 Therefore the Lord shall set up the adversaries of Rezin against him, and join his enemies together;

72 The Syrians before, and the Philistines behind: and they shall devour Israel with open mouth. For all this his anger is not turned away, but his hand stretched out still.

73 ¶For the people turneth not unto him that smiteth them, neither do they seek the Lord of hosts.

74 Therefore, will the Lord cut off from Israel head and tail, branch and rush in one day.

75 The ancient, he is the head; and the prophet that teacheth lies, he is the tail.

76 For the leaders of this people cause them to err; and they that are led of them are destroyed.

77 Therefore the Lord shall have no joy in their young men, neither shall have mercy on their fatherless and widows: for every one of them is a hypocrite and an evil doer, and every mouth speaketh folly. For all this his anger is not turned away, but his hand stretched out still.

78 ¶For wickedness burneth as the fire; it shall devour the briers and thorns, and shall kindle in the thickets of the forests, and they shall mount up like the lifting up of smoke.

79 Through the wrath of the Lord of hosts is the land darkened, and the people shall be as the fuel of the fire; no man shall spare his brother.

80 And he shall snatch on the right hand, and be hungry; and he shall eat on the left hand, and they shall not be satisfied; they shall eat every man the flesh of his own arm:

81 Manasseh, Ephraim; and Ephraim, Manasseh; they

together shall be against Judah. For all this his anger is not turned away, but his hand stretched out still.

82 ¶ Wo unto them that decree unrighteous decrees, and that write grievousness which they have prescribed;

83 To turn aside the needy from judgment, and to take away the right from the poor of my people, that widows may be their prey, and that they may rob the fatherless!

84 And what will ye do in the day of visitation, and in the desolation which shall come from far? To whom will ye flee for help? and where will ye leave your glory?

85 Without me they shall bow down under the prisoners, and they shall fall under the slain. For all this his anger is not turned away, but his hand stretched out still.

86 ¶ O Assyrian, the rod of mine anger, and the staff in their hand is their indignation.

87 I will send him against a hypocritical nation, and against the people of my wrath will I give him a charge, to take the spoil, and to take the prey, and to tread them down like the mire of the streets.

88 Howbeit he meaneth not so, neither doth his heart think so; but in his heart it is to destroy and cut off nations not a few.

89 For he saith, Are not my princes altogether kings?

90 Is not Calno as Carchemish? Is not Hamath as Arpad? Is not Samaria as Damascus?

91 As my hand hath founded the kingdoms of the idols, and whose graven images did excel them of Jerusalem and of Samaria;

92 Shall I not, as I have done unto Samaria and her idols, so do to Jerusalem and to her idols?

93 Wherefore it shall come to pass, that when the Lord hath performed his whole work upon mount Zion and upon Jerusalem, I will punish the fruit of the stout heart of the king of Assyria, and the glory of his high looks.

94 For he saith, By the strength of my hand and by my wisdom I have done these things: for I am prudent; and I

⁵Isaiah 10.

have moved the borders of the people, and have robbed their treasures, and I have put down the inhabitants like a valiant man;

95 And my hand hath found as a nest the riches of the people; and as one gathereth eggs that are left, have I gathered all the earth: and there was none that moved the wing, or opened the mouth, or peeped.

96 Shall the axe boast itself against him that heweth therewith? Shall the saw magnify itself against him that shaketh it? as if the rod should shake itself against them that lift it up, or as if the staff should lift up itself, as if it were no wood.

97 Therefore shall the Lord, the Lord of hosts, send among his fat ones, leanness: and under his glory he shall kindle a burning like the burning of a fire.

98 And the light of Israel shall be for a fire, and his Holy One for a flame, and shall burn and shall devour his thorns and his briers in one day;

99 And shall consume the glory of his forest, and of his fruitful field, both soul and body; and they shall be as when a standard-bearer fainteth.

100 And the rest of the trees of his forest shall be few, that a child may write them.

101 ¶And it shall come to pass in that day, that the remnant of Israel, and such as are escaped of the house of Jacob, shall no more again stay upon him that smote them: but shall stay upon the Lord, the Holy One of Israel, in truth.

102 The remnant shall return, yea, even the remnant of Jacob, unto the mighty God.

103 For though thy people Israel be as the sand of the sea, yet a remnant of them shall return; the consumption decreed shall overflow with righteousness.

104 For the Lord God of hosts shall make a consumption, even determined, in all the land.

105 ¶Therefore, thus saith the Lord God of hosts, O my people, that dwellest in Zion, be not afraid of the Assyrian: he shall smite thee with a rod, and shall lift up his staff against thee, after the manner of Egypt.

106 For yet a very little while, and the indignation shall cease, and mine anger in their destruction.

107 And the Lord of hosts shall stir up a scourge for him according to the slaughter of Midian at the rock of Oreb: and as his rod was upon the sea, so shall he lift it up after the manner of Egypt.

108 And it shall come to pass in that day, that his burden shall be taken away from off thy shoulder, and his yoke from off thy neck, and the yoke shall be destroyed because of the anointing.

109 He is come to Aiath, he is passed to Migron; at Michmash he hath laid upon his carriages;

110 They are gone over the passage; they have taken up their lodging at Geba; Ramath is afraid; Gibeah of Saul is fled.

111 Lift up the voice, O daughter of Gallim: cause it to be heard unto Laish, O poor Anathoth.

112 Madmenah is removed: the inhabitants of Gebim gather themselves to flee.

113 As yet shall he remain at Nob that day; he shall shake his hand against the mount of the daughter of Zion, the hill of Jerusalem.

114 Behold, the Lord, the Lord of hosts shall lop the bough with terror: and the high ones of stature shall be hewn down: and the haughty shall be humbled.

115 And he shall cut down the thickets of the forests with iron, and Lebanon shall fall by a mighty one.

116 ¶[6]And there shall come forth a rod out of the stem of Jesse, and a branch shall grow out of his roots;

117 And the Spirit of the Lord shall rest upon him, the spirit of wisdom and understanding, the spirit of counsel and might, the spirit of knowledge and of the fear of the Lord;

118 And shall make him of quick understanding in the fear of the Lord: and he shall not judge after the sight of his eyes, neither reprove after the hearing of his ears;

119 But with righteousness shall he judge the poor, and

[6]Isaiah 11.

reprove with equity for the meek of the earth: and he shall smite the earth with the rod of his mouth, and with the breath of his lips shall he slay the wicked.

120 And righteousness shall be the girdle of his loins, and faithfulness the girdle of his reins.

121 The wolf also shall dwell with the lamb, and the leopard shall lie down with the kid; and the calf and the young lion and the fatling together; and a little child shall lead them.

122 And the cow and the bear shall feed; their young ones shall lie down together; and the lion shall eat straw like the ox.

123 And the sucking child shall play on the hole of the asp, and the weaned child shall put his hand on the cockatrice's den.

124 They shall not hurt nor destroy in all my holy mountain: for the earth shall be full of the knowledge of the Lord, as the waters cover the sea.

125 ¶And in that day there shall be a root of Jesse, which shall stand for an ensign of the people: to it shall the Gentiles seek: and his rest shall be glorious.

126 And it shall come to pass in that day, that the Lord shall set his hand again the second time to recover the remnant of his people, which shall be left from Assyria, and from Egypt, and from Pathros, and from Cush, and from Elam, and from Shinar, and from Hamath, and from the islands of the sea.

127 And he shall set up an ensign for the nations, and shall assemble the outcasts of Israel, and gather together the dispersed of Judah from the four corners of the earth.

128 The envy of Ephraim also shall depart, and the adversaries of Judah shall be cut off: Ephraim shall not envy Judah, and Judah shall not vex Ephraim.

129 But they shall fly upon the shoulders of the Philistines toward the west; they shall spoil them of the east together; they shall lay their hand upon Edom and Moab; and the children of Ammon shall obey them.

130 And the Lord shall utterly destroy the tongue of the

Egyptian sea; and with his mighty wind he shall shake his hand over the river, and shall smite it in the seven streams, and make men go over dry shod.

131 And there shall be a highway for the remnant of his people, which shall be left, from Assyria, like as it was to Israel in the day that he came up out of the land of Egypt.

132 ¶[7]And in that day thou shalt say, O Lord, I will praise thee: though thou wast angry with me, thine anger is turned away, and thou comfortedst me.

133 Behold, God is my salvation; I will trust, and not be afraid: for the Lord, JEHOVAH is my strength and my song; he also is become my salvation.

134 Therefore, with joy shall ye draw water out of the wells of salvation.

135 And in that day shall ye say, Praise the Lord, call upon his name, declare his doings among the people, make mention that his name is exalted.

136 Sing unto the Lord; for he hath done excellent things: this is known in all the earth.

137 Cry out and shout, thou inhabitant of Zion; for great is the Holy One of Israel in the midst of thee.

CHAPTER 10.

1 ¶[1]The burden of Babylon, which Isaiah the son of Amoz did see.

2 Lift ye up a banner upon the high mountain, exalt the voice unto them, shake the hand, that they may go into the gates of the nobles.

3 I have commanded my sanctified ones, I have also called my mighty ones, for mine anger is not upon them that rejoice in my highness.

4 The noise of the multitude in the mountains like as of a great people; a tumultuous noise of the kingdoms of nations

[7]Isaiah 12.
[1]Isaiah 13.

gathered together: the Lord of hosts mustereth the hosts of the battle.

5 They come from a far country, from the end of heaven, yea, the Lord, and the weapons of his indignation, to destroy the whole land.

6 ¶Howl ye; for the day of the Lord is at hand: it shall come as a destruction from the Almighty.

7 Therefore, shall all hands be faint, every man's heart shall melt;

8 And they shall be afraid; pangs and sorrows shall take hold of them; they shall be amazed one at another; their faces shall be as flames:

9 Behold, the day of the Lord cometh, cruel both with wrath and fierce anger, to lay the land desolate: and he shall destroy the sinners thereof out of it.

10 For the stars of heaven and the constellations thereof shall not give their light; the sun shall be darkened in his going forth, and the moon shall not cause her light to shine.

11 And I will punish the world for evil, and the wicked for their iniquity; I will cause the arrogancy of the proud to cease, and will lay down the haughtiness of the terrible;

12 I will make a man more precious than fine gold; even a man than the golden wedge of Ophir.

13 Therefore, I will shake the heavens, and the earth shall remove out of her place, in the wrath of the Lord of hosts, and in the day of his fierce anger.

14 And it shall be as the chased roe, and as a sheep that no man taketh up: they shall every man turn to his own people, and flee every one into his own land.

15 Every one that is proud shall be thrust through; yea, and every one that is joined to the wicked, shall fall by the sword.

16 Their children also shall be dashed to pieces before their eyes; their houses shall be spoiled and their wives ravished.

17 Behold, I will stir up the Medes against them, which shall not regard silver and gold, nor they shall not delight in it.

18 Their bows shall also dash the young men to pieces; and

they shall have no pity on the fruit of the womb; their eyes shall not spare children.

19 ¶And Babylon, the glory of kingdoms, the beauty of the Chaldee's excellency, shall be as when God overthrew Sodom and Gomorrah.

20 It shall never be inhabited, neither shall it be dwelt in from generation to generation: neither shall the Arabian pitch tent there; neither shall the shepherds make their fold there:

21 But wild beasts of the desert shall lie there; and their houses shall be full of doleful creatures; and owls shall dwell there, and satyrs shall dance there.

22 And the wild beasts of the islands shall cry in their desolate houses, and dragons in their pleasant palaces: and her time is near to come, and her day shall not be prolonged. For I will destroy her speedily; yea, for I will be merciful unto my people: but the wicked shall perish.

23 ¶²For the Lord will have mercy on Jacob, and will yet choose Israel, and set them in their own land: and the strangers shall be joined with them, and they shall cleave to the house of Jacob.

24 And the people shall take them, and bring them to their place; yea, from far unto the ends of the earth; and they shall return to their lands of promise. And the house of Israel shall possess them, and the land of the Lord shall be for servants and handmaids; and they shall take them captives, unto whom they were captives; and they shall rule over their oppressors.

25 And it shall come to pass in that day that the Lord shall give thee rest, from thy sorrow, and from thy fear, and from the hard bondage wherein thou wast made to serve.

26 ¶And it shall come to pass in that day that thou shalt take up this proverb against the king of Babylon, and say, How hath the oppressor ceased, the golden city ceased!

27 The Lord hath broken the staff of the wicked, the scepters of the rulers.

²Isaiah 14.

28 He who smote the people in wrath with a continual stroke, he that ruled the nations in anger, is persecuted, and none hindereth.

29 The whole earth is at rest, and is quiet: they break forth into singing.

30 Yea, the fir-trees rejoice at thee, and also the cedars of Lebanon, saying, Since thou art laid down, no feller is come up against us.

31 Hell from beneath is moved for thee to meet thee at thy coming; it stirreth up the dead for thee, even all the chief ones of the earth: it hath raised up from their thrones all the kings of the nations.

32 All they shall speak and say unto thee, Art thou also become weak as we? Art thou become like unto us?

33 Thy pomp is brought down to the grave; the noise of thy viols is not heard: the worm is spread under thee, and the worms cover thee.

34 How art thou fallen from heaven, O Lucifer, son of the morning! Art thou cut down to the ground, which did weaken the nations!

35 For thou hast said in thy heart, I will ascend into heaven, I will exalt my throne above the stars of God: I will sit also upon the mount of the congregation, in the sides of the north;

36 I will ascend above the heights of the clouds; I will be like the Most High.

37 Yet thou shalt be brought down to hell, to the sides of the pit.

38 They that see thee shall narrowly look upon thee, and shall consider thee, and shall say, Is this the man that made the earth to tremble, that did shake kingdoms,

39 And made the world as a wilderness, and destroyed the cities thereof, and opened not the house of his prisoners?

40 All the kings of the nations, yea, all of them, lie in glory, every one of them in his own house.

41 But thou art cast out of thy grave like an abominable branch, and the remnant of those that are slain, thrust

through with a sword, that go down to the stones of the pit; as a carcass trodden under feet.

42 Thou shalt not be joined with them in burial, because thou hast destroyed thy land, and slain thy people: the seed of evil doers shall never be renowned.

43 Prepare slaughter for his children for the iniquities of their fathers; that they do not rise, nor possess the land, nor fill the face of the world with cities.

44 For I will rise up against them, saith the Lord of hosts, and cut off from Babylon the name, and remnant, and son, and nephew, saith the Lord.

45 I will also make it a possession for the bittern, and pools of water: and I will sweep it with the besom of destruction, saith the Lord of hosts.

46 ¶The Lord of hosts hath sworn, saying, Surely as I have thought, so shall it come to pass; and as I have purposed, so shall it stand:

47 That I will bring the Assyrian in my land, and upon my mountains tread him under foot: then shall his yoke depart from off them, and his burden depart from off their shoulders.

48 This is the purpose that is purposed upon the whole earth: and this is the hand that is stretched out upon all nations.

49 For the Lord of Hosts hath purposed, and who shall disannul? And his hand stretched out, and who shall turn it back?

50 In the year that King Ahaz died was this burden.

51 ¶Rejoice not thou, whole Palestina, because the rod of him that smote thee is broken: for out of the serpent's root shall come forth a cockatrice, and his fruit shall be a fiery flying serpent.

52 And the first born of the poor shall feed, and the needy shall lie down in safety: and I will kill thy root with famine, and he shall slay thy remnant.

53 Howl, O gate; cry, O city; thou, whole Palestina, art dissolved: for there shall come from the north a smoke, and none shall be alone in his appointed times.

54 What shall then answer the messengers of the nations? That the Lord hath founded Zion, and the poor of his people shall trust in it.

CHAPTER 11.

1 ¶Now I, Nephi, do speak somewhat concerning the words which I have written, which have been spoken by the mouth of Isaiah.

2 For behold, Isaiah spake many things which were hard for many of my people to understand; for they know not concerning the manner of prophesying among the Jews.

3 For I, Nephi, have not taught them many things concerning the manner of the Jews; for their works were works of darkness, and their doings were doings of abomination.

4 Wherefore, I write unto my people, unto all those that shall receive hereafter these things which I write, that they may know the judgments of God, that they come upon all nations, according to the word which he hath spoken.

5 Wherefore hearken, O my people, which are of the house of Israel, and give ear unto my words: for because the words of Isaiah are not plain unto you, nevertheless they are plain unto all those that are filled with the spirit of prophecy.

6 But I give unto you a prophecy, according to the spirit which is in me; wherefore I shall prophesy according to the plainness which hath been with me from the time that I came out from Jerusalem with my father:

7 For behold, my soul delighteth in plainness unto my people, that they may learn;

8 Yea, and my soul delighteth in the words of Isaiah, for I came out from Jerusalem, and mine eyes hath beheld the things of the Jews, and I know that the Jews do understand the things of the prophets, and there is none other people that understand the things which were spoken unto the Jews, like unto them, save it be that they are taught after the manner of the things of the Jews.

9 But behold, I, Nephi, have not taught my children after the manner of the Jews; but behold, I, of myself, have dwelt

at Jerusalem, wherefore I know concerning the regions round about;

10 And I have made mention unto my children concerning the judgments of God, which hath come to pass among the Jews, unto my children, according to all that which Isaiah hath spoken, and I do not write them.

11 But behold, I proceed with mine own prophecy, according to my plainness; in the which I know that no man can err;

12 Nevertheless, in the days that the prophecies of Isaiah shall be fulfilled, men shall know of a surety, at the times when they shall come to pass;

13 Wherefore, they are of worth unto the children of men, and he that supposeth that they are not, unto them will I speak particularly, and confine the words unto mine own people:

14 For I know that they shall be of great worth unto them in the last days; for in that day shall they understand them; wherefore, for their good have I written them.

15 And as one generation hath been destroyed among the Jews, because of iniquity, even so have they been destroyed from generation to generation, according to their iniquities;

16 And never hath any of them been destroyed, save it were foretold them by the prophets of the Lord.

17 Wherefore, it hath been told them concerning the destruction which should come upon them, immediately after my father left Jerusalem;

18 Nevertheless, they hardened their hearts; and according to my prophecy, they have been destroyed, save it be those which are carried away captive into Babylon.

19 And now this I speak because of the spirit which is in me.

20 And notwithstanding they have been carried away, they shall return again, and possess the land of Jerusalem; wherefore they shall be restored again to the lands of their inheritance.

21 But, behold, they shall have wars, and rumors of wars; and when the day cometh that the Only Begotten of the

Father, yea, even the Father of heaven and of earth, shall manifest himself unto them in the flesh, behold, they will reject him, because of their iniquities, and the hardness of their hearts, and the stiffness of their necks.

22 Behold, they will crucify him, and after he is laid in a sepulcher for the space of three days, he shall rise from the dead, with healing in his wings, and all those who shall believe on his name, shall be saved in the kingdom of God;

23 Wherefore, my soul delighteth to prophesy concerning him, for I have seen his day, and my heart doth magnify his holy name.

24 ¶And behold, it shall come to pass, that after the Messiah hath risen from the dead, and hath manifested himself unto his people, unto as many as will believe on his name, behold, Jerusalem shall be destroyed again: for wo unto them that fight against God and the people of his church.

25 Wherefore, the Jews shall be scattered among all nations; yea, and also Babylon shall be destroyed; wherefore, the Jews shall be scattered by other nations;

26 And after they have been scattered, and the Lord God hath scourged them by other nations, for the space of many generations, yea, even down from generation to generation, until they shall be persuaded to believe in Christ, the Son of God, and the atonement, which is infinite for all mankind;

27 And when that day shall come, that they shall believe in Christ, and worship the Father in his name, with pure hearts, and clean hands, and look not forward any more for another Messiah, then, at that time, the day will come that it must needs be expedient that they should believe these things,

28 And the Lord will set his hand again the second time to restore his people from their lost and fallen state.

29 Wherefore, he will proceed to do a marvelous work, and a wonder among the children of men.

30 ¶Wherefore, he shall bring forth his words unto them, which words shall judge them at the last day;

31 For they shall be given them for the purpose of convincing them of the true Messiah, who was rejected by them;

32 And unto the convincing of them that they need not look forward any more for a Messiah to come,

33 For there should not any come, save it should be a false Messiah, which should deceive the people:

34 For there is save one Messiah spoken of by the prophets, and that Messiah is he who should be rejected of the Jews.

35 For according to the words of the prophets, the Messiah cometh in six hundred years from the time that my father left Jerusalem;

36 And according to the words of the prophets, and also the word of the angel of God, his name shall be Jesus Christ, the Son of God.

37 ¶And now my brethren, I have spoken plain, that ye can not err;

38 And as the Lord God liveth, that brought Israel up out of the land of Egypt, and gave unto Moses power that he should heal the nations, after they had been bitten by the poisonous serpents, if they would cast their eyes unto the serpent which he did raise up before them, and also gave him power that he should smite the rock, and the water should come forth;

39 Yea, behold, I say unto you, that as these things are true, and as the Lord God liveth, there is none other name given under heaven, save it be this Jesus Christ of which I have spoken, whereby man can be saved.

40 ¶Wherefore, for this cause hath the Lord God promised unto me that these things which I write, shall be kept and preserved, and handed down unto my seed, from generation to generation, that the promise may be fulfilled unto Joseph, that his seed should never perish as long as the earth should stand.

41 Wherefore, these things shall go from generation to generation as long as the earth shall stand; and they shall go according to the will and pleasure of God;

42 And the nations which shall possess them, shall be judged of them according to the words which are written;

43 For we labor diligently to write, to persuade our chil-

dren, and also our brethren, to believe in Christ, and to be reconciled to God;

44 For we know that it is by grace that we are saved, after all we can do.

45 ¶And notwithstanding we believe in Christ, we keep the law of Moses, and look forward with steadfastness unto Christ, until the law shall be fulfilled; for, for this end was the law given;

46 Wherefore, the law hath become dead unto us, and we are made alive in Christ, because of our faith;

47 Yet we keep the law because of the commandments;

48 And we talk of Christ, we rejoice in Christ, we preach of Christ, we prophesy of Christ, and we write according to our prophecies, that our children may know to what source they may look for a remission of their sins.

49 Wherefore, we speak concerning the law, that our children may know the deadness of the law;

50 And they, by knowing the deadness of the law, may look forward unto that life which is in Christ, and know for what end the law was given.

51 And after the law is fulfilled in Christ, that they need not harden their hearts against him, when the law ought to be done away.

52 ¶And now behold, my people, ye are a stiff-necked people; wherefore, I have spoken plain unto you, that ye can not misunderstand.

53 And the words which I have spoken, shall stand as a testimony against you; for they are sufficient to teach any man the right way:

54 For the right way is to believe in Christ and deny him not; for by denying him, ye also deny the prophets and the law.

55 ¶And now behold I say unto you, that the right way is to believe in Christ, and deny him not; and Christ is the Holy One of Israel:

56 Wherefore ye must bow down before him, and worship him with all your might, mind and strength, and your whole soul, and if ye do this, ye shall in no wise be cast out.

57 And inasmuch as it shall be expedient, ye must keep the performances and ordinances of God, until the law shall be fulfilled which was given unto Moses.

58 ¶And after Christ shall have risen from the dead, he shall shew himself unto you, my children, and my beloved brethren;

59 And the words which he shall speak unto you, shall be the law which ye shall do.

60 For behold, I say unto you, that I have beheld that many generations shall pass away, and there shall be great wars and contentions among my people.

61 And after the Messiah shall come, there shall be signs given unto my people of his birth, and also of his death and resurrection;

62 And great and terrible shall that day be unto the wicked; for they shall perish;

63 And they perish because they cast out the prophets, and the saints, and stone them, and slay them:

64 Wherefore the cry of the blood of the saints shall ascend up to God from the ground, against them.

65 Wherefore all those who are proud, and that do wickedly, the day that cometh shall burn them up, saith the Lord of hosts, for they shall be as stubble;

66 And they that kill the prophets, and the saints, the depths of the earth shall swallow them up, saith the Lord of hosts:

67 And mountains shall cover them, and whirlwinds shall carry them away, and buildings shall fall upon them, and crush them to pieces and grind them to powder;

68 And they shall be visited with thunderings, and lightnings, and earthquakes, and all manner of destructions;

69 For the fire of the anger of the Lord shall be kindled against them, and they shall be as stubble, and the day that cometh shall consume them, saith the Lord of hosts.

70 ¶O the pain, and the anguish of my soul for the loss of the slain of my people!

71 For I, Nephi, hath seen it, and it well nigh consumeth

me before the presence of the Lord: but I must cry unto my God, Thy ways are just.

72 But behold, the righteous, that hearken unto the words of the prophets, and destroy them not, but look forward unto Christ with steadfastness for the signs which are given, notwithstanding all persecutions; behold they are they which shall not perish.

73 But the Son of Righteousness shall appear unto them; and he shall heal them, and they shall have peace with him, until three generations shall have passed away, and many of the fourth generation shall have passed away in righteousness.

74 And when these things shall have passed away, a speedy destruction cometh unto my people; for, notwithstanding the pains of my soul, I have seen it; wherefore, I know that it shall come to pass;

75 And they sell themselves for nought; for, for the reward of their pride, and their foolishness, they shall reap destruction;

76 For because they yield unto the devil, and choose works of darkness rather than light; therefore they must go down to hell, for the Spirit of the Lord will not always strive with man.

77 And when the Spirit ceaseth to strive with man, then cometh speedy destruction; and this grieveth my soul.

78 ¶And as I spake concerning the convincing of the Jews, that Jesus is the very Christ, it must needs be that the Gentiles be convinced also, that Jesus is the Christ, the Eternal God; and that he manifesteth himself unto all those who believe in him, by the power of the Holy Ghost;

79 Yea, unto every nation, kindred, tongue, and people, working mighty miracles, signs and wonders, among the children of men, according to their faith.

80 ¶But behold, I prophesy unto you concerning the last days; concerning the days when the Lord God shall bring these things forth unto the children of men.

81 After my seed, and the seed of my brethren shall have

dwindled in unbelief, and shall have been smitten by the Gentiles;

82 Yea, after the Lord God shall have camped against them round about, and shall have laid siege against them with a mount, and raised forts against them;

83 And after they shall have been brought down low in the dust, even that they are not, yet the words of the righteous shall be written, and the prayers of the faithful shall be heard, and all those who have dwindled in unbelief, shall not be forgotten;

84 For those who shall be destroyed shall speak unto them out of the ground, and their speech shall be low out of the dust, and their voice shall be as one that hath a familiar spirit;

85 For the Lord God will give unto him power, that he may whisper concerning them, even as it were out of the ground; and their speech shall whisper out of the dust.

86 For thus saith the Lord God: They shall write the things which shall be done among them, and they shall be written and sealed up in a book, and those who have dwindled in unbelief shall not have them, for they seek to destroy the things of God;

87 Wherefore, as those who have been destroyed, have been destroyed speedily: and the multitude of their terrible ones shall be as chaff that passeth away.

88 Yea, thus saith the Lord God: It shall be at an instant, suddenly.

89 ¶And it shall come to pass, that those who have dwindled in unbelief, shall be smitten by the hand of the Gentiles.

90 And the Gentiles are lifted up in the pride of their eyes, and have stumbled, because of the greatness of their stumbling block, that they have built up many churches;

91 Nevertheless they put down the power and the miracles of God, and preach up unto themselves, their own wisdom, and their own learning, that they may get gain, and grind upon the face of the poor;

92 And there are many churches built up which cause envyings, and strifes, and malice;

93 And there are also secret combinations, even as in times of old, according to the combinations of the devil, for he is the foundation of all these things; yea, the foundation of murder, and works of darkness;

94 Yea, and he leadeth them by the neck with a flaxen cord, until he bindeth them with his strong cords for ever.

95 ¶For behold, my beloved brethren, I say unto you, that the Lord God worketh not in darkness.

96 He doeth not anything save it be for the benefit of the world; for he loveth the world, even that he layeth down his own life, that he may draw all men unto him.

97 Wherefore, he commandeth none that they shall not partake of his salvation.

98 Behold, doth he cry unto any, saying, Depart from me?

99 Behold, I say unto you, Nay; but he saith, Come unto me all ye ends of the earth, buy milk and honey, without money and without price.

100 Behold, hath he commanded any that they should depart out of the synagogues, or out of the houses of worship?

101 Behold, I say unto you, Nay.

102 Hath he commanded any that they should not partake of his salvation?

103 Behold, I say unto you, Nay; but he hath given it free for all men; and he hath commanded his people that they should persuade all men to repentance.

104 Behold, hath the Lord commanded any that they should not partake of his goodness?

105 Behold, I say unto you, Nay; but all men are privileged the one like unto the other, and none are forbidden.

106 He commandeth that there shall be no priestcrafts; for, behold, priestcrafts are that men preach and set themselves up for a light unto the world, that they may get gain, and praise of the world; but they seek not the welfare of Zion.

107 Behold, the Lord hath forbidden this thing; wherefore, the Lord God hath given a commandment, that all men should have charity, which charity is love.

108 And except they should have charity, they were noth-

ing: wherefore, if they should have charity, they would not suffer the laborer in Zion to perish.

109 But the laborer in Zion shall labor for Zion; for if they labor for money, they shall perish.

110 And, again, the Lord God hath commanded that men should not murder; that they should not lie; that they should not steal; that they should not take the name of the Lord their God in vain; that they should not envy; that they should not have malice; that they should not contend one with another; that they should not commit whoredoms; and that they should do none of these things;

111 For whoso doeth them shall perish; for none of these iniquities come of the Lord; for he doeth that which is good among the children of men;

112 And he doeth nothing save it be plain unto the children of men;

113 And he inviteth them all to come unto him, and partake of his goodness;

114 And he denieth none that come unto him, black and white, bond and free, male and female;

115 And he remembereth the heathen, and all are alike unto God, both Jew and Gentile.

116 But behold, in the last days, or in the days of the Gentiles; yea, behold all the nations of the Gentiles, and also the Jews, both those who shall come upon this land, and those who shall be upon other lands; yea, even upon all the lands of the earth; behold, they will be drunken with iniquity, and all manner of abominations;

117 And when that day shall come, they shall be visited of the Lord of hosts, with thunder and with earthquake, and with a great noise, and with storm and with tempest, and with the flame of devouring fire;

118 And all the nations that fight against Zion, and that distress her, shall be as a dream of a night vision;

119 Yea, it shall be unto them even as unto a hungry man, which dreameth, and behold he eateth, but he awaketh and his soul is empty;

120 Or like unto a thirsty man which dreameth, and behold

he drinketh, but he awaketh, and behold he is faint, and his soul hath appetite:

121 Yea, even so shall the multitude of all the nations be that fight against mount Zion:

122 For behold, all ye that do iniquity, stay yourselves and wonder; for ye shall cry out, and cry, yea, ye shall be drunken, but not with wine; ye shall stagger, but not with strong drink;

123 For behold, the Lord hath poured out upon you the spirit of deep sleep.

124 For behold, ye have closed your eyes, and ye have rejected the prophets, and your rulers, and the seers hath he covered because of your iniquity.

125 ¶And it shall come to pass, that the Lord God shall bring forth unto you the words of a book, and they shall be the words of them which have slumbered.

126 And behold the book shall be sealed: and in the book shall be a revelation from God, from the beginning of the world to the ending thereof.

127 Wherefore, because of the things which are sealed up, the things which are sealed, shall not be delivered in the day of the wickedness and abominations of the people.

128 Wherefore the book shall be kept from them.

129 But the book shall be delivered unto a man, and he shall deliver the words of the book, which are the words of those who have slumbered in the dust; and he shall deliver these words unto another; but the words which are sealed, he shall not deliver, neither shall he deliver the book.

130 For the book shall be sealed by the power of God, and the revelation which was sealed, shall be kept in the book until the own due time of the Lord, that they may come forth: for, behold, they reveal all things from the foundation of the world unto the end thereof.

131 And the day cometh that the words of the book which were sealed, shall be read upon the housetops; and they shall be read by the power of Christ;

132 And all things shall be revealed unto the children of

men which ever have been among the children of men, and which ever will be, even unto the end of the earth.

133 Wherefore, at that day when the book shall be delivered unto the man of whom I have spoken, the book shall be hid from the eyes of the world, that the eyes of none shall behold it, save it be that three witnesses shall behold it, by the power of God, besides him to whom the book shall be delivered; and they shall testify to the truth of the book and the things therein.

134 And there is none other which shall view it, save it be a few, according to the will of God, to bear testimony of his word unto the cnildren of men: for the Lord God hath said, that the words of the faithful should speak as if it were from the dead.

135 Wherefore, the Lord God will proceed to bring forth the words of the book; and in the mouth of as many witnesses as seemeth him good, will he establish his word; and wo be unto him that rejecteth the word of God.

136 ¶But behold, it shall come to pass that the Lord God shall say unto him to whom he shall deliver the book, Take these words which are not sealed, and deliver them to another, that he may shew them unto the learned, saying, Read this, I pray thee.

137 And the learned shall say, Bring hither the book, and I will read them:

138 And now, because of the glory of the world, and to get gain, will they say this, and not for the glory of God.

139 And the man shall say, I can not bring the book, for it is sealed.

140 Then shall the learned say, I can not read it.

141 Wherefore it shall come to pass, that the Lord God will deliver again the book and the words thereof, to him that is not learned; and the man that is not learned, shall say, I am not learned.

142 Then shall the Lord God say unto him, The learned shall not read them, for they have rejected them, and I am able to do mine own work; wherefore, thou shalt read the words which I shall give unto thee.

CHAP. 11.] SECOND BOOK OF NEPHI. 151

143 Touch not the things which are sealed, for I will bring them forth in mine own due time: for I will shew unto the children of men, that I am able to do mine own work.

144 Wherefore, when thou hast read the words which I have commanded thee, and obtained the witnesses which I have promised unto thee, then shalt thou seal up the book again, and hide it up unto me, that I may preserve the words which thou hast not read, until I shall see fit in mine own wisdom, to reveal all things unto the children of men.

145 For behold, I am God; and I am a God of miracles; and I will shew unto the world that I am the same yesterday, to-day, and for ever; and I work not among the children of men, save it be according to their faith.

146 ¶And again it shall come to pass, that the Lord shall say unto him that shall read the words that shall be delivered him, Forasmuch as this people draw near unto me with their mouth, and with their lips do honor me, but have removed their hearts far from me, and their fear towards me is taught by the precepts of men, therefore, I will proceed to do a marvelous work among this people;

147 Yea, a marvelous work, and a wonder, for the wisdom of their wise and learned shall perish, and the understanding of their prudent shall be hid.

148 And wo unto them that seek deep to hide their counsel from the Lord.

149 And their works are in the dark; and they say, Who seeth us; and who knoweth us?

150 And they also say, Surely, your turning of things upside down, shall be esteemed as the potter's clay.

151 But behold, I will shew unto them, saith the Lord of hosts, that I know all their works.

152 For shall the work say of him that made it, He made me not?

153 Or shall the thing framed say of him that framed it, He had no understanding?

154 But behold, saith the Lord of hosts, I will shew unto the children of men, that it is not yet a very little while, and

Lebanon shall be turned into a fruitful field; and the fruitful field shall be esteemed as a forest.

155 And in that day shall the deaf hear the words of the book; and the eyes of the blind shall see out of obscurity and out of darkness:

156 And the meek also shall increase, and their joy shall be in the Lord; and the poor among men shall rejoice in the Holy One of Israel.

157 For assuredly as the Lord liveth, they shall see that the terrible one is brought to nought, and the scorner is consumed, and all that watch for iniquity are cut off; and they that make a man an offender for a word, and lay a snare for him that reproveth in the gate, and turn aside the just for a thing of nought.

158 Therefore thus saith the Lord, who redeemed Abraham, concerning the house of Jacob, Jacob shall not now be ashamed, neither shall his face now wax pale.

159 But when he seeth his children, the work of my hands, in the midst of him, they shall sanctify my name, and sanctify the Holy One of Jacob, and shall fear the God of Israel.

160 They also that erred in spirit shall come to understanding, and they that murmured shall learn doctrine.

CHAPTER 12.

1 ¶ And now, behold, my brethren, I have spoken unto you according as the Spirit hath constrained me; wherefore, I know that they must surely come to pass.

2 And the things which shall be written out of the book shall be of great worth unto the children of men, and especially unto our seed, which is a remnant of the house of Israel.

3 For it shall come to pass in that day, that the churches which are built up, and not unto the Lord, when the one shall say unto the other, Behold, I, I am the Lord's; and the other shall say, I, I am the Lord's.

4 And thus shall every one say, that hath built up churches, and not unto the Lord;

5 And they shall contend one with another; and their priests shall contend one with another; and they shall teach with their learning, and deny the Holy Ghost, which giveth utterance.

6 And they deny the power of God, the Holy One of Israel; and they say unto the people, Hearken unto us, and hear ye our precept;

7 For behold, there is no God to-day, for the Lord and the Redeemer hath done his work, and he hath given his power unto men.

8 Behold, hearken ye unto my precept: if they shall say there is a miracle wrought, by the hand of the Lord, believe it not; for this day he is not a God of miracles; he hath done his work.

9 Yea, and there shall be many which shall say, Eat, drink, and be merry, for to-morrow we die: and it shall be well with us.

10 And there shall also be many which shall say, Eat, drink, and be merry; nevertheless, fear God, he will justify in committing a little sin: yea, lie a little, take the advantage of one because of his words, dig a pit for thy neighbor; there is no harm in this.

11 And do all these things, for to-morrow we die; and if it so be that we are guilty, God will beat us with a few stripes, and at last we shall be saved in the kingdom of God.

12 Yea, and there shall be many which shall teach after this manner, false, and vain, and foolish doctrines, and shall be puffed up in their hearts, and shall seek deep to hide their counsels from the Lord; and their works shall be in the dark; and the blood of the saints shall cry from the ground against them.

13 Yea, they have all gone out of the way; they have become corrupted.

14 Because of pride, and because of false teachers, and false doctrine, their churches have become corrupted; and their churches are lifted up; because of pride, they are puffed up.

15 They rob the poor, because of their fine sanctuaries;

they rob the poor, because of their fine clothing; and they persecute the meek, and the poor in heart; because in their pride, they are puffed up.

16 They wear stiff necks and high heads; yea, and because of pride, and wickedness, and abominations, and whoredoms, they have all gone astray, save it be a few, who are the humble followers of Christ;

17 Nevertheless, they are led, that in many instances they do err, because they are taught by the precepts of men.

18 ¶O the wise, and the learned, and the rich, that are puffed up in the pride of their hearts, and all those who preach false doctrines, and all those who commit whoredoms, and pervert the right way of the Lord; wo, wo, wo be unto them, saith the Lord God Almighty, for they shall be thrust down to hell.

19 ¶Wo unto them that turn aside the just for a thing of nought, and revile against that which is good, and say that it is of no worth:

20 For the day shall come that the Lord God will speedily visit the inhabitants of the earth; and in that day that they are fully ripe in iniquity, they shall perish.

21 But behold, if the inhabitants of the earth shall repent of their wickedness and abominations, they shall not be destroyed, saith the Lord of hosts.

22 But behold, that great and abominable church, the whore of all the earth, must tumble to the earth; and great must be the fall thereof:

23 For the kingdom of the devil must shake, and they which belong to it must needs be stirred up unto repentance, or the devil will grasp them with his everlasting chains, and they be stirred up to anger and perish:

24 For behold, at that day shall he rage in the hearts of the children of men, and stir them up to anger against that which is good;

25 And others will he pacify, and lull them away into carnal security, that they will say, All is well in Zion; yea, Zion prospereth, all is well;

26 And thus the devil cheateth their souls, and leadeth them away carefully down to hell.

27 And behold, others he flattereth away, and telleth them there is no hell; and he saith unto them, I am no devil, for there is none:

28 And thus he whispereth in their ears, until he grasps them with his awful chains, from whence there is no deliverance.

29 Yea, they are grasped with death and hell; and death, and hell, and the devil, and all that have been seized therewith, must stand before the throne of God and be judged according to their works, from whence they must go into the place prepared for them, even a lake of fire and brimstone, which is endless torment.

30 Therefore, wo be unto him that is at ease in Zion.

31 Wo be unto him that crieth, All is well; yea, wo be unto him that hearkeneth unto the precepts of men, and denieth the power of God, and the gift of the Holy Ghost.

32 Yea, wo be unto him that saith, We have received, and we need no more.

33 And in fine, wo unto all those who tremble, and are angry because of the truth of God.

34 For behold, he that is built upon the rock, receiveth it with gladness: and he that is built upon a sandy foundation, trembleth, lest he shall fall.

35 ¶Wo be unto him that shall say, We have received the word of God, and we need no more of the word of God, for we have enough.

36 For behold, thus saith the Lord God: I will give unto the children of men line upon line, precept upon precept, here a little and there a little:

37 And blessed are those who hearken unto my precepts, and lend an ear unto my counsel, for they shall learn wisdom;

38 For unto him that receiveth, I will give more: and from them that shall say, We have enough, shall be taken away even that which they have.

39 Cursed is he that putteth his trust in man, or maketh flesh his arm, or shall hearken unto the precepts of men, save

their precepts shall be given by the power of the Holy Ghost.

40 ¶Wo be unto the Gentiles, saith the Lord God of hosts; for notwithstanding I shall lengthen out mine arm unto them from day to day, they will deny me;

41 Nevertheless, I will be merciful unto them, saith the Lord God, if they will repent and come unto me; for mine arm is lengthened out all the day long, saith the Lord God of hosts.

42 ¶But behold, there shall be many at that day, when I shall proceed to do a marvelous work among them, that I may remember my covenants which I have made unto the children of men, that I may set my hand again the second time to recover my people, which are of the house of Israel;

43 And also, that I may remember the promises which I have made unto thee, Nephi, and also unto thy father, that I would remember your seed; and that the words of your seed should proceed forth out of my mouth unto your seed.

44 And my words shall hiss forth unto the ends of the earth, for a standard unto my people, which are of the house of Israel.

45 And because my words shall hiss forth, many of the Gentiles shall say, A bible, a bible, we have got a bible, and there can not be any more bible.

46 But thus saith the Lord God: O fools, they shall have a bible; and it shall proceed forth from the Jews, mine ancient covenant people.

47 And what thank they the Jews for the bible which they received from them?

48 Yea, what do the Gentiles mean?

49 Do they remember the travels, and the labors, and the pains of the Jews, and their diligence unto me, in bringing forth salvation unto the Gentiles?

50 ¶O ye Gentiles, have ye remembered the Jews, mine ancient covenant people?

51 Nay; but ye have cursed them, and have hated them, and have not sought to recover them.

52 But behold, I will return all these things upon your own heads; for I, the Lord, hath not forgotten my people.

53 Thou fool, that shall say, A bible, we have got a bible, and we need no more bible.

54 Have ye obtained a bible, save it were by the Jews?

55 Know ye not that there are more nations than one?

56 Know ye not that I, the Lord your God, have created all men, and that I remember those who are upon the isles of the sea; and that I rule in the heavens above, and in the earth beneath;

57 And I bring forth my word unto the children of men, yea, even upon all the nations of the earth?

58 Wherefore murmur ye, because that ye shall receive more of my word?

59 Know ye not that the testimony of two nations is a witness unto you that I am God, that I remember one nation like unto another?

60 Wherefore, I speak the same words unto one nation like unto another.

61 And when the two nations shall run together, the testimony of the two nations shall run together also.

62 And I do this that I may prove unto many, that I am the same yesterday, to-day, and for ever; and that I speak forth my words according to mine own pleasure.

63 And because that I have spoken one word, ye need not suppose that I can not speak another; for my work is not yet finished; neither shall it be, until the end of man; neither from that time henceforth and for ever.

64 ¶Wherefore, because that ye have a bible, ye need not suppose that it contains all my words; neither need ye suppose that I have not caused more to be written:

65 For I command all men, both in the east, and in the west, and in the north, and in the south, and in the islands of the sea, that they shall write the words which I speak unto them:

66 For out of the books which shall be written, I will judge the world, every man according to their works, according to that which is written.

67 For behold, I shall speak unto the Jews, and they shall write it:

68 And I shall also speak unto the Nephites, and they shall write it;

69 And I shall also speak unto the other tribes of the house of Israel, which I have led away, and they shall write it;

70 And I shall also speak unto all nations of the earth, and they shall write it.

71 ¶And it shall come to pass that the Jews shall have the words of the Nephites, and the Nephites shall have the words of the Jews:

72 And the Nephites and the Jews shall have the words of the lost tribes of Israel; and the lost tribes of Israel shall have the words of the Nephites and the Jews.

73 ¶And it shall come to pass that my people which are of the house of Israel, shall be gathered home unto the lands of their possessions; and my word also shall be gathered in one.

74 And I will shew unto them that fight against my word and against my people, who are of the house of Israel, that I am God, and that I covenanted with Abraham, that I would remember his seed for ever.

75 ¶And now, behold, my beloved brethren, I would speak unto you: for I, Nephi, would not suffer that ye should suppose that ye are more righteous than the Gentiles shall be.

76 For behold, except ye shall keep the commandments of God ye shall all likewise perish; and because of the words which have been spoken ye need not suppose that the Gentiles are utterly destroyed.

77 For behold, I say unto you, That as many of the Gentiles as will repent, are the covenant people of the Lord; and as many of the Jews as will not repent, shall be cast off;

78 For the Lord covenanteth with none, save it be with them that repent and believe in his Son, who is the Holy One of Israel.

79 ¶And now, I would prophesy somewhat more concerning the Jews and the Gentiles.

80 For after the book of which I have spoken shall come forth, and be written unto the Gentiles, and sealed up again unto the Lord, there shall be many which shall believe the

words which are written; and they shall carry them forth unto the remnant of our seed.

81 And then shall the remnant of our seed know concerning us, how that we came out from Jerusalem, and that they are descendants of the Jews.

82 And the gospel of Jesus Christ shall be declared among them; wherefore, they shall be restored unto the knowledge of their fathers, and also to the knowledge of Jesus Christ, which was had among their fathers.

83 And then shall they rejoice; for they shall know that it is a blessing unto them from the hand of God;

84 And their scales of darkness shall begin to fall from their eyes: and many generations shall not pass away among them, save they shall be a white and a delightsome people.

85 ¶And it shall come to pass that the Jews which are scattered, also shall begin to believe in Christ: and they shall begin to gather in upon the face of the land;

86 And as many as shall believe in Christ, shall also become a delightsome people.

87 ¶And it shall come to pass that the Lord God shall commence his work, among all nations, kindreds, tongues, and people, to bring about the restoration of his people upon the earth.

88 And with righteousness shall the Lord God judge the poor, and reprove with equity, for the meek of the earth.

89 And he shall smite the earth with the rod of his mouth; and with the breath of his lips shall he slay the wicked;

90 For the time speedily cometh, that the Lord God shall cause a great division among the people; and the wicked will he destroy; and he will spare his people, yea, even if it so be that he must destroy the wicked by fire.

91 And righteousness shall be the girdle of his loins, and faithfulness the girdle of his reins.

92 And then shall the wolf dwell with the lamb, and the leopard shall lie down with the kid; and the calf, and the young lion, and the fatling, together; and a little child shall lead them.

93 And the cow and the bear shall feed; their young ones

shall lie down together; and the lion shall eat straw like the ox.

94 And the sucking child shall play on the hole of the asp, and the weaned child shall put his hand on the cockatrice's den.

95 They shall not hurt nor destroy in all my holy mountain; for the earth shall be full of the knowledge of the Lord, as the waters cover the sea.

96 Wherefore, the things of all nations shall be made known: yea, all things shall be made known unto the children of men.

97 There is nothing which is secret, save it shall be revealed; there is no work of darkness, save it shall be made manifest in the light; and there is nothing which is sealed upon the earth, save it shall be loosed.

98 Wherefore, all things which have been revealed unto the children of men, shall at that day be revealed;

99 And Satan shall have power over the hearts of the children of men no more, for a long time.

100 And now my beloved brethren, I must make an end of my sayings.

CHAPTER 13.

1 ¶And now I, Nephi, make an end of my prophesying unto you, my beloved brethren.

2 And I can not write but a few things, which I know must surely come to pass; neither can I write but a few of the words of my brother Jacob.

3 Wherefore the things which I have written, sufficeth me, save it be a few words which I must speak, concerning the doctrine of Christ; wherefore I shall speak unto you plainly, according to the plainness of my prophesying.

4 For my soul delighteth in plainness: for after this manner doth the Lord God work among the children of men.

5 For the Lord God giveth light unto the understanding: for he speaketh unto men according to their language, unto their understanding.

6 Wherefore, I would that ye should remember that I have spoken unto you, concerning that prophet which the Lord shewed unto me, that should baptize the Lamb of God, which should take away the sin of the world.

7 ¶And now, if the Lamb of God, he being holy, should have need to be baptized by water to fulfill all righteousness, O then, how much more need have we, being unholy, to be baptized, yea, even by water.

8 And now, I would ask of you, my beloved brethren, wherein the Lamb of God did fulfill all righteousness in being baptized by water? Know ye not that he was holy?

9 But notwithstanding he being holy, he sheweth unto the children of men, that according to the flesh, he humbleth himself before the Father, and witnesseth unto the Father that he would be obedient unto him in keeping his commandments;

10 Wherefore, after he was baptized with water, the Holy Ghost descended upon him in the form of a dove.

11 And again: It sheweth unto the children of men the straightness of the path, and the narrowness of the gate, by which they should enter, he having set the example before them.

12 And he said unto the children of men, Follow thou me.

13 Wherefore, my beloved brethren, can we follow Jesus, save we shall be willing to keep the commandments of the Father?

14 And the Father said, Repent ye, repent ye, and be baptized in the name of my beloved Son.

15 And also, the voice of the Son came unto me, saying, He that is baptized in my name, to him will the Father give the Holy Ghost, like unto me; wherefore, follow me, and do the things which ye have seen me do.

16 Wherefore, my beloved brethren, I know that if ye shall follow the Son with full purpose of heart, acting no hypocrisy and no deception before God, but with real intent, repenting of your sins, witnessing unto the Father that ye are willing to take upon you the name of Christ, by baptism: yea, by following your Lord and your Savior down into the

water, according to his word; behold, then shall ye receive the Holy Ghost;

17 Yea, then cometh the baptism of fire and of the Holy Ghost; and then can ye speak with the tongue of angels, and shout praises unto the Holy One of Israel.

18 ¶But behold, my beloved brethren, thus came the voice f the Son unto me, saying, After ye have repented of your sins, and witnessed unto the Father that ye are willing to keep my commandments, by the baptism of water, and have received the baptism of fire and of the Holy Ghost, and can speak with a new tongue, yea, even with the tongue of angels, and after this, should deny me, it would have been better for you, that ye had not known me.

19 ¶And I heard a voice from the Father, saying, Yea, the words of my beloved, are true and faithful.

20 He that endureth to the end, the same shall be saved.

21 And now, my beloved brethren, I know by this, that unless a man shall endure to the end, in following the example of the Son of the living God, he can not be saved;

22 Wherefore, do the things which I have told you I have seen, that your Lord and your Redeemer should do:

23 For, for this cause have they been shewn unto me, that ye might know the gate by which ye should enter.

24 For the gate by which ye should enter is repentance and baptism by water: and then cometh a remission of your sins by fire, and by the Holy Ghost.

25 And then are ye in this straight and narrow path which leads to eternal life; yea, ye have entered in by the gate; ye have done according to the commandments of the Father and the Son;

26 And ye have received the Holy Ghost, which witnesses of the Father and the Son, unto the fulfilling of the promise which he hath made, that if ye entered in by the way, ye should receive.

27 ¶And now, my beloved brethren, after ye have gotten into this straight and narrow path, I would ask, if all is done?

28 Behold, I say unto you, Nay; for ye have not come

thus far, save it were by the word of Christ, with unshaken faith in him, relying wholly upon the merits of him who is mighty to save;

29 Wherefore, ye must press forward with a steadfastness in Christ, having a perfect brightness of hope, and a love of God and of all men.

30 Wherefore, if ye shall press forward, feasting upon the word of Christ, and endure to the end, behold, thus saith the Father: Ye shall have eternal life.

31 ¶And now behold, my beloved brethren, this is the way; and there is none other way nor name given under heaven, whereby man can be saved in the kingdom of God.

32 And now behold, this is the doctrine of Christ, and the only and true doctrine of the Father, and of the Son, and of the Holy Ghost, which is one God, without end. Amen.

CHAPTER 14.

1 ¶And now behold, my beloved brethren, I suppose that ye ponder somewhat in your hearts, concerning that which ye should do, after ye have entered in by the way.

2 But behold, why do ye ponder these things in your hearts? Do ye not remember that I said unto you, that after ye had received the Holy Ghost, ye could speak with the tongue of angels?

3 And now, how could ye speak with the tongue of angels, save it were by the Holy Ghost? Angels speak by the power of the Holy Ghost; wherefore, they speak the words of Christ.

4 Wherefore, I said unto you, Feast upon the words of Christ; for behold the words of Christ will tell you all things what ye should do.

5 Wherefore, now after I have spoken these words, if ye can not understand them, it will be because ye ask not, neither do ye knock; wherefore, ye are not brought into the light, but must perish in the dark.

6 For behold, again I say unto you, that if ye will enter in

by the way and receive the Holy Ghost, it will shew unto you all things what ye should do.

7 Behold, this the doctrine of Christ; and there will be no more doctrine given, until after he shall manifest himself unto you in the flesh.

8 And when he shall manifest himself unto you in the flesh, the things which he shall say unto you, shall ye observe to do.

9 ¶And now I, Nephi, can not say more: the Spirit stoppeth mine utterance, and I am left to mourn because of the unbelief, and the wickedness, and the ignorance, and the stiffneckedness of men: for they will not search knowledge, nor understand great knowledge, when it is given unto them in plainness, even as plain as word can be.

10 ¶And now, my beloved brethren, I perceive that ye ponder still in your hearts; and it grieveth me that I must speak concerning this thing.

11 For if ye would hearken unto the spirit which teacheth a man to pray, ye would know that ye must pray: for the evil spirit teacheth not a man to pray, but teacheth him that he must not pray.

12 But behold I say unto you, that ye must pray always, and not faint: that ye must not perform anything unto the Lord, save in the first place ye shall pray unto the Father in the name of Christ, that he will consecrate thy performance unto thee, that thy performance may be for the welfare of thy soul.

CHAPTER 15.

1 ¶And now I, Nephi, can not write all the things which were taught among my people; neither am I mighty in writing, like unto speaking: for when a man speaketh by the power of the Holy Ghost, the power of the Holy Ghost carrieth it unto the hearts of the children of men.

2 But behold, there are many that harden their hearts against the Holy Spirit, that it hath no place in them; where-

fore, they cast many things away which are written, and esteem them as things of nought.

3 But I, Nephi, have written what I have written; and I esteem it as of great worth, and especially unto my people.

4 For I pray continually for them by day, and mine eyes water my pillow by night, because of them; and I cry unto my God in faith, and I know that he will hear my cry; and I know that the Lord God will consecrate my prayers, for the gain of my people.

5 And the words which I have written in weakness, will he make strong unto them; for it persuadeth them to do good; it maketh known unto them of their fathers; and it speaketh of Jesus, and persuadeth them to believe in him, and to endure to the end, which is life eternal.

6 And it speaketh harsh against sin, according to the plainness of the truth; wherefore, no man will be angry at the words which I have written, save he shall be of the spirit of the devil.

7 I glory in plainness; I glory in truth; I glory in my Jesus, for he hath redeemed my soul from hell.

8 I have charity for my people, and great faith in Christ, that I shall meet many souls spotless at his judgment seat.

9 I have charity for the Jew: I say Jew, because I mean them from whence I came. I also have charity for the Gentiles.

10 But behold, for none of these can I hope, except they shall be reconciled unto Christ, and enter into the narrow gate, and walk in the straight path, which leads to life, and continue in the path until the end of the day of probation.

11 ¶And now, my beloved brethren, and also Jew, and all ye ends of the earth, hearken unto these words, and believe in Christ; and if ye believe not in these words, believe in Christ.

12 And if ye shall believe in Christ, ye will believe in these words; for they are the words of Christ, and he hath given them unto me; and they teach all men that they should do good.

13 And if they are not the words of Christ, judge ye: for

Christ will shew unto you, with power and great glory, that they are his words, at the last day;

14 And you and I shall stand face to face before his bar; and ye shall know that I have been commanded of him to write these things, notwithstanding my weakness:

15 And I pray the Father in the name of Christ, that many of us, if not all, may be saved in his kingdom, at that great and last day.

16 ¶And now, my beloved brethren, all those who are of the house of Israel, and all ye ends of the earth, I speak unto you, as the voice of one crying from the dust: Farewell until that great day shall come;

17 And you that will not partake of the goodness of God, and respect the words of the Jews, and also my words, and the words which shall proceed forth out of the mouth of the Lamb of God, behold, I bid you an everlasting farewell, for these words shall condemn you at the last day;

18 For what I seal on earth, shall be brought against you at the judgment bar; for thus hath the Lord commanded me, and I must obey. Amen.

THE BOOK OF JACOB.

THE BROTHER OF NEPHI.

CHAPTER 1.

The words of his preaching unto his brethren. He confoundeth a man who seeketh to overthrow the doctrine of Christ. A few words concerning the history of the people of Nephi.

1 ¶For behold, it came to pass that fifty and five years had passed away, from the time that Lehi left Jerusalem; wherefore, Nephi gave me, Jacob, a commandment concerning these small plates, upon which these things are engraven.

2 And he gave me, Jacob, a commandment that I should

write upon these plates, a few of the things which I considered to be most precious: that I should not touch, save it were lightly, concerning the history of this people, which are called the people of Nephi.

3 For he said that the history of his people should be engraven upon his other plates, and that I should preserve these plates, and hand them down unto my seed, from generation to generation.

4 And if there were preaching which was sacred, or revelation which was great, or prophesying, that I should engraven the heads of them upon these plates, and touch upon them as much as it were possible, for Christ's sake, and for the sake of our people:

5 For because of faith and great anxiety, it truly had been made manifest unto us concerning our people, what things should happen unto them.

6 And we also had many revelations, and the spirit of much prophecy; wherefore, we knew of Christ and his kingdom, which should come.

7 Wherefore, we labored diligently among our people, that we might persuade them to come unto Christ, and partake of the goodness of God, that they might enter into his rest, lest by any means he should swear in his wrath they should not enter in, as in the provocation in the days of temptation, while the children of Israel were in the wilderness.

8 Wherefore, we would to God that we could persuade all men not to rebel against God, to provoke him to anger, but that all men would believe in Christ, and view his death, and suffer his cross, and bear the shame of the world; wherefore, I, Jacob, take it upon me to fulfill the commandment of my brother Nephi.

9 ¶Now Nephi began to be old, and he saw that he must soon die; wherefore, he anointed a man to be a king and a ruler over his people now, according to the reigns of the kings.

10 The people having loved Nephi exceedingly, he having been a great protector for them, having wielded the sword of Laban in their defense, and having labored in all his days

for their welfare; wherefore, the people were desirous to retain in remembrance his name.

11 And whoso should reign in his stead, were called by the people, second Nephi, third Nephi, etc., according to the reigns of the kings; and thus they were called by the people, let them be of whatever name they would.

12 ¶And it came to pass that Nephi died.

13 Now the people which were not Lamanites, were Nephites; nevertheless, they were called Nephites, Jacobites, Josephites, Zoramites, Lamanites, Lemuelites, and Ishmaelites.

14 But I, Jacob, shall not hereafter distinguish them by these names, but I shall call them Lamanites, that seek to destroy the people of Nephi; and those who are friendly to Nephi, I shall call Nephites, or the people of Nephi, according to the reigns of the kings.

15 ¶And now it came to pass that the people of Nephi, under the reign of the second king, began to grow hard in their hearts, and indulge themselves somewhat in wicked practices, such as like unto David of old, desiring many wives and concubines, and also Solomon, his son:

16 Yea, and they also began to search much gold and silver, and began to be lifted up somewhat in pride;

17 Wherefore, I, Jacob, gave unto them these words as I taught them in the temple, having firstly obtained mine errand from the Lord.

18 For I, Jacob, and my brother Joseph, had been consecrated priests, and teachers of this people by the hand of Nephi.

19 And we did magnify our office unto the Lord, taking upon us the responsibility, answering the sins of the people upon our own heads, if we did not teach them the word of God with all diligence;

20 Wherefore, by laboring with our mights, their blood might not come upon our garments; otherwise, their blood would come upon our garments, and we would not be found spotless at the last day.

CHAPTER 2.

1 ¶The words which Jacob, the brother of Nephi, spake unto the people of Nephi, after the death of Nephi:

2 Now, my beloved brethren, I, Jacob, according to the responsibility which I am under to God, to magnify mine office with soberness, and that I might rid my garments of your sins, I come up into the temple this day, that I might declare unto you the word of God;

3 And ye yourselves know, that I have hitherto been diligent in the office of my calling; but I this day am weighed down with much more desire and anxiety for the welfare of your souls, than I have hitherto been.

4 For behold, as yet, ye have been obedient unto the word of the Lord, which I have given unto you.

5 But behold, hearken ye unto me, and know that by the help of the all-powerful Creator of heaven and earth, I can tell you concerning your thoughts, how that ye are beginning to labor in sin, which sin appeareth very abominable unto me, yea, and abominable unto God.

6 Yea, it grieveth my soul and causeth me to shrink with shame before the presence of my Maker, that I must testify unto you concerning the wickedness of your hearts;

7 And also, it grieveth me that I must use so much boldness of speech, concerning you, before your wives and your children, many of whose feelings are exceeding tender, and chaste, and delicate before God, which thing is pleasing unto God;

8 And it supposeth me that they have come up hither to hear the pleasing word of God, yea, the word which healeth the wounded soul.

9 ¶Wherefore, it burdeneth my soul, that I should be constrained because of the strict commandment which I have received from God, to admonish you, according to your crimes, to enlarge the wounds of those which are already wounded, instead of consoling and healing their wounds;

10 And those which have not been wounded, instead of

feasting upon the pleasing word of God, have daggers placed to pierce their souls, and wound their delicate minds.

11 But, notwithstanding the greatness of the task, I must do according to the strict commands of God, and tell you concerning your wickedness and abominations, in the presence of the pure in heart, and the broken heart, and under the glance of the piercing eye of the Almighty God.

12 ¶Wherefore, I must tell you the truth, according to the plainness of the word of God.

13 For behold, as I inquired of the Lord, thus came the word unto me, saying, Jacob, get thou up into the temple on the morrow, and declare the word which I shall give thee, unto this people.

14 ¶And now behold, my brethren, this is the word which I declare unto you, that many of you have begun to search for gold, and for silver, and all manner of precious ores, in the which this land, which is a land of promise unto you, and to your seed, doth abound most plentifully.

15 And the hand of providence hath smiled upon you most pleasingly, that you have obtained many riches;

16 And because some of you have obtained more abundantly than that of your brethren, ye are lifted up in the pride of your hearts, and wear stiff necks, and high heads, because of the costliness of your apparel, and persecute your brethren, because ye suppose that ye are better than they.

17 ¶And now my brethren, do ye suppose that God justifieth you in this thing? Behold, I say unto you, Nay.

18 But he condemneth you, and if ye persist in these things, his judgments must speedily come unto you.

19 O that he would shew you that he can pierce you, and with one glance of his eye, he can smite you to the dust.

20 O that he would rid you from this iniquity and abomination.

21 And, O that ye would listen unto the word of his commands, and let not this pride of your hearts destroy your souls.

22 Think of your brethren, like unto yourselves, and be

familiar with all, and free with your substance, that they may be rich like unto you.

23 But before ye seek for riches, seek ye for the kingdom of God.

24 And after ye have obtained a hope in Christ, ye shall obtain riches, if ye seek them; and ye will seek them, for the intent to do good; to clothe the naked, and to feed the hungry, and to liberate the captive, and administer relief to the sick, and the afflicted.

25 ¶And now my brethren, I have spoken unto you concerning pride; and those of you which have afflicted your neighbor, and persecuted him, because ye were proud in your hearts, of the things which God hath given you, what say ye of it?

26 Do ye not suppose that such things are abominable unto him, who created all flesh?

27 And the one being is as precious in his sight as the other.

28 And all flesh is of the dust; and for the self-same end hath he created them, that they should keep his commandments, and glorify him for ever.

29 And now I make an end of speaking unto you concerning this pride.

30 And were it not that I must speak unto you concerning a grosser crime, my heart would rejoice exceedingly, because of you.

31 But the word of God burthens me because of your grosser crimes.

32 For behold, thus saith the Lord, This people begin to wax in iniquity; they understand not the scriptures: for they seek to excuse themselves in committing whoredoms, because of the things which were written concerning David, and Solomon his son.

33 Behold, David and Solomon truly had many wives and concubines, which thing was abominable before me, saith the Lord,

34 Wherefore, thus saith the Lord, I have led this people forth out of the land of Jerusalem, by the power of mine

arm, that I might raise up unto me a righteous branch from the fruit of the loins of Joseph.

35 Wherefore, I, the Lord God, will not suffer that this people shall do like unto them of old.

36 Wherefore, my brethren, hear me, and hearken to the word of the Lord: For there shall not any man among you have save it be one wife; and concubines he shall have none: For I, the Lord God, delighteth in the chastity of women.

37 And whoredoms are an abomination before me: thus saith the Lord of hosts.

38 Wherefore, this people shall keep my commandments, saith the Lord of hosts, or cursed be the land for their sakes.

39 For if I will, saith the Lord of hosts, raise up seed unto me, I will command my people: otherwise, they shall hearken unto these things.

40 For behold, I, the Lord, have seen the sorrow, and heard the mourning of the daughters of my people in the land of Jerusalem; yea, and in all the lands of my people, because of the wickedness and abominations of their husbands.

41 And I will not suffer, saith the Lord of hosts, that the cries of the fair daughters of this people, which I have led out of the land of Jerusalem, shall come up unto me, against the men of my people, saith the Lord of hosts;

42 For they shall not lead away captive, the daughters of my people, because of their tenderness, save I shall visit them with a sore curse, even unto destruction;

43 For they shall not commit whoredoms, like unto them of old, saith the Lord of hosts.

44 ¶And now behold, my brethren, ye know that these commandments were given to our father Lehi; wherefore, ye have known them before; and ye have come unto great condemnation: for ye have done these things, which ye ought not to have done.

45 Behold, ye have done greater iniquity than the Lamanites, our brethren.

46 Ye have broken the hearts of your tender wives, and lost the confidence of your children, because of your bad ex-

amples before them; and the sobbings of their hearts ascend up to God against you.

47 And because of the strictness of the word of God, which cometh down against you, many hearts died, pierced with deep wounds.

48 ¶But behold, I, Jacob, would speak unto you that are pure in heart.

49 Look unto God with firmness of mind, and pray unto him with exceeding faith, and he will console you in your afflictions, and he will plead your cause, and send down justice upon those who seek your destruction.

50 ¶O all ye that are pure in heart, lift up your heads and receive the pleasing word of God, and feast upon his love; for ye may, if your minds are firm for ever.

51 But wo, wo, unto you that are not pure in heart; that are filthy this day before God; for except ye repent, the land is cursed for your sakes;

52 And the Lamanites which are not filthy like unto you, (nevertheless, they are cursed with a sore cursing,) shall scourge you even unto destruction.

53 And the time speedily cometh, that except ye repent, they shall possess the land of your inheritance, and the Lord God will lead away the righteous out from among you.

54 Behold, the Lamanites, your brethren, whom ye hate, because of their filthiness and the cursings which hath come upon their skins, are more righteous than you;

55 For they have not forgotten the commandments of the Lord, which was given unto our fathers, that they should have, save it were one wife: and concubines they should have none; and there should not be whoredoms committed among them.

56 And now this commandment they observe to keep; wherefore because of this observance in keeping this commandment, the Lord God will not destroy them, but will be merciful unto them; and one day they shall become a blessed people.

57 Behold, their husbands love their wives, and their wives

love their husbands, and their husbands and their wives love their children;

58 And their unbelief and their hatred towards you, is because of the iniquity of their fathers; wherefore, how much better are you than they, in the sight of your great Creator?

59 ¶O my brethren, I fear, that unless ye shall repent of your sins, that their skins will be whiter than yours, when ye shall be brought with them before the throne of God.

60. Wherefore, a commandment I give unto you, which is the word of God, that ye revile no more against them, because of the darkness of their skins; neither shall ye revile against them because of their filthiness;

61 But ye shall remember your own filthiness, and remember that their filthiness came because of their fathers.

62 Wherefore, ye shall remember your children, how that ye have grieved their hearts because of the example that ye have set before them;

63 And also, remember that ye may, because of your filthiness, bring your children unto destruction, and their sins be heaped upon your heads at the last day.

64 ¶O my brethren, hearken unto my word; arouse the faculties of your soul; shake yourselves, that ye may awake from the slumber of death;

65 And loose yourselves from the pains of hell, that ye may not become angels to the devil, to be cast into that lake of fire and brimstone, which is the second death.

66 And now I, Jacob, spake many more things unto the people of Nephi, warning them against fornication, and lasciviousness, and every kind of sin, telling them the awful consequences of them;

67 And a hundredth part of the proceedings of this people, which now began to be numerous, can not be written upon these plates;

68 But many of their proceedings are written upon the larger plates, and their wars, and their contentions, and the reigns of their kings.

69 These plates are called the plates of Jacob; and they were made by the hand of Nephi.

70 And I make an end of speaking these words.

CHAPTER 3.

1 ¶Now behold, it came to pass, that I, Jacob, having ministered much unto my people, in word, (and I can not write but little of my words, because of the difficulty of engraving our words upon plates,) and we know that the things which we write upon plates must remain;

2 But whatsoever things we write upon anything save it be upon plates, must perish and vanish away; but we can write a few words upon plates, which will give our children, and also our beloved brethren, a small degree of knowledge concerning us, or concerning their fathers.

3 Now in this thing we do rejoice; and we labor diligently to engraven these words upon plates, hoping that our beloved brethren, and our children, will receive them with thankful hearts, and look upon them, that they may learn with joy, and not with sorrow, neither with contempt concerning their first parents:

4 For, for this intent have we written these things, that they may know that we knew of Christ, and we had a hope of his glory, many hundred years before his coming, and not only we, ourselves, had a hope of his glory, but also all the holy prophets which were before us.

5 ¶Behold, they believed in Christ, and worshiped the Father in his name; and also, we worship the Father in his name.

6 And for this intent, we keep the law of Moses, it pointing our souls to him; and for this cause, it is sanctified unto us, for righteousness, even as it was accounted unto Abraham in the wilderness, to be obedient unto the commands of God, in offering up his son Isaac, which is a similitude of God and his only begotten Son.

7 Wherefore, we search the prophets; and we have many

revelations, and the spirit of prophecy, and having all these witnesses, we obtain a hope, and our faith becometh unshaken, insomuch that we truly can command in the name of Jesus, and the very trees obey us, or the mountains, or the waves of the sea;

8 Nevertheless, the Lord God sheweth us our weakness, that we may know that it is by his grace, and his great condescensions unto the children of men, that we have power to do these things.

9 ¶Behold, great and marvelous are the works of the Lord.

10 How unsearchable are the depths of the mysteries of him; and it is impossible that man should find out all his ways.

11 And no man knoweth of his ways, save it be revealed unto him; wherefore, brethren, despise not the revelations of God.

12 For behold, by the power of his word, man came upon the face of the earth; which earth was created by the power of his word.

13 Wherefore, if God, being able to speak, and the world was; and to speak, and man was created, O then, why not able to command the earth, or the workmanship of his hands upon the face of it, according to his will and pleasure.

14 Wherefore, brethren, seek not to counsel the Lord, but to take counsel from his hand.

15 For behold, ye yourselves know, that he counseleth in wisdom, and in justice, and in great mercy, over all his works;

16 Wherefore, beloved brethren, be reconciled unto him, through the atonement of Christ, his only begotten Son,

17 That ye may obtain a resurrection, according to the power of the resurrection which is in Christ, and be presented as the first fruits of Christ, unto God, having faith, and obtained a good hope of glory in him, before he manifesteth himself in the flesh.

18 ¶And now, beloved, marvel not that I tell you these things; for why not speak of the atonement of Christ, and attain to a perfect knowledge of him, as to attain to the knowledge of a resurrection and the world to come?

19 Behold, my brethren, he that prophesieth, let him prophesy to the understanding of men; for the Spirit speaketh the truth, and lieth not.

20 Wherefore, it speaketh of things as they really are, and of things as they really will be; wherefore, these things are manifested unto us plainly, for the salvation of our souls.

21 But behold, we are not witnesses alone in these things; for God also spake them unto prophets of old.

22 ¶But behold, the Jews were a stiff-necked people; and they despised the words of plainness, and killed the prophets, and sought for things that they could not understand.

23 Wherefore, because of their blindness, which blindness came by looking beyond the mark, they must needs fall:

24 For God hath taken away his plainness from them, and delivered unto them many things which they can not understand, because they desired it.

25 And because they desired it, God hath done it, that they may stumble.

26 ¶And now I, Jacob, am led on by the Spirit unto prophesying: for I perceive by the workings of the Spirit which is in me, that by the stumbling of the Jews, they will reject the stone upon which they might build, and have safe foundation.

27 But behold, according to the scriptures, this stone shall become the great, and the last, and the only sure foundation, upon which the Jews can build.

28 And now, my beloved, how is it possible that these, after having rejected the sure foundation, can ever build upon it, that it may become the head of their corner?

29 Behold, my beloved brethren, I will unfold this mystery unto you; if I do not, by any means get shaken from my firmness in the Spirit, and stumble because of my overanxiety for you.

30 ¶Behold, my brethren, do ye not remember to have read the words of the prophet Zenos, which spake unto the house of Israel, saying: Hearken, O ye house of Israel, and hear the words of me, a prophet of the Lord:

31 For behold, thus saith the Lord, I will liken thee, O house of Israel, like unto a tame olive tree, which a man

took and nourished in his vineyard: and it grew, and waxed old, and began to decay.

32 And it came to pass that the master of the vineyard went forth, and he saw that his olive tree began to decay; and he said, I will prune it, and dig about it, and nourish it, that perhaps it may shoot forth young and tender branches, and it perish not.

33 And it came to pass that he pruned it, and digged about it, and nourished it, according to his word.

34 And it came to pass that after many days, it began to put forth somewhat a little, young and tender branches; but behold, the main top thereof began to perish.

35 And it came to pass that the master of the vineyard saw it, and he said unto his servant, It grieveth me that I should lose this tree;

36 Wherefore, go and pluck the branches from a wild olive tree, and bring them hither unto me; and we will pluck off those main branches which are beginning to wither away, and we will cast them into the fire, that they may be burned.

37 And behold, saith the Lord of the vineyard, I take away many of these young and tender branches, and I will graft them whithersoever I will;

38 And it mattereth not that if it so be, that the root of this tree will perish, I may preserve the fruit thereof unto myself;

39 Wherefore, I will take these young and tender branches, and I will graft them whithersoever I will.

40 Take thou the branches of the wild olive tree, and graft them in, in the stead thereof;

41 And these which I have plucked off, I will cast into the fire, and burn them, that they may not cumber the ground of my vineyard.

42 ¶And it came to pass that the servant of the Lord of the vineyard, did according to the word of the Lord of the vineyard, and grafted in the branches of the wild olive tree.

43 And the Lord of the vineyard caused that it should be digged about, and pruned, and nourished, saying unto his servant, It grieveth me that I should lose this tree;

44 Wherefore, that perhaps I might preserve the roots thereof that they perish not, that I might preserve them unto myself I have done this thing.

45 Wherefore, go thy way; watch the tree, and nourish it, according to my words.

46 And these will I place in the nethermost part of my vineyard, whithersoever I will, it mattereth not unto thee;

47 And I do it, that I may preserve unto myself the natural branches of the tree; and also, that I may lay up fruit thereof, against the season, unto myself: for it grieveth me that I should lose this tree, and the fruit thereof.

48 ¶And it came to pass that the Lord of the vineyard went his way, and hid the natural branches of the tame olive tree in the nethermost parts of the vineyard; some in one, and some in another, according to his will and pleasure.

49 And it came to pass that a long time passed away, and the Lord of the vineyard said unto his servant, Come, let us go down into the vineyard, that we may labor in the vineyard.

50 ¶And it came to pass that the Lord of the vineyard, and also the servant, went down into the vineyard to labor.

51 And it came to pass that the servant said unto his master, Behold, look here; behold the tree.

52 And it came to pass that the Lord of the vineyard looked and beheld the tree, in the which the wild olive branches had been grafted; and it had sprang forth, and began to bear fruit.

53 And he beheld that it was good: and the fruit thereof was like unto the natural fruit.

54 And he said unto the servant, Behold, the branches of the wild tree hath taken hold of the moisture of the root thereof, that the root thereof hath brought forth much strength;

55 And because of the much strength of the root thereof, the wild branches have brought forth tame fruit:

56 Now, if we had not grafted in these branches, the tree thereof would have perished.

57 And now, behold, I shall lay up much fruit, which the

tree thereof hath brought forth; and the fruit thereof I shall lay up, against the season, unto mine own self.

58 ¶And it came to pass that the Lord of the vineyard said unto the servant, Come, let us go to the nethermost parts of the vineyard, and behold if the natural branches of the tree hath not brought forth much fruit also, that I may lay up of the fruit thereof, against the season, unto mine own self.

59 And it came to pass that they went forth whither the master of the vineyard had hid the natural branches of the tree, and he said unto the servant, Behold these:

60 And he beheld the first, that it had brought forth much fruit; and he beheld also, that it was good.

61 And he said unto the servant, Take of the fruit thereof, and lay it up, against the season, that I may preserve it unto mine own self;

62 For behold, said he, this long time have I nourished it, and it hath brought forth much fruit.

63 ¶And it came to pass that the servant said unto his master, How comest thou hither to plant this tree, or this branch of the tree? for behold, it was the poorest spot in all the land of thy vineyard.

64 And the Lord of the vineyard said unto him, Counsel me not: I knew that it was a poor spot of ground; wherefore, I said unto thee, I have nourished it this long time; and thou beholdest that it hath brought forth much fruit.

65 ¶And it came to pass that the Lord of the vineyard said unto his servant, Look hither: behold, I have planted another branch of the tree also; and thou knowest that this spot of ground was poorer than the first.

66 But, behold the tree: I have nourished it this long time, and it hath brought forth much fruit; therefore, gather it, and lay it up, against the season, that I may preserve it unto mine own self.

67 ¶And it came to pass that the Lord of the vineyard said again unto his servant, Look hither, and behold another branch also, which I have planted; behold that I have nourished it also, and it hath brought forth fruit.

68 And he said unto the servant, Look hither, and behold

the last: behold, this have I planted in a good spot of ground; and I have nourished it this long time, and only a part of the tree hath brought forth tame fruit; and the other part of the tree hath brought forth wild fruit: behold, I have nourished this tree like unto the others.

69 ¶And it came to pass that the Lord of the vineyard said unto the servant, Pluck off the branches that have not brought forth good fruit, and cast them into the fire.

70 But behold, the servant said unto him, Let us prune it, and dig about it, and nourish it a little longer, that perhaps it may bring forth good fruit unto thee, that thou canst lay it up against the season.

71 And it came to pass that the Lord of the vineyard, and the servant of the Lord of the vineyard, did nourish all the fruit of the vineyard.

72 ¶And it came to pass that a long time had passed away, and the Lord of the vineyard said unto his servant, Come, let us go down into the vineyard, that we may labor again in the vineyard.

73 For behold, the time draweth near, and the end soon cometh: wherefore, I must lay up fruit, against the season, unto mine own self.

74 ¶And it came to pass that the Lord of the vineyard, and the servant, went down into the vineyard; and they came to the tree whose natural branches had been broken off, and the wild branches had been grafted in; and behold, all sorts of fruit did cumber the tree.

75 ¶And it came to pass that the Lord of the vineyard did taste of the fruit, every sort according to its number.

76 And the Lord of the vineyard said, Behold, this long time have we nourished this tree, and I have laid up unto myself against the season, much fruit.

77 But behold, this time it hath brought forth much fruit, and there is none of it which is good.

78 And behold, there are all kinds of bad fruit; and it profiteth me nothing, notwithstanding all our labor: and now, it grieveth me that I should lose this tree.

79 And the Lord of the vineyard said unto the servant,

What shall we do unto the tree, that I may preserve again good fruit thereof unto mine own self?

80 And the servant said unto his master, Behold, because thou didst graft in the branches of the wild olive tree, they have nourished the roots, that they are alive, and they have not perished; wherefore, thou beholdest that they are yet good.

81 ¶And it came to pass that the Lord of the vineyard said unto his servant, The tree profiteth me nothing; and the roots thereof profiteth me nothing, so long as it shall bring forth evil fruit.

82 Nevertheless, I know that the roots are good; and for mine own purpose I have preserved them; and because of their much strength, they have hitherto brought forth from the wild branches good fruit.

83 But behold, the wild branches have grown, and have overran the roots thereof: and because that the wild branches have overcome the roots thereof, it hath brought forth much evil fruit;

84 And because that it hath brought forth so much evil fruit, thou beholdest that it beginneth to perish: and it will soon become ripened, that it may be cast into the fire, except we should do something for it to preserve it.

85 ¶And it came to pass that the Lord of the vineyard said unto his servant, Let us go down into the nethermost parts of the vineyard, and behold if the natural branches have also brought forth evil fruit.

86 And it came to pass that they went down into the nethermost parts of the vineyard.

87 And it came to pass that they beheld that the fruit of the natural branches had become corrupt also; yea, the first, and the second, and also the last; and they had all become corrupt.

88 And the wild fruit of the last, had overcome that part of the tree which brought forth good fruit, even that the branch had withered away and died.

89 ¶And it came to pass that the Lord of the vineyard

wept, and said unto the servant, What could I have done more for my vineyard?

90 Behold, I knew that all the fruit of the vineyard, save it were these, had' become corrupted.

91 And now, these which have once brought forth good fruit, have also become corrupted.

92 And now, all the trees of my vineyard are good for nothing, save it be to be hewn down and cast into the fire.

93 And behold, this last, whose branch hath withered away, I did plant in a good spot of ground; yea, even that which was choice unto me, above all other parts of the land of my vineyard.

94 And thou beheldest that I also cut down that which cumbered this spot of ground, that I might plant this tree in the stead thereof.

95 And thou beheldest that a part thereof, brought forth good fruit; and a part thereof, brought forth wild fruit.

96 And because I plucked not the branches thereof, and cast them into the fire, behold, they have overcome the good branch, that it has withered away.

97 And now behold, notwithstanding all the care which we have taken of my vineyard, the trees thereof have become corrupted, that they bring forth no good fruit:

98 And these I had hoped to preserve, to have laid up fruit thereof, against the season, unto mine own self.

99 But behold, they have become like unto the wild olive tree; and they are of no worth, but to be hewn down and cast into the fire: and it grieveth me that I should lose them.

100 But what could I have done more in my vineyard?

101 Have I slackened my hand, that I have not nourished it?

102 Nay; I have nourished it, and I have digged about it, and I have pruned it, and I have dunged it; and I have stretched forth mine hand almost all the day long; and the end draweth nigh.

103 And it grieveth me that I should hew down all the trees of my vineyard, and cast them into the fire, that they should be burned.

104 Who is it that has corrupted my vineyard?

105 ¶And it came to pass that the servant said unto his master, Is it not the loftiness of thy vineyard?

106 Has not the branches thereof overcome the roots, which are good?

107 And because the branches have overcome the roots thereof, behold, they grew faster than the strength of the roots, taking strength unto themselves.

108 Behold, I say, Is not this the cause that the trees of thy vineyard have become corrupted?

109 ¶And it came to pass that the Lord of the vineyard said unto the servant, Let us go to, and hew down the trees of the vineyard, and cast them into the fire, that they shall not cumber the ground of my vineyard: for I have done all; what could I have done more for my vineyard?

110 But behold, the servant said unto the Lord of the vineyard, Spare it a little longer.

111 And the Lord said, Yea, I will spare it a little longer: for it grieveth me that I should lose the trees of my vineyard.

112 Wherefore let us take of the branches of these which I have planted in the nethermost parts of my vineyard, and let us graft them into the tree from whence they came;

113 And let us pluck from the tree those branches whose fruit is most bitter, and graft in the natural branches of the tree in the stead thereof.

114 And this will I do, that the tree may not perish, that perhaps I may preserve unto myself the roots thereof, for mine own purpose.

115 And behold, the roots of the natural branches of the tree which I planted whithersoever I would, are yet alive;

116 Wherefore, that I may preserve them also, for mine own purpose, I will take of the branches of this tree, and I will graft them in unto them.

117 Yea, I will graft in unto them the branches of their mother tree, that I may preserve the roots also unto mine own self, that when they shall be sufficiently strong, perhaps they may bring forth good fruit unto me, and I may yet have glory in the fruit of my vineyard.

118 ¶And it came to pass that they took from the natural tree which had become wild, and grafted in unto the natural trees, which also had become wild:

119 And they also took of the natural trees which had become wild, and grafted into their mother tree.

120 And the Lord of the vineyard said unto the servant, Pluck not the wild branches from the trees, save it be those which are most bitter; and in them ye shall graft, according to that which I have said.

121 And we will nourish again the trees of the vineyard, and we will trim up the branches thereof; and we will pluck from the trees those branches which are ripened that must perish, and cast them into the fire.

122 And this I do, that perhaps the roots thereof may take strength, because of their goodness; and because of the change of the branches, that the good may overcome the evil;

123 And because that I have preserved the natural branches, and the roots thereof; and that I have grafted in the natural branches again, into their mother tree; and have preserved the roots of their mother tree, that perhaps the trees of my vineyard may bring forth again good fruit;

124 And that I may have joy again in the fruit of my vineyard; and perhaps that I may rejoice exceedingly, that I have preserved the roots and the branches of the first fruit.

125 Wherefore, go to, and call servants, that we may labor diligently with our mights in the vineyard, that we may prepare the way, that I may bring forth again the natural fruit, which natural fruit is good, and the most precious above all other fruit.

126 Wherefore, let us go to, and labor with our mights, this last time; for behold the end draweth nigh: and this is for the last time that I shall prune my vineyard.

127 Graft in the branches; begin at the last, that they may be first, and that the first may be last, and dig about the trees, both old and young, the first and the last, and the last and the first, that all may be nourished once again for the last time.

128 Wherefore, dig about them, and prune them, and dung

them once more, for the last time: for the end draweth nigh.

129 And if it so be that these last grafts shall grow, and bring forth the natural fruit, then shall ye prepare the way for them, that they may grow;

130 And as they begin to grow, ye shall clear away the branches which bring forth bitter fruit, according to the strength of the good and the size thereof;

131 And ye shall not clear away the bad thereof, all at once, lest the roots thereof should be too strong for the graft, and the graft thereof shall perish, and I lose the trees of my vineyard.

132 For it grieveth me that I should lose the trees of my vineyard; wherefore, ye shall clear away the bad, according as the good shall grow, that the root and the top may be equal in strength, until the good shall overcome the bad, and the bad be hewn down and cast into the fire, that they cumber not the ground of my vineyard; and thus will I sweep away the bad out of my vineyard.

133 And the branches of the natural tree will I graft in again, into the natural tree; and the branches of the natural tree will I graft into the natural branches of the tree;

134 And thus will I bring them together again, that they shall bring forth the natural fruit; and they shall be one.

135 And the bad shall be cast away; yea, even out of all the land of my vineyard; for behold, only this once will I prune my vineyard.

136 ¶And it came to pass that the Lord of the vineyard sent his servant; and the servant went and did as the Lord had commanded him, and brought other servants; and they were few.

137 And the Lord of the vineyard said unto them, Go to, and labor in the vineyard, with your mights.

138 For behold, this is the last time that I shall nourish my vineyard: for the end is nigh at hand, and the season speedily cometh;

139 And if ye labor with your mights with me, ye shall have joy in the fruit which I shall lay up unto myself, against the time which will soon come.

140 ¶And it came to pass that the servants did go, and labor with their mights; and the Lord of the vineyard labored also with them; and they did obey the commandments of the Lord of the vineyard, in all things.

141 And there began to be the natural fruit again in the vineyard; and the natural branches began to grow and thrive exceedingly;

142 And the wild branches began to be plucked off, and to be cast away; and they did keep the root and the top thereof equal, according to the strength thereof.

143 And thus they labored, with all diligence, according to the commandments of the Lord of the vineyard, even until the bad had been cast away out of the vineyard, and the Lord had preserved unto himself, that the trees had become again the natural fruit;

144 And they became like unto one body; and the fruit were equal; and the Lord of the vineyard had preserved unto himself the natural fruit, which was most precious unto him from the beginning.

145 ¶And it came to pass that when the Lord of the vineyard saw that his fruit was good, and that his vineyard was no more corrupt, he called up his servants and said unto them, Behold, for this last time have we nourished my vineyard; and thou beholdest that I have done according to my will;

146 And I have preserved the natural fruit, that it is good, even like as it was in the beginning; and blessed art thou.

147 For because ye have been diligent in laboring with me in my vineyard, and have kept my commandments, and have brought unto me again the natural fruit, that my vineyard is no more corrupted, and the bad is cast away, behold, ye shall have joy with me, because of the fruit of my vineyard.

148 For behold, for a long time will I lay up of the fruit of my vineyard unto mine own self, against the season, which speedily cometh;

149 And for the last time have I nourished my vineyard, and pruned it, and dug about it, and dunged it;

150 Wherefore I will lay up unto mine own self of the fruit for a long time, according to that which I have spoken.

151 And when the time cometh that evil fruit shall again come into my vineyard, then will I cause the good and the bad to be gathered:

152 And the good will I preserve unto myself; and the bad will I cast away into its own place.

153 And then cometh the season and the end; and my vineyard will I cause to be burned with fire.

CHAPTER 4.

1 ¶And now, behold, my brethren, as I said unto you that I would prophesy, behold, this is my prophecy:

2 That the things which this prophet Zenos spake, concerning the house of Israel, in the which he likened them unto a tame olive tree, must surely come to pass.

3 And in the day that he shall set his hand again the second time to recover his people, is the day, yea, even the last time, that the servants of the Lord shall go forth in his power, to nourish and prune his vineyard; and after that, the end soon cometh.

4 And how blessed are they who have labored diligently in his vineyard; and how cursed are they who shall be cast out into their own place!

5 And the world shall be burned with fire.

6 And how merciful is our God unto us; for he remembereth the house of Israel, both roots and branches; and he stretches forth his hands unto them, all the day long;

7 And they are a stiff-necked, and a gainsaying people; but as many as will not harden their hearts, shall be saved in the kingdom of God.

8 Wherefore, my beloved brethren, I beseech of you in words of soberness, that ye would repent, and come with full purpose of heart, and cleave unto God as he cleaveth unto you.

9 And while his arm of mercy is extended towards you in the light of the day, harden not your hearts.

10 Yea, to-day if ye will hear his voice, harden not your hearts: for why will ye die?

11 For behold, after ye have been nourished by the good word of God all the day long, will ye bring forth evil fruit, that ye must be hewn down and cast into the fire?

12 Behold, will ye reject these words?

13 Will ye reject the words of the prophets? and will ye reject all the words which have been spoken concerning Christ, after so many have spoken concerning him? and deny the good word of Christ, and the power of God, and the gift of the Holy Ghost, and quench the Holy Spirit? and make a mock of the great plan of redemption, which hath been laid for you?

14 Know ye not that if ye will do these things, that the power of the redemption and the resurrection which is in Christ, will bring you to stand with shame and awful guilt before the bar of God?

15 And according to the power of justice, for justice can not be denied, ye must go away into that lake of fire and brimstone, whose flames are unquenchable, and whose smoke ascendeth up for ever and ever, which lake of fire and brimstone, is endless torment.

16 O then, my beloved brethren, repent ye, and enter in at the straight gate, and continue in the way which is narrow, until ye shall obtain eternal life.

17 O be wise: what can I say more?

18 Finally, I bid you farewell, until I shall meet you before the pleasing bar of God, which bar striketh the wicked with awful dread and fear.   Amen.

CHAPTER 5.

1 ¶And now it came to pass after some years had passed away, there came a man among the people of Nephi, whose name was Sherem.

2 And it came to pass that he began to preach among the

people, and to declare unto them that there should be no Christ.

3 And he preached many things which were flattering unto the people; and this he did that he might overthrow the doctrine of Christ.

4 And he labored diligently that he might lead away the hearts of the people, insomuch that he did lead away many hearts;

5 And he knowing that I, Jacob, had faith in Christ who should come, he sought much opportunity that he might come unto me.

6 And he was learned, that he had a perfect knowledge of the language of the people; wherefore, he could use much flattery, and much power of speech, according to the power of the devil.

7 And he had hope to shake me from the faith, notwithstanding the many revelations, and the many things which I had seen concerning these things; for I truly had seen angels, and they had ministered unto me.

8 And also, I had heard the voice of the Lord speaking unto me in very word, from time to time; wherefore, I could not be shaken.

9 ¶And it came to pass that he came unto me; and on this wise did he speak unto me, saying: Brother Jacob, I have sought much opportunity that I might speak unto you: for I have heard and also know, that thou goest about much, preaching that which ye call the gospel, or the doctrine of Christ;

10 And ye have led away much of this people, that they pervert the right way of God, and keep not the law of Moses, which is the right way; and convert the law of Moses into the worship of a being, which ye say shall come many hundred years hence.

11 And now behold, I, Sherem, declare unto you, that this is blasphemy; for no man knoweth of such things: for he can not tell of things to come.

12 And after this manner did Sherem contend against me.

13 But behold, the Lord God poured in his Spirit into my soul, insomuch that I did confound him in all his words.

14 And I said unto him, Deniest thou the Christ which shall come?

15 And he said, If there should be a Christ, I would not deny him; but I know that there is no Christ, neither has been, nor ever will be.

16 And I said unto him, Believest thou the scriptures?

17 And he said, Yea.

18 And I said unto him, Then ye do not understand them; for they truly testify of Christ.

19 Behold, I say unto you, that none of the prophets have written, nor prophesied, save they have spoken concerning this Christ.

20 And this is not all: it has been made manifest unto me, for I have heard and seen; and it also has been made manifest unto me by the power of the Holy Ghost;

21 Wherefore, I know if there should be no atonement made, all mankind must be lost.

22 ¶And it came to pass that he said unto me, Shew me a sign by this power of the Holy Ghost, in the which ye know so much.

23 And I said unto him, What am I, that I should tempt God to shew unto thee a sign, in the thing which thou knowest to be true?

24 Yet thou wilt deny it, because thou art of the devil.

25 Nevertheless, not my will be done; but if God shall smite thee, let that be a sign unto thee that he has power, both in heaven and in earth; and also, that Christ shall come.

26 And thy will, O Lord, be done, and not mine.

27 ¶And it came to pass that when I, Jacob, had spoken these words, the power of the Lord came upon him, insomuch that he fell to the earth.

28 And it came to pass that he was nourished for the space of many days.

29 And it came to pass that he said unto the people, Gather together on the morrow, for I shall die; wherefore, I desire to speak unto the people, before I shall die.

30 ¶And it came to pass that on the morrow, the multitude were gathered together; and he spake plainly unto them, and

denied the things which he had taught them; and confessed the Christ, and the power of the Holy Ghost, and the ministering of angels.

31 And he spake plainly unto them, that he had been deceived by the power of the devil.

32 And he spake of hell, and of eternity, and of eternal punishment.

33 And he said, I fear lest I have committed the unpardonable sin, for I have lied unto God: for I denied the Christ, and said that I believed the scriptures; and they truly testify of him.

34 And because I have thus lied unto God, I greatly fear lest my case shall be awful; but I confess unto God.

35 ¶And it came to pass that when he had said these words, he could say no more; and he gave up the ghost.

36 And when the multitude had witnessed that he spake these things as he was about to give up the ghost, they were astonished exceedingly; insomuch, that the power of God came down upon them, and they were overcome, that they fell to the earth.

37 Now, this thing was pleasing unto me, Jacob; for I had requested it of my Father who was in heaven: for he had heard my cry, and answered my prayer.

38 ¶And it came to pass that peace and the love of God was restored again among the people; and they searched the scriptures, and hearkened no more to the words of this wicked man.

39 And it came to pass that many means were devised, to reclaim and restore the Lamanites, to the knowledge of the truth; but it all were vain: for they delighted in wars and bloodshed; and they had an eternal hatred against us, their brethren.

40 And they sought by the power of their arms to destroy us continually;

41 Wherefore, the people of Nephi did fortify against them with their armies, and with all their might, trusting in the God and rock of their salvation; wherefore, they became as yet, conquerors of their enemies.

42 ¶And it came to pass that I, Jacob, began to be old; and the record of this people being kept on the other plates of Nephi, wherefore, I conclude this record, declaring that I have written according to the best of my knowledge, by saying,

43 That the time passed away with us, and also our lives passed away, like as it were unto us a dream, we being a lonesome and a solemn people, wanderers, cast out from Jerusalem;

44 Born in tribulation, in a wilderness, and hated of our brethren, which caused wars and contentions; wherefore, we did mourn out our days.

45 ¶And I, Jacob, saw that I must soon go down to my grave; wherefore, I said unto my son Enos, Take these plates.

46 And I told him the things which my brother Nephi had commanded me; and he promised obedience unto the commands.

47 And I make an end of my writing upon these plates, which writing has been small;

48 And to the reader I bid farewell, hoping that many of my brethren may read my words. Brethren, adieu.

THE BOOK OF ENOS.

CHAPTER 1.

1 ¶Behold, it came to pass that I, Enos, knowing my father, that he was a just man: for he taught me in his language, and also in the nurture and admonition of the Lord.

2 And blessed be the name of my God for it.

3 And I will tell you of the wrestle which I had before God, before I received a remission of my sins:

4 Behold I went to hunt beasts in the forest; and the words which I had often heard my father speak, concerning eternal life, and the joy of the saints, sunk deep into my heart.

5 And my soul hungered; and I kneeled down before my Maker, and I cried unto him in mighty prayer and supplication, for mine own soul;

6 And all the day long did I cry unto him; yea, and when the night came, I did still raise my voice high, that it reached the heavens.

7 And there came a voice unto me saying, Enos, thy sins are forgiven thee, and thou shalt be blessed.

8 And I, Enos, knew that God could not lie; wherefore, my guilt was swept away.

9 And I said, Lord, how is it done?

10 And he said unto me, because of thy faith in Christ, whom thou hast never before heard nor seen.

11 And many years pass away, before he shall manifest himself in the flesh; wherefore, go to, thy faith hath made thee whole.

12 ¶Now, it came to pass that when I had heard these words, I began to feel a desire for the welfare of my brethren, the Nephites; wherefore, I did pour out my whole soul unto God for them.

13 And while I was thus struggling in the spirit, behold, the voice of the Lord came into my mind again, saying,

14 I will visit thy brethren, according to their diligence in keeping my commandments.

15 I have given unto them this land; and it is a holy land; and I curse it not, save it be for the cause of iniquity;

16 Wherefore, I will visit thy brethren; according as I have said; and their transgressions will I bring down with sorrow upon their own heads.

17 And after I, Enos, had heard these words, my faith began to be unshaken in the Lord; and I prayed unto him with many long strugglings for my brethren, the Lamanites.

18 ¶And it came to pass, that after I had prayed, and labored with all diligence, the Lord said unto me, I will grant unto thee according to thy desires, because of thy faith.

19 And now behold, this was the desire which I desired of him: that if it should so be, that my people, the Nephites, should fall into transgression, and by any means be destroyed,

and the Lamanites should not be destroyed, that the Lord God would preserve a record of my people, the Nephites;

20 Even if it so be, by the power of his holy arm, that it might be brought forth, at some future day, unto the Lamanites, that perhaps they might be brought unto salvation:

21 For at the present, our strugglings were vain, in restoring them to the true faith.

22 And they swore in their wrath, that if it were possible, they would destroy our records and us; and, also, all the traditions of our fathers.

23 ¶Wherefore, I knowing that the Lord God was able to preserve our records, I cried unto him continually;

24 For he had said unto me, Whatsoever thing ye shall ask in faith, believing that ye shall receive in the name of Christ, ye shall receive it.

25 And I had faith, and I did cry unto God, that he would preserve the records;

26 And he covenanted with me that he would bring them forth unto the Lamanites, in his own due time.

27 And I, Enos, knew it would be according to the covenant which he had made; wherefore, my soul did rest.

28 And the Lord said unto me, Thy fathers have also required of me this thing; and it shall be done unto them according to their faith, for their faith was like unto thine.

29 ¶And now it came to pass, that I, Enos, went about among the people of Nephi, prophesying of things to come, and testifying of the things which I had heard and seen.

30 And I bear record that the people of Nephi did seek diligently to restore the Lamanites unto the true faith in God.

31 But our labors were vain; their hatred was fixed, and they were led by their evil nature, that they became wild, and ferocious, and a bloodthirsty people; full of idolatry, and filthiness;

32 Feeding upon beasts of prey, dwelling in tents, and wandering about in the wilderness, with a short skin girted about their loins, and their heads shaven; and their skill was in the bow, and the cimeter, and the ax.

33 And many of them did eat nothing save it was raw meat; and they were continually seeking to destroy us.

34 ¶And it came to pass that the people of Nephi did till the land, and raise all manner of grain, and of fruit, and flocks of herds, and flocks of all manner of cattle, of every kind, and goats, and wild goats, and also many horses.

35 And there were exceeding many prophets among us.

36 And the people were a stiff-necked people, hard to understand.

37 And there was nothing save it was exceeding harshness, preaching and prophesying of wars, and contentions, and destructions, and continually reminding them of death, and the duration of eternity, and the judgments and the power of God;

38 And all these things stirring them up continually, to keep them in the fear of the Lord.

39 I say there was nothing short of these things, and exceeding great plainness of speech, would keep them from going down speedily to destruction.

40 And after this manner do I write concerning them.

41 And I saw wars between the Nephites and the Lamanites, in the course of my days.

42 ¶And it came to pass that I began to be old, and an hundred and seventy and nine years had passed away from the time that our father Lehi left Jerusalem.

43 And as I saw that I must soon go down to my grave, having been wrought upon by the power of God that I must preach and prophesy unto this people, and declare the word according to the truth which is in Christ.

44 And I have declared it, in all my days; and have rejoiced in it, above that of the world.

45 And I soon go to the place of my rest, which is with my Redeemer; for I know that in him I shall rest:

46 And I rejoice in the day when my mortal shall put on immortality, and shall stand before him: then shall I see his face with pleasure, and he will say unto me, Come unto me ye blessed, there is a place prepared for you in the mansions of my Father. Amen.

THE BOOK OF JAROM.

CHAPTER 1.

1 ¶Now behold, I, Jarom, write a few words, according to the commandment of my father Enos, that our genealogy may be kept.

2 And as these plates are small, and as these things are written for the intent of the benefit of our brethren, the Lamanites, wherefore, it must needs be that I write a little; but I shall not write the things of my prophesying, nor of my revelations.

3 For what could I write more than my fathers have written?

4 For have not they revealed the plan of salvation?

5 I say unto you, Yea; and this sufficeth me.

6 ¶Behold, it is expedient that much should be done among this people, because of the hardness of their hearts, and the deafness of their ears, and the blindness of their minds, and the stiffness of their necks;

7 Nevertheless, God is exceeding merciful unto them, and has not as yet swept them off from the face of the land.

8 And there are many among us who have many revelations: for they are not all stiff-necked.

9 And as many as are not stiff-necked, and have faith, have communion with the Holy Spirit, which maketh manifest unto the children of men, according to their faith.

10 ¶And now, behold, two hundred years had passed away, and the people of Nephi had waxed strong in the land.

11 They observed to keep the law of Moses, and the Sabbath day holy unto the Lord.

12 And they profaned not; neither did they blaspheme.

13 And the laws of the land were exceeding strict.

14 And they were scattered upon much of the face of the land; and the Lamanites also.

15 And they were exceeding more numerous than were they of the Nephites; and they loved murder, and would drink the blood of beasts.

16 ¶And it came to pass that they came many times against us, the Nephites, to battle.

17 But our kings and our leaders were mighty men in the faith of the Lord; and they taught the people the ways of the Lord;

18 Wherefore, we withstood the Lamanites, and swept them away, out of our lands, and began to fortify our cities, or whatsoever place of our inheritance.

19 And we multiplied exceedingly, and spread upon the face of the land, and became exceeding rich in gold, and in silver, and in precious things, and in fine workmanship of wood, in buildings, and in machinery, and also in iron, and copper, and brass, and steel, making all manner of tools of every kind to till the ground, and weapons of war;

20 Yea, the sharp pointed arrow, and the quiver, and the dart, and the javelin, and all preparations for war;

21 And thus being prepared to meet the Lamanites, they did not prosper against us.

22 But the word of the Lord was verified, which he spake unto our fathers, saying, That inasmuch as ye will keep my commandments, ye shall prosper in the land.

23 ¶And it came to pass that the prophets of the Lord did threaten the people of Nephi, according to the word of God, that if they did not keep the commandments, but should fall into transgression, they should be destroyed from off the face of the land;

24 Wherefore, the prophets, and the priests, and the teachers, did labor diligently, exhorting with all long suffering, the people to diligence; teaching the law of Moses, and the intent for which it was given;

25 Persuading them to look forward unto the Messiah, and believe in him to come, as though he already was.

26 And after this manner did they teach them.

27 And it came to pass, that by so doing they kept them from being destroyed upon the face of the land:

28 For they did prick their hearts with the word, continually stirring them up unto repentance.

29 ¶And it came to pass that two hundred and thirty and eight years had passed away, after the manner of wars, and contentions, and dissensions, for the space of much of the time.

30 And I, Jarom, do not write more, for the plates are small.

31 But behold, my brethren, ye can go to the other plates of Nephi: for behold, upon them the record of our wars are engraven, according to the writings of the kings, or those which they caused to be written.

32 And I deliver these plates into the hands of my son Omni, that they may be kept according to the commandments of my fathers.

THE BOOK OF OMNI.

CHAPTER 1.

1 ¶Behold, it came to pass that I, Omni, being commanded by my father Jarom, that I should write somewhat upon these plates, to preserve our genealogy;

2 Wherefore, in my days, I would that ye should know that I fought much with the sword, to preserve my people, the Nephites, from falling into the hands of their enemies, the Lamanites.

3 But behold, I, of myself, am a wicked man, and I have not kept the statutes and the commandments of the Lord, as I ought to have done.

4 ¶And it came to pass that two hundred and seventy and six years had passed away, and we had many seasons of peace; and we had many seasons of serious war and bloodshed.

5 Yea, and in fine, two hundred and eighty and two years had passed away, and I had kept these plates according to the commandments of my fathers; and I conferred them upon my son Amaron. And I make an end.

6 ¶And now I, Amaron, write the things whatsoever I write, which are few, in the book of my father.

7 Behold, it came to pass that three hundred and twenty years had passed away, and the more wicked part of the Nephites were destroyed:

8 For the Lord would not suffer, after he had led them out of the land of Jerusalem, and kept and preserved them from falling into the hands of their enemies; yea, he would not suffer that the words should not be verified, which he spake unto our fathers, saying, That inasmuch as ye will not keep my commandments, ye shall not prosper in the land.

9 Wherefore, the Lord did visit them in great judgment; nevertheless, he did spare the righteous, that they should not perish, but did deliver them out of the hands of their enemies.

10 And it came to pass that I did deliver the plates unto my brother Chemish.

11 ¶Now I, Chemish, write what few things I write, in the same book with my brother: for behold, I saw the last which he wrote, that he wrote it with his own hand; and he wrote it in the day that he delivered them unto me.

12 And after this manner we keep the records, for it is according to the commandments of our fathers. And I make an end.

13 ¶Behold, I, Abinadom, am the son of Chemish.

14 Behold, it came to pass that I saw much war and contention between my people, the Nephites, and the Lamanites:

15 And I, with mine own sword, have taken the lives of many of the Lamanites, in the defense of my brethren.

16 And behold, the record of this people is engraven upon plates which is had by the kings, according to the generations;

17 And I know of no revelation, save that which has been written, neither prophecy; wherefore, that which is sufficient is written. And I make an end.

18 ¶Behold, I am Amaleki, the son of Abinadom.

19 Behold, I will speak unto you somewhat concerning Mosiah, who was made king over the land of Zarahemla:

20 For behold, he being warned of the Lord that he should flee out of the land of Nephi, and as many as would hearken unto the voice of the Lord, should also depart out of the land with him, into the wilderness.

21 And it came to pass that he did according as the Lord had commanded him.

22 And they departed out of the land into the wilderness, as many as would hearken unto the voice of the Lord; and they were led by many preachings and prophesyings.

23 And they were admonished continually by the word of God: and they were led by the power of his arm, through the wilderness, until they came down into the land which is called the land of Zarahemla.

24 And they discovered a people, who were called the people of Zarahemla.

25 Now, there was great rejoicing among the people of Zarahemla; and also, Zarahemla did rejoice exceedingly, because the Lord had sent the people of Mosiah with the plates of brass which contained the record of the Jews.

26 ¶Behold, it came to pass that Mosiah discovered that the people of Zarahemla, came out from Jerusalem, at the time that Zedekiah, king of Judah, was carried away captive into Babylon.

27 And they journeyed in the wilderness, and were brought by the hand of the Lord, across the great waters, into the land where Mosiah discovered them; and they had dwelt there from that time forth.

28 And at the time that Mosiah discovered them, they had become exceeding numerous.

29 Nevertheless, they had had many wars and serious contentions, and had fallen by the sword from time to time;

30 And their language had become corrupted; and they had brought no records with them:

31 And they denied the being of their Creator; and Mosiah, nor the people of Mosiah, could understand them.

32 ¶But it came to pass that Mosiah caused that they should be taught in his language.

33 And it came to pass that after they were taught in the language of Mosiah, Zarahemla gave a genealogy of his fathers, according to his memory; and they are written, but not in these plates.

34 ¶And it came to pass that the people of Zarahemla, and of Mosiah, did unite together; and Mosiah was appointed to be their king.

35 And it came to pass in the days of Mosiah, there was a large stone brought unto him, with engravings on it; and he did interpret the engravings, by the gift and power of God.

36 ¶And they gave an account of one Coriantumr, and the slain of his people.

37 And Coriantumr was discovered by the people of Zarahemla; and he dwelt with them for the space of nine moons.

38 It also spake a few words concerning his fathers.

39 And his first parents came out from the tower, at the time the Lord confounded the language of the people; and the severity of the Lord fell upon them, according to his judgments, which are just; and their bones lay scattered in the land northward:

40 ¶Behold, I, Amaleki, was born in the days of Mosiah; and I have lived to see his death; and Benjamin, his son, reigneth in his stead.

41 And behold, I have seen in the days of King Benjamin, a serious war, and much bloodshed, between the Nephites and the Lamanites.

42 But behold, the Nephites did obtain much advantage over them; yea, insomuch that King Benjamin did drive them out of the land of Zarahemla.

43 ¶And it came to pass that I began to be old; and, having no seed, and knowing King Benjamin to be a just man before the Lord, wherefore, I shall deliver up these plates unto him, exhorting all men to come unto God, the Holy One of Israel,

44 And believe in prophesying, and in revelations, and in the ministering of angels, and in the gift of speaking with

tongues, and in the gift of interpreting languages, and in all things which are good:

45 For there is nothing which is good, save it comes from the Lord; and that which is evil, cometh from the devil.

46 ¶And now, my beloved brethren, I would that ye should come unto Christ, who is the Holy One of Israel, and partake of his salvation, and the power of his redemption.

47 Yea, come unto him, and offer your whole souls as an offering unto him, and continue in fasting and praying, and endure to the end; and as the Lord liveth, ye will be saved.

48 ¶And now, I would speak somewhat concerning a certain number who went up into the wilderness, to return to the land of Nephi:

49 For there was a large number who were desirous to possess the land of their inheritance; wherefore, they went up into the wilderness.

50 And their leader being a strong and a mighty man, and a stiff-necked man, wherefore he caused a contention among them; and they were all slain, save fifty, in the wilderness, and they returned again to the land of Zarahemla.

51 ¶And it came to pass that they also took others, to a considerable number, and took their journey again into the wilderness.

52 And I, Amaleki, had a brother, who also went with them; and I have not since known concerning them.

53 And I am about to lie down in my grave; and these plates are full.

54 And I make an end of my speaking.

THE WORDS OF MORMON.

CHAPTER 1.

1 ¶And now I, Mormon, being about to deliver up the record which I have been making, into the hands of my son Moroni, behold, I have witnessed almost all the destruction of my people, the Nephites.

2 And it is many hundred years after the coming of Christ, that I deliver these records into the hands of my son; and it supposeth me that he will witness the entire destruction of my people.

3 But may God grant that he may survive them, that he may write somewhat concerning them, and somewhat concerning Christ, that perhaps some day it may profit them.

4 ¶And now, I speak somewhat concerning that which I have written: for after I had made an abridgment from the plates of Nephi, down to the reign of this King Benjamin, of whom Amaleki spake,

5 I searched among the records which had been delivered into my hands, and I found these plates, which contained this small account of the prophets, from Jacob, down to the reign of this King Benjamin: and also many of the words of Nephi.

6 And the things which are upon these plates pleasing me, because of the prophecies of the coming of Christ; and my fathers knowing that many of them have been fulfilled;

7 Yea, and I also know that as many things as have been prophesied concerning us down to this day, have been fulfilled; and as many as go beyond this day, must surely come to pass;

8 Wherefore, I chose these things, to finish my record upon them, which remainder of my record I shall take from the plates of Nephi; and I can not write the hundredth part of the things of my people.

9 ¶But behold, I shall take these plates, which contain these prophesyings and revelations, and put them with the remainder of my record, for they are choice unto me; and I know they will be choice unto my brethren.

10 And I do this for a wise purpose; for thus it whispereth me, according to the workings of the Spirit of the Lord which is in me.

11 And now, I do not know all things; but the Lord knoweth all things which are to come; wherefore, he worketh in me to do according to his will.

12 And my prayer to God, is concerning my brethren, that they may once again come to the knowledge of God; yea, the redemption of Christ; that they may once again be a delightsome people.

13 ¶And now I, Mormon, proceed to finish out my record, which I take from the plates of Nephi; and I make it according to the knowledge and the understanding which God has given me.

14 Wherefore, it came to pass that after Amaleki had delivered up these plates into the hands of King Benjamin, he took them and put them with the other plates, which contained records which had been handed down by the kings, from generation to generation, until the days of King Benjamin;

15 And they were handed down from King Benjamin, from generation to generation, until they have fallen into my hands.

16 And I, Mormon, pray to God that they may be preserved, from this time henceforth.

17 And I know that they will be preserved: for there are great things written upon them, out of which my people and their brethren, shall be judged at the great and last day, according to the word of God which is written.

18 ¶And now, concerning this King Benjamin: he had somewhat contentions among his own people.

19 And it came to pass also, that the armies of the Lamanites came down out of the land of Nephi, to battle against his people.

20 But behold, King Benjamin gathered together his armies, and he did stand against them; and he did fight with the strength of his own arm, with the sword of Laban;

21 And in the strength of the Lord they did contend against their enemies, until they had slain many thousands of the Lamanites.

22 And it came to pass that they did contend against the Lamanites, until they had driven them out of all the lands of their inheritance.

23 ¶And it came to pass that after there had been false Christs, and their mouths had been shut, and they punished according to their crimes;

24 And after there had been false prophets, and false preachers and teachers among the people, and all these having been punished according to their crimes;

25 And after there having been much contentions and many dissensions, away unto the Lamanites, behold, it came to pass that King Benjamin, with the assistance of the holy prophets who were among his people; for behold, King Benjamin was a holy man, and he did reign over his people in righteousness.

26 And there were many holy men in the land; and they did speak the word of God, with power and with authority; and they did use much sharpness because of the stiff-neckedness of the people;

27 Wherefore, with the help of these, King Benjamin, by laboring with all the might of his body and the faculty of his whole soul, and also the prophets, did once more establish peace in the land.

THE BOOK OF MOSIAH.

CHAPTER 1.

1 ¶And now there was no more contention in all the land of Zarahemla, among all the people who belonged to King Benjamin, so that King Benjamin had continual peace all the remainder of his days.

2 And it came to pass that he had three sons; and he called their names Mosiah, and Helorum, and Helaman.

3 And he caused that they should be taught in all the language of his fathers, that thereby they might become men of understanding; and that they might know concerning the prophecies which had been spoken by the mouths of their fathers, which were delivered them by the hand of the Lord.

4 And he also taught them concerning the records which were engraven on the plates of brass, saying, My sons, I would that ye should remember, that were it not for these plates, which contain these records and these commandments, we must have suffered in ignorance, even at this present time, not knowing the mysteries of God:

5 For it were not possible that our father Lehi could have remembered all these things, to have taught them to his children, except it were for the help of these plates:

6 For he having been taught in the language of the Egyptians, therefore he could read these engravings, and teach them to his children, that thereby they could teach them to their children, and so fulfilling the commandments of God, even down to this present time.

7 I say unto you, my sons, Were it not for these things, which have been kept and preserved by the hand of God, that we might read and understand of his mysteries, and have his commandments always before our eyes, that even our fathers would have dwindled in unbelief,

8 And we should have been like unto our brethren, the Lamanites, who know nothing concerning these things, or even do not believe them when they are taught them, because of the traditions of their fathers, which are not correct.

9 O my sons, I would that ye should remember that these sayings are true; and also, that these records are true.

10 And behold, also the plates of Nephi, which contain the records and the sayings of our fathers from the time they left Jerusalem, until now; and they are true; and we can know of their surety, because we have them before our eyes.

11 And now, my sons, I would that ye should remember to search them diligently, that ye may profit thereby;

12 And I would that ye should keep the commandments of God, that ye may prosper in the land, according to the promises which the Lord made unto our fathers.

13 And many more things did King Benjamin teach his sons, which are not written in this book.

14 ¶And it came to pass that after King Benjamin had made an end of teaching his sons that he waxed old; and he saw that he must very soon go the way of all the earth; therefore, he thought it expedient that he should confer the kingdom upon one of his sons.

15 Therefore, he had Mosiah brought before him; and these are the words which he spake unto him, saying: My son, I would that ye should make a proclamation throughout all this land, among all this people, or the people of Zarahemla, and the people of Mosiah, who dwell in this land, that thereby they may be gathered together:

16 For on the morrow, I shall proclaim unto this my people, out of mine own mouth, that thou art a king and a ruler over this people, whom the Lord our God hath given us.

17 And moreover, I shall give this people a name, that thereby they may be distinguished above all the people which the Lord God hath brought out of the land of Jerusalem; and this I do, because they have been a diligent people in keeping the commandments of the Lord.

18 And I give unto them a name, that never shall be blotted out, except it be through transgression.

19 Yea, and moreover I say unto you, that if this highly favored people of the Lord should fall into transgression, and become a wicked and an adulterous people, that the Lord will deliver them up, that thereby they become weak, like unto their brethren;

20 And he will no more preserve them, by his matchless and marvelous power, as he has hitherto preserved our fathers.

21 For I say unto you, that if he had not extended his arm in the preservation of our fathers, they must have fallen into the hands of the Lamanites, and become victims to their hatred.

22 ¶And it came to pass that after King Benjamin had made an end of these sayings to his son, that he gave him charge concerning all the affairs of the kingdom.

23 And moreover, he also gave him charge concerning the records which were engraven on the plates of brass; and also, the plates of Nephi;

24 And also, the sword of Laban, and the ball or director, which led our fathers through the wilderness, which was prepared by the hand of the Lord, that thereby they might be led, every one according to the heed and diligence which they gave unto him.

25 Therefore, as they were unfaithful, they did not prosper nor progress in their journey, but were driven back, and incurred the displeasure of God upon them;

26 And therefore, they were smitten with famine and sore afflictions, to stir them up in remembrance of their duty.

27 ¶And now, it came to pass that Mosiah went and did as his father had commanded him, and proclaimed unto all the people who were in the land of Zarahemla, that thereby they might gather themselves together, to go up to the temple, to hear the words which his father should speak unto them.

28 ¶And it came to pass that after Mosiah had done as his father had commanded him, and had made a proclamation throughout all the land, that the people gathered themselves together throughout all the land, that they might go up to

the temple to hear the words which King Benjamin should speak unto them.

29 And there were a great number, even so many that they did not number them; for they had multiplied exceedingly, and waxed great in the land.

30 And they also took of the firstlings of their flocks, that they might offer sacrifice and burnt offerings, according to the law of Moses;

31 And also, that they might give thanks to the Lord their God, who had brought them out of the land of Jerusalem, and who had delivered them out of the hands of their enemies, and had appointed just men to be their teachers, and also, a just man to be their king,

32 Who had established peace in the land of Zarahemla, and who had taught them to keep the commandments of God, that thereby they might rejoice, and be filled with love towards God, and all men.

33 ¶And it came to pass that when they came up to the temple, they pitched their tents round about, every man according to his family, consisting of his wife, and his sons, and his daughters, and their sons, and their daughters, from the eldest down to the youngest, every family being separate, one from another;

34 And they pitched their tents round about the temple, every man having his tent with the door thereof towards the temple, that thereby they might remain in their tents, and hear the words which King Benjamin should speak unto them;

35 For the multitude being so great, that King Benjamin could not teach them all within the walls of the temple; therefore he caused a tower to be erected; that thereby his people might hear the words which he should speak unto them.

36 ¶And it came to pass that he began to speak to his people from the tower; and they could not all hear his words, because of the greatness of the multitude;

37 Therefore, he caused that the words which he spake, should be written and sent forth among those that were not

under the sound of his voice, that they might also receive his words.

28 And these are the words which he spake and caused to be written, saying: My brethren, all ye that have assembled yourselves together, you that can hear my words which I shall speak unto you this day:

39 For I have not commanded you to come up hither to trifle with the words which I shall speak, but that you should hearken unto me, and open your ears that ye may hear, and your hearts that ye may understand, and your minds that the mysteries of God may be unfolded to your view.

40 I have not commanded you to come up hither, that ye should fear me, or that ye should think that I, of myself, am more than a mortal man;

41 But I am like as yourselves, subject to all manner of infirmities in body and mind;

42 Yet, as I have been chosen by this people, and was consecrated by my father, and was suffered by the hand of the Lord that I should be a ruler, and a king over this people; and have been kept and preserved by his matchless power, to serve thee with all the might, mind, and strength which the Lord hath granted unto me;

43 I say unto you, that as I have been suffered to spend my days in your service, even up to this time, and have not sought gold nor silver, nor any manner of riches of you;

44 Neither have I suffered that ye should be confined in dungeons, nor that ye should make slaves one of another, or that ye should murder, or plunder, or steal, or commit adultery,

45 Or even I have not suffered that ye should commit any manner of wickedness, and have taught you that ye should keep the commandments of the Lord, in all things which he hath commanded you;

46 And even I, myself, have labored with mine own hands, that I might serve you, and that ye should not be laden with taxes, and that there should nothing come upon you which was grievous to be borne; and of all these things which I have spoken, ye yourselves are witnesses this day.

47 Yet, my brethren, I have not done these things that I might boast, neither do I tell these things that thereby I might accuse you; but I tell you these things that ye may know that I can answer a clear conscience before God this day.

48 Behold, I say unto you, that because I said unto you that I had spent my days in your service, I do not desire to boast, for I have only been in the service of God.

49 And behold, I tell you these things that ye may learn wisdom; that ye may learn that when ye are in the service of your fellow beings, ye are only in the service of your God.

50 Behold, ye have called me your king; and if I, whom ye call your king, do labor to serve you, then had not ye ought to labor to serve one another?

51 And behold, also, if I, whom ye call your king, who has spent his days in your service, and yet has been in the service of God, doth merit any thanks from you, O how had you ought to thank your heavenly King!

52 I say unto you, my brethren, that if you should render all the thanks and praise which your whole souls have power to possess, to that God who has created you, and has kept and preserved you, and has caused that ye should rejoice, and has granted that ye should live in peace one with another;

53 I say unto you, that if ye should serve him who has created you from the beginning, and art preserving you from day to day, by lending you breath, that ye may live and move, and do according to your own will, and even supporting you from one moment to another;

54 I say, if ye should serve him with all your whole soul, yet ye would be unprofitable servants.

55 And behold, all that he requires of you, is to keep his commandments; and he has promised you that if ye would keep his commandments, ye should prosper in the land;

56 And he never doth vary from that which he hath said; therefore, if ye do keep his commandments, he doth bless you, and prosper you.

57 ¶And now, in the first place, he hath created you, and

granted unto you your lives, for which ye are indebted unto him.

58 And secondly: he doth require that ye should do as he hath commanded you, for which if ye do, he doth immediately bless you; and therefore, he hath paid you.

59 And ye are still indebted unto him; and are, and will be, for ever and ever; therefore, of what have ye to boast?

60 And now I ask, Can ye say aught of yourselves? I answer you, Nay.

61 Ye can not say that ye are even as much as the dust of the earth: yet ye were created of the dust of the earth: but behold, it belongeth to him who created you.

62 And I, even I, whom ye call your king, am no better than ye yourselves are; for I am also of the dust.

63 And ye behold that I am old, and am about to yield up this mortal frame to its mother earth;

64 Therefore, as I said unto you that I had served you, walking with a clear conscience before God, even so I at this time have caused that ye should assemble yourselves together, that I might be found blameless, and that your blood should not come upon me, when I shall stand to be judged of God of the things whereof he hath commanded me concerning you.

65 I say unto you, that I have caused that ye should assemble yourselves together, that I might rid my garments of your blood, at this period of time when I am about to go down to my grave,

66 That I might go down in peace, and my immortal spirit may join the choirs above in singing the praises of a just God.

67 And moreover, I say unto you, that I have caused that ye should assemble yourselves together, that I might declare unto you that I can no longer be your teacher, nor your king;

68 For even at this time, my whole frame doth tremble exceedingly, while attempting to speak unto you;

69 But the Lord God doth support me, and hath suffered me, that I should speak unto you, and hath commanded me,

that I should declare unto you this day, that my son Mosiah, is a king and a ruler over you.

70 ¶And now, my brethren, I would that ye should do as ye have hitherto done.

71 As ye have kept my commandments, and also the commandments of my father, and have prospered, and have been kept from falling into the hands of your enemies,

72 Even so if ye shall keep the commandments of my son, or the commandments of God, which shall be delivered unto you by him, ye shall prosper in the land, and your enemies shall have no power over you.

73 But O my people, beware lest there shall arise contentions among you, and ye list to obey the evil spirit, which was spoken of by my father Mosiah.

74 For behold, there is a wo pronounced upon him who listeth to obey that spirit: for if he listeth to obey him, and remaineth and dieth in his sins, the same drinketh damnation to his own soul;

75 For he receiveth for his wages an everlasting punishment, having transgressed the law of God, contrary to his own knowledge.

76 I say unto you, that there are not any among you, except it be your little children, that have not been taught concerning these things, but what knoweth that ye are eternally indebted to your heavenly Father,

77 To render to him all that you have, and are, and also have been taught, concerning the records which contain the prophecies which have been spoken by the holy prophets, even down to the time our father Lehi left Jerusalem; and also, all that has been spoken by our fathers, until now.

78 And behold, also, they spake that which was commanded them of the Lord; therefore, they are just and true.

79 ¶And now, I say unto you, my brethren, that after ye have known and have been taught all these things, if ye should transgress, and go contrary to that which has been spoken, that ye do withdraw yourselves from the Spirit of the Lord, that it may have no place in you to guide you in

wisdom's paths, that ye may be blessed, prospered, and preserved.

80 I say unto you, that the man that doeth this, the same cometh out in open rebellion against God;

81 Therefore he listeth to obey the evil spirit, and becometh an enemy to all righteousness;

82 Therefore, the Lord has no place in him, for he dwelleth not in unholy temples.

83 Therefore, if that man repenteth not, and remaineth and dieth an enemy to God, the demands of divine justice doth awaken his immortal soul to a lively sense of his own guilt,

84 Which doth cause him to shrink from the presence of the Lord, and doth fill his breast with guilt, and pain, and anguish, which is like an unquenchable fire, whose flames ascendeth up for ever and ever.

85 And now I say unto you, that mercy hath no claim on that man; therefore, his final doom is to endure a never ending torment.

86 ¶O all ye old men, and also ye young men, and you little children, who can understand my words, (for I have spoken plain unto you, that ye might understand,)

87 I pray that ye should awake to a remembrance of the awful situation of those that have fallen into transgression;

88 And moreover, I would desire that ye should consider on the blessed and happy state of those that keep the commandments of God.

89 For behold, they are blessed in all things, both temporal and spiritual;

90 And if they hold out faithful to the end, they are received into heaven, that thereby they may dwell with God in a state of never ending happiness.

91 O remember, remember that these things are true; for the Lord God hath spoken it.

92 ¶And again, my brethren, I would call your attention, for I have somewhat more to speak unto you:

93 For behold, I have things to tell you, concerning that which is to come; and the things which I shall tell you, are made known unto me, by an angel from God.

94 And he said unto me, Awake; and I awoke, and behold, he stood before me.

95 And he said unto me, Awake, and hear the words which I shall tell thee: for behold, I am come to declare unto thee glad tidings of great joy.

96 For the Lord hath heard thy prayers, and hath judged of thy righteousness, and hath sent me to declare unto thee that thou mayest rejoice; and that thou mayest declare unto thy people, that they may also be filled with joy.

97 For behold, the time cometh, and is not far distant, that with power, the Lord Omnipotent who reigneth, who was, and is from all eternity to all eternity, shall come down from heaven, among the children of men, and shall dwell in a tabernacle of clay,

98 And shall go forth amongst men, working mighty miracles, such as healing the sick, raising the dead, causing the lame to walk, the blind to receive their sight, and the deaf to hear, and curing all manner of diseases;

99 And he shall cast out devils, or the evil spirits which dwell in the hearts of the children of men.

100 And lo, he shall suffer temptations, and pain of body, hunger, thirst, and fatigue, even more than man can suffer, except it be unto death;

101 For behold, blood cometh from every pore, so great shall be his anguish for the wickedness and the abominations of his people.

102 And he shall be called Jesus Christ, the Son of God, the Father of heaven and earth, the Creator of all things, from the beginning; and his mother shall be called Mary.

103 And lo, he cometh unto his own, that salvation might come unto the children of men, even through faith, on his name;

104 And even after all this, they shall consider him a man, and say that he hath a devil, and shall scourge him, and shall crucify him.

105 And he shall rise the third day from the dead; and behold, he standeth to judge the world.

106 And behold, all these things are done, that a righteous judgment might come upon the children of men.

107 For behold, and also his blood atoneth for the sins of those who have fallen by the transgression of Adam, who have died, not knowing the will of God concerning them, or who have ignorantly sinned.

108 But wo, wo unto him who knoweth that he rebelleth against God; for salvation cometh to none such, except it be through repentance and faith on the Lord Jesus Christ.

109 And the Lord God hath sent his holy prophets among all the children of men to declare these things to every kindred, nation, and tongue, that thereby whosoever should believe that Christ should come, the same might receive remission of their sins, and rejoice with exceeding great joy, even as though he had already come among them.

110 Yet the Lord God saw that his people were a stiffnecked people, and he appointed unto them a law, even the law of Moses.

111 And many signs, and wonders, and types, and shadows shewed he unto them, concerning his coming:

112 And also holy prophets spake unto them concerning his coming;

113 And yet they hardened their hearts, and understood not that the law of Moses availeth nothing, except it were through the atonement of his blood;

114 And even if it were possible that little children could sin, they could not be saved; but I say unto you, they are blessed;

115 For behold as in Adam, or by nature they fall, even so the blood of Christ atoneth for their sins.

116 And moreover, I say unto you, that there shall be no other name given, nor any other way nor means whereby salvation can come unto the children of men, only in and through the name of Christ, the Lord Omnipotent.

117 For behold, he judgeth, and his judgment is just, and the infant perisheth not, that dieth in his infancy;

118 But men drink damnation to their own souls, except they humble themselves, and become as little children, and

believe that salvation was, and is, and is to come, in and through the atoning blood of Christ, the Lord Omnipotent:

119 For the natural man is an enemy to God, and has been, from the fall of Adam, and will be, for ever and ever;

120 But if he yields to the enticings of the Holy Spirit, and putteth off the natural man, and becometh a saint, through the atonement of Christ, the Lord, and becometh as a child, submissive, meek, humble, patient, full of love, willing to submit to all things which the Lord seeth fit to inflict upon him, even as a child doth submit to his father.

121 And moreover, I say unto you, that the time shall come, when the knowledge of a Savior shall spread throughout every nation, kindred, tongue, and people.

122 And behold, when that time cometh, none shall be found blameless before God, except it be little children, only through repentance and faith on the name of the Lord God Omnipotent;

123 And even at this time, when thou shalt have taught thy people the things which the Lord thy God hath commanded thee, even then are they found no more blameless in the sight of God, only according to the words which I have spoken unto thee.

124 ¶And now, I have spoken the words which the Lord God hath commanded me.

125 And thus saith the Lord: They shall stand as a bright testimony against this people, at the judgment day;

126 Whereof, they shall be judged, every man, according to his works, whether they be good, or whether they be evil;

127 And if they be evil, they are consigned to an awful view of their own guilt and abominations, which doth cause them to shrink from the presence of the Lord, into a state of misery and endless torment, from whence they can no more return: therefore, they have drunk damnation to their own souls.

128 Therefore, they have drunk out of the cup of the wrath of God, which justice could no more deny unto them than it could deny that Adam should fall, because of his par-

taking of the forbidden fruit; therefore, mercy could have claim on them no more for ever.

129 And their torment is as a lake of fire and brimstone, whose flames are unquenchable, and whose smoke ascendeth up for ever and ever.

130 Thus hath the Lord commanded me. Amen.

CHAPTER 2.

1 ¶And now, it came to pass that when King Benjamin had made an end of speaking the words which had been delivered unto him by the angel of the Lord, that he cast his eyes round about on the multitude, and behold they had fallen to the earth, for the fear of the Lord had come upon them;

2 And they had viewed themselves in their own carnal state, even less than the dust of the earth.

3 And they all cried aloud with one voice, saying, O have mercy, and apply the atoning blood of Christ, that we may receive forgiveness of our sins, and our hearts may be purified:

4 For we believe in Jesus Christ, the Son of God, who created heaven and earth, and all things, who shall come down among the children of men.

5 ¶And it came to pass that after they had spoken these words, the Spirit of the Lord came upon them, and they were filled with joy,

6 Having received a remission of their sins, and having peace of conscience, because of the exceeding faith which they had in Jesus Christ who should come, according to the words which King Benjamin had spoken unto them.

7 And King Benjamin again opened his mouth, and began to speak unto them, saying, My friends and my brethren, my kindred and my people, I would again call your attention, that ye may hear and understand the remainder of my words which I shall speak unto you;

8 For behold, if the knowledge of the goodness of God at

this time, has awakened you to a sense of your nothingness, and your worthless and fallen state;

9 I say unto you, if ye have come to a knowledge of the goodness of God, and his matchless power, and his wisdom, and his patience, and his long suffering towards the children of men,

10 And also, the atonement which has been prepared from the foundation of the world, that thereby salvation might come to him that should put his trust in the Lord, and should be diligent in keeping his commandments, and continue in the faith even unto the end of his life; I mean the life of the mortal body;

11 I say, that this is the man who receiveth salvation, through the atonement which was prepared from the foundation of the world, for all mankind, which ever were, ever since the fall of Adam, or who are or who ever shall be, even unto the end of the world; and this is the means whereby salvation cometh.

12 And there is none other salvation, save this which hath been spoken of; neither is there any conditions whereby man can be saved, except the conditions which I have told you.

13 Believe in God; believe that he is, and that he created all things, both in heaven and in earth;

14 Believe that he has all wisdom, and all power, both in heaven and in earth;

15 Believe that man doth not comprehend all things which the Lord can comprehend.

16 And again: Believe that ye must repent of your sins and forsake them, and humble yourselves before God; and ask in sincerity of heart that he would forgive you:

17 And now, if you believe all these things, see that ye do them.

18 And again I say unto you as I have said before, that as ye have come to the knowledge of the glory of God,

19 Or if ye have known of his goodness, and have tasted of his love, and have received a remission of your sins, which causeth such exceeding great joy in your souls,

20 Even so I would that ye should remember, and always

retain in remembrance, the greatness of God, and your own nothingness, and his goodness and long suffering towards you unworthy creatures,

21 And humble yourselves even in the depths of humility, calling on the name of the Lord daily, and standing steadfastly in the faith of that which is to come, which was spoken by the mouth of the angel;

22 And behold, I say unto you, that if ye do this, ye shall always rejoice, and be filled with the love of God, and always retain a remission of your sins;

23 And ye shall grow in the knowledge of the glory of him that created you, or in the knowledge of that which is just and true.

24 And ye will not have a mind to injure one another, but to live peaceably, and to render to every man according to that which is his due.

25 And ye will not suffer your children, that they go hungry, or naked;

26 Neither will ye suffer that they transgress the laws of God, and fight and quarrel one with another, and serve the devil, who is the master of sin, or who is the evil spirit which hath been spoken of by our fathers; he being an enemy to all righteousness;

27 But ye will teach them to walk in the ways of truth and soberness; ye will teach them to love one another, and to serve one another;

28 And also, ye yourselves will succor those that stand in need of your succor; ye will administer of your substance unto him that standeth in need;

29 And ye will not suffer that the beggar putteth up his petition to you in vain, and turn him out to perish.

30 Perhaps thou shalt say, The man has brought upon himself his misery; therefore I will stay my hand, and will not give unto him of my food, nor impart unto him of my substance, that he may not suffer, for his punishments are just.

31 But I say unto you, O man, whosoever doeth this, the same hath great cause to repent; and except he repenteth of

that which he hath done, he perisheth for ever, and hath no interest in the kingdom of God.

32 For behold, are we not all beggars? Do we not all depend upon the same being, even God, for all the substance which we have; for both food, and raiment, and for gold, and for silver, and for all the riches which we have of every kind?

33 And behold, even at this time, ye have been calling on his name, and begging for a remission of your sins.

34 And has he suffered that ye have begged in vain?

35 Nay; he has poured out his Spirit upon you, and has caused that your hearts should be filled with joy, and has caused that your mouths should be stopped, that ye could not find utterance, so exceeding great was your joy.

36 And now, if God, who has created you, on whom you are dependent for your lives, and for all that ye have and are, doth grant unto you whatsoever ye ask that is right, in faith, believing that ye shall receive, O then, how had ye ought to impart of the substance that ye have, one to another?

37 And if ye judge the man who putteth up his petition to you for your substance, that he perish not, and condemn him, how much more just will be your condemnation, for withholding your substance, which doth not belong to you, but to God, to whom also, your life belongeth;

38 And yet ye put up no petition, nor repent of the thing which thou hast done.

39 I say unto you, wo be unto that man, for his substance shall perish with him; and now, I say these things unto those who are rich, as pertaining to the things of this world.

40 And again, I say unto the poor, ye who have not and yet have sufficient, that ye remain from day to day; I mean all you who deny the beggar, because ye have not; I would that ye say in your hearts, that I give not because I have not; but if I had, I would give.

41 And now, if ye say this in your hearts, ye remain guiltless, otherwise ye are condemned, and your condemnation is just; for ye covet that which ye have not received.

42 ¶And now, for the sake of these things which I have

spoken unto you; that is, for the sake of retaining a remission of your sins from day to day, that ye may walk guiltless before God,

43 I would that ye should impart of your substance to the poor, every man according to that which he hath, such as feeding the hungry, clothing the naked, visiting the sick, and administering to their relief, both spiritually and temporally, according to their wants,

44 And see that all these things are done in wisdom and order: for it is not requisite that a man should run faster than he has strength.

45 And again: it is expedient that he should be diligent, that thereby he might win the prize: therefore, all things must be done in order.

46 And I would that ye should remember, that whosoever among you that borroweth of his neighbor, should return the thing that he borroweth, according as he doth agree,

47 Or else thou shalt commit sin, and perhaps thou shalt cause thy neighbor to commit sin also.

48 And finally, I can not tell you all the things whereby ye may commit sin: for there are divers ways and means, even so many, that I can not number them.

49 But this much I can tell you, that if ye do not watch yourselves, and your thoughts, and your words, and your deeds, and observe to keep the commandments of God, and continue in the faith of what ye have heard concerning the coming of our Lord, even unto the end of your lives, ye must perish.

50 And now, O man, remember, and perish not.

CHAPTER 3.

1 ¶And now, it came to pass that when King Benjamin had thus spoken to his people, he sent among them, desiring to know of his people, if they believed the words which he had spoken unto them.

2 And they all cried with one voice, saying, Yea, we believe all the words which thou hast spoken unto us;

3 And also, we know of their surety and truth, because of the Spirit of the Lord Omnipotent, which has wrought a mighty change in us, or in our hearts, that we have no more disposition to do evil, but to do good continually.

4 And we, ourselves, also, through the infinite goodness of God, and the manifestations of his Spirit, have great views of that which is to come; and were it expedient, we could prophesy of all things.

5 And it is the faith which we have had on the things which our king has spoken unto us, and has brought us to this great knowledge, whereby we do rejoice with such exceeding great joy;

6 And we are willing to enter into a covenant with our God, to do his will, and to be obedient to his commandments in all things that he shall command us, all the remainder of our days, that we may not bring upon ourselves a never ending torment, as has been spoken by the angel, that we may not drink out of the cup of the wrath of God.

7 ¶And now, these are the words which King Benjamin desired of them; and therefore he said unto them, Ye have spoken the words that I desired; and the covenant which ye have made, is a righteous covenant.

8 And now, because of the covenant which ye have made, ye shall be called the children of Christ, his sons, and his daughters:

9 For behold, this day he hath spiritually begotten you; for ye say that your hearts are changed through faith on his name; therefore, ye are born of him, and have become his sons and his daughters.

10 And under this head ye are made free; and there is no other head whereby ye can be made free.

11 There is no other name given, whereby salvation cometh; therefore, I would that ye should take upon you the name of Christ, all you that have entered into the covenant with God, that ye should be obedient unto the end of your lives.

12 And it shall come to pass that whosoever doeth this, shall be found at the right hand of God, for he shall know the

name by which he is called; for he shall be called by the name of Christ.

13 ¶And now, it shall come to pass that whosoever shall not take upon them the name of Christ, must be called by some other name; therefore, he findeth himself on the left hand of God.

14 And I would that ye should remember also, that this is the name that I said I should give unto you, that never should be blotted out, except it be through transgression;

15 Therefore, take heed that ye do not transgress, that the name be not blotted out of your hearts.

16 I say unto you, I would that ye should remember to retain the name written always in your hearts, that ye are not found on the left hand of God, but that ye hear and know the voice by which ye shall be called, and also, the name by which he shall call you:

17 For, how knoweth a man the master whom he has not served, and who is a stranger unto him, and is far from the thoughts and intents of his heart?

18 And again: Doth a man take an ass which belongeth to his neighbor, and keep him?

19 I say unto you, Nay; he will not even suffer that he shall feed among his flocks, but will drive him away, and cast him out.

20 I say unto you, that even so shall it be among you, if ye know not the name by which ye are called.

21 Therefore, I would that ye should be steadfast and immovable, always abounding in good works, that Christ, the Lord God Omnipotent, may seal you his, that you may be brought to heaven, that ye may have everlasting salvation and eternal life, through the wisdom, and power, and justice, and mercy of him, who created all things, in heaven and in earth, who is God above all.   Amen.

CHAPTER 4.

1 ¶And now, King Benjamin thought it was expedient, after having finished speaking to the people, that he should take the names of all those who had entered into a covenant with God, to keep his commandments.

2 And it came to pass that there was not one soul, except it were little children, but what had entered into the covenant, and had taken upon them the name of Christ.

3 And again: It came to pass that when King Benjamin had made an end of all these things, and had consecrated his son Mosiah, to be a ruler and a king over his people, and had given him all the charges concerning the kingdom,

4 And also had appointed priests to teach the people, that thereby they might hear and know the commandments of God, and to stir them up in remembrance of the oath which they had made, he dismissed the multitude, and they returned, every one according to their families, to their own houses.

5 ¶And Mosiah began to reign in his father's stead.

6 And he began to reign in the thirtieth year of his age, making in the whole, about four hundred and seventy-six years from the time that Lehi left Jerusalem.

7 And King Benjamin lived three years and he died.

8 And it came to pass that King Mosiah did walk in the ways of the Lord, and did observe his judgments, and his statutes, and did keep his commandments in all things whatsoever he commanded him.

9 ¶And King Mosiah did cause his people that they should till the earth.

10 And he also, himself did till the earth, that thereby he might not become burthensome to his people, that he might do according to that which his father had done, in all things.

11 And there was no contention among all his people, for the space of three years.

CHAPTER 5.

1 ¶And now, it came to pass that after King Mosiah had had continual peace, for the space of three years, he was desirous to know concerning the people who went up to dwell in the land of Lehi-Nephi, or in the city of Lehi-Nephi:

2 For his people had heard nothing from them, from the time they left the land of Zarahemla; therefore, they wearied him with their teasings.

3 ¶And it came to pass that King Mosiah granted that sixteen of their strong men might go up to the land of Lehi-Nephi, to inquire concerning their brethren.

4 And it came to pass that on the morrow, they started to go up, having with them one Ammon, he being a strong and mighty man, and a descendant of Zarahemla; and he was also their leader.

5 And now, they knew not the course they should travel in the wilderness, to go up to the land of Lehi-Nephi; therefore, they wandered many days in the wilderness, even forty days did they wander.

6 And when they had wandered forty days, they came to a hill, which is north of the land of Shilom, and there they pitched their tents.

7 And Ammon took three of his brethren, and their names were Amaleki, Helem, and Hem, and they went down into the land of Nephi;

8 And behold, they met the king of the people, who was in the land of Nephi, and in the land of Shilom;

9 And they were surrounded by the king's guard, and were taken, and were bound, and were committed to prison.

10 And it came to pass when they had been in prison two days, they were again brought before the king, and their bands were loosed;

11 And they stood before the king, and were permitted, or rather commanded that they should answer the questions which he should ask them.

12 And he said unto them, Behold I am Limhi, the son of Noah, who was the son of Zeniff, who came up out of the

land of Zarahemla to inherit this land, which was the land of their fathers, who was made a king by the voice of the people.

13 And now, I desire to know the cause whereby ye were so bold as to come near the walls of the city, when I, myself, was with my guards, without the gate?

14 And now, for this cause have I suffered that ye should be preserved, that I might inquire of you, or else I should have caused that my guards should have put you to death. Ye are permitted to speak.

15 ¶And now, when Ammon saw that he was permitted to speak, he went forth and bowed himself before the king; and rising again he said, O king, I am very thankful before God this day, that I am yet alive, and am permitted to speak;

16 And I will endeavor to speak with boldness; for I am assured that if ye had known me, ye would not have suffered that I should have wore these bands.

17 For I am Ammon, and am a descendant of Zarahemla, and have come up out of the land of Zarahemla, to inquire concerning our brethren, whom Zeniff brought up out of that land.

18 ¶And now, it came to pass that after Limhi had heard the words of Ammon, he was exceeding glad, and said, Now, I know of a surety that my brethren who were in the land of Zarahemla, are yet alive.

19 And now, I will rejoice; and on the morrow, I will cause that my people shall rejoice also.

20 For behold, we are in bondage to the Lamanites, and are taxed with a tax which is grievous to be borne.

21 And now, behold, our brethren will deliver us out of our bondage, or out of the hands of the Lamanites, and we will be their slaves:

22 For it is better that we be slaves to the Nephites, than to pay tribute to the king of the Lamanites.

23 ¶And now, King Limhi commanded his guards that they should no more bind Ammon, nor his brethren, but caused that they should go to the hill which was north of Shilom, and bring their brethren into the city, that thereby they might

eat, and drink, and rest themselves from the labors of their journey;

24 For they had suffered many things; they had suffered hunger, thirst, and fatigue.

25 ¶And now, it came to pass on the morrow, that King Limhi sent a proclamation among all his people, that thereby they might gather themselves together to the temple, to hear the words which he should speak unto them.

26 And it came to pass that when they had gathered themselves together, that he spake unto them in this wise, saying,

27 O ye my people, lift up your heads and be comforted: for behold, the time is at hand, or is not far distant, when we shall no longer be in subjection to our enemies, notwithstanding our many strugglings, which have been in vain; yet I trust there remaineth an effectual struggle to be made.

28 Therefore, lift up your heads, and rejoice, and put your trust in God, in that God who was the God of Abraham, and Isaac, and Jacob;

29 And also, that God who brought the children of Israel out of the land of Egypt, and caused that they should walk through the Red Sea on dry ground, and fed them with manna, that they might not perish in the wilderness; and many more things did he do for them.

30 And again: that same God has brought our fathers out of the land of Jerusalem, and has kept and preserved his people, even until now.

31 And behold, it is because of our iniquities and abominations, that has brought us into bondage.

32 And ye all are witnesses this day, that Zeniff, who was made king over this people, he being over-zealous to inherit the land of his fathers,

33 Therefore being deceived by the cunning and craftiness of King Laman, who having entered into a treaty with King Zeniff, and having yielded up into his hands the possessions of a part of the land, or even the city of Lehi-Nephi, and the city of Shilom; and the land round about;

34 And all this he did, for the sole purpose of bringing this people into subjection, or into bondage.

35 And behold, we at this time do pay tribute to the king of the Lamanites, to the amount of one half of our corn, and our barley, and even all our grain of every kind, and one half of the increase of our flocks, and our herds;

36 And even one half of all we have or possess, the king of the Lamanites doth exact of us, or our lives.

37 And now, is not this grievous to be borne?

38 And is not this, our affliction great?

39 Now behold, how great reason have we to mourn.

40 Yea, I say unto you, great are the reasons which we have to mourn: for behold, how many of our brethren have been slain, and their blood has been spilt in vain, and all because of iniquity.

41 For if this people had not fallen into transgression, the Lord would not have suffered that this great evil should come upon them.

42 But behold, they would not hearken unto his words; but there arose contentions among them, even so much that they did shed blood among themselves.

43 And a prophet of the Lord have they slain; yea, a chosen man of God, who told them of their wickedness and abominations, and prophesied of many things which are to come, yea, even the coming of Christ.

44 And because he said unto them, that Christ was the God, the Father of all things, and said that he should take upon him the image of man, and it should be the image after which man was created in the beginning;

45 Or in other words, he said that man was created after the image of God, and that God should come down among the children of men, and take upon him flesh and blood, and go forth upon the face of the earth;

46 And now because he said this, they did put him to death; and many more things did they do, which brought down the wrath of God upon them.

47 Therefore, who wondereth that they are in bondage, and that they are smitten with sore afflictions?

48 For behold, the Lord has said, I will not succor my people in the day of their transgression; but I will hedge up

their ways, that they prosper not; and their doings shall be as a stumbling block before them.

49 And again, he saith, If my people shall sow filthiness, they shall reap the chaff thereof, in the whirlwind; and the effects thereof, is poison.

50 And again, he saith, If my people shall sow filthiness, they shall reap the east wind, which bringeth immediate destruction.

51 And now, behold, the promise of the Lord is fulfilled; and ye are smitten, and afflicted.

52 But if ye will turn to the Lord with full purpose of heart, and put your trust in him, and serve him with all diligence of mind; if ye do this, he will, according to his own will and pleasure, deliver you out of bondage.

53 ¶And it came to pass that after King Limhi had made an end of speaking to his people, for he spake many things unto them, and only a few of them have I written in this book, he told his people all the things concerning their brethren who were in the land of Zarahemla;

54 And he caused that Ammon should stand up before the multitude, and rehearse unto them all that had happened unto their brethren, from the time that Zeniff went up out of the land, even until the time that he himself came up out of the land.

55 And he also rehearsed unto them the last words which King Benjamin had taught them, and explained them to the people of King Limhi, so that they might understand all the words which he spake.

56 And it came to pass that after he had done all this, that King Limhi dismissed the multitude, and caused that they should return, every one unto his own house.

57 ¶And it came to pass that he caused that the plates which contained the record of his people, from the time that they left the land of Zarahemla, should be brought before Ammon, that he might read them.

58 Now, as soon as Ammon had read the record, the king inquired of him to know if he could interpret languages.

59 And Ammon told him that he could not.

60 And the king said unto him, Being grieved for the afflictions of my people, I caused that forty and three of my people should take a journey into the wilderness, that thereby they might find the land of Zarahemla; that we might appeal unto our brethren to deliver us out of bondage;

61 And they were lost in the wilderness, for the space of many days, yet they were diligent, and found not the land of Zarahemla, but returned to this land, having traveled in a land among many waters;

62 Having discovered a land which was covered with bones of men, and of beasts, etc., and was also covered with ruins of buildings of every kind:

63 Having discovered a land which had been peopled with a people who were as numerous as the hosts of Israel.

64 And for a testimony that the things that they have said are true, they have brought twenty-four plates, which are filled with engravings; and they are of pure gold.

65 And behold, also, they have brought breast-plates, which are large; and they are of brass, and of copper, and are perfectly sound.

66 And again, they have brought swords, the hilts thereof have perished, and the blades thereof were cankered with rust;

67 And there is no one in the land that is able to interpret the language or the engravings that are on the plates.

68 Therefore, I said unto thee, Canst thou translate?

69 And I say unto thee again, Knowest thou of any one that can translate? for I am desirous that these records should be translated into our language.

70 For, perhaps they will give us a knowledge of a remnant of the people who have been destroyed, from whence these records came;

71 Or, perhaps they will give us a knowledge of this very people who have been destroyed; and I am desirous to know the cause of their destruction.

72 ¶Now Ammon said unto him, I can assuredly tell thee, O king, of a man that can translate the records: for he has

wherewith that he can look, and translate all records that are of ancient date: and it is a gift from God.

73 And the things are called interpreters; and no man can look in them, except he be commanded, lest he should look for that he ought not, and he should perish.

74 And whosoever is commanded to look in them, the same is called seer.

75 And behold, the king of the people who is in the land of Zarahemla, is the man that is commanded to do these things, and who has this high gift from God.

76 And the king said, that a seer is greater than a prophet.

77 And Ammon said, that a seer is a revelator, and a prophet also; and a gift which is greater, can no man have, except he should possess the power of God, which no man can; yet a man may have great power given him from God.

78 But a seer can know of things which have past, and also of things which are to come;

79 And by them shall all things be revealed, or rather, shall secret things be made manifest, and hidden things shall come to light, and things which are not known, shall be made known by them;

80 And also, things shall be made known by them, which otherwise could not be known.

81 Thus God has provided a means that man, through faith, might work mighty miracles; therefore, he becometh a great benefit to his fellow beings.

82 ¶And now, when Ammon had made an end of speaking these words, the king rejoiced exceedingly, and gave thanks to God, saying,

83 Doubtless, a great mystery is contained within these plates; and these interpreters were doubtless prepared for the purpose of unfolding all such mysteries to the children of men.

84 O how marvelous are the works of the Lord, and how long doth he suffer with his people;

85 Yea, and how blind and impenetrable are the under-

standings of the children of men: for they will not seek wisdom, neither do they desire that she should rule over them.

86 Yea, they are as a wild flock, which fleeth from the shepherd, and scattereth, and are driven, and are devoured by the beasts of the forest.

CHAPTER 6.

THE RECORD OF ZENIFF.—*An account of his people, from the time they left the land of Zarahemla, until the time that they were delivered out of the hands of the Lamanites.*

1 ¶I, Zeniff, having been taught in all the language of the Nephites, and having had a knowledge of the land of Nephi, or of the land of our fathers' first inheritance, and having been sent as a spy among the Lamanites, that I might spy out their forces, that our army might come upon them and destroy them;

2 But when I saw that which was good among them, I was desirous that they should not be destroyed; therefore, I contended with my brethren in the wilderness: for I would that our ruler should make a treaty with them.

3 But he being an austere and a bloodthirsty man, commanded that I should be slain; but I was rescued by the shedding of much blood:

4 For father fought against father, and brother against brother, until the greatest number of our army was destroyed in the wilderness;

5 And we returned, those of us that were spared, to the land of Zarahemla, to relate that tale to their wives, and their children.

6 And yet, I being over zealous to inherit the land of our fathers, collected as many as were desirous to go up to possess the land, and started again on our journey into the wilderness, to go up to the land; but we were smitten with famine and sore afflictions; for we were slow to remember the Lord our God.

7 Nevertheless, after many days' wandering in the wilder-

ness, we pitched our tents in the place where our brethren were slain, which was near to the land of our fathers.

8 ¶And it came to pass that I went again with four of my men, into the city, in unto the king, that I might know of the disposition of the king; and that I might know if I might go in with my people, and possess the land in peace.

9 And I went in unto the king, and he covenanted with me, that I might possess the land of Lehi-Nephi, and the land of Shilom.

10 And he also commanded that his people should depart out of that land, and I and my people went into the land, that we might possess it.

11 And we began to build buildings, and to repair the walls of the city, yea, even the walls of the city of Lehi-Nephi, and the city of Shilom.

12 And we began to till the ground, yea, even with all manner of seeds, with seeds of corn, and of wheat, and of barley, and with neas, and with sheum, and with seeds of all manner of fruits; and we did begin to multiply and prosper in the land.

13 Now, it was the cunning and the craftiness of King Laman, to bring my people into bondage, that he yielded up the land, that we might possess it.

14 ¶Therefore, it came to pass that after we had dwelt in the land for the space of twelve years, that King Laman began to grow uneasy, lest by any means my people should wax strong in the land, and that they could not overpower them and bring them into bondage.

15 Now, they were a lazy, and an idolatrous people; therefore, they were desirous to bring us into bondage, that they might glut themselves with the labors of our hands; yea, that they might feast themselves upon the flocks of our fields.

16 ¶Therefore, it came to pass that King Laman began to stir up his people, that they should contend with my people; therefore, there began to be wars and contentions in the land.

17 For, in the thirteenth year of my reign in the land of Nephi, away on the south of the land of Shilom, when my people were watering and feeding their flocks, and tilling

their lands, a numerous host of Lamanites came upon them, and began to slay them, and to take of their flocks, and the corn of their fields.

18 Yea, and it came to pass that they fled, all that were not overtaken, even into the city of Nephi, and did call upon me for protection.

19 ¶And it came to pass that I did arm them with bows, and with arrows, with swords, and with cimeters, and with clubs, and with slings, and with all manner of weapons which we could invent, and I and my people did go forth against the Lamanites, to battle;

20 Yea, in the strength of the Lord did we go forth to battle against the Lamanites;

21 For I and my people did cry mightily to the Lord, that he would deliver us out of the hands of our enemies, for we were awakened to a remembrance of the deliverance of our fathers.

22 And God did hear our cries, and did answer our prayers; and we did go forth in his might.

23 Yea, we did go forth against the Lamanites; and in one day and a night we did slay three thousand and forty-three; we did slay them, even until we had driven them out of our land.

24 And I, myself, with mine own hands, did help bury their dead.

25 And behold, to our great sorrow and lamentation, two hundred and seventy-nine of our brethren were slain.

26 ¶And it came to pass that we again began to establish the kingdom; and we again began to possess the land in peace.

27 And I caused that there should be weapons of war made, of every kind, that thereby I might have weapons for my people, against the time the Lamanites should come up again to war against my people.

28 And I set guards round about the land that the Lamanites might not come upon us again unawares, and destroy us;

29 And thus I did guard my people, and my flocks, and keep them from falling into the hands of our enemies.

30 ¶And it came to pass that we did inherit the land of our

fathers, for many years; yea, for the space of twenty and two years.

31 And I did cause that the men should till the ground, and raise all manner of grain, and all manner of fruit, of every kind.

32 And I did cause that the women should spin, and toil, and work; and work all manner of fine linen; yea, and cloth of every kind, that we might clothe our nakedness;

33 And thus we did prosper in the land; thus we did have continual peace in the land, for the space of twenty and two years.

34 ¶And it came to pass that King Laman died, and his son began to reign in his stead.

35 And he began to stir his people up in rebellion against my people; therefore, they began to prepare for war, and to come up to battle against my people.

36 But I had sent my spies out round about the land of Shemlon, that I might discover their preparations, that I might guard against them, that they might not come upon my people and destroy them.

37 ¶And it came to pass that they came up upon the north of the land of Shilom, with their numerous hosts, men armed with bows, and with arrows, and with swords, and with cimeters, and with stones, and with slings;

38 And they had their heads shaved, that they were naked; and they were girded with a leathern girdle about their loins.

39 ¶And it came to pass that I caused that the women and children of my people should be hid in the wilderness;

40 And I also caused that all my old men that could bear arms, and also all my young men that were able to bear arms, should gather themselves together, to go to battle against the Lamanites; and I did place them in their ranks, every man according to his age.

41 ¶And it came to pass that we did go up to battle against the Lamanites.

42 And I, even I, in my old age, did go up to battle against the Lamanites.

43 And it came to pass that we did go up in the strength of the Lord, to battle.

44 ¶Now, the Lamanites knew nothing concerning the Lord, nor the strength of the Lord; therefore they depended upon their own strength.

45 Yet tney were a strong people, as to the strength of men; they were a wild, and ferocious, and a bloodthirsty people, believing in the tradition of their fathers, which is this:

46 Believing that they were driven out of the land of Jerusalem, because of the iniquities of their fathers, and that they were wronged in the wilderness by their brethren; and they were also wronged, while crossing the sea.

47 And again: that they were wronged while in the land of their first inheritance, after they had crossed the sea;

48 And all this, because that Nephi was more faithful in keeping the commandments of the Lord; therefore he was favored of the Lord, for the Lord heard his prayers and answered them, and he took the lead of their journey in the wilderness.

49 And his brethren were wroth with him, because they understood not the dealings of the Lord;

50 They were also wroth with him upon the waters, because they hardened their hearts against the Lord.

51 And again: they were wroth with him when they had arrived to the promised land, because they said that he had taken the ruling of the people out of their hands; and they sought to kill him.

52 And again: they were wroth with him, because he departed into the wilderness as the Lord had commanded him, and took the records which were engraven on the plates of brass; for they said that he robbed them.

53 And thus they have taught their children, that they should hate them, and that they should murder them, and that they should rob and plunder them, and do all they could to destroy them; therefore, they have an eternal hatred towards the children of Nephi.

54 For this very cause has King Laman, by his cunning and lying craftiness, and his fair promises, deceived me, that

I have brought this, my people, up into this land, that they may destroy them; yea, and we have suffered this many years in the land.

55 ¶And now I, Zeniff, after having told all these things unto my people concerning the Lamanites, I did stimulate them to go to battle with their might, putting their trust in the Lord; therefore, we did contend with them, face to face.

56 And it came to pass that we did drive them again out of our land; and we slew them with a great slaughter, even so many that we did not number them.

57 ¶And it came to pass that we returned again to our own land, and my people again began to tend their flocks, and to till their ground.

58 And now, I being old, did confer the kingdom upon one of my sons; therefore, I say no more. And may the Lord bless my people. Amen.

CHAPTER 7.

1 ¶And now it came to pass that Zeniff conferred the kingdom upon Noah, one of his sons; therefore Noah began to reign in his stead; and he did not walk in the ways of his father.

2 For behold, he did not keep the commandments of God, but he did walk after the desires of his own heart.

3 And he had many wives and concubines.

4 And did cause his people to commit sin, and do that which was abominable in the sight of the Lord.

5 Yea, and they did commit whoredoms, and all manner of wickedness.

6 And he laid a tax of one fifth part of all they possessed; a fifth part of their gold and of their silver, and a fifth part of their ziff, and of their copper, and of their brass and their iron; and a fifth part of their fatlings; and also, a fifth part of all their grain.

7 And all this did he take, to support himself, and his wives, and his concubines, and also, his priests, and their

wives, and their concubines; thus he had changed the affairs of the kingdom.

8 For he put down all the priests that had been consecrated by his father, and consecrated new ones in their stead, such as were lifted up in the pride of their hearts.

9 Yea, and thus they were supported in their laziness, and in their idolatry, and in their whoredoms, by the taxes which King Noah had put upon his people; thus did the people labor exceedingly, to support iniquity.

10 Yea, and they also became idolatrous, because they were deceived by the vain and flattering words of the king and priests: for they did speak flattering things unto them.

11 ¶And it came to pass that King Noah built many elegant and spacious buildings; and he ornamented them with fine work of wood, and of all manner of precious things, of gold, and of silver, and of iron, and of brass, and of ziff, and of copper;

12 And he also built him a spacious palace, and a throne in the midst thereof, all of which was of fine wood, and was ornamented with gold, and silver, and with precious things.

13 And he also caused that his workmen should work all manner of fine work within the walls of the temple, of fine wood, and of copper, and of brass;

14 And the seats which were set apart for the high priests, which were above all the other seats, he did ornament with pure gold;

15 And he caused a breastwork to be built before them, that they might rest their bodies and their arms upon, while they should speak lying and vain words to his people.

16 ¶And it came to pass that he built a tower near the temple; yea, a very high tower, even so high that he could stand upon the top thereof and overlook the land of Shilom, and also the land of Shemlon, which was possessed by the Lamanites; and he could even look over all the land round about.

17 ¶And it came to pass that he caused many buildings to be built in the land Shilom:

18 And he caused a great tower to be built on the hill north

of the land Shilom, which had been a resort for the children of Nephi, at the time they fled out of the land;

19 And thus he did do with the riches which he obtained by the taxation of his people.

20 ¶And it came to pass that he placed his heart upon his riches, and he spent his time in riotous living with his wives and his concubines; and so did also his priests spend their time with harlots.

21 And it came to pass that he planted vineyards round about in the land; and he built wine presses, and made wine in abundance; and therefore he became a wine bibber, and also his people.

22 ¶And it came to pass that the Lamanites began to come in upon his people, upon small numbers, and to slay them in their fields, and while they were tending their flocks.

23 And King Noah sent guards round about the land to keep them off; but he did not send a sufficient number, and the Lamanites came upon them and killed them, and drove many of their flocks out of the land;

24 Thus the Lamanites began to destroy them, and to exercise their hatred upon them.

25 ¶And it came to pass that King Noah sent his armies against them, and they were driven back, or they drove them back for a time; therefore, they returned rejoicing in their spoil.

26 And now, because of this great victory, they were lifted up in the pride of their hearts; they did boast in their own strength, saying, that their fifty could stand against thousands of the Lamanites;

27 And thus they did boast, and did delight in blood, and the shedding of the blood of their brethren, and this because of the wickedness of their king and priests.

28 ¶And it came to pass that there was a man among them, whose name was Abinadi; and he went forth among them, and began to prophesy, saying,

29 Behold, thus saith the Lord, and thus hath he commanded me, saying,

30 Go forth and say unto this people, Thus saith the Lord:

31 Wo be unto this people, for I have seen their abominations, and their wickedness, and their whoredoms: and except they repent, I will visit them in mine anger.

32 And except they repent, and turn to the Lord their God, behold, I will deliver them into the hands of their enemies;

33 Yea, and they shall be brought into bondage; and they shall be afflicted by the hand of their enemies.

34 And it shall come to pass that they shall know that I am the Lord their God, and am a jealous God, visiting the iniquities of my people.

35 And it shall come to pass that except this people repent, and turn unto the Lord their God, they shall be brought into bondage; and none shall deliver them, except it be the Lord, the Almighty God.

36 Yea, and it shall come to pass that when they shall cry unto me, I will be slow to hear their cries; yea, and I will suffer them that they be smitten by their enemies.

37 And except they repent in sackcloth and ashes, and cry mightily to the Lord their God, I will not hear their prayers, neither will I deliver them out of their afflictions;

38 And thus saith the Lord, and thus hath he commanded me.

39 ¶Now it came to pass that when Abinadi had spoken these words unto them, they were wroth with him, and sought to take away his life; but the Lord delivered him out of their hands.

40 Now when King Noah had heard of the words which Abinadi had spoken unto the people, he was also wroth;

41 And he said, Who is Abinadi, that I and my people should be judged of him? or who is the Lord, that shall bring upon my people such great affliction?

42 I command you to bring Abinadi hither, that I may slay him; for he has said these things, that he might stir up my people to anger, one with another, and to raise contentions among my people; therefore I will slay him.

43 Now the eyes of the people were blinded; therefore, they hardened their hearts against the words of Abinadi, and they sought from that time forward to take him.

44 And King Noah hardened his heart against the word of the Lord; and he did not repent of his evil doings.

45 ¶And it came to pass that after the space of two years, that Abinadi came among them in disguise, that they knew him not, and began again to prophesy among them, saying,

46 Thus hath the Lord commanded me, saying, Abinadi, go and prophesy unto this my people, for they have hardened their hearts against my words; they have repented not of their evil doings;

47 Therefore, I will visit them in my anger, yea, in my fierce anger will I visit them in their iniquities and abominations; yea, wo be unto this generation.

48 And the Lord said unto me, Stretch forth thy hand, and prophesy, saying, Thus saith the Lord: It shall come to pass that this generation, because of their iniquities, shall be brought into bondage, and shall be smitten on the cheek;

49 Yea, and shall be driven by men, and shall be slain; and the vultures of the air, and the dogs, yea, and the wild beasts, shall devour their flesh.

50 ¶And it shall come to pass that the life of King Noah shall be valued even as a garment in a hot furnace; for he shall know that I am the Lord.

51 And it shall come to pass that I will smite this my people with sore afflictions; yea, with famine and with pestilence; and I will cause that they shall howl all the day long.

52 Yea, and I will cause that they shall have burdens lashed upon their backs; and they shall be driven before, like a dumb ass.

53 ¶And it shall come to pass that I will send forth hail among them, and it shall smite them; and they shall also be smitten with the east wind; and insects shall pester their land also, and devour their grain.

54 And they shall be smitten with a great pestilence; and all this will I do, because of their iniquities and abominations.

55 ¶And it shall come to pass that except they repent, I will utterly destroy them from off the face of the earth;

56 Yet they shall leave a record behind them, and I will

preserve them for other nations which shall possess the land;

57 Yea, even this will I do, that I may discover the abominations of this people to other nations.

58 And many things did Abinadi prophesy against this people.

59 ¶And it came to pass that they were angry with him; and they took him and carried him bound before the king, and said unto the king,

60 Behold, we have brought a man before thee who has prophesied evil concerning thy people, and saith that God will destroy them;

61 And he also prophesieth evil concerning thy life, and saith that thy life shall be as a garment in a furnace of fire.

62 And again, he saith that thou shalt be as a stalk, even as a dry stalk of the field, which is ran over by the beasts and trodden under foot.

63 And again, he saith thou shalt be as the blossoms of a thistle, which when it is fully ripe, if the wind bloweth, it is driven forth upon the face of the land; and he pretendeth the Lord hath spoken it.

64 And he saith all this shall come upon thee except thou repent; and this because of thine iniquities.

65 And now, O king, what great evil hast thou done, or what great sins have thy people committed, that we should be condemned of God or judged of this man?

66 And now, O king, behold, we are guiltless, and thou, O king, hast not sinned; therefore, this man has lied concerning you, and he has prophesied in vain.

67 And behold, we are strong, we shall not come into bondage, or be taken captive by our enemies; yea, and thou hast prospered in the land, and thou shalt also prosper.

68 Behold, here is the man, we deliver him into thy hands; thou mayest do with him as seemeth thee good.

69 ¶And it came to pass that King Noah caused that Abinadi should be cast into prison;

70 And he commanded that the priests should gather themselves together, that he might hold a council with them what he should do with him.

CHAP. 7.] BOOK OF MOSIAH. 245

71 And it came to pass that they said unto the king, Bring him hither, that we may question him.

72 And the king commanded that he should be brought before them.

73 And they began to question him, that they might cross him, that thereby they might have wherewith to accuse him;

74 But he answered them boldly, and withstood all their questions, yea, to their astonishment:

75 For he did withstand them in all their questions, and did confound them in all their words.

76 ¶And it came to pass that one of them said unto him, What meaneth the words which are written, and which have been taught by our fathers, saying:

77 How beautiful upon the mountains are the feet of him that bringeth good tidings; that publisheth peace; that bringeth good tidings of good; that publisheth salvation; that saith unto Zion, thy God reigneth;

78 Thy watchman shall lift up the voice; with the voice together shall they sing, for they shall see eye to eye, when the Lord shall bring again Zion.

79 Break forth into joy; sing together, ye waste places of Jerusalem: for the Lord hath comforted his people; he hath redeemed Jerusalem.

80 The Lord hath made bare his holy arm in the eyes of all the nations; and all the ends of the earth shall see the salvation of our God.

81 And now Abinadi said unto them, Are you priests, and pretend to teach this people, and to understand the spirit of prophesying, and yet desire to know of me what these things mean?

82 I say unto you, Wo be unto you for perverting the ways of the Lord. For if ye understand these things, ye have not taught them; therefore ye have perverted the ways of the Lord.

83 Ye have not applied your hearts to understanding; therefore, ye have not been wise. Therefore, what teach ye this people?

84 And they said, We teach the law of Moses.

85 And again, he said unto them, If ye teach the law of Moses, why do ye not keep it?

86 Why do ye set your hearts upon riches?

87 Why do ye commit whoredoms, and spend your strength with harlots, yea, and cause this people to commit sin, that the Lord has cause to send me to prophesy against this people, yea, even a great evil against this people?

88 Know ye not that I speak the truth?

89 Yea, ye know that I speak the truth; and you ought to tremble before God.

90 ¶And it shall come to pass that ye shall be smitten for your iniquities: for ye have said that ye teach the law of Moses.

91 And what know ye concerning the law of Moses?

92 Doth salvation come by the law of Moses? What say ye?

93 And they answered and said, that salvation did come by the law of Moses.

94 But now Abinadi said unto them, I know if ye keep the commandments of God, ye shall be saved;

95 Yea, if ye keep the commandments which the Lord delivered unto Moses, in the mount of Sinai, saying: I am the Lord thy God, who has brought thee out of the land of Egypt, out of the house of bondage.

96 Thou shalt have no other God before me.

97 Thou shalt not make unto thee any graven image, or any likeness of anything in heaven above, or things which are in the earth beneath.

98 Now Abinadi said unto them, Have ye done all this? I say unto you, Nay, ye have not.

99 And have ye taught this people that they should do all these things? I say unto you, Nay, ye have not.

100 ¶And now when the king had heard these words, he said unto his priests, Away with this fellow, and slay him: for what have we to do with him, for he is mad.

101 And they stood forth and attempted to lay their hands on him: but he withstood them, and said unto them, Touch me not, for God shall smite you if ye lay your hands upon me,

for I have not delivered the message which the Lord sent me to deliver;

102 Neither have I told you that which ye requested that I should tell: therefore, God will not suffer that I shall be destroyed at this time.

103 But I must fulfill the commandments wherewith God has commanded me, and because I have told you the truth, ye are angry with me.

104 And again, because I have spoken the word of God, ye have judged me that I am mad.

105 ¶Now it came to pass after Abinadi had spoken these words, that the people of King Noah durst not lay their hands on him;

106 For the Spirit of the Lord was upon him: and his face shone with exceeding luster, even as Moses' did while in the mount of Sinai, while speaking with the Lord.

107 And he spake with power and authority from God; and he continued his words, saying, Ye see that ye have not power to slay me, therefore I finish my message.

108 Yea, and I perceive that it cuts you to your hearts, because I tell you the truth concerning your iniquities: yea, and my words fill you with wonder and amazement, and with anger.

109 But I finish my message; and then it matters not whither I go, if it so be that I am saved.

110 But this much I tell you: What you do with me, after this, shall be as a type and a shadow of things which are to come.

111 And now I read unto you the remainder of the commandments of God, for I perceive that they are not written in your hearts;

112 I perceive that ye have studied and taught iniquity the most part of your lives.

113 ¶And now, ye remember that I said unto you, Thou shalt not make unto thee any graven image, or any likeness of things which are in heaven above, or which are in the earth beneath, or which are in the water under the earth.

114 And again: Thou shalt not bow down thyself unto

them, nor serve them: for I the Lord thy God am a jealous God, visiting the iniquities of the fathers upon the children, unto the third and fourth generations of them that hate me; and showing mercy unto thousands of them that love me, and keep my commandments.

115 Thou shalt not take the name of the Lord thy God in vain: for the Lord will not hold him guiltless that taketh his name in vain.

116 Remember the Sabbath day, to keep it holy.

117 Six days shalt thou labor, and do all thy work; but the seventh day, the Sabbath of the Lord thy God, thou shalt not do any work, thou, nor thy son, nor thy daughter, thy man servant, nor thy maid servant, nor thy cattle, nor thy stranger that is within thy gates:

118 For in six days the Lord made heaven and earth, and the sea and all that in them is: wherefore the Lord blessed the Sabbath day and hallowed it.

119 Honor thy father and thy mother, that thy days may be long upon the land which the Lord thy God giveth thee.

120 Thou shalt not kill.

121 Thou shalt not commit adultery.

122 Thou shalt not steal.

123 Thou shalt not bear false witness against thy neighbor.

124 Thou shalt not covet thy neighbor's house, thou shalt not covet thy neighbor's wife, nor his man servant, nor his maid servant, nor his ox, nor his ass, nor anything that is thy neighbor's.

CHAPTER 8.

1 ¶And it came to pass that after Abinadi had made an end of these sayings, that he said unto them, Have ye taught this people that they should observe to do all these things? for to keep these commandments?

2 I say unto you, Nay; for if you had, the Lord would not have caused me to come forth and to prophesy evil concerning this people.

3 And now ye have said that salvation cometh by the law of Moses.

4 I say unto you that it is expedient that ye should keep the law of Moses as yet; but I say unto you, that the time shall come when it shall no more be expedient to keep the law of Moses.

5 And moreover, I say unto you, that salvation doth not come by the law alone; and were it not for the atonement which God himself shall make for the sins and iniquities of his people, that they must unavoidably perish, notwithstanding the law of Moses.

6 And now I say unto you, that it was expedient that there should be a law given to the children of Israel, yea, even a very strict law: for they were a stiff-necked people: quick to do iniquity, and slow to remember the Lord their God;

7 Therefore there was a law given them, yea, a law of performances and of ordinances, a law which they were to observe strictly, from day to day, to keep them in remembrance of God, and their duty towards him.

8 But behold, I say unto you, that all these things were types of things to come.

9 And now, did they understand the law?

10 I say unto you, Nay, they did not all understand the law; and this because of the hardness of their hearts: for they understood not that there could not any man be saved, except it were through the redemption of God.

11 For behold, did not Moses prophesy unto them concerning the coming of the Messiah, and that God should redeem his people, yea, and even all the prophets who have prophesied ever since the world began?

12 Have they not spoken more or less concerning these things?

13 Have they not said that God himself should come down among the children of men, and take upon him the form of man, and go forth in mighty power upon the face of the earth?

14 Yea, and have they not said also, that he should bring

to pass the resurrection of the dead, and that he, himself, should be oppressed and afflicted?

15 Yea, even doth not Isaiah say,

16 [1]Who hath believed our report, and to whom is the arm of the Lord revealed?

17 For he shall grow up before him as a tender plant, and as a root out of dry ground; he hath no form nor comeliness: and when we shall see him, there is no beauty that we should desire him.

18 He is despised and rejected of men; a man of sorrows, and acquainted with grief: and we hid as it were our face from him; he was despised, and we esteemed him not.

19 ¶Surely he has borne our griefs: and carried our sorrows: yet we did esteem him stricken, smitten of God, and afflicted.

20 But he was wounded for our transgressions, he was bruised for our iniquities; the chastisement of our peace was upon him; and with his stripes we are healed.

21 All we, like sheep, have gone astray; we have turned every one to his own way; and the Lord hath laid on him the iniquities of us all.

22 He was oppressed, and he was afflicted, yet he opened not his mouth: he is brought as a lamb to the slaughter, and as a sheep before her shearers is dumb, so he opened not his mouth.

23 He was taken from prison and from judgment; and who shall declare his generation? for he was cut off out of the land of the living: for the transgressions of my people was he stricken.

24 And he made his grave with the wicked, and with the rich in his death; because he had done no evil, neither was any deceit in his mouth.

25 ¶Yet it pleased the Lord to bruise him; he hath put him to grief; when thou shalt make his soul an offering for sin, he shall see his seed, he shall prolong his days, and the pleasure of the Lord shall prosper in his hand.

[1]Isaiah 53.

26 He shall see of the travail of his soul, and shall be satisfied: by his knowledge shall my righteous servant justify many; for he shall bear their iniquities.

27 Therefore will I divide him a portion with the great, and he shall divide the spoil with the strong; because he hath poured out his soul unto death: and he was numbered with the transgressors: and he bare the sins of many, and made intercession for the transgressors.

28 ¶And now Abinadi said unto them, I would that ye should understand that God himself shall come down among the children of men, and shall redeem his people;

29 And because he dwelleth in flesh, he shall be called the Son of God:

30 And having subjected the flesh to the will of the Father, being the Father and the Son; the Father because he was conceived by the power of God; and the Son, because of the flesh; thus becoming the Father and Son:

31 And they are one God, yea, the very eternal Father of heaven and of earth;

32 And thus the flesh becoming subject to the Spirit, or the Son to the Father, being one God, suffereth temptation, and yieldeth not to the temptation, but suffereth himself to be mocked, and scourged, and cast out, and disowned by his people.

33 And after all this, and after working many mighty miracles among the children of men, he shall be led, yea, even as Isaiah said, as a sheep before the shearer is dumb, so he opened not his mouth;

34 Yea, even so he shall be led, crucified and slain, the flesh becoming subject even unto death, the will of the Son being swallowed up in the will of the Father;

35 And thus God breaketh the bands of death; having gained the victory over death; giving the Son power to make intercession for the children of men:

36 Having ascended into heaven; having the bowels of mercy; being filled with compassion toward the children of men;

37 Standing betwixt them and justice; having broken the

bands of death, taken upon himself their iniquity and their transgressions; having redeemed them, and satisfied the demands of justice.

38 And now I say unto you, Who shall declare his generation?

39 Behold, I say unto you, that when his soul has been made an offering for sin, he shall see his seed.

40 And now what say ye? And who shall be his seed?

41 Behold, I say unto you, that whosoever has heard the words of the prophets, yea, all the holy prophets who have prophesied concerning the coming of the Lord:

42 I say unto you, that all those who have hearkened unto their words, and believed that the Lord would redeem his people, and have looked forward to that day for a remission of their sins;

43 I say unto you, that these are his seed, or they are heirs of the kingdom of God:

44 For these are they whose sins he has borne; these are they for whom he has died, to redeem them from their transgressions.

45 And now, are they not his seed?

46 Yea, and are not the prophets, every one that has opened his mouth to prophesy, that has not fallen into transgression; I mean all the holy prophets ever since the world began?

47 I say unto you that they are his seed; and these are they who have published peace, who have brought good tidings of good, who have published salvation; and said unto Zion, Thy God reigneth!

48 And O how beautiful upon the mountains were their feet!

49 And again, how beautiful upon the mountains are the feet of those that are still publishing peace!

50 And again, how beautiful upon the mountains are the feet of those who shall hereafter publish peace, yea, from this time henceforth and for ever!

51 And behold, I say unto you, This is not all: for O how beautiful upon the mountains are the feet of him that bringeth good tidings, that is the founder of peace;

52 Yea, even the Lord, who has redeemed his people; yea, him who has granted salvation unto his people:

53 For were it not for the redemption which he hath made for his people, which was prepared from the foundation of the world; I say unto you, were it not for this, all mankind must have perished.

54 But behold, the bands of death shall be broken, and the Son reigneth, and hath power over the dead; therefore, he bringeth to pass the resurrection of the dead.

55 And there cometh a resurrection, even a first resurrection; yea, even a resurrection of those that have been, and who are, and who shall be, even until the resurrection of Christ: for so shall he be called.

56 And now, the resurrection of all the prophets, and all those that have believed in their words, or all those that have kept the commandments of God, shall come forth in the first resurrection; therefore, they are the first resurrection.

57 They are raised to dwell with God who has redeemed them: thus they have eternal life through Christ, who has broken the bands of death.

58 And these are those who have part in the first resurrection; and these are they that have died before Christ came, in their ignorance, not having salvation declared unto them.

59 And thus the Lord bringeth about the restoration of these; and they have a part in the first resurrection, or have eternal life, being redeemed by the Lord.

60 And little children also have eternal life.

61 But behold, and fear, and tremble before God; for ye ought to tremble: for the Lord redeemeth none such that rebel against him, and die in their sins;

62 Yea, even all those that have perished in their sins ever since the world began, that have willfully rebelled against God, that have known the commandments of God, and would not keep them; these are they that have no part in the first resurrection.

63 Therefore had ye not ought to tremble?

64 For salvation cometh to none such; for the Lord hath redeemed none such;

65 Yea, neither can the Lord redeem such: for he can not deny himself; for he can not deny justice when it has its claim.

66 ¶And now I say unto you, that the time shall come that the salvation of the Lord shall be declared to every nation, kindred, tongue, and people,

67 Yea, Lord, thy watchmen shall lift up their voice; with the voice together shall they sing: for they shall see eye to eye, when the Lord shall bring again Zion.

68 Break forth into joy, sing together, ye waste places of Jerusalem: for the Lord hath comforted his people, he hath redeemed Jerusalem.

69 The Lord hath made bare his holy arm in the eyes of all the nations: and all the ends of the earth shall see the salvation of our God.

70 ¶And now it came to pass that after Abinadi had spoken these words, he stretched forth his hand and said, The time shall come when all shall see the salvation of the Lord;

71 When every nation, kindred, tongue and people, shall see eye to eye, and shall confess before God that his judgments are just;

72 And then shall the wicked be cast out, and they shall have cause to howl, and weep, and wail, and gnash their teeth;

73 And this because they would not hearken unto the voice of the Lord; therefore the Lord redeemeth them not, for they are carnal and devilish, and the devil has power over them;

74 Yea, even that old serpent that did beguile our first parents, which was the cause of their fall;

75 Which was the cause of all mankind becoming carnal, sensual, devilish, knowing evil from good, subjecting themselves to the devil.

76 Thus all mankind were lost; and behold, they would have been endlessly lost, were it not that God redeemed his people from their lost and fallen state.

77 But remember, that he that persists in his own carnal nature, and goes on in the ways of sin and rebellion against

God, remaineth in his fallen state, and the devil hath all power over him.

78 Therefore he is as though there was no redemption made; being an enemy to God; and also is the devil an enemy to God.

79 And now if Christ had not come into the world, speaking of things to come, as though they had already come, there could have been no redemption.

80 And if Christ had not risen from the dead, or have broken the bands of death, that the grave should have no victory, and that death should have no sting, there could have been no resurrection.

81 But there is a resurrection, therefore the grave hath no victory, and the sting of death is swallowed up in Christ.

82 He is the light and the life of the world; yea, a light that is endless, that can never be darkened; yea, and also a life which is endless, that there can be no more death.

83 Even this mortal shall put on immortality, and this corruption shall put on incorruption, and shall be brought to stand before the bar of God, to be judged of him according to their works, whether they be good or whether they be evil.

84 If they be good, to the resurrection of endless life and happiness, and if they be evil, to the resurrection of endless damnation;

85 Being delivered up to the devil, who hath subjected them, which is damnation;

86 Having gone according to their own carnal wills and desires; having never called upon the Lord while the arms of mercy were extended towards them;

87 For the arms of mercy were extended towards them, and they would not; they being warned of their iniquities, and yet they would not depart from them;

88 And they were commanded to repent, and yet they would not repent.

89 And now had ye not ought to tremble and repent of your sins, and remember only in and through Christ ye can be saved?

90 Therefore, if ye teach the law of Moses, also teach that it is a shadow of those things which are to come;

91 Teach them that redemption cometh through Christ the Lord, who is the very eternal Father. Amen.

CHAPTER 9.

1 ¶And now it came to pass that when Abinadi had finished these sayings, that the king commanded that the priests should take him and cause that he should be put to death.

2 But there was one among them, whose name was Alma, he also being a descendant of Nephi.

3 And he was a young man, and he believed the words which Abinadi had spoken, for he knew concerning the iniquity which Abinadi had testified against them:

4 Therefore he began to plead with the king that he would not be angry with Abinadi, but suffer that he might depart in peace.

5 But the king was more wroth, and caused that Alma should be cast out from among them, and sent his servants after him, that they might slay him.

6 But he fled from before them, and hid himself, that they found him not.

7 And he, being concealed for many days, did write all the words which Abinadi had spoken.

8 ¶And it came to pass that the king caused that his guards should surround Abinadi, and take him; and they bound him and cast him into prison.

9 And after three days, having counseled with his priests, he caused that he should again be brought before him.

10 And he said unto him, Abinadi, we have found an accusation against thee, and thou art worthy of death.

11 For thou hast said that God himself should come down among the children of men;

12 And now for this cause thou shalt be put to death, unless thou wilt recall all the words which thou hast spoken evil concerning me and my people.

13 ¶Now Abinadi said unto him: I say unto you, I will not recall the words which I have spoken unto you concerning this people, for they are true;

14 And that ye may know of their surety, I have suffered myself that I have fallen into your hands.

15 Yea, and I will suffer even until death, and I will not recall my words, and they shall stand as a testimony against you.

16 And if ye slay me, ye will shed innocent blood, and this shall also stand as a testimony against you at the last day.

17 ¶And now King Noah was about to release him, for he feared his word; for he feared that the judgments of God would come upon him.

18 But the priests lifted up their voices against him, and began to accuse him, saying: He has reviled the king.

19 Therefore the king was stirred up in anger against him, and he delivered him up, that he might be slain.

20 ¶And it came to pass that they took him, and bound him, and scourged his skin with fagots, yea, even unto death.

21 And now when the flames began to scorch him, he cried unto them, saying: Behold, even as ye have done unto me, so shall it come to pass that thy seed shall cause that many shall suffer the pains that I do suffer, even the pains of death, by fire; and this because they believe in the salvation of the Lord their God.

22 And it will come to pass that ye shall be afflicted with all manner of diseases, because of your iniquities.

23 Yea, and ye shall be smitten on every hand, and shall be driven and scattered to and fro, even as a wild flock is driven by wild and ferocious beasts.

24 And in that day ye shall be hunted, and ye shall be taken by the hand of your enemies, and then ye shall suffer, as I suffer, the pains of death by fire.

25 Thus God executeth vengeance upon those that destroy his people.

26 O God, receive my soul.

27 And now when Abinadi had said these words, he fell, having suffered death by fire; yea, having been put to death

because he would not deny the commandments of God: having sealed the truth of his words by his death.

28 ¶And now it came to pass that Alma, who had fled from the servants of King Noah, repented of his sins and iniquities, and went about privately among the people, and began to teach the words of Abinadi;

29 Yea, concerning that which was to come, and also concerning the resurrection of the dead, and the redemption of the people, which was to be brought to pass through the power, and sufferings, and death of Christ, and his resurrection and ascension into heaven.

30 And as many as would hear his word he did teach.

31 And he taught them privately, that it might not come to the knowledge of the king. And many did believe his words.

32 And it came to pass that as many as did believe him, did go forth to a place which was called Mormon, having received its name from the king, being in the borders of the land having been infested, by times, or at seasons, by wild beasts.

33 Now there was in Mormon a fountain of pure water, and Alma resorted thither, there being near the water a thicket of small trees, where he did hide himself in the day time, from the searches of the king.

34 And it came to pass that as many as believed him, went thither to hear his words.

35 And it came to pass after many days, there were a goodly number gathered together to the place of Mormon, to hear the words of Alma.

36 Yea, all were gathered together that believed on his word, to hear him.

37 And he did teach them, and did preach unto them repentance, and redemption, and faith on the Lord.

38 ¶And it came to pass that he said unto them, Behold, here are the waters of Mormon; for thus were they called.

39 And now, as ye are desirous to come into the fold of God, and to be called his people, and are willing to bear one another's burdens, that they may be light;

40 Yea, and are willing to mourn with those that mourn; yea, and comfort those that stand in need of comfort, and to stand as witnesses of God at all times, and in all things, and in all places that ye may be in, even until death, that ye may be redeemed of God, and be numbered with those of the first resurrection, that ye may have eternal life:

41 Now I say unto you, If this be the desire of your hearts, what have you against being baptized in the name of the Lord, as a witness before him that ye have entered into a covenant with him that ye will serve him and keep his commandments, that he may pour out his Spirit more abundantly upon you?

42 And now when the people had heard these words, they clapped their hands for joy, and exclaimed, This is the desire of our hearts.

43 ¶And now it came to pass that Alma took Helam, he being one of the first, and went and stood forth in the water, and cried, saying, O Lord, pour out thy Spirit upon thy servant, that he may do this work with holiness of heart.

44 And when he had said these words, the Spirit of the Lord was upon him, and he said, Helam, I baptize thee, having authority from the Almighty God, as a testimony that ye have entered into a covenant to serve him until you are dead, as to the mortal body; and may the Spirit of the Lord be poured out upon you; and may he grant unto you eternal life, through the redemption of Christ, whom he has prepared from the foundation of the world.

45 And after Alma had said these words, both Alma and Helam were buried in the water; and they arose and came forth out of the water rejoicing, being filled with the Spirit.

46 And again, Alma took another, and went forth a second time into the water, and baptized him according to the first, only he did not bury himself again in the water.

47 And after this manner he did baptize every one that went forth to the place of Mormon: and they were in number about two hundred and four souls;

48 Yea, and they were baptized in the waters of Mormon, and were filled with the grace of God:

49 And they were called the church of God, or the church of Christ, from that time forward.

50 ¶And it came to pass that whosoever was baptized by the power and authority of God, was added to his church.

51 ¶And it came to pass that Alma, having authority from God, ordained priests; even one priest to every fifty of their number did he ordain to preach unto them, and to teach them concerning the things pertaining to the kingdom of God.

52 And he commanded them that they should teach nothing save it were the things which he had taught, and which had been spoken by the mouth of the holy prophets.

53 Yea, even he commanded them that they should preach nothing save it were repentance and faith on the Lord, who had redeemed his people.

54 And he commanded them that there should be no contention one with another, but that they should look forward with one eye, having one faith and one baptism; having their hearts knit together in unity and in love, one towards another.

55 And thus he commanded them to preach. And thus they became the children of God.

56 And he commanded them that they should observe the Sabbath day, and keep it holy, and also every day they should give thanks to the Lord their God.

57 And he also commanded them that the priests, whom he had ordained, should labor with their own hands for their support;

58 And there was one day in every week that was set apart that they should gather themselves together to teach the people, and to worship the Lord their God, and also as often as it was in their power, to assemble themselves together.

59 And the priests were not to depend upon the people for their support; but for their labor they were to receive the grace of God, that they might wax strong in the Spirit, having the knowledge of God, that they might teach with power and authority from God.

60 And again, Alma commanded that the people of the

church should impart of their substance, every one according to that which he had;

61 If he have more abundantly, he should impart more abundantly; and he that had but little, but little should be required; and to him that had not should be given.

62 And thus they should impart of their substance, of their own free will and good desires towards God, and to those priests that stood in need, yea, and to every needy, naked soul.

63 And this he said unto them, having been commanded of God;

64 And they did walk uprightly before God, imparting to one another, both temporally and spiritually, according to their needs and their wants.

65 ¶And now it came to pass that all this was done in Mormon; yea, by the waters of Mormon, in the forest that was near the waters of Mormon:

66 Yea, the place of Mormon, the waters of Mormon, the forest of Mormon, how beautiful are they to the eyes of them who there came to the knowledge of their Redeemer;

67 Yea, and how blessed are they, for they shall sing to his praise for ever.

68 And these things were done in the borders of the land, that they might not come to the knowledge of the king.

69 But behold, it came to pass that the king, having discovered a movement among the people, sent his servants to watch them.

70 Therefore on the day that they were assembling themselves together to hear the word of the Lord, they were discovered unto the king.

71 And now the king said that Alma was stirring up the people to rebellion against him; therefore he sent his army to destroy them.

72 And it came to pass that Alma, and the people of the Lord, were apprised of the coming of the king's army; therefore they took their tents and their families, and departed into the wilderness.

73 And they were in number about four hundred and fifty souls.

74 ¶And it came to pass that the army of the king returned, having searched in vain for the people of the Lord.

75 And now behold, the forces of the king were small, having been reduced, and there began to be a division among the remainder of the people.

76 And the lesser part began to breathe out threatenings against the king, and there began to be a great contention among them.

77 And now there was a man among them whose name was Gideon, and he being a strong man, and an enemy to the king, therefore he drew his sword and swore in his wrath, that he would slay the king.

78 And it came to pass that he fought with the king; and when the king saw that he was about to overpower him, he fled and ran and got upon the tower, which was near the temple.

79 And Gideon pursued after him, and was about to get upon the tower to slay the king, and the king cast his eyes round about towards the land of Shemlon, and behold, the army of the Lamanites were within the borders of the land.

80 And now the king cried out in the anguish of his soul, saying, Gideon, spare me, for the Lamanites are upon us, and they will destroy them; yea, they will destroy my people.

81 And now the king was not so much concerned about his people, as he was about his own life; nevertheless, Gideon did spare his life.

82 And the king commanded the people that they should flee before the Lamanites, and he himself did go before them, and they did flee into the wilderness with their women and their children.

83 And it came to pass that the Lamanites did pursue them, and did overtake them, and began to slay them.

84 ¶And it came to pass that the king commanded them that all the men should leave their wives and their children, and flee before the Lamanites.

85 Now there were many that would not leave them, but had rather stay and perish with them.

86 And the rest left their wives and their children and fled.

87 ¶And it came to pass that those who tarried with their wives and their children, caused that their fair daughters should stand forth and plead with the Lamanites, that they would not slay them.

88 And it came to pass that the Lamanites had compassion on them, for they were charmed with the beauty of their women;

89 Therefore the Lamanites did spare their lives, and took them captives, and carried them back to the land of Nephi, and granted unto them that they might possess the land, under the conditions that they would deliver up King Noah into the hands of the Lamanites, and deliver up their property,

90 Even one half of all they possessed; one half of their gold, and their silver, and all their precious things; and thus they should pay tribute to the king of the Lamanites, from year to year.

91 And now there was one of the sons of the king among those that were taken captive, whose name was Limhi.

92 And now Limhi was desirous that his father should not be destroyed; nevertheless, Limhi was not ignorant of the iniquities of his father, he himself being a just man.

93 ¶And it came to pass that Gideon sent men into the wilderness secretly, to search for the king, and those that were with him.

94 And it came to pass that they met the people in the wilderness, all save the king and his priests.

95 Now they had sworn in their hearts that they would return to the land of Nephi, and if their wives and their children were slain, and also those that had tarried with them, that they would seek revenge, and also perish with them.

96 And the king commanded them that they should not return; and they were angry with the king, and caused that he should suffer, even unto death by fire.

97 And they were about to take the priests also to put them to death, and they fled before them.

98 ¶And it came to pass that they were about to return to the land of Nephi, and they met the men of Gideon.

99 And the men of Gideon told them of all that had happened to their wives and their children; and that the Lamanites had granted unto them that they might possess the land by paying a tribute to the Lamanites of one half of all they possessed.

100 And the people told the men of Gideon that they had slain the king, and his priests had fled from them farther into the wilderness.

101 And it came to pass that after they had ended the ceremony, that they returned to the land of Nephi, rejoicing, because their wives and their children were not slain; and they told Gideon what they had done to the king.

102 ¶And it came to pass that the king of the Lamanites made an oath unto them that his people should not slay them.

103 And also Limhi, being the son of the king, having the kingdom conferred upon him by the people, made oath unto the king of the Lamanites, that his people should pay tribute unto him; even one half of all they possessed.

104 ¶And it came to pass that Limhi began to establish the kingdom, and to establish peace among his people.

105 And the king of the Lamanites set guards round about the land, that he might keep the people of Limhi in the land, that they might not depart into the wilderness;

106 And he did support his guards out of the tribute which he did receive from the Nephites.

107 And now King Limhi did have continual peace in his kingdom, for the space of two years, that the Lamanites did not molest them nor seek to destroy them.

108 ¶Now there was a place in Shemlon, where the daughters of the Lamanites did gather themselves together to sing, and to dance, and to make themselves merry.

109 And it came to pass that there was one day a small number of them gathered together to sing and to dance.

110 And now the priests of King Noah, being ashamed to return to the city of Nephi, yea, and also fearing that the

CHAP. 9.] BOOK OF MOSIAH. 265

people would slay them, therefore they durst not return to their wives and their children.

111 And having tarried in the wilderness, and having discovered the daughters of the Lamanites, they laid and watched them; and when there were but few of them gathered together to dance, they came forth out of their secret places, and took them and carried them into the wilderness;

112 Yea, twenty and four of the daughters of the Lamanites they carried into the wilderness.

113 ¶And it came to pass that when the Lamanites found that their daughters had been missing, they were angry with the people of Limhi; for they thought it was the people of Limhi.

114 Therefore they sent their armies forth; yea, even the king himself went before his people; and they went up to the land of Nephi, to destroy the people of Limhi.

115 And now Limhi had discovered them from the tower; even all their preparations for war did he discover; therefore he gathered his people together, and laid wait for them in the fields, and in the forests.

116 And it came to pass that when the Lamanites had come up, that the people of Limhi began to fall upon them from their waiting places, and began to slay them.

117 ¶And it came to pass that the battle became exceeding sore, for they fought like lions for their prey.

118 And it came to pass that the people of Limhi began to drive the Lamanites before them, yet they were not half so numerous as the Lamanites.

119 But they fought for their lives, and for their wives, and for their children; therefore they exerted themselves, and like dragons did they fight.

120 ¶And it came to pass that they found the king of the Lamanites among the number of their dead; yet he was not dead, having been wounded and left upon the ground, so speedy was the flight of his people.

121 And they took him and bound up his wounds, and brought him before Limhi, and said, Behold, here is the king of the Lamanites; he having received a wound, has fallen

among their dead, and they have left him; and behold, we have brought him before you; and now let us slay him.

122 But Limhi said unto them, Ye shall not slay him, but bring him hither, that I may see him. And they brought him.

123 And Limhi said unto him, What cause have ye to come up to war against my people?

124 Behold, my people have not broken the oath that I made unto you; therefore, why should ye break the oath which ye made unto my people?

125 And now the king said, I have broken the oath, because thy people did carry away the daughters of my people; therefore in my anger I did cause my people to come up to war against thy people.

126 Now Limhi had heard nothing concerning this matter; therefore he said, I will search among my people, and whosoever has done this thing shall perish.

127 Therefore he caused a search to be made among his people.

128 Now when Gideon had heard these things, he being the king's captain, he went forth and said unto the king, I pray thee forbear, and do not search this people, and lay not this thing to their charge.

129 For do ye not remember the priests of thy father, whom this people sought to destroy?

130 And are they not in the wilderness? And are not they the ones who have stolen the daughters of the Lamanites?

131 And now behold, and tell the king of these things, that he may tell his people, that they may be pacified towards us: for behold they are already preparing to come against us; and behold also, there are but few of us.

132 And behold, they come with their numerous hosts; and except the king doth pacify them towards us, we must perish.

133 For are not the words of Abinadi fulfilled, which he prophesied against us? and all this because we would not hearken unto the word of the Lord, and turn from our iniquities?

134 And now let let us pacify the king, and we fulfill the

oath which we have made unto him: for it is better that we should be in bondage, than that we should lose our lives; therefore, let us put a stop to the shedding of so much blood.

135 And now Limhi told the king all the things concerning his father, and the priests that had fled into the wilderness, and attributed the carrying away of their daughters to them.

136 ¶And it came to pass that the king was pacified towards his people; and he said unto them, Let us go forth to meet my people, without arms; and I swear unto you with an oath, that my people shall not slay thy people.

137 And it came to pass that they followed the king, and went forth without arms to meet the Lamanites.

138 And it came to pass that they did meet the Lamanites; and the king of the Lamanites did bow himself down before them, and did plead in behalf of the people of Limhi.

139 And when the Lamanites saw the people of Limhi, that they were without arms, they had compassion on them, and were pacified towards them, and returned with their king in peace to their own land.

140 ¶And it came to pass that Limhi and his people returned to the city of Nephi, and began to dwell in the land again in peace.

141 And it came to pass that after many days, the Lamanites began again to be stirred up in anger against the Nephites; and they began to come into the borders of the land round about.

142 Now they durst not slay them, because of the oath which their king had made unto Limhi; but they would smite them on their cheeks, and exercise authority over them; and began to put heavy burdens upon their backs, and drive them as they would a dumb ass; yea, all this was done, that the word of the Lord might be fulfilled.

143 And now the afflictions of the Nephites were great; and there was no way that they could deliver themselves out of their hands, for the Lamanites had surrounded them on every side.

144 ¶And it came to pass that the people began to murmur

with the king, because of their afflictions; and they began to be desirous to go against them to battle.

145 And they did afflict the king sorely with their complaints; therefore he granted unto them that they should do according to their desires.

146 And they gathered themselves together again, and put on their armor, and went forth against the Lamanites, to drive them out of their land.

147 And it came to pass that the Lamanites did beat them, and drove them back, and slew many of them.

148 And now there was a great mourning and lamentation among the people of Limhi: the widow mourning for her husband; the son and the daughter mourning for their father; and the brothers for their brethren.

149 Now there were a great many widows in the land; and they did cry mightily from day to day, for a great fear of the Lamanites had come upon them.

150 And it came to pass that their continual cries did stir up the remainder of the people of Limhi to anger, against the Lamanites.

151 And they went again to battle; but they were driven back again, suffering much loss.

152 Yea, they went again, even the third time, and suffered in the like manner; and those that were not slain, returned again to the city of Nephi.

153 And they did humble themselves even to the dust, subjecting themselves to the yoke of bondage, submitting themselves to be smitten, and to be driven to and fro, and burdened, according to the desires of their enemies.

154 And they did humble themselves even in the depths of humility; and they did cry mightily to God; yea, even all the day long did they cry unto their God, that he would deliver them out of their afflictions.

155 And now the Lord was slow to hear their cry, because of their iniquities;

156 Nevertheless the Lord did hear their cries, and began to soften the hearts of the Lamanites, that they began to ease

their burdens; yet the Lord did not see fit to deliver them out of bondage.

157 ¶And it came to pass that they began to prosper by degrees in the land, and began to raise grain more abundantly, and flocks, and herds, that they did not suffer with hunger.

158 Now there was a great number of women more than there was of men; therefore King Limhi commanded that every man should impart to the support of the widows and their children, that they might not perish with hunger; and this they did, because of the greatness of their number that had been slain.

159 Now the people of Limhi kept together in a body as much as it was possible, and secure their grain, and their flocks;

160 And the king himself did not trust his person without the walls of the city, unless he took his guards with him, fearing that he might by some means fall into the hands of the Lamanites.

161 And he caused that his people should watch the land round about, that by some means they might take those priests that fled into the wilderness, who had stolen the daughters of the Lamanites, and that had caused such a great destruction to come upon them;

162 For they were desirous to take them, that they might punish them: for they had come into the land of Nephi by night, and carried off their grain, and many of their precious things; therefore they laid wait for them.

163 ¶And it came to pass that there was no more disturbance between the Lamanites and the people of Limhi, even until the time that Ammon and his brethren came into the land.

164 And the king having been without the gates of the city with his guard, discovered Ammon and his brethren; and supposing them to be priests of Noah, therefore he caused that they should be taken, and bound, and cast into prison.

165 And had they been the priests of Noah, he would have caused that they should be put to death; but when he found that they were not, but that they were his brethren, and had

come from the land of Zarahemla, he was filled with exceeding great joy.

166 Now King Limhi had sent, previous to the coming of Ammon, a small number of men to search for the land of Zarahemla; but they could not find it, and they were lost in the wilderness.

167 Nevertheless they did find a land which had been peopled; yea, a land which was covered with dry bones; yea, a land which had been peopled, and which had been destroyed;

168 And they having supposed it to be the land of Zarahemla, returned to the land of Nephi, having arrived in the borders of the land not many days before the coming of Ammon.

169 And they brought a record with them, even a record of the people whose bones they had found; and they were engraven on plates of ore.

170 And now Limhi was again filled with joy, on learning from the mouth of Ammon that King Mosiah had a gift from God, whereby he could interpret such engravings; yea, and Ammon also did rejoice.

171 Yet Ammon and his brethren were filled with sorrow, because so many of their brethren had been slain; and also that King Noah and his priests had caused the people to commit so many sins and iniquities against God;

172 And they also did mourn for the death of Abinadi; and also for the departure of Alma, and the people that went with him, who had formed a church of God through the strength and power of God, and faith on the words which had been spoken by Abinadi;

173 Yea, they did mourn for their departure, for they knew not whither they had fled.

174 Now they would have gladly joined with them, for they themselves had entered into a covenant with God, to serve him, and keep his commandments.

175 And now since the coming of Ammon, King Limhi had also entered into a covenant with God, and also many of his people, to serve him, and keep his commandments.

176 ¶And it came to pass that King Limhi and many of his

people were desirous to be baptized; but there was none in the land that had authority from God.

177 And Ammon declined doing this thing, considering himself an unworthy servant; therefore they did not at that time form themselves into a church, waiting upon the Spirit of the Lord.

178 Now they were desirous to become even as Alma and his brethren, who had fled into the wilderness.

179 They were desirous to be baptized, as a witness and a testimony that they were willing to serve God with all their hearts;

180 Nevertheless they did prolong the time; and an account of their baptism shall be given hereafter.

181 And now all the study of Ammon and his people, and King Limhi and his people, was to deliver themselves out of the hands of the Lamanites and from bondage.

CHAPTER 10.

1 ¶And now it came to pass that Ammon and King Limhi began to consult with the people how they should deliver themselves out of bondage;

2 And even they did cause that all the people should gather themselves together; and this they did that they might have the voice of the people concerning the matter.

3 And it came to pass that they could find no way to deliver themselves out of bondage, except it were to take their women and children, and their flocks and their herds, and their tents, and depart into the wilderness;

4 For the Lamanites being so numerous that it was impossible for the people of Limhi to contend with them, thinking to deliver themselves out of bondage by the sword.

5 ¶Now it came to pass that Gideon went forth and stood before the king, and said unto him, Now O king, thou hast hitherto hearkened unto my words many times when we have been contending with our brethren, the Lamanites.

6 And now O king, if thou hast not found me to be an

unprofitable servant, or if thou hast hitherto listened to my words in any degree, and they have been of service to thee, even so I desire that thou wouldst listen to my words at this time, and I will be thy servant, and deliver this people out of bondage.

7 And the king granted unto him that he might speak.

8 And Gideon said unto him, Behold the back pass through the back wall, on the back side of the city.

9 The Lamanites, or the guards of the Lamanites, by night, are drunken; therefore let us send a proclamation among all this people, that they gather together their flocks and herds, that they may drive them into the wilderness by night.

10 And I will go according to thy command, and pay the last tribute of wine to the Lamanites, and they will be drunken; and we will pass through the secret pass on the left of their camp, when they are drunken and asleep;

11 Thus we will depart with our women and our children, our flocks and our herds, into the wilderness; and we will travel around the land of Shilom.

12 And it came to pass that the king hearkened unto the words of Gideon.

13 And King Limhi caused that his people should gather their flocks together; and he sent the tribute of wine to the Lamanites; and he also sent more wine, as a present unto them; and they did drink freely of the wine which King Limhi did send unto them.

14 ¶And it came to pass that the people of King Limhi did depart by night into the wilderness with their flocks and their herds, and they went round about the land of Shilom in the wilderness, and bent their course towards the land of Zarahemla, being led by Ammon and his brethren.

15 And they had taken all their gold, and silver, and their precious things, which they could carry; and also their provisions with them, into the wilderness; and they pursued their journey.

16 And after being many days in the wilderness, they arrived in the land of Zarahemla, and joined his people, and became his subjects.

17 And it came to pass that Mosiah received them with joy; and he also received their records, and also the records which had been found by the people of Limhi.

18 And now it came to pass when the Lamanites had found that the people of Limhi had departed out of the land by night, that they sent an army into the wilderness to pursue them;

19 And after they had pursued them two days, they could no longer follow their tracks; therefore they were lost in the wilderness.

CHAPTER 11.

An account of Alma and the people of the Lord, who were driven into the wilderness by the people of King Noah.

1 ¶Now Alma, having been warned of the Lord that the armies of King Noah would come upon them, and had made it known to his people, therefore they gathered together their flocks, and took of their grain, and departed into the wilderness before the armies of King Noah.

2 And the Lord did strengthen them, that the people of King Noah could not overtake them, to destroy them.

3 And they fled eight days' journey into the wilderness.

4 And they came to a land, yea, even a very beautiful and pleasant land; a land of pure water.

5 And they pitched their tents, and began to till the ground, and began to build buildings, etc.; yea, they were industrious, and did labor exceedingly.

6 And the people were desirous that Alma should be their king, for he was beloved by his people.

7 But he said unto them, Behold, it is not expedient that we should have a king; for thus saith the Lord: Ye shall not esteem one flesh above another, or one man shall not think himself above another; therefore I say unto you, It is not expedient that ye should have a king.

8 Nevertheless, if it were possible that ye could always have just men to be your kings, it would be well for you to have a king.

9 But remember the iniquity of King Noah and his priests; and I myself was caught in a snare, and did many things which were abominable in the sight of the Lord, which caused me sore repentance;

10 Nevertheless, after much tribulation, the Lord did hear my cries, and did answer my prayers, and has made me an instrument in his hands, in bringing so many of you to a knowledge of his truth.

11 Nevertheless, in this I do not glory, for I am unworthy to glory of myself.

12 And now I say unto you, ye have been oppressed by King Noah, and have been in bondage to him and his priests, and have been brought into iniquity by them; therefore ye were bound with the bands of iniquity.

13 And now as ye have been delivered, by the power of God, out of these bonds;

14 Yea, even out of the hands of King Noah and his people, and also from the bonds of iniquity, even so I desire that ye should stand fast in this liberty wherewith ye have been made free, and that ye trust no man to be a king over you;

15 And also trusting no one to be your teacher nor your minister, except he be a man of God, walking in his ways and keeping his commandments.

16 Thus did Alma teach his people, that every man should love his neighbor as himself; that there should be no contention among them.

17 And now Alma was their high priest, he being the founder of their church.

18 And it came to pass that none received authority to preach or to teach, except it were by him from God.

19 Therefore he consecrated all their priests, and all their teachers, and none were consecrated except they were just men.

20 Therefore they did watch over their people, and did nourish them with things pertaining to righteousness.

21 And it came to pass that they began to prosper exceedingly in the land; and they called the land Helam.

22 And it came to pass that they did multiply and prosper

exceedingly in the land of Helam; and they built a city, which they called the city of Helam.

23 Nevertheless the Lord seeth fit to chasten his people; yea, he trieth their patience and their faith.

24 Nevertheless, whosoever putteth his trust in him, the same shall be lifted up at the last day.

25 Yea, and thus it was with this people.

26 For behold, I will shew unto you that they were brought into bondage, and none could deliver them but the Lord their God; yea, even the God of Abraham, and of Isaac, and of Jacob.

27 And it came to pass that he did deliver them, and he did shew forth his mighty power unto them, and great were their rejoicings.

28 For behold, it came to pass that while they were in the land of Helam, yea, in the city of Helam, while tilling the land round about, behold an army of the Lamanites were in the borders of the land.

29 Now it came to pass that the brethren of Alma fled from their fields, and gathered themselves together into the city of Helam; and they were much frightened because of the appearance of the Lamanites.

30 But Alma went forth and stood among them, and exhorted them that they should not be frightened, but that they should remember the Lord their God, and he would deliver them;

31 Therefore they hushed their fears, and began to cry unto the Lord, that he would soften the hearts of the Lamanites, that they would spare them, and their wives, and their children.

32 And it came to pass that the Lord did soften the hearts of the Lamanites.

33 And Alma and his brethren went forth and delivered themselves up into their hands; and the Lamanites took possession of the land of Helam.

34 Now the armies of the Lamanites which had followed after the people of King Limhi, had been lost in the wilderness for many days.

35 And behold, they had found those priests of King Noah, in a place which they called Amulon; and they had began to possess the land of Amulon, and had began to till the ground.

36 Now the name of the leader of those priests was Amulon.

37 And it came to pass that Amulon did plead with the Lamanites; and he also sent forth their wives, who were the daughters of the Lamanites, to plead with their brethren, that they should not destroy their husbands.

38 And the Lamanites had compassion on Amulon and his brethren, and did not destroy them, because of their wives.

39 And Amulon and his brethren did join the Lamanites, and they were traveling in the wilderness in search of the land of Nephi, when they discovered the land of Helam, which was possessed by Alma and his brethren.

40 And it came to pass that the Lamanites promised unto Alma and his brethren, that if they would shew them the way which led to the land of Nephi, that they would grant unto them their lives and their liberty.

41 But after Alma had shewn them the way that led to the land of Nephi, the Lamanites would not keep their promise; but they set guards round about the land of Helam, over Alma and his brethren.

42 And the remainder of them went to the land of Nephi; and a part of them returned to the land of Helam, and also brought with them the wives and the children of the guards who had been left in the land.

43 And the king of the Lamanites had granted unto Amulon that he should be a king and a ruler over his people, who were in the land of Helam; nevertheless he should have no power to do anything contrary to the will of the king of the Lamanites.

44 ¶And it came to pass that Amulon did gain favor in the eyes of the king of the Lamanites; therefore the king of the Lamanites granted unto him and his brethren, that they should be appointed teachers over his people;

45 Yea, even over the people who were in the land of Shemlon, and in the land of Shilom, and in the land of Amulon:

46 For the Lamanites had taken possession of all these lands; therefore the king of the Lamanites had appointed kings over all these lands.

47 And now the name of the king of the Lamanites was Laman, being called after the name of his father; and therefore he was called King Laman.

48 And he was king over a numerous people; and he appointed teachers of the brethren of Amulon, in every land which was possessed by his people;

49 And thus the language of Nephi began to be taught among all the people of the Lamanites.

50 And they were a people friendly one with another; nevertheless they knew not God; neither did the brethren of Amulon teach them anything concerning the Lord their God, neither the law of Moses;

51 Nor did they teach them the words of Abinadi; but they taught them that they should keep their record, and that they might write one to another.

52 And thus the Lamanites began to increase in riches, and began to trade one with another, and wax great, and began to be a cunning and a wise people, as to the wisdom of the world;

53 Yea, a very cunning people; delighting in all manner of wickedness and plunder except it were among their own brethren.

54 ¶And now it came to pass that Amulon began to exercise authority over Alma and his brethren, and began to persecute him, and cause that his children should persecute their children:

55 For Amulon knew Alma, that he had been one of the king's priests, and that it was he that believed the words of Abinadi, and was driven out before the king; and therefore he was wroth with him, for he was subject to King Laman;

56 Yet he exercised authority over them, and put tasks upon them, and put task-masters over them.

57 And it came to pass that so great were their afflictions, that they began to cry mightily to God.

58 And Amulon commanded them that they should stop

their cries; and he put guards over them to watch them, that whosoever should be found calling upon God, should be put to death.

59 And Alma and his people did not raise their voices to the Lord their God, but did pour out their hearts to him; and he did know the thoughts of their hearts.

60 ¶And it came to pass that the voice of the Lord came to them in their afflictions, saying, Lift up your heads and be of good comfort, for I know of the covenant which ye have made unto me; and I will covenant with this my people, and deliver them out of bondage.

61 And I will also ease the burdens which are put upon your shoulders, that even you can not feel them upon your backs, even while you are in bondage;

62 And this will I do, that ye may stand as witnesses for me hereafter, and that ye may know of a surety that I, the Lord God, do visit my people in their afflictions.

63 And now it came to pass that the burdens which were laid upon Alma and his brethren, were made light;

64 Yea, the Lord did strengthen them that they could bear up their burdens with ease, and they did submit cheerfully and with patience to all the will of the Lord.

65 ¶And it came to pass that so great was their faith and their patience, that the voice of the Lord came unto them again, saying, Be of good comfort, for on the morrow I will deliver you out of bondage.

66 And he said unto Alma, Thou shalt go before this people, and I will go with thee, and deliver this people out of bondage.

67 ¶Now it came to pass that Alma and his people in the night time, gathered their flocks together, and also of their grain; yea, even all the night time were they gathering their flocks together.

68 And in the morning the Lord caused a deep sleep to come upon the Lamanites, yea, and all their task-masters were in a profound sleep.

69 And Alma and his people departed into the wilderness; and when they had traveled all day, they pitched their tents

in a valley, and they called the valley Alma, because he led their way in the wilderness;

70 Yea, and in the valley of Alma they poured out their thanks to God because he had been merciful unto them, and eased their burdens, and had delivered them out of bondage;

71 For they were in bondage, and none could deliver them, except it were the Lord their God.

72 And they gave thanks to God, yea, all their men, and all their women, and all their children, that could speak, lifted their voices in the praises of their God.

73 ¶And now the Lord said unto Alma, Haste thee and get thou and this people out of this land, for the Lamanites have awoke and do pursue thee;

74 Therefore get thee out of this land, and I will stop the Lamanites in this valley, that they come no further in pursuit of this people.

75 And it came to pass that they departed out of the valley, and took their journey into the wilderness.

76 And after they had been in the wilderness twelve days, they arrived to the land of Zarahemla; and King Mosiah did also receive them with joy.

77 And now King Mosiah caused that all the people should be gathered together.

78 Now there were not so many of the children of Nephi, or so many of those who were descendants of Nephi, as there were of the people of Zarahemla, who was a descendant of Mulok, and those who came with him into the wilderness;

79 And there were not so many of the people of Nephi and of the people of Zarahemla as there were of the Lamanites: yea, they were not half so numerous.

80 And now all the people of Nephi were assembled together, and also all the people of Zarahemla, and they were gathered together in two bodies.

81 ¶And it came to pass that Mosiah did read, and caused to be read, the records of Zeniff to his people; yea, he read the records of the people of Zeniff, from the time they left the land of Zarahemla until they returned again.

82 And he also read the account of Alma and his brethren,

and all their afflictions, from the time they left the land of Zarahemla, until the time they returned again.

83 And now when Mosiah had made an end of reading the records, his people who tarried in the land were struck with wonder and amazement, for they knew not what to think;

84 For when they beheld those that had been delivered out of bondage, they were filled with exceeding great joy.

85 And again, when they thought of their brethren who had been slain by the Lamanites, they were filled with sorrow, and even shed many tears of sorrow;

86 And again, when they thought of the immediate goodness of God, and his power in delivering Alma and his brethren out of the hands of the Lamanites, and of bondage, they did raise their voices, and give thanks to God.

87 And again, when they thought upon the Lamanites, who were their brethren, of their sinful and polluted state, they were filled with pain and anguish, for the welfare of their souls.

88 ¶And it came to pass that those who were the children of Amulon and his brethren, who had taken to wife the daughters of the Lamanites, were displeased with the conduct of their fathers,

89 And they would no longer be called by the names of their fathers, therefore they took upon themselves the name of Nephi, that they might be called the children of Nephi, and be numbered among those who were called Nephites.

90 And now all the people of Zarahemla were numbered with the Nephites, and this because the kingdom had been conferred upon none but those who were descendants of Nephi.

91 ¶And now it came to pass that when Mosiah had made an end of speaking and reading to the people, he desired that Alma should also speak to the people.

92 And Alma did speak unto them, when they were assembled together in large bodies, and he went from one body to another preaching unto the people repentance and faith on the Lord.

93 And he did exhort the people of Limhi and his brethren,

all those that had been delivered out of bondage, that they should remember that it was the Lord that did deliver them.

94 And it came to pass that after Alma had taught the people many things, and had made an end of speaking to them, that King Limhi was desirous that he might be baptized; and all his people were desirous that they might be baptized also.

95 Therefore Alma did go forth into the water, and did baptize them; yea, he did baptize them after the manner he did his brethren in the waters of Mormon;

96 Yea, and as many as he did baptize did belong to the church of God; and this because of their belief on the words of Alma.

97 ¶And it came to pass that King Mosiah granted unto Alma, that he might establish churches throughout all the land of Zarahemla; and gave him power to ordain priests and teachers over every church.

98 Now this was done because there were so many people that they could not all be governed by one teacher; neither could they all hear the word of God in one assembly; therefore they did assemble themselves together in different bodies, being called churches;

99 Every church having their priests and their teachers, and every priest preaching the word according as it was delivered to him by the mouth of Alma;

100 And thus, notwithstanding there being many churches they were all one church; yea, even the church of God:

101 For there was nothing preached in all the churches except it were repentance and faith in God.

102 And now there were seven churches in the land of Zarahemla.

103 And it came to pass that whosoever were desirous to take upon them the name of Christ, or of God, they did join the churches of God; and they were called the people of God.

104 And the Lord did pour out his Spirit upon them, and they were blessed, and prospered in the land.

105 ¶Now it came to pass that there were many of the rising generation that could not understand the words of King

Benjamin, being little children at the time he spake unto his people; and they did not believe the tradition of their fathers.

106 They did not believe what had been said concerning the resurrection of the dead; neither did they believe concerning the coming of Christ.

107 And now because of their unbelief, they could not understand the word of God; and their hearts were hardened.

108 And they would not be baptized; neither would they join the church.

109 And they were a separate people as to their faith, and remained so ever after, even in their carnal and sinful state; for they would not call upon the Lord their God.

110 And now in the reign of Mosiah, they were not half so numerous as the people of God; but because of the dissensions among the brethren, they became more numerous.

111 For it came to pass that they did deceive many with their flattering words, who were in the church, and did cause them to commit many sins;

112 Therefore it became expedient that those who committed sin that were in the church, should be admonished by the church.

113 ¶And it came to pass that they were brought before the priests, and delivered up unto the priests by the teachers; and the priests brought them before Alma, who was the high priest.

114 Now King Mosiah had given Alma the authority over the church.

115 And it came to pass that Alma did not know concerning them, for there were many witnesses against them; yea, the people stood and testified of their iniquity in abundance.

116 Now there had not any such thing happened before, in the church; therefore Alma was troubled in his spirit, and he caused that they should be brought before the king.

117 And he said unto the king, Behold, here are many whom we have brought before thee, who are accused of their brethren; yea, and they have been taken in divers iniquities.

118 And they do not repent of their iniquities; therefore

we have brought them before thee, that thou mayest judge them according to their crimes.

119 But King Mosiah said unto Alma, Behold, I judge them not; therefore I deliver them into thy hands to be judged.

120 And now the spirit of Alma was again troubled; and he went and inquired of the Lord what he should do concerning this matter, for he feared that he should do wrong in the sight of God.

121 ¶And it came to pass that after he had poured out his whole soul to God, the voice of the Lord came to him, saying, Blessed art thou, Alma, and blessed are they who were baptized in the waters of Mormon.

122 Thou art blessed because of thy exceeding faith in the words alone of my servant, Abinadi.

123 And blessed are they because of their exceeding faith in the words alone which thou hast spoken unto them.

124 And blessed art thou because thou hast established a church among this people; and they shall be established, and they shall be my people.

125 Yea, blessed is this people, who are willing to bear my name; for in my name shall they be called; and they are mine.

126 And because thou hast inquired of me concerning the transgressor, thou art blessed.

127 Thou art my servant: and I covenant with thee, that thou shalt have eternal life; and thou shalt serve me, and go forth in my name, and shall gather together my sheep.

128 And he that will hear my voice, shall be my sheep; and him shall ye receive into the church; and him will I also receive.

129 For behold, this is my church: whosoever is baptized, shall be baptized unto repentance.

130 And whosoever ye receive, shall believe in my name; and him will I freely forgive:

131 For it is I that taketh upon me the sins of the world; for it is I that hath created them; and it is I that granteth unto him that believeth in the end, a place at my right hand.

132 For behold, in my name are they called; and if they

know me, they shall come forth, and shall have a place eternally at my right hand.

133 And it shall come to pass that when the second trump shall sound, then shall they that never knew me come forth, and shall stand before me;

134 And then shall they know that I am the Lord their God, that I am their Redeemer; but they would not be redeemed.

135 And then will I confess unto them, that I never knew them; and they shall depart into everlasting fire, prepared for the devil and his angels.

136 Therefore I say unto you, that he that will not hear my voice, the same shall ye not receive into my church, for him I will not receive at the last day:

137 Therefore I say unto you, Go; and whosoever transgresseth against me, him shall ye judge according to the sins which he has committed;

138 And if he confess his sins before thee and me, and repenteth in the sincerity of his heart, him shall ye forgive, and I will forgive him also;

139 Yea, and as often as my people repent, will I forgive them their trespasses against me.

140 And ye shall also forgive one another your trespasses: for verily I say unto you, He that forgiveth not his neighbor's trespasses, when he says that he repents, the same hath brought himself under condemnation.

141 Now I say unto you, Go; and whosoever will not repent of his sins, the same shall not be numbered among my people: and this shall be observed from this time forward.

142 ¶And it came to pass when Alma had heard these words, he wrote them down, that he might have them, and that he might judge the people of that church, according to the commandments of God.

143 ¶And it came to pass that Alma went and judged those that had been taken in iniquity, according to the word of the Lord.

144 And whosoever repented of their sins and did confess them, them he did number among the people of the church;

CHAP. 11.] BOOK OF MOSIAH. 285

145 And those that would not confess their sins and repent of their iniquity, the same were not numbered among the people of the church, and their names were blotted out.

146 And it came to pass that Alma did regulate all the affairs of the church;

147 And they began again to have peace and to prosper exceedingly in the affairs of the church; walking circumspectly before God; receiving many, and baptizing many.

148 And now all these things did Alma and his fellow laborers do, who were over the church; walking in all diligence; teaching the word of God in all things, suffering all manner of afflictions; being persecuted by all those who did not belong to the church of God.

149 And they did admonish their brethren; and they were also admonished, every one, by the word of God, according to his sins, or to the sins which he had committed; being commanded of God to pray without ceasing, and to give thanks in all things.

150 And now it came to pass that the persecutions which were inflicted on the church by the unbelievers, became so great, that the church began to murmur, and complain to their leaders concerning the matter; and they did complain to Alma.

151 And Alma laid the case before their King Mosiah. And Mosiah consulted with his priests.

152 ¶And it came to pass that King Mosiah sent a proclamation throughout the land round about, that there should not any unbeliever persecute any of those who belonged to the church of God:

153 And there was a strict command throughout all the churches, that there should be no persecutions among them, that there should be an equality among all men; that they should let no pride nor haughtiness disturb their peace;

154 That every man should esteem his neighbor as himself, laboring with their own hands for their support;

155 Yea, and all their priests and teachers should labor with their own hands for their support, in all cases save it

were in sickness, or in much want: and doing these things they did abound in the grace of God.

156 And there began to be much peace again in the land; and the people began to be very numerous, and began to scatter abroad upon the face of the earth;

157 Yea, on the north and on the south, on the east and on the west, building large cities and villages in all quarters of the land.

158 And the Lord did visit them, and prosper them, and they became a large and a wealthy people.

159 ¶Now the sons of Mosiah were numbered among the unbelievers; and also one of the sons of Alma was numbered among them, he being called Alma, after his father; nevertheless he became a very wicked and an idolatrous man.

160 And he was a man of many words, and did speak much flattery to the people: therefore he led many of the people to do after the manner of his iniquities.

161 And he became a great hinderment to the prosperity of the church of God; stealing away the hearts of the people, causing much dissension among the people; giving a chance for the enemy of God to exercise his power over them.

162 ¶And now it came to pass that while he was going about to destroy the church of God: for he did go about secretly with the sons of Mosiah, seeking to destroy the church, and to lead astray the people of the Lord, contrary to the commandments of God, or even the king;

163 And as I said unto you, as they were going about rebelling against God, behold, the angel of the Lord appeared unto them; and he descended as it were in a cloud; and he spake as it were with a voice of thunder, which caused the earth to shake upon which they stood;

164 And so great was their astonishment, that they fell to the earth, and understood not the words which he spake unto them.

165 Nevertheless he cried again, saying, Alma, arise, and stand forth, for why persecuteth thou the church of God?

166 For the Lord hath said, This is my church, and I will

establish it; and nothing shall overthrow it, save it is the transgression of my people.

167 And again, the angel said, Behold, the Lord hath heard the prayers of his people, and also the prayers of his servant Alma, who is thy father:

168 For he has prayed with much faith concerning thee, that thou mightest be brought to the knowledge of the truth;

169 Therefore for this purpose have I come to convince thee of the power and authority of God, that the prayers of his servants might be answered according to their faith.

170 And now behold, can ye dispute the power of God?

171 For behold, doth not my voice shake the earth?

172 And can ye not also behold me before you?

173 And I am sent from God.

174 Now I say unto thee, Go, and remember the captivity of thy fathers in the land of Helam, and in the land of Nephi; and remember how great things he has done for them: for they were in bondage, and he has delivered them.

175 And now I say unto thee, Alma, go thy way, and seek to destroy the church no more, that their prayers may be answered; and this even if thou wilt of thyself be cast off.

176 ¶And now it came to pass that these were the last words which the angel spake unto Alma, and he departed.

177 And now Alma, and those that were with him, fell again to the earth, for great was their astonishment; for with their own eyes they had beheld an angel of the Lord; and his voice was as thunder, which shook the earth;

178 And they knew that there was nothing save the power of God, that could shake the earth and cause it to tremble, as though it would part asunder.

179 And now the astonishment of Alma was so great, that he became dumb, that he could not open his mouth; yea, and he became weak, even that he could not move his hands:

180 Therefore he was taken by those that were with him, and carried helpless, even until he was laid before his father.

181 And they rehearsed unto his father all that had happened unto them; and his father rejoiced, for he knew that it was the power of God.

182 And he caused that a multitude should be gathered together, that they might witness what the Lord had done for his son, and also for those that were with him.

183 And he caused that the priests should assemble themselves together; and they began to fast, and to pray to the Lord their God, that he would open the mouth of Alma, that he might speak;

184 And also that his limbs might receive their strength, that the eyes of the people might be opened to see and know of the goodness and glory of God.

185 ¶And it came to pass after they had fasted and prayed for the space of two days and two nights, the limbs of Alma received their strength, and he stood up and began to speak unto them, bidding them to be of good comfort:

186 For, said he, I have repented of my sins, and have been redeemed of the Lord; behold, I am born of the Spirit.

187 And the Lord said unto me, Marvel not that all mankind, yea, men, and women, all nations, kindreds, tongues and people, must be born again;

188 Yea, born of God, changed from their carnal and fallen state, to a state of righteousness, being redeemed of God, becoming his sons and daughters; and thus they become new creatures; and unless they do this, they can in no wise inherit the kingdom of God.

189 I say unto you, Unless this be the case, they must be cast off; and this I know, because I was like to be cast off.

190 Nevertheless, after wading through much tribulation, repenting nigh unto death, the Lord in mercy hath seen fit to snatch me out of an everlasting burning, and I am born of God;

191 My soul hath been redeemed from the gall of bitterness and bonds of iniquity.

192 I was in the darkest abyss; but now I behold the marvelous light of God.

193 My soul was wrecked with eternal torment; but I am snatched, and my soul is pained no more.

194 I rejected my Redeemer, and denied that which had been spoken of by our fathers;

195 But now that they may foresee that he will come, and that he remembereth every creature of his creating;

196 He will make himself manifest unto all; yea, every knee shall bow, and every tongue confess before him.

197 Yea, even at the last day, when all men shall stand to be judged of him, then shall they confess that he is God;

198 Then shall they confess, who live without God in the world, that the judgment of an everlasting punishment is just upon them;

199 And they shall quake, and tremble, and shrink beneath the glance of his all-searching eye.

200 ¶And now it came to pass that Alma began from this time forward, to teach the people, and those who were with Alma at the time the angel appeared unto them:

201 Traveling round about through all the land, publishing to all the people the things which they had heard and seen, and preaching the word of God in much tribulation, being greatly persecuted by those who were unbelievers, being smitten by many of them;

202 But notwithstanding all this, they did impart much consolation to the church, confirming their faith, and exhorting them with longsuffering and much travail, to keep the commandments of God.

203 And four of them were the sons of Mosiah; and their names were Ammon, and Aaron, and Omner, and Himni; these were the names of the sons of Mosiah.

204 And they traveled throughout all the land of Zarahemla, and among all the people who were under the reign of King Mosiah, zealously striving to repair all the injuries which they had done to the church:

205 Confessing all their sins, and publishing all the things which they had seen, and explaining the prophecies and the scriptures to all who desired to hear them:

206 And thus they were instruments in the hands of God, in bringing many to the knowledge of the truth, yea, to the knowledge of their Redeemer.

207 And how blessed are they! For they did publish peace; they did publish good tidings of good; and they did declare unto the people that the Lord reigneth.

CHAPTER 12.

1 ¶Now it came to pass that after the sons of Mosiah had done all these things, they took a small number with them, and returned to their father, the king, and desired of him that he would grant unto them, that they might, with those whom they had selected, go up to the land of Nephi,

2 That they might preach the things which they had heard, and that they might impart the word of God to their brethren, the Lamanites, that perhaps they might bring them to the knowledge of the Lord their God, and convince them of the iniquity of their fathers;

3 And that perhaps they might cure them of their hatred towards the Nephites, that they might also be brought to rejoice in the Lord their God,

4 That they might become friendly to one another, and that there should be no more contentions in all the land which the Lord their God had given them.

5 Now they were desirous that salvation should be declared to every creature, for they could not bear that any human soul should perish;

6 Yea, even the very thoughts that any soul should endure endless torment, did cause them to quake and tremble.

7 And thus did the Spirit of the Lord work upon them, for they were the very vilest of sinners.

8 And the Lord saw fit in his infinite mercy to spare them; nevertheless they suffered much anguish of soul, because of their iniquities; and suffering much, fearing that they should be cast off for ever.

9 ¶And it came to pass that they did plead with their father many days, that they might go up to the land of Nephi.

10 And King Mosiah went and inquired of the Lord, if he

should let his sons go up among the Lamanites to preach the word.

11 And the Lord said unto Mosiah, Let them go up, for many shall believe on their words, and they shall have eternal life; and I will deliver thy sons out of the hands of the Lamanites.

12 ¶And it came to pass that Mosiah granted that they might go, and do according to their request;

13 And they took their journey into the wilderness, to go up to preach the word among the Lamanites: and I shall give an account of their proceedings hereafter.

14 Now King Mosiah had no one to confer the kingdom upon, for there was not any of his sons who would accept of the kingdom;

15 Therefore he took the records which were engraven on the plates of brass, and also the plates of Nephi, and all the things which he had kept and preserved, according to the commandments of God,

16 After having translated and caused to be written the records which were on the plates of gold, which had been found by the people of Limhi, which were delivered to him by the hand of Limhi;

17 And this he did, because of the great anxiety of his people, for they were desirous beyond measure, to know concerning those people who had been destroyed.

18 And now he translated them by the means of those two stones which were fastened into the two rims of a bow.

19 Now these things were prepared from the beginning, and were handed down from generation to generation, for the purpose of interpreting languages;

20 And they have been kept and preserved by the hand of the Lord, that he should discover to every creature who should possess the land, the iniquities and abominations of his people;

21 And whosoever has these things, is called seer, after the manner of old times.

22 ¶Now after Mosiah had finished translating these records, behold, it gave an account of the people who were de-

stroyed, from the time that they were destroyed, back to the building of the great tower, at the time the Lord confounded the language of the people;

23 And they were scattered abroad upon the face of all the earth, yea, and even from that time until the creation of Adam.

24 Now this account did cause the people of Mosiah to mourn exceedingly; yea, they were filled with sorrow;

25 Nevertheless it gave them much knowledge, in the which they did rejoice.

26 And this account shall be written hereafter; for behold, it is expedient that all people should know the things which are written in this account.

CHAPTER 13.

1 ¶And now, as I said unto you, that after King Mosiah had done these things, he took the plates of brass, and all the things which he had kept, and conferred them upon Alma, who was the son of Alma;

2 Yea, all the records, and also the interpreters, and conferred them upon him, and commanded him that he should keep and preserve them, and also keep a record of the people, handing them down from one generation to another, even as they had been handed down from the time that Lehi left Jerusalem.

3 Now when Mosiah had done this, he sent out through all the land, among all the people, desiring to know their will concerning who should be their king.

4 And it came to pass that the voice of the people came, saying, We are desirous that Aaron, thy son, should be our king, and our ruler.

5 Now Aaron had gone up to the land of Nephi, therefore the king could not confer the kingdom upon him; neither would Aaron take upon him the kingdom;

6 Neither were any of the sons of Mosiah willing to take upon them the kingdom, therefore King Mosiah sent again

among the people, yea, even a written word sent he among the people.

7 And these were the words that were written; saying: Behold, O ye my people, or my brethren, for I esteem you as such; for I desire that ye should consider the cause which ye are called to consider; for ye are desirous to have a king.

8 Now I declare unto you, that he to whom the kingdom doth rightly belong, has declined, and will not take upon him the kingdom.

9 And now if there should be another appointed in his stead, behold I fear there would rise contentions among you;

10 And who knoweth but what my son, to whom the kingdom doth belong, should turn to be angry, and draw away a part of this people after him, which would cause wars and contentions among you; which would be the cause of shedding much blood, and perverting the way of the Lord; yea, and destroy the souls of many people.

11 Now I say unto you, Let us be wise and consider these things, for we have no right to destroy my son, neither should we have any right to destroy another, if he should be appointed in his stead.

12 And if my son should turn again to his pride and vain things, he would recall the things which he had said, and claim his right to the kingdom, which would cause him and also this people to commit much sin.

13 And now let us be wise and look forward to these things, and do that which will make for the peace of this people.

14 Therefore I will be your king the remainder of my days;

15 Nevertheless, let us appoint judges, to judge this people according to our law, and we will newly arrange the affairs of this people, for we will appoint wise men to be judges, that will judge this people according to the commandments of God.

16 Now it is better that a man should be judged of God than of man, for the judgments of God are always just, but the judgments of man are not always just;

17 Therefore, if it were possible that ye could have just

men to be your kings, who would establish the laws of God, and judge this people according to his commandments; yea, if ye could have men for your kings, who would do even as my father Benjamin did for this people, I say unto you, If this could always be the case, then it would be expedient that ye should always have kings to rule over you.

18 And even I myself have labored with all the power and faculties which I have possessed, to teach you the commandments of God, and to establish peace throughout the land,

19 That there should be no wars nor contentions, no stealing, nor plundering, nor murdering, nor any manner of iniquity;

20 And whosoever has committed iniquity, him have I punished according to the crime which he has committed, according to the law which has been given to us by our fathers.

21 ¶Now I say unto you, that because all men are not just, it is not expedient that ye should have a king or kings to rule over you.

22 For behold, how much iniquity doth one wicked king cause to be committed! yea, and what great destruction!

23 Yea, remember King Noah, his wickedness and his abominations; and also the wickedness and abominations of his people.

24 Behold what great destruction did come upon them; and also because of their iniquities, they were brought into bondage.

25 And were it not for the interposition of their all-wise Creator, and this because of their sincere repentance, they must unavoidably remained in bondage until now.

26 But behold, he did deliver them because they did humble themselves before him; and because they cried mightily unto him, he did deliver them out of bondage:

27 And thus doth the Lord work with his power in all cases among the children of men, extending the arm of mercy towards them that put their trust in him.

28 And behold, now I say unto you, Ye can not dethrone an iniquitous king, save it be through much contention, and the shedding of much blood.

29 For behold, he has his friends in iniquity, and he keepeth his guards about him; and he teareth up the laws of those who have reigned in righteousness before him: and he trampleth under his feet the commandments of God;

30 And he enacteth laws, and sendeth them forth among his people; yea, laws after the manner of his own wickedness; and whosoever doth not obey his laws, he causeth to be destroyed;

31 And whosoever doth rebel against him, he will send his armies against them to war, and if he can, he will destroy them;

32 And thus an unrighteous king doth pervert the ways of all righteousness.

33 And now behold I say unto you, It is not expedient that such abominations should come upon you;

34 Therefore choose you by the voice of this people, judges, that ye may be judged according to the laws which have been given you by our fathers, which are correct, and which were given them by the hand of the Lord.

35 Now it is not common that the voice of the people desireth anything contrary to that which is right; but it is common for the lesser part of the people to desire that which is not right;

36 Therefore this shall ye observe, and make it your law to do your business by the voice of the people.

37 And if the time comes that the voice of the people doth choose iniquity, then is the time that the judgments of God will come upon you;

38 Yea, then is the time he will visit you with great destruction, even as he has hitherto visited this land.

39 And now if ye have judges, and they do not judge you according to the law which has been given, ye can cause that they may be judged of a higher judge;

40 If your higher judges do not judge righteous judgments, ye shall cause that a small number of your lower judges should be gathered together, and they shall judge your higher judges, according to the voice of the people.

41 And I command you to do these things in the fear of the Lord;

42 And I command you to do these things, and that ye have no king: that if these people commit sins and iniquities, they shall be answered upon their own heads.

43 For behold I say unto you, The sins of many people have been caused by the iniquities of their kings; therefore their iniquities are answered upon the heads of their kings.

44 And now I desire that this inequality should be no more in this land, especially among this my people;

45 But I desire that this land be a land of liberty, and every man may enjoy his rights and privileges alike, so long as the Lord sees fit, that we may live and inherit the land;

46 Yea, even as long as any of our posterity remains upon the face of the land.

47 And many more things did King Mosiah write unto them, unfolding unto them all the trials and troubles of a righteous king;

48 Yea, all the travails of soul for their people, and also all the murmurings of the people to their king; and he explained it all unto them.

49 And he told them that these things ought not to be; but that the burden should come upon all the people, that every man might bear his part.

50 And he also unfolded unto them all the disadvantages they labored under, by having an unrighteous king to rule over them;

51 Yea, all his iniquities and abominations, and all the wars, and contentions, and bloodshed, and the stealing, and the plundering, and the committing of whoredoms, and all manner of iniquities, which can not be enumerated,

52 Telling them that these things ought not to be; that they were expressly repugnant to the commandments of God.

53 ¶And now it came to pass, after King Mosiah had sent these things forth among the people, they were convinced of the truth of his words;

54 Therefore they relinquished their desires for a king, and

became exceedingly anxious that every man should have an equal chance throughout all the land;

55 Yea, and every man expressed a willingness to answer for his own sins.

56 Therefore it came to pass that they assembled themselves together in bodies throughout the land, to cast in their voices concerning who should be their judges, to judge them according to the law which had been given them;

57 And they were exceedingly rejoiced, because of the liberty which had been granted unto them.

58 And they did wax strong in love towards Mosiah; yea, they did esteem him more than any other man:

59 For they did not look upon him as a tyrant, who was seeking for gain, yea, for that lucre which doth corrupt the soul,

60 For he had not exacted riches of them, neither had he delighted in the shedding of blood; but he had established peace in the land, and he had granted unto his people that they should be delivered from all manner of bondage;

61 Therefore they did esteem him, yea, exceedingly, beyond measure.

62 And it came to pass that they did appoint judges to rule over them, or to judge them according to the law; and this they did throughout all the land.

63 ¶And it came to pass that Alma was appointed to be the chief judge; he being also the high priest; his father having conferred the office upon him, and had given him the charge concerning all the affairs of the church.

64 And now it came to pass that Alma did walk in the ways of the Lord, and he did keep his commandments, and he did judge righteous judgments; and there was continual peace through the land;

65 And thus commenced the reign of the judges throughout all the land of Zarahemla, among all the people who were called the Nephites: and Alma was the first and chief judge.

66 And now it came to pass that his father died, being

eighty and two years old, having lived to fulfill the commandments of God.

67 ¶And it came to pass that Mosiah died also, in the thirty and third year of his reign, being sixty and three years old, making in the whole, five hundred and nine years from the time Lehi left Jerusalem;

68 And thus ended the reign of the kings over the people of Nephi; and thus ended the days of Alma, who was the founder of their church.

THE BOOK OF ALMA,
THE SON OF ALMA.

CHAPTER 1.

The account of Alma, who was the son of Alma, the First and Chief Judge over the people of Nephi, and also the High Priest over the Church. An account of the reign of the Judges, and the wars and contentions among the people. And also an account of a war between the Nephites and the Lamanites, according to the record of Alma the First, and Chief Judge.

1 ¶Now it came to pass that in the first year of the reign of the Judges over the people of Nephi, from this time forward, King Mosiah having gone the way of all the earth, having warred a good warfare, walking uprightly before God, leaving none to reign in his stead;

2 Nevertheless he established laws, and they were acknowledged by the people; therefore they were obliged to abide by the laws which he had made.

3 ¶And it came to pass that in the first year of the reign of Alma in the judgment seat, there was a man brought before him to be judged; a man who was large, and was noted for his much strength;

4 And he had gone about among the people, preaching to them that which he termed to be the word of God, bearing down against the church;

5 Declaring unto the people that every priest and teacher ought to become popular; and they ought not to labor with their own hands, but that they ought to be supported by the people;

6 And he also testified unto the people that all mankind should be saved at the last day, and that they need not fear nor tremble, but that they might lift up their heads and rejoice;

7 For the Lord had created all men, and had also redeemed all men; and in the end, all men should have eternal life.

8 And it came to pass that he did teach these things so much, that many did believe on his words, even so many that they began to support him and give him money;

9 And he began to be lifted up in the pride of his heart, and to wear very costly apparel; yea, and even began to establish a church, after the manner of his preaching.

10 ¶And it came to pass as he was going to preach to those who believed on his word, he met a man who belonged to the church of God, yea, even one of their teachers;

11 And he began to contend with him sharply, that he might lead away the people of the church; but the man withstood him, admonishing him with the words of God.

12 Now the name of the man was Gideon; and it was he who was an instrument in the hands of God, in delivering the people of Limhi out of bondage.

13 Now because Gideon withstood him with the words of God, he was wroth with Gideon, and drew his sword and began to smite him.

14 Now Gideon being stricken with many years therefore he was not able to withstand his blows, therefore he was slain by the sword;

15 And the man who slew him was taken by the people of the church, and was brought before Alma, to be judged according to the crime which he had committed.

16 And it came to pass that he stood before Alma, and plead for himself with much boldness.

17 But Alma said unto him, Behold, this is the first time that priestcraft has been introduced among this people.

18 And behold, thou art not only guilty of priestcraft, but hast endeavored to enforce it by the sword; and were priestcraft to be enforced among this people, it would prove their entire destruction.

19 And thou hast shed the blood of a righteous man, yea, a man who has done much good among this people; and were we to spare thee, his blood would come upon us for vengeance;

20 Therefore thou art condemned to die, according to the law which has been given us by Mosiah, our last king;

21 And they have been acknowledged by this people; therefore this people must abide by the law.

22 ¶And it came to pass that they took him; and his name was Nehor; and they carried him upon the top of the hill Manti,

23 And there he was caused, or rather did acknowledge, between the heavens and the earth, that what he had taught to the people was contrary to the word of God; and there he suffered an ignominious death.

24 Nevertheless this did not put an end to the spreading of priestcraft through the land; for there were many who loved the vain things of the world, and they went forth preaching false doctrines, and this they did for the sake of riches and honor.

25 Nevertheless they durst not lie, if it were known, for fear of the law, for liars were punished; therefore they pretended to preach according to their belief:

26 And now the law could have no power on any man for his belief.

27 And they durst not steal, for fear of the law; for such were punished; neither durst they rob, nor murder: for he that murdered was punished unto death.

28 ¶But it came to pass that whosoever did not belong to the church of God, began to persecute those that did be-

long to the church of God, and had taken upon them the name of Christ;

29 Yea, they did persecute them, and afflict them with all manner of words, and this because of their humility;

30 Because they were not proud in their own eyes, and because they did impart the word of God, one with another, without money and without price.

31 Now there was a strict law among the people of the church, that there should not any man, belonging to the church, arise and persecute those that did not belong to the church, and that there should be no persecution among themselves.

32 Nevertheless, there were many among them who began to be proud, and began to contend warmly with their adversaries, even unto blows; yea, they would smite one another with their fists.

33 Now this was in the second year of the reign of Alma, and it was a cause of much affliction to the church; yea, it was the cause of much trial with the church;

34 For the hearts of many were hardened, and their names were blotted out, that they were remembered no more among the people of God.

35 And also many withdrew themselves from among them.

36 Now this was a great trial to those that did stand fast in the faith; nevertheless, they were steadfast and immovable in keeping the commandments of God, and they bore with patience the persecution which was heaped upon them.

37 And when the priests left their labor, to impart the word of God unto the people, the people also left their labors to hear the word of God.

38 And when the priest had imparted unto them the word of God, they all returned again diligently unto their labors;

39 And the priest, not esteeming himself above his hearers; for the preacher was no better than the hearer, neither was the teacher any better than the learner: and thus they were all equal, and they did all labor, every man according to his strength;

40 And they did impart of their substance every man ac-

cording to that which he had, to the poor, and the needy, and the sick, and the afflicted;

41 And they did not wear costly apparel, yet they were neat and comely;

42 And thus they did establish the affairs of the church; and thus they began to have continual peace again, notwithstanding all their persecutions.

43 And now because of the steadiness of the church, they began to be exceeding rich; having abundance of all things whatsoever they stood in need;

44 An abundance of flocks, and herds, and fatlings of every kind, and also abundance of grain, and of gold, and of silver, and of precious things; and abundance of silk and fine twined linen, and all manner of good homely cloth.

45 And thus in their prosperous circumstances they did not send away any who were naked, or that were hungry, or that were athirst, or that were sick, or that had not been nourished;

46 And they did not set their hearts upon riches; therefore they were liberal to all, both old and young, both bond and free, both male and female, whether out of the church or in the church, having no respect to persons as to those who stood in need;

47 And thus they did prosper and become far more wealthy than those who did not belong to their church.

48 For those who did not belong to their church did indulge themselves in sorceries, and in idolatry or idleness, and in babblings, and in envyings and strife;

49 And wearing costly apparel; being lifted up in the pride of their own eyes; persecuting, lying, thieving, robbing, committing whoredoms, and murdering, and all manner of wickedness;

50 Nevertheless, the law was put in force upon all those who did transgress it, inasmuch as it were possible.

51 ¶And it came to pass that by thus exercising the law upon them, every man suffering according to that which he had done, they become more still, and durst not commit any wickedness, if it were known:

52 Therefore there was much peace among the people of Nephi, until the fifth year of the reign of the Judges.

53 And it came to pass in the commencement of the fifth year of their reign, there began to be a contention among the people, for a certain man, being called Amlici; he being a very cunning man, yea, a wise man, as to the wisdom of the world; he being after the order of the man that slew Gideon by the sword, who was executed according to the law.

54 Now this Amlici had, by his cunning, drawn away much people after him; even so much that they began to be very powerful; and they began to endeavor to establish Amlici to be a king over the people.

55 Now this was alarming to the people of the church, and also to all those who had not been drawn away after the persuasions of Amlici:

56 For they knew that according to their law that such things must be established by the voice of the people;

57 Therefore, if it were possible that Amlici should gain the voice of the people, he being a wicked man, would deprive them of their rights and privileges of the church, etc.; for it was his intent to destroy the church of God.

58 ¶And it came to pass that the people assembled themselves together throughout all the land, every man according to his mind, whether it were for or against Amlici, in separate bodies, having much dispute and wonderful contentions, one with another;

59 And thus they did assemble themselves together, to cast in their voices concerning the matter: and they were laid before the Judges.

60 And it came to pass that the voice of the people came against Amlici, that he was not made king over the people.

61 Now this did cause much joy in the hearts of those who were against him; but Amlici did stir up those who were in his favor, to anger against those who were not in his favor.

62 ¶And it came to pass that they gathered themselves together, and did consecrate Amlici to be their king.

63 Now when Amlici was made king over them, he commanded them that they should take up arms against their

brethren; and this he did, that he might subject them to him.

64 Now the people of Amlici were distinguished by the name of Amlici, being called Amlicites; and the remainder were called Nephites, or the people of God:

65 Therefore the people of the Nephites were aware of the intent of the Amlicites, and therefore they did prepare to meet them;

66 Yea, they did arm themselves with swords, and with cimeters, and with bows, and with arrows, and with stones, and with slings, and with all manner of weapons of war, of every kind;

67 And thus they were prepared to meet the Amlicites at the time of their coming.

68 And there were appointed captains, and higher captains, and chief captains, according to their numbers.

69 ¶And it came to pass that Amlici did arm his men with all manner of weapons of war, of every kind; and he also appointed rulers and leaders over his people, to lead them to war against their brethren.

70 And it came to pass that the Amlicites came upon the hill of Amnihu, which was east of the river Sidon, which ran by the land of Zarahemla, and there they began to make war with the Nephites.

71 Now Alma, being the chief judge, and the governor of the people of Nephi, therefore he went up with his people, yea, with his captains, and chief captains, yea, at the head of his armies, against the Amlicites to battle; and they began to slay the Amlicites upon the hill east of Sidon.

72 And the Amlicites did contend with the Nephites with great strength, insomuch that many of the Nephites did fall before the Amlicites;

73 Nevertheless the Lord did strengthen the hand of the Nephites, that they slew the Amlicites with a great slaughter, that they began to flee before them.

74 And it came to pass that the Nephites did pursue the Amlicites all that day, and did slay them with much slaughter, insomuch that there was slain of the Amlicites twelve thousand five hundred thirty and two souls;

75 And there was slain of the Nephites, six thousand five hundred sixty and two souls.

76 ¶And it came to pass that when Alma could pursue the Amlicites no longer, he caused that his people should pitch their tents, in the valley of Gideon, the valley being called after that Gideon who was slain by the hand of Nehor with the sword; and in this valley the Nephites did pitch their tents for the night.

77 And Alma sent spies to follow the remnant of the Amlicites, that he might know of their plans and their plots, whereby he might guard himself against them, that he might preserve his people from being destroyed.

78 Now those whom he had sent out to watch the camp of the Amlicites, were called Zeram, and Amnor, and Manti, and Limher; these were they who went out with their men to watch the camp of the Amlicites.

79 ¶And it came to pass that on the morrow they returned into the camp of the Nephites, in great haste, being greatly astonished, and struck with much fear, saying,

80 Behold, we followed the camp of the Amlicites, and to our great astonishment, in the land of Minon, above the land of Zarahemla, in the course of the land of Nephi, we saw a numerous host of the Lamanites;

81 And behold, the Amlicites have joined them, and they are upon our brethren in that land; and they are fleeing before them with their flocks, and their wives, and their children, towards our city;

82 And except we make haste, they obtain possession of our city; and our fathers, and our wives, and our children be slain.

83 ¶And it came to pass that the people of Nephi took their tents, and departed out of the valley of Gideon towards their city, which was the city of Zarahemla.

84 And behold, as they were crossing the river Sidon, the Lamanites and the Amlicites, being as numerous almost, as it were, as the sands of the sea, came upon them to destroy them;

85 Nevertheless the Nephites, being strengthened by the

hand of the Lord, having prayed mightily to him that he would deliver them out of the hands of their enemies;

86 Therefore the Lord did hear their cries, and did strengthen them, and the Lamanites and Amlicites did fall before them.

87 And it came to pass that Alma fought with Amlici with the sword, face to face; and they did contend mightily, one with another.

88 ¶And it came to pass that Alma, being a man of God, being exercised with much faith, cried saying, O Lord, have mercy and spare my life, that I may be an instrument in thy hands, to save and protect this people.

89 Now when Alma had said these words, he contended again with Amlici; and he was strengthened, insomuch that he slew Amlici with the sword.

90 And he also contended with the king of the Lamanites: but the king of the Lamanites fled back from before Alma, and sent his guards to contend with Alma.

91 But Alma, with his guards, contended with the guards of the king of the Lamanites, until he slew and drove them back;

92 And thus he cleared the ground, or rather the bank, which was on the west of the river Sidon, throwing the bodies of the Lamanites who had been slain, into the waters of Sidon, that thereby his people might have room to cross and contend with the Lamanites and the Amlicites on the west side of the river Sidon.

93 ¶And it came to pass that when they had all crossed the river Sidon that the Lamanites and the Amlicites began to flee before them, notwithstanding they were so numerous that they could not be numbered;

94 And they fled before the Nephites, towards the wilderness which was west and north, away beyond the borders of the land;

95 And the Nephites did pursue them with their might, and did slay them; yea, they were met on every hand, and slain, and driven, until they were scattered on the west, and

on the north, until they had reached the wilderness, which was called Hermounts;

96 And it was that part of the wilderness which was infested by wild and ravenous beasts.

97 And it came to pass that many died in the wilderness of their wounds, and were devoured by those beasts, and also the vultures of the air: and their bones have been found, and have been heaped upon the earth.

98 ¶And it came to pass that the Nephites, who were not slain by the weapons of war, after having buried those who had been slain: now the number of the slain were not numbered, because of the greatness of their number; after they had finished burying their dead, they all returned to their lands, and to their houses, and their wives, and their children.

99 Now many women and children had been slain with the sword, and also many of their flocks and their herds;

100 And also many of their fields of grain were destroyed, for they were trodden down by the hosts of men.

101 And now as many of the Lamanites and the Amlicites who had been slain upon the bank of the river Sidon, were cast into the waters of Sidon; and behold, their bones are in the depths of the sea, and they are many.

102 And the Amlicites were distinguished from the Nephites; for they had marked themselves with red in their foreheads, after the manner of the Lamanites; nevertheless they had not shorn their heads like unto the Lamanites.

103 Now the heads of the Lamanites were shorn; and they were naked, save it were skin, which was girded about their loins, and also their armor, which was girded about them, and their bows, and their arrows, and their stones, and their slings, etc.

104 And the skins of the Lamanites were dark, according to the mark which was set upon their fathers, which was a curse upon them because of their transgression and their rebellion against their brethren, who consisted of Nephi, Jacob, and Joseph, and Sam, who were just and holy men.

105 And their brethren sought to destroy them; therefore they were cursed; and the Lord God set a mark upon them,

yea, upon Laman and Lemuel, and also the sons of Ishmael, and the Ishmaelitish women;

106 And this was done, that their seed might be distinguished from the seed of their brethren, that thereby the Lord God might preserve his people, that they might not mix and believe in incorrect traditions which would prove their destruction.

107 ¶And it came to pass that whosoever did mingle his seed with that of the Lamanites, did bring the same curse upon his seed;

108 Therefore whosoever suffered himself to be led away by the Lamanites, was called under that head, and there was a mark set upon him.

109 And it came to pass that whosoever would not believe in the tradition of the Lamanites, but believed those records which were brought out of the land of Jerusalem, and also in the tradition of their fathers, which were correct, who believed in the commandments of God, and kept them, were called the Nephites, or the people of Nephi, from that time forth;

110 And it is they who have kept the records which are true of their people, and also of the people of the Lamanites.

111 Now we will return again to the Amlicites, for they also had a mark set upon them; yea, they set the mark upon themselves, yea, even a mark of red upon their foreheads.

112 Thus the word of God is fulfilled, for these are the words which he said to Nephi:

113 Behold, the Lamanites have I cursed; and I will set a mark upon them, that they and their seed may be separated from thee and thy seed, from this time henceforth and for ever, except they repent of their wickedness and turn to me, that I may have mercy upon them.

114 And again: I will set a mark upon him that mingleth his seed with thy brethren, that they may be cursed also.

115 And again: I will set a mark upon him that fighteth against thee and thy seed.

116 And again I say, He that departeth from thee, shall no more be called thy seed; and I will bless thee, etc., and whom-

soever shall be called thy seed, henceforth and for ever: and these were the promises of the Lord unto Nephi, and to his seed.

117 Now the Amlicites knew not that they were fulfilling the words of God, when they began to mark themselves in their foreheads;

118 Nevertheless they had come out in open rebellion against God; therefore it was expedient that the curse should fall upon them.

119 Now I would that ye should see that they brought upon themselves the curse;

120 And even so doth every man that is cursed, bring upon himself his own condemnation.

121 ¶Now it came to pass that not many days after the battle which was fought in the land of Zarahemla, by the Lamanites and the Amlicites, that there was another army of the Lamanites came in upon the people of Nephi, in the same place, where the first army met the Amlicites.

122 And it came to pass that there was an army sent to drive them out of their land.

123 Now Alma himself being afflicted with a wound, did not go up to battle at this time against the Lamanites; but he sent up a numerous army against them;

124 And they went up and slew many of the Lamanites, and drove the remainder of them out of the borders of their land;

125 And then they returned again, and began to establish peace in the land, being troubled no more for a time with their enemies.

126 Now all these things were done, yea, all these wars and contentions were commenced and ended, in the fifth year of the reign of the Judges;

127 And in one year were thousands and tens of thousands of souls sent to the eternal world,

128 That they might reap their rewards according to their works, whether they were good or whether they were bad, to reap eternal happiness or eternal misery, according to the

spirit which they listed to obey, whether it be a good spirit or a bad one;

129 For every man receiveth wages of him whom he listeth to obey, and this according to the words of the spirit of prophecy; therefore let it be according to the truth.

130 And thus ended the fifth year of the reign of the Judges.

CHAPTER 2.

1 ¶Now it came to pass in the sixth year of the reign of the Judges over the people of Nephi, there were no contentions nor wars in the land of Zarahemla;

2 But the people were afflicted, yea, greatly afflicted for the loss of their brethren, and also for the loss of their flocks and herds, and also for the loss of their fields of grain, which were trodden under foot and destroyed by the Lamanites,

3 And so great were their afflictions, that every soul had cause to mourn; and they believed that it was the judgments of God sent upon them, because of their wickedness and their abominations; therefore they were awakened to a remembrance of their duty.

4 And they began to establish the church more fully; yea, and many were baptized in the waters of Sidon, and were joined to the church of God;

5 Yea, they were baptized by the hand of Alma, who had been consecrated the high priest over the people of the church, by the hand of his father Alma.

6 ¶And it came to pass in the seventh year of the reign of the Judges, there were about three thousand five hundred souls that united themselves to the church of God, and were baptized.

7 And thus ended the seventh year of the reign of the Judges over the people of Nephi; and there was continual peace in all that time.

8 ¶And it came to pass in the eighth year of the reign of the Judges, that the people of the church began to wax proud,

because of their exceeding riches, and their fine silks, and their fine twined linen,

9 And because of their many flocks and herds, and their gold, and their silver, and all manner of precious things, which they had obtained by their industry;

10 And in all these things were they lifted up in the pride of their eyes, for they began to wear very costly apparel.

11 Now this was the cause of much affliction to Alma, yea, and to many of the people whom Alma had consecrated to be teachers, and priests, and elders, over the church;

12 Yea, many of them were sorely grieved for the wickedness which they saw had begun to be among their people.

13 For they saw and beheld with great sorrow, that the people of the church began to be lifted up in the pride of their eyes, and to set their hearts upon riches and upon the vain things of the world;

14 That they began to be scornful, one towards another, and they began to persecute those that did not believe according to their own will and pleasure.

15 And thus in this eighth year of the reign of the Judges, there began to be great contentions among the people of the church;

16 Yea, there were envyings, and strifes, and malice, and persecutions, and pride, even to exceed the pride of those who did not belong to the church of God.

17 And thus ended the eighth year of the reign of the Judges; and the wickedness of the church was a great stumbling block to those who did not belong to the church; and thus the church began to fail in its progress.

18 ¶And it came to pass in the commencement of the ninth year, Alma saw the wickedness of the church, and he saw also that the example of the church began to lead those who were unbelievers, on from one piece of iniquity to another, thus bringing on the destruction of the people;

19 Yea, he saw great inequality among the people, some lifting themselves up with their pride, despising others, turning their backs upon the needy, and the naked, and those

who were hungry, and those who were athirst, and those who were sick and afflicted.

20 Now this was a great cause for lamentations among the people, while others were abasing themselves, succoring those who stood in need of their succor, such as imparting their substance to the poor and the needy; feeding the hungry; and suffering all manner of afflictions, for Christ's sake, who should come according to the spirit of prophecy, looking forward to that day, thus retaining a remission of their sins;

21 Being filled with great joy, because of the resurrection of the dead, according to the will, and power, and deliverance of Jesus Christ from the bands of death.

22 ¶And now it came to pass that Alma, having seen the afflictions of the humble followers of God, and the persecutions which were heaped upon them by the remainder of his people, and seeing all their inequality, began to be very sorrowful; nevertheless the Spirit of the Lord did not fail him.

23 And he selected a wise man who was among the elders of the church, and gave him power according to the voice of the people, that he might have power to enact laws according to the laws which had been given, and to put them in force, according to the wickedness and the crimes of the people.

24 Now this man's name was Nephihah, and he was appointed chief judge; and he sat in the judgment seat, to judge and to govern the people.

25 Now Alma did not grant unto him the office of being high priest over the church, but he retained the office of high priest unto himself; but he delivered the judgment seat unto Nephihah:

26 And this he did, that he himself might go forth among his people, or among the people of Nephi, that he might preach the word of God unto them, to stir them up in remembrance of their duty,

27 And that he might pull down, by the word of God, all the pride and craftiness, and all the contentions which were among his people, seeing no way that he might reclaim them, save it were in bearing down in pure testimony against them.

28 And thus in the commencement of the ninth year of the

reign of the Judges over the people of Nephi, Alma delivered up the judgment seat to Nephihah, and confined himself wholly to the high priesthood of the holy order of God, to the testimony of the word, according to the spirit of revelation and prophecy.

CHAPTER 3.

The words which Alma, the High Priest, according to the holy order of God, delivered to the people in their cities and villages throughout the land.

1 ¶Now it came to pass that Alma began to deliver the word of God unto the people, first in the land of Zarahemla, and from thence throughout all the land.

2 And these are the words which he spake to the people in the church which was established in the city of Zarahemla, according to his own record, saying:

3 I, Alma, having been consecrated by my father Alma, to be a high priest over the church of God, he having power and authority from God to do these things, behold, I say unto you, that he began to establish a church in the land which was in the borders of Nephi;

4 Yea, the land which was called the land of Mormon; yea, and he did baptize his brethren in the waters of Mormon.

5 And behold, I say unto you, They were delivered out of the hands of the people of King Noah, by the mercy and power of God.

6 And behold, after that, they were brought into bondage by the hands of the Lamanites, in the wilderness; yea, I say unto you, They were in captivity, and again the Lord did deliver them out of bondage by the power of his word;

7 And we were brought into this land and here we began to establish the church of God throughout this land also.

8 And now behold, I say unto you, my brethren, you that belong to this church, Have you sufficiently retained in remembrance the captivity of your fathers?

9 Yea, and have you sufficiently retained in remembrance his mercy and long suffering towards them?

10 And moreover, have ye sufficiently retained in remembrance that he has delivered their souls from hell?

11 Behold, he changed their hearts; yea, he awaked them out of a deep sleep, and they awoke unto God.

12 Behold they were in the midst of darkness; nevertheless, their souls were illuminated by the light of the everlasting word;

13 Yea, they were encircled about by the bands of death, and the chains of hell, and an everlasting destruction did await them.

14 And now I ask of you my brethren, Were they destroyed?

15 Behold, I say unto you, Nay, they were not.

16 And again I ask, Were the bands of death broken, and the chains of hell which encircled them about, were they loosed?

17 I say unto you, Yea, they were loosed, and their souls did expand, and they did sing redeeming love.

18 And I say unto you that they are saved.

19 And now I ask of you on what conditions are they saved? Yea, what grounds had they to hope for salvation?

20 What is the cause of their being loosed from the bands of death? Yea, and also, the chains of hell?

21 Behold, I can tell you: Did not my father Alma believe in the words which were delivered by the mouth of Abinadi? And was he not a holy prophet?

22 Did he not speak the words of God, and my father Alma believe them?

23 And according to his faith there was a mighty change wrought in his heart.

24 Behold I say unto you, that this is all true.

25 And behold, he preached the word unto your fathers, and a mighty change was also wrought in their hearts; and they humbled themselves, and put their trust in the true and living God.

26 And behold, they were faithful until the end; therefore they were saved.

27 And now behold, I ask of you, my brethren of the church, Have ye spiritually been born of God?

28 Have ye received his image in your countenances?

29 Have ye experienced this mighty change in your hearts?

30 Do ye exercise faith in the redemption of him who created you?

31 Do you look forward with an eye of faith, and view this mortal body raised in immortality, and this corruption raised in incorruption, to stand before God, to be judged according to the deeds which have been done in the mortal body?

32 I say unto you, Can you imagine to yourselves that ye hear the voice of the Lord, saying unto you, in that day, Come unto me ye blessed, for behold, your works have been the works of righteousness upon the face of the earth?

33 Or do ye imagine to yourselves that ye can lie unto the Lord in that day, and say, Lord, our works have been righteous works upon the face of the earth, and that he will save you?

34 Or otherwise, can ye imagine yourselves brought before the tribunal of God, with your souls filled with guilt and remorse; having a remembrance of all your guilt;

35 Yea, a perfect remembrance of all your wickedness; yea, a remembrance that ye have set at defiance the commandments of God?

36 I say unto you, Can ye look up to God at that day with a pure heart and clean hands?

37 I say unto you, Can you look up, having the image of God engraven upon your countenances?

38 I say unto you, Can ye think of being saved when you have yielded yourselves to become subjects to the devil?

39 I say unto you, Ye will know at that day, that ye can not be saved: for there can no man be saved except his garments are washed white:

40 Yea, his garments must be purified until they are cleansed from all stain, through the blood of him of whom it has been spoken by our fathers who should come to redeem his people from their sins.

41 And now I ask of you, my brethren, How will any of

you feel, if ye shall stand before the bar of God, having your garments stained with blood, and all manner of filthiness?

42 Behold, what will these things testify against you?

43 Behold, will they not testify that ye are murderers, yea, and also that ye are guilty of all manner of wickedness?

44 Behold, my brethren, do ye suppose that such an one can have a place to sit down in the kingdom of God, with Abraham, with Isaac, and with Jacob, and also all the holy prophets, whose garments are cleansed, and are spotless, pure, and white?

45 I say unto you, Nay, except ye make our Creator a liar from the beginning, or suppose that he is a liar from the beginning, ye can not suppose that such can have place in the kingdom of heaven, but they shall be cast out, for they are the children of the kingdom of the devil.

46 And now behold, I say unto you my brethren, If ye have experienced a change of heart, and if ye have felt to sing the song of redeeming love, I would ask, Can ye feel so now?

47 Have ye walked, keeping yourselves blameless before God?

48 Could ye say, if ye were called to die at this time, within yourselves, that ye have been sufficiently humble?

49 That your garments have been cleansed and made white, through the blood of Christ, who will come to redeem his people from their sins?

50 Behold, are ye stripped of pride? I say unto you, If ye are not, ye are not prepared to meet God.

51 Behold ye must prepare quickly, for the kingdom of heaven is soon at hand, and such an one hath not eternal life.

52 Behold, I say, Is there one among you who is not stripped of envy?

53 I say unto you, that such an one is not prepared, and I would that he should prepare quickly, for the hour is close at hand, and he knoweth not when the time shall come; for such an one is not found guiltless.

54 And again I say unto you, Is there one among you that doth make a mock of his brother, or that heapeth upon him persecutions?

55 Wo unto such an one, for he is not prepared, and the time is at hand that he must repent, or he can not be saved;

56 Yea, even wo unto all ye workers of iniquity; repent, repent, for the Lord God hath spoken it.

57 Behold, he sendeth an invitation unto all men; for the arms of mercy are extended towards them, and he saith, Repent, and I will receive you;

58 Yea, he saith, Come unto me and ye shall partake of the fruit of the tree of life; yea, ye shall eat and drink of the bread and the waters of life freely;

59 Yea, come unto me and bring forth works of righteousness, and ye shall not be hewn down and cast into the fire;

60 For behold, the time is at hand that whosoever bringeth forth not good fruit, or whosoever doeth not the works of righteousness, the same have cause to wail and mourn.

61 O ye workers of iniquity; ye that are puffed up in the vain things of the world; ye that have professed to have known the ways of righteousness; nevertheless have gone astray, as sheep having no shepherd, notwithstanding a shepherd hath called after you, and art still calling after you, but ye will not hearken unto his voice.

62 Behold, I say unto you, that the good shepherd doth call you; yea, and in his own name he doth call you, which is the name of Christ;

63 And if ye will not hearken unto the voice of the good shepherd, to the name by which ye are called, behold, ye are not the sheep of the good shepherd.

64 And now if ye are not the sheep of the good shepherd, of what fold are ye?

65 Behold, I say unto you, that the devil is your shepherd, and ye are of his fold; and now who can deny this?

66 Behold, I say unto you, Whosoever denieth this, is a liar and a child of the devil;

67 For I say unto you, that whatsoever is good, cometh from God, and whatsoever is evil, cometh from the devil;

68 Therefore, if a man bringeth forth good works, he hearkeneth unto the voice of the good shepherd; and he doth follow him;

69 But whosoever bringeth forth evil works, the same becometh a child of the devil; for he hearkeneth unto his voice, and doth follow him.

70 And whosoever doeth this must receive his wages of him; therefore, for his wages he receiveth death, as to things pertaining unto righteousness, being dead unto all good works.

71 And now my brethren, I would that ye should hear me, for I speak in the energy of my soul;

72 For behold, I have spoken unto you plain, that ye can not err, or have spoken according to the commandments of God.

73 For I am called to speak after this manner, according to the holy order of God, which is in Christ Jesus:

74 Yea, I am commanded to stand and testify unto this people the things which have been spoken by our fathers, concerning the things which are to come.

75 And this is not all. Do ye not suppose that I know of these things myself?

76 Behold, I testify unto you, that I do know that these things whereof I have spoken, are true.

77 And how do ye suppose that I know of their surety?

78 Behold, I say unto you, They are made known unto me by the Holy Spirit of God.

79 Behold, I have fasted and prayed many days, that I might know these things of myself.

80 And now I do know of myself that they are true; for the Lord God hath made them manifest unto me by his Holy Spirit; and this is the spirit of revelation which is in me.

81 And moreover, I say unto you, that as it has thus been revealed unto me, that the words which have been spoken by our fathers, are true,

82 Even so according to the spirit of prophecy, which is in me, which is also by the manifestation of the Spirit of God, I say unto you, that I know of myself that whatsoever I shall say unto you concerning that which is to come, is true,

83 And I say unto you, that I know that Jesus Christ shall

come; yea, the Son, the only begotten of the Father, full of grace, and mercy, and truth.

84 And behold, it is he that cometh to take away the sins of the world; yea, the sins of every man who steadfastly believeth on his name.

85 ¶And now I say unto you, that this is the order after which I am called; yea, to preach unto my beloved brethren; yea, and every one that dwelleth in the land;

86 Yea, to preach unto all, both old and young, both bond and free; yea, I say unto you, the aged, and also the middle aged, and the rising generation; yea, to cry unto them that they must repent and be born again;

87 Yea, thus saith the Spirit, Repent all ye ends of the earth, for the kingdom of heaven is soon at hand; yea, the Son of God cometh in his glory, in his might, majesty, power and dominion.

88 Yea, my beloved brethren, I say unto you, that the Spirit saith, Behold, the glory of the King of all the earth; and also the King of heaven shall very soon shine forth among all the children of men;

89 And also the Spirit saith unto me, yea, crieth unto me with a mighty voice, saying, Go forth and say unto this people, Repent, for except ye repent, ye can in no wise inherit the kingdom of heaven.

90 And again I say unto you, the Spirit saith, Behold, the ax is laid at the root of the tree; therefore every tree that bringeth not forth good fruit, shall be hewn down and cast into the fire; yea, a fire which can not be consumed; even an unquenchable fire.

91 Behold, and remember, the Holy One hath spoken it.

92 And now my beloved brethren, I say unto you, Can ye withstand these sayings; yea, can ye lay aside these things, and trample the Holy One under your feet;

93 Yea, can ye be puffed up in the pride of your hearts; yea, will ye still persist in the wearing of costly apparel, and setting your hearts upon the vain things of the world, upon your riches;

94 Yea, will ye persist in supposing that ye are better one than another;

95 Yea, will ye persist in the persecutions of your brethren, who humble themselves, and do walk after the holy order of God, wherewith they have been brought into this church, having been sanctified by the Holy Spirit; and they do bring forth works which are meet for repentance;

96 Yea, and will you persist in turning your backs upon the poor, and the needy, and in withholding your substance from them?

97 And finally, all ye that will persist in your wickedness, I say unto you, that these are they who shall be hewn down and cast into the fire, except they speedily repent.

98 ¶And now I say unto you, all you that are desirous to follow the voice of the good shepherd, come ye out from the wicked, and be ye separate, and touch not their unclean things;

99 And behold, their names shall be blotted out, that the names of the wicked shall not be numbered among the names of the righteous, that the word of God may be fulfilled, which saith, The names of the wicked shall not be mingled with the names of my people.

100 For the names of the righteous shall be written in the book of life; and unto them will I grant an inheritance at my right hand.

101 And now my brethren, What have ye to say against this?

102 I say unto you, If ye speak against it, it matters not, for the word of God must be fulfilled.

103 For what shepherd is there among you having many sheep, doth not watch over them, that the wolves enter not and devour his flock?

104 And behold, if a wolf enter his flock, doth he not drive him out? Yea, and at the last, if he can, he will destroy him.

105 And now I say unto you, that the good shepherd doth call after you; and if you will hearken unto his voice, he will bring you into his fold, and ye are his sheep;

106 And he commandeth you that ye suffer no ravenous wolf to enter among you, that ye may not be destroyed.

107 ¶And now, I, Alma, do command you in the language of him who hath commanded me, that ye observe to do the words which I have spoken unto you.

108 I speak by way of command unto you that belong to the church; and unto those who do not belong to the church, I speak by way of invitation, saying, Come, and be baptized unto repentance, that ye also may be partakers of the fruit of the tree of life.

CHAPTER 4.

1 ¶And now it came to pass that after Alma had made an end of speaking unto the people of the church, which was established in the city of Zarahemla, he ordained priests and elders, by laying on his hands according to the order of God, to preside and watch over the church.

2 And it came to pass that whosoever did not belong to the church who repented of their sins, were baptized unto repentance, and were received into the church.

3 And it also came to pass that whosoever did belong to the church, that did not repent of their wickedness, and humble themselves before God;

4 I mean those who were lifted up in the pride of their hearts; the same were rejected, and their names were blotted out, that their names were not numbered among those of the righteous; and thus they began to establish the order of the church in the city of Zarahemla.

5 Now I would that ye should understand that the word of God was liberal unto all; that none were deprived of the privilege of assembling themselves together to hear the word of God;

6 Nevertheless the children of God were commanded that they should gather themselves together oft, and join in fasting and mighty prayer, in behalf of the welfare of the souls of those who knew not God.

7 ¶And now it came to pass that when Alma had made

these regulations, he departed from them, yea, from the church which was in the city of Zarahemla,

8 And went over upon the east of the river Sidon, into the valley of Gideon, there having been a city built which was called the city of Gideon, which was in the valley that was called Gideon, being called after the man who was slain by the hand of Nehor with the sword.

9 And Alma went and began to declare the word of God unto the church which was established in the valley of Gideon, according to the revelation of the truth of the word which had been spoken by his fathers,

10 And according to the spirit of prophecy which was in him, according to the testimony of Jesus Christ, the Son of God, who should come to redeem his people from their sins, and the holy order by which he was called. And thus it is written. Amen.

CHAPTER 5.

The words of Alma which he delivered to the people in Gideon, according to his own record.

1 ¶Behold my beloved brethren, seeing that I have been permitted to come unto you, therefore I attempt to address you in my language;

2 Yea, by my own mouth, seeing that it is the first time that I have spoken unto you by the words of my mouth, I having been wholly confined to the judgment seat, having had much business that I could not come unto you;

3 And even I could not have come now at this time, were it not that the judgment seat hath been given to another to reign in my stead; and the Lord in much mercy hath granted that I should come unto you.

4 And behold, I have come, having great hopes and much desire that I should find that ye had humbled yourselves before God, and that ye had continued in the supplicating of his grace, that I should find that ye were blameless before him;

5 That I should find that ye were not in the awful dilemma that our brethren were in at Zarahemla:

6 But blessed be the name of God, that he hath given me to know, yea, hath given unto me the exceeding great joy of knowing that they are established again in the way of his righteousness.

7 And I trust, according to the Spirit of God which is in me, that I shall also have joy over you;

8 Nevertheless I do not desire that my joy over you should come by the cause of so much afflictions and sorrow which I have had for the brethren at Zarahemla;

9 For behold, my joy cometh over them after wading through much afflictions and sorrow.

10 But behold, I trust that ye are not in a state of so much unbelief as were your brethren:

11 I trust that ye are not lifted up in the pride of your hearts; yea, I trust that ye have not set your hearts upon riches, and the vain things of the world;

12 Yea, I trust that you do not worship idols, but that ye do worship the true and the living God, and that ye look forward for the remission of your sins with an everlasting faith which is to come.

13 For behold, I say unto you, There be many things to come; and behold, there is one thing which is of more importance than they all:

14 For behold, the time is not far distant, that the Redeemer liveth and cometh among his people.

15 Behold, I do not say that he will come among us at the time of his dwelling in his mortal tabernacle; for behold, the Spirit hath not said unto me that this should be the case.

16 Now as to this thing I do not know; but this much I do know, that the Lord God hath power to do all things which are according to his word.

17 But behold, the Spirit hath said this much unto me, saying: Cry unto this people, saying, Repent ye, repent ye and prepare the way of the Lord, and walk in his paths, which are straight:

18 For behold, the kingdom of heaven is at hand, and the Son of God cometh upon the face of the earth.

19 And behold, he shall be born of Mary at Jerusalem,

which is the land of our forefathers, she being a virgin, a precious and chosen vessel, who shall be overshadowed, and conceive by the power of the Holy Ghost, and bring forth a son, yea, even the Son of God;

20 And he shall go forth, suffering pains, and afflictions, and temptations of every kind;

21 And this that the word might be fulfilled which saith, He will take upon him the pains and the sicknesses of his people; and he will take upon him death, that he may loose the bands of death which bind his people:

22 And he will take upon him their infirmities, that his bowels may be filled with mercy, according to the flesh, that he may know according to the flesh how to succor his people according to their infirmities.

23 Now the Spirit knoweth all things; nevertheless the Son of God suffereth according to the flesh, that he might take upon him the sins of his people, that he might blot out their transgressions, according to the power of his deliverance; and now behold, this is the testimony which is in me.

24 Now I say unto you, that ye must repent, and be born again: for the Spirit saith, If ye are not born again, ye can not inherit the kingdom of heaven;

25 Therefore come and be baptized unto repentance, that ye may be washed from your sins, that ye may have faith on the Lamb of God, who taketh away the sins of the world, who is mighty to save and to cleanse from all unrighteousness;

26 Yea, I say unto you, Come and fear not, and lay aside every sin, which easily doth beset you, which doth bind you down to destruction;

27 Yea, come and go forth, and shew unto your God that ye are willing to repent of your sins, and enter into a covenant with him to keep his commandments, and witness it unto him this day, by going into the waters of baptism;

28 And whosoever doeth this, and keepeth the commandments of God from thenceforth, the same will remember that I say unto him, yea, he will remember that I have said unto him, he shall have eternal life, according to the testimony of the Holy Spirit, which testifieth in me.

29 And now my beloved brethren, do you believe these things?

30 Behold, I say unto you, Yea, I know that ye believe them; and the way that I know that ye believe them, is by the manifestation of the Spirit which is in me.

31 And now because your faith is strong concerning that, yea, concerning the things which I have spoken, great is my joy.

32 For as I said unto you from the beginning, that I had much desire that ye were not in the state of dilemma like your brethren, even so I have found that my desires have been gratified.

33 For I perceive that ye are in the paths of righteousness: I perceive that ye are in the path which leads to the kingdom of God;

34 Yea, I perceive that ye are making his paths straight, I perceive that it has been made known unto you by the testimony of his word, that he can not walk in crooked paths;

35 Neither doth he vary from that which he hath said; neither hath he a shadow of turning from the right to the left, or from that which is right to that which is wrong; therefore, his course is one eternal round.

36 And he doth not dwell in unholy temples; neither can filthiness, or anything which is unclean be received into the kingdom of God;

37 Therefore I say unto you, The time shall come, yea, and it shall be at the last day, that he who is filthy, shall remain in his filthiness.

38 ¶And now my beloved brethren, I have said these things unto you, that I might awaken you to a sense of your duty to God, that ye may walk blameless before him; that ye may walk after the holy order of God, after which ye have been received.

39 And now I would that ye should be humble, and be submissive, and gentle; easy to be entreated; full of patience and long suffering; being temperate in all things; being diligent in keeping the commandments of God at all times;

40 Asking for whatsoever things ye stand in need, both

spiritual and temporal; always returning thanks unto God for whatsoever things ye do receive,

41 And see that ye have faith, hope and charity, and then ye will always abound in good works;

42 And may the Lord bless you, and keep your garments spotless, that ye may at last be brought to sit down with Abraham, Isaac and Jacob, and the holy prophets who have been ever since the world began, having your garments spotless, even as their garments are spotless in the kingdom of heaven, to go no more out.

43 ¶And now my beloved brethren, I have spoken these words unto you, according to the Spirit which testifieth in me; and my soul doth exceedingly rejoice, because of the exceeding diligence and heed which ye have given unto my word.

44 And now, may the peace of God rest upon you, and upon your houses and lands, and upon your flocks and herds, and all that you possess; your women and your children, according to your faith and good works, from this time forth and for ever. And thus I have spoken. Amen.

CHAPTER 6.

1 ¶And now it came to pass that Alma returned from the land of Gideon, after having taught the people of Gideon many things which can not be written, having established the order of the church, according as he had before done in the land of Zarahemla;

2 Yea, he returned to his own house at Zarahemla to rest himself from the labors which he had performed.

3 And thus ended the ninth year of the reign of the Judges over the people of Nephi.

4 ¶And it came to pass in the commencement of the tenth year of the reign of the Judges over the people of Nephi, that Alma departed from thence, and took his journey over into the land of Melek, on the west of the river Sidon, on the west, by the borders of the wilderness;

5 And he began to teach the people in the land of Melek,

according to the holy order of God by which he had been called; and he began to teach the people throughout all the land of Melek.

6 ¶And it came to pass that the people came to him throughout all the borders of the land which was by the wilderness side.

7 And they were baptized throughout all the land, so that when he had finished his work at Melek, he departed thence, and traveled three days' journey on the north of the land of Melek; and he came to a city which was called Ammonihah.

8 Now it was the custom of the people of Nephi, to call their lands, and their cities, and their villages, yea, even all their small villages, after the name of him who first possessed them; and thus it was with the land of Ammonihah.

9 ¶And it came to pass that when Alma had come to the city of Ammonihah, he began to preach the word of God unto them.

10 Now Satan had gotten great hold upon the hearts of the people of the city of Ammonihah; therefore they would not hearken unto the words of Alma.

11 Nevertheless Alma labored much in the spirit, wrestling with God in mighty prayer, that he would pour out his Spirit upon the people who were in the city: that he would also grant that he might baptize them unto repentance;

12 Nevertheless, they hardened their hearts, saying unto him, Behold, we know that thou art Alma; and we know that thou art high priest over the church which thou hast established in many parts of the land, according to your tradition;

13 And we are not of thy church, and we do not believe in such foolish traditions.

14 And now we know that because we are not of thy church, we know that thou hast no power over us;

15 And thou hast delivered up the judgment seat unto Nephihah; therefore thou art not the chief judge over us.

16 Now when the people had said this, and had withstood all his words, and reviled him, and spit upon him, and caused that he should be cast out of their city, he departed thence and took his journey towards the city which was called Aaron.

17 ¶And it came to pass that while he was journeying thither, being weighed down with sorrow, wading through much tribulation and anguish of soul, because of the wickedness of the people who were in the city of Ammonihah,

18 It came to pass that while Alma was thus weighed down with sorrow, behold an angel of the Lord appeared unto him, saying, Blessed art thou, Alma; therefore lift up thy head and rejoice, for thou hast great cause to rejoice:

19 For thou hast been faithful in keeping the commandments of God from the time which thou received thy first message from him.

20 Behold, I am he that delivered it unto you; and behold, I am sent to command thee that thou return to the city of Ammonihah, and preach again unto the people of the city; yea, preach unto them.

21 Yea, say unto them, except they repent, the Lord God will destroy them.

22 For behold, they do study at this time that they may destroy the liberty of thy people, (for thus saith the Lord,) which is contrary to the statutes, and judgments, and commandments which he has given unto his people.

23 ¶Now it came to pass that after Alma had received his message from the angel of the Lord, he returned speedily to the land of Ammonihah.

24 And he entered the city by another way, yea, by the way which is on the south of the city of Ammonihah.

25 And as he entered the city he was an hungered, and he said to a man, Will ye give to an humble servant of God something to eat?

26 And the man said unto him, I am a Nephite, and I know that thou art a holy prophet of God, for thou art the man whom an angel said in a vision, Thou shalt receive;

27 Therefore go with me into my house, and I will impart unto thee of my food; and I know that thou will be a blessing unto me and my house.

28 And it came to pass that the man received him into his house; and the man was called Amulek; and he brought forth bread and meat, and sat before Alma.

29 ¶And it came to pass that Alma ate bread and was filled; and he blessed Amulek and his house, and he gave thanks unto God.

30 And after he had eat and was filled, he said unto Amulek, I am Alma, and am the high priest over the church of God throughout the land.

31 And behold, I have been called to preach the word of God among all this people, according to the spirit of revelation and prophecy;

32 And I was in this land, and they would not receive me, but they cast me out, and I was about to set my back towards this land for ever.

33 But behold, I have been commanded that I should turn again and prophesy unto this people, yea, and to testify against them concerning their iniquities.

34 And now Amulek, because thou hast fed me and took me in, thou art blessed; for I was an hungered, for I had fasted many days.

35 And Alma tarried many days with Amulek, before he began to preach unto the people.

36 ¶And it came to pass that the people did wax more gross in their iniquities.

37 And the word came to Alma, saying, Go; and also say unto my servant Amulek, Go forth and prophesy unto this people, saying, Repent ye, for thus saith the Lord, Except ye repent, I will visit this people in mine anger; yea, and I will not turn my fierce anger away.

38 And Alma went forth, and also Amulek, among the people to declare the words of God unto them; and they were filled with the Holy Ghost;

39 And they had power given unto them, insomuch that they could not be confined in dungeons; neither were it possible that any man could slay them;

40 Nevertheless they did not exercise their power until they were bound in bands and cast into prison.

41 Now this was done that the Lord might shew forth his power in them.

42 ¶And it came to pass that they went forth and began to preach and to prophesy unto the people, according to the spirit and power which the Lord had given them.

CHAPTER 7.

The words of Alma, and also the words of Amulek which were declared unto the people who were in the land of Ammonihah. And also they are cast into prison, and delivered by the miraculous power of God which was in them, according to the record of Alma.

1 ¶And again: I, Alma, having been commanded of God that I should take Amulek and go forth and preach again unto this people, or the people who were in the city of Ammonihah, it came to pass as I began to preach unto them, they began to contend with me, saying, Who art thou?

2 Suppose ye that we shall believe the testimony of one man, although he should preach unto us that the earth should pass away?

3 Now they understood not the words which they spake: for they knew not that the earth should pass away.

4 And they said also, We will not believe thy words, if thou shouldst prophesy that this great city should be destroyed in one day.

5 Now they knew not that God could do such marvelous works, for they were a hard-hearted and stiff-necked people.

6 And they said, Who is God, that sendeth no more authority than one man among this people, to declare unto them the truth of such great and marvelous things?

7 And they stood forth to lay their hands on me; but behold, they did not.

8 And I stood with boldness to declare unto them, yea, I did boldly testify unto them, saying: Behold, O ye wicked and perverse generation, how have ye forgotten the tradition of your fathers; yea, how soon ye have forgotten the commandments of God.

9 Do ye not remember that our father Lehi was brought out of Jerusalem by the hand of God?

10 Do ye not remember that they were all led by him through the wilderness?

11 And have ye forgotten so soon how many times he delivered our fathers out of the hands of their enemies, and preserved them from being destroyed, even by the hands of their own brethren?

12 Yea, and if it had not been for his matchless power, and his mercy, and his long suffering towards us, we should unavoidably have been cut off from the face of the earth, long before this period of time, and perhaps been consigned to a state of endless misery and wo.

13 Behold, now I say unto you, that he commandeth you to repent; and except ye repent, ye can in no wise inherit the kingdom of God.

14 But behold, this is not all: he has commanded you to repent, or he will utterly destroy you from off the face of the earth; yea, he will visit you in his anger, and in his fierce anger he will not turn away.

15 Behold, do ye not remember the words which he spake unto Lehi, saying, that inasmuch as ye shall keep my commandments ye shall prosper in the land?

16 And again it is said, that inasmuch as ye will not keep my commandments, ye shall be cut off from the presence of the Lord.

17 Now I would that ye should remember, that inasmuch as the Lamanites have not kept the commandments of God, they have been cut off from the presence of the Lord.

18 Now we see that the word of the Lord has been verified in this thing, and the Lamanites have been cut off from his presence, from the beginning of their transgressions in the land.

19 Nevertheless I say unto you, that it shall be more tolerable for them in the day of judgment than for you, if ye remain in your sins;

20 Yea, and even more tolerable for them in this life, than

for you, except ye repent, for there are many promises which are extended to the Lamanites:

21 For it is because of the traditions of their fathers that cause them to remain in their state of ignorance; therefore the Lord will be merciful unto them, and prolong their existence in the land.

22 And at some period of time they will be brought to believe in his word, and to know of the incorrectness of the traditions of their fathers;

23 And many of them will be saved, for the Lord will be merciful unto all who call on his name.

24 But behold, I say unto you, that if ye persist in your wickedness, that your days shall not be prolonged in the land, for the Lamanites shall be sent upon you;

25 And if ye repent not, they shall come in a time when you know not, and ye shall be visited with utter destruction;

26 And it shall be according to the fierce anger of the Lord; for he will not suffer you that ye shall live in your iniquities to destroy his people.

27 I say unto you, Nay; he would rather suffer that the Lamanites might destroy all this people who are called the people of Nephi, if it were possible that they could fall into sins and transgressions, after having had so much light and so much knowledge given unto them of the Lord their God;

28 Yea, after having been such a highly favored people of the Lord; yea, after having been favored above every other nation, kindred, tongue or people;

29 After having had all things made known unto them, according to their desires, and their faith, and prayers, of that which has been, and which is, and which is to come;

30 Having been visited by the Spirit of God; having conversed with angels, and having been spoken unto by the voice of the Lord;

31 And having the spirit of prophecy, and the spirit of revelation, and also many gifts; the gift of speaking with tongues, and the gift of preaching, and the gift of the Holy Ghost, and the gift of translation:

32 Yea, and after having been delivered of God out of the land of Jerusalem, by the hand of the Lord;

33 Having been saved from famine, and from sickness, and all manner of diseases of every kind;

34 And they having been waxed strong in battle, that they might not be destroyed; having been brought out of bondage time after time, and having been kept and preserved until now; and they have been prospered until they are rich in all manner of things.

35 And now behold I say unto you, that if this people, who have received so many blessings from the hand of the Lord, should transgress, contrary to the light and knowledge which they do have;

36 I say unto you, that if this be the case; that if they should fall into transgression, that it would be far more tolerable for the Lamanites than for them.

37 For behold, the promises of the Lord are extended to the Lamanites, but they are not unto you, if ye transgress;

38 For has not the Lord expressly promised and firmly decreed, that if ye will rebel against him, that ye shall utterly be destroyed from off the face of the earth?

39 And now for this cause, that ye may not be destroyed, the Lord has sent his angel to visit many of his people, declaring unto them that they must go forth and cry mightily unto this people, saying, Repent ye, repent ye, for the kingdom of heaven is nigh at hand;

40 And not many days hence, the Son of God shall come in his glory; and his glory shall be the glory of the Only Begotten of the Father, full of grace, equity and truth, full of patience, mercy, and long suffering, quick to hear the cries of his people, and to answer their prayers.

41 And behold, he cometh to redeem those who will be baptized unto repentance, through faith on his name;

42 Therefore prepare ye the way of the Lord, for the time is at hand that all men shall reap a reward of their works, according to that which they have been:

43 If they have been righteous, they shall reap the salva-

tion of their souls, according to the power and deliverance of Jesus Christ;

44 And if they have been evil, they shall reap the damnation of their souls, according to the power and captivation of the devil.

45 Now behold, this is the voice of the angel, crying unto the people.

46 And now my beloved brethren, for ye are my brethren, and ye had ought to be beloved, and ye had ought to bring forth works which are meet for repentance, seeing that your hearts have been grossly hardened against the word of God, and seeing that ye are a lost and a fallen people.

47 ¶Now it came to pass that when I, Alma, had spoken these words, behold, the people were wroth with me, because I said unto them that they was a hard-hearted and a stiffnecked people;

48 And also because I said unto them that they were a lost and a fallen people, they were angry with me, and sought to lay their hands upon me, that they might cast me into prison;

49 But it came to pass that the Lord did not suffer them that they should take me at that time and cast me into prison.

50 ¶And it came to pass that Amulek went and stood forth, and began to preach unto them also.

51 And now the words of Amulek are not all written; nevertheless a part of his words are written in this boook.

CHAPTER 8.

1 ¶Now these are the words which Amulek preached unto the people who were in the land of Ammonihah, saying: I am Amulek; I am the son of Giddonah, who was the son of Ishmael, who was a descendant of Aminadi:

2 And it was that same Aminadi who interpreted the writing which was upon the wall of the temple, which was written by the finger of God.

3 And Aminadi was a descendant of Nephi, who was the

son of Lehi, who came out of the land of Jerusalem, who was a descendant of Manasseh, who was the son of Joseph, who was sold into Egypt by the hands of his brethren.

4 And behold, I am also a man of no small reputation among all those who know me;

5 Yea, and behold, I have many kindred and friends, and I have also acquired much riches by the hand of my industry;

6 Nevertheless, after all this, I never have known much of the ways of the Lord, and his mysteries and marvelous power.

7 I said I never had known much of these things; but behold I mistake, for I have seen much of his mysteries and his miraculous power; yea, even in the preservation of the lives of this people;

8 Nevertheless, I did harden my heart, for I was called many times, and I would not hear; therefore I knew concerning these things, yet I would not know;

9 Therefore I went on rebelling against God, in the wickedness of my heart, even until the fourth day of this seventh month, which is in the tenth year of the reign of the Judges.

10 As I was journeying to see a very near kindred, behold an angel of the Lord appeared unto me, and said, Amulek, return to thine own house, for thou shalt feed a prophet of the Lord; yea, a holy man, who is a chosen man of God;

11 For he has fasted many days because of the sins of this people, and he is an hungered, and thou shalt receive him into thy house and feed him, and he shall bless thee and thy house; and the blessing of the Lord shall rest upon thee and thy house.

12 ¶And it came to pass that I obeyed the voice of the angel, and returned towards my house.

13 And as I was going thither, I found the man whom the angel said unto me, Thou shalt receive into thy house; and behold it was this same man who has been speaking unto you concerning the things of God.

14 And the angel said unto me, He is a holy man; wherefore I know he is a holy man, because it was said by an angel of God.

15 And again, I know that the things whereof he hath tes-

tified are true; for behold, I say unto you that as the Lord liveth, even so he has sent his angel to make these things manifest unto me; and this he has done while this Alma hath dwelt at my house;

16 For behold, he hath blessed mine house, he hath blessed me, and my women, and my children, and my father, and my kinsfolks;

17 Yea, even all my kindred hath he blessed, and the blessing of the Lord hath rested upon us according to the words which he spake.

18 ¶And now when Amulek had spoken these words, the people began to be astonished, seeing there was more than one witness who testified of the things whereof they were accused, and also of the things which were to come, according to the spirit of prophecy which was in them;

19 Nevertheless, there were some among them who thought to question them, that by their cunning devices they might catch them in their words, that they might find witness against them, that they might deliver them to the Judges,

20 That they might be judged according to the law, and that they might be slain or cast into prison, according to the crime which they could make appear, or witness against them.

21 Now it was those men who sought to destroy them, who were lawyers, who were hired or appointed by the people to administer the law at their times of trials, or at the trials of the crimes of the people, before the Judges.

22 Now these lawyers were learned in all the arts and cunning of the people; and this was to enable them that they might be skillful in their profession.

23 And it came to pass that they began to question Amulek, that thereby they might make him cross his words, or contradict the words which he should speak.

24 Now they knew not that Amulek could know of their designs.

25 But it came to pass as they began to question him, he perceived their thoughts, and he said unto them, O ye wicked and perverse generation; ye lawyers and hypocrites; for ye are laying the foundations of the devil;

26 For ye are laying traps and snares to catch the holy ones of God; ye are laying plans to pervert the ways of the righteous, and to bring down the wrath of God upon your heads, even to the utter destruction of this people;

27 Yea, well did Mosiah say, who was our last king, when he was about to deliver up the kingdom, having no one to confer it upon, causing that this people should be governed by their own voices;

28 Yea, well did he say, that if the time should come that the voice of this people should choose iniquity; that is, if the time should come that this people should fall into transgression, they would be ripe for destruction.

29 And now I say unto you, that well doth the Lord judge of your iniquities; well doth he cry unto this people, by the voice of his angels, Repent ye, repent, for the kingdom of heaven is at hand.

30 Yea, well doth he cry, by the voice of his angels, that I will come down among my people, with equity and justice in my hands.

31 Yea, and I say unto you, that if it were not for the prayers of the righteous, who are now in the land, that ye would even now be visited with utter destruction;

32 Yet it would not be by flood, as were the people in the days of Noah, but it would be by famine, and by pestilence, and the sword.

33 But it is by the prayers of the righteous that ye are spared; now therefore if ye will cast out the righteous from among you, then will not the Lord stay his hand, but in his fierce anger he will come out against you;

34 Then ye shall be smitten by famine, and by pestilence, and by the sword; and the time is soon at hand, except ye repent.

35 ¶And now it came to pass that the people were more angry with Amulek, and they cried out saying: This man doth revile against our laws, which are just, and our wise lawyers whom we have selected.

36 But Amulek stretched forth his hand, and cried the mightier unto them, saying: O ye wicked and perverse gene-

ration; why hath Satan got such great hold upon your hearts?

37 Why will ye yield yourselves unto him that he may have power over you, to blind your eyes, that ye will not understand the words which are spoken, according to their truth?

38 For behold, have I testified against your law?

39 Ye do not understand; ye say that I have spoken against your law; but I have not; but I have spoken in favor of your law, to your condemnation.

40 And now behold, I say unto you, that the foundation of the destruction of this people is beginning to be laid by the unrighteousness of your lawyers and your judges.

41 ¶And now it came to pass that when Amulek had spoken these words, the people cried out against him, saying, Now we know that this man is a child of the devil, for he hath lied unto us; for he hath spoken against our law.

42 And now he says that he has not spoken against it.

43 And again; he has reviled against our lawyers, and our judges, etc.

44 And it came to pass that the lawyers put it into their hearts that they should remember these things against him.

45 And there was one among them whose name was Zeezrom.

46 Now he was the foremost to accuse Amulek and Alma, he being one of the most expert among them, having much business to do among the people.

47 Now the object of these lawyers was to get gain; and they got gain according to their employ.

48 ¶Now it was in the law of Mosiah that every man who was a judge of the law, or those who were appointed to be judges should receive wages according to the time which they labored to judge those who were brought before them to be judged.

49 ¶Now if a man owed another, and he would not pay that which he did owe, he was complained of to the judge;

50 And the judge executed authority, and sent forth officers that the man should be brought before him;

51 And he judged the man according to the law and the evidences which were brought against him, and thus the man

CHAP. 8.]   BOOK OF ALMA.   339

was compelled to pay that which he owed, or be striped, or be cast out from among the people, as a thief and a robber.

52 And the judge received for his wages according to his time: a senine of gold for a day, or a senum of silver, which is equal to a senine of gold; and this is according to the law which was given.

53 Now these are the names of the different pieces of their gold, and of their silver, according to their value.

54 And the names are given by the Nephites; for they did not reckon after the manner of the Jews who were at Jerusalem; neither did they measure after the manner of the Jews,

55 But they altered their reckoning and their measure, according to the minds and the circumstances of the people, in every generation, until the reign of the Judges; they having been established by King Mosiah.

56 Now the reckoning is thus: a senine of gold, a seon of gold, a shum of gold, and a limnah of gold.

57 A senum of silver, an amnor of silver, an ezrom of silver, and an onti of silver.

58 A senum of silver was equal to a senine of gold; and either for a measure of barley, and also for a measure of every kind of grain.

59 Now the amount of a seon of gold was twice the value of a senine; and a shum of gold was twice the value of a seon; and a limnah of gold was the value of them all;

60 And an amnor of silver was as great as two senums; and an ezrom of silver was as great as four senums; and an onti was as great as them all.

61 Now this is the value of the lesser numbers of their reckoning, a shiblon is half of a senum: therefore a shiblon for half a measure of barley; and a shiblum is a half of a shiblon; and a leah is the half of a shiblum.

62 Now an antion of gold is equal to three shiblons.

63 Now this is their number, according to their reckoning.

64 ¶Now it was for the sole purpose to get gain, because they received their wages according to their employ;

65 Therefore they did stir up the people to riotings, and

all manner of disturbances and wickedness, that they might have more employ;

66 That they might get money according to the suits which were brought before them; therefore they did stir up the people against Alma and Amulek.

67 And this Zeezrom began to question Amulek, saying: Will ye answer me a few questions which I shall ask you?

68 Now Zeezrom was a man who was expert in the devices of the devil, that he might destroy that which was good; therefore he said unto Amulek, Will ye answer the questions which I shall put unto you?

69 And Amulek said unto him, Yea, I will if it be according to the Spirit of the Lord which is in me; for I shall say nothing which is contrary to the Spirit of the Lord.

70 And Zeezrom said unto him, Behold here are six onties of silver, and all these will I give thee if thou wilt deny the existence of a supreme being.

71 Now Amulek said, O thou child of hell, why tempt ye me?

72 Knowest thou that the righteous yieldeth to no such temptations?

73 Believest thou that there is no God?

74 I say unto you, Nay; thou knowest that there is a God, but thou lovest that lucre more than him.

75 And now thou hast lied before God unto me.

76 Thou saidst unto me, Behold these six onties which are of great worth, I will give unto thee, when thou had it in thy heart to retain them from me;

77 And it was only thy desire that I should deny the true and living God, that thou mightest have cause to destroy me.

78 And now behold, for this great evil thou shalt have thy reward.

79 And Zeezrom said unto him, Thou sayest there is a true and living God?

80 And Amulek said, Yea, there is a true and a living God.

81 Now Zeezrom said, Is there more than one God?

82 And he answereth, No.

83 Now Zeezrom said unto him again, How knowest thou these things?

84 And he said, An angel hath made them known unto me.

85 And Zeezrom said again, Who is he that shall come? Is it the Son of God?

86 And he said unto him, Yea.

87 And Zeezrom said again, Shall he save his people in their sins?

88 And Amulek answered and said unto him, I say unto you he shall not, for it is impossible for him to deny his word.

89 ¶Now Zeezrom said unto the people, See that ye remember these things; for he said there is but one God; yet he saith that the Son of God shall come, but he shall not save his people, as though he had authority to command God.

90 Now Amulek saith again unto him, Behold thou hast lied, for thou sayest that I spake as though I had authority to command God, because I said he shall not save his people in their sins.

91 And I say unto you again, that he can not save them in their sins; for I can not deny his word, and he hath said that no unclean thing can inherit the kingdom of heaven;

92 Therefore how can ye be saved, except ye inherit the kingdom of heaven? Therefore ye can not be saved in your sins.

93 Now Zeezrom saith again unto him, Is the Son of God the very eternal Father?

94 And Amulek said unto him, Yea, he is the very eternal Father of heaven and of earth, and all things which in them is;

95 He is the beginning and the end, the first and the last;

96 And he shall come into the world to redeem his people; and he shall take upon him the transgressions of those who believe on his name; and these are they that shall have eternal life, and salvation cometh to none else;

97 Therefore the wicked remain as though there had been no redemption made, except it be the loosing of the bands of death;

98 For behold, the day cometh that all shall rise from the

dead and stand before God, and be judged according to their works.

99 Now there is a death which is called a temporal death; and the death of Christ shall loose the bands of this temporal death, that all shall be raised from this temporal death;

100 The spirit and the body shall be reunited again, in its perfect form; both limb and joint shall be restored to its proper frame, even as we now are at this time;

101 And we shall be brought to stand before God, knowing even as we know now, and have a bright recollection of all our guilt.

102 Now this restoration shall come to all, both old and young, both bond and free, both male and female, both the wicked and the righteous;

103 And even there shall not so much as a hair of their heads be lost; but all things shall be restored to its perfect frame, as it is now, or in the body,

104 And shall be brought and be arraigned before the bar of Christ the Son, and God the Father, and the Holy Spirit, which is one eternal God, to be judged according to their works, whether they be good or whether they be evil.

105 ¶Now behold I have spoken unto you concerning the death of the mortal body, and also concerning the resurrection of the mortal body.

106 I say unto you, that this mortal body is raised to an immortal body; that is from death; even from the first death, unto life, that they can die no more; their spirits uniting with their bodies, never to be divided;

107 Thus the whole becoming spiritual and immortal, that they can no more see corruption.

108 ¶Now when Amulek had finished these words, the people began again to be astonished, and also Zeezrom began to tremble.

109 And thus ended the words of Amulek, or this is all that I have written.

CHAPTER 9.

1 ¶Now Alma, seeing that the words of Amulek had silenced Zeezrom, for he beheld that Amulek had caught him in his lying and deceiving, to destroy him, and seeing that he began to tremble under a consciousness of his guilt, he opened his mouth and began to speak unto him, and to establish the words of Amulek, and to explain things beyond, or to unfold the scriptures beyond that which Amulek had done.

2 Now the words that Alma spake unto Zeezrom, were heard by the people round about; for the multitude was great, and he spake on this wise:

3 Now Zeezrom, seeing that thou hast been taken in thy lying and craftiness, for thou hast not lied unto men only, but thou hast lied unto God;

4 For behold, he knows all thy thoughts; and thou seest that thy thoughts are made known unto us by his Spirit;

5 And thou seest that we know that thy plan was a very subtle plan, as to the subtlety of the devil, for to lie and to deceive this people, that thou mightest set them against us, to revile us and to cast us out.

6 Now this was a plan of thine adversary, and he hath exercised his power in thee.

7 Now I would that ye should remember that what I say unto thee, I say unto all.

8 And behold, I say unto you all, that this was a snare of the adversary, which he has laid to catch this people,

9 That he might bring you into subjection unto him, that he might encircle you about with his chains, that he might chain you down to everlasting destruction, according to the power of his captivity.

10 ¶Now when Alma had spoken these words, Zeezrom began to tremble more exceedingly, for he was convinced more and more of the power of God;

11 And he was also convinced that Alma and Amulek had a knowledge of him, for he was convinced that they knew the thoughts and intents of his heart:

12 For power was given unto them that they might know of these things, according to the spirit of prophecy.

13 And Zeezrom began to inquire of them diligently, that he might know more concerning the kingdom of God.

14 And he said unto Alma, What does this mean which Amulek hath spoken concerning the resurrection of the dead, that all shall rise from the dead, both the just and the unjust, and are brought to stand before God, to be judged according to their works?

15 And now Alma began to expound these things unto him, saying, It is given unto many to know the mysteries of God;

16 Nevertheless they are laid under a strict command, that they shall not impart only according to the portion of his word, which he doth grant unto the children of men; according to the heed and diligence which they give unto him;

17 And therefore he that will harden his heart, the same receiveth the lesser portion of the word;

18 And he that will not harden his heart, to him is given the greater portion of the word, until it is given unto him to know the mysteries of God, until they know them in full;

19 And they that will harden their hearts, to them is given the lesser portion of the word, until they know nothing concerning his mysteries;

20 And then they are taken captive by the devil, and led by his will down to destruction.

21 Now this is what is meant by the chains of hell; and Amulek hath spoken plainly concerning death, and being raised from this mortality to a state of immortality, and being brought before the bar of God, to be judged according to our works.

22 Then if our hearts have been hardened, yea, if we have hardened our hearts against the word, insomuch that it has not been found in us, then will our state be awful, for then we shall be condemned;

23 For our words will condemn us, yea, all our works will condemn us; we shall not be found spotless:

24 And our thoughts will also condemn us; and in this awful state, we shall not dare look up to our God;

25 And we would fain be glad if we could command the rocks and the mountains to fall upon us, to hide us from his presence.

26 But this can not be: we must come forth and stand before him in his glory, and in his power, and in his might, majesty, and dominion, and acknowledge to our everlasting shame, that all his judgments are just:

27 That he is just in all his works, and that he is merciful unto the children of men, and that he has all power to save every man that believeth on his name, and bringeth forth fruit meet for repentance.

28 ¶And now behold I say unto you, then cometh a death, even a second death, which is a spiritual death;

29 Then is a time that whosoever dieth in his sins, as to a temporal death, shall also die a spiritual death: yea, he shall die as to things pertaining unto righteousness;

30 Then is the time when their torments shall be as a lake of fire and brimstone, whose flames ascendeth up for ever and ever;

31 And then is the time that they shall be chained down to an everlasting destruction, according to the power and captivity of Satan: he having subjected them according to his will.

32 Then I say unto you, They shall be as though there had been no redemption made; for they can not be redeemed according to God's justice; and they can not die, seeing there is no more corruption.

33 ¶Now it came to pass that when Alma had made an end of speaking these words, the people began to be more astonished;

34 But there was one Antionah, who was a chief ruler among them, came forth and said unto him, What is this that thou hast said, that man should rise from the dead and be changed from this mortal to an immortal state, that the soul can never die?

35 What does the scripture mean, which saith that God

placed cherubims and a flaming sword on the east of the garden of Eden, lest our first parents should enter and partake of the fruit of the tree of life, and live for ever?

36 And thus we see that there was no possible chance that they should live for ever.

37 Now Alma said unto him, This is the thing which I was about to explain.

38 Now we see that Adam did fall by the partaking of the forbidden fruit, according to the word of God; and thus we see, that by his fall, all mankind became a lost and a fallen people.

39 And now behold, I say unto you, that if it had been possible for Adam to have partaken of the fruit of the tree of life at that time, there would have been no death, and the word would have been void, making God a liar: for he said, If thou eat, thou shall surely die.

40 And we see that death comes upon mankind, yea, the death which has been spoken of by Amulek, which is the temporal death; nevertheless there was a space granted unto man, in which he might repent;

41 Therefore this life became a probationary state; a time to prepare to meet God; a time to prepare for that endless state, which has been spoken of by us, which is after the resurrection of the dead.

42 Now if it had not been for the plan of redemption, which was laid from the foundation of the world, there could have been no resurrection of the dead;

43 But there was a plan of redemption laid, which shall bring to pass the resurrection of the dead, of which has been spoken.

44 And now behold, if it were possible that our first parents could have went forth and partaken of the tree of life, they would have been for ever miserable, having no preparatory state;

45 And thus the plan of redemption would have been frustrated, and the word of God would have been void, taking none effect.

46 But behold, it was not so; but it was appointed unto

man that they must die; and after death, they must come to judgment; even that same judgment of which we have spoken, which is the end.

47 And after God had appointed that these things should come unto man, behold, then he saw that it was expedient that man should know concerning the things whereof he had appointed unto them;

48 Therefore he sent angels to converse with them, who caused men to behold of his glory.

49 And they began from that time forth to call on his name; therefore God conversed with men, and made known unto them the plan of redemption, which had been prepared from the foundation of the world;

50 And this he made known unto them according to their faith and repentance, and their holy works;

51 Wherefore he gave commandments unto men, they having first transgressed the first commandments as to things which were temporal, and becoming as gods, knowing good from evil, placing themselves in a state to act, or being placed in a state to act according to their wills and pleasures, whether to do evil or to do good;

52 Therefore God gave unto them commandments, after having made known unto them the plan of redemption, that they should not do evil, the penalty thereof being a second death, which was an everlasting death as to things pertaining unto righteousness;

53 For on such the plan of redemption could have no power, for the works of justice could not be destroyed, according to the supreme goodness of God.

54 But God did call on men, in the name of his Son, (this being the plan of redemption which was laid,) saying: If ye will repent, and harden not your hearts, then will I have mercy upon you, through mine only begotten Son;

55 Therefore, whosoever repenteth, and hardeneth not his heart, he shall have claim on mercy through mine only begotten Son, unto a remission of his sins; and these shall enter into my rest.

56 And whosoever will harden his heart, and will do iniq-

uity, behold, I swear in my wrath that he shall not enter into my rest.

57 And now my brethren, behold I say unto you, that if ye will harden your hearts, ye shall not enter into the rest of the Lord;

58 Therefore your iniquity provoketh him, that he sendeth down his wrath upon you as in the first provocation,

59 Yea, according to his word in the last provocation, as well as the first, to the everlasting destruction of your souls; therefore, according to his word, unto the last death, as well as the first.

60 ¶And now my brethren, seeing we know these things, and they are true, let us repent, and harden not our hearts, that we provoke not the Lord our God to pull down his wrath upon us in these his second commandments which he has given unto us;

61 But let us enter into the rest of God, which is prepared according to his word.

62 And again: my brethren, I would cite your minds forward to the time which the Lord God gave these commandments unto his children;

63 And I would that ye should remember that the Lord God ordained priests, after his holy order, which was after the order of his Son, to teach these things unto the people;

64 And those priests were ordained after the order of his Son, in a manner that thereby the people might know in what manner to look forward to his Son for redemption.

65 And this is the manner after which they were ordained: being called and prepared from the foundation of the world, according to the foreknowledge of God, on account of their exceeding faith and good works; in the first place being left to choose good or evil;

66 Therefore they having chosen good, and exercising exceeding great faith, are called with a holy calling, yea, with that holy calling which was prepared with, and according to, a preparatory redemption for such;

67 And thus they have been called to this holy calling on account of their faith, while others would reject the Spirit

of God on account of the hardness of their hearts and blindness of their minds, while, if it had not been for this, they might had as great privilege as their brethren.

68 Or in fine: in the first place they were on the same standing with their brethren; thus this holy calling being prepared from the foundation of the world for such as would not harden their hearts, being in and through the atonement of the only begotten Son, who was prepared;

69 And thus being called by this holy calling, and ordained unto the high priesthood of the holy order of God, to teach his commandments unto the children of men, that they also might enter into his rest,

70 This high priesthood being after the order of his Son, which order was from the foundation of the world:

71 Or in other words, being without beginning of days or end of years, being prepared from eternity to all eternity, according to his foreknowledge of all things.

72 Now they were ordained after this manner: Being called with a holy calling, and ordained with a holy ordinance, and taking upon them the high priesthood of the holy order, which calling, and ordinance, and high priesthood, is without beginning or end;

73 Thus they become high priests for ever, after the order of the Son, the only begotten of the Father, who is without beginning of days or end of years, who is full of grace, equity, and truth. And thus it is. Amen.

CHAPTER 10.

1 ¶Now as I said concerning the holy order of this high priesthood: there were many who were ordained and became high priests of God;

2 And it was on account of their exceeding faith and repentance, and their righteousness before God, they choosing to repent and work righteousness, rather than to perish;

3 Therefore they were called after this holy order, and were sanctified, and their garments were washed white, through the blood of the Lamb.

4 Now they, after being sanctified by the Holy Ghost, having their garments made white, being pure and spotless before God, could not look upon sin, save it were with abhorrence;

5 And there were many, exceeding great many, who were made pure, and entered into the rest of the Lord their God.

6 And now, my brethren, I would that ye should humble yourselves before God, and bring forth fruit meet for repentance, that ye may also enter into that rest;

7 Yea, humble yourselves even as the people in the days of Melchisedec, who was also a high priest after this same order which I have spoken, who also took upon him the high priesthood for ever.

8 And it was this same Melchisedec to whom Abraham paid tithes: yea, even our father Abraham paid tithes of one tenth part of all that he possessed.

9 Now these ordinances were given after this manner, that thereby the people might look forward on the Son of God, it being a type of his order, or it being his order;

10 And this, that they might look forward to him for a remission of their sins, that they might enter into the rest of the Lord.

11 ¶Now this Melchisedec was a king over the land of Salem; and his people had waxed strong in iniquity and abominations; yea, they had all gone astray: they were full of all manner of wickedness;

12 But Melchisedec having exercised mighty faith, and received the office of the high priesthood, according to the holy order of God, did preach repentance unto his people.

13 And behold, they did repent; and Melchisedec did establish peace in the land in his days;

14 Therefore he was called the prince of peace, for he was the king of Salem; and he did reign under his father.

15 Now there were many before him, and also there were many afterwards, but none were greater; therefore of him they have more particularly made mention.

16 Now I need not rehearse the matter; what I have said, may suffice.

17 Behold, the scriptures are before you; if ye will wrest them it shall be to your own destruction.

18 ¶And now it came to pass that when Alma had said these words unto them, he stretched forth his hand unto them and cried with a mighty voice, saying, Now is the time to repent, for the day of salvation draweth nigh;

19 Yea, and the voice of the Lord, by the mouth of angels, doth declare it, unto all nations: yea, doth declare it, that they may have glad tidings of great joy;

20 Yea, and he doth sound these glad tidings among all his people, yea, even to them that are scattered abroad upon the face of the earth; wherefore they have come unto us.

21 And they are made known unto us in plain terms, that we may understand, that we can not err; and this because of our being wanderers in a strange land:

22 Therefore we are thus highly favored, for we have these glad tidings declared unto us in all parts of our vineyard.

23 For behold, angels are declaring it unto many at this time in our land; and this is for the purpose of preparing the hearts of the children of men to receive his word, at the time of his coming in his glory.

24 And now we only wait to hear the joyful news declared unto us by the mouth of angels, of his coming; for the time cometh we know not how soon.

25 Would to God that it might be in my day; but let it be sooner or later, in it I will rejoice.

26 And it shall be made known unto just and holy men, by the mouth of angels, at the time of his coming, that the words of our fathers may be fulfilled, according to that which they have spoken concerning him, which was according to the spirit of prophecy which was in them.

27 ¶And now my brethren, I wish from the inmost part of my heart, yea, with great anxiety, even unto pain, that ye would hearken unto my words, and cast off your sins, and not procrastinate the day of your repentance;

28 But that ye would humble yourselves before the Lord, and call on his holy name, and watch and pray continually, that ye may not be tempted above that which ye can bear, and

thus be led by the Holy Spirit, becoming humble, meek, submissive, patient, full of love and all long suffering; having faith on the Lord;

29 Having a hope that ye shall receive eternal life; having the love of God always in your hearts, that ye may be lifted up at the last day, and enter into his rest;

30 And may the Lord grant unto you repentance, that ye may not bring down his wrath upon you, that ye may not be bound down by the chains of hell, that ye may not suffer the second death.

31 And Alma spake many more words unto the people, which are not written in this book.

32 ¶And it came to pass after he had made an end of speaking unto the people, many of them did believe on his words, and began to repent and to search the scriptures;

33 But the more part of them were desirous that they might destroy Alma and Amulek; for they were angry with Alma, because of the plainness of his words unto Zeezrom;

34 And they also said that Amulek had lied unto them, and had reviled against their law, and also against their lawyers and judges.

35 And they were also angry with Alma and Amulek; and because they had testified so plainly against their wickedness, they sought to put them away privily.

36 But it came to pass that they did not; but they took them and bound them with strong cords, and took them before the chief judge of the land.

37 And the people went forth and witnessed against them, testifying that they had reviled against the law, and their lawyers and judges of the land, and also all the people that were in the land;

38 And also testified that there was but one God, and that he should send his Son among the people, but he should not save them; and many such things did the people testify against Alma and Amulek.

39 Now this was done before the chief judge of the land.

40 And it came to pass that Zeezrom was astonished at the words which had been spoken; and he also knew concerning

the blindness of the minds which he had caused among the people, by his lying words;

41 And his soul began to be harrowed up, under a consciousness of his own guilt; yea, he began to be encircled about by the pains of hell.

42 ¶And it came to pass that he began to cry unto the people, saying: Behold I am guilty, and these men are spotless before God.

43 And he began to plead for them, from that time forth; but they reviled him, saying: Art thou also possessed with the devil?

44 And they spit upon him, and cast him out from among them, and also all those who believed in the words which had been spoken by Alma and Amulek; and they cast them out, and sent men to cast stones at them.

45 And they brought their wives and children together, and whosoever believed or had been taught to believe in the word of God, they caused that they should be cast into the fire;

46 And they also brought forth their records, which contained the holy scriptures, and cast them into the fire also, that they might be burned and destroyed by fire.

47 ¶And it came to pass that they took Alma and Amulek, and carried them forth to the place of martyrdom, that they might witness the destruction of those who were consumed by fire.

48 And when Amulek saw the pains of the women and children who were consuming in the fire, he was also pained; and he said unto Alma, How can we witness this awful scene?

49 Therefore let us stretch forth our hands, and exercise the power of God which is in us, and save them from the flames.

50 But Alma said unto him, The Spirit constraineth me that I must not stretch forth mine hand; for behold, the Lord receiveth them up unto himself, in glory;

51 And he doth suffer that they may do this thing, or that the people may do this thing unto them, according to the hardness of their hearts, that the judgments which he shall exercise upon them in his wrath, may be just;

52 And the blood of the innocent shall stand as a witness against them, yea, and cry mightily against them at the last day.

53 Now Amulek said unto Alma, Behold, perhaps they will burn us also.

54 And Alma said, Be it according to the will of the Lord. But behold, our work is not finished; therefore they burn us not.

55 ¶Now it came to pass that when the bodies of those who had been cast into the fire, were consumed, and also the records which were cast in with them, the chief judge of the land came and stood before Alma and Amulek, as they were bound;

56 And he smote them with his hand upon their cheeks, and said unto them, After what ye have seen, will ye preach again unto this people, that they shall be cast into a lake of fire and brimstone?

57 Behold, ye see that ye had not power to save these who had been cast into the fire; neither has God saved them, because they were of thy faith.

58 And the judge smote them upon their cheeks, and asked, What say ye for yourselves?

59 Now this judge was after the order and faith of Nehor, who slew Gideon.

60 And it came to pass that Alma and Amulek answered him nothing; and he smote them again, and delivered them to the officers to be cast into prison.

61 And when they had been cast into prison three days, there came many lawyers, and judges, and priests, and teachers, who were of the profession of Nehor;

62 And they came in unto the prison to see them, and they questioned them about many words; but they answered them nothing.

63 And it came to pass that the judge stood before them, and said, Why do ye not answer the words of this people?

64 Know ye not that I have power to deliver ye up unto the flames?

65 And he commanded them to speak; but they answered nothing.

66 ¶And it came to pass that they departed and went their ways, but came again on the morrow; and the judge also smote them again on their cheeks.

67 And many came forth also, and smote them, saying, Will ye stand again, and judge this people, and condemn our law?

68 If ye have such great power, why do ye not deliver yourselves?

69 And many such things did they say unto them, gnashing their teeth upon them, and spitting upon them, and saying, How shall we look when we are damned?

70 And many such things, yea, all manner of such things did they say unto them; and thus they did mock them, for many days.

71 And they did withhold food from them, that they might hunger, and water, that they might thirst;

72 And they also did take from them their clothes, that they were naked; and thus they were bound with strong cords, and confined in prison.

73 ¶And it came to pass after they had thus suffered for many days, (and it was on the twelfth day, in the tenth month, in the tenth year of the reign of the Judges over the people of Nephi,) that the chief judge over the land of Ammonihah, and many of their teachers and their lawyers, went in unto the prison where Alma and Amulek were bound with cords.

74 And the chief judge stood before them, and smote them again, and said unto them, If ye have the power of God, deliver yourselves from these bands, and then we will believe that the Lord will destroy this people according to your words.

75 And it came to pass that they all went forth and smote them, saying the same words, even until the last;

76 And when the last had spoken unto them, the power of God was upon Alma and Amulek, and they arose and stood

upon their feet; and Alma cried, saying, How long shall we suffer these great afflictions, O Lord?

77 O Lord, give us strength according to our faith which is in Christ, even unto deliverance; and they brake the cords with which they were bound; and when the people saw this, they began to flee, for the fear of destruction had come upon them.

78 ¶And it came to pass that so great was their fear, that they fell to the earth, and did not obtain the outer door of the prison;

79 And the earth shook mightily, and the walls of the prison were rent in twain, so that they fell to the earth:

80 And the chief judge, and the lawyers, and priests, and teachers, who smote upon Alma and Amulek, were slain by the fall thereof.

81 And Alma and Amulek came forth out of the prison, and they were not hurt; for the Lord had granted unto them power, according to their faith which was in Christ.

82 And they straightway came forth out of the prison; and they were loosed from their bands:

83 And the prison had fallen to the earth, and every soul who was within the walls thereof, save it were Alma and Amulek, were slain; and they straightway came forth into the city.

84 Now the people having heard a great noise, came running together by multitudes, to know the cause of it;

85 And when they saw Alma and Amulek coming forth out of the prison, and the walls thereof had fallen to the earth, they were struck with great fear and fled from the presence of Alma and Amulek, even as a goat fleeth with her young from two lions; and thus they did flee from the presence of Alma and Amulek.

86 ¶And it came to pass that Alma and Amulek were commanded to depart out of that city; and they departed, and came out even into the land of Sidom;

87 And behold, there they found all the people who had departed out of the land of Ammonihah, who had been cast out and stoned, because they believed in the words of Alma:

88 And they related unto them all that had happened unto their wives and children, and also concerning themselves, and of their power of deliverance.

89 And also Zeezrom lay sick at Sidom, with a burning fever, which was caused by the great tribulations of his mind, on account of his wickedness, for he supposed that Alma and Amulek were no more; and he supposed that they had been slain, by the cause of his iniquity.

90 And this great sin, and his many other sins, did harrow up his mind, until it did become exceeding sore, having no deliverance; therefore he began to be scorched with a burning heat.

91 Now when he heard that Alma and Amulek were in the land of Sidom, his heart began to take courage; and he sent a message immediately unto them, desiring them to come unto him.

92 ¶And it came to pass that they went immediately, obeying the message which he had sent unto them; and they went in unto the house unto Zeezrom;

93 And they found him upon his bed sick, being very low with a burning fever; and his mind also was exceeding sore, because of his iniquities;

94 And when he saw them, he stretched forth his hand, and besought them that they would heal him.

95 ¶And it came to pass that Alma said unto him, taking him by the hand, Believest thou in the power of Christ unto salvation?

96 And he answered and said, Yea, I believe all the words that thou hast taught.

97 And Alma said, If thou believest in the redemption of Christ, thou canst be healed.

98 And he said, Yea, I believe according to thy words.

99 And then Alma cried unto the Lord, saying, O Lord our God, have mercy on this man, and heal him according to his faith which is in Christ.

100 And when Alma had said these words, Zeezrom leaped upon his feet, and began to walk;

101 And this was done to the great astonishment of all the

people; and the knowledge of this went forth throughout all the land of Sidom.

102 And Alma baptized Zeezrom unto the Lord; and he began from that time forth to preach unto the people.

103 And Alma established a church in the land of Sidom, and consecrated priests and teachers in the land, to baptize unto the Lord whosoever were desirous to be baptized.

104 ¶And it came to pass that they were many; for they did flock in from all the region round about Sidom, and were baptized;

105 But as to the people that were in the land of Ammonihah, they yet remained a hard-hearted and a stiff-necked people;

106 And they repented not of their sins, ascribing all the power of Alma and Amulek to the devil: for they were of the profession of Nehor, and did not believe in the repentance of their sins.

107 ¶And it came to pass that Alma and Amulek, Amulek having forsaken all his gold, and silver, and his precious things, which were in the land of Ammonihah, for the word of God, he being rejected by those who were once his friends, and also by his father and his kindred;

108 Therefore, after Alma having established the church at Sidom, seeing a great check, yea, seeing that the people were checked as to the pride of their hearts, and began to humble themselves before God,

109 And began to assemble themselves together at their sanctuaries to worship God before the altar, watching and praying continually, that they might be delivered from Satan, and from death, and from destruction:

110 Now as I said, Alma having seen all these things, therefore he took Amulek and came over to the land of Zarahemla, and took him to his own house, and did administer unto him in his tribulations, and strengthened him in the Lord.

111 And thus ended the tenth year of the reign of the Judges over the people of Nephi.

CHAPTER 11.

1 ¶And it came to pass in the eleventh year of the reign of the Judges over the people of Nephi, on the fifth day of the second month, there having been much peace in the land of Zarahemla; there having been no wars nor contentions for a certain number of years; even until the fifth day of the second month, in the eleventh year, there was a cry of war heard throughout the land;

2 For behold, the armies of the Lamanites had come in upon the wilderness side, into the borders of the land, even into the city of Ammonihah, and began to slay the people, and to destroy the city.

3 ¶And now it came to pass before the Nephites could raise a sufficient army to drive them out of the land, they had destroyed the people who were in the city of Ammonihah, and also some around the borders of Noah, and taking others captive into the wilderness.

4 ¶Now it came to pass that the Nephites were desirous to obtain those who had been carried away captive into the wilderness;

5 Therefore he that had been appointed chief captain over the armies of the Nephites, (and his name was Zoram, and he had two sons, Lehi and Aha):

6 Now Zoram and his two sons, knowing that Alma was high priest over the church, and having heard that he had the spirit of prophecy,

7 Therefore they went unto him and desired of him to know whether the Lord would that they should go into the wilderness in search of their brethren, who had been taken captive by the Lamanites.

8 ¶And it came to pass that Alma inquired of the Lord concerning the matter.

9 And Alma returned and said unto them, Behold, the Lamanites will cross the river Sidon, in the south wilderness, away up beyond the borders of the land of Manti.

10 And behold there shall ye meet them, on the east of the river Sidon, and there the Lord will deliver unto thee

thy brethren who have been taken captive by the Lamanites.

11 ¶And it came to pass that Zoram and his sons crossed over the river Sidon with their armies, and marched away beyond the borders of Manti, into the south wilderness, which was on the east side of the river Sidon.

12 And they came upon the armies of the Lamanites, and the Lamanites were scattered and driven into the wilderness; that they took their brethren who had been taken captive by the Lamanites, and there was not one soul of them who had been lost, that were taken captive.

13 And they were brought by their brethren to possess their own lands.

14 And thus ended the eleventh year of the Judges, the Lamanites having been driven out of the land, and the people of Ammonihah were destroyed;

15 Yea, every living soul of the Ammonihahites were destroyed, and also their great city, which they said God could not destroy, because of its greatness.

16 But behold, in one day it was left desolate; and the carcasses were mangled by dogs and wild beasts of the wilderness;

17 Nevertheless, after many days, their dead bodies were heaped up upon the face of the earth, and they were covered with a shallow covering.

18 And now so great was the scent thereof, that the people did not go in to possess the land of Ammonihah for many years.

19 And it was called Desolation of Nehors; for they were of the profession of Nehor, who were slain; and their lands remained desolate.

20 And the Lamanites did not come again to war against the Nephites until the fourteenth year of the reign of the Judges over the people of Nephi.

21 And thus for three years did the people of Nephi have continual peace in all the land.

22 ¶And Alma and Amulek went forth preaching repentance to the people in their temples, and in their sanctuaries,

and also in their synagogues, which were built after the manner of the Jews.

23 And as many as would hear their words, unto them they did impart the word of God, without any respect of persons, continually.

24 And thus did Alma and Amulek go forth, and also many more who had been chosen for the work, to preach the word throughout all the land.

25 And the establishment of the church became general throughout the land, in all the region round about, among all the people of the Nephites.

26 ¶And there was no inequality among them, for the Lord did pour out his Spirit on all the face of the land, to prepare the minds of the children of men, or to prepare their hearts to receive the word which should be taught among them at the time of his coming,

27 That they might not be hardened against the word, that they might not be unbelieving, and go on to destruction,

28 But that they might receive the word with joy, and as a branch be grafted into the true vine, that they might enter into the rest of the Lord their God.

29 ¶Now those priests who did go forth among the people, did preach against all lyings, and deceivings, and envyings, and strifes, and malice, and revilings, and stealing, robbing, plundering, murdering, committing adultery, and all manner of lasciviousness, crying that these things ought not so to be;

30 Holding forth things which must shortly come; yea, holding forth the coming of the Son of God, his sufferings and death, and also the resurrection of the dead.

31 And many of the people did inquire concerning the place where the Son of God should come; and they were taught that he would appear unto them after his resurrection; and this the people did hear with great joy and gladness.

32 And now after the church having been established throughout all the land, having got the victory over the devil, and the word of God being preached in its purity in all the

land; and the Lord pouring out his blessings upon the people;

33 Thus ended the fourteenth year of the reign of the Judges, over the people of Nephi.

CHAPTER 12.

An account of the sons of Mosiah, who rejected their rights to the kingdom, for the word of God, and went up to the land of Nephi, to preach to the Lamanites. Their sufferings and deliverance, according to the record of Alma.

1 ¶And now it came to pass that as Alma was journeying from the land of Gideon, southward, away to the land of Manti, behold, to his astonishment, he met the sons of Mosiah, journeying towards the land of Zarahemla.

2 Now these sons of Mosiah were with Alma at the time the angel first appeared unto him; therefore Alma did rejoice exceedingly, to see his brethren;

3 And what added more to his joy, they were still his brethren in the Lord; yea, and they had waxed strong in the knowledge of the truth;

4 For they were men of a sound understanding, and they had searched the scriptures diligently, that they might know the word of God.

5 But this is not all: they had given themselves to much prayer, and fasting, therefore they had the spirit of prophecy, and the spirit of revelation, and when they taught, they taught with power and authority, even as with the power and authority of God.

6 And they had been teaching the word of God for the space of fourteen years, among the Lamanites, having had much success in bringing many to the knowledge of the truth;

7 Yea, by the power of their words, many were brought before the altar of God, to call on his name, and confess their sins before him.

8 Now these are the circumstances which attended them in their journeyings, for they had many afflictions;

9 They did suffer much, both in body and in mind; such as hunger, thirst, and fatigue, and also much labor in the spirit.

10 Now these were their journeyings: Having taken leave of their father Mosiah, in the first year of the reign of the Judges; having refused the kingdom which their father was desirous to confer upon them; and also this was the mind of the people;

11 Nevertheless they departed out of the land of Zarahemla, and took their swords, and their spears, and their bows, and their arrows, and their slings;

12 And this they did that they might provide food for themselves while in the wilderness:

13 And thus they departed into the wilderness, with their numbers which they had selected, to go up to the land of Nephi, to preach the word of God unto the Lamanites.

14 ¶And it came to pass that they journeyed many days in the wilderness, and they fasted much, and prayed much, that the Lord would grant unto them a portion of his Spirit to go with them, and abide with them,

15 That they might be an instrument in the hands of God, to bring, if it were possible, their brethren, the Lamanites, to the knowledge of the truth;

16 To the knowledge of the baseness of the traditions of their fathers, which were not correct.

17 ¶And it came to pass that the Lord did visit them with his Spirit, and said unto them, Be comforted; and they were comforted.

18 And the Lord said unto them also, Go forth among the Lamanites, thy brethren, and establish my word;

19 Yet ye shall be patient in long suffering and afflictions, that ye may shew forth good examples unto them in me, and I will make an instrument of thee in my hands, unto the salvation of many souls.

20 ¶And it came to pass that the hearts of the sons of Mosiah, and also those who were with them, took courage to go forth unto the Lamanites, to declare unto them the word of God.

21 ¶And it came to pass when they had arrived in the borders of the land of the Lamanites, that they separated themselves, and departed one from another, trusting in the

Lord, that they should meet again at the close of their harvest: for they supposed that great was the work which they had undertaken.

22 And assuredly it was great, for they had undertaken to preach the word of God to a wild, and a hardened, and a ferocious people; a people who delighted in murdering the Nephites, and robbing, and plundering them;

23 And their hearts were set upon riches, or upon gold, and silver, and precious stones;

24 Yet they sought to obtain these things by murdering and plundering, that they might not labor for them with their own hands:

25 Thus they were a very indolent people, many of whom did worship idols, and the curse of God had fallen upon them because of the traditions of their fathers; notwithstanding, the promises of the Lord were extended unto them, on the conditions of repentance;

26 Therefore this was the cause for which the sons of Mosiah had undertaken the work, that perhaps they might bring them unto repentance; that perhaps they might bring them to know of the plan of redemption:

27 Therefore they separated themselves one from another, and went forth among them, every man alone, according to the word and power of God, which was given unto him.

28 ¶Now Ammon being the chief among them, or rather he did minister unto them; and he departed from them, after having blessed them according to their several stations, having imparted the word of God unto them, or administered unto them before his departure: and thus they took their several journeys throughout the land.

29 And Ammon went to the land of Ishmael, the land being called after the sons of Ishmael, who also became Lamanites.

30 And as Ammon entered the land of Ishmael, the Lamanites took him and bound him, as was their custom, to bind all the Nephites who fell into their hands, and carry them before the king;

31 And thus it was left to the pleasure of the king to slay them, or to retain them in captivity, or to cast them into

prison, or to cast them out of his land, according to his will and pleasure;

32 And thus Ammon was carried before the king who was over the land of Ishmael; and his name was Lamoni; and he was a descendant of Ishmael.

33 And the king inquired of Ammon if it were his desire to dwell in the land among the Lamanites, or among his people?

34 And Ammon said unto him, Yea, I desire to dwell among this people for a time; yea, and perhaps until the day I die.

35 ¶And it came to pass that King Lamoni was much pleased with Ammon, and caused that his bands should be loosed; and he would that Ammon should take one of his daughters to wife.

36 But Ammon said unto him, Nay, but I will be thy servant; therefore Ammon became a servant to King Lamoni.

37 And it came to pass that he was set, among other servants, to watch the flocks of Lamoni, according to the custom of the Lamanites.

38 And after he had been in the service of the king three days, as he was with the Lamanitish servants, going forth with their flocks to the place of water, which was called the water of Sebus; (and all the Lamanites drive their flocks hither, that they may have water;)

39 Therefore as Ammon and the servants of the king were driving forth their flocks to this place of water, behold a certain number of the Lamanites who had been with their flocks to water, stood and scattered the flocks of Ammon, and the servants of the king, and they scattered them insomuch that they fled many ways.

40 ¶Now the servants of the king began to murmur, saying, Now the king will slay us, as he has our brethren, because their flocks were scattered by the wickedness of these men.

41 And they began to weep exceedingly, saying, Behold our flocks are scattered already.

42 Now they wept because of the fear of being slain.

43 Now when Ammon saw this, his heart was swollen

within him, with joy; for, said he, I will shew forth my power unto these my fellow servants, or the power which is in me, in restoring these flocks unto the king, that I may win the hearts of these my fellow servants, that I may lead them to believe in my words.

44 Now these were the thoughts of Ammon, when he saw the afflictions of those whom he termed to be his brethren.

45 ¶And it came to pass that he flattered them by his words, saying, My brethren be of good cheer and let us go in search of the flocks, and we will gather them together, and bring them back unto the place of water;

46 And thus we will reserve the flocks unto the king, and he will not slay us.

47 ¶And it came to pass that they went in search of the flocks, and they did follow Ammon, and they rushed forth with much swiftness, and did head the flocks of the king, and did gather them together again, to the place of water.

48 And those men again stood to scatter their flocks; but Ammon said unto his brethren, Encircle the flocks round about that they flee not: and I go and contend with these men who do scatter our flocks.

49 Therefore they did as Ammon commanded them, and he went forth and stood to contend with those who stood by the waters of Sebus;

50 And they were in number not a few; therefore they did not fear Ammon, for they supposed that one of their men could slay him, according to their pleasure, for they knew not that the Lord had promised Mosiah that he would deliver his sons out of their hands; neither did they know anything concerning the Lord;

51 Therefore they delighted in the destruction of their brethren; and for this cause they stood to scatter the flocks of the king.

52 ¶But Ammon stood forth and began to cast stones at them with his sling; yea, with mighty power he did sling stones amongst them;

53 And thus he slew a certain number of them, insomuch that they began to be astonished at his power;

54 Nevertheless they were angry because of the slain of their brethren, and they were determined that he should fall;

55 Therefore, seeing that they could not hit him with their stones, they came forth with clubs to slay him.

56 But behold, every man that lifted his club to smite Ammon, he smote off their arms with his sword;

57 For he did withstand their blows by smiting their arms with the edge of his sword, insomuch that they began to be astonished, and began to flee before him;

58 Yea, and they were not few in number: and he caused them to flee by the strength of his arm.

59 Now six of them had fallen by the sling, but he slew none save it were their leader, with his sword; and he smote off as many of their arms as were lifted against him, and they were not a few.

60 And when he had driven them afar off, he returned, and they watered their flocks and returned them to the pasture of the king, and then went in unto the king, bearing the arms which had been smote off by the sword of Ammon, of those who sought to slay him;

61 And they were carried in unto the king, for a testimony of the things which they had done.

62 ¶And it came to pass that King Lamoni caused that his servants should stand forth and testify to all the things which they had seen, concerning the matter.

63 And when they had all testified to the things which they had seen, and he had learned of the faithfulness of Ammon in preserving his flocks, and also of his great power in contending against those who sought to slay him, he was astonished exceedingly, and said, Surely this is more than a man.

64 Behold, is not this the Great Spirit who doth send such great punishments upon this people, because of their murders?

65 And they answered the king, and said, Whether he be the Great Spirit or a man, we know not, but this much we do know, that he can not be slain by the enemies of the king;

66 Neither can they scatter the king's flock when he is with

us, because of his expertness and great strength; therefore, we know that he is a friend to the king.

67 And now, O king, we do not believe that a man has such great power, for we know that he can not be slain.

68 And now when the king heard these words, he said unto them, Now I know that it is the Great Spirit; and he has come down at this time to preserve your lives, that I might not slay you as I did your brethren.

69 Now this is the Great Spirit of whom our fathers have spoken.

70 Now this was the tradition of Lamoni, which he had received from his father, that there was a Great Spirit.

71 Notwithstanding they believed in a Great Spirit, they supposed that whatsoever they did, was right;

72 Nevertheless Lamoni began to fear exceedingly, with fear lest he had done wrong in slaying his servants;

73 For he had slain many of them, because their brethren had scattered their flocks at the place of water; and thus because they had had their flocks scattered, they were slain.

74 Now it was the practice of the Lamanites to stand by the waters of Sebus, to scatter the flocks of the people, that thereby they might drive away many that were scattered unto their own land, it being a practice of plunder among them.

75 ¶And it came to pass that King Lamoni inquired of his servants, saying, Where is this man that has such great power?

76 And they said unto him, Behold, he is feeding thy horses.

77 Now the king had commanded his servants previous to the time of the watering of their flocks, that they should prepare his horses and chariots, and conduct him forth to the land of Nephi:

78 For there had been a great feast appointed at the land of Nephi, by the father of Lamoni, who was king over all the land.

79 Now when King Lamoni heard that Ammon was preparing his horses and his chariots, he was more astonished, because of the faithfulness of Ammon, saying,

80 Surely, there has not been any servant among all my

servants, that has been so faithful as this man; for even he doth remember all my commandments to execute them.

81 Now I surely know that this is the Great Spirit; and I would desire him that he come in unto me, but I durst not.

82 ¶And it came to pass that when Ammon had made ready the horses and the chariots for the king and his servants, he went in unto the king, and he saw that the countenance of the king was changed; therefore he was about to return out of his presence;

83 And one of the king's servants said unto him, Rabbanah, which is, being interpreted, powerful or great king, considering their kings to be powerful:

84 And thus he said unto him, Rabbanah, the king desireth thee to stay;

85 Therefore Ammon turned himself unto the king, and said unto him, What wilt thou that I should do for thee, O king!

86 And the king answered him not for the space of an hour, according to their time, for he knew not what he should say unto him.

87 And it came to pass that Ammon said unto him again, What desirest thou of me? But the king answered him not.

88 ¶And it came to pass that Ammon, being filled with the Spirit of God, therefore he perceived the thoughts of the king.

89 And he said unto him, Is it because thou hast heard that I defended thy servants and thy flocks, and slew seven of their brethren with the sling, and with the sword, and smote off the arms of others, in order to defend thy flocks and thy servants: behold, is it this that causeth thy marvelings?

90 I say unto you, What is it, that thy marvelings are so great?

91 Behold, I am a man, and am thy servant; therefore, whatsoever thou desirest which is right, that will I do.

92 Now when the king had heard these words, he marveled again, for he beheld that Ammon could discern his thoughts;

93 But notwithstanding this, King Lamoni did open his mouth; and said unto him, Who art thou? Art thou that Great Spirit who knows all things?

94 Ammon answered and said unto him, I am not.

95 And the king said, How knowest thou the thoughts of my heart?

96 Thou mayest speak boldly, and tell me concerning these things; and also tell me by what power ye slew and smote off the arms of my brethren, that scattered my flocks.

97 And now if thou wilt tell me concerning these things, whatsoever thou desirest, I will give unto thee:

98 And if it were needed, I would guard thee with my armies; but I know that thou art more powerful than all they: nevertheless, whatsoever thou desirest of me, I will grant it unto thee.

99 Now Ammon being wise, yet harmless, he said unto Lamoni, Wilt thou hearken unto my words, if I tell thee by what power I do these things? And this is the thing that I desire of thee.

100 And the king answered him and said, Yea, I will believe all thy words; and thus he was caught with guile.

101 And Ammon began to speak unto him with boldness, and said unto him, Believest thou that there is a God?

102 And he answered, and said unto him, I do not know what that meaneth.

103 And then Ammon said, Believest thou that there is a Great Spirit?

104 And he said, Yea.

105 And Ammon said, This is God.

106 And Ammon said unto him again, Believest thou that this Great Spirit, who is God, created all things, which are in heaven and in the earth?

107 And he said, Yea, I believe that he created all things which are in the earth; but I do not know the heavens.

108 And Ammon said unto him, The heavens is a place where God dwells, and all his holy angels.

109 And King Lamoni said, Is it above the earth?

110 And Ammon said, Yea, and he looketh down upon all the children of men: and he knows all the thoughts and intents of the heart: for by his hand were they all created from the beginning.

111 And King Lamoni said, I believe all these things which thou hast spoken. Art thou sent from God?

112 Ammon said unto him, I am a man; and man in the beginning, was created after the image of God, and I am called by his Holy Spirit to teach these things unto this people, that they may be brought to a knowledge of that which is just and true;

113 And a portion of that Spirit dwelleth in me, which giveth me knowledge, and also power, according to my faith and desires which are in God.

114 Now when Ammon had said these words, he began to the creation of the world, and also the creation of Adam, and told him all the things concerning the fall of man,

115 And rehearsed and laid before him the records and the holy scriptures of the people, which had been spoken by the prophets, even down to the time that their father Lehi left Jerusalem;

116 And he also rehearsed unto them, (for it was unto the king and to his servants,) all the journeyings of their fathers in the wilderness, and all their sufferings with hunger and thirst, and their travel, etc.:

117 And he also rehearsed unto them concerning the rebellions of Laman and Lemuel, and the sons of Ishmael, yea, all their rebellions did he relate unto them;

118 And he expounded unto them all the records and scriptures, from the time that Lehi left Jerusalem, down to the present time;

119 But this is not all; for he expounded unto them the plan of redemption, which was prepared from the foundation of the world;

120 And he also made known unto them concerning the coming of Christ; and all the works of the Lord did he make known unto them.

121 ¶And it came to pass that after he had said all these things, and expounded them to the king, that the king believed all his words.

122 And he began to cry unto the Lord, saying: O Lord

have mercy; according to thy abundant mercy which thou hast had upon the people of Nephi, have upon me and my people.

123 And now when he had said this, he fell unto the earth, as if he were dead.

124 And it came to pass that his servants took him and carried him in unto his wife, and laid him upon a bed; and he lay as if he were dead, for the space of two days and two nights;

125 And his wife, and his sons, and his daughters mourned over him, after the manner of the Lamanites, greatly lamenting his loss.

126 ¶And it came to pass that after two days and two nights, they were about to take his body and lay it in a sepulcher which they had made for the purpose of burying their dead.

127 Now the queen having heard of the fame of Ammon, therefore she sent and desired that he should come in unto her.

128 And it came to pass that Ammon did as he was commanded, and went in unto the queen, and desired to know what she would that he should do.

129 And she said unto him, The servants of my husband have made it known unto me, that thou art a prophet of a holy God, and that thou hast power to do many mighty works in his name;

130 Therefore, if this is the case, I would that ye should go in and see my husband, for he has been laid upon his bed for the space of two days and two nights;

131 And some say that he is not dead, but others say that he is dead, and that he stinketh, and that he ought to be placed in a sepulcher; but as for myself, to me he doth not stink.

132 Now this was what Ammon desired, for he knew that King Lamoni was under the power of God;

133 He knew that the dark veil of unbelief being cast away from his mind, and the light which did light up his mind, which was the light of the glory of God, which was a marvelous light of his goodness;

134 Yea, this light had infused such joy into his soul, the cloud of darkness having been dispelled, and that the light of everlasting light was lit up in his soul;

135 Yea, he knew that this had overcome his natural frame, and he was carried away in God; therefore, what the queen desired of him, was his only desire.

136 Therefore he went in to see the king, according as the queen had desired him; and he saw the king, and he knew that he was not dead.

137 And he said unto the queen, He is not dead, but he sleepeth in God, and on the morrow he shall rise again; therefore bury him not.

138 And Ammon said unto her, Believest thou this?

139 And she said unto him, I have had no witness, save thy word, and the word of our servants; nevertheless, I believe that it shall be according as thou hast said.

140 And Ammon said unto her, Blessed art thou, because of thy exceeding faith; I say unto thee, woman, there has not been such great faith among all the people of the Nephites.

141 ¶And it came to pass that she watched over the bed of her husband, from that time, even until that time on the morrow which Ammon had appointed that he should rise.

142 And it came to pass that he arose, according to the words of Ammon; and as he arose, he stretched forth his hand unto the woman, and said, Blessed be the name of God, and blessed art thou;

143 For as sure as thou livest, behold, I have seen my Redeemer; and he shall come forth and be born of a woman, and he shall redeem all mankind who believe on his name.

144 Now when he had said these words, his heart was swollen within him, and he sunk again with joy: and the queen also sunk down, being overpowered by the Spirit.

145 Now Ammon seeing the Spirit of the Lord poured out according to his prayers upon the Lamanites, his brethren; who had been the cause of so much mourning among the Nephites, or among all the people of God, because of their iniquities and their traditions,

146 He fell upon his knees, and began to pour out his soul in prayer and thanksgiving to God, for what he had done for his brethren:

147 And he was also overpowered with joy; and thus they all three had sunk to the earth.

148 Now when the servants of the king had seen that they had fallen, they also began to cry unto God, for the fear of the Lord had come upon them also,

149 For it was they who had stood before the king, and testified unto him concerning the great power of Ammon.

150 ¶And it came to pass that they did call on the name of the Lord, in their might, even till they had all fallen to the earth, save it were one of the Lamanitish women, whose name was Abish, she having been converted unto the Lord for many years, on account of a remarkable vision of her father; thus having been converted to the Lord, never had made it known;

151 Therefore when she saw that all the servants of Lamoni had fallen to the earth, and also her mistress, the queen, and the king, and Ammon lay prostrate upon the earth, she knew that it was the power of God;

152 And supposing that this opportunity, by making known unto the people what had happened among them, that by beholding this scene, it would cause them to believe in the power of God,

153 Therefore she ran forth from house to house, making it known unto the people; and they began to assemble themselves together unto the house of the king.

154 And there came a multitude, and to their astonishment, they beheld the king, and the queen, and their servants, prostrate upon the earth, and they all lay there as though they were dead;

155 And they also saw Ammon, and behold he was a Nephite.

156 And now the people began to murmur among themselves; some saying, that it was a great evil that had come upon them, or upon the king and his house, because he had suffered that the Nephite should remain in the land.

157 But others rebuked them, saying, The king hath brought this evil upon his house, because he slew his servants who had had their flocks scattered at the waters of Sebus:

158 And they were also rebuked by those men who had stood at the waters of Sebus, and scattered the flocks which belonged to the king,

159 For they were angry with Ammon because of the number which he had slain of their brethren at the waters of Sebus, while defending the flocks of the king.

160 Now one of them, whose brother had been slain with the sword of Ammon, being exceeding angry with Ammon, drew his sword and went forth that he might let it fall upon Ammon, to slay him; and as he lifted the sword to smite him, behold he fell dead.

161 Now we see that Ammon could not be slain, for the Lord had said unto Mosiah, his father, I will spare him, and it shall be unto him according to thy faith; therefore Mosiah trusted him unto the Lord.

162 ¶And it came to pass that when the multitude beheld that the man had fallen dead, who lifted the sword to slay Ammon, fear came upon them all, and they durst not put forth their hands to touch him, or any of those who had fallen;

163 And they began to marvel again among themselves what could be the cause of this great power, or what all these things could mean.

164 ¶And it came to pass that there were many among them, who said that Ammon was the Great Spirit, and others said he was sent by the Great Spirit;

165 But others rebuked them all, saying, that he was a monster, who had been sent from the Nephites to torment us;

166 And there were some who said that Ammon was sent by the Great Spirit to afflict them, because of their iniquities; and that it was the Great Spirit that had always attended the Nephites; who had ever delivered them out of their hands;

167 And they said that it was this Great Spirit who had destroyed so many of their brethren, the Lamanites; and thus the contention began to be exceeding sharp among them.

168 And while they were thus contending, the woman serv-

ant who had caused the multitude to be gathered together, came; and when she saw the contention which was among the multitude, she was exceeding sorrowful, even unto tears.

169 ¶And it came to pass that she went and took the queen by the hand, that perhaps she might raise her from the ground: and as soon as she touched her hand, she arose and stood upon her feet, and cried with a loud voice, saying,

170 O blessed Jesus, who has saved me from an awful hell! O blessed God, have mercy upon this people.

171 And when she had said this, she clapped her hands, being filled with joy, speaking many words which were not understood;

172 And when she had done this, she took the king, Lamoni, by the hand, and behold he arose and stood upon his feet;

173 And he immediately, seeing the contention among his people, went forth and began to rebuke them, and to teach them the words which he had heard from the mouth of Ammon; and as many as heard his words, believed, and were converted unto the Lord.

174 But there were many among them who would not hear his words; therefore they went their way.

175 ¶And it came to pass that when Ammon arose, he also administered unto them, and also did all the servants of Lamoni;

176 And they did all declare unto the people the self-same thing; that their hearts had been changed; that they had no more desire to do evil.

177 And behold, many did declare unto the people that they had seen angels, and had conversed with them; and thus they had told them things of God, and of his righteousness.

178 And it came to pass that there were many that did believe in their words: and as many as did believe, were baptized; and they became a righteous people, and they did establish a church among them;

179 And thus the work of the Lord did commence among

the Lamanites; thus the Lord did begin to pour out his Spirit upon them;

180 And we see that his arm is extended to all people who will repent and believe on his name.

181 ¶And it came to pass that when they had established a church in that land, that King Lamoni desired that Ammon should go with him to the land of Nephi, that he might shew him unto his father.

182 And the voice of the Lord came to Ammon, saying, Thou shalt not go up to the land of Nephi, for behold the king will seek thy life; but thou shalt go to the land of Middoni; for behold, thy brother Aaron, and also Muloki and Ammah are in prison.

183 ¶Now it came to pass that when Ammon had heard this, he said unto Lamoni, Behold, my brother and brethren are in prison at Middoni, and I go that I may deliver them.

184 Now Lamoni said unto Ammon, I know, in the strength of the Lord, thou canst do all things. But behold, I will go with thee to the land of Middoni, for the king of the land of Middoni, whose name is Antiomno, is a friend unto me;

185 Therefore I go to the land of Middoni, that I may flatter the king of the land; and he will cast thy brethren out of prison.

186 Now Lamoni said unto him, Who told thee that thy brethren were in prison?

187 And Ammon said unto him, No one hath told me, save it be God; and he said unto me, Go and deliver thy brethren, for they are in prison in the land of Middoni.

188 Now when Lamoni had heard this, he caused that his servants should make ready his horses, and his chariots.

189 And he said unto Ammon, Come, I will go with thee down to the land of Middoni, and there I will plead with the king, that he will cast thy brethren out of prison.

190 ¶And it came to pass that as Ammon and Lamoni were journeying thither, that they met the father of Lamoni, who was king over all the land.

191 And behold, the father of Lamoni said unto him, Why

did ye not come to the feast, on that great day when I made a feast unto my sons, and unto my people?

192 And he also said, Whither art thou going with this Nephite, who is one of the children of a liar?

193 And it came to pass that Lamoni rehearsed unto him whither he was going, for he feared to offend him.

194 And he also told him all the cause of his tarrying in his own kingdom, that he did not go unto his father, to the feast which he had prepared.

195 And now when Lamoni had rehearsed unto him all these things, behold to his astonishment his father was angry with him, and said, Lamoni, thou art going to deliver these Nephites, who are sons of a liar.

196 Behold, he robbed our fathers; and now his children are also come amongst us, that they may, by their cunning and their lyings, deceive us, that they again may rob us of our property.

197 Now the father of Lamoni commanded him that he should slay Ammon, with the sword.

198 And he also commanded him that he should not go to the land of Middoni, but that he should return with him, to the land of Ishmael.

199 But Lamoni said unto him, I will not slay Ammon, neither will I return to the land of Ishmael, but I go to the land of Middoni, that I may release the brethren of Ammon, for I know that they are just men, and holy prophets of the true God.

200 Now when his father had heard these words, he was angry with him, and he drew his sword that he might smite him to the earth.

201 But Ammon stood forth and said unto him, Behold thou shalt not slay thy son; nevertheless, it were better that he should fall than thee:

202 For behold he has repented of his sins; but if thou shouldst fall at this time, in thine anger, thy soul could not be saved.

203 And again, it is expedient that thou shouldst forbear; for if thou shouldst slay thy son, (he being an innocent man,)

[CHAP. 12.] BOOK OF ALMA. 379

his blood would cry from the ground, to the Lord his God, for vengeance to come upon thee; and perhaps thou wouldst lose thy soul.

204 Now when Ammon had said these words unto him, he answered him saying, I know that if I should slay my son, that I should shed innocent blood; for it is thou that hast sought to destroy him: and he stretched forth his hand to slay Ammon.

205 But Ammon withstood his blows, and also smote his arm that he could not use it.

206 Now when the king saw that Ammon could slay him, he began to plead with Ammon, that he would spare his life.

207 But Ammon raised his sword, and said unto him, Behold, I will smite thee, except thou wilt grant unto me that my brethren may be cast out of prison.

208 Now the king, fearing that he should lose his life, said, If thou wilt spare me, I will grant unto thee whatsoever thou wilt ask, even to the half of the kingdom.

209 ¶Now when Ammon saw that he had wrought upon the old king according to his desire, he said unto him, If thou wilt grant that my brethren may be cast out of prison, and also that Lamoni may retain his kingdom, and that ye be not displeased with him, but grant that he may do according to his own desires, in whatsoever thing he thinketh, then will I spare thee; otherwise I will smite thee to the earth.

210 Now when Ammon had said these words, the king began to rejoice because of his life.

211 And when he saw that Ammon had no desire to destroy him, and when he also saw the great love he had for his son, Lamoni, he was astonished exceedingly, and said,

212 Because this is all that thou hast desired, that I would release thy brethren, and suffer that my son Lamoni should retain his kingdom, behold, I will grant unto you that my son may retain his kingdom from this time and for ever; and I will govern him no more.

213 And I will also grant unto thee that thy brethren may be cast out of prison, and thou and thy brethren may come

unto me, in my kingdom; for I shall greatly desire to see thee:

214 For the king was greatly astonished at the words which he had spoken, and also at the words which had been spoken by his son Lamoni; therefore he was desirous to learn them.

215 ¶And it came to pass that Ammon and Lamoni proceeded on their journey towards the land of Middoni.

216 And Lamoni found favor in the eyes of the king of the land; therefore the brethren of Ammon were brought forth out of prison.

217 And when Ammon did meet them, he was exceeding sorrowful, for behold, they were naked, and their skins were worn exceedingly, because of being bound with strong cords.

218 And they also had suffered hunger, thirst, and all kind of affliction; nevertheless they were patient in all their sufferings.

219 And as it happened, it was their lot to have fallen into the hands of a more hardened and a more stiff-necked people;

220 Therefore they would not hearken unto their words, and they had cast them out, and had smitten them, and had driven them from house to house, and from place to place, even until they had arrived to the land of Middoni;

221 And there they were taken and cast into prison, and bound with strong cords, and kept in prison for many days; and were delivered by Lamoni and Ammon.

CHAPTER 13.

An account of the preaching of Aaron and Muloki, and their brethren, to the Lamanites.

1 ¶Now when Ammon and his brethren separated themselves in the borders of the land of the Lamanites, behold, Aaron took his journey towards the land which was called by the Lamanites, Jerusalem; calling it after the land of their fathers' nativity; and it was away joining the borders of Mormon.

2 Now the Lamanites, and the Amalekites, and the people of Amulon, had built a great city, which was called Jerusalem.

3 Now the Lamanites, of themselves, were sufficiently hardened, but the Amalekites, and the Amulonites, were still harder; therefore they did cause the Lamanites that they should harden their hearts, that they should wax strong in wickedness, and their abominations.

4 ¶And it came to pass that Aaron came to the city of Jerusalem, and firstly began to preach to the Amalekites.

5 And he began to preach to them in their synagogues, for they had built synagogues after the order of the Nehors; for many of the Amalekites and the Amulonites were after the order of the Nehors.

6 Therefore, as Aaron entered into one of their synagogues to preach unto the people, and as he was speaking unto them, behold there arose an Amalekite, and began to contend with him, saying,

7 What is that thou hast testified? Hast thou seen an angel? Why do not angels appear unto us? Behold, are not this people as good as thy people? Thou also sayest, except we repent, we shall perish.

8 How knowest thou the thought and intent of our heart? How knowest thou that we have cause to repent? How knowest thou that we are not a righteous people?

9 Behold, we have built sanctuaries, and we do assemble ourselves together to worship God. We do believe that God will save all men.

10 ¶Now Aaron said unto him, Believest thou that the Son of God shall come to redeem mankind from their sins?

11 And the man said unto him, We do not believe that thou knowest any such thing. We do not believe in these foolish traditions.

12 We do not believe that thou knowest of things to come, neither do we believe that thy fathers, and also that our fathers did know concerning the things which they spake, of that which is to come.

13 ¶Now Aaron began to open the scriptures unto them,

concerning the coming of Christ, and also concerning the resurrection of the dead, and that there could be no redemption for mankind, save it were through the death and sufferings of Christ, and the atonement of his blood.

14 And it came to pass as he began to expound these things unto them, they were angry with him, and began to mock him; and they would not hear the words which he spake;

15 Therefore, when he saw that they would not hear his words, he departed out of their synagogue, and came over to a village which was called Ani-anti, and there he found Muloki preaching the word unto them; and also Ammah, and his brethren. And they contended with many about the word.

16 And it came to pass that they saw that the people would harden their hearts; therefore they departed, and came over into the land of Middoni.

17 And they did preach the word unto many, and few believed on the words which they taught.

18 Nevertheless, Aaron, and a certain number of his brethren, were taken and cast into prison, and the remainder of them fled out of the land of Middoni, unto the regions round about.

19 And those who were cast into prison suffered many things, and they were delivered by the hand of Lamoni and Ammon: and they were fed and clothed.

20 And they went forth again to declare the word; and thus they were delivered for the first time out of prison; and thus they had suffered.

21 And they went forth whithersoever they were led by the Spirit of the Lord, preaching the word of God in every synagogue of the Amalekites, or in every assembly of the Lamanites where they could be admitted.

22 ¶And it came to pass that the Lord began to bless them, insomuch that they brought many to the knowledge of the truth; yea, they did convince many of their sins, and of the tradition of their fathers, which were not correct.

23 ¶And it came to pass that Ammon and Lamoni returned from the land of Middoni, to the land of Ishmael, which was the land of their inheritance.

24 And King Lamoni would not suffer that Ammon should serve him, or be his servant; but he caused that there should be synagogues built in the land of Ishmael; and he caused that his people, or the people who were under his reign, should assemble themselves together.

25 And he did rejoice over them, and he did teach them many things.

26 And he did also declare unto them that they were a people who were under him, and that they were a free people; that they were free from the oppressions of the king, his father; for that his father had granted unto him that he might reign over the people who were in the land of Ishmael, and in all the land round about.

27 And he also declared unto them that they might have the liberty of worshiping the Lord their God, according to their desires, in whatsoever place they were in, if it were in the land which was under the reign of King Lamoni.

28 And Ammon did preach unto the people of King Lamoni. And it came to pass that he did teach them all things concerning things pertaining to righteousness.

29 And he did exhort them daily, with all diligence; and they gave heed unto his word, and they were zealous for keeping the commandments of God.

30 Now as Ammon was thus teaching the people of Lamoni continually, we will return to the account of Aaron and his other brethren;

31 For after he departed from the land of Middoni, he was led by the Spirit to the land of Nephi; even to the house of the king which was over all the land, save it were the land of Ishmael: and he was the father of Lamoni.

32 ¶And it came to pass that he went in unto him into the king's palace, with his brethren, and bowed himself before the king, and said unto him, Behold, O king, we are the brethren of Ammon, whom thou hast delivered out of prison. And now, O king, if thou wilt spare our lives, we will be thy servants.

33 And the king said unto them, Arise for I will grant unto you your lives, and I will not suffer that ye shall be my

servants; but I will insist that ye shall administer unto me;

34 For I have been somewhat troubled in mind, because of the generosity, and the greatness of the words of thy brother Ammon; and I desire to know the cause why he has not come up out of Middoni with thee.

35 And Aaron said unto the king, Behold the Spirit of the Lord has called him another way; he has gone to the land of Ishmael, to teach the people of Lamoni.

36 Now the king said unto them, What is this that ye have said concerning the Spirit of the Lord? Behold, this is the thing which doth trouble me.

37 And also, what is this that Ammon said: If ye will repent ye shall be saved, and if ye will not repent, ye shall be cast off at the last day?

38 And Aaron answered him and said unto him, Believest thou that there is a God?

39 And the king said, I know that the Amalekites say that there is a God, and I have granted unto them that they should build sanctuaries, that they may assemble themselves together, to worship him. And if now thou sayest there is a God, behold, I will believe.

40 ¶And now when Aaron heard this, his heart began to rejoice, and he said, Behold, assuredly, as thou livest, O king, there is a God.

41 And the king said, Is God that Great Spirit that brought our fathers out of the land of Jerusalem?

42 And Aaron said unto him, Yea, he is that Great Spirit, and he created all things, both in heaven and in earth: believest thou this?

43 And he said, Yea, I believe that the Great Spirit created all things, and I desire that ye should tell me concerning all these things, and I will believe thy words.

44 ¶And it came to pass that when Aaron saw that the king would believe his words, he began from the creation of Adam, reading the scriptures unto the king; how God created man after his own image, and that God gave him commandments, and that because of transgression, man had fallen.

45 And Aaron did expound unto him the scriptures, from

the creation of Adam, laying the fall of man before him, and their carnal state, and also the plan of redemption, which was prepared from the foundation of the world, through Christ, for all whosoever would believe on his name.

46 And since man had fallen, he could not merit anything of himself; but the sufferings and death of Christ atoneth for their sins, through faith and repentance, etc.:

47 And that he breaketh the bands of death, that the grave shall have no victory, and that the sting of death should be swallowed up in the hopes of glory: and Aaron did expound all these things unto the king.

48 And it came to pass that after Aaron had expounded these things unto him, the king said, What shall I do, that I may have this eternal life of which thou hast spoken?

49 Yea, what shall I do that I may be born of God, having this wicked spirit rooted out of my breast, and receive his Spirit, that I may be filled with joy, that I may not be cast off at the last day?

50 Behold, said he, I will give up all that I possess; yea, I will forsake my kingdom, that I may receive this great joy.

51 But Aaron said unto him, If thou desirest this thing, if thou wilt bow down before God, yea, if thou wilt repent of all thy sins, and will bow down before God, and call on his name in faith, believing that ye shall receive, then shalt thou receive the hope which thou desirest.

52 ¶And it came to pass that when Aaron had said these words, the king did bow down before the Lord, upon his knees; yea, even he did prostrate himself upon the earth, and cried mightily, saying, O God, Aaron hath told me that there is a God;

53 And if there is a God, and if thou art God, wilt thou make thyself known unto me, and I will give away all my sins to know thee, and that I may be raised from the dead, and be saved at the last day.

54 And now when the king had said these words, he was struck as if he were dead.

55 ¶And it came to pass that his servants ran and told the queen all that had happened unto the king.

56 And she came in unto the king; and when she saw him lay as if he were dead, and also Aaron and his brethren standing as though they had been the cause of his fall, she was angry with them, and commanded that her servants, or the servants of the king, should take them and slay them.

57 Now the servants had seen the cause of the king's fall, therefore they durst not lay their hands on Aaron and his brethren;

58 And they plead with the queen, saying, Why commandest thou that we should slay these men, when behold, one of them is mightier than us all? Therefore we shall fall before them.

59 Now when the queen saw the fear of the servants, she also began to fear exceedingly, lest there should some evil come upon her.

60 And she commanded her servants that they should go and call the people, that they might slay Aaron and his brethren.

61 Now when Aaron saw the determination of the queen, and he also knowing the hardness of the hearts of the people, feared lest that a multitude should assemble themselves together, and there should be a great contention, and a disturbance among them;

62 Therefore he put forth his hand and raised the king from the earth, and said unto him, Stand: and he stood upon his feet, receiving his strength.

63 Now this was done in the presence of the queen, and many of the servants. And when they saw it, they greatly marveled, and began to fear.

64 And the king stood forth and began to minister unto them. And he did minister unto them insomuch that his whole household were converted unto the Lord.

65 Now there was a multitude gathered together because of the commandment of the queen, and there began to be great murmurings among them, because of Aaron and his brethren.

66 But the king stood forth among them, and administered

unto them. And they were pacified towards Aaron, and those who were with him.

67 ¶And it came to pass that when the king saw that the people were pacified, he caused that Aaron and his brethren should stand forth in the midst of the multitude, and that they should preach the word unto them.

68 And it came to pass that the king sent a proclamation throughout all the land, amongst all his people who were in all his land, who were in all the regions round about, which was bordering even to the sea, on the east, and on the west, and which was divided from the land of Zarahemla by a narrow strip of wilderness,

69 Which ran from the sea east, even to the sea west, and round about on the borders of the sea-shore, and the borders of the wilderness which was on the north, by the land of Zarahemla, through the borders of Manti, by the head of the river Sidon, running from the east towards the west; and thus were the Lamanites and the Nephites divided.

70 Now the more idle part of the Lamanites lived in the wilderness, and dwelt in tents; and they were spread through the wilderness, on the west, in the land of Nephi:

71 Yea, and also on the west of the land of Zarahemla, in the borders, by the sea-shore, and on the west, in the land of Nephi, in the place of their fathers' first inheritance, and thus bordering along by the sea-shore.

72 And also there were many Lamanites on the east by the sea-shore, whither the Nephites had driven them. And thus the Nephites were nearly surrounded by the Lamanites;

73 Nevertheless the Nephites had taken possession of all the northern parts of the land, bordering on the wilderness, at the head of the river Sidon, from the east to the west, round about on the wilderness side; on the north, even until they came to the land which they called Bountiful.

74 And it bordered upon the land which they called Desolation; it being so far northward, that it came into the land which had been peopled, and been destroyed, of whose bones we have spoken, which was discovered by the people of Zara-

hemla; it being the place of their first landing. And they came from there up into the south wilderness.

75 Thus the land on the northward was called Desolation, and the land on the southward was called Bountiful; it being the wilderness which is filled with all manner of wild animals of every kind; a part of which had come from the land northward, for food.

76 And now it was only the distance of a day and a half's journey for a Nephite, on the line Bountiful, and the land Desolation, from the east to the west sea;

77 And thus the land of Nephi, and the land of Zarahemla, were nearly surrounded by water; there being a small neck of land between the land northward, and the land southward.

78 ¶And it came to pass that the Nephites had inhabited the land Bountiful, even from the east unto the west sea,

79 And thus the Nephites in their wisdom, with their guards and their armies, had hemmed in the Lamanites on the south, that thereby they should have no more possession on the north, that they might not overrun the land northward;

80 Therefore the Lamanites could have no more possessions only in the land of Nephi, and the wilderness round about.

81 Now this was wisdom in the Nephites; as the Lamanites were an enemy to them, they would not suffer their afflictions on every hand, and also that they might have a country whither they might flee, according to their desires.

82 And now I, after having said this, return again to the account of Ammon, and Aaron, Omner, and Himni, and their brethren.

CHAPTER 14.

1 ¶Behold, now it came to pass that the king of the Lamanites sent a proclamation among all his people, that they should not lay their hands on Ammon, or Aaron, or Omner, or Himni, nor neither of their brethren who should go forth

preaching the word of God, in whatsoever place they should be, in any part of their land;

2 Yea, he sent a decree among them, that they should not lay their hands on them to bind them, or to cast them into prison; neither should they spit upon them, nor smite them, nor cast them out of their synagogues, nor scourge them;

3 Neither should they cast stones at them, but that they should have free access to their houses, and also their temples, and their sanctuaries;

4 And thus they might go forth and preach the word according to their desires, for the king had been converted unto the Lord, and all his household:

5 Therefore he sent this proclamation throughout the land unto his people, that the word of God might have no obstruction, but that it might go forth throughout all the land, that his people might be convinced concerning the wicked traditions of their fathers,

6 And that they might be convinced that they were all brethren, and that they ought not to murder, nor to plunder, nor to steal, nor to commit adultery, nor to commit any manner of wickedness.

7 And now it came to pass that when the king had sent forth this proclamation, that Aaron and his brethren went forth from city to city, and from one house of worship to another,

8 Establishing churches, and consecrating priests and teachers throughout the land among the Lamanites, to preach and to teach the word of God among them; and thus they began to have great success.

9 And thousands were brought to the knowledge of the Lord, yea, thousands were brought to believe in the traditions of the Nephites; and they were taught the records and the prophecies which were handed down, even to the present time;

10 And as sure as the Lord liveth, so sure as many as believed, or as many as were brought to the knowledge of the truth, through the preaching of Ammon and his brethren,

according to the spirit of revelation and of prophecy, and the power of God, working miracles in them;

11 Yea, I say unto you, As the Lord liveth, as many of the Lamanites as believed in their preaching, and were converted unto the Lord, never did fall away, for they became a righteous people:

12 They did lay down the weapons of their rebellion, that they did not fight against God any more, neither against any of their brethren.

13 Now these are they who were converted unto the Lord: The people of the Lamanites who were in the land of Ishmael, and also of the people of the Lamanites who were in the land of Middoni, and also of the people of the Lamanites who were in the city of Nephi, and also of the people of the Lamanites who were in the land of Shilom, and who were in the land of Shemlon, and in the city of Lemuel, and in the city of Shimnilom;

14 And these are the names of the cities of the Lamanites which were converted unto the Lord; and these are they that laid down the weapons of their rebellion, yea, all their weapons of war; and they were all Lamanites.

15 And the Amalekites were not converted, save only one; neither were any of the Amulonites; but they did harden their hearts, and also the hearts of the Lamanites in that part of the land wheresoever they dwelt; yea, and all their villages and all their cities;

16 Therefore we have named all the cities of the Lamanites in which they did repent and come to the knowledge of the truth, and were converted.

17 ¶And now it came to pass that the king and those who were converted, were desirous that they might have a name, that thereby they might be distinguished from their brethren;

18 Therefore the king consulted with Aaron and many of their priests, concerning the name that they should take upon them, that they might be distinguished.

19 And it came to pass that they called their name Anti-

Nephi-Lehies; and they were called by this name, and were no more called Lamanites.

20 And they began to be a very industrious people; yea, and they were friendly with the Nephites; therefore they did open a correspondence with them, and the curse of God did no more follow them.

21 ¶And it came to pass that the Amalekites, and the Amulonites, and the Lamanites who were in the land of Amulon, and also in the land of Helam, and who were in the land of Jerusalem, and in fine, in all the land round about, who had not been converted, and had not taken upon them the name of Anti-Nephi-Lehi, were stirred up by the Amalekites, and by the Amulonites, to anger against their brethren;

22 And their hatred became exceeding sore against them, even insomuch that they began to rebel against their king, insomuch that they would not that he should be their king; therefore they took up arms against the people of Anti-Nephi-Lehi.

23 ¶Now the king conferred the kingdom upon his son and he called his name Anti-Nephi-Lehi.

24 And the king died in that self-same year that the Lamanites began to make preparations for war against the people of God.

25 Now when Ammon and his brethren, and all those who had come up with him, saw the preparations of the Lamanites to destroy their brethren, they came forth to the land of Midian, and there Ammon met all his brethren;

26 And from thence they came to the land of Ishmael, that they might hold a council with Lamoni, and also with his brother Anti-Nephi-Lehi, what they should do to defend themselves against the Lamanites.

27 Now there was not one soul among all the people who had been converted unto the Lord, that would take up arms against their brethren;

28 Nay, they would not even make any preparations for war; yea, and also their king commanded them that they should not

29 Now these are the words which he said unto the people concerning the matter: I thank my God, my beloved people, that our great God has in goodness sent these our brethren, the Nephites, unto us to preach unto us, and to convince us of the traditions of our wicked fathers.

30 And behold, I thank my great God that he has given us a portion of his Spirit to soften our hearts, that we have opened a correspondence with these brethren, the Nephites;

31 And behold, I also thank my God that by opening this correspondence we have been convinced of our sins; and of the many murders which we have committed;

32 And I also thank my God, yea, my great God, that he hath granted unto us that we might repent of these things, and also that he hath forgiven us of those our many sins and murders which we have committed, and took away the guilt from our hearts, through the merits of his Son.

33 And now behold, my brethren, since it has been all that we could do, (as we were the most lost of all mankind,) to repent of all our sins and the many murders which we have committed, and to get God to take them away from our hearts, for it was all we could do to repent sufficiently before God, that he would take away our stain.

34 Now my best beloved brethren, since God hath taken away our stains, and our swords have become bright, then let us stain our swords no more with the blood of our brethren.

35 Behold, I say unto you, Nay, let us retain our swords, that they be not stained with the blood of our brethren:

36 For perhaps if we should stain our swords again, they can no more be washed bright through the blood of the Son of our great God, which shall be shed for the atonement of our sins.

37 And the great God has had mercy on us, and made these things known unto us, that we might not perish:

38 Yea, and he has made these things known unto us beforehand, because he loveth our souls as well as he loveth our children; therefore in his mercy he doth visit us by his angels, that the plan of salvation might be made known unto

us as well as unto future generations. O how merciful is our God!

39 And now behold, since it has been as much as we could do to get our stains taken away from us, and our swords are made bright,

40 Let us hide them away that they may be kept bright, as a testimony to our God at the last day, or at the day that we shall be brought to stand before him to be judged, that we have not stained our swords in the blood of our brethren since he imparted his word unto us, and has made us clean thereby.

41 And now my brethren, if our brethren seek to destroy us, behold, we will hide away our swords; yea, even we will bury them deep in the earth, that they may be kept bright, as a testimony that we have never used them, at the last day; and if our brethren destroy us, behold, we shall go to our God and shall be saved.

42 ¶And now it came to pass that when the king had made an end of these sayings, and all the people were assembled together, they took their swords, and all the weapons which were used for the shedding of man's blood, and they did bury them up deep in the earth;

43 And this they did, it being in their view a testimony to God, and also to men, that they never would use weapons again for the shedding of man's blood;

44 And this they did, vouching and covenanting with God, that rather than shed the blood of their brethren, they would give up their own lives;

45 And rather than take away from a brother, they would give unto him; and rather than spend their days in idleness, they would labor abundantly with their hands;

46 And thus we see that when these Lamanites were brought to believe and to know the truth, they were firm, and would suffer even unto death, rather than commit sin:

47 And thus we see, that they buried the weapons of peace, or they buried the weapons of war, for peace.

48 ¶And it came to pass that their brethren the Lamanites, made preparations for war, and came up to the land of Ne-

phi, for the purpose of destroying the king, and to place another in his stead, and also of destroying the people of Anti-Nephi-Lehi out of the land.

49 Now when the people saw that they were coming against them, they went out to meet them, and prostrated themselves before them to the earth, and began to call on the name of the Lord;

50 And thus they were in this attitude when the Lamanites began to fall upon them, and began to slay them with the sword; and thus without meeting any resistance, they did slay a thousand and five of them; and we know that they are blessed, for they have gone to dwell with their God.

51 Now when the Lamanites saw that their brethren would not flee from the sword, neither would they turn aside to the right hand or to the left, but that they would lie down and perish, and praised God even in the very act of perishing under the sword; now when the Lamanites saw this, they did forbear from slaying them;

52 And there were many whose hearts had swollen in them for those of their brethren who had fallen under the sword, for they repented of the things which they had done.

53 ¶And it came to pass that they threw down their weapons of war, and they would not take them again, for they were stung for the murders which they had committed: and they came down even as their brethren, relying upon the mercies of those whose arms were lifted to slay them.

54 ¶And it came to pass that the people of God were joined that day by more than the number who had been slain; and those who had been slain were righteous people; therefore we have no reason to doubt but what they are saved.

55 And there was not a wicked man slain among them; but there were more than a thousand brought to the knowledge of the truth; thus we see that the Lord worketh in many ways to the salvation of his people.

56 Now the greatest number of those of the Lamanites who slew so many of their brethren, were Amalekites and Amulonites, the greatest number of whom were after the order of the Nehors.

57 Now among those who joined the people of the Lord, there were none who were Amalekites or Amulonites or who were of the order of Nehor, but they were actual descendants of Laman and Lemuel:

58 And thus we can plainly discern, that after a people have been once enlightened by the Spirit of God, and have had great knowledge of things pertaining to righteousness, and then have fallen away into sin and transgression, they become more hardened, and thus their state becomes worse than though they had never known these things.

59 ¶And behold, now it came to pass that those Lamanites were more angry, because they had slain their brethren; therefore they swore vengeance upon the Nephites;

60 And they did no more attempt to slay the people of Anti-Nephi-Lehi at that time; but they took their armies and went over into the borders of the land of Zarahemla, and fell upon the people who were in the land of Ammonihah, and destroyed them.

61 And after that, they had many battles with the Nephites, in the which they were driven and slain;

62 And among the Lamanites who were slain, were almost all the seed of Amulon and his brethren, who were the priests of Noah, and they were slain by the hands of the Nephites;

63 And the remainder having fled into the east wilderness, and having usurped the power and authority over the Lamanites, caused that many of the Lamanites should perish by fire, because of their belief:

64 For many of them, after having suffered much loss and so many afflictions, began to be stirred up in remembrance of the words which Aaron and his brethren had preached to them in their land:

65 Therefore they began to disbelieve the traditions of their fathers, and to believe in the Lord, and that he gave great power unto the Nephites; and thus there were many of them converted in the wilderness.

66 ¶And it came to pass that those rulers who were the remnant of the children of Amulon, caused that they should be put to death, yea, all those that believed in these things.

67 Now this martyrdom caused that many of their brethren should be stirred up to anger; and there began to be contention in the wilderness; and the Lamanites began to hunt the seed of Amulon and his brethren, and began to slay them, and they fled into the east wilderness.

68 And behold they are hunted at this day, by the Lamanites: thus the words of Abinadi were brought to pass, which he said concerning the seed of the priests who caused that he should suffer death by fire.

69 For he said unto them, What ye shall do unto me, shall be a type of things to come.

70 And now Abinadi was the first that suffered death by fire, because of his belief in God: now this is what he meant, that many should suffer death by fire, according as he had suffered.

71 And he said unto the priests of Noah, that their seed should cause many to be put to death, in the like manner as he was, and that they should be scattered abroad and slain, even as a sheep having no shepherd is driven and slain by wild beasts;

72 And now behold, these words were verified, for they were driven by the Lamanites, and they were hunted, and they were smitten.

73 ¶And it came to pass that when the Lamanites saw that they could not overpower the Nephites, they returned again to their own land; and many of them came over to dwell in the land of Ishmael and the land of Nephi, and did join themselves to the people of God, who were the people of Anti-Nephi-Lehi;

74 And they did also bury their weapons of war, according as their brethren had, and they began to be a righteous people; and they did walk in the ways of the Lord, and did observe to keep his commandments, and his statutes, yea, and they did keep the law of Moses; for it was expedient that they should keep the law of Moses as yet, for it was not all fulfilled.

75 But notwithstanding the law of Moses, they did look forward to the coming of Christ, considering that the law of

CHAP. 14.] BOOK OF ALMA. 397

Moses was a type of his coming, and believing that they must keep those outward performances, until the time that he should be revealed unto them.

76 Now they did not suppose that salvation came by the law of Moses; but the law of Moses did serve to strengthen their faith in Christ;

77 And thus they did retain a hope through faith, unto eternal salvation, relying upon the spirit of prophecy, which spake of those things to come.

78 And now behold, Ammon, and Aaron, and Omner, and Himni, and their brethren, did rejoice exceedingly, for the success which they had had among the Lamanites, seeing that the Lord had granted unto them according to their prayers, and that he had also verified his word unto them in every particular.

79 And now, these are the words of Ammon to his brethren, which say thus: My brothers and my brethren, behold I say unto you, How great reason have we to rejoice: for could we have supposed, when we started from the land of Zarahemla, that God would have granted unto us such great blessings?

80 And now I ask, What great blessings has he bestowed upon us? Can ye tell?

81 Behold, I answer for you; for our brethren, the Lamanites, were in darkness, yea, even in the darkest abyss; but behold, how many of them are brought to behold the marvelous light of God!

82 And this is the blessing which hath been bestowed upon us, that we have been made instruments in the hands of God, to bring about this great work.

83 Behold, thousands of them do rejoice, and have been brought into the fold of God.

84 Behold, the field was ripe, and blessed are ye, for ye did thrust in the sickle, and did reap with your mights, yea, all the day long did ye labor;

85 And behold the number of your sheaves, and they shall be gathered into the garners, that they are not wasted; yea, they shall not be beaten down by the storm, at the last day;

86 Yea, neither shall they be harrowed up by the whirlwinds; but when the storm cometh, they shall be gathered together in their place, that the storm can not penetrate to them; yea, neither shall they be driven with fierce winds, whithersoever the enemy listeth to carry them.

87 But behold, they are in the hands of the Lord of the harvest, and they are his; and he will raise them up at the last day.

88 Blessed be the name of our God; let us sing to his praise, yea, let us give thanks to his holy name, for he doth work righteousness for ever.

89 For if we had not come up out of the land of Zarahemla, these our dearly beloved brethren, who have so dearly beloved us, would still have been racked with hatred against us, yea, and they would also have been strangers to God.

90 ¶And it came to pass that when Ammon had said these words, his brother Aaron rebuked him, saying: Ammon, I fear that thy joy doth carry thee away unto boasting.

91 But Ammon said unto him, I do not boast in my own strength, or in my own wisdom; but behold, my joy is full, yea, my heart is brim with joy, and I will rejoice in my God;

92 Yea, I know that I am nothing; as to my strength, I am weak; therefore I will not boast of myself, but I will boast of my God; for in his strength I can do all things; yea, behold, many mighty miracles we have wrought in this land, for which we will praise his name for ever.

93 Behold, how many thousands of our brethren has he loosed from the pains of hell; and they are brought to sing redeeming love; and this because of the power of his word which is in us; therefore have we not great reason to rejoice?

94 Yea, we have reason to praise him for ever, for he is the most high God, and has loosed our brethren from the chains of hell.

95 Yea, they were encircled about with everlasting darkness and destruction; but behold, he has brought them into his

everlasting light, yea, into everlasting salvation; and they are encircled about with the matchless bounty of his love:

96 Yea, and we have been instruments in his hands, of doing this great and marvelous work; therefore let us glory, yea, we will glory in the Lord; yea, we will rejoice, for our joy is full; yea, we will praise our God for ever.

97 Behold, who can glory too much in the Lord? Yea, who can say too much of his great power, and of his mercy, and of his long suffering towards the children of men? Behold I say unto you, I can not say the smallest part which I feel.

98 Who could have supposed that our God would have been so merciful as to have snatched us from our awful, sinful, and polluted state?

99 Behold, we went forth even in wrath, with mighty threatenings to destroy his church. O then, why did he not consign us to an awful destruction; yea, why did he not let the sword of his justice fall upon us, and doom us to eternal despair?

100 O my soul, almost as it were fleeth at the thought.

101 Behold, he did not exercise his justice upon us, but in his great mercy hath brought us over that everlasting gulf of death and misery, even to the salvation of our souls.

102 And now behold, my brethren, what natural man is there, that knoweth these things? I say unto you, there is none that knoweth these things, save it be the penitent;

103 Yea, he that repenteth and exerciseth faith, and bringeth forth good works, and prayeth continually without ceasing: unto such it is given to know the mysteries of God; yea, unto such it shall be given to reveal things which never have been revealed;

104 Yea, and it shall be given unto such, to bring thousands of souls to repentance, even as it has been given unto us to bring these our brethren to repentance.

105 Now do ye remember, my brethren, that we said unto our brethren in the land of Zarahemla, We go up to the land of Nephi, to preach unto our brethren, the Lamanites, and they laughed us to scorn?

106 For they said unto us, Do ye suppose that ye can bring the Lamanites to the knowledge of the truth?

107 Do ye suppose that ye can convince the Lamanites of the incorrectness of the traditions of their fathers, as stiffnecked a people as they are; whose hearts delight in the shedding of blood; whose days have been spent in the grossest iniquity; whose ways have been the ways of a transgressor, from the beginning?

108 Now my brethren, ye remember that this was their language.

109 And moreover, they did say, Let us take up arms against them, that we destroy them and their iniquity out of the land, lest they overrun us, and destroy us.

110 But behold, my beloved brethren, we came into the wilderness not with the intent to destroy our brethren, but with the intent that perhaps we might save some few of their souls.

111 Now when our hearts were depressed, and we were about to turn back, behold, the Lord comforted us, and said, Go amongst thy brethren, the Lamanites, and bear with patience thine afflictions, and I will give unto you success.

112 And now behold, we have come, and been forth amongst them; and we have been patient in our sufferings, and we have suffered every privation; yea, we traveled from house to house, relying upon the mercies of the world; not upon the mercies of the world alone, but upon the mercies of God.

113 And we have entered into their houses and taught them, and we have taught them in their streets; yea, and we taught them upon their hills: and we have also entered into their temples and their synagogues and taught them;

114 And we have been cast out, and mocked, and spit upon, and smote upon our cheeks; and we have been stoned, and taken and bound with strong cords, and cast into prison; and through the power and wisdom of God, we have been delivered again:

115 And we have suffered all manner of afflictions, and all this, that perhaps we might be the means of saving some soul;

and we supposed that our joy would be full, if perhaps we could be the means of saving some.

116 Now behold, we can look forth and see the fruits of our labors; and are they few?

117 I say unto you, Nay, they are many; yea, and we can witness of their sincerity, because of their love towards their brethren, and also towards us.

118 For behold, they had rather sacrifice their lives than even to take the life of their enemy; and they have buried their weapons of war deep in the earth, because of their love towards their brethren.

119 And now behold I say unto you, Has there been so great love in all the land?

120 Behold, I say unto you, Nay, there has not, even among the Nephites.

121 For behold, they would take up arms against their brethren; they would not suffer themselves to be slain.

122 But behold, how many of these have laid down their lives, and we know that they have gone to their God, because of their love, and of their hatred to sin.

123 Now have we not reason to rejoice? Yea, I say unto you, there never were men that had so great reason to rejoice as we, since the world began:

124 Yea, and my joy is carried away, even unto boasting in my God; for he has all power, all wisdom, and all understanding; he comprehendeth all things, and he is a merciful Being even unto salvation, to those who will repent and believe on his name.

125 Now if this is boasting, even so will I boast; for this is my life and my light, my joy and my salvation, and my redemption from everlasting wo.

126 Yea, blessed is the name of my God, who has been mindful of this people, who are a branch of the tree of Israel, and has been lost from its body, in a strange land; yea, I say, blessed be the name of my God, who has been mindful of us wanderers in a strange land.

127 Now my brethren, we see that God is mindful of every people, in whatsoever land they may be in; yea, he number-

eth his people, and his bowels of mercy are over all the earth.

128 Now this is my joy, and my great thanksgiving; yea, and I will give thanks unto my God for ever. Amen.

CHAPTER 15.

1 ¶Now it came to pass that when those Lamanites who had gone to war against the Nephites, had found after their many struggles to destroy them, that it was in vain to seek their destruction, they returned again to the land of Nephi.

2 And it came to pass that the Amalekites, because of their loss, were exceeding angry.

3 And when they saw that they could not seek revenge from the Nephites, they began to stir up the people in anger against their brethren, the people of Anti-Nephi-Lehi; therefore they began again to destroy them.

4 Now this people again refused to take their arms, and they suffered themselves to be slain according to the desires of their enemies.

5 Now when Ammon and his brethren saw this work of destruction among those who they so dearly beloved, and among those who had so dearly beloved them; for they were treated as though they were angels sent from God to save them from everlasting destruction;

6 Therefore when Ammon and his brethren saw this great work of destruction, they were moved with compassion, and they said unto the king, Let us gather together this people of the Lord, and let us go down to the land of Zarahemla, to our brethren, the Nephites, and flee out of the hands of our enemies, that we be not destroyed.

7 But the king said unto them, Behold, the Nephites will destroy us, because of the many murders and sins we have committed against them.

8 And Ammon said, I will go and inquire of the Lord, and if he say unto us, Go down unto our brethren, will ye go?

9 And the king said unto him, Yea: if the Lord saith unto us, Go, we will go down unto our brethren, and we will

be their slaves until we repair unto them the many murders and sins which we have committed against them.

10 But Ammon said unto him, It is against the law of our brethren, which was established by my father, that there should be any slaves among them; therefore let us go down and rely upon the mercies of our brethren.

11 But the king said unto him, Inquire of the Lord, and if he saith unto us, Go, we will go; otherwise we will perish in the land.

12 ¶And it came to pass that Ammon went and inquired of the Lord, and the Lord said unto him, Get this people out of this land, that they perish not, for Satan has great hold on the hearts of the Amalekites, who do stir up the Lamanites to anger against their brethren, to slay them; therefore get thee out of this land; and blessed are this people in this generation; for I will preserve them.

13 ¶And now it came to pass that Ammon went and told the king all the words which the Lord had said unto him.

14 And they gathered together all their people; yea, all the people of the Lord, and did gather together all their flocks and herds, and departed out of the land, and came into the wilderness which divided the land of Nephi from the land of Zarahemla, and came over near the borders of the land.

15 ¶And it came to pass that Ammon said unto them, Behold, I and my brethren will go forth into the land of Zarahemla, and ye shall remain here until we return; and we will try the hearts of our brethren, whether they will that ye shall come into their land.

16 ¶And it came to pass that as Ammon was going forth into the land, that he and his brethren met Alma, over in the place of which has been spoken; and behold, this was a joyful meeting.

17 Now the joy of Ammon was so great, even that he was full, yea, he was swallowed up in the joy of his God, even to the exhausting of his strength; and he fell again to the earth.

18 Now was not this exceeding joy? Behold, this is joy which none receiveth save it be the truly penitent and humble seeker of happiness.

19 Now the joy of Alma in meeting his brethren was truly great, and also the joy of Aaron, of Omner, and Himni: but behold, their joy was not that to exceed their strength.

20 ¶And now it came to pass that Alma conducted his brethren back to the land of Zarahemla; even to his own house.

21 And they went and told the chief judge all the things that had happened unto them in the land of Nephi among their brethren, the Lamanites.

22 ¶And it came to pass that the chief judge sent a proclamation throughout all the land, desiring the voice of the people concerning the admitting their brethren, who were the people of Anti-Nephi-Lehi.

23 And it came to pass that the voice of the people came, saying: Behold, we will give up the land of Jershon, which is on the east by the sea, which joins the land Bountiful, which is on the south of the land Bountiful; and this land Jershon is the land which we will give unto our brethren for an inheritance.

24 And behold, we will set our armies between the land Jershon and the land Nephi, that we may protect our brethren in the land Jershon;

25 And this we do for our brethren, on account of their fear to take up arms against their brethren, lest they should commit sin: and this their great fear came, because of their sore repentance which they had, on account of their many murders, and their awful wickedness.

26 And now behold, this will we do unto our brethren, that they may inherit the land Jershon; and we will guard them from their enemies with our armies, on conditions they will give us a portion of their substance to assist us, that we may maintain our armies.

27 ¶Now it came to pass that when Ammon had heard this, he returned to the people of Anti-Nephi-Lehi, and also Alma with him, into the wilderness, where they had pitched their tents, and made known unto them all these things.

28 And Alma also related unto them his conversion with

Ammon, and Aaron and his brethren. And it came to pass that it did cause great joy among them.

29 And they went down into the land of Jershon, and took possession of the land of Jershon; and they were called by the Nephites the people of Ammon;

30 Therefore they were distinguished by that name ever after; and they were among the people of Nephi, and also numbered among the people who were of the church of God.

31 And they were also distinguished for their zeal towards God, and also towards men; for they were perfectly honest and upright in all things; and they were firm in the faith of Christ, even unto the end.

32 And they did look upon shedding the blood of their brethren with the greatest abhorrence; and they never could be prevailed upon to take up arms against their brethren:

33 And they never did look upon death with any degree of terror for their hope and views of Christ and the resurrection; therefore death was swallowed up to them by the victory of Christ over it;

34 Therefore they would suffer death in the most aggravating and distressing manner which could be inflicted by their brethren, before they would take the sword or the cimeter to smite them.

35 And thus they were a zealous and beloved people, a highly favored people of the Lord.

36 ¶And now it came to pass that after the people of Ammon were established in the land of Jershon, and a church also established in the land of Jershon; and the armies of the Nephites were set round about the land of Jershon; yea, in all the borders round about the land of Zarahemla; behold the armies of the Lamanites had followed their brethren into the wilderness.

37 And thus there was a tremendous battle; yea, even such an one as never had been known among all the people in the land from the time Lehi left Jerusalem; yea, and tens of thousands of the Lamanites were slain and scattered abroad.

38 Yea, and also there was a tremendous slaughter among the people of Nephi; nevertheless, the Lamanites were driven

and scattered, and the people of Nephi returned again to their land.

39 And now this was a time that there was a great mourning and lamentation heard throughout all the land among all the people of Nephi;

40 Yea, the cry of widows mourning for their husbands, and also of fathers mourning for their sons, and the daughter for the brother; yea, the brother for the father:

41 And thus the cry of mourning was heard among every one of them: mourning for their kindred who had been slain.

42 And now surely this was a sorrowful day; yea, a time of solemnity and a time of much fasting and prayer: and thus ended the fifteenth year of the reign of the Judges of the people of Nephi;

43 And this is the account of Ammon and his brethren, their journeyings in the land of Nephi, their sufferings in the land, their sorrows, and their afflictions, and their incomprehensible joy, and the reception and safety of the brethren in the land of Jershon.

44 And now may the Lord, the Redeemer of all men, bless their souls for ever.

45 And this is the account of the wars and contentions among the Nephites, and also the wars between the Nephites and the Lamanites; and the fifteenth year of the reign of the Judges is ended;

46 And from the first year to the fifteenth, has brought to pass the destruction of many thousand lives; yea, it has brought to pass an awful scene of bloodshed;

47 And the bodies of many thousands are laid low in the earth, while the bodies of many thousands are mouldering in heaps upon the face of the earth;

48 Yea, and many thousands are mourning for the loss of their kindred, because they have reason to fear, according to the promises of the Lord, that they are consigned to a state of endless wo;

49 While many thousands of others truly mourn for the loss of their kindred, yet they rejoice and exult in the hope, yea, and even know, according to the promises of the Lord,

that they are raised to dwell at the right hand of God, in a state of never ending happiness;

50 And thus we see how great the inequality of man is because of sin and transgression, and the power of the devil, which comes by the cunning plans which he hath devised to ensnare the hearts of men:

51 And thus we see the great call of the diligence of men to labor in the vineyards of the Lord; and thus we see the great reason of sorrow, and also of rejoicing; sorrow because of death and destruction among men, and joy because of the light of Christ unto life.

52 O that I were an angel, and could have the wish of mine heart, that I might go forth and speak with the trump of God, with a voice to shake the earth, and cry repentance unto every people;

53 Yea, I would declare unto every soul, as with the voice of thunder, repentance, and the plan of redemption, that they should repent and come unto our God, that there might be no more sorrow upon all the face of the earth.

54 But behold, I am a man, and do sin in my wish; for I ought to be content with the things which the Lord hath allotted unto me.

55 I ought not to harrow up in my desires, the firm decree of a just God, for I know that he granteth unto men according to their desire, whether it be unto death or unto life; yea, I know that he allotteth unto men, yea, decreeth unto them decrees which are unalterable, according to their wills; whether they be unto salvation or unto destruction;

56 Yea, and I know that good and evil have come before all men; or he that knoweth not good from evil is blameless; but he that knoweth good and evil, to him it is given according to his desires; whether he desireth good or evil, life or death, joy or remorse of conscience.

57 Now seeing that I know these things, why should I desire more than to perform the work to which I have been called?

58 Why should I desire that I was an angel, that I could speak unto all the ends of the earth?

59 For behold, the Lord doth grant unto all nations, of their own nation and tongue, to teach his word; yea, in wisdom, all that he seeth fit that they should have; therefore we see that the Lord doth counsel in his wisdom, according to that which is just and true.

60 I know that which the Lord hath commanded me, and I glory in it: I do not glory of myself, but I glory in that which the Lord hath commanded me;

61 Yea, and this is my glory, that perhaps I may be an instrument in the hands of God, to bring some soul to repentance; and this is my joy.

62 And behold, when I see many of my brethren truly penitent, and coming to the Lord their God, then is my soul filled with joy; then do I remember what the Lord has done for me; yea, even that he hath heard my prayer; yea, then do I remember his merciful arm which he extended towards me;

63 Yea, and I also remember the captivity of my fathers; for I surely do know that the Lord did deliver them out of bondage, and by this did establish his church; yea, the Lord God, the God of Abraham, the God of Isaac, and the God of Jacob, did deliver them out of bondage;

64 Yea, I have always remembered the captivity of my fathers; and that same God who delivered them out of the hands of the Egyptians, did deliver them out of bondage; yea, and that same God did establish his church among them;

65 Yea, and that same God hath called me by a holy calling, to preach the word unto this people, and hath given me much success, in the which my joy is full; but I do not joy in my own success alone, but my joy is more full because of the success of my brethren, who have been up to the land of Nephi.

66 Behold, they have labored exceedingly, and have brought forth much fruit; and how great shall be their reward.

67 Now when I think of the success of these my brethren, my soul is carried away, even to the separation of it from the body, as it were, so great is my joy.

68 ¶And now may God grant unto these my brethren, that they may sit down in the kingdom of God; yea, and also all

those who are the fruit of their labors that they may go no more out, but that they may praise him for ever.

69 And may God grant that it may be done according to my words, even as I have spoken. Amen.

CHAPTER 16.

1 ¶Behold, now it came to pass that after the people of Ammon were established in the land of Jershon, yea, and also after the Lamanites were driven out of the land, and their dead were buried by the people of the land.

2 Now their dead were not numbered, because of the greatness of their numbers, neither were the dead of the Nephites numbered.

3 But it came to pass after they had buried their dead, and also after the days of fasting, and mourning, and prayer, (and it was in the sixteenth year of the reign of the Judges over the people of Nephi,) there began to be continual peace throughout all the land, yea, and the people did observe to keep the commandments of the Lord;

4 And they were strict in observing the ordinances of God, according to the law of Moses; for they were taught to keep the law of Moses, until it should be fulfilled;

5 And thus the people did have no disturbance in all the sixteenth year of the reign of the Judges over the people of Nephi.

6 ¶And it came to pass in the seventeenth year of the reign of the Judges, there was continual peace.

7 But it came to pass in the latter end of the seventeenth year, there came a man into the land of Zarahemla; and he was Anti-christ, for he began to preach unto the people against the prophecies which had been spoken by the prophets concerning the coming of Christ.

8 Now there was no law against a man's belief; for it was strictly contrary to the commands of God, that there should be a law which should bring men on to unequal grounds.

9 For thus saith the scripture, Choose ye this day whom ye will serve.

10 Now if a man desired to serve God, it was his privilege, or rather if he believed in God, it was his privilege to serve him; but if he did not believe in him, there was no law to punish him.

11 But if he murdered, he was punished unto death; and if he robbed, he was also punished; and if he stole, he was also punished; and if he committed adultery, he was also punished; yea, for all this wickedness, they were punished; for there was a law that men should be judged according to their crimes.

12 Nevertheless, there was no law against a man's belief; therefore, a man was punished only for the crimes which he had done; therefore all men were on equal grounds.

13 And this Anti-christ, whose name was Korihor, (and the law could have no hold upon him,) began to preach unto the people, that there should be no Christ.

14 And after this manner did he preach, saying: O ye that are bound down under a foolish and a vain hope, why do ye yoke yourselves with such foolish things? Why do ye look for a Christ? For no man can know of anything which is to come.

15 Behold, these things which ye call prophecies, which ye say are handed down by holy prophets, behold, they are foolish traditions of your fathers. How do ye know of their surety?

16 Behold, ye can not know of things which ye do not see; therefore ye can not know that there shall be a Christ.

17 Ye look forward and say, that ye see a remission of your sins. But behold, it is the effect of a frenzied mind: and this derangement of your minds comes because of the tradition of your fathers, which lead you away into a belief of things which are not so.

18 And many more such things did he say unto them, telling them that there could be no atonement made for the sins of men, but every man fared in this life, according to the management of the creature; therefore every man prospered according to his genius, and that every man conquered ac-

cording to his strength; and whatsoever a man did, was no crime.

19 And thus he did preach unto them, leading away the hearts of many, causing them to lift up their heads in their wickedness; yea, leading away many women, and also men, to commit whoredoms; telling them that when a man was dead, that was the end thereof.

20 ¶Now this man went over to the land of Jershon also, to preach these things among the people of Ammon, who were once the people of the Lamanites.

21 But behold, they were more wise than many of the Nephites; for they took him, and bound him, and carried him before Ammon, who was a high priest over that people.

22 ¶And it came to pass that he caused that he should be carried out of the land.

23 And he came over into the land of Gideon, and began to preach unto them also; and here he did not have much success, for he was taken and bound, and carried before the high priest, and also the chief judge over the land.

24 ¶And it came to pass that the high priest said unto him, Why do ye go about perverting the ways of the Lord?

25 Why do ye teach this people that there shall be no Christ, to interrupt their rejoicings?

26 Why do ye speak against all the prophecies of the holy prophets?

27 Now the high priest's name was Giddonah.

28 And Korihor said unto him, Because I do not teach the foolish traditions of your fathers, and because I do not teach this people to bind themselves down under the foolish ordinances and performances which are laid down by ancient priests, to usurp power and authority over them, to keep them in ignorance, that they may not lift up their heads, but be brought down according to thy words.

29 Ye say that this people is a free people. Behold, I say tney are in bondage.

30 Ye say that those ancient prophecies are true. Behold, I say that ye do not know that they are true.

31 Ye say that this people is a guilty and a fallen people,

because of the transgression of a parent. Behold, I say that a child is not guilty because of its parents.

32 And ye also say that Christ shall come. But behold, I say that ye do not know that there shall be a Christ.

33 And ye say also, that he shall be slain for the sins of the world; and thus ye lead away this people after the foolish traditions of your fathers, and according to your own desires;

34 And ye keep them down, even as it were, in bondage, that ye may glut yourselves with the labors of their hands, that they durst not look up with boldness, and that they durst not enjoy their rights and privileges;

35 Yea, they durst not make use of that which is their own, lest they should offend their priests, who do yoke them according to their desires, and have brought them to believe by their traditions, and their dreams, and their whims, and their visions, and their pretended mysteries, that they should, if they did not do according to their words, offend some unknown being, who they say is God; a being who never has been seen nor known, who never was nor ever will be.

36 Now when the high priest and the chief judge saw the hardness of his heart; yea, when they saw that he would revile even against God, they would not make any reply to his words;

37 But they caused that he should be bound; and they delivered him up into the hands of the officers, and sent him to the land of Zarahemla, that he might be brought before Alma and the chief judge, who was governor over all the land.

38 ¶And it came to pass that when he was brought before Alma and the chief judge, he did go on in the same manner as he did in the land of Gideon; yea, he went on to blaspheme.

39 And he did rise up in great swelling words before Alma, and did revile against the priests and teachers, accusing them of leading away the people after the silly traditions of their fathers, for the sake of glutting in the labors of the people.

40 Now Alma said unto him, Thou knowest that we do not

glut ourselves upon the labors of this people; for behold, I have labored even from the commencement of the reign of the Judges, until now, with mine own hands, for my support, notwithstanding my many travels round about the land, to declare the word of God unto my people.

41 And notwithstanding the many labors which I have performed in the church, I have never received so much as even one senine for my labor; neither has any of my brethren, save it were in the judgment seat; and then we have received only according to law, for our time.

42 And now if we do not receive anything for our labors in the church, what doth it profit us to labor in the church, save it were to declare the truth, that we may have rejoicings in the joy of our brethren?

43 Then why sayest thou that we preach unto this people to get gain, when thou of thyself knowest that we receive no gain?

44 And now, believest thou that we deceive this people, that causes such joy in their hearts?

45 And Korihor answered him, Yea.

46 And then Alma said unto him, Believest thou that there is a God? And he answered, Nay.

47 Now Alma said unto him, Will ye deny again that there is a God, and also deny the Christ? for behold, I say unto you, I know there is a God, and also that Christ shall come.

48 And now, what evidence have ye that there is no God, or that Christ cometh not? I say unto you that ye have none, save it be your word only.

49 But behold, I have all things as a testimony that these things are true; and ye also have all things as a testimony unto you that they are true; and will ye deny them?

50 Believest thou that these things are true?

51 Behold, I know that thou believest, but thou art possessed with a lying spirit, and ye have put off the Spirit of God, that it may have no place in you; but the devil has power over you, and he doth carry you about, working devices, that he may destroy the children of God.

52 And now Korihor said unto Alma, If thou wilt shew

me a sign, that I may be convinced that there is a God, yea, shew unto me that he hath power, and then will I be convinced of the truth of thy words.

53 But Alma said unto him, Thou hast had signs enough; will ye tempt your God? Will ye say, Shew unto me a sign, when ye have the testimony of all these thy brethren, and also all the holy prophets?

54 The scriptures are laid before thee, yea, and all things denote there is a God; yea, even the earth, and all things that are upon the face of it, yea, and its motion;

55 Yea, and also all the planets which move in their regular form, doth witness that there is a Supreme Creator: and yet do ye go about, leading away the hearts of this people, testifying unto them there is no God? And yet will ye deny against all these witnesses?

56 And he said, Yea, I will deny, except ye shall shew me a sign.

57 ¶And now it came to pass that Alma said unto him, Behold, I am grieved because of the hardness of your heart; yea, that ye will still resist the spirit of the truth, that thy soul may be destroyed.

58 But behold, it is better that thy soul should be lost, than that thou shouldst be the means of bringing many souls down to destruction, by thy lying and by thy flattering words;

59 Therefore if thou shalt deny again, behold, God shall smite thee, that thou shalt become dumb, that thou shalt never open thy mouth any more, that thou shalt not deceive this people any more.

60 Now Korihor said unto him, I do not deny the existence of a God, but I do not believe that there is a God; and I say also, that ye do not know that there is a God; and except ye shew me a sign, I will not believe.

61 Now Alma said unto him, This will I give unto thee for a sign, that thou shalt be struck dumb, according to my words; and I say, that in the name of God, ye shall be struck dumb, that ye shall no more have utterance.

62 Now when Alma had said these words, Korihor was

struck dumb, that he could not have utterance according to the words of Alma.

63 And now when the chief judge saw this, he put forth his hand and wrote unto Korihor, saying: Art thou convinced of the power of God?

64 In whom did ye desire that Alma should shew forth his sign? Would ye that he should afflict others, to shew unto thee a sign?

65 Behold, he has shewed unto you a sign; and now will ye dispute more?

66 And Korihor put forth his hand, and wrote, saying: I know that I am dumb, for I can not speak; and I know that nothing, save it were the power of God, could bring this upon me; yea, and I also knew that there was a God.

67 But, behold the devil hath deceived me; for he appeared unto me in the form of an angel, and said unto me, Go and reclaim this people, for they have all gone astray after an unknown God.

68 And he said unto me, There is no God; yea, and he taught me that which I should say. And I have taught his words; and I taught them, because they were pleasing unto the carnal mind;

69 And I taught them, even until I had much success, insomuch that I verily believed that they were true; and for this cause, I withstood the truth, even until I have brought this great curse upon me.

70 Now when he had said this, he besought that Alma should pray unto God, that the curse might be taken from him.

71 But Alma said unto him, If this curse should be taken from thee, thou wouldest again lead away the hearts of this people; therefore, it shall be unto thee, even as the Lord will.

72 ¶And it came to pass that the curse was not taken off of Korihor; but he was cast out, and went about from house to house, begging for his food.

73 Now the knowledge of what had happened unto Korihor, was immediately published throughout all the land; yea, the proclamation was sent forth by the chief judge, to all the

people in the land, declaring unto those who had believed in the words of Korihor, that they must speedily repent, lest the same judgments would come unto them.

74 ¶And it came to pass that they were all convinced of the wickedness of Korihor; therefore they were all converted again unto the Lord; and this put an end to the iniquity after the manner of Korihor.

75 And Korihor did go about from house to house, begging food for his support.

76 ¶And it came to pass that as he went forth among the people, yea, among a people who had separated themselves from the Nephites, and called themselves Zoramites, being led by a man whose name was Zoram; and as he went forth amongst them, behold, he was run upon, and trodden down, even until he was dead;

77 And thus we see the end of him who perverteth the ways of the Lord; and thus we see that the devil will not support his children at the last day, but doth speedily drag them down to hell.

78 ¶Now it came to pass that after the end of Korihor, Alma having received tidings that the Zoramites were perverting the ways of the Lord, and that Zoram, who was their leader, was leading the hearts of the people to bow down to dumb idols, etc., his heart again began to sicken, because of the iniquity of the people;

79 For it was the cause of great sorrow to Alma, to know of iniquity among his people: therefore his heart was exceeding sorrowful, because of the separation of the Zoramites from the Nephites.

80 Now the Zoramites had gathered themselves together in a land which they called Antionum, which was east of the land of Zarahemla, which lay nearly bordering upon the seashore, which was south of the land of Jershon, which also bordered upon the wilderness south, which wilderness was full of the Lamanites.

81 Now the Nephites greatly feared that the Zoramites would enter into a correspondence with the Lamanites, and

that it would be the means of great loss on the part of the Nephites.

82 And now, as the preaching of the word had had a greater tendency to lead the people to do that which was just; yea, it had had more powerful effect upon the minds of the people than the sword, or anything else, which had happened unto them; therefore Alma thought it was expedient that they should try the virtue of the word of God.

83 Therefore he took Ammon, and Aaron, and Omner; and Himni he did leave in the church in Zarahemla; but the former three he took with him, and also Amulek and Zeezrom, who were at Melek; and he also took two of his sons.

84 Now the eldest of his sons he took not with him; and his name was Helaman; but the names of those whom he took with him, were Shiblon and Corianton; and these are the names of those who went with him among the Zoramites, to preach unto them the word.

85 ¶Now the Zoramites were dissenters from the Nephites; therefore they had the word of God preached unto them.

86 But they had fallen into great errors, for they would not observe to keep the commandments of God, and his statutes, according to the law of Moses;

87 Neither would they observe the performances of the church, to continue in prayer and supplication to God daily, that they might not enter into temptation; yea, in fine, they did pervert the ways of the Lord in very many instances; therefore, for this cause, Alma and his brethren went into the land, to preach the word unto them.

88 ¶Now when they had come into the land, behold, to their astonishment, they found that the Zoramites had built synagogues, and that they did gather themselves together on one day of the week, which day they did call the day of the Lord;

89 And they did worship after a manner which Alma and his brethren had never beheld; for they had a place built up in the center of their synagogue, a place for standing, which was high above the head; and the top thereof would only admit one person.

90 Therefore, whosoever desired to worship, must go forth

and stand upon the top thereof, and stretch forth his hands towards heaven; and cry with a loud voice, saying: Holy, holy, God; we believe that thou art God, and we believe that thou art holy, and that thou wast a spirit, and that thou art a spirit, and that thou wilt be a spirit for ever.

91 Holy God, we believe that thou hast separated us from our brethren; and we do not believe in the tradition of our brethren, which was handed down to them by the childishness of their fathers; but we believe that thou hast elected us to be thy holy children;

92 And also thou hast made it known unto us that there shall be no Christ; but thou art the same, yesterday, to-day, and for ever; and thou hast elected us, that we shall be saved, whilst all around us are elected to be cast by thy wrath down to hell; for the which holiness, O God, we thank thee;

93 And we also thank thee, that thou hast elected us, that we may not be led away after the foolish traditions of our brethren, which doth bind them down to a belief of Christ, which doth lead their hearts to wander far from thee, our God.

94 And again we thank thee, O God, that we are a chosen and a holy people. Amen.

95 ¶Now it came to pass that after Alma and his brethren, and his sons, had heard these prayers, they were astonished beyond all measure.

96 For behold every man did go forth and offer up the same prayers.

97 Now the place was called by them Rameumptom, which being interpreted, is the Holy Stand.

98 Now from this stand, they did offer up, every man, the selfsame prayer unto God, thanking their God that they were chosen of him, and that he did not lead them away after the tradition of their brethren; and that their hearts were not stolen away to believe in things to come, which they knew nothing about.

99 ¶Now after the people had all offered up thanks after this manner, they returned to their homes, never speaking of their God again, until they had assembled themselves to-

gether again, to the holy stand, to offer up thanks after their manner.

100 Now when Alma saw this, his heart was grieved: for he saw that they were a wicked and a perverse people; yea, he saw that their hearts were set upon gold, and upon silver, and upon all manner of fine goods.

101 Yea, and he also saw that their hearts were lifted up unto great boasting, in their pride.

102 And he lifted up his voice to heaven, and cried, saying: O how long, O Lord, wilt thou suffer that thy servants shall dwell here below in the flesh, to behold such gross wickedness among the children of men.

103 Behold, O God, they cry unto thee, and yet their hearts are swallowed up in their pride.

104 Behold, O God, they cry unto thee with their mouths, while they are puffed up, even to greatness, with the vain things of the world.

105 Behold, O my God, their costly apparel, and their ringlets, and their bracelets, and their ornaments of gold, and all their precious things which they are ornamented with;

106 And behold, their hearts are set upon them, and yet they cry unto thee and say, We thank thee, O God, for we are a chosen people unto thee, while others shall perish.

107 Yea, and they say that thou hast made it known unto them, that there shall be no Christ.

108 O Lord God, how long wilt thou suffer that such wickedness and iniquity shall be among this people?

109 O Lord, wilt thou give me strength, that I may bear with mine infirmities? For I am infirm, and such wickedness among this people doth pain my soul.

110 O Lord, my heart is exceeding sorrowful; wilt thou comfort my soul in Christ?

111 O Lord, wilt thou grant unto me that I may have strength, that I may suffer with patience these afflictions which shall come upon me, because of the iniquity of this people?

112 O Lord, wilt thou comfort my soul, and give unto me success, and also my fellow laborers who are with me; yea,

Ammon, and Aaron, and Omner, and also Amulek, and Zeezrom, and also my two sons; yea, even all these wilt thou comfort, O Lord? Yea, wilt thou comfort their souls in Christ?

113 Wilt thou grant unto them that they may have strength, that they may bear their afflictions which shall come upon them, because of the iniquities of this people?

114 O Lord, wilt thou grant unto us that we may have success in bringing them again unto thee, in Christ?

115 Behold, O Lord, their souls are precious, and many of them are our near brethren, therefore, give unto us, O Lord, power and wisdom, that we may bring these, our brethren, again unto thee.

116 ¶Now it came to pass, that when Alma had said these words, that he clapped his hands upon all them who were with him.

117 And behold, as he clapped his hands upon them, they were filled with the Holy Spirit.

118 And after that, they did separate themselves one from another; taking no thought for themselves what they should eat, or what they should drink, or what they should put on.

119 And the Lord provided for them that they should hunger not, neither should they thirst; yea, and he also gave them strength, that they should suffer no manner of afflictions, save it were swallowed up in the joy of Christ.

120 Now this was according to the prayer of Alma; and this because he prayed in faith.

121 ¶And it came to pass that they did go forth, and began to preach the word of God unto the people, entering into their synagogues, and into their houses; yea, and even they did preach the word in their streets.

122 And it came to pass that after much labor among them, they began to have success among the poor class of people; for behold, they were cast out of the synagogues, because of the coarseness of their apparel;

123 Therefore they were not permitted to enter into their synagogues to worship God, being esteemed as filthiness; therefore they were poor; yea, they were esteemed by their

brethren as dross; therefore they were poor as to things of the world; and also they were poor in heart.

124 ¶Now as Alma was teaching and speaking unto the people upon the hill Onidah, there came a great multitude unto him, who were those of whom we have been speaking of, who were poor in heart, because of their poverty as to the things of the world.

125 And they came unto Alma; and the one who was the most foremost among them, said unto him, Behold, what shall these my brethren do, for they are despised of all men, because of their poverty; yea, and more especially by our priests;

126 For they have cast us out of our synagogues, which we have labored abundantly to build, with our own hands; and they have cast us out because of our exceeding poverty, and we have no place to worship our God; and behold, what shall we do?

127 And now when Alma heard this, he turned him about, his face immediately towards him, and he beheld, with great joy; for he beheld that their afflictions had truly humbled them, and that they were in a preparation to hear the word;

128 Therefore he did say no more to the other multitude, but he stretched forth his hand, and cried unto those whom he beheld, who were truly penitent, and said unto them, I behold that ye are lowly in heart; and if so, blessed are ye.

129 Behold thy brother hath said, What shall we do? for we are cast out of our synagogues, that we can not worship our God.

130 Behold, I say unto you, Do ye suppose that ye can not worship God, save it be in your synagogues only?

131 And moreover, I would ask, Do ye suppose that ye must not worship God only once in a week?

132 I say unto you, It is well that ye are cast out of your synagogues, that ye may be humble, and that ye may learn wisdom; for it is necessary that ye should learn wisdom;

133 For it is because that ye are cast out, that ye are despised of your brethren, because of your exceeding poverty,

that ye are brought to a lowliness of heart; for ye are necessarily brought to be humble.

134 And now because ye are compelled to be humble, blessed are ye; for a man sometimes, if he is compelled to be humble, seeketh repentance;

135 And now surely, whosoever repenteth shall find mercy; and he that findeth mercy and endureth to the end, the same shall be saved.

136 And now as I said unto you, that because ye were compelled to be humble, ye were blessed, do ye not suppose that they are more blessed who truly humble themselves because of the word?

137 Yea, he that truly humbleth himself and repenteth of his sins, and endureth to the end, the same shall be blessed; yea, much more blessed than they who are compelled to be humble, because of their exceeding poverty; therefore blessed are they who humble themselves without being compelled to be humble;

138 Or rather, in other words, Blessed is he that believeth in the word of God, and is baptized without stubbornness of heart; yea, without being brought to know the word, or even compelled to know, before they will believe.

139 Yea, there are many who do say, If thou wilt shew unto us a sign from heaven, then we shall know of a surety; then we shall believe.

140 Now I ask, Is this faith? Behold, I say unto you, Nay; for if a man knoweth a thing, he hath no cause to believe, for he knoweth it.

141 And now how much more cursed is he that knoweth the will of God and doeth it not, than he that only believeth, or only hath cause to believe, and falleth into transgression? Now of this thing, ye must judge.

142 Behold, I say unto you, that it is on the one hand, even as it is on the other; and it shall be unto every man according to his work.

143 ¶And now as I said concerning faith: Faith, is not to have a perfect knowledge of things; therefore if ye have faith, ye hope for things which are not seen, which are true.

144 And now, behold, I say unto you; and I would that ye should remember that God is merciful unto all who believe on his name: therefore he desireth, in the first place, that ye should believe, yea, even on his word.

145 And now, he imparteth his word by angels, unto men; yea, not only men, but women also.

146 Now this is not all: little children do have words given unto them many times, which confound the wise and the learned.

147 ¶And now, my beloved brethren, as ye have desired to know of me what ye shall do because ye are afflicted and cast out: now I do not desire that ye should suppose that I mean to judge you only according to that which is true;

148 For I do not mean that ye all of you have been compelled to humble yourselves; for I verily believe that there are some among you who would humble themselves, let them be in whatsoever circumstances they might.

149 Now as I said concerning faith—that it was not a perfect knowledge, even so it is with my words.

150 Ye can not know of their surety at first, unto perfection, any more than faith is a perfect knowledge.

151 But behold, if ye will awake and arouse your faculties, even to an experiment upon my words, and exercise a particle of faith; yea, even if ye can no more than desire to believe, let this desire work in you, even until ye believe in a manner that ye can give place for a portion of my words.

152 Now we will compare the word unto a seed.

153 Now if ye give place, that a seed may be planted in your heart, behold, if it be a true seed, or a good seed, if ye do not cast it out by your unbelief, that ye will resist the Spirit of the Lord, behold, it will begin to swell within your breasts;

154 And when you feel these swelling motions, ye will begin to say within yourselves, It must needs be that this is a good seed, or that the word is good, for it beginneth to enlarge my soul; yea, it beginneth to enlighten my understanding; yea, and it beginneth to be delicious to me.

155 Now behold, would not this increase your faith? I

say unto you, Yea; nevertheless it hath not grown up to a perfect knowledge.

156 But behold, as the seed swelleth, and sprouteth, and beginneth to grow, then ye must needs say, that the seed is good; for behold it swelleth, and sprouteth, and beginneth to grow.

157 And now behold, will not this strengthen your faith? Yea, it will strengthen your faith, for ye will say, I know that this is a good seed, for behold, it sprouteth and beginneth to grow.

158 And now behold, are ye sure that this is a good seed? I say unto you, Yea; for every seed bringeth forth unto its own likeness; therefore, if a seed groweth, it is good, but if it groweth not, behold, it is not good; therefore it is cast away.

159 And now, behold, because ye have tried the experiment, and planted the seed, and it swelleth, and sprouteth, and beginneth to grow, ye must needs know that the seed is good.

160 And now behold, is your knowledge perfect? Yea, your knowledge is perfect in that thing, and your faith is dormant;

161 And this because you know; for ye know that the word hath swelled your souls, and ye also know that it hath sprouted up, that your understanding doth begin to be enlightened, and your mind doth begin to expand.

162 O then, is not this real? I say unto you, Yea; because it is light; and whatsoever is light, is good, because it is discernible; therefore ye must know that it is good.

163 And now behold, after ye have tasted this light, is your knowledge perfect? Behold, I say unto you, Nay; neither must ye lay aside your faith, for ye have only exercised your faith to plant the seed, that ye might try the experiment, to know if the seed was good.

164 And behold, as the tree beginneth to grow, ye will say, Let us nourish it with great care, that it may get root, that it may grow up and bring forth fruit unto us.

165 And now behold, if ye nourish it with much care, it will get root, and grow up, and bring forth fruit.

166 But if ye neglect the tree, and take no thought for its

nourishment, behold, it will not get any root; and when the heat of the sun cometh and scorcheth it, because it hath no root, it withers away, and ye pluck it up and cast it out.

167 Now this is not because the seed was not good, neither is it because the fruit thereof would not be desirable.

168 But it is because your ground is barren, and ye will not nourish the tree; therefore ye can not have the fruit thereof.

169 And thus it is if ye will not nourish the word, looking forward with an eye of faith to the fruit thereof, ye can never pluck of the fruit of the tree of life.

170 But if ye will nourish the word, yea, nourish the tree as it beginneth to grow, by your faith with great diligence, and with patience, looking forward to the fruit thereof, it shall take root; and behold, it shall be a tree springing up unto everlasting life;

171 And because of your diligence, and your faith, and your patience with the word, in nourishing it, that it may take root in you, behold, by and by, ye shall pluck the fruit thereof, which is most precious, which is sweet above all that is sweet, and which is white above all that is white; yea, and pure above all that is pure;

172 And ye shall feast upon this fruit, even until ye are filled, that ye hunger not, neither shall ye thirst.

173 Then my brethren ye shall reap the rewards of your faith, and your diligence, and patience, and long suffering, waiting for the tree to bring forth fruit unto you.

174 ¶Now after Alma had spoken these words, they sent forth unto him desiring to know whether they should believe in one God, that they might obtain this fruit of which he had spoken, or how they should plant the seed, or the word, of which he had spoken, which he said must be planted in their hearts; or in what manner they should begin to exercise their faith?

175 And Alma said unto them, Behold, ye have said that ye could not worship your God, because ye are cast out of your synagogues.

176 But behold, I say unto you, If ye suppose that ye can not worship God, ye do greatly err, and ye ought to search

the scriptures; if ye suppose that they have taught you this, ye do not understand them.

177 Do ye remember to have read what Zenos, the prophet of old, has said concerning prayer or worship?

178 For he said, Thou art merciful O God, for thou hast heard my prayer, even when I was in the wilderness: yea, thou wast merciful when I prayed concerning those who were mine enemies, and thou didst turn them to me:

179 Yea, O God, and thou wast merciful unto me when I did cry unto thee in my field; when I did cry unto thee in my prayer, and thou didst hear me.

180 And again, O God, when I did turn to my house thou didst hear me in my prayer.

181 And when I did turn unto my closet, O Lord, and prayed unto thee, thou didst hear me; yea, thou art merciful unto thy children when they cry unto thee to be heard of thee, and not of men, and thou wilt hear them;

182 Yea, O God, thou hast been merciful unto me and heard my cries in the midst of thy congregations; yea, and thou hast also heard me when I have been cast out, and have been despised by mine enemies;

183 Yea, thou didst hear my cries, and wast angry with mine enemies, and thou didst visit them in thine anger, with speedy destruction; and thou didst hear me because of mine afflictions and my sincerity;

184 And it is because of thy Son that thou hast been thus merciful unto me; therefore I will cry unto thee in all mine afflictions; for in thee is my joy; for thou hast turned thy judgments away from me, because of thy Son.

185 ¶And now Alma said unto them, Do ye believe those scriptures which have been written by them of old?

186 Behold, if ye do, ye must believe what Zenos said; for behold, he said, Thou hast turned away thy judgments, because of thy Son.

187 Now, behold, my brethren, I would ask, if ye have read the scriptures? If ye have, how can ye disbelieve on the Son of God?

188 For it is not written that Zenos alone spake of these

things, but Zenock also spake of these things; for behold, he said, Thou art angry, O Lord, with this people, because they will not understand of thy mercies which thou hast bestowed upon them, because of thy Son.

189 And now my brethren, ye see that a second prophet of old has testified of the Son of God; and because the people would not understand his words, they stoned him to death.

190 But behold, this is not all; these are not the only ones who have spoken concerning the Son of God.

191 Behold, he was spoken of by Moses; yea, and behold, a type was raised up in the wilderness, that whosoever would look upon it might live. And many did look and live.

192 But few understood the meaning of those things, and this because of the hardness of their hearts.

193 But there were many who were so hardened that they would not look; therefore they perished.

194 Now the reason they would not look, was because they did not believe that it would heal them.

195 O my brethren, if ye could be healed by merely casting about your eyes, that ye might be healed, would ye not behold quickly, or would ye rather harden your hearts in unbelief, and be slothful, that ye would not cast about your eyes, that ye might perish?

196 If so, wo shall come upon you; but if not so, then cast about your eyes and begin to believe in the Son of God, that he will come to redeem his people, and that he shall suffer and die to atone for their sins;

197 And that he shall rise again from the dead, which shall bring to pass the resurrection, that all men shall stand before him, to be judged, at the last and judgment day, according to their works.

198 And now my brethren, I desire that ye shall plant this word in your hearts, and as it beginneth to swell, even so nourish it by your faith.

199 And behold, it will become a tree, springing up in you unto everlasting life.

200 And then may God grant unto you that your burdens

may be light, through the joy of his Son. And even all this can ye do, if ye will. Amen.

201 ¶And now it came to pass that after Alma had spoken these words unto them, he sat down upon the ground, and Amulek arose and began to teach them, saying, My brethren, I think that it is impossible that ye should be ignorant of the things which have been spoken concerning the coming of Christ, who is taught by us to be the Son of God;

202 Yea, I know that these things were taught unto you, bountifully, before your dissension from among us, and as ye have desired of my beloved brother, that he should make known unto you what ye should do, because of your afflictions; and he hath spoken somewhat unto you to prepare your minds; yea, and he hath exhorted you unto faith, and to patience;

203 Yea, even that ye would have so much faith as even to plant the word in your hearts, that ye may try the experiment of its goodness; and we have beheld that the great question which is in your minds, is whether the word be in the Son of God, or whether there shall be no Christ.

204 And ye also beheld that my brother has proven unto you, in many instances, that the word is in Christ, unto salvation.

205 My brother has called upon the words of Zenos, that redemption cometh through the Son of God, and also upon the words of Zenock: and also he has appealed unto Moses, to prove that these things are true.

206 And now behold, I will testify unto you of myself, that these things are true.

207 Behold, I say unto you, that I do know that Christ shall come among the children of men, to take upon him the transgressions of his people, and that he shall atone for the sins of the world; for the Lord God has spoken it;

208 For it is expedient that an atonement should be made; for according to the great plan of the eternal God, there must be an atonement made, or else all mankind must unavoidably perish;

209 Yea, all are hardened; yea, all are fallen, and are lost,

and must perish except it be through the atonement which it is expedient should be made;

210 For it is expedient that there should be a great and last sacrifice; yea, not a sacrifice of man, neither of beast, neither of any manner of fowl; for it shall not be a human sacrifice: but it must be an infinite and eternal sacrifice.

211 Now there is not any man that can sacrifice his own blood, which will atone for the sins of another.

212 Now if a man murdereth, behold, will our law, which is just, take the life of his brother? I say unto you, Nay.

213 But the law requireth the life of him who hath murdered; therefore there can be nothing, which is short of an infinite atonement, which will suffice for the sins of the world; therefore it is expedient that there should be a great and last sacrifice;

214 And then shall there be, or it is expedient there should be, a stop to the shedding of blood; then shall the law of Moses be fulfilled; yea, it shall all be fulfilled; every jot and tittle, and none shall have passed away.

215 And behold, this is the whole meaning of the law; every whit pointing to that great and last sacrifice; and that great and last sacrifice will be the Son of God; yea, infinite and eternal; and thus he shall bring salvation to all those who shall believe on his name;

216 This being the intent of this last sacrifice, to bring about the bowels of mercy, which overpowereth justice and bringeth about means unto men that they may have faith unto repentance.

217 And thus mercy can satisfy the demands of justice, and encircles them in the arms of safety, while he that exercises no faith unto repentance, is exposed to the whole law of the demands of justice; therefore, only unto him that has faith unto repentance, is brought about the great and eternal plan of redemption.

218 Therefore may God grant unto you, my brethren, that ye may begin to exercise your faith unto repentance, that ye begin to call upon his holy name, that he would have mercy

upon you; yea, cry unto him for mercy; for he is mighty to save;

219 Yea, humble yourselves, and continue in prayer unto him; cry unto him when ye are in your fields; yea, over all your flocks; cry unto him in your houses, yea, over all your household, both morning, mid-day, and evening; yea, cry unto him against the power of your enemies; yea, cry unto him against the devil, who is an enemy to all righteousness.

220 Cry unto him over the crops of your fields, that ye may prosper in them: cry over the flocks of your fields, that they may increase.

221 But this is not all: ye must pour out your souls in your closets, and your secret places, and in your wilderness;

222 Yea, and when you do not cry unto the Lord, let your hearts be full, drawn out in prayer unto him continually for your welfare, and also for the welfare of those who are around you.

223 ¶And now behold, my brethren, I say unto you, Do not suppose that this is all; for after ye have done all these things, if ye turn away the needy, and the naked, and visit not the sick and afflicted, and impart of your substance if ye have, to those who stand in need;

224 I say unto you, If ye do not any of these things, behold, your prayer is vain, and availeth you nothing, and ye are as hypocrites who do deny the faith;

225 Therefore if ye do not remember to be charitable, ye are as dross, which the refiners do cast out, (it being of no worth,) and is trodden under foot of men.

226 ¶And now, my brethren, I would that after ye have received so many witnesses, seeing that the holy scriptures testify of these things, come forth and bring fruit unto repentance;

227 Yea, I would that ye would come forth and harden not your hearts any longer; for behold, now is the time, and the day of your salvation; and therefore, if ye will repent and harden not your hearts, immediately shall the great plan of redemption be brought about unto you.

228 For behold, this life is the time for men to prepare to

meet God: yea, behold, the day of this life is the day for men to perform their labors.

229 And now as I said unto you before, as ye have had so many witnesses, therefore I beseech of you, that ye do not procrastinate the day of your repentance until the end;

230 For after this day of life, which is given us to prepare for eternity, behold, if we do not improve our time while in this life, then cometh the night of darkness, wherein there can be no labor performed.

231 Ye can not say, when ye are brought to that awful crisis, that I will repent, that I will return to my God.

232 Nay, ye can not say this; for that same spirit which doth possess your bodies at the time that ye go out of this life, that same spirit will have power to possess your body in that eternal world.

233 For behold, if ye have procrastinated the day of your repentance, even until death, behold, ye have become subjected to the spirit of the devil, and he doth seal you his;

234 Therefore the Spirit of the Lord hath withdrawn from you, and hath no place in you, and the devil hath all power over you; and this is the final state of the wicked.

235 And this I know, because the Lord has said, he dwelleth not in unholy temples, but in the hearts of the righteous doth he dwell;

236 Yea, and he has also said, that the righteous shall sit down in his kingdom, to go no more out; but their garments should be made white, through the blood of the Lamb.

237 ¶And now my beloved brethren, I desire that ye should remember these things, and that ye should work out your salvation with fear before God, and that ye should no more deny the coming of Christ; that ye contend no more against the Holy Ghost, but that ye receive it, and take upon you the name of Christ; that ye humble yourselves even to the dust, and worship God in whatsoever place ye may be in, in spirit and in truth;

238 And that ye live in thanksgiving daily, for the many mercies and blessings which he doth bestow upon you; yea, and I also exhort you my brethren, that ye be watchful unto

prayer continually, that ye may not be led away by the temptation of the devil, that he may not overpower you, that ye may not become his subjects at the last day: for behold, he rewardeth you no good thing.

239 And now my beloved brethren, I would exhort you to have patience, and that ye bear with all manner of afflictions; that ye do not revile against those who do cast you out because of your exceeding poverty, lest ye become sinners like unto them; but that ye have patience, and bear with those afflictions, with a firm hope that ye shall one day rest from all your afflictions.

240 ¶Now it came to pass that after Amulek had made an end of these words, they withdrew themselves from the multitude, and came over into the land of Jershon;

241 Yea, and the rest of the brethren, after they had preached the word unto the Zoramites, also came over into the land of Jershon.

242 ¶And it came to pass that after the more popular part of the Zoramites had consulted together concerning the words which had been preached unto them, they were angry because of the word, for it did destroy their craft; therefore they would not hearken unto the words.

243 And they sent and gathered together throughout all the land, all the people, and consulted with them concerning the words which had been spoken.

244 Now their rulers, and their priests, and their teachers, did not let the people know concerning their desires; therefore they found out privily the minds of all the people.

245 ¶And it came to pass that after they had found out the minds of all the people, those who were in favor of the words which had been spoken by Alma and his brethren, were cast out of the land; and they were many, and they came over also into the land of Jershon.

246 ¶And it came to pass that Alma and his brethren did minister unto them.

247 Now the people of the Zoramites were angry with the people of Ammon who were in Jershon, and the chief ruler of the Zoramites being a very wicked man, sent over unto the

CHAP. 16.] BOOK OF ALMA. 433

people of Ammon desiring them that they should cast out of their land all those who came over from them into their land.

248 And he breathed out many threatenings against them.

249 And now the people of Ammon did not fear their words, therefore they did not cast them out, but they did receive all the poor of the Zoramites that came over unto them;

250 And they did nourish them, and did clothe them, and did give unto them lands for their inheritance; and they did administer unto them according to their wants.

251 Now this did stir up the Zoramites to anger against the people of Ammon, and they began to mix with the Lamanites, and to stir them up also to anger against them;

252 And thus the Zoramites and the Lamanites began to make preparations for war against the people of Ammon, and also against the Nephites.

253 And thus ended the seventeenth year of the reign of the Judges, over the people of Nephi.

254 ¶And the people of Ammon departed out of the land of Jershon, and came over into the land of Melek, and gave place in the land of Jershon for the armies of the Nephites, that they might contend with the armies of the Lamanites, and the armies of the Zoramites;

255 And thus commenced a war betwixt the Lamanites and the Nephites, in the eighteenth year of the reign of the Judges; and an account shall be given of their wars hereafter.

256 And Alma, and Ammon, and their brethren, and also the two sons of Alma, returned to the land of Zarahemla, after having been instruments in the hands of God of bringing many of the Zoramites to repentance; and as many as were brought to repentance, were driven out of their land;

257 But they have lands for their inheritance in the land of Jershon, and they have taken up arms to defend themselves, and their wives, and children, and their lands.

258 Now Alma, being grieved for the iniquity of his people, yea for the wars, and the bloodsheds, and the contentions which were among them; and having been to declare the word, or sent to declare the word, among all the people in every city;

259 And seeing that the hearts of the people began to wax hard, and that they began to be offended because of the strictness of the word, his heart was exceeding sorrowful;

260 Therefore, he caused that his sons should be gathered together that he might give unto them every one his charge, separately, concerning the things pertaining unto righteousness.

261 And we have an account of his commandments, which he gave unto them according to his own record.

CHAPTER 17.

The commandments of Alma, to his son, Helaman.

1 ¶My son, give ear to my words; for I swear unto you, that inasmuch as ye shall keep the commandments of God, ye shall prosper in the land.

2 I would that ye should do as I have done, in remembering the captivity of our fathers; for they were in bondage, and none could deliver them, except it was the God of Abraham, and the God of Isaac, and the God of Jacob: and he surely did deliver them in their afflictions.

3 And now, O my son Helaman, behold thou art in thy youth, and therefore I beseech of thee that thou wilt hear my words, and learn of me; for I do know that whosoever shall put their trust in God, shall be supported in their trials, and their troubles, and their afflictions, and shall be lifted up at the last day;

4 And I would not that ye think that I know of myself, not of the temporal, but of the spiritual; not of the carnal mind, but of God.

5 Now behold I say unto you, If I had not been born of God, I should not have known these things; but God has by the mouth of his holy angel, made these things known unto me, not of any worthiness of myself, for I went about with the sons of Mosiah, seeking to destroy the church of God; but behold, God sent his holy angel to stop us by the way.

6 And behold, he spake unto us, as it were the voice of

thunder, and the whole earth did tremble beneath our feet, and we all fell to the earth, for the fear of the Lord came upon us.

7 But behold, the voice said unto me, Arise. And I arose and stood up, and beheld the angel. And he said unto me, If thou wilt of thyself be destroyed, seek no more to destroy the church of God.

8 ¶And it came to pass that I fell to the earth; and it was for the space of three days and three nights, that I could not open my mouth; neither had I the use of my limbs.

9 And the angel spake more things unto me, which were heard by my brethren, but I did not hear them; for when I heard the words, If thou wilt be destroyed of thyself, seek no more to destroy the church of God, I was struck with such great fear and amazement, lest perhaps I should be destroyed, that I fell to the earth, and I did hear no more;

10 But I was racked with eternal torment, for my soul was harrowed up to the greatest degree, and racked with all my sins. Yea, I did remember all my sins and iniquities, for which I was tormented with the pains of hell;

11 Yea, I saw that I had rebelled against my God, and that I had not kept his holy commandments; yea, and I had murdered many of his children, or rather led them away unto destruction;

12 Yea, and in fine, so great had been my iniquities, that the very thoughts of coming into the presence of my God, did rack my soul with inexpressible horror.

13 O, thought I, that I could be banished and become extinct both soul and body, that I might not be brought to stand in the presence of my God, to be judged of my deeds.

14 And now, for three days and for three nights was I racked, even with the pains of a damned soul.

15 ¶And it came to pass that as I was thus racked with torment, while I was harrowed up by the memory of my many sins, behold, I remembered also to have heard my father prophesy unto the people, concerning the coming of one Jesus Christ, a Son of God, to atone for the sins of the world.

16 Now as my mind caught hold upon this thought, I cried

within my heart, O Jesus, thou Son of God, have mercy on me, who art in the gall of bitterness, and art encircled about by the everlasting chains of death.

17 And now behold, when I thought this, I could remember my pains no more; yea, I was harrowed up by the memory of my sins no more.

18 And O, what joy, and what marvelous light I did behold; yea, my soul was filled with joy as exceeding as was my pain; yea, I say unto you, my son, that there could be nothing so exquisite and so bitter as was my pains.

19 Yea, and again I say unto you, my son, that on the other hand, there can be nothing so exquisite and sweet as was my joy;

20 Yea, methought I saw even as our father Lehi saw, God sitting upon his throne, surrounded with numberless concourses of angels, in the attitude of singing and praising their God; yea, and my soul did long to be there.

21 But behold, my limbs did receive their strength again, and I stood upon my feet, and did manifest unto the people that I had been born of God;

22 Yea, and from that time, even until now, I have labored without ceasing, that I might bring souls unto repentance; that I might bring them to taste of the exceeding joy of which I did taste; that they might also be born of God, and be filled with the Holy Ghost.

23 Yea, and now behold, O my son, the Lord doth give me exceeding great joy in the fruit of my labors; for because of the word which he has imparted unto me, behold, many have been born of God, and have tasted as I have tasted, and have seen eye to eye, as I have seen;

24 Therefore they do know of these things of which I have spoken, as I do know; and the knowledge which I have is of God.

25 And I have been supported under trials and troubles of every kind, yea, and in all manner of afflictions; yea, God has delivered me from prison, and from bonds, and from death; yea, and I do put my trust in him, and he will still deliver me;

26 And I know that he will raise me up at the last day, to

dwell with him in glory; yea, and I will praise him for ever, for he has brought our fathers out of Egypt, and he has swallowed up the Egyptians in the Red Sea; and he led them by his power into the promised land;

27 Yea, and he has delivered them out of bondage and captivity, from time to time; yea, and he has also brought our fathers out of the land of Jerusalem; and he has also by his everlasting power, delivered them out of bondage and captivity, from time to time, even down to the present day;

28 And I have always retained in remembrance their captivity: yea, and ye also ought to retain in remembrance, as I have done, their captivity.

29 But behold, my son, this is not all; for ye ought to know, as I do know, that inasmuch as ye shall keep the commandments of God, ye shall prosper in the land;

30 And ye ought to know also, that inasmuch as ye will not keep the commandments of God, ye shall be cut off from his presence. Now this is according to his word.

31 ¶And now my son Helaman, I command you that ye take the records which have been entrusted with me; and I also command you that ye keep a record of this people, according as I have done, upon the plates of Nephi, and keep all these things sacred which I have kept, even as I have kept them: for it is for a wise purpose that they are kept;

32 And these plates of brass which contain these engravings, which have the records of the holy scriptures upon them, which have the genealogy of our forefathers, even from the beginning.

33 And behold, it has been prophesied by our fathers, that they should be kept and handed down from one generation to another, and be kept and preserved by the hand of the Lord, until they should go forth unto every nation, kindred, tongue and people, that they shall know of the mysteries contained thereon.

34 And now behold, if they are kept, they must retain their brightness; yea, and they will retain their brightness; yea, and also shall all the plates which do contain that which is holy writ.

35 Now ye may suppose that this is foolishness in me; but behold I say unto you, that by small and simple things, are great things brought to pass; and small means in many instances, doth confound the wise.

36 And the Lord God doth work by means to bring about his great and eternal purposes; and by very small means the Lord doth confound the wise, and bringeth about the salvation of many souls.

37 And now, it has hitherto been wisdom in God, that these things should be preserved: for behold, they have enlarged the memory of this people, yea, and convinced many of the error of their ways, and brought them to the knowledge of their God, unto the salvation of their souls.

38 Yea, I say unto you, were it not for these things that these records do contain, which are on these plates, Ammon and his brethren could not have convinced so many thousands of the Lamanites, of the incorrect tradition of their fathers;

39 Yea, these records and their words, brought them unto repentance; that is, they brought them to the knowledge of the Lord their God, and to rejoice in Jesus Christ their Redeemer.

40 And who knoweth but what they will be the means of bringing many thousands of them, yea, and also many thousands of our stiff-necked brethren, the Nephites, who are now hardening their hearts, in sins and iniquities, to the knowledge of their Redeemer.

41 Now these mysteries are not yet fully made known unto me; therefore I shall forbear.

42 And it may suffice, if I only say, they are preserved for a wise purpose, which purpose is known unto God: for he doth counsel in wisdom over all his works, and his paths are straight and his course is one eternal round.

43 O remember, remember, my son Helaman, how strict are the commandments of God.

44 And he said, If ye will keep my commandments, ye shall prosper in the land; but if ye keep not his commandments, ye shall be cut off from his presence.

45 And now remember, my son, that God has entrusted

you with these things, which are sacred, which he has kept sacred, and also which he will keep and preserve for a wise purpose in him, that he may shew forth his power unto future generations.

46 ¶And now behold, I tell you by the spirit of prophecy, that if ye transgress the commandments of God, behold, these things which are sacred, shall be taken away from you by the power of God, and ye shall be delivered up unto Satan, that he may sift you as chaff before the wind;

47 But if ye keep the commandments of God, and do with these things which are sacred, according to that which the Lord doth command you, (for you must appeal unto the Lord for all things whatsoever ye must do with them,) behold no power of earth or hell can take them from you, for God is powerful to the fulfilling of all his words:

48 For he will fulfill all his promises which he shall make unto you, for he has fulfilled his promises which he has made unto our fathers.

49 For he promised unto them that he would reserve these things for a wise purpose in him, that he might shew forth his power unto future generations.

50 ¶And now behold, one purpose hath he fulfilled, even to the restoration of many thousands of the Lamanites to the knowledge of the truth; and he hath shewn forth his power in them, and he will also still shew forth his power in them, unto future generations; therefore they shall be preserved;

51 Therefore I command you, my son Helaman, that ye be diligent in fulfilling all my words, and that ye be diligent in keeping the commandments of God, as they are written.

52 ¶And now, I will speak unto you concerning those twenty-four plates, that ye keep them, that the mysteries and the works of darkness, and their secret works, or the secret works of those people, who have been destroyed, may be made manifest unto this people;

53 Yea, all their murders, and robbings, and their plunderings, and all their wickedness, and abominations, may be made manifest unto this people; yea, and that ye preserve these directors.

54 For, behold, the Lord saw that his people began to work in darkness, yea, work secret murders and abominations; therefore the Lord said, if they did not repent, they should be destroyed from off the face of the earth.

55 And the Lord said, I will prepare unto my servant Gazelem, a stone, which shall shine forth in darkness unto light, that I may discover unto my people who serve me, that I may discover unto them the works of their brethren; yea, their secret works, their works of darkness, and their wickedness and abominations.

56 And now my son, these directors were prepared, that the word of God might be fulfilled, which he spake, saying: I will bring forth out of darkness unto light, all their secret works and their abominations:

57 And except they repent, I will destroy them from off the face of the earth; and I will bring to light all their secrets and abominations, unto every nation that shall hereafter possess the land.

58 And now my son, we see that they did not repent; therefore they have been destroyed; and thus far the word of God has been fulfilled; yea, their secret abominations have been brought out of darkness, and made known unto us.

59 ¶And now my son, I command you that ye retain all their oaths, and their covenants, and their agreements in their secret abominations; yea, and all their signs and their wonders ye shall retain from this people, that they know them not, lest peradventure they should fall into darkness also, and be destroyed.

60 For behold, there is a curse upon all this land, that destruction shall come upon all those workers of darkness, according to the power of God, when they are fully ripe; therefore I desire that this people might not be destroyed.

61 Therefore ye shall keep these secret plans of their oaths and their covenants from this people, and only their wickedness, and their murders, and their abominations, shall ye make known unto them:

62 And ye shall teach them to abhor such wickedness, and abominations, and murders; and ye shall also teach them,

that these people were destroyed on account of their wickedness, and abominations, and their murders.

63 For behold, they murdered all the prophets of the Lord who came among them to declare unto them concerning their iniquities; and the blood of those whom they murdered, did cry unto the Lord their God, for vengeance upon those who were their murderers;

64 And thus the judgments of God did come upon these workers of darkness and secret combinations; yea, and cursed be the land for ever and ever unto those workers of darkness and secret combinations, even unto destruction, except they repent before they are fully ripe.

65 ¶And now my son, remember the words which I have spoken unto you: trust not those secret plans unto this people, but teach them an everlasting hatred against sin and iniquity;

66 Preach unto them repentance, and faith on the Lord Jesus Christ: teach them to humble themselves, and to be meek and lowly in heart; teach them to withstand every temptation of the devil, with their faith on the Lord Jesus Christ;

67 Teach them to never be weary of good works, but to be meek and lowly in heart: for such shall find rest to their souls.

68 O remember my son, and learn wisdom in thy youth; yea, learn in thy youth to keep the commandments of God; yea, and cry unto God for all thy support;

69 Yea, let all thy doings be unto the Lord, and whithersoever thou goest, let it be in the Lord; yea, let thy thoughts be directed unto the Lord; yea, let the affections of thy heart be placed upon the Lord for ever; counsel the Lord in all thy doings, and he will direct thee for good:

70 Yea, when thou liest down at night, lie down unto the Lord, that he may watch over you in your sleep; and when thou risest in the morning, let thy heart be full of thanks unto God; and if ye do these things, ye shall be lifted up at the last day.

71 And now my son, I have somewhat to say concerning the thing which our fathers call a ball, or director; or our fathers called it liahona, which is, being interpreted, a compass; and the Lord prepared it.

72 And behold, there can not any man work after the manner of so curious a workmanship.

73 And behold, it was prepared to shew unto our fathers the course which they should travel in the wilderness; and it did work for them according to their faith in God;

74 Therefore if they had faith to believe that God could cause that those spindles should point the way they should go, behold, it was done; therefore they had this miracle, and also many other miracles wrought by the power of God, day by day;

75 Nevertheless, because those miracles were worked by small means, it did shew unto them marvelous works.

76 They were slothful, and forgot to exercise their faith and diligence, and then those marvelous works ceased, and they did not progress in their journey:

77 Therefore they tarried in the wilderness, or did not travel a direct course, and were afflicted with hunger and thirst, because of their transgressions.

78 ¶And now my son, I would that ye should understand that these things are not without a shadow; for as our fathers were slothful to give heed to this compass, (now these things were temporal,) they did not prosper; even so it is with things which are spiritual.

79 For behold, it is as easy to give heed to the word of Christ, which will point to you a straight course to eternal bliss, as it was for our fathers to give heed to this compass, which would point unto them a straight course, to the promised land.

80 And now I say, Is there not a type in this thing? For just as surely as this director did bring our fathers, by following its course, to the promised land, shall the words of Christ, if we follow their course, carry us beyond this vale of sorrow, into a far better land of promise.

81 ¶O my son, do not let us be slothful because of the easiness of the way; for so was it with our fathers; for so was it prepared for them, that if they would look, they might live; even so it is with us.

82 The way is prepared, and if we will look, we may live for ever.

83 And now my son, see that ye take care of these sacred things; yea, see that ye look to God and live.

84 Go unto this people, and declare the word, and be sober. My son, farewell.

CHAPTER 18.

The commandments of Alma, to his son, Shiblon.

1 ¶My son, give ear to my words; for I say unto you, even as I said unto Helaman, that inasmuch as ye shall keep the commandments of God, ye shall prosper in the land; and inasmuch as ye will not keep the commandments of God, ye shall be cast off from his presence.

2 And now my son, I trust that I shall have great joy in you, because of your steadiness and your faithfulness unto God; for as you have commenced in your youth, to look to the Lord your God, even so I hope that you will continue in keeping his commandments: for blessed is he that endureth to the end.

3 I say unto you my son, that I have had great joy in thee already, because of thy faithfulness, and thy diligence, and thy patience, and thy long suffering among the people of the Zoramites.

4 For I knew that thou wast in bonds; yea, and I also knew that thou wast stoned for the word's sake; and thou didst bear all these things with patience, because the Lord was with thee; and now thou knowest that the Lord did deliver thee.

5 ¶And now my son Shiblon, I would that ye should remember that as much as ye shall put your trust in God, even so much ye shall be delivered out of your trials, and your troubles, and your afflictions; and ye shall be lifted up at the last day.

6 Now my son, I would not that ye should think that I know these things of myself, but it is the Spirit of God which is in me, which maketh these things known unto me: for if I

had not been born of God, I should not have known these things.

7 But behold, the Lord in his great mercy sent his angel to declare unto me, that I must stop the work of destruction among his people;

8 Yea, and I have seen an angel face to face; and he spake with me, and his voice was as thunder, and it shook the whole earth.

9 ¶And it came to pass that I was three days and three nights in the most bitter pain and anguish of soul: and never, until I did cry out unto the Lord Jesus Christ for mercy, did I receive a remission of my sins.

10 But behold, I did cry unto him, and I did find peace to my soul.

11 And now my son, I have told you this, that ye may learn wisdom, that ye may learn of me that there is no other way nor means whereby man can be saved, only in and through Christ.

12 Behold, he is the life and the light of the world. Behold, he is the word of truth and righteousness.

13 And now, as ye have begun to teach the word, even so I would that ye should continue to teach; and I would that ye would be diligent and temperate in all things.

14 See that ye are not lifted up unto pride: yea, see that ye do not boast in your own wisdom, nor of your much strength; use boldness, but not overbearance;

15 And also see that ye bridle all your passions, that ye may be filled with love; see that ye refrain from idleness; do not pray as the Zoramites do, for ye have seen that they pray to be heard of men, and to be praised for their wisdom.

16 Do not say, O God, I thank thee that we are better than our brethren; but rather say, O Lord, forgive my unworthiness, and remember my brethren in mercy; yea, acknowledge your unworthiness before God at all times.

17 And may the Lord bless your soul, and receive you at the last day into his kingdom, to sit down in peace.

18 Now go, my son, and teach the word unto this people. Be sober. My son, farewell.

CHAPTER 19.

The commandments of Alma, to his son, Corianton.

1 ¶And now my son, I have somewhat more to say unto thee than what I said unto thy brother: for behold, have ye not observed the steadiness of thy brother, his faithfulness, and his diligence in keeping the commandments of God.

2 Behold, has he not set a good example for thee?

3 For thou didst not give so much heed unto my words as did thy brother, among the people of the Zoramites.

4 Now this is what I have against thee; thou didst go on unto boasting in thy strength, and thy wisdom.

5 And this is not all, my son. Thou didst do that which was grievous unto me; for thou didst forsake the ministry, and did go over into the land of Siron, among the borders of the Lamanites, after the harlot Isabel; yea, she did steal away the hearts of many; but this was no excuse for thee, my son.

6 Thou shouldst have tended to the ministry, wherewith thou wast entrusted.

7 Know ye not, my son, that these things are an abomination in the sight of the Lord; yea, most abominable above all sins, save it be the shedding of innocent blood, or denying the Holy Ghost?

8 For behold, if ye deny the Holy Ghost when it once has had place in you, and ye know that ye deny it; behold, this is a sin which is unpardonable;

9 Yea, and whosoever murdereth against the light and knowledge of God, it is not easy for him to obtain forgiveness; yea, I say unto you, my son, that it is not easy for him to obtain a forgiveness.

10 And now my son, I would to God that ye had not been guilty of so great a crime.

11 I would not dwell upon your crimes, to harrow up your soul, if it were not for your good.

12 But behold, ye can not hide your crimes from God; and except ye repent, they will stand as a testimony against you at the last day.

13 Now, my son, I would that ye should repent, and forsake your sins, and go no more after the lusts of your eyes, but cross yourself in all these things; for except ye do this, ye can in no wise inherit the kingdom of God.

14 O remember, and take it upon you, and cross yourself in these things.

15 And I command you to take it upon you to counsel your elder brothers in your undertakings; for behold, thou art in thy youth, and ye stand in need to be nourished by your brothers.

16 And give heed to their counsel; suffer not yourself to be led away by any vain or foolish thing; suffer not that the devil lead away your heart again, after those wicked harlots.

17 Behold, O my son, how great iniquity ye brought upon the Zoramites: for when they saw your conduct, they would not believe in my words.

18 And now the Spirit of the Lord doth say unto me, Command thy children to do good, lest they lead away the hearts of many people to destruction:

19 Therefore I command you, my son, in the fear of God, that you refrain from your iniquities; that ye turn to the Lord with all your mind, might and strength; that ye lead away the hearts of no more, to do wickedly;

20 But rather return unto them, and acknowledge your faults, and retain that wrong which ye have done; seek not after riches, nor the vain things of this world; for behold, you can not carry them with you.

21 ¶And now, my son, I would say somewhat unto you concerning the coming of Christ.

22 Behold, I say unto you, that it is he that surely shall come, to take away the sins of the world; yea, he cometh to declare glad tidings of salvation unto his people.

23 And now my son, this was the ministry unto which ye were called, to declare these glad tidings unto this people, to prepare their minds; or rather that salvation might come unto them, that they may prepare the minds of their children to hear the word at the time of his coming.

24 And now I will ease your mind somewhat on this sub-

CHAP. 19.]   BOOK OF ALMA.   447

ject. Behold, you marvel why these things should be known so long beforehand.

25 Behold, I say unto you, Is not a soul at this time as precious unto God, as a soul will be at the time of his coming?

26 Is it not as necessary that the plan of redemption should be made known unto this people, as well as unto their children?

27 Is it not as easy at this time, for the Lord to send his angel to declare these glad tidings unto us, as unto our children; or as after the time of his coming?

28 Now my son, here is somewhat more I would say unto thee: for I perceive that thy mind is worried concerning the resurrection of the dead.

29 Behold, I say unto you, that there is no resurrection; or I would say in other words, that this mortal does not put on immortality; this corruption does not put on incorruption, until after the coming of Christ.

30 Behold, he bringeth to pass the resurrection of the dead. But behold, my son, the resurrection is not yet.

31 Now I unfold unto you a mystery: nevertheless, there are many mysteries, which are kept, that no one knoweth them, save God himself.

32 But I shew unto you one thing, which I have inquired diligently of God, that I might know; that is, concerning the resurrection.

33 Behold, there is a time appointed that all shall come forth from the dead.

34 Now when this time cometh, no one knows; but God knoweth the time which is appointed.

35 Now whether there shall be one time, or a second time, or a third time, that men shall come forth from the dead, it mattereth not; for God knoweth all these things; and it sufficeth me to know that this is the case; that there is a time appointed that all shall rise from the dead.

36 Now there must needs be a space betwixt the time of death, and the time of the resurrection.

37 And now I would inquire what becometh of the souls of

men, from this time of death, to the time appointed for the resurrection?

38 Now whether there is more than one time appointed for men to rise, it mattereth not: for all do not die at once: and this mattereth not; all is as one day, with God; and time only is measured unto men;

39 Therefore there is a time appointed unto men, that they shall rise from the dead; and there is a space between the time of death and the resurrection.

40 And now concerning this space of time. What becometh of the souls of men, is the thing which I have inquired diligently of the Lord to know; and this is the thing of which I do know.

41 And when the time cometh when all shall rise, then shall they know that God knoweth all the times which are appointed unto man.

42 Now concerning the state of the soul between death and the resurrection.

43 Behold, it has been made known unto me, by an angel, that the spirits of all men, as soon as they are departed from this mortal body; yea, the spirits of all men, whether they be good or evil, are taken home to that God who gave them life.

44 And then shall it come to pass that the spirits of those who are righteous, are received into a state of happiness, which is called paradise; a state of rest; a state of peace, where they shall rest from all their troubles, and from all care, and sorrow, etc.

45 And then shall it come to pass, that the spirits of the wicked, yea, who are evil; for behold, they have no part nor portion of the Spirit of the Lord: for behold they choose evil works, rather than good: therefore the spirit of the devil did enter into them, and take possession of their house;

46 And these shall be cast out into outer darkness; there shall be weeping, and wailing and gnashing of teeth; and this because of their own iniquity; being led captive by the will of the devil.

47 Now this is the state of the souls of the wicked; yea, in darkness, and a state of awful, fearful, looking for, of the

fiery indignation of the wrath of God upon them; thus they remain in this state, as well as the righteous in paradise, until the time of their resurrection.

48 Now there are some that have understood that this state of happiness, and this state of misery of the soul, before the resurrection, was a first resurrection.

49 Yea, I admit it may be termed a resurrection; the raising of the spirit or the soul, and their consignation to happiness or misery, according to the words which have been spoken.

50 And behold, again it hath been spoken, that there is a first resurrection; a resurrection of all those who have been, or who are, or who shall be, down to the resurrection of Christ from the dead.

51 Now we do not suppose that this first resurrection which is spoken of in this manner, can be the resurrection of the souls, and their consignation to happiness or misery. Ye can not suppose that this is what it meaneth.

52 Behold, I say unto you, Nay; but it meaneth the reuniting of the soul with the body of those from the days of Adam, down to the resurrection of Christ.

53 Now whether the souls and the bodies of those of whom have been spoken, shall all be reunited at once, the wicked as well as the righteous, I do not say;

54 Let it suffice, that I say that they all come forth; or in other words, their resurrection cometh to pass before the resurrection of those who die after the resurrection of Christ.

55 Now my son, I do not say that their resurrection cometh at the resurrection of Christ; but behold, I give it as my opinion, that the souls and the bodies are reunited, of the righteous at the resurrection of Christ, and his ascension into heaven.

56 But whether it be at his resurrection, or after, I do not say; but this much I say, that there is a space between death and the resurrection of the body, and a state of the soul in happiness or in misery, until the time which is appointed of God that the dead shall come forth and be reunited, both soul

and body, and be brought to stand before God, and be judged according to their works;

57 Yea, this bringeth about the restoration of those things of which have been spoken by the mouths of the prophets.

58 The soul shall be restored to the body, and the body to the soul; yea, and every limb and joint shall be restored to its body; yea, even a hair of the head shall not be lost, but all things shall be restored to their proper and perfect frame.

59 And now my son, this is the restoration of which has been spoken by the mouths of the prophets. And then shall the righteous shine forth in the kingdom of God.

60 But behold, an awful death cometh upon the wicked; for they die as to things pertaining to things of righteousness; for they are unclean, and no unclean thing can inherit the kingdom of God;

61 But they are cast out, and consigned to partake of the fruits of their labors or their works, which have been evil; and they drink the dregs of a bitter cup.

62 ¶And now my son, I have somewhat to say concerning the restoration of which has been spoken: for behold, some have wrested the scriptures, and have gone far astray, because of this thing.

63 And I perceive that thy mind has been worried also concerning this thing. But behold, I will explain it unto thee.

64 I say unto thee, my son, that the plan of restoration is requisite with the justice of God; for it is requisite that all things should be restored to their proper order.

65 Behold it is requisite and just, according to the power and resurrection of Christ, that the soul of man should be restored to its body, and that every part of the body should be restored to itself.

66 And it is requisite with the justice of God, that men should be judged according to their works; and if their works were good in this life, and the desires of their hearts were good, that they should also, at the last day, be restored unto that which is good;

67 And if their works are evil, they shall be restored unto him for evil: therefore, all things shall be restored to their

proper order; everything to its natural frame; mortality raised to immortality; corruption to incorruption; raised to endless happiness, to inherit the kingdom of God, or to endless misery, to inherit the kingdom of the devil;

68 The one on the one hand, the other on the other; the one raised to happiness, according to his desires of happiness; or good, according to his desires of good; and the other to evil, according to his desires of evil; for as he has desired to do evil all the day long, even so shall he have his reward of evil, when the night cometh.

69 And so it is on the other hand. If he hath repented of his sins, and desired righteousness until the end of his days, even so shall he be rewarded unto righteousness.

70 These are they that are redeemed of the Lord; yea, these are they that are taken out, that are delivered from that endless night of darkness; and thus they stand or fall; for behold, they are their own judges, whether to do good or do evil.

71 Now the decrees of God are unalterable; therefore the way is prepared, that whosoever will, may walk therein and be ,saved.

72 And now behold, my son, do not risk one more offense against your God upon those points of doctrine, which ye have hitherto risked to commit sin.

73 Do not suppose, because it has been spoken concerning restoration, that ye shall be restored from sin to happiness.

74 Behold, I say unto you, Wickedness never was happiness.

75 And now, my son, all men that are in a state of nature, or I would say, in a carnal state, are in the gall of bitterness, and in the bonds of iniquity; they are without God in the world, and they have gone contrary to the nature of God; therefore they are in a state contrary to the nature of happiness.

76 And now behold, is the meaning of the word restoration, to take a thing of a natural state, and place it in an unnatural state, or to place it in a state opposite to its nature?

77 O, my son, this is not the case; but the meaning of the word restoration, is to bring back again evil for evil, or carnal for carnal, or devilish for devilish; good for that which is

good; righteous for that which is righteous; just for that which is just; merciful for that which is merciful;

78 Therefore, my son, see that ye are merciful unto your brethren; deal justly, judge righteously, and do good continually; and if ye do all these things, then shall ye receive your reward;

79 Yea, ye shall have mercy restored unto you again; ye shall have justice restored unto you again; ye shall have a righteous judgment restored unto you again;

80 And ye shall have good rewarded unto you again; for that which ye do send out, shall return unto you again, and be restored; therefore the word restoration, more fully condemneth the sinner, and justifieth him not at all.

81 ¶And now, my son, I perceive there is somewhat more which doth worry your mind, which ye can not understand, which is concerning the justice of God, in the punishment of the sinner: for ye do try to suppose that it is injustice that the sinner should be consigned to a state of misery.

82 Now behold, my son, I will explain this thing unto thee: for behold, after the Lord God sent our first parents forth from the garden of Eden to till the ground, from whence they were taken; yea, he drew out the man, and he placed at the east end of the garden of Eden, cherubim, and a flaming sword which turned every way, to keep the tree of life.

83 Now we see that the man had become as God, knowing good and evil; and lest he should put forth his hand, and take also of the tree of life, and eat, and live for ever, the Lord God placed cherubim and the flaming sword, that he should not partake of the fruit;

84 And thus we see, that there was a time granted unto man, to repent, yea, a probationary time, a time to repent and serve God.

85 For behold, if Adam had put forth his hand immediately, and partook of the tree of life, he would have lived for ever, according to the word of God, having no space for repentance;

86 Yea, and also the word of God would have been void, and the great plan of salvation would have been frustrated.

87 But behold it was appointed unto man to die; therefore as they were cut off from the tree of life, they should be cut off from the face of the earth; and man became lost for ever; yea, they became fallen man.

88 And now we see by this, that our first parents were cut off, both temporally and spiritually, from the presence of the Lord; and thus we see they became subjects to follow after their own will.

89 Now behold, it was not expedient that man should be reclaimed from this temporal death, for that would destroy the great plan of happiness;

90 Therefore, as the soul could never die, and the fall had brought upon all mankind a spiritual death as well as a temporal; that is, they were cut off from the presence of the Lord; therefore it was expedient that mankind should be reclaimed from this spiritual death;

91 Therefore as they had been carnal, sensual and devilish, by nature, this probationary state became a state for them to prepare; it became a preparatory state.

92 And now remember, my son, if it were not for the plan of redemption, (laying it aside,) as soon as they were dead, their souls were miserable, being cut off from the presence of the Lord.

93 And now there was no means to reclaim men from this fallen state which man had brought upon himself, because of his own disobedience;

94 Therefore, according to justice, the plan of redemption could not be brought about, only, on conditions of repentance of men in this probationary state; yea, this preparatory state; for except it were for these conditions, mercy could not take effect except it should destroy the work of justice.

95 Now the work of justice could not be destroyed: if so God would cease to be God.

96 And thus we see that all mankind were fallen, and they were in the grasp of justice; yea, the justice of God, which consigned them for ever to be cut off from his presence.

97 And now the plan of mercy could not be brought about, except an atonement should be made; therefore God himself

atoneth for the sins of the world, to bring about the plan of mercy, to appease the demands of justice, that God might be a perfect, just God, and a merciful God also.

98 Now repentance could not come unto men, except there were a punishment, which also was as eternal as the life of the soul should be, affixed opposite to the plan of happiness, which was as eternal also as the life of the soul.

99 Now, how could a man repent, except he should sin? How could he sin, if there was no law? How could there be a law, save there was a punishment?

100 Now there was a punishment affixed, and a just law given, which brought remorse of conscience unto man.

101 Now if there was no law given, if a man murdered he should die, would he be afraid he should die if he should murder?

102 And also, if there was no law given against sin, men would not be afraid to sin.

103 And if there was no law given if men sinned, what could justice do, or mercy either: for they would have no claim upon the creature.

104 But there is a law given and a punishment affixed, and repentance granted; which repentance, mercy claimeth: otherwise, justice claimeth the creature, and executeth the law, and the law inflicteth the punishment; if not so, the works of justice would be destroyed, and God would cease to be God.

105 But God ceaseth not to be God, and mercy claimeth the penitent, and mercy cometh because of the atonement; and the atonement bringeth to pass the resurrection of the dead: and the resurrection of the dead bringeth back men into the presence of God;

106 And thus they are restored into his presence; to be judged according to their works; according to the law and justice; for behold, justice exerciseth all his demands, and also mercy claimeth all which is her own; and thus, none but the truly penitent are saved.

107 What, do ye suppose that mercy can rob justice? I say unto you, Nay; not one whit. If so, God would cease to be God.

108 And thus God bringeth about his great and eternal purposes, which were prepared from the foundation of the world.

109 And thus cometh about the salvation and redemption of men, and also their destruction and misery; therefore, O my son, whosoever will come, may come, and partake of the waters of life freely;

110 And whosoever will not come, the same is not compelled to come; but in the last day it shall be restored unto him, according to his deeds.

111 If he has desired to do evil, and has not repented in his days, behold evil shall be done unto him, according to the restoration of God.

112 And now, my son, I desire that ye should let these things trouble you no more, and only let your sins trouble you, with that trouble which shall bring you down unto repentance.

113 O my son, I desire that ye should deny the justice of God no more.

114 Do not endeavor to excuse yourself in the least point, because of your sins, by denying the justice of God, but do you let the justice of God, and his mercy, and his long suffering, have full sway in your heart; but let it bring you down to the dust in humility.

115 And now, O my son, ye are called of God to preach the word unto this people.

116 And now, my son, go thy way, declare the word with truth and soberness, that thou mayest bring souls unto repentance, that the great plan of mercy may have claim upon them.

117 And may God grant unto you even according to my words. Amen.

CHAPTER 20.

1 ¶And now it came to pass, that the sons of Alma did go forth among the people, to declare the word unto them. And Alma also, himself, could not rest, and he also went forth.

2 Now we shall say no more concerning their preaching, except that they preached the word, and the truth, according to the spirit of prophecy and revelation: and they preached after the holy order of God, by which they were called.

3 ¶And now I return to an account of the wars between the Nephites and the Lamanites, in the eighteenth year of the reign of the Judges.

4 For behold, it came to pass that the Zoramites became Lamanites; therefore in the commencement of the eighteenth year, the people of the Nephites saw that the Lamanites were coming upon them; therefore they made preparations for war; yea, they gathered together their armies in the land of Jershon.

5 And it came to pass that the Lamanites came with their thousands; and they came into the land of Antionum, which was the land of the Zoramites; and a man by the name of Zerahemnah was their leader.

6 And now as the Amalekites were of a more wicked and murderous disposition than the Lamanites were, in and of themselves, therefore Zerahemnah appointed chief captains over the Lamanites, and they were all the Amalekites and the Zoramites.

7 Now this he did, that he might preserve their hatred towards the Nephites; that he might bring them into subjection, to the accomplishment of his designs;

8 For behold, his designs were to stir up the Lamanites to anger against the Nephites; this he did that he might usurp great power over them; and also that he might gain power over the Nephites by bringing them into bondage, etc.

9 And now the design of the Nephites was to support their lands, and their houses, and their wives and their children, that they might preserve them from the hands of their enemies, and also that they might preserve their rights and their privileges;

10 Yea, and also their liberty, that they might worship God according to their desires; for they knew that if they should fall into the hands of the Lamanites, that whosoever should

worship God, in spirit and in truth, the true and the living God, the Lamanites would destroy;

11 Yea, and they also knew the extreme hatred of the Lamanites towards their brethren, who were the people of Anti-Nephi-Lehi; who were called the people of Ammon;

12 And they would not take up arms; yea, they had entered into a covenant, and they would not break it; therefore if they should fall into the hands of the Lamanites, they would be destroyed.

13 And the Nephites would not suffer that they should be destroyed; therefore they gave them lands for their inheritance.

14 And the people of Ammon did give unto the Nephites a large portion of their substance, to support their armies;

15 And thus the Nephites were compelled, alone, to withstand against the Lamanites, who were a compound of Laman and Lemuel, and the sons of Ishmael, and all those who had dissented from the Nephites, who were Amalekites, and Zoramites, and the descendants of the priests of Noah.

16 Now those descendants were as numerous, nearly, as were the Nephites; and thus the Nephites were obliged to contend with their brethren, even unto bloodshed.

17 ¶And it came to pass as the armies of the Lamanites had gathered together in the land of Antionum, behold the armies of the Nephites were prepared to meet them in the land of Jershon.

18 Now the leader of the Nephites, or the man who had been appointed to be the chief captain over the Nephites: now the chief captain took the command of all the armies of the Nephites: and his name was Moroni;

19 And Moroni took all the command, and the governments of their wars. And he was only twenty and five years old when he was appointed chief captain over the armies of the Nephites.

20 ¶And it came to pass that he met the Lamanites in the borders of Jershon, and his people were armed with swords, and with cimeters, and all manner of weapons of war.

21 And when the armies of the Lamanites saw that the

people of Nephi, or that Moroni had prepared his people with breastplates, and with arm-shields; yea, and also shields to defend their heads; and also they were dressed with thick clothing.

22 Now the army of Zerahemnah was not prepared with any such thing.

23 They had only their swords, and their cimeters, their bows and their arrows, their stones and their slings; but they were naked, save it were a skin which was girded about their loins; yea, all were naked, save it were the Zoramites and the Amalekites.

24 But they were not armed with breastplates, nor shields; therefore they were exceeding afraid of the armies of the Nephites, because of their armor, notwithstanding their number being so much greater than the Nephites.

25 ¶Behold, now it came to pass, that they durst not come against the Nephites in the borders of Jershon; therefore they departed out of the land of Antionum, into the wilderness, and took their journey round about in the wilderness, away by the head of the river Sidon, that they might come into the land of Manti, and take possession of the land; for they did not suppose that the armies of Moroni would know whither they had gone.

26 But it came to pass, as soon as they had departed into the wilderness, Moroni sent spies into the wilderness, to watch their camp; and Moroni, also, knowing of the prophecies of Alma, sent certain men unto him, desiring him that he should inquire of the Lord whither the armies of the Nephites should go, to defend themselves against the Lamanites.

27 And it came to pass that the word of the Lord came unto Alma, and Alma informed the messenger of Moroni that the armies of the Lamanites were marching round about in the wilderness, that they might come over into the land of Manti, that they might commence an attack upon the more weak part of the people.

28 And those messengers went and delivered the message unto Moroni.

29 ¶Now Moroni, leaving a part of his army in the land

of Jershon, lest by any means, a part of the Lamanites should come into that land and take possession of the city, took the remainder part of his army and marched over into the land of Manti.

30 And he caused that all the people in that quarter of the land, should gather themselves together to battle, against the Lamanites, to defend their lands and their country, their rights and their liberties; therefore they were prepared against the time of the coming of the Lamanites.

31 And it came to pass, that Moroni caused that his army should be secreted in the valley which was near the bank of the river Sidon, which was on the west of the river Sidon, in the wilderness.

32 And Moroni placed spies round about, that he might know when the camp of the Lamanites should come.

33 ¶And now as Moroni knew the intention of the Lamanites, that it was their intention to destroy their brethren, or to subject them and bring them into bondage, that they might establish a kingdom unto themselves, over all the land;

34 And he also knowing that it was the only desire of the Nephites to preserve their lands, their liberty, and their church, therefore he thought it no sin that he should defend them by stratagem; therefore he found, by his spies, which course the Lamanites were to take.

35 Therefore he divided his army, and brought a part over into the valley, and concealed them on the east, and on the south of the hill Riplah; and the remainder he concealed in the west valley, on the west of the river Sidon, and so down into the borders of the land Manti.

36 And thus having placed his army according to his desire, he was prepared to meet them.

37 ¶And it came to pass that the Lamanites came up on the north of the hill where a part of the army of Moroni was concealed.

38 And as the Lamanites had passed the hill Riplah, and come into the valley, and began to cross the river Sidon, the army which was concealed on the south of the hill, which was led by a man whose name was Lehi; and he led his army

forth and encircled the Lamanites about, on the east in their rear.

39 ¶And it came to pass that the Lamanites, when they saw the Nephites coming upon them in their rear, turned them about, and began to contend with the army of Lehi; and the work of death commenced, on both sides;

40 But it was more dreadful on the part of the Lamanites; for their nakedness was exposed to the heavy blows of the Nephites, with their swords and their cimeters, which brought death almost at every stroke; while on the other hand, there was now and then a man fell among the Nephites, by their swords and the loss of blood;

41 They being shielded from the more vital parts of the body, or the more vital parts of the body being shielded from the strokes of the Lamanites, by their breastplates, and their arm-shields, and their head-plates; and thus the Nephites did carry on the work of death among the Lamanites.

42 And it came to pass that the Lamanites became frightened, because of the great destruction among them, even until they began to flee towards the river Sidon.

43 And they were pursued by Lehi and his men, and they were driven by Lehi into the waters of Sidon; and they crossed the waters of Sidon.

44 And Lehi retained his armies upon the bank of the river Sidon, that they should not cross.

45 ¶And it came to pass that Moroni and his army met the Lamanites in the valley, on the other side of the river Sidon, and began to fall upon them, and to slay them.

46 And the Lamanites did flee again before them, towards the land of Manti; and they were met again by the armies of Moroni.

47 Now in this case, the Lamanites did fight exceedingly; yea, never had the Lamanites been known to fight with such exceeding great strength and courage; no, not even from the beginning:

48 And they were inspired by the Zoramites, and the Amalekites, who were their chief captains and leaders, and

by Zerahemnah, who was their chief captain, or their chief leader and commander;

49 Yea, they did fight like dragons; and many of the Nephites were slain by their hands; yea, for they did smite in two many of their head-plates; and they did pierce many of their breastplates; and they did smite off many of their arms; and thus the Lamanites did smite in their fierce anger.

50 Nevertheless, the Nephites were inspired by a better cause; for they were not fighting for monarchy nor power; but they were fighting for their homes, and their liberties, their wives, and their children, and their all; yea, for their rites of worship, and their church;

51 And they were doing that which they felt was the duty which they owed to their God; for the Lord had said unto them, and also unto their fathers, That inasmuch as ye are not guilty of the first offense, neither the second, ye shall not suffer yourselves to be slain by the hands of your enemies.

52 And again, the Lord has said that ye shall defend your families, even unto bloodshed; therefore for this cause were the Nephites contending with the Lamanites, to defend themselves, and their families, and their lands, their country, and their rights, and their religion.

53 ¶And it came to pass that when the men of Moroni saw the fierceness and the anger of the Lamanites, they were about to shrink and flee from them.

54 And Moroni, perceiving their intent, sent forth and inspired their hearts, with these thoughts; yea, the thoughts of their lands, their liberty, yea, their freedom from bondage.

55 And it came to pass that they turned upon the Lamanites, and they cried with one voice unto the Lord their God, for their liberty, and their freedom from bondage.

56 And they began to stand against the Lamanites with power; and in the selfsame hour that they cried unto the Lord for their freedom, the Lamanites began to flee before them; and they fled even to the waters of Sidon.

57 Now the Lamanites were more numerous; yea, by more than double the number of the Nephites; nevertheless, they

were driven insomuch that they were gathered together in one body, in the valley, upon the bank, by the river Sidon;

58 Therefore the armies of Moroni encircled them about; yea, even on both sides of the river; for behold, on the east, were the men of Lehi;

59 Therefore when Zerahemnah saw the men of Lehi on the east of the river Sidon, and the armies of Moroni on the west of the river Sidon, that they were encircled about by the Nephites, they were struck with terror.

60 Now Moroni, when he saw their terror, commanded his men that they should stop shedding their blood.

61 ¶And it came to pass that they did stop, and withdrew a pace from them.

62 And Moroni said unto Zerahemnah, Behold, Zerahemnah, that we do not desire to be men of blood.

63 Ye know that ye are in our hands, yet we do not desire to slay you.

64 Behold, we have not come out to battle against you, that we might shed your blood, for power; neither do we desire to bring any one to the yoke of bondage.

65 But this is the very cause for which ye have come against us; yea, and ye are angry with us because of our religion.

66 But now ye behold that the Lord is with us; and ye behold that he has delivered you into our hands.

67 And now I would that ye should understand that this is done unto us because of our religion and our faith in Christ. And now ye see that ye can not destroy this our faith.

68 Now ye see that this is the true faith of God; yea, ye see that God will support, and keep, and preserve us, so long as we are faithful unto him, and unto our faith, and our religion;

69 And never will the Lord suffer that we shall be destroyed, except we should fall into transgression, and deny our faith.

70 And now, Zerahemnah, I command you, in the name of that all-powerful God, who has strengthened our arms, that we have gained power over you by our faith, by our religion,

and by our rites of worship, and by our church, and by the sacred support which we owe to our wives and our children, by that liberty which binds us to our lands and our country; yea, and also by the maintenance of the sacred word of God, to which we owe all our happiness;

71 And by all that is most dear unto us; yea, and this is not all; I command you by all the desires which ye have for life, that ye deliver up your weapons of war unto us, and we will seek not your blood, but we will spare your lives, if ye will go your way, and come not again to war against us.

72 And now if ye do not this, behold, ye are in our hands, and I will command my men that they shall fall upon you, and inflict the wounds of death in your bodies, that ye may become extinct;

73 And then we will see who shall have power over this people; yea, we shall see who will be brought into bondage.

74 ¶And now it came to pass that when Zerahemnah had heard these sayings, he came forth and delivered up his sword and his cimeter, and his bow into the hands of Moroni, and said unto him,

75 Behold, here are our weapons of war; we will deliver them up unto you, and we will not suffer ourselves to take an oath unto you, which we know that we shall break, and also our children; but take our weapons of war, and suffer that we may depart into the wilderness; otherwise we will retain our swords, and we will perish or conquer.

76 Behold, we are not of your faith; we do not believe that it is God that has delivered us into your hands; but we believe that it is your cunning that has preserved you from our swords.

77 Behold, it is your breastplates and your shields that have preserved you.

78 And now when Zerahemnah had made an end of speaking these words, Moroni returned the sword, and the weapons of war which he had received, unto Zerahemnah, saying, Behold, we will end the conflict.

79 Now I can not retain the words which I have spoken; therefore as the Lord liveth, ye shall not depart, except ye

depart with an oath, that ye will not return again against us to war.

80 Now as ye are in our hands, we will spill your blood upon the ground, or ye shall submit to the conditions to which I have proposed.

81 And now when Moroni had said these words, Zerahemnah retained his sword, and he was angry with Moroni and he rushed forward that he might slay Moroni;

82 But as he raised his sword, behold, one of Moroni's soldiers smote it even to the earth; and it broke by the hilt; and he also smote Zerahemnah, that he took off his scalp, and it fell to the earth.

83 And Zerahemnah withdrew from before them, into the midst of his soldiers.

84 ¶And it came to pass that the soldier who stood by, who smote off the scalp of Zerahemnah, took up the scalp from off the ground, by the hair, and laid it upon the point of his sword, and he stretched it forth unto them, saying unto them with a loud voice, .

85 Even as this scalp has fallen to the earth, which is the scalp of your chief, so shall ye fall to the earth, except ye will deliver up your weapons of war, and depart, with a covenant of peace.

86 ¶Now there were many, when they heard these words, and saw the scalp which was upon the sword, that were struck with fear, and many came forth and threw down their weapons of war, at the feet of Moroni, and entered into a covenant of peace.

87 And as many as entered into a covenant, they suffered to depart into the wilderness.

88 ¶Now it came to pass that Zerahemnah was exceeding wroth, and he did stir up the remainder of his soldiers to anger, to contend more powerfully against the Nephites.

89 And now Moroni was angry, because of the stubbornness of the Lamanites; therefore he commanded his people that they should fall upon them and slay them.

90 And it came to pass that they began to slay them: yea,

and the Lamanites did contend with their swords and their mights.

91 But behold, their naked skins, and their bare heads, were exposed to the sharp swords of the Nephites; yea, behold, they were pierced and smitten;

92 Yea, and did fall exceeding fast before the swords of the Nephites; and they began to be swept down, even as the soldier of Moroni had prophesied.

93 Now Zerahemnah, when he saw that they were all about to be destroyed, cried mightily unto Moroni, promising that he would covenant, and also his people, with them, if they would spare the remainder of their lives, that they never would come to war against them.

94 And it came to pass that Moroni caused that the work of death should cease again among the people.

95 And he took the weapons of war from the Lamanites; and after they had entered into a covenant with him of peace, they were suffered to depart into the wilderness.

96 Now the number of their dead were not numbered, because of the greatness of the number; yea, the number of their dead were exceeding great, both on the Nephites, and on the Lamanites.

97 And it came to pass that they did cast their dead into the waters of Sidon; and they have gone forth, and are buried in the depths of the sea.

98 And the armies of the Nephites, or of Moroni, returned, and came to their houses, and their lands.

99 And thus ended the eighteenth year of the reign of the Judges over the people of Nephi.

100 And thus ended the record of Alma, which was written upon the plates of Nephi.

CHAPTER 21.

The account of the people of Nephi, and their wars and dissensions, in the days of Helaman, according to the record of Helaman, which he kept in his days.

1 ¶Behold, now it came to pass that the people of Nephi

were exceedingly rejoiced, because the Lord had again delivered them out of the hands of their enemies;

2 Therefore they gave thanks unto the Lord their God: yea, and they did fast much and pray much, and they did worship God with exceeding great joy.

3 ¶And it came to pass in the nineteenth year of the reign of the Judges over the people of Nephi, that Alma came unto his son Helaman, and said unto him, Believest thou the words which I spake unto thee concerning those records which have been kept?

4 And Helaman said unto him, Yea, I believe.

5 And Alma said again, Believest thou in Jesus Christ, who shall come? And he said, Yea, I believe all the words which thou hast spoken.

6 And Alma said unto him again, Will ye keep my commandments? And he said, Yea, I will keep thy commandments with all my heart.

7 Then Alma said unto him, Blessed art thou: and the Lord shall prosper thee in this land.

8 But behold, I have somewhat to prophesy unto thee; but what I prophesy unto thee, ye shall not make known; yea, what I prophesy unto thee shall not be made known, even until the prophecy is fulfilled; therefore write the words which I shall say.

9 And these are the words: Behold, I perceive that this very people, the Nephites, according to the spirit of revelation which is in me, in four hundred years from the time that Jesus Christ shall manifest himself unto them, shall dwindle in unbelief;

10 Yea, and then shall they see wars and pestilences, yea, famines and bloodshed, even until the people of Nephi shall become extinct;

11 Yea, and this because they shall dwindle in unbelief, and fall into the works of darkness and lasciviousness, and all manner of iniquities;

12 Yea, I say unto you, that because they shall sin against so great light and knowledge; yea, I say unto you, that from

that day, even the fourth generation shall not all pass away, before this great iniquity shall come;

13 And when that great day cometh, behold, the time very soon cometh that those who are now, or the seed of those who are now numbered among the people of the Nephites, shall no more be numbered among the people of Nephi;

14 But whosoever remaineth, and is not destroyed in that great and dreadful day, shall be numbered among the Lamanites, and shall become like unto them, all, save it be a few, who shall be called the disciples of the Lord;

15 And them shall the Lamanites pursue, even until they shall become extinct. And now, because of iniquity, this prophecy shall be fulfilled.

16 ¶And now it came to pass that after Alma had said these things to Helaman, he blessed him, and also his other sons; and he also blessed the earth for the righteous' sake.

17 And he said, Thus saith the Lord God: Cursed shall be the land, yea, this land, unto every nation, kindred, tongue, and people, unto destruction, which do wickedly, when they are fully ripe;

18 And as I have said, so shall it be: for this is the cursing and the blessing of God upon the land, for the Lord can not look upon sin with the least degree of allowance.

19 And, now when Alma had said these words, he blessed the church, yea, all those who should stand fast in the faith, from that time henceforth;

20 And when Alma had done this, he departed out of the land of Zarahemla, as if to go into the land of Melek. And it came to pass that he was never heard of more; as to his death or burial, we know not of.

21 Behold, this we know, that he was a righteous man; and the saying went abroad in the church, that he was taken up by the Spirit, or buried by the hand of the Lord, even as Moses.

22 But behold, the scripture saith the Lord took Moses unto himself; and we suppose that he has also received Alma in the spirit, unto himself; therefore, for this cause we know nothing concerning his death and burial.

23 ¶And now it came to pass in the commencement of the nineteenth year of the reign of the Judges over the people of Nephi, that Helaman went forth among the people to declare the word unto them;

24 For behold, because of their wars with the Lamanites, and the many little dissensions and disturbances, which had been among the people, it became expedient that the word of God should be declared among them; yea, and that a regulation should be made throughout the church;

25 Therefore Helaman and his brethren went forth to establish the church again in all the land, yea, in every city throughout all the land which was possessed by the people of Nephi.

26 And it came to pass that they did appoint priests and teachers throughout all the land, over all the churches.

27 ¶And now it came to pass that after Helaman and his brethren had appointed priests and teachers over the churches, that there arose a dissension among them, and they would not give heed to the words of Helaman and his brethren;

28 But they grew proud, being lifted up in their hearts, because of their exceeding great riches; therefore they grew rich in their own eyes, and would not give heed to their words, to walk uprightly before God.

29 ¶And it came to pass that as many as would not hearken to the words of Helaman and his brethren, were gathered together against their brethren.

30 And now behold, they were exceeding wroth, insomuch that they were determined to slay them.

31 Now the leader of those who were wroth against their brethren, was a large and a strong man; and his name was Amalickiah.

32 And Amalickiah was desirous to be a king; and those people who were wroth, were also desirous that he should be their king; and they were the greater part of them the lower judges of the land; and they were seeking for power.

33 And they had been led by the flatteries of Amalickiah, that if they would support him, and establish him to be their king, that he would make them rulers over the people.

34 Thus they were led away by Amalickiah, to dissensions, notwithstanding the preaching of Helaman and his brethren; yea, notwithstanding their exceeding great care over the church, for they were high priests over the church.

35 And there were many in the church who believed in the flattering words of Amalickiah, therefore they dissented even from the church;

36 And thus were the affairs of the people of Nephi exceeding precarious and dangerous, notwithstanding their great victory which they had had over the Lamanites, and their great rejoicings which they had had, because of their deliverance by the hands of the Lord.

37 Thus we see how quick the children of men do forget the Lord their God; yea, how quick to do iniquity, and to be led away by the evil one; yea, and we also see the great wickedness one very wicked man can cause to take place among the children of men;

38 Yea, we see that Amalickiah, because he was a man of cunning devices, and a man of many flattering words, that he led away the hearts of many people to do wickedly;

39 Yea, and to seek to destroy the church of God, and to destroy the foundation of liberty which God had granted unto them, or which blessing God had sent upon the face of the land, for the righteous' sake.

40 ¶And now it came to pass that when Moroni, who was the chief commander of the armies of the Nephites, had heard of these dissensions, he was angry with Amalickiah.

41 And it came to pass that he rent his coat; and he took a piece thereof, and wrote upon it, In memory of our God, our religion, and freedom, and our peace, our wives, and our children; and he fastened it upon the end of a pole thereof.

42 And he fastened on his head-plate, and his breastplate, and his shields, and girded on his armor about his loins; and he took the pole, which had on the end thereof his rent coat (and he called it the title of liberty),

43 And he bowed himself to the earth, and he prayed mightily unto his God for the blessings of liberty to rest upon

his brethren so long as there should a band of christians remain to possess the land;

44 For thus were all the true believers of Christ, who belonged to the church of God, called, by those who did not belong to the church; and those who did belong to the church, were faithful;

45 Yea, all those who were true believers in Christ, took upon them, gladly, the name of Christ, or christians, as they were called, because of their belief in Christ, who should come; and therefore, at this time, Moroni prayed that the cause of the christians, and the freedom of the land might be favored.

46 ¶And it came to pass that when he had poured out his soul to God, he gave all the land which was south of the land Desolation: yea, and in fine, all the land, both on the north and south, a chosen land, and the land of liberty.

47 And he said, Surely God shall not suffer that we, who are despised because we take upon us the name of Christ, shall be trodden down and destroyed, until we bring it upon us by our own transgressions.

48 And when Moroni had said these words, he went forth among the people, waving the rent of his garment in the air, that all might see the writing which he had written upon the rent, and crying with a loud voice, saying,

49 Behold, whosoever will maintain this title upon the land, let them come forth in the strength of the Lord, and enter into a covenant that they will maintain their rights, and their religion, that the Lord God may bless them.

50 ¶And it came to pass that when Moroni had proclaimed these words, behold, the people came running together, with their armor girded about their loins, rending their garments in token, or as a covenant, that they would not forsake the Lord their God;

51 Or, in other words, if they should transgress the commandments of God, or fall into transgression, and be ashamed to take upon them the name of Christ, the Lord should rend them even as they had rent their garments.

52 Now this was the covenant which they made; and they

cast their garments at the feet of Moroni, saying, We covenant with our God, that we shall be destroyed, even as our brethren in the land northward, if we shall fall into transgression;

53 Yea, he may cast us at the feet of our enemies, even as we have cast our garments at thy feet, to be trodden under foot, if we shall fall into transgression.

54 Moroni said unto them, Behold, we are a remnant of the seed of Jacob; yea, we are a remnant of the seed of Joseph, whose coat was rent by his brethren, into many pieces;

55 Yea, and now behold, let us remember to keep the commandments of God, or our garments shall be rent by our brethren, and we be cast into prison, or be sold, or be slain: yea, let us preserve our liberty, as a remnant of Joseph;

56 Yea, let us remember the words of Jacob, before his death; for behold he saw that a part of the remnant of the coat of Joseph was preserved, and had not decayed.

57 And he said, Even as this remnant of garment of my son's hath been preserved, so shall a remnant of the seed of my sons be preserved by the hand of God, and be taken unto himself, while the remainder of the seed of Joseph shall perish, even as the remnant of his garment.

58 Now behold, this giveth my soul sorrow: nevertheless, my soul hath joy in my son, because that part of his seed which shall be taken unto God.

59 Now behold, this was the language of Jacob.

60 And now who knoweth but what the remnant of the seed of Joseph, which shall perish as his garment, are those who have dissented from us; yea, and even it shall be us, if we do not stand fast in the faith of Christ.

61 ¶And now it came to pass that when Moroni had said these words, he went forth and also sent forth in all the parts of the land where there were dissensions, and gathered together all the people who were desirous to maintain their liberty, to stand against Amalickiah, and those who had dissented, who were called Amalickiahites.

62 ¶And it came to pass that when Amalickiah saw that the people of Moroni were more numerous than the Amalickiah-

ites; and he also saw that his people were doubtful concerning the justice of the cause in which they had undertaken; therefore, fearing that he should not gain the point, he took those of his people who would, and departed into the land of Nephi.

63 ¶Now Moroni thought it was not expedient that the Lamanites should have any more strength; therefore he thought to cut off the people of Amalickiah, or to take them and bring them back, and put Amalickiah to death;

64 Yea, for he knew that they would stir up the Lamanites to anger against them, and cause them to come to battle against them; and this he knew that Amalickiah would do, that he might obtain his purposes:

65 Therefore Moroni thought it was expedient that he should take his armies, who had gathered themselves together, and armed themselves, and entered into a covenant to keep the peace:

66 And it came to pass that he took his army, and marched out into the wilderness, to cut off the course of Amalickiah in the wilderness.

67 ¶And it came to pass that he did according to his desires, and marched forth into the wilderness, and headed the armies of Amalickiah.

68 And it came to pass that Amalickiah fled with a small number of his men, and the remainder were delivered up into the hands of Moroni, and were taken back into the land of Zarahemla.

69 Now Moroni being a man who was appointed by the chief judges and the voice of the people, therefore he had power according to his will, with the armies of the Nephites, to establish and to exercise authority over them.

70 ¶And it came to pass that whomsoever of the Amalickiahites that would not enter into a covenant to support the cause of freedom, that they might maintain a free government, he caused to be put to death; and there was but few who denied the covenant of freedom.

71 ¶And it came to pass also, that he caused the title of liberty to be hoisted upon every tower which was in all the

land, which was possessed by the Nephites; and thus Moroni planted the standard of liberty among the Nephites.

72 And they began to have peace again in the land; and thus they did maintain peace in the land, until nearly the end of the nineteenth year of the reign of the Judges.

73 And Helaman and the high priests did also maintain order in the church; yea, even for the space of four years, did they have much peace and rejoicing in the church.

74 ¶And it came to pass that there were many who died, firmly believing that their souls were redeemed by the Lord Jesus Christ; thus they went out of the world rejoicing.

75 And there were some who died with fevers, which at some seasons of the year was very frequent in the land;

76 But not so much so with fevers, because of the excellent qualities of the many plants and roots which God had prepared, to remove the cause of diseases to which man was subject by the nature of the climate.

77 But there were many who died with old age; and those who died in the faith of Christ, are happy in him, as we must needs suppose.

78 Now we will return in our record, to Amalickiah and those who had fled with him into the wilderness: for behold, he had taken those who went with him, and went up into the land of Nephi, among the Lamanites, and did stir up the Lamanites to anger against the people of Nephi, insomuch that the king of the Lamanites, sent a proclamation throughout all his land, among all his people, that they should gather themselves together again, to go to battle against the Nephites.

79 ¶And it came to pass that when the proclamation had gone forth among them, they were exceeding fraid; yea, they feared to displease the king, and they also feared to go to battle against the Nephites, lest they should lose their lives.

80 And it came to pass that they would not, or the more part of them, would not obey the commandments of the king.

81 ¶And now it came to pass that the king was wroth, because of their disobedience; therefore he gave Amalickiah the command of that part of his army which was obedient unto

his commands, and commanded him that he should go forth and compel them to arms.

82 Now behold, this was the desire of Amalickiah: for he being a very subtile man to do evil, therefore he laid the plan in his heart to dethrone the king of the Lamanites.

83 And now he had got the command of those parts of the Lamanites who were in favor of the king; and he sought to gain favor of those who were not obedient;

84 Therefore he went forward to the place which was called Onidah, for thither had all the Lamanites fled; for they discovered the army coming, and supposing that they were coming to destroy them, therefore they fled to Onidah, to the place of arms.

85 And they had appointed a man to be a king and a leader over them, being fixed in their minds with a determined resolution that they would not be subjected to go against the Nephites.

86 ¶And it came to pass that they had gathered themselves together upon the top of the mount which was called Antipas, in preparation to battle.

87 Now it was not Amalickiah's intention to give them battle, according to the commandments of the king; but behold, it was his intention to gain favor with the armies of the Lamanites, that he might place himself at their head, and dethrone the king, and take possession of the kingdom.

88 And behold, it came to pass that he caused his army to pitch their tents in the valley which was near the mount Antipas.

89 And it came to pass that when it was night, he sent a secret embassy into the mount Antipas, desiring that the leader of those who were upon the mount, whose name was Lehonti, that he should come down to the foot of the mount, for he desired to speak with him.

90 ¶And it came to pass that when Lehonti received the message, he durst not go down to the foot of the mount.

91 And it came to pass that Amalickiah sent again the second time, desiring him to come down. And it came to pass that Lehonti would not: and he sent again the third time.

92 And it came to pass that when Amalickiah found that he could not get Lehonti to come down off from the mount, he went up into the mount, nearly to Lehonti's camp; and he sent again the fourth time, his message unto Lehonti, desiring that he would come down, and that he would bring his guards with him.

93 ¶And it came to pass that when Lehonti had come down with his guards to Amalickiah, that Amalickiah desired him to come down with his army in the night time, and surround those men in their camp, over whom the king had gave him command, and that he would deliver them up into Lehonti's hands, if he would make him, (Amalickiah,) a second leader over the whole army.

94 ¶And it came to pass that Lehonti came down with his men, and surrounded the men of Amalickiah, so that before they awoke at the dawn of the day, they were surrounded by the armies of Lehonti.

95 And it came to pass that when they saw they were surrounded, they plead with Amalickiah that he would suffer them to fall in with their brethren, that they might not be destroyed.

96 Now this was the very thing which Amalickiah desired. ¶And it came to pass that he delivered his men, contrary to the commands of the king.

97 Now this was the thing that Amalickiah desired, that he might accomplish his designs in dethroning the king.

98 Now it was the custom among the Lamanites, if their chief leader was killed, to appoint the second leader to be their chief leader.

99 ¶Now it came to pass that Amalickiah caused that one of his servants should administer poison, by degrees to Lehonti, that he died.

100 Now when Lehonti was dead, the Lamanites appointed Amalickiah to be their leader and chief commander.

101 And it came to pass that Amalickiah marched with his armies (for he had gained his desires) to the land of Nephi, to the city of Nephi, which was the chief city.

102 And the king came out to meet him, with his guards:

for he supposed that Amalickiah had fulfilled his commands, and that Amalickiah had gathered together so great an army to go against the Nephites to battle.

103 But behold, as the king came out to meet him, Amalickiah caused that his servants should go forth to meet the king.

104 And they went and bowed themselves before the king, as if to reverence him, because of his greatness.

105 And it came to pass that the king put forth his hand to raise them, as was the custom with the Lamanites, as a token of peace, which custom they had taken from the Nephites.

106 And it came to pass that when he had raised the first from the ground, behold he stabbed the king to the heart; and he fell to the earth.

107 Now the servants of the king fled; and the servants of Amalickiah raised a cry, saying, Behold the servants of the king have stabbed him to the heart, and he has fell, and they have fled; behold, come and see.

108 ¶And it came to pass that Amalickiah commanded that his armies should march forth, and see what had happened to the king:

109 And when they had come to the spot, and found the king lying in his gore, Amalickiah pretended to be wroth, and said, Whosoever loved the king, let him go forth and pursue his servants, that they may be slain.

110 ¶And it came to pass that when all they who loved the king, when they heard these words, came forth and pursued after the servants of the king.

111 Now when the servants of the king saw an army pursuing after them, they were frightened again, and fled into the wilderness, and came over in the land of Zarahemla, and joined the people of Ammon;

112 And the army which pursued after them, returned, having pursued after them in vain: and thus Amalickiah, by his fraud, gained the hearts of the people.

113 ¶And it came to pass on the morrow, he entered the city Nephi, with his armies, and took possession of the city.

[CHAP. 21.] BOOK OF ALMA. 477

114 And now it came to pass that the queen, when she had heard that the king was slain: for Amalickiah had sent an embassy to the queen, informing her that the king had been slain by his servants; that he had pursued them with his army, but it was in vain, and they had made their escape,

115 Therefore when the queen had received this message, she sent unto Amalickiah, desiring him that he would spare the people of the city; and she also desired him that he should come in unto her; and she also desired him that he should bring witnesses with him, to testify concerning the death of the king.

116 ¶And it came to pass that Amalickiah took the same servant that slew the king, and all they who were with him, and went in unto the queen, unto the place where she sat;

117 And they all testified unto her that the king was slain by his own servants; and they said also, They have fled; does not this testify against them?

118 And thus they satisfied the queen concerning the death of the king.

119 ¶And it came to pass that Amalickiah sought the favor of the queen, and took her unto him to wife; and thus by his fraud, and by the assistance of his cunning servants, he obtained the kingdom;

120 Yea, he was acknowledged king throughout all the land, among all the people of the Lamanites, who were composed of the Lamanites, and the Lemuelites, and the Ishmaelites, and all the dissenters of the Nephites, from the reign of Nephi down to the present time.

121 Now these dissenters, having the same instruction and the same information of the Nephites; yea, having been instructed in the same knowledge of the Lord; nevertheless, it is strange to relate, not long after their dissensions, they became more hardened and impenitent, and more wild, wicked and ferocious, than the Lamanites;

122 Drinking in with the traditions of the Lamanites, giving way to indolence, and all manner of lasciviousness; yea, entirely forgetting the Lord their God.

123 ¶And now it came to pass that as soon as Amalickiah

had obtained the kingdom, he began to inspire the hearts of the Lamanites against the people of Nephi; yea, he did appoint men to speak unto the Lamanites from their towers, against the Nephites;

124 And thus he did inspire their hearts against the Nephites, insomuch, that in the latter end of the nineteenth year of the reign of the Judges, he having accomplished his designs thus far; yea, having been made king over the Lamanites, he sought also to reign over all the land;

125 Yea, and all the people who were in the land, the Nephites as well as the Lamanites, therefore he had accomplished his design, for he had hardened the hearts of the Lamanites, and blinded their minds, and stirred them up to anger, insomuch that he had gathered together a numerous host, to go to battle against the Nephites, for he was determined, because of the greatness of the number of his people, to overpower the Nephites, and to bring them into bondage;

126 And thus he did appoint chief captains of the Zoramites, they being the most acquainted with the strength of the Nephites, and their places of resort, and the weakest parts of their cities; therefore he appointed them to be chief captains over his armies.

127 ¶And it came to pass that they took their camp, and moved forth towards the land of Zarahemla, in the wilderness.

128 Now it came to pass that while Amalickiah had thus been obtaining power by fraud and deceit, Moroni, on the other hand, had been preparing the minds of the people to be faithful unto the Lord their God;

129 Yea, he had been strengthening the armies of the Nephites, and erecting small forts, or places of resort; throwing up banks of earth round about to enclose his armies, and also building walls of stone to encircle them about, round about their cities, and the borders of their lands; yea, all round about the land;

130 And in their weakest fortifications, he did place the greater number of men; and thus he did fortify and strengthen the land which was possessed by the Nephites.

131 And thus he was preparing to support their liberty,

CHAP. 21.] BOOK OF ALMA. 479

their lands, their wives, and their children, and their peace, and that they might live unto the Lord their God, and that they might maintain that which was called by their enemies the cause of christians.

132 And Moroni was a strong and a mighty man; he was a man of a perfect understanding; yea, a man that did not delight in bloodshed; a man whose soul did joy in the liberty and the freedom of his country, and his brethren from bondage and slavery;

133 Yea, a man whose heart did swell with thanksgiving to his God, for the many privileges and blessings which he bestowed upon his people; a man who did labor exceedingly for the welfare and safety of his people:

134 Yea, and he was a man who was firm in the faith of Christ, and he had sworn with an oath, to defend his people, his rights, and his country, and his religion, even to the loss of his blood.

135 Now the Nephites were taught to defend themselves against their enemies, even to the shedding of blood, if it were necessary;

136 Yea, and they were also taught never to give an offense; yea, and never to raise the sword, except it were against an enemy, except it were to preserve their lives;

137 And this was their faith, that by so doing, God would prosper them in the land; or in other words, if they were faithful in keeping the commandments of God, that he would prosper them in the land; yea, warn them to flee, or to prepare for war, according to their danger;

138 And also that God would make it known unto them, whither they should go to defend themselves against their enemies; and by so doing, the Lord would deliver them, and this was the faith of Moroni;

139 And his heart did glory in it; not in the shedding of blood, but in doing good, in preserving his people; yea, in keeping the commandments of God; yea, and resisting iniquity.

140 Yea, verily, verily I say unto you, if all men had been, and were, and ever would be, like unto Moroni, behold, the

very powers of hell would have been shaken for ever; yea, the devil would never have power over the hearts of the children of men.

141 Behold, he was a man like unto Ammon, the son of Mosiah, yea, and even the other sons of Mosiah; yea, and also Alma and his sons, for they were all men of God.

142 Now behold, Helaman and his brethren were no less serviceable unto the people, than was Moroni; for they did preach the word of God, and they did baptize unto repentance, all men whosoever would hearken unto their words.

143 And thus they went forth, and the people did humble themselves because of their words, insomuch that they were highly favored of the Lord; and thus they were free from wars and contentions among themselves; yea, even for the space of four years.

144 But as I have said in the latter end of the nineteenth; yea, notwithstanding their peace amongst themselves, they were compelled reluctantly to contend with their brethren, the Lamanites;

145 Yea, and in fine, their wars never did cease for the space of many years with the Lamanites, notwithstanding their much reluctance.

146 Now they were sorry to take up arms against the Lamanites, because they did not delight in the shedding of blood; yea, and this was not all; they were sorry to be the means of sending so many of their brethren out of this world into an eternal world unprepared to meet their God;

147 Nevertheless, they could not suffer to lay down their lives, that their wives and their children should be massacred by the barbarous cruelty of those who were once their brethren, yea, and had dissented from their church, and had left them, and had gone to destroy them, by joining the Lamanites;

148 Yea, they could not bear that their brethren should rejoice over the blood of the Nephites, so long as there were any who should keep the commandments of God, for the promise of the Lord was, if they should keep his commandments, they should prosper in the land.

149 ¶And now it came to pass, in the eleventh month of the nineteenth year, on the tenth day of the month, the armies of the Lamanites were seen approaching towards the land of Ammonihah.

150 And behold, the city had been rebuilt, and Moroni had stationed an army by the borders of the city, and they had cast up dirt round about, to shield them from the arrows and the stones of the Lamanites: for behold, they fought with stones, and with arrows.

151 Behold, I said that the city of Ammonihah had been rebuilt. I say unto you, yea, that it was in part rebuilt, and because the Lamanites had destroyed it once because of the iniquity of the people, they supposed that it would again become an easy prey for them.

152 But behold, how great was their disappointment; for behold, the Nephites had dug up a ridge of earth round about them, which was so high that the Lamanites could not cast their stones and arrows at them, that they might take effect, neither could they come upon them, save it was by their place of entrance.

153 Now at this time, the chief captains of the Lamanites were astonished exceedingly, because of the wisdom of the Nephites in preparing their places of security.

154 Now the leaders of the Lamanites had supposed, because of the greatness of their numbers; yea, they supposed that they should be privileged to come upon them as they had hitherto done;

155 Yea, and they had also prepared themselves with shields, and with breastplates; and they had also prepared themselves with garments of skins; yea, very thick garments, to cover their nakedness.

156 And being thus prepared, they supposed that they should easily overpower and subject their brethren to the yoke of bondage, or slay and massacre them according to their pleasure.

157 But behold, to their uttermost astonishment, they were prepared for them, in a manner which never had been known among all the children of Lehi.

158 Now they were prepared for the Lamanites, to battle, after the manner of the instructions of Moroni.

159 And it came to pass that the Lamanites, or the Amalickiahites, were exceedingly astonished at their manner of preparation for war.

160 Now if King Amalickiah had come down out of the land of Nephi, at the head of his army, perhaps he would have caused the Lamanites to have attacked the Nephites at the city of Ammonihah; for behold, he did care not for the blood of his people.

161 But behold, Amalickiah did not come down himself to battle.

162 And behold, his chief captains durst not attack the Nephites at the city of Ammonihah, for Moroni had altered the management of affairs among the Nephites, insomuch that the Lamanites were disappointed in their places of retreat, and they could not come upon them;

163 Therefore they retreated into the wilderness, and took their camp, and marched towards the land of Noah, supposing that to be the next best place for them to come against the Nephites;

164 For they knew not that Moroni had fortified or had built forts of security for every city in all the land round about;

165 Therefore they marched forward to the land of Noah, with a firm determination; yea, their chief captains came forward, and took an oath that they would destroy the people of that city.

166 But behold, to their astonishment, the city of Noah, which had hitherto been a weak place, had now, by the means of Moroni, become strong; yea, even to exceed the strength of the city Ammonihah.

167 And now behold, this was wisdom in Moroni; for he had supposed that they would be frightened at the city Ammonihah; and as the city of Noah had hitherto been the weakest part of the land, therefore they would march thither to battle; and thus it was, according to his desires.

168 And behold, Moroni had appointed Lehi to be chief

captain over the men of that city; and it was that same Lehi who fought with the Lamanites in the valley, on the east of the river Sidon.

169 ¶And now behold, it came to pass, that when the Lamanites had found that Lehi commanded the city, they were again disappointed, for they feared Lehi exceedingly; nevertheless, their chief captains had sworn with an oath, to attack the city; therefore they brought up their armies.

170 Now behold, the Lamanites could not get into their forts of security, by any other way save by the entrance, because of the highness of the bank which had been thrown up, and the depth of the ditch which had been dug round about, save it were by the entrance.

171 And thus were the Nephites prepared to destroy all such as should attempt to climb up to enter the fort by any other way, by casting over stones and arrows at them.

172 Thus they were prepared; yea, a body of their most strong men, with their swords and their slings, to smite down all who should attempt to come into their place of security, by the place of entrance; and thus were they prepared to defend themselves against the Lamanites.

173 And it came to pass that the captains of the Lamanites brought up their armies before the place of entrance, and began to contend with the Nephites, to get into their place of security;

174 But behold, they were driven back from time to time, insomuch that they were slain, with an immense slaughter.

175 Now when they found that they could not obtain power over the Nephites by the pass, they began to dig down their banks of earth, that they might obtain a pass to their armies, that they might have an equal chance to fight;

176 But behold, in these attempts, they were swept off by the stones and the arrows which were thrown at them; and instead of filling up their ditches by pulling down the banks of earth, they were filled up in a measure, with their dead and wounded bodies.

177 Thus the Nephites had all power over their enemies;

and thus the Lamanites did attempt to destroy the Nephites, until their chief captains were all slain;

178 Yea, and more than a thousand of the Lamanites were slain; while on the other hand, there was not a single soul of the Nephites which was slain.

179 There were about fifty who were wounded, who had been exposed to the arrows of the Lamanites through the pass, but they were shielded by their shields, and their breastplates, and their head-plates, insomuch that their wounds were upon their legs: many of which were very severe.

180 ¶And it came to pass, that when the Lamanites saw that their chief captains were all slain, they fled into the wilderness.

181 And it came to pass that they returned to the land of Nephi, to inform their king, Amalickiah, who was a Nephite by birth, concerning their great loss.

182 And it came to pass that he was exceeding angry with his people, because he had not obtained his desire over the Nephites; he had not subjected them to the yoke of bondage;

183 Yea, he was exceeding wroth, and he did curse God, and also Moroni, and swearing with an oath that he would drink his blood; and this because Moroni had kept the commandments of God in preparing for the safety of his people.

184 And it came to pass, that on the other hand, the people of Nephi did thank the Lord their God, because of his matchless power in delivering them from the hands of their enemies.

185 And thus ended the nineteenth year of the reign of the Judges over the people of Nephi; yea, and there was continual peace among them, and exceeding great prosperity in the church, because of their heed and diligence which they gave unto the word of God, which was declared unto them by Helaman, and Shiblon, and Corianton, and Ammon, and his brethren, etc.;

186 Yea, and by all those who had been ordained by the holy order of God, being baptized unto repentance, and sent forth to preach among the people, etc.

CHAPTER 22.

1 ¶And now it came to pass that Moroni did not stop making preparations for war, or to defend his people against the Lamanites; for he caused that his armies should commence in the commencement of the twentieth year of the reign of the Judges, that they should commence in digging up heaps of earth round about all the cities, throughout all the land which was possessed by the Nephites;

2 And upon the top of these ridges of earth he caused that there should be timbers; yea, works of timbers built up to the height of a man, round about the cities.

3 And he caused that upon those works of timbers, there should be a frame of pickets built upon the timbers, round about; and they were strong and high; and he caused towers to be erected that overlooked those works of pickets;

4 And he caused places of security to be built upon those towers, that the stones and the arrows of the Lamanites could not hurt them.

5 And they were prepared, that they could cast stones from the top thereof, according to their pleasure and their strength, and slay him who should attempt to approach near the walls of the city.

6 Thus Moroni did prepare strongholds against the coming of their enemies, round about every city in all the land.

7 ¶And it came to pass that Moroni caused that his armies should go forth into the east wilderness; yea, and they went forth, and drove all the Lamanites who were in the east wilderness into their own lands, which were south of the land of Zarahemla;

8 And the land of Nephi did run in a straight course from the east sea to the west.

9 And it came to pass that when Moroni had driven all the Lamanites out of the east wilderness, which was north of the lands of their own possessions, he caused that the inhabitants who were in the land of Zarahemla, and in the land round about, should go forth into the east wilderness, even to the borders, by the sea-shore, and possess the land.

10 And he also placed armies on the south, in the borders of their possessions, and caused them to erect fortifications, that they might secure their armies and their people from the hands of their enemies.

11 And thus he cut off all the strongholds of the Lamanites, in the east wilderness: yea, and also on the west, fortifying the line between the Nephites and the Lamanites, between the land of Zarahemla and the land of Nephi; from the west sea, running by the head of the river Sidon;

12 The Nephites possessing all the land northward; yea, even all the land which was northward of the land Bountiful, according to their pleasure.

13 Thus Moroni, with his armies, which did increase daily, because of the assurance of protection which his works did bring forth unto them; therefore they did seek to cut off the strength and the power of the Lamanites, from off the lands of their possessions, that they should have no power upon the lands of their possessions.

14 ¶And it came to pass that the Nephites began the foundation of a city; and they called the name of the city Moroni; and it was by the east sea; and it was on the south by the line of the possessions of the Lamanites.

15 And they also began a foundation for a city between the city of Moroni and the city of Aaron, joining the borders of Aaron and Moroni; and they called the name of the city, or the land, Nephihah.

16 And they also began, in that same year, to build many cities on the north; one in a particular manner which they called Lehi, which was in the north, by the borders of the sea-shore. And thus ended the twentieth year.

17 And in these prosperous circumstances were the people of Nephi, in the commencement of the twenty and first year of the reign of the Judges over the people of Nephi.

18 And they did prosper exceedingly, and they became exceeding rich; yea, and they did multiply, and wax strong in the land.

19 And thus we see how merciful and just are all the deal-

ings of the Lord, to the fulfilling of all his words unto the children of men;

20 Yea, we can behold that his words are verified, even at this time, which he spake unto Lehi, saying, Blessed art thou and thy children; and they shall be blessed; inasmuch as they shall keep my commandments, they shall prosper in the land.

21 But remember, inasmuch as they will not keep my commandments, they shall be cut off from the presence of the Lord.

22 And we see that these promises have been verified to the people of Nephi; for it has been their quarrelings and their contentions, yea, their murderings, and their plunderings, their idolatry, their whoredoms, and their abominations, which were among themselves, which brought upon them their wars and their destructions.

23 And those who were faithful in keeping the commandments of the Lord, were delivered at all times, whilst thousands of their wicked brethren have been consigned to bondage, or to perish by the sword, or to dwindle in unbelief, and mingle with the Lamanites.

24 But behold, there never was a happier time among the people of Nephi, since the days of Nephi, than in the days of Moroni; yea, even at this time, in the twenty and first year of the reign of the Judges.

25 And it came to pass that the twenty and second year of the reign of the Judges, also ended in peace; yea, and also the twenty and third year.

26 ¶And it came to pass that in the commencement of the twenty and fourth year of the reign of the Judges, there would also have been peace among the people of Nephi, had it not been for a contention which took place among them concerning the land of Lehi, and the land of ·Morianton, which joined upon the borders of Lehi; both of which were on the borders by the sea-shore.

27 For behold, the people who possessed the land of Morianton did claim a part of the land of Lehi; therefore there began to be a warm contention between them, insomuch that

the people of Morianton took up arms against their brethren, and they were determined by the sword to slay them.

28 But behold, the people who possessed the land of Lehi, fled to the camp of Moroni, and appealed unto him for assistance; for behold, they were not in the wrong.

29 ¶And it came to pass that when the people of Morianton, who were led by a man whose name was Morianton, found that the people of Lehi had fled to the camp of Moroni, they were exceeding fearful lest the army of Moroni should come upon them, and destroy them;

30 Therefore, Morianton put it into their hearts that they should flee to the land which was northward, which was covered with large bodies of water, and take possession of the land which was northward.

31 And behold, they would have carried this plan into effect, (which would have been a cause to have been lamented,) but behold, Morianton, being a man of much passion, therefore he was angry with one of his maid-servants, and he fell upon her, and beat her much.

32 And it came to pass that she fled, and came over to the camp of Moroni, and told Moroni all things concerning the matter; and also concerning their intentions to flee into the land northward.

33 Now behold, the people who were in the land Bountiful, or rather Moroni, feared that they would hearken to the words of Morianton, and unite with his people, and thus he would obtain possession of those parts of the land, which would lay a foundation for serious consequences among the people of Nephi; yea, which consequences would lead to the overthrow of their liberty;

34 Therefore Moroni sent an army, with their camp, to head the people of Morianton, to stop their flight into the land northward.

35 And it came to pass that they did not head them, until they had come to the borders of the land Desolation: and there they did head them, by the narrow pass which led by the sea into the land northward; yea, by the sea, on the west, and on the east.

[CHAP. 22.] BOOK OF ALMA. 489

36 ¶And it came to pass that the army which was sent by Moroni, which was led by a man whose name was Teancum, did meet the people of Morianton;

37 And so stubborn were the people of Morianton, (being inspired by his wickedness and his flattering words,) that a battle commenced between them, in the which Teancum did slay Morianton, and defeat his army, and took them prisoners, and returned to the camp of Moroni.

38 And thus ended the twenty and fourth year of the reign of the Judges over the people of Nephi. And thus was the people of Morianton brought back.

39 And upon their covenanting to keep the peace, they were restored to the land of Morianton, and a union took place between them and the people of Lehi; and they were also restored to their lands.

40 ¶And it came to pass that in the same year that the people of Nephi had peace restored unto them, that Nephihah, the second chief judge, died, having filled the judgment seat with perfect uprightness before God;

41 Nevertheless, he had refused Alma to take possession of those records and those things which were esteemed by Alma and his fathers to be most sacred; therefore Alma had conferred them upon his son Helaman.

42 ¶Behold, it came to pass that the son of Nephihah was appointed to fill the judgment seat, in the stead of his father; yea, he was appointed chief judge, and governor over the people, with an oath, and sacred ordinance to judge righteously, and to keep the peace, and the freedom of the people, and to grant unto them their sacred privileges to worship the Lord their God;

43 Yea, to support and maintain the cause of God all his days, and to bring the wicked to justice, according to their crime. Now behold, his name was Pahoran.

44 And Pahoran did fill the seat of his father, and did commence his reign in the end of the twenty and fourth year, over the people of Nephi.

CHAPTER 23.

1 ¶And now it came to pass in the commencement of the twenty and fifth year of the reign of the Judges over the people of Nephi, they having established peace between the people of Lehi and the people of Morianton concerning their lands, and having commenced the twenty and fifth year in peace;

2 Nevertheless, they did not long maintain an entire peace in the land, for there began to be a contention among the people concerning the chief judge, Pahoran; for behold, there were a part of the people who desired that a few particular points of the law should be altered.

3 But behold, Pahoran would not alter, nor suffer the law to be altered; therefore he did not hearken to those who had sent in their voices with their petitions, concerning the altering of the law;

4 Therefore those who were desirous that the law should be altered, were angry with him, and desired that he should no longer be chief judge over the land; therefore there arose a warm dispute concerning the matter; but not unto bloodshed.

5 ¶And it came to pass that those who were desirous that Pahoran should be dethroned from the judgment seat, were called king-men, for they were desirous that the law should be altered in a manner to overthrow the free government, and to establish a king over the land.

6 And those who were desirous that Pahoran should remain chief judge over the land, took upon them the name of freemen; and thus was the division among them; for the freemen had sworn or covenanted to maintain their rights, and the privileges of their religion, by a free government.

7 ¶And it came to pass that this matter of their contention was settled, by the voice of the people.

8 And it came to pass that the voice of the people came in favor of the freemen, and Pahoran retained the judgment seat, which caused much rejoicing among the brethren of Pahoran, and also many of the people of liberty; who also

put the king-men to silence, that they durst not oppose, but were obliged to maintain the cause of freedom.

9 Now those who were in favor of kings, were those of high birth; and they sought to be kings; and they were supported by those who sought power and authority over the people.

10 But behold, this was a critical time for such contentions to be among the people of Nephi; for behold, Amalickiah had again stirred up the hearts of the people of the Lamanites, against the people of the Nephites, and he was gathering together soldiers, from all parts of his land, and arming them, and preparing for war, with all diligence, for he had sworn to drink the blood of Moroni.

11 But behold, we shall see that his promise which he made, was rash; nevertheless, he did prepare himself and his armies, to come to battle against the Nephites.

12 Now his armies were not so great as they had hitherto been, because of the many thousands who had been slain by the hand of the Nephites;

13 But notwithstanding their great loss, Amalickiah had gathered together a wonderful great army, insomuch that he feared not to come down to the land of Zarahemla.

14 Yea, even Amalickiah did himself come down, at the head of the Lamanites.

15 And it was in the twenty and fifth year of the reign of the Judges; and it was at the same time that they had began to settle the affairs of their contentions concerning the chief judge, Pahoran.

16 ¶And it came to pass that when the men who were called king-men, had heard that the Lamanites were coming down to battle against them, they were glad in their hearts, and they refused to take up arms; for they were so wroth with the chief judge, and also with the people of liberty, that they would not take up arms to defend their country.

17 And it came to pass that when Moroni saw this, and also saw that the Lamanites were coming into the borders of the land, he was exceeding wroth, because of the stubbornness of those people, whom he had labored with so much dili-

gence to preserve; yea, he was exceeding wroth; his soul was filled with anger against them.

18 And it came to pass that he sent a petition, with the voice of the people, unto the governor of the land, desiring that he should read it, and give him, (Moroni,) power to compel those dissenters to defend their country, or to put them to death;

19 For it was his first care to put an end to such contentions, and dissensions among the people; for behold, this had been hitherto a cause of all their destruction.

20 And it came to pass that it was granted, according to the voice of the people.

21 ¶And it came to pass that Moroni commanded that his army should go against those king-men, to pull down their pride and their nobility, and level them with the earth, or they should take up arms and support the cause of liberty.

22 And it came to pass that the armies did march forth against them; and they did pull down their pride and their nobility, insomuch, that as they did lift their weapons of war to fight against the men of Moroni, they were hewn down, and leveled to the earth.

23 And it came to pass that there were four thousand of those dissenters, who were hewn down by the sword; and those of their leaders who were not slain in battle, were taken and cast into prison, for there was no time for their trials at this period;

24 And the remainder of those dissenters, rather than to be smote down to the earth by the sword, yielded to the standard of liberty, and were compelled to hoist the title of liberty upon their towers, and in their cities, and to take up arms in defense of their country.

25 And thus Moroni put an end to those king-men, that there were not any known by the appellation of king-men; and thus he put an end to the stubbornness, and the pride of those people who professed the blood of nobility;

26 But they were brought down to humble themselves like unto their brethren, and to fight valiantly for their freedom from bondage.

27 ¶Behold, it came to pass that while Moroni was thus breaking down the wars and contentions among his own people, and subjecting them to peace and civilization, and making regulations to prepare for war against the Lamanites, behold, the Lamanites had come into the land of Moroni, which was in the borders by the sea-shore.

28 ¶And it came to pass that the Nephites were not sufficiently strong in the city of Moroni; therefore Amalickiah did drive them, slaying many.

29 And it came to pass that Amalickiah took possession of the city; yea, possession of all their fortifications.

30 And those who fled out of the city of Moroni, came to the city of Nephihah; and also the people of the city of Lehi gathered themselves together, and made preparations, and were ready to receive the Lamanites to battle.

31 ¶But it came to pass that Amalickiah would not suffer the Lamanites to go against the city of Nephihah to battle, but kept them down by the sea-shore, leaving men in every city to maintain and defend it;

32 And thus he went on, taking possession of many cities: the city of Nephihah, and the city of Lehi, and the city of Morianton, and the city of Omner, and the city of Gid, and the city of Mulek, all of which were on the east borders, by the sea-shore.

33 And thus had the Lamanites obtained, by the cunning of Amalickiah, so many cities, by their numberless hosts, all of which were strongly fortified, after the manner of the fortifications of Moroni; all of which afforded strongholds for the Lamanites.

34 ¶And it came to pass that they marched to the borders of the land Bountiful, driving the Nephites before them, and slaying many.

35 But it came to pass that they were met by Teancum, who had slain Morianton, and had headed his people in his flight.

36 And it came to pass that he headed Amalickiah also, as he was marching forth with his numerous army, that he

might take possession of the land Bountiful, and also the land northward.

37 But behold, he met with a disappointment, by being repulsed by Teancum and his men, for they were great warriors: for every man of Teancum did exceed the Lamanites in their strength, and in their skill of war, insomuch that they did gain advantage over the Lamanites.

38 ¶And it came to pass that they did harass them, insomuch that they did slay them even until it was dark.

39 And it came to pass that Teancum and his men did pitch their tents in the borders of the land Bountiful; and Amalickiah did pitch his tents in the borders on the beach by the sea-shore, and after this manner were they driven.

40 ¶And it came to pass that when the night had come, Teancum and his servant stole forth and went out by night, and went into the camp of Amalickiah; and behold, sleep had overpowered them, because of their much fatigue, which was caused by the labors and heat of the day.

41 ¶And it came to pass that Teancum stole privily into the tent of the king, and put a javelin to his heart; and he did cause the death of the king immediately, that he did not awake his servants.

42 And he returned again privily to his own camp, and behold, his men were asleep; and he awoke them, and told them all the things that he had done.

43 And he caused that his armies should stand in readiness, lest the Lamanites had awoke, and should come upon them.

44 And thus ended the twenty and fifth year of the reign of the Judges over the people of Nephi; and thus ended the days of Amalickiah.

CHAPTER 24.

1 ¶And now it came to pass in the twenty and sixth year of the reign of the Judges over the people of Nephi, behold, when the Lamanites awoke on the first morning of the first month, behold, they found Amalickiah was dead in his own

tent; and they also saw that Teancum was ready to give them battle on that day.

2 And now when the Lamanites saw this, they were affrighted; and they abandoned their design in marching into the land northward, and retreated with all their army into the city of Mulek, and sought protection in their fortifications.

3 And it came to pass that the brother of Amalickiah was appointed king over the people; and his name was Ammoron; thus King Ammoron, the brother of King Amalickiah, was appointed to reign in his stead.

4 ¶And it came to pass that he did command that his people should maintain those cities which they had taken by the shedding of blood; for they had not taken any cities, save they had lost much blood.

5 And now Teancum saw that the Lamanites were determined to maintain those cities which they had taken, and those parts of the land which they had obtained possession of;

6 And also seeing the enormity of their number, Teancum thought it was not expedient that he should attempt to attack them in their forts; but he kept his men round about, as if making preparations for war;

7 Yea, and truly he was preparing to defend himself against them, by casting up walls round about, and preparing places of resort.

8 ¶And it came to pass that he kept thus preparing for war, until Moroni had sent a large number of men to strengthen his army;

9 And Moroni also sent orders unto him, that he should retain all the prisoners who fell into his hands; for as the Lamanites had taken many prisoners, that he should retain all the prisoners of the Lamanites, as a ransom for those whom the Lamanites had taken.

10 And he also sent orders unto him, that he should fortify the land Bountiful, and secure the narrow pass which led into the land northward, lest the Lamanites should obtain that point, and should have power to harass them on every side.

11 And Moroni also sent unto him, desiring him that he

would be faithful in maintaining that quarter of the land, and that he would seek every opportunity to scourge the Lamanites in that quarter, as much as was in his power,

12 That perhaps he might take again, by stratagem or some other way, those cities which had been taken out of their hands; and that he also would fortify and strengthen the cities round about, which had not fallen into the hands of the Lamanites.

13 And he also said unto him, I would come unto you, but behold, the Lamanites are upon us in the borders of the land by the west sea; and behold, I go against them, therefore I can not come unto you.

14 ¶Now the king (Ammoron) had departed out of the land of Zarahemla, and had made known unto the queen concerning the death of his brother, and had gathered together a large number of men, and had marched forth against the Nephites, on the borders by the west sea;

15 And thus he was endeavoring to harass the Nephites and to draw away a part of their forces to that part of the land, while he had commanded those whom he had left to possess the cities which he had taken, that they should also harass the Nephites on the borders by the east sea; and should take possession of their lands as much as it was in their power, according to the power of their armies.

16 And thus were the Nephites in those dangerous circumstances, in the ending of the twenty and sixth year of the reign of the Judges over the people of Nephi.

17 ¶But behold, it came to pass in the twenty and seventh year of the reign of the Judges, that Teancum, by the command of Moroni, who had established armies to protect the south and the west borders of the land, had began his march towards the land Bountiful, that he might assist Teancum with his men, in retaking the cities which they had lost.

18 And it came to pass that Teancum had received orders to make an attack upon the city of Mulek, and retake it if it were possible.

19 ¶And it came to pass that Teancum made preparations to make an attack upon the city of Mulek, and march forth

with his army against the Lamanites; but he saw that it was impossible that he could overpower them while they were in their fortifications;

20 Therefore he abandoned his designs, and returned again to the city Bountiful, to wait for the coming of Moroni that he might receive strength to his army.

21 ¶And it came to pass that Moroni did arrive with his army to the land of Bountiful, in the latter end of the twenty and seventh year of the reign of the Judges over the people of Nephi.

22 And in the commencement of the twenty and eighth year, Moroni and Teancum, and many of the chief captains, held a council of war, what they should do to cause the Lamanites to come out against them to battle;

23 Or that they might by some means, flatter them out of their strongholds, that they might gain advantage over them, and take again the city of Mulek.

24 ¶And it came to pass that they sent embassies to the army of the Lamanites, which protected the city of Mulek, to their leader, whose name was Jacob, desiring him that he would come out with his armies to meet them upon the plains, between the two cities.

25 But behold, Jacob, who was a Zoramite, would not come out with his army to meet them upon the plains.

26 ¶And it came to pass that Moroni, having no hopes of meeting them upon fair grounds, therefore he resolved upon a plan that he might decoy the Lamanites out of their strongholds.

27 Therefore he caused that Teancum should take a small number of men, and march down near the sea-shore; and Moroni and his army, by night, marched into the wilderness, on the west of the city Mulek;

28 And thus, on the morrow, when the guards of the Lamanites had discovered Teancum, they ran and told it unto Jacob, their leader.

29 ¶And it came to pass that the armies of the Lamanites did march forth against Teancum, supposing by their num-

bers to overpower Teancum, because of the smallness of his numbers.

30 And as Teancum saw the armies of the Lamanites coming out against him, he began to retreat down by the seashore northward.

31 ¶And it came to pass that when the Lamanites saw that he began to flee, they took courage and pursued them with vigor.

32 And while Teancum was thus leading away the Lamanites who were pursuing them in vain, behold, Moroni commanded that a part of his army who were with him, should march forth into the city, and take possession of it.

33 And thus they did, and slew all those who had been left to protect the city; yea, all those who would not yield up their weapons of war.

34 And thus Moroni had obtained possession of the city Mulek, with a part of his army, while he marched with the remainder to meet the Lamanites, when they should return from the pursuit of Teancum.

35 ¶And it came to pass that the Lamanites did pursue Teancum until they came near the city Bountiful, and then they were met by Lehi, and a small army, which had been left to protect the city Bountiful.

36 And now behold, when the chief captains of the Lamanites had beheld Lehi, with his army, coming against them, they fled in much confusion, lest perhaps they should not obtain the city Mulek, before Lehi should overtake them; for they were wearied because of their march, and the men of Lehi were fresh.

37 Now the Lamanites did not know that Moroni had been in their rear with his army; and all they feared, was Lehi and his men.

38 Now Lehi was not desirous to overtake them, till they should meet Moroni and his army.

39 And it came to pass that before the Lamanites had retreated far, they were surrounded by the Nephites; by the men of Moroni on one hand, and the men of Lehi on the other,

all of whom were fresh and full of strength; but the Lamanites were wearied, because of their long march.

40 And Moroni commanded his men that they should fall upon them, until they had given up their weapons of war.

41 ¶And it came to pass that Jacob, being their leader, being also a Zoramite, and having an unconquerable spirit, he led the Lamanites forth to battle, with exceeding fury against Moroni.

42 Moroni being in their course of march, therefore Jacob was determined to slay them, and cut his way through to the city of Mulek.

43 But behold, Moroni and his men were more powerful; therefore they did not give way before the Lamanites.

44 ¶And it came to pass that they fought on both hands with exceeding fury; and there were many slain on both sides; yea, and Moroni was wounded, and Jacob was killed.

45 And Lehi pressed upon their rear with such fury, with his strong men, that the Lamanites in the rear delivered up their weapons of war; and the remainder of them, being much confused, knew not whether to go or to strike.

46 Now Moroni seeing their confusion, he said unto them, If ye will bring forth your weapons of war, and deliver them up, behold we will forbear shedding your blood.

47 And it came to pass that when the Lamanites had heard these words, their chief captains, all those who were not slain, came forth and threw down their weapons of war at the feet of Moroni, and also commanded their men that they should do the same:

48 But behold, there were many that would not; and those who would not deliver up their swords, were taken and bound, and their weapons of war were taken from them, and they were compelled to march with their brethren forth into the land Bountiful.

49 And now the number of prisoners who were taken, exceeded more than the number of those who had been slain; yea, more than those who had been slain on both sides.

50 ¶And it came to pass that they did set guards over the prisoners of the Lamanites, and did compel them to go forth

and bury their dead; yea, and also the dead of the Nephites who were slain; and Moroni placed men over them to guard them while they should perform their labor.

51 And Moroni went to the city of Mulek with Lehi, and took command of the city, and gave it unto Lehi.

52 Now behold this Lehi was a man who had been with Moroni in the more part of all his battles; and he was a man like unto Moroni; and they rejoiced in each other's safety; yea, they were beloved by each other, and also beloved by all the people of Nephi.

53 ¶And it came to pass that after the Lamanites had finished burying their dead, and also the dead of the Nephites, they were marched back into the land Bountiful;

54 And Teancum, by the orders of Moroni, caused that they should commence laboring in digging a ditch round about the land, or the city Bountiful;

55 And he caused that they should build a breastwork of timbers upon the inner bank of the ditch; and they cast up dirt out of the ditch against the breastwork of timbers;

56 And thus they did cause the Lamanites to labor, until they had encircled the city of Bountiful round about with a strong wall of timbers and earth, to an exceeding height.

57 And this city became an exceeding stronghold ever after; and in this city they did guard the prisoners of the Lamanites; yea, even within a wall, which they had caused them to build with their own hands.

58 Now Moroni was compelled to cause the Lamanites to labor, because it were easy to guard them while at their labor; and he desired all his forces, when he should make an attack upon the Lamanites.

59 ¶And it came to pass that Moroni had thus gained a victory over one of the greatest of the armies of the Lamanites, and had obtained possession of the city Mulek, which was one of the strongest holds of the Lamanites in the land of Nephi; and thus he had also built a stronghold to retain his prisoners.

60 And it came to pass that he did no more attempt a battle with the Lamanites in that year; but he did employ his

men in preparing for war: yea, and in making fortifications to guard against the Lamanites; yea, and also delivering their women and their children from famine and affliction, and providing food for their armies.

61 ¶And now it came to pass that the armies of the Lamanites, on the west sea, south, while in the absence of Moroni, on account of some intrigue amongst the Nephites, which caused dissensions amongst them, had gained some ground over the Nephites, yea, insomuch that they had obtained possession of a number of their cities in that part of the land;

62 And thus because of iniquity amongst themselves, yea, because of dissension and intrigue among themselves, they were placed in the most dangerous circumstances.

63 ¶And now behold, I have somewhat to say concerning the people of Ammon, who, in the beginning were Lamanites; but by Ammon and his brethren, or rather by the power and word of God, they had been converted unto the Lord;

64 And they had been brought down into the land of Zarahemla, and had ever since been protected by the Nephites; and because of their oath, they had been kept from taking up arms against their brethren;

65 For they had taken an oath, that they never would shed blood more; and according to their oath, they would have perished; yea, they would have suffered themselves to have fallen into the hands of their brethren, had it not been for the pity and the exceeding love which Ammon and his brethren had had for them;

66 And for this cause, they were brought down into the land of Zarahemla; and they ever had been protected by the Nephites.

67 ¶But it came to pass that when they saw the danger, and the many afflictions and tribulations which the Nephites bore for them, they were moved with compassion, and were desirous to take up arms in defense of their country.

68 But behold, as they were about to take their weapons of war, they were overpowered by the persuasions of Hela-

man and his brethren, for they were about to break the oath which they had made;

69 And Helaman feared lest by so doing, they should lose their souls; therefore all those who had entered into this covenant, were compelled to behold their brethren wade through their afflictions, in their dangerous circumstances, at this time.

70 But behold, it came to pass they had many sons, who had not entered into a covenant that they would not take their weapons of war to defend themselves against their enemies;

71 Therefore they did assemble themselves together at this time, as many as were able to take up arms; and they called themselves Nephites;

72 And they entered into a covenant, to fight for the liberty of the Nephites; yea, to protect the land unto the laying down of their lives;

73 Yea, even they covenanted that they never would give up their liberty, but they would fight in all cases to protect the Nephites and themselves from bondage.

74 ¶Now behold, there were two thousand of those young men who entered into this covenant, and took their weapons of war to defend their country.

75 And now behold, as they never had hitherto been a disadvantage to the Nephites, they became now at this period of time also a great support, for they took their weapons of war, and they would that Helaman should be their leader.

76 And they were all young men, and they were exceeding valiant for courage, and also for strength and activity; but behold, this was not all: they were men who were true at all times in whatsoever thing they were entrusted;

77 Yea, they were men of truth and soberness, for they had been taught to keep the commandments of God, and to walk uprightly before him.

78 ¶And now it came to pass that Helaman did march at the head of his two thousand stripling soldiers, to the support of the people in the borders of the land on the south by the west sea.

79 And thus ended the twenty and eighth year of the reign of the Judges over the people of Nephi, etc.

CHAPTER 25.

1 ¶And now it came to pass in the twenty and ninth year of the Judges, that Ammoron sent unto Moroni, desiring that he would exchange prisoners.

2 And it came to pass that Moroni felt to rejoice exceedingly at this request, for he desired the provisions which were imparted for the support of the Lamanite prisoners, for the support of his own people; and he also desired his own people for the strengthening of his army.

3 Now the Lamanites had taken many women and children; and there was not a woman nor a child among all the prisoners of Moroni; or the prisoners whom Moroni had taken;

4 Therefore Moroni resolved upon a stratagem, to obtain as many prisoners of the Nephites from the Lamanites, as it were possible; therefore he wrote an epistle, and sent it by the servant of Ammoron, the same who had brought an epistle to Moroni.

5 Now these are the words which he wrote unto Ammoron, saying, Behold, Ammoron, I have written unto you somewhat concerning this war which ye have waged against my people, or rather which thy brother hath waged against them, and which ye are still determined to carry on after his death.

6 Behold I would tell you something concerning the justice of God, and the sword of his Almighty wrath, which doth hang over you, except ye repent and withdraw your armies into your own lands, or the lands of your possessions, which is the land of Nephi; yea, I would tell you these things, if ye were capable of hearkening unto them;

7 Yea, I would tell you concerning that awful hell that awaits to receive such murderers as thou and thy brother have been, except ye repent and withdraw your murderous purposes, and return with your armies to your own lands;

8 But as ye have once rejected these things, and have

fought against the people of the Lord, even so I may expect you will do it again.

9 ¶And now behold, we are prepared to receive you; yea, and except ye withdraw your purposes, behold, ye will pull down the wrath of that God whom you have rejected, upon you, even to your utter destruction;

10 But as the Lord liveth, our armies shall come upon you, except ye withdraw, and ye shall soon be visited with death, for we will retain our cities and our lands; yea, and we will maintain our religion and the cause of our God.

11 But behold, it supposeth me that I talk to you concerning these things in vain; or it supposeth me that thou art a child of hell; therefore, I will close my epistle, by telling you that I will not exchange prisoners, save it be on conditions that ye will deliver up a man, and his wife, and his children, for one prisoner; if this be the case that ye will do it, I will exchange.

12 And behold, if ye do not this, I will come against you with my armies; yea, even I will arm my women and my children, and I will come against you, and I will follow you even into your own land, which is the land of our first inheritance; yea, and it shall be blood for blood; yea, life for life; and I will give you battle, even until you are destroyed from off the face of the earth.

13 Behold, I am in my anger, and also my people; ye have sought to murder us, and we have only sought to defend ourselves.

14 But behold, if ye seek to destroy us more, we will seek to destroy you; yea, and we will seek our land, the lands of our first inheritance.

15 Now I close my epistle. I am Moroni; I am a leader of the people of the Nephites.

16 ¶Now it came to pass that Ammoron, when he had received this epistle he was angry; and he wrote another epistle unto Moroni; and these are the words which he wrote, saying, I am Ammoron the king of the Lamanites; I am the brother of Amalickiah, whom ye have murdered.

17 Behold, I will avenge his blood upon you; yea, and I

will come upon you with my armies, for I fear not your threatenings.

18 For behold, your fathers did wrong their brethren, insomuch that they did rob them of their right to the government, when it rightly belonged unto them.

19 And now behold, if ye will lay down your arms, and subject yourselves to be governed by those to whom the government doth rightly belong, then will I cause that my people shall lay down their weapons, and shall be at war no more.

20 Behold, ye have breathed out many threatenings against me and my people: but behold, we fear not your threatenings;

21 Nevertheless, I will grant to exchange prisoners according to your request, gladly, that I may preserve my food for my men of war;

22 And we will wage a war which shall be eternal, either to the subjecting the Nephites to our authority, or to their eternal extinction.

23 And as concerning that God whom ye say we have rejected, behold, we know not such a being; neither do ye; but if it so be that there is such a being, we know not but that he hath made us as well as you;

24 And if it so be that there is a devil and a hell, behold, will he not send you there, to dwell with my brother, whom ye have murdered, whom ye have hinted that he hath gone to such a place? But behold, these things mattereth not.

25 I am Ammoron, and a descendant of Zoram, whom your fathers pressed and brought out of Jerusalem. And behold, now, I am a bold Lamanite.

26 Behold, this war hath been waged, to avenge their wrongs, and to maintain and to obtain their rights to the government; and I close my epistle to Moroni.

27 ¶Now it came to pass that when Moroni had received this epistle, he was more angry, because he knew that Ammoron had a perfect knowledge of his fraud; yea, he knew that Ammoron knew that it was not a just cause that had caused him to wage a war against the people of Nephi.

28 And he said, Behold, I will not exchange prisoners with

Ammoron, save he will withdraw his purpose, as I have stated in my epistle; for I will not grant unto him that he shall have any more power than what he hath got.

29 Behold, I know the place where the Lamanites doth guard my people, whom they have taken prisoners; and as Ammoron would not grant unto me mine epistle, behold, I will give unto him according to my words; yea, I will seek death among them, until they shall sue for peace.

30 And now it came to pass that when Moroni had said these words, he caused that a search should be made among his men, that perhaps he might find a man who was a descendant of Laman among them.

31 ¶And it came to pass that they found one, whose name was Laman; and he was one of the servants of the king who was murdered by Amalickiah.

32 Now Moroni caused that Laman and a small number of his men, should go forth unto the guards who were over the Nephites.

33 Now the Nephites were guarded in the city of Gid; therefore Moroni appointed Laman, and caused that a small number of men should go with him.

34 ¶And when it was evening, Laman went to the guards who were over the Nephites, and behold, they saw him coming, and they hailed him.

35 But he saith unto them, Fear not. Behold, I am a Lamanite. Behold we have escaped from the Nephites, and they sleepeth; and behold, we have took of their wine, and brought with us.

36 Now when the Lamanites heard these words, they received him with joy. And they said unto him, Give us of your wine, that we may drink; we are glad that ye have thus taken wine with you, for we are weary.

37 But Laman said unto them, Let us keep of our wine, till we go against the Nephites to battle. But this saying only made them more desirous to drink of the wine.

38 For, said they, We are weary; therefore let us take of the wine, and by and by we shall receive wine for our rations, which will strengthen us to go against the Nephites. And

Laman said unto them, You may do according to your desires.

39 And it came to pass that they did take of the wine freely, and it was pleasant to their taste; therefore they took of it more freely; and it was strong, having been prepared in its strength.

40 ¶And it came to pass that they did drink and were merry, and by and by they were all drunken.

41 And now when Laman and his men saw that they were all drunken, and were in a deep sleep, they returned to Moroni, and told him all the things that had happened. And now this was according to the design of Moroni.

42 And Moroni had prepared his men with weapons of war; and he sent to the city of Gid, while the Lamanites were in a deep sleep, and drunken, and cast in the weapons of war in unto the prisoners, insomuch that they were all armed; yea, even to their women, and all those of their children, as many as were able to use a weapon of war; when Moroni had armed all those prisoners.

43 And all those things were done in a profound silence. But had they awoke the Lamanites, behold they were drunken, and the Nephites could have slain them.

44 But behold this was not the desire of Moroni. He did not delight in murder or bloodshed; but he delighted in the saving of his people from destruction; and for this cause he might not bring upon him injustice, he would not fall upon the Lamanites and destroy them in their drunkenness.

45 But he had obtained his desires; for he had armed those prisoners of the Nephites who were within the wall of the city, and had gave them power to gain possession of those parts which were within the walls;

46 And then he caused the men who were with him, to withdraw a pace from them, and surround the armies of the Lamanites.

47 Now behold, this was done in the night time, so that when the Lamanites awoke in the morning, they beheld that they were surrounded by the Nephites without, and that their prisoners were armed within.

48 And thus they saw that the Nephites had power over

them; and in these circumstances they found that it was not expedient that they should fight with the Nephites;

49 Therefore their chief captains demanded their weapons of war, and they brought them forth, and cast them at the feet of the Nephites, pleading for mercy. Now behold, this was the desire of Moroni.

50 He took them prisoners of war, and took possession of the city, and caused that all the prisoners should be liberated, who were Nephites; and they did join the army of Moroni, and were a great strength to his army.

51 ¶And it came to pass that he did cause the Lamanites whom he had taken prisoners, that they should commence a labor in strengthening the fortifications round about the city Gid.

52 And it came to pass that when he had fortified the city Gid, according to his desires, he caused that his prisoners should be taken to the city Bountiful.

53 And he also guarded that city with an exceeding strong force.

54 And it came to pass that they did, notwithstanding all the intrigues of the Lamanites, keep and protect all the prisoners whom they had taken, and also maintain all the ground and the advantage which they had retaken.

55 And it came to pass that the Nephites began again to be victorious, and to reclaim their rights and their privileges.

56 Many times did the Lamanites attempt to encircle them about by night, but in these attempts they did lose many prisoners.

57 And many times did they attempt to administer of their wine to the Nephites, that they might destroy them with poison or with drunkenness.

58 But behold, the Nephites were not slow to remember the Lord their God, in this their times of affliction.

59 They could not be taken in their snares; yea, they would not partake of their wine; yea, they would not partake of wine, save they had firstly given to some of the Lamanite prisoners.

60 And they were thus cautious, that no poison should be

administered among them; for if their wine would poison a Lamanite, it would also poison a Nephite; and thus they did try all their liquors.

61 And now it came to pass that it was expedient for Moroni to make preparations to attack the city Morianton.

62 For behold, the Lamanites had, by their labors, fortified the city Morianton until it had become an exceeding stronghold; and they were continually bringing new forces into that city, and also new supplies of provisions.

63 And thus ended the twenty and ninth year of the reign of the Judges over the people of Nephi.

CHAPTER 26.

1 ¶And now it came to pass in the commencement of the thirtieth year of the reign of the Judges, in the second day, on the first month, Moroni received an epistle from Helaman, stating the affairs of the people in that quarter of the land.

2 And these are the words which he wrote, saying, My dearly beloved brother, Moroni, as well in the Lord as in the tribulations of our warfare; behold, my beloved brother, I have somewhat to tell you concerning our warfare in this part of the land.

3 Behold, two thousand of the sons of those men whom Ammon brought down out of the land of Nephi.

4 Now ye have known that these were a descendant of Laman, who was the eldest son of our father Lehi.

5 Now I need not rehearse unto you concerning their traditions or their unbelief, for thou knowest concerning all these things; therefore it supposeth me that I tell you that two thousand of these young men have taken their weapons of war, and would that I should be their leader; and we have come forth to defend our country.

6 And now ye also know concerning the covenant which their fathers made, that they would not take up their weapons of war against their brethren, to shed blood.

7 But in the twenty and sixth year, when they saw our afflictions and our tribulations for them, they were about to

break the covenant which they had made, and take up their weapons of war in our defense.

8 But I would not suffer them that they should break this covenant which they had made, supposing that God would strengthen us, insomuch that we should not suffer more because of the fulfilling the oath which they had taken.

9 But behold, here is one thing in which we may have great joy.

10 For behold, in the twenty and sixth year, I Helaman, did march at the head of these two thousand young men, to the city of Judea, to assist Antipus, whom ye had appointed a leader over the people of that part of the land.

11 And I did join my two thousand sons (for they are worthy to be called sons) to the army of Antipus; in which strength Antipus did rejoice exceedingly; for behold, his army had been reduced by the Lamanites because their forces had slain a vast number of our men; for which cause we have to mourn.

12 Nevertheless, we may console ourselves in this point: that they have died in the cause of their country and of their God, yea, and they are happy.

13 And the Lamanites had also retained many prisoners, all of whom are chief captains; for none other have they spared alive.

14 And we suppose that they are now at this time in the land of Nephi; it is so if they are not slain.

15 And now these are the cities which the Lamanites have obtained possession, by the shedding of the blood of so many of our valiant men: The land of Manti, or the city of Manti, and the city of Zeezrom, and the city of Cumeni, and the city of Antiparah.

16 And these are the cities which they possessed when I arrived at the city of Judea; and I found Antipus and his men toiling with their mights to fortify the city;

17 Yea, and they were depressed in body as well as in spirit; for they had fought valiantly by day, and toiled by night, to maintain their cities; and thus they had suffered great afflictions of every kind.

18 And now they were determined to conquer in this place, or die; therefore you may well suppose that this little force which I brought with me; yea, those sons of mine, gave them great hopes and much joy.

19 ¶And now it came to pass that when the Lamanites saw that Antipus had received a greater strength to his army, they were compelled, by the orders of Ammoron, to not come against the city of Judea, or against us, to battle.

20 And thus were we favored of the Lord: for had they come upon us in this our weakness, they might have perhaps destroyed our little army: but thus were we preserved.

21 They were commanded by Ammoron to maintain those cities which they had taken. And thus ended the twenty and sixth year.

22 And in the commencement of the twenty and seventh year, we had prepared our city and ourselves for defense.

23 Now we were desirous that the Lamanites should come upon us; for we were not desirous to make an attack upon them in their strongholds.

24 And it came to pass that we kept spies out round about, to watch the movements of the Lamanites, that they might not pass us by night, nor by day, to make an attack upon our other cities, which were on the northward;

25 For we knew in those cities they were not sufficiently strong to meet them; therefore we were desirous, if they should pass by us, to fall upon them in their rear, and thus bring them up in the rear, at the same time they were met in the front.

26 We supposed that we could overpower them; but behold, we were disappointed in this our desire.

27 They durst not pass by us with their whole army; neither durst they with a part, lest they should not be sufficiently strong, and they should fall.

28 Neither durst they march down against the city of Zarahemla; neither durst they cross the head of Sidon, over to the city of Nephihah.

29 And thus, with their forces, they were determined to maintain those cities which they had taken.

30 ¶And now it came to pass, in the second month of this year, there was brought unto us many provisions, from the fathers of those my two thousand sons.

31 And also there was sent two thousand men unto us, from the land of Zarahemla.

32 And thus we were prepared with ten thousand men, and provisions for them, and also for their wives, and their children.

33 And the Lamanites, thus seeing our forces increase daily, and provisions arrive for our support, they began to be fearful, and began to sally forth, if it were possible, to put an end to our receiving provisions and strength.

34 Now when we saw that the Lamanites began to grow uneasy on this wise, we were desirous to bring a stratagem into effect upon them:

35 Therefore Antipus ordered that I should march forth with my little sons, to a neighboring city, as if we were carrying provisions to a neighboring city.

36 And we were to march near the city of Antiparah, as if we were going to the city beyond, in the borders by the seashore.

37 And it came to pass that we did march forth, as if with our provisions, to go to that city.

38 And it came to pass that Antipus did march forth, with a part of his army, leaving the remainder to maintain the city.

39 But he did not march forth, until I had gone forth with my little army, and came near the city Antiparah.

40 And now in the city Antiparah, were stationed the strongest army of the Lamanites; yea, the most numerous.

41 And it came to pass that when they had been informed by their spies, they came forth with their army, and marched against us.

42 ¶And it came to pass that we did flee before them, northward.

43 And thus we did lead away the most powerful army of the Lamanites; yea, even to a considerable distance, insomuch that when they saw the army of Antipus pursuing them, with

their mights, they did not turn to the right nor to the left, but pursued their march in a straight course after us:

44 And, as we suppose, it was their intent to slay us before Antipus should overtake them, and this that they might not be surrounded by our people.

45 And now Antipus, beholding our danger, did speed the march of his army.

46 But behold, it was night; therefore they did not overtake us, neither did Antipus overtake them; therefore we did camp for the night.

47 ¶And it came to pass that before the dawn of the morning, behold, the Lamanites were pursuing us.

48 Now we were not sufficiently strong to contend with them; yea, I would not suffer that my little sons should fall into their hands; therefore we did continue our march; and we took our march into the wilderness.

49 Now they durst not turn to the right nor to the left, lest they should be surrounded: neither would I turn to the right or to the left, lest they should overtake me, and we could not stand against them, but be slain, and they would make their escape; and thus we did flee all that day into the wilderness, even until it was dark.

50 ¶And it came to pass that again when the light of the morning came, we saw the Lamanites upon us, and we did flee before them.

51 But it came to pass that they did not pursue us far, before they halted; and it was in the morning of the third day, on the seventh month.

52 And now whether they were overtaken by Antipus, we knew not; but I said unto my men, Behold, we know not but they have halted for the purpose that we should come against them, that they might catch us in their snare; therefore what say ye, my sons, will ye go against them to battle?

53 And now I say unto you my beloved brother, Moroni, that never had I seen so great courage, nay, not amongst all the Nephites.

54 For as I had ever called them my sons, (for they were all of them very young,) even so they said unto me, Father,

behold, our God is with us, and he will not suffer that we shall fall; then let us go forth;

55 We would not slay our brethren, if they would let us alone; therefore let us go, lest they should overpower the army of Antipus.

56 Now they never had fought, yet they did not fear death: and they did think more upon the liberty of their fathers, than they did upon their lives; yea, they had been taught by their mothers, that if they did not doubt, that God would deliver them.

57 And they rehearsed unto me the words of their mothers, saying, We do not doubt our mothers knew.

58 ¶And it came to pass that I did return with my two thousand, against these Lamanites who had pursued us.

59 And now behold, the armies of Antipus had overtaken them, and a terrible battle had commenced.

60 The army of Antipus being weary, because of their long march in so short a space of time, were about to fall into the hands of the Lamanites; and had I not returned with my two thousand, they would have obtained their purpose;

61 For Antipus had fallen by the sword, and many of his leaders, because of their weariness, which was occasioned by the speed of their march; therefore the men of Antipus being confused, because of the fall of their leaders, began to give way before the Lamanites.

62 ¶And it came to pass that the Lamanites took courage, and began to pursue them; and thus were the Lamanites pursuing them with great vigor, when Helaman came upon their rear with his two thousand, and began to slay them exceedingly, insomuch that the whole army of the Lamanites halted, and turned upon Helaman.

63 Now when the people of Antipus saw that the Lamanites had turned them about, they gathered together their men, and came again upon the rear of the Lamanites.

64 ¶And now it came to pass that we, the people of Nephi, the people of Antipus, and I with my two thousand, did surround the Lamanites, and did slay them; yea, insomuch

that they were compelled to deliver up their weapons of war, and also themselves as prisoners of war.

65 ¶And now it came to pass that when they had surrendered themselves up unto us, behold, I numbered those young men who had fought with me, fearing lest there were many of them slain.

66 But behold, to my great joy, there had not one soul of them fallen to the earth; yea, and they had fought as if with the strength of God; yea, never was men known to have fought with such miraculous strength;

67 And with such mighty power did they fall upon the Lamanites, that they did frighten them; and for this cause did the Lamanites deliver themselves up as prisoners of war.

68 And as we had no place for our prisoners, that we could guard them to keep them from the armies of the Lamanites, therefore we sent them to the land of Zarahemla, and a part of those men who were not slain of Antipus, with them;

69 And the remainder I took and joined them to my stripling Ammonites, and took our march back to the city of Judea.

70 ¶And now it came to pass that I received an epistle from Ammoron, the king, stating that if I would deliver up those prisoners of war whom we had taken, that he would deliver up the city of Antiparah unto us.

71 But I sent an epistle unto the king, that we were sure our forces were sufficient to take the city of Antiparah by our force; and by delivering up the prisoners for that city, we should suppose ourselves unwise, and that we would only deliver up our prisoners on exchange.

72 And Ammoron refused mine epistle, for he would not exchange prisoners; therefore we began to make preparations to go against the city of Antiparah.

73 But the people of Antiparah did leave the city, and fled to their other cities which they had possession of, to fortify them; and thus the city of Antiparah fell into our hands.

74 And thus ended the twenty and eighth year of the reign of the Judges.

75 ¶And it came to pass that in the commencement of the

twenty and ninth year, we received a supply of provisions, and also an addition to our army, from the land of Zarahemla, and from the land round about, to the number of six thousand men, besides sixty of the sons of the Ammonites, who had come to join their brethren, my little band of two thousand.

76 And now behold, we were strong; yea, and we had also a plenty of provisions brought unto us.

77 ¶And it came to pass that it was our desire to wage a battle with the army which was placed to protect the city Cumeni.

78 And now behold, I will shew unto you that we soon accomplished our desire; yea, with our strong force, or with a part of our strong force, we did surround, by night, the city Cumeni, a little before they were to receive a supply of provisions.

79 And it came to pass that we did camp round about the city for many nights; but we did sleep upon our swords, and keep guards, that the Lamanites could not come upon us by night, and slay us, which they attempted many times; but as many times as they attempted this, their blood was spilt.

80 At length their provisions did arrive, and they were about to enter the city by night.

81 And we, instead of being Lamanites, were Nephites; therefore, we did take them and their provisions.

82 And notwithstanding the Lamanites being cut off from their support after this manner, they were still determined to maintain the city;

83 Therefore it became expedient that we should take those provisions and send them to Judea and our prisoners to the land of Zarahemla.

84 ¶And it came to pass that not many days had passed away, before the Lamanites began to lose all hopes of succor; therefore they yielded up the city into our hands; and thus we had accomplished our designs, in obtaining the city Cumeni.

85 But it came to pass that our prisoners were so numerous, that notwithstanding the enormity of our numbers, we

were obliged to employ all our force to keep them, or to put them to death.

86 For behold they would break out in great numbers, and would fight with stones, and with clubs, or whatsoever things they could get into their hands, insomuch that we did slay upwards of two thousand of them, after they had surrendered themselves prisoners of war;

87 Therefore it became expedient for us, that we should put an end to their lives, or guard them, sword in hand, down to the land of Zarahemla;

88 And also our provisions were not any more than sufficient for our own people, notwithstanding that which we had taken from the Lamanites.

89 And now, in those critical circumstances, it became a very serious matter to determine concerning these prisoners of war, nevertheless, we did resolve to send them down to the land of Zarahemla;

90 Therefore we selected a part of our men, and gave them charge over our prisoners, to go down to the land of Zarahelma. ¶But it came to pass that on the morrow, they did return.

91 And now behold, we did not inquire of them concerning the prisoners; for behold, the Lamanites were upon us, and they returned in season to save us from falling into their hands.

92 For behold, Ammoron had sent to their support a new supply of provisions, and also a numerous army of men.

93 ¶And it came to pass that those men whom we sent with the prisoners, did arrive in season to check them, as they were about to overpower us.

94 But behold, my little band of two thousand and sixty, fought most desperately; yea, they were firm before the Lamanites, and did administer death unto all those who opposed them;

95 And as the remainder of our army were about to give way before the Lamanites, behold, those two thousand and sixty were firm and undaunted; yea, and they did obey and observe to perform every word of command with exactness;

96 Yea, and even according to their faith, it was done unto them; and I did remember the words which they said unto me that their mothers had taught them.

97 And now behold, it was these, my sons, and those men who had been selected to convey the prisoners, to whom we owe this great victory; for it was they who did beat the Lamanites; therefore they were driven back to the city of Manti.

98 And we retained our city Cumeni, and were not all destroyed by the sword; nevertheless, we had suffered great loss.

99 ¶And it came to pass that after the Lamanites had fled, I immediately gave orders that my men who had been wounded, should be taken from among the dead, and caused that their wounds should be dressed.

100 And it came to pass that there were two hundred, out of my two thousand and sixty, who had fainted because of the loss of blood;

101 Nevertheless, according to the goodness of God, and to our great astonishment, and also the joy of our whole army, there was not one soul of them who did perish; yea, and neither was there one soul among them who had not received many wounds.

102 And now, their preservation was astonishing to our whole army; yea, that they should be spared, while there was a thousand of our brethren who were slain.

103 And we do justly ascribe it to the miraculous power of God, because of their exceeding faith in that which they had been taught to believe, that there was a just God; and whosoever did not doubt, that they should be preserved by his marvelous power.

104 Now this was the faith of these of whom I have spoken; they are young, and their minds are firm; and they do put their trust in God continually.

105 ¶And now it came to pass that after we had thus taken care of our wounded men, and had buried our dead, and also the dead of the Lamanites, who were many, behold, we did inquire of Gid concerning the prisoners whom they had started to go down to the land of Zarahemla with.

106 Now Gid was the chief captain over the band which was appointed to guard them down to the land.

107 And now, these are the words which Gid said unto me, Behold, we did start to go down to the land of Zarahemla with our prisoners.

108 And it came to pass that we did meet the spies of our armies, who had been sent out to watch the camp of the Lamanites.

109 And they cried unto us, saying, Behold, the armies of the Lamanites are marching towards the city of Cumeni; and behold, they will fall upon them, yea, and will destroy our people.

110 ¶And it came to pass that our prisoners did hear their cries, which caused them to take courage; and they did rise up in rebellion against us.

111 And it came to pass because of their rebellion, we did cause that our swords should come upon them.

112 And it came to pass that they did, in a body, run upon our swords, in the which, the greater number of them were slain; and the remainder of them broke through and fled from us.

113 And behold, when they had fled, and we could not overtake them, we took our march with speed towards the city Cumeni; and behold, we did arrive in time that we might assist our brethren in preserving the city.

114 And behold, we are again delivered out of the hands of our enemies.

115 And blessed is the name of our God: for behold, it is he that has delivered us; yea, that has done this great thing for us.

116 ¶Now it came to pass that when I, Helaman, had heard these words of Gid, I was filled with exceeding joy, because of the goodness of God in preserving us, that we might not all perish;

117 Yea, and I trust that the souls of them who have been slain, have entered into the rest of their God.

118 ¶And behold, now it came to pass that our next object was to obtain the city of Manti; but behold, there was no

way that we could lead them out of the city, by our small bands.

119 For behold they remembered that which we had hitherto done; therefore we could not decoy them away from their strongholds;

120 And they were so much more numerous than was our army, that we durst not go forth and attack them in their strongholds.

121 Yea, and it became expedient that we should employ our men, to the maintaining those parts of the land, of the which we had retained of our possessions;

122 Therefore it became expedient that we should wait, that we might receive more strength from the land of Zarahemla, and also a new supply of provisions.

123 ¶And it came to pass that I thus did send an embassy to the governor of our land, to acquaint him concerning the affairs of our people.

124 And it came to pass that we did wait to receive provisions and strength, from the land of Zarahemla.

125 But behold, this did not profit us but little: for the Lamanites were also receiving great strength, from day to day, and also many provisions; and thus were our circumstances at this period of time.

126 And the Lamanites were sallying forth against us, from time to time, resolving by stratagem to destroy us; nevertheless, we could not come to battle with them, because of their retreats and their strongholds.

127 ¶And it came to pass that we did wait in these difficult circumstances, for the space of many months, even until we were about to perish for the want of food.

128 But it came to pass that we did receive food, which was guarded to us by an army of two thousand men, to our assistance;

129 And this is all the assistance which we did receive, to defend ourselves and our country from falling into the hands of our enemies; yea, to contend with an enemy which was innumerable.

130 And now the cause of these our embarrassments, or

the cause why they did not send more strength unto us, we knew not; therefore we were grieved, and also filled with fear, lest by any means the judgments of God should come upon our land, to our overthrow and utter destruction;

131 Therefore we did pour out our souls in prayer to God, that he would strengthen us and deliver us out of the hands of our enemies; yea, and also give us strength, that we might retain our cities, and our lands, and our possessions, for the support of our people.

132 Yea, and it came to pass that the Lord our God did visit us with assurances, that he would deliver us; yea, insomuch that he did speak peace to our souls, and did grant unto us great faith, and did cause us that we should hope for our deliverance in him;

133 And we did take courage with our small force which we had received, and were fixed with a determination to conquer our enemies, and to maintain our lands, and our possessions, and our wives, and our children, and the cause of our liberty.

134 And thus we did go forth with all our might against the Lamanites, who were in the city of Manti; and we did pitch our tents by the wilderness side, which was near to the city.

135 And it came to pass that on the morrow, that when the Lamanites saw that we were in the borders by the wilderness which was near the city, that they sent out their spies round about us, that they might discover the number and the strength of our army.

136 ¶And it came to pass that when they saw that we were not strong, according to our numbers, and fearing that we should cut them off from their support, except they should come out to battle against us, and kill us,

137 And also supposing that they could easily destroy us with their numerous hosts, therefore they began to make preparations to come out against us to battle.

138 And when we saw that they were making preparations to come out against us, behold, I caused that Gid, with a small number of men, should secrete himself in the wilder-

ness, and also that Teomner should, with a small number of men, secrete themselves also in the wilderness.

139 Now Gid and his men were on the right, and the others on the left; and when they had thus secreted themselves, behold, I remained with the remainder of my army, in that same place where we had first pitched our tents, against the time that the Lamanites should come out to battle.

140 ¶And it came to pass that the Lamanites did come out with their numerous army against us.

141 And when they had come and were about to fall upon us with the sword, I caused that my men, those who were with me, should retreat into the wilderness.

142 ¶And it came to pass that the Lamanites did follow after us with great speed, for they were exceedingly desirous to overtake us, that they might slay us; therefore they did follow us into the wilderness;

143 And we did pass by in the midst of Gid and Teomner, insomuch that they were not discovered by the Lamanites.

144 ¶And it came to pass that when the Lamanites had passed by, or when the army had passed by, Gid and Teomner did rise up from their secret places, and did cut off the spies of the Lamanites, that they should not return to the city.

145 And it came to pass that when they had cut them off, they ran to the city, and fell upon the guards who were left to guard the city, insomuch that they did destroy them, and did take possession of the city.

146 Now this was done because the Lamanites did suffer their whole army, save a few guards only, to be led away into the wilderness.

147 ¶And it came to pass that Gid and Teomner, by this means, had obtained possession of their strongholds.

148 And it came to pass that we took our course, after having traveled much in the wilderness, towards the land of Zarahemla.

149 And when the Lamanites saw that they were marching towards the land of Zarahemla, they were exceeding fraid, lest there was a plan laid to lead them on to destruction; therefore they began to retreat into the wilderness

again, yea, even back by the same way which they had come.

150 And behold, it was night, and they did pitch their tents; for the chief captains of the Lamanites had supposed that the Nephites were weary, because of their march; and supposing that they had driven their whole army, therefore they took no thought concerning the city of Manti.

151 ¶Now it came to pass that when it was night, that I caused that my men should not sleep, but that they should march forward by another way, towards the land of Manti.

152 And because of this our march in the night time, behold, on the morrow, we were beyond the Lamanites, insomuch that we did arrive before them to the city of Manti.

153 And thus it came to pass, that by this stratagem, we did take possession of the city of Manti, without the shedding of blood.

154 ¶And it came to pass that when the armies of the Lamanites did arrive near the city, and saw that we were prepared to meet them, they were astonished exceedingly, and struck with great fear, insomuch that they did flee into the wilderness.

155 Yea, and it came to pass that the armies of the Lamanites did flee out of all this quarter of the land.

156 But behold, they have carried with them many women and children out of the land.

157 And those cities which had been taken by the Lamanites, all of them are at this period of time in our possession; and our fathers, and our women, and our children, are returning to their homes, all save it be those who have been taken prisoners and carried off by the Lamanites.

158 But behold, our armies are small, to maintain so great a number of cities, and so great possessions.

159 But behold, we trust that our God, who has given us victory over those lands, insomuch that we have obtained those cities and those lands, which were our own.

160 Now we do not know the cause that the government does not grant us more strength; neither do those men who came up unto us, know why we have not received greater strength.

161 Behold, we do not know but what ye are unsuccessful, and ye have drawn away the forces into that quarter of the land; if so, we do not desire to murmur.

162 And if it is not so, behold, we fear that there is some faction in the government, that they do not send more men to our assistance; for we know that they are more numerous than that which they have sent.

163 But behold, it mattereth not; we trust God will deliver us, notwithstanding the weakness of our armies, yea, and deliver us out of the hands of our enemies.

164 Behold, this is the twenty and ninth year, in the latter end, and we are in the possession of our lands; and the Lamanites have fled to the land of Nephi.

165 And those sons of the people of Ammon of whom I have so highly spoken, are with me in the city of Manti; and the Lord has supported them, yea, and kept them from falling by the sword, insomuch that even one soul has not been slain.

166 But behold they have received many wounds; nevertheless they stand fast in that liberty wherewith God has made them free;

167 And they are strict to remember the Lord their God, from day to day; yea, they do observe to keep his statutes, and his judgments, and his commandments continually; and their faith is strong in the prophecies concerning that which is to come.

168 And now my beloved brother Moroni, that the Lord our God who has redeemed us and made us free, may keep you continually in his presence;

169 Yea, and that he may favor this people, even that ye may have success in obtaining the possession of all that which the Lamanites have taken from us, which was for our support.

170 And now behold, I close mine epistle. I am Helaman, the son of Alma.

CHAPTER 27.

1 ¶Now it came to pass in the thirtieth year of the reign of the Judges over the people of Nephi, after Moroni had received and had read Helaman's epistle, he was exceedingly rejoiced because of the welfare, yea, the exceeding success which Helaman had had, in obtaining those lands which were lost;

2 Yea, and he did make it known unto all his people in all the land round about in that part where he was, that they might rejoice also.

3 ¶And it came to pass that he immediately sent an epistle to Pahoran, desiring that he should cause men to be gathered together, to strengthen Helaman, or the armies of Helaman, insomuch that he might with ease maintain that part of the land which he had been so miraculously prospered in retaining.

4 And it came to pass when Moroni had sent this epistle to the land of Zarahemla, he began again to lay a plan, that he might obtain the remainder of those possessions and cities which the Lamanites had taken from them.

5 And it came to pass that while Moroni was thus making preparations to go against the Lamanites to battle, behold, the people of Nephihah who were gathered together from the city of Moroni, and the city of Lehi, and the city of Morianton, were attacked by the Lamanites;

6 Yea, even those who had been compelled to flee from the land of Manti, and from the land round about, had come over and joined the Lamanites in this part of the land;

7 And thus being exceeding numerous, yea, and receiving strength from day to day, by the command of Ammoron, they came forth against the people of Nephihah, and they did begin to slay them with an exceeding great slaughter.

8 And their armies were so numerous, that the remainder of the people of Nephihah were obliged to flee before them; and they came even and joined the army of Moroni.

9 And now as Moroni had supposed that there should be men sent to the city of Nephihah, to the assistance of the

people to maintain that city, and knowing that it was easier to keep the city from falling into the hands of the Lamanites, than to retake it from them, he supposed that they would easily maintain that city;

10 Therefore he retained all his force to maintain those places which he had recovered.

11 ¶And now when Moroni saw that the city of Nephihah was lost, he was exceeding sorrowful, and began to doubt, because of the wickedness of the people, whether they should not fall into the hands of their brethren.

12 Now this was the case with all his chief captains. They doubted and marveled also, because of the wickedness of the people; and this because of the success of the Lamanites over them.

13 And it came to pass that Moroni was angry with the government, because of their indifference concerning the freedom of their country.

14 ¶And it came to pass that he wrote again to the governor of the land, who was Pahoran, and these are the words which he wrote, saying, Behold, I direct mine epistle to Pahoran, in the city of Zarahemla, who is the chief judge and the governor over the land, and also to all those who have been chosen by this people to govern and manage the affairs of this war;

15 For behold, I have somewhat to say unto them by the way of condemnation; for behold, ye yourselves know that ye have been appointed to gather together men, and arm them with swords, and with cimeters, and all manner of weapons of war, of every kind, and send forth against the Lamanites, in whatsoever parts they should come into our land.

16 And now behold, I say unto you, that myself, and also my men, and also Helaman and his men, have suffered exceeding great sufferings; yea, even hunger, thirst, and fatigue, and all manner of afflictions of every kind.

17 But behold, were this all we had suffered, we would not murmur nor complain; but behold, great has been the slaughter among our people:

18 Yea, thousands have fallen by the sword, while it might

have otherwise been, if ye had rendered unto our armies sufficient strength and succor for them.

19 Yea, great has been your neglect towards us. And now behold, we desire to know the cause of this exceeding great neglect; yea, we desire to know the cause of your thoughtless state.

20 Can you think to sit upon your thrones, in a state of thoughtless stupor, while your enemies are spreading the work of death around you?

21 Yea, while they are murdering thousands of your brethren; yea, even they who have looked up to you for protection, yea, have placed you in a situation that ye might have succored them;

22 Yea, ye might have sent armies unto them, to have strengthened them, and have saved thousands of them from falling by the sword!

23 But behold, this is not all, ye have withheld your provisions from them, insomuch that many have fought and bled out their lives because of their great desires which they had for the welfare of this people;

24 Yea, and this they have done, when they were about to perish with hunger, because of your exceeding great neglect towards them.

25 And now, my beloved brethren; for ye had ought to be beloved; yea, and ye had ought to have stirred yourselves more diligently for the welfare and the freedom of this people;

26 But behold, ye have neglected them, insomuch that the blood of thousands shall come upon your heads for vengeance; yea, for known unto God were all their cries, and all their sufferings.

27 Behold, could ye suppose that ye could sit upon your thrones, and because of the exceeding goodness of God, ye could do nothing, and he would deliver you? Behold, if ye have supposed this, ye have supposed in vain.

28 Do ye suppose that; because so many of your brethren have been killed because of their wickedness? I say unto you, If ye have supposed this, ye have supposed in vain; for

I say unto you, There are many who have fallen by the sword;

29 And behold, it is to your condemnation; for the Lord suffereth the righteous to be slain, that his justice and judgment may come upon the wicked; therefore ye need not suppose that the righteous are lost because they are slain; but behold, they do enter into the rest of the Lord their God.

30 And now behold, I say unto you, I fear exceedingly that the judgments of God will come upon this people, because of their exceeding slothfulness; yea, even the slothfulness of our government, and their exceeding great neglect towards their brethren, yea, towards those who have been slain:

31 For were it not for the wickedness which first commenced at our head, we could have withstood our enemies, that they could have gained no power over us; yea, had it not been for the war which broke out among ourselves;

32 Yea were it not for those king-men, who caused so much bloodshed among ourselves; yea, at the time we were contending among ourselves, if we had united our strength, as we hitherto have done;

33 Yea, had it not been for the desire of power and authority which those king-men had over us; had they been true to the cause of our freedom, and united with us, and gone forth against our enemies, instead of taking up their swords against us, which was the cause of so much bloodshed among ourselves;

34 Yea, if we had gone forth against them, in the strength of the Lord, we should have dispersed our enemies; for it would have been done according to the fulfilling of his word.

35 But behold, now the Lamanites are coming upon us, and they are murdering our people with the sword; yea, our women and our children; taking possession of our lands, and also carrying them away captive; causing them that they should suffer all manner of afflictions; and this because of the great wickedness of those who are seeking for power and authority; yea, even those king-men.

36 But why should I say much concerning this matter, for we know not but what ye yourselves are seeking for au-

thority? We know not but what ye are also traitors to your country?

37 Or is it that ye have neglected us because ye are in the heart of our country, and ye are surrounded by security, that ye do not cause food to be sent unto us, and also men to strengthen our armies?

38 Have ye forgot the commandments of the Lord your God? Yea, have ye forgot the captivity of our fathers?

39 Have ye forgot the many times we have been delivered out of the hands of our enemies?

40 Or do ye suppose that the Lord will still deliver us, while we sit upon our thrones, and do not make use of the means which the Lord has provided for us?

41 Yea, will ye sit in idleness, while ye are surrounded with thousands of those, yea, and tens of thousands, who do also sit in idleness, while there are thousands round about in the borders of the land, who are falling by the sword, yea, wounded and bleeding?

42 Do ye suppose that God will look upon you as guiltless, while ye sit still and behold these things? Behold, I say unto you, Nay.

43 Now I would that ye should remember that God has said that the inward vessel shall be cleansed first, and then shall the outer vessel be cleansed also.

44 And now except ye do repent of that which ye have done, and begin to be up and doing, and send forth food and men unto us, and also unto Helaman, that he may support those parts of our country which he has retained, and that we may also recover the remainder of our possessions in these parts, behold, it will be expedient that we contend no more with the Lamanites until we have first cleansed our inward vessel; yea, even the great head of our government;

45 And except ye grant mine epistle, and come out and shew unto me a true spirit of freedom, and strive to strengthen and fortify our armies, and grant unto them food for their support, behold, I will leave a part of my freemen to maintain this part of our land, and I will leave the strength and the blessings of God upon them, that none other power

can operate against them; and this because of their exceeding faith and their patience in their tribulations;

46 And I will come unto you, and if there be any among you that has a desire for freedom, yea, if there be even a spark of freedom remaining, behold I will stir up insurrections among you, even until those who have desires to usurp power and authority, shall become extinct;

47 Yea, behold I do not fear your power nor your authority, but it is my God whom I fear, and it is according to his commandments that I do take my sword to defend the cause of my country, and it is because of your iniquity that we have suffered so much loss.

48 Behold it is time; yea, the time is now at hand, that except ye do bestir yourselves in the defense of your country and your little ones, the sword of justice doth hang over you: yea, and it shall fall upon you and visit you even to your utter destruction.

49 Behold, I wait for assistance from you, and except ye do administer unto our relief, behold I come unto you even into the land of Zarahemla, and smite you with the sword, insomuch that ye can have no more power to impede the progress of this people in the cause of our freedom;

50 For behold the Lord will not suffer that ye shall live and wax strong in your iniquities, to destroy his righteous people.

51 Behold, can you suppose that the Lord will spare you and come out in judgment against the Lamanites, when it is the tradition of their fathers that has caused their hatred;

52 Yea, and it has been redoubled by those who have dissented from us, while your iniquity is for the cause of your love of glory, and the vain things of the world?

53 Ye know that ye do transgress the laws of God, and ye do know that ye do trample them under your feet.

54 Behold, the Lord saith unto me, If those whom ye have appointed your governors, do not repent of their sins and iniquities, ye shall go up to battle against them.

55 And now behold, I Moroni am constrained, according to the covenant which I have made to keep the commandments

of my God; therefore I would that ye should adhere to the word of God, and send speedily unto me of your provisions and of your men, and also to Helaman.

56 And behold if ye will not do this, I come unto you speedily; for behold, God will not suffer that we should perish with hunger; therefore he will give unto us of your food, even if it must be by the sword.

57 Now see that ye fulfill the word of God.

58 Behold, I am Moroni, your chief captain. I seek not for power but to pull it down.

59 I seek not for honor of the world, but for the glory of my God, and the freedom and welfare of my country. And thus I close mine epistle.

CHAPTER 28.

1 ¶Behold, now it came to pass that soon after Moroni had sent his epistle unto the chief governor, he received an epistle from Pahoran, the chief governor.

2 And these are the words which he received: I, Pahoran, who am the chief governor of this land, do send these words unto Moroni, the chief captain over the army: Behold I say unto you, Moroni, that I do not joy in your great afflictions; yea, it grieves my soul.

3 But behold, there are those who do joy in your afflictions; yea, insomuch that they have risen up in rebellion against me, and also those of my people who are freemen; yea, and those who have risen up are exceeding numerous.

4 And it is those who have sought to take away the judgment seat from me, that have been the cause of this great iniquity;

5 For they have used great flattery; and they have led away the hearts of many people, which will be the cause of sore affliction among us; they have withheld our provisions, and have daunted our freemen, that they have not come unto you.

6 And behold, they have driven me out before them, and I

have fled to the land of Gideon, with as many men as it were possible that I could get.

7 And behold, I have sent a proclamation throughout this part of the land; and behold, they are flocking to us daily, to their arms, in the defense of their country, and their freedom, and to avenge our wrongs.

8 And they have come unto us, insomuch that those who have risen up in rebellion against us, are set at defiance; yea, insomuch that they do fear us, and durst not come out against us to battle.

9 They have got possession of the land, or the city of Zarahemla: they have appointed a king over them, and he hath written unto the king of the Lamanites, in the which he hath joined an alliance with him;

10 In the which alliance, he hath agreed to maintain the city of Zarahemla, which maintenance he supposeth will enable the Lamanites to conquer the remainder of the land, and he shall be placed king over this people, when they shall be conquered under the Lamanites.

11 And now, in your epistle you have censured me; but it mattereth not, I am not angry, but do rejoice in the greatness of your heart.

12 I, Pahoran, do not seek for power, save only to retain my judgment seat, that I may preserve the rights and the liberty of my people.

13 My soul standeth fast in that liberty, in the which God hath made us free.

14 ¶And now behold we will resist wickedness, even unto bloodshed.

15 We would not shed the blood of the Lamanites, if they would stay in their own land.

16 We would not shed the blood of our brethren, if they would not rise up in rebellion and take the sword against us.

17 We would subject ourselves to the yoke of bondage, if it were requisite with the justice of God, or if he should command us so to do.

18 But behold he doth not command us that we shall sub-

ject ourselves to our enemies, but that we should put our trust in him and he will deliver us.

19 Therefore my beloved brother Moroni, let us resist evil; and whatsoever evil we can not resist with our words, yea, such as rebellions and dissensions, let us resist them with our swords, that we may retain our freedom, that we may rejoice in the great privilege of our church and in the cause of our Redeemer and our God.

20 Therefore come unto me speedily, with a few of your men, and leave the remainder in the charge of Lehi and Teancum; give unto them power to conduct the war in that part of the land, according to the Spirit of God, which is also the spirit of freedom which is in them.

21 Behold I have sent a few provisions unto them, that they may not perish until ye can come unto me.

22 Gather together whatsoever force ye can upon your march hither, and we will go speedily against those dissenters, in the strength of our God, according to the faith which is in us.

23 And we will take possession of the city of Zarahemla, that we may obtain more food to send forth unto Lehi and Teancum; yea, we will go forth against them in the strength of the Lord, and we will put an end to this great iniquity.

24 ¶And now, Moroni, I do joy in receiving your epistle; for I was somewhat worried concerning what we should do, whether it should be just in us to go against our brethren.

25 But ye have said, Except they repent, the Lord hath commanded you that ye should go against them.

26 See that ye strengthen Lehi and Teancum in the Lord; tell them to fear not, for God will deliver them; yea, and also all those who stand fast in that liberty wherewith God hath made them free.

27 And now I close mine epistle to my beloved brother Moroni.

CHAPTER 29.

1 ¶And now it came to pass that when Moroni had received this epistle, his heart did take courage, and was filled with exceeding great joy, because of the faithfulness of Pahoran, that he was not also a traitor to the freedom and cause of his country.

2 But he did also mourn exceedingly, because of the iniquity of those who have driven Pahoran from the judgment seat; yea, in fine, because of those who had rebelled against their country and also their God.

3 ¶And it came to pass that Moroni took a small number of men according to the desire of Pahoran, and gave Lehi and Teancum command over the remainder of his army, and took his march towards the land of Gideon.

4 And he did raise the standard of liberty in whatsoever place he did enter, and gained whatsoever force he could in all his march towards the land of Gideon.

5 ¶And it came to pass that thousands did flock unto his standard, and did take up their swords in the defense of their freedom, that they might not come into bondage.

6 And thus when Moroni had gathered together whatsoever men he could in all his march, he came to the land of Gideon; and uniting his forces with that of Pahoran, they became exceeding strong, even stronger than the men of Pachus, who was the king of those dissenters who had driven out the freemen out of the land of Zarahemla, and had taken possession of the land.

7 ¶And it came to pass that Moroni and Pahoran went down with their armies into the land of Zarahemla, and went forth against the city, and did meet the men of Pachus, insomuch that they did come to battle.

8 And behold, Pachus was slain, and his men were taken prisoners; and Pahoran was restored to his judgment seat.

9 And the men of Pachus received their trial, according to the law, and also those king-men who had been taken and cast into prison; and they were executed according to the law;

10 Yea, those men of Pachus, and those king-men, whoso-

ever would not take up arms in the defense of their country, but would fight against it, were put to death.

11 And thus it became expedient that this law should be strictly observed, for the safety of their country; yea, and whosoever was found denying their freedom, was speedily executed according to the law.

12 And thus ended the thirtieth year of the reign of the Judges over the people of Nephi: Moroni and Pahoran having restored peace to the land of Zarahemla, among their own people, having inflicted death upon all those who were not true to the cause of freedom.

13 ¶And it came to pass in the commencement of the thirty and first year of the reign of the Judges over the people of Nephi, Moroni immediately caused that provisions should be sent, and also an army of six thousand men should be sent unto Helaman, to assist him in preserving that part of the land;

14 And he also caused that an army of six thousand men, with a sufficient quantity of food, should be sent to the armies of Lehi and Teancum.

15 And it came to pass that this was done, to fortify the land against the Lamanites.

16 ¶And it came to pass that Moroni and Pahoran, leaving a large body of men in the land of Zarahemla, took their march with a large body of men towards the land of Nephihah, being determined to overthrow the Lamanites in that city.

17 ¶And it came to pass that as they were marching towards the land, they took a large body of men of the Lamanites, and slew many of them, and took their provisions, and their weapons of war.

18 And it came to pass after they had took them, they caused them to enter into a covenant, that they would no more take up their weapons of war against the Nephites.

19 And when they had entered into this covenant, they sent them to dwell with the people of Ammon; and they were in number about four thousand who had not been slain.

20 ¶And it came to pass that when they had sent them

away, they pursued their march towards the land of Nephihah.

21 And it came to pass that when they had come to the city Nephihah, they did pitch their tents in the plains of Nephihah, which is near the city Nephihah.

22 Now Moroni was desirous that the Lamanites should come out to battle against them, upon the plains; but the Lamanites knowing of their exceeding great courage, and beholding the greatness of their numbers, therefore they durst not come out against them; therefore they did not come to battle in that day.

23 And when the night came, Moroni went forth in the darkness of the night, and came upon the top of the wall to spy out in what part of the city the Lamanites did camp with their army.

24 ¶And it came to pass that they were on the east, by the entrance; and they were all asleep.

25 And now Moroni returned to his army, and caused that they should prepare in haste strong cords and ladders, to be let down from the top of the wall into the inner part of the wall.

26 ¶And it came to pass that Moroni caused that his men should march forth and come upon the top of the wall, and let themselves down into that part of the city, yea, even on the west, where the Lamanites did not camp with their armies.

27 ¶And it came to pass that they were all let down into the city by night, by the means of their strong cords and their ladders; thus when the morning came, they were all within the walls of the city.

28 And now when the Lamanites awoke, and saw that the armies of Moroni were within the walls, they were affrighted exceedingly, insomuch that they did flee out by the pass.

29 And now when Moroni saw that they were fleeing before him, he did cause that his men should march forth against them, and slew many, and surrounded many others and took them prisoners; and the remainder of them fled into the land of Moroni, which was in the borders of the sea-shore.

30 Thus had Moroni and Pahoran obtained the possession

of the city of Nephihah, without the loss of one soul; and there were many of the Lamanites who were slain.

31 ¶Now it came to pass that many of the Lamanites who were prisoners, were desirous to join the people of Ammon, and become a free people.

32 And it came to pass that as many as were desirous, unto them it was granted, according to their desires; therefore all the prisoners of the Lamanites did join the people of Ammon, and did begin to labor exceedingly, tilling the ground, raising all manner of grain, and flocks, and herds of every kind;

33 And thus were the Nephites relieved from a great burthen; yea, insomuch that they were relieved from all the prisoners of the Lamanites.

34 ¶Now it came to pass that Moroni, after he had obtained possession of the city of Nephihah, having taken many prisoners, which did reduce the armies of the Lamanites exceedingly, and having retained many of the Nephites who had been taken prisoners, which did strengthen the army of Moroni exceedingly; therefore Moroni went forth from the land of Nephihah to the land of Lehi.

35 ¶And it came to pass that when the Lamanites saw that Moroni was coming against them, they were again frightened, and fled before the army of Moroni.

36 And it came to pass that Moroni and his army did pursue them from city to city, until they were met by Lehi and Teancum; and the Lamanites fled from Lehi and Teancum, even down upon the borders by the sea-shore, until they came to the land of Moroni.

37 And the armies of the Lamanites were all gathered together, insomuch that they were all in one body, in the land of Moroni.

38 Now Ammoron, the king of the Lamanites, was also with them.

39 ¶And it came to pass that Moroni, and Lehi, and Teancum, did encamp with their armies round about in the borders of the land of Moroni, insomuch that the Lamanites were encircled about in the borders by the wilderness, on the south,

and in the borders by the wilderness, on the east; and thus they did encamp for the night.

40 For behold, the Nephites and the Lamanites also, were weary because of the greatness of the march; therefore they did not resolve upon any stratagem in the night time, save it were Teancum:

41 For he was exceeding angry with Ammoron, insomuch that he considered that Ammoron and Amalickiah his brother, had been the cause of this great and lasting war between them and the Lamanites, which had been the cause of so much war and bloodshed, yea, and so much famine.

42 ¶And it came to pass that Teancum in his anger did go forth into the camp of the Lamanites, and did let himself down over the walls of the city.

43 And he went forth with a cord, from place to place, insomuch that he did find the king; and he did cast a javelin at him, which did pierce him near the heart.

44 But behold, the king did awake his servant before he died, insomuch that they did pursue Teancum, and slew him.

45 ¶Now it came to pass that when Lehi and Moroni knew that Teancum was dead, they were exceeding sorrowful: for behold, he had been a man who had fought valiantly for his country, yea, a true friend to liberty; and he had suffered very many exceeding sore afflictions.

46 But behold, he was dead, and had gone the way of all the earth.

47 ¶Now it came to pass that Moroni marched forth on the morrow, and came upon the Lamanites, insomuch that they did slay them with a great slaughter; and they did drive them out of the land: and they did flee, even that they did not return at that time against the Nephites.

48 And thus ended the thirty and first year of the reign of the Judges over the people of Nephi; and thus they had had wars, and bloodsheds, and famine, and affliction for the space of many years.

49 And there had been murders, and contentions, and dissensions, and all manner of iniquity among the people of Ne-

phi; nevertheless, for the righteous' sake, yea, because of the prayers of the righteous, they were spared.

50 But behold, because of the exceeding great length of the war between the Nephites and the Lamanites, many had become hardened, because of the exceeding great length of the war;

51 And many were softened, because of their afflictions, insomuch that they did humble themselves before God, even in the depth of humility.

52 ¶And it came to pass that after Moroni had fortified those parts of the land which were most exposed to the Lamanites, until they were sufficiently strong, he returned to the city of Zarahemla, and also Helaman returned to the place of his inheritance; and there was once more peace established among the people of Nephi.

53 And Moroni yielded up the command of his armies into the hands of his son, whose name was Moronihah; and he retired to his own house that he might spend the remainder of his days in peace.

54 And Pahoran did return to his judgment seat; and Helaman did take upon him again to preach unto the people the word of God: for because of so many wars and contentions, it had become expedient that a regulation should be made again in the church;

55 Therefore Helaman and his brethren went forth, and did declare the word of God with much power, unto the convincing of many people of their wickedness, which did cause them to repent of their sins, and to be baptized unto the Lord their God.

56 ¶And it came to pass that they did establish again the church of God, throughout all the land; yea, and regulations were made concerning the law.

57 And their judges, and their chief judges were chosen.

58 And the people of Nephi began to prosper again in the land, and began to multiply and to wax exceeding strong again in the land.

59 And they began to grow exceeding rich; but notwithstanding their riches, or their strength, or their prosperity,

they were not lifted up in the pride of their eyes; neither were they slow to remember the Lord their God: but they did humble themselves exceedingly before him;

60 Yea, they did remember how great things the Lord had done for them, that he had delivered them from death, and from bonds, and from prisons, and from all manner of afflictions; and he had delivered them out of the hands of their enemies.

61 And they did pray unto the Lord their God continually, insomuch that the Lord did bless them according to his word, so that they did wax strong, and prosper in the land.

62 And it came to pass that all these things were done.

63 And Helaman died, in the thirty and fifth year of the reign of the Judges over the people of Nephi.

CHAPTER 30.

1 ¶And it came to pass in the commencement of the thirty and sixth year of the reign of the Judges over the people of Nephi, that Shiblon took possession of those sacred things which had been delivered unto Helaman by Alma;

2 And he was a just man, and he did walk uprightly before God; and he did observe to do good continually, to keep the commandments of the Lord his God; and also did his brother.

3 ¶And it came to pass that Moroni died also.

4 And thus ended the thirty and sixth year of the reign of the Judges.

5 And it came to pass that in the thirty and seventh year of the reign of the Judges, there was a large company of men, even to the amount of five thousand and four hundred men, with their wives and their children, departed out of the land of Zarahemla, into the land which was northward.

6 ¶And it came to pass that Hagoth, he being an exceeding curious man, therefore he went forth, and built him an exceeding large ship, on the borders of the land Bountiful, by the land Desolation, and launched it forth into the west sea, by the narrow neck which led into the land northward.

7 And behold there were many of the Nephites who did enter therein, and did sail forth with much provisions, and also many women and children; and they took their course northward.

8 And thus ended the thirty and seventh year.

9 And in the thirty and eighth year, this man built other ships.

10 And the first ship did also return, and many more people did enter into it; and they also took much provisions, and set out again to the land northward.

11 ¶And it came to pass that they were never heard of more. And we suppose that they were drowned up in the depths of the sea.

12 And it came to pass that one other ship also did sail forth; and whither she did go we know not.

13 And it came to pass that in this year, there were many people who went forth into the land northward. And thus ended the thirty and eighth year.

14 ¶And it came to pass in the thirty and ninth year of the reign of the Judges, Shiblon died also, and Corianton had gone forth to the land northward, in a ship, to carry forth provisions unto the people who had gone forth into that land;

15 Therefore it became expedient for Shiblon to confer those sacred things, before his death, upon the son of Helaman, who was called Helaman, being called after the name of his father.

16 Now behold, all those engravings which were in the possession of Helaman, were written and sent forth among the children of men throughout all the land, save it were those parts which had been commanded by Alma should not go forth.

17 Nevertheless these things were to be kept sacred, and handed down from one generation to another; therefore, in this year they had been conferred upon Helaman, before the death of Shiblon.

18 And it came to pass also in this year, that there were some dissenters who had gone forth unto the Lamanites; and they were stirred up again to anger against the Nephites.

19 And also in this same year, they came down with a numerous army to war against the people of Moronihah, or against the army of Moronihah, in the which they were beaten, and driven back again to their own lands, suffering great loss.

20 And thus ended the thirty and ninth year of the reign of the Judges over the people of Nephi.

21 And thus ended the account of Alma, and Helaman his son, and also Shiblon, who was his son.

THE BOOK OF HELAMAN.

CHAPTER 1.

An account of the Nephites. Their wars and contentions, and their dissensions. And also the prophecies of many holy prophets, before the coming of Christ, according to the record of Helaman, who was the son of Helaman, and also according to the records of his sons, even down to the coming of Christ. And also many of the Lamanites are converted. An account of their conversion. An account of the righteousness of the Lamanites, and the wickedness and abominations of the Nephites, according to the record of Helaman and his sons, even down to the coming of Christ, which is called the book of Helaman, etc.

1 ¶And now behold, it came to pass in the commencement of the fortieth year of the reign of the Judges over the people of Nephi, there began to be a serious difficulty among the people of the Nephites.

2 For behold, Pahoran had died, and gone the way of all the earth; therefore there began to be a serious contention concerning who should have the judgment seat among the brethren, who were the sons of Pahoran.

3 Now these are their names who did contend for the judg-

ment seat, who did also cause the people to contend: Pahoran, Paanchi, and Pacumeni.

4 Now these are not all the sons of Pahoran, (for he had many,) but these are they who did contend for the judgment seat; therefore, they did cause three divisions among the people.

5 Nevertheless, it came to pass that Pahoran was appointed by the voice of the people to be chief judge and a governor over the people of Nephi.

6 ¶And it came to pass that Pacumeni, when he saw that he could not obtain the judgment seat, he did unite with the voice of the people.

7 But behold, Paanchi, and that part of the people that were desirous that he should be their governor, was exceeding wroth; therefore, he was about to flatter away those people to rise up in rebellion against their brethren.

8 ¶And it came to pass as he was about to do this, behold, he was taken, and was tried according to the voice of the people, and condemned unto death; for he had raised up in rebellion, and sought to destroy the liberty of the people.

9 Now when those people who were desirous that he should be their governor, saw that he was condemned unto death, therefore they were angry; and behold they sent forth one Kishkumen, even to the judgment seat of Pahoran, and murdered Pahoran as he sat upon the judgment seat.

10 And he was pursued by the servants of Pahoran; but behold, so speedy was the flight of Kishkumen, that no man could overtake him.

11 And he went unto those that sent him, and they all entered into a covenant, yea, swearing by their everlasting Maker, that they would tell no man that Kishkumen had murdered Pahoran; therefore Kishkumen was not known among the people of Nephi, for he was in disguise at the time that he murdered Pahoran.

12 And Kishkumen, and his band who had covenanted with him, did mingle themselves among the people, in a manner that they all could not be found; but as many as were found, were condemned unto death.

13 And now behold, Pacumeni was appointed, according to the voice of the people, to be a chief judge and a governor over the people, to reign in the stead of his brother Pahoran: and it was according to his right.

14 And all this was done, in the fortieth year of the reign of the Judges; and it had an end.

15 ¶And it came to pass in the forty and first year of the reign of the Judges, that the Lamanites had gathered together an innumerable army of men, and armed them with swords, and with cimeters, and with bows, and with arrows, and with head-plates, and with breastplates, and with all manner of shields of every kind; and they came down again, that they might pitch battle against the Nephites.

16 And they were led by a man whose name was Coriantumr; and he was a descendant of Zarahemla; and he was a dissenter from among the Nephites; and he was a large and a mighty man;

17 Therefore the king of the Lamanites, whose name was Tubaloth, who was the son of Ammoron, supposing that Coriantumr, being a mighty man, could stand against the Nephites, insomuch with his strength and also with his great wisdom, that by sending him forth, he should gain power over the Nephites;

18 Therefore he did stir them up to anger, and he did gather together his armies, and he did appoint Coriantumr to be their leader, and did cause that they should march down to the land of Zarahemla, to battle against the Nephites.

19 ¶And it came to pass that because of so much contention and so much difficulty in the government, that they had not kept sufficient guards in the land of Zarahemla; for they had supposed that the Lamanites durst not come into the heart of their lands to attack that great city Zarahemla.

20 But it came to pass that Coriantumr did march forth at the head of his numerous host, and came upon the inhabitants of the city, and their march was with such exceeding great speed, that there was no time for the Nephites to gather together their armies;

21 Therefore Coriantumr did cut down the watch by the

entrance of the city, and did march forth with his whole army into the city, and they did slay every one who did oppose them, insomuch that they did take possession of the whole city.

22 And it came to pass that Pacumeni, who was the chief judge, did flee before Coriantumr, even to the walls of the city.

23 And it came to pass that Coriantumr did smite him against the wall, insomuch that he died. And thus ended the days of Pacumeni.

24 And now when Coriantumr saw that he was in possession of the city of Zarahemla, and saw that the Nephites had fled before them, and were slain, and were taken, and were cast into prison, and that he had obtained the possession of the strongest hold in all the land, his heart took courage, insomuch that he was about to go forth against all the land.

25 And now he did not tarry in the land of Zarahemla, but he did march forth with a large army, even towards the city of Bountiful; for it was his determination to go forth and cut his way through with the sword, that he might obtain the north parts of the land,

26 And supposing that their greatest strength was in the center of the land, therefore he did march forth, giving them no time to assemble themselves together, save it were in small bodies; and in this manner they did fall upon them and cut them down to the earth.

27 But behold, this march of Coriantumr through the center of the land, gave Moronihah great advantage over them, notwithstanding the greatness of the number of the Nephites who were slain;

28 For behold, Moronihah had supposed that the Lamanites durst not come into the center of the land, but that they would attack the cities round about in the borders as they had hitherto done; therefore Moronihah had caused that their strong armies should maintain those parts round about by the borders.

29 But behold, the Lamanites were not frightened according to his desire, but they had come into the center of the land, and had taken the capital city, which was the city of Zarahemla, and were marching through the most capital parts

of the land, slaying the people with a great slaughter, both men, women and children, taking possession of many cities and of many strongholds.

30 But when Moronihah had discovered this, he immediately sent forth Lehi with an army round about to head them, before they should come to the land Bountiful.

31 And thus he did; and he did head them, before they came to the land Bountiful, and gave unto them battle insomuch that they began to retreat back towards the land of Zarahemla.

32 And it came to pass that Moronihah did head them in their retreat, and did give unto them battle insomuch that it became an exceeding bloody battle; yea, many were slain; and among the number who were slain, Coriantumr was also found.

33 And now behold the Lamanites could not retreat either way; neither on the north, nor on the south, nor on the east, nor on the west, for they were surrounded on every hand by the Nephites.

34 And thus had Coriantumr plunged the Lamanites into the midst of the Nephites, insomuch that they were in the power of the Nephites, and he himself was slain, and the Lamanites did yield themselves into the hands of the Nephites.

35 ¶And it came to pass that Moronihah took possession of the city of Zarahemla again, and caused that the Lamanites who had been taken prisoners should depart out of the land in peace.

36 And thus ended the forty and first year of the reign of the Judges.

37 ¶And it came to pass in the forty and second year of the reign of the Judges, after Moronihah had established again peace between the Nephites and the Lamanites, behold there was no one to fill the judgment seat; therefore there began to be a contention among the people concerning who should fill the judgment seat.

38 And it came to pass that Helaman, who was the son of

Helaman, was appointed to fill the judgment seat, by the voice of the people;

39 But behold, Kishkumen, who had murdered Pahoran, did lay wait to destroy Helaman also; and he was upheld by his band, who had entered into a covenant that no one should know his wickedness;

40 For there was one Gadianton who was exceeding expert in many words, and also in his craft, to carry on the secret work of murder and of robbery; therefore he became the leader of the band of Kishkumen;

41 Therefore he did flatter them, and also Kishkumen, that if they would place him in the judgment seat, he would grant unto those who belonged to his band that they should be placed in power and authority among the people; therefore Kishkumen sought to destroy Helaman.

42 ¶And it came to pass as he went forth towards the judgment seat, to destroy Helaman, behold one of the servants of Helaman, having been out by night, and having obtained, through disguise, a knowledge of those plans which had been laid by his band to destroy Helaman.

43 And it came to pass that he met Kishkumen and he gave unto him a sign; therefore Kishkumen made known unto him the object of his desire, desiring that he would conduct him to the judgment seat, that he might murder Helaman;

44 And when the servant of Helaman had known all the heart of Kishkumen, and how that it was his object to murder, and also that it was the object of all those who belonged to his band, to murder, and to rob, and to gain power, (and this was their secret plan and their combination,) the servant of Helaman saith unto Kishkumen, Let us go forth unto the judgment seat.

45 Now this did please Kishkumen exceedingly, for he did suppose that he should accomplish his design; but behold, the servant of Helaman, as they were going forth unto the judgment seat, did stab Kishkumen, even to the heart that he fell dead without a groan.

46 And he ran and told Helaman all the things which he had seen, and heard, and done.

47 ¶And it came to pass that Helaman did send forth to take this band of robbers and secret murderers, that they might be executed according to the law.

48 But behold, when Gadianton had found that Kishkumen did not return, he feared lest that he should be destroyed; therefore he caused that his band should follow him.

49 And they took their flight out of the land, by a secret way, into the wilderness; and thus when Helaman sent forth to take them, they could nowhere be found. And more of this Gadianton shall be spoken hereafter.

50 And thus ended the forty and second year of the reign of the Judges over the people of Nephi.

51 And behold, in the end of this book, ye shall see that this Gadianton did prove the overthrow, yea, almost the entire destruction of the people of Nephi.

52 Behold I do not mean the end of the book of Helaman, but I mean the end of the book of Nephi, from which I have taken all the account which I have written.

CHAPTER 2.

1 ¶And now it came to pass in the forty and third year of the reign of the Judges, there was no contention among the people of Nephi, save it were a little pride which was in the church, which did cause some little dissensions among the people, which affairs were settled in the ending of the forty and third year.

2 And there was no contention among the people in the forty and fourth year; neither was there much contention in the forty and fifth year.

3 And it came to pass in the forty and sixth, yea, there were much contentions and many dissensions; in the which there were an exceeding great many who departed out of the land of Zarahemla, and went forth unto the land northward, to inherit the land;

4 And they did travel to an exceeding great distance, insomuch that they came to large bodies of water, and many rivers;

CHAP. 2.] BOOK OF HELAMAN. 549

5 Yea, and even they did spread forth into all parts of the land, into whatever parts it had not been rendered desolate, and without timber, because of the many inhabitants who had before inherited the land.

6 And now no part of the land was desolate, save it were for timber, etc.; but because of the greatness of the destruction of the people who had before inhabited the land, it was called desolate.

7 And there being but little timber upon the face of the land, nevertheless the people who went forth became exceeding expert in the working of cement: therefore they did build houses of cement, in the which they did dwell.

8 ¶And it came to pass that they did multiply and spread, and did go forth from the land southward to the land northward, and did spread insomuch that they began to cover the face of the whole earth, from the sea south, to the sea north, from the sea west, to the sea east.

9 And the people who were in the land northward, did dwell in tents, and in houses of cement, and they did suffer whatsoever tree should spring up upon the face of the land, that it should grow up, that in time they might have timber to build their houses, yea, their cities and their temples, and their synagogues, and their sanctuaries, and all manner of their buildings.

10 ¶And it came to pass as timber was exceeding scarce in the land northward, they did send forth much by the way of shipping; and thus they did enable the people in the land northward, that they might build many cities, both of wood and of cement.

11 And it came to pass that there were many of the people of Ammon who were Lamanites by birth, did also go forth into this land.

12 ¶And now there are many records kept of the proceedings of this people, by many of this people, which are particular and very large, concerning them;

13 But behold a hundredth part of the proceedings of this people, yea, the account of the Lamanites, and of the Nephites, and their wars, and contentions, and dissensions, and

their preaching, and their prophecies, and their shipping, and their building of ships, and their building of temples, and of synagogues, and their sanctuaries, and their righteousness, and their wickedness, and their murders, and their robbings, and their plundering, and all manner of abominations and whoredoms, can not be contained in this work;

14 But behold, there are many books and many records of every kind, and they have been kept chiefly by the Nephites; and they have been handed down from one generation to another, by the Nephites, even until they have fallen into transgression, and have been murdered, plundered and hunted, and driven forth, and slain, and scattered upon the face of the earth, and mixed with the Lamanites until they are no more called the Nephites, becoming wicked, and wild, and ferocious, yea, even becoming Lamanites.

15 ¶And now I return again to mine account; therefore what I have spoken had passed after there had been great contentions, and disturbances, and wars, and dissensions among the people of Nephi.

16 The forty and sixth year of the reign of the Judges ended.

17 And it came to pass that there was still great contentions in the land, yea, even in the forty and seventh year, and also in the forty and eighth year;

18 Nevertheless, Helaman did fill the judgment seat with justice and equity; yea, he did observe to keep the statutes, and the judgments, and the commandments of God; and he did do that which was right in the sight of God continually; and he did walk after the ways of his father, insomuch that he did prosper in the land.

19 And it came to pass that he had two sons. He gave unto the eldest the name of Nephi, and unto the youngest the name of Lehi. And they began to grow up unto the Lord.

20 And it came to pass that the wars and contentions began to cease, in a small degree, among the people of the Nephites, in the latter end of the forty and eighth year of the reign of the Judges over the people of Nephi.

21 And it came to pass in the forty and ninth year of the

reign of the Judges, there was continual peace established in the land, all save it were the secret combinations which Gadianton the robber had established, in the more settled parts of the land, which at that time were not known unto those who were at the head of government; therefore they were not destroyed out of the land.

22 ¶And it came to pass that in this same year, there was exceeding great prosperity in the church, insomuch that there were thousands who did join themselves unto the church, and were baptized unto repentance;

23 And so great was the prosperity of the church, and so many the blessings which were poured out upon the people, that even the high priests and the teachers were themselves astonished beyond measure.

24 And it came to pass that the work of the Lord did prosper unto the baptizing and uniting to the church of God, many souls; yea, even tens of thousands.

25 Thus we may see that the Lord is merciful unto all who will in the sincerity of their hearts, call upon his holy name; yea, thus we see that the gate of heaven is open unto all, even to those who will believe on the name of Jesus Christ, who is the Son of God;

26 Yea, we see that whosoever will lay hold upon the word of God which is quick and powerful, which shall divide asunder all the cunning, and the snares, and the wiles of the devil, and lead the man of Christ in a straight and narrow course across that everlasting gulf of misery which is prepared to engulf the wicked, and land their souls, yea, their immortal souls, at the right hand of God, in the kingdom of heaven, to sit down with Abraham, and Isaac, and with Jacob, and with all our holy fathers, to go no more out.

27 And in this year there were continual rejoicing in the land of Zarahemla, and in all the regions round about, even in all the land which was possessed by the Nephites.

28 And it came to pass that there was peace and exceeding great joy in the remainder of the forty and ninth year; yea, and also there was continual peace and great joy in the fiftieth year of the reign of the Judges.

29 And in the fifty and first year of the reign of the Judges, there was peace also, save it were the pride which began to enter into the church; not into the church of God, but into the hearts of the people who professed to belong to the church of God; and they were lifted up in pride, even to the persecution of many of their brethren.

30 Now this was a great evil, which did cause the more humble part of the people to suffer great persecutions, and to wade through much affliction;

31 Nevertheless, they did fast and pray oft, and did wax stronger and stronger in their humility, and firmer and firmer in the faith of Christ, unto the filling their souls with joy and consolation, yea, even to the purifying and the sanctification of their hearts, which sanctification cometh because of their yielding their hearts unto God.

32 And it came to pass that the fifty and second year ended in peace also, save it were the exceeding great pride which had gotten into the hearts of the people; and it was because of their exceeding great riches, and their prosperity in the land; and it did grow upon them from day to day.

33 ¶And it came to pass in the fifty and third year of the reign of the Judges, Helaman died, and his eldest son Nephi began to reign in his stead.

34 And it came to pass that he did fill the judgment seat with justice and equity; yea, he did keep the commandments of God, and did walk in the ways of his father.

35 And it came to pass in the fifty and fourth year, there were many dissensions in the church, and there was also a contention among the people, insomuch that there was much bloodshed; and the rebellious part were slain and driven out of the land, and they did go unto the king of the Lamanites.

36 ¶And it came to pass that they did endeavor to stir up the Lamanites to war against the Nephites; but behold, the Lamanites were exceeding fraid, insomuch that they would not hearken to the words of those dissenters.

37 But it came to pass in the fifty and sixth year of the reign of the Judges, there were dissenters who went up from the Nephites unto the Lamanites; and they succeeded with

CHAP. 2.] BOOK OF HELAMAN. 553

those others in stirring them up to anger against the Nephites; and they were all that year preparing for war.

38 And in the fifty and seventh year, they did come down against the Nephites to battle; and they did commence the work of death; yea, insomuch that in the fifty and eighth year of the reign of the Judges, they succeeded in obtaining possession of the land of Zarahemla: yea, and also all the lands, even unto the land which was near the land Bountiful;

39 And the Nephites, and the armies of Moronihah, were driven even into the land of Bountiful; and there they did fortify against the Lamanites, from the west sea, even unto the east; it being a day's journey for a Nephite, on the line which they had fortified and stationed their armies to defend their north country.

40 And thus those dissenters of the Nephites, with the help of a numerous army of the Lamanites, had obtained all the possession of the Nephites which was in the land southward.

41 And all this was done in the fifty and eighth and ninth years of the reign of the Judges.

42 ¶And it came to pass in the sixtieth year of the reign of the Judges, Moronihah did succeed with his armies, in obtaining many parts of the land; yea, they retained many cities which had fallen into the hands of the Lamanites.

43 ¶And it came to pass in the sixty and first year of the reign of the Judges, they succeeded in retaining even the half of all their possessions.

44 Now this great loss of the Nephites, and the great slaughter which was among them, would not have happened, had it not been for their wickedness and their abomination which was among them; yea, and it was among those also who professed to belong to the church of God:

45 And it was because of the pride of their hearts, because of their exceeding riches, yea, it was because of their oppression to the poor, withholding their food from the hungry, withholding their clothing from the naked, and smiting their humble brethren upon the cheek, making a mock of that which was sacred, denying the spirit of prophecy and of revelation, murdering, plundering, lying, stealing, committing adultery,

rising up in great contentions, and deserting away into the land of Nephi, among the Lamanites;

46 And because of this their great wickedness, and their boastings in their own strength, they were left in their own strength; therefore they did not prosper, but were afflicted and smitten, and driven before the Lamanites, until they had lost possession of almost all their lands.

47 But behold, Moronihah did preach many things unto the people, because of their iniquity, and also Nephi and Lehi, who were the sons of Helaman, did preach many things unto the people;

48 Yea, and did prophesy many things unto them concerning their iniquities, and what should come unto them if they did not repent of their sins.

49 And it came to pass that they did repent, and inasmuch as they did repent, they did begin to prosper;

50 For when Moronihah saw that they did repent, he did venture to lead them forth from place to place, and from city to city, even until they had retained the one half of their property, and the one half of all their lands.

51 And thus ended the sixty and first year of the reign of the Judges.

52 ¶And it came to pass in the sixty and second year of the reign of the Judges, that Moronihah could obtain no more possessions over the Lamanites;

53 Therefore they did abandon their design to obtain the remainder of their lands, for so numerous were the Lamanites that it became impossible for the Nephites to obtain more power over them; therefore Moronihah did employ all his armies in maintaining those parts which he had taken.

54 ¶And it came to pass because of the greatness of the number of the Lamanites, the Nephites were in great fear, lest they should be overpowered, and trodden down, and slain, and destroyed;

55 Yea, they began to remember the prophecies of Alma, and also the words of Mosiah; and they saw that they had been a stiff-necked people, and that they had set at nought the commandments of God;

56 And that they had altered and trampled under their feet the laws of Mosiah, or that which the Lord commanded him to give unto the people;

57 And thus seeing that their laws had become corrupted, and that they had become a wicked people, insomuch that they were wicked even like unto the Lamanites.

58 And because of their iniquity, the church had began to dwindle; and they began to disbelieve in the spirit of prophecy, and in the spirit of revelation; and the judgments of God did stare them in the face.

59 And they saw that they had become weak, like unto their brethren, the Lamanites, and that the Spirit of the Lord did no more preserve them; yea, it had withdrawn from them, because the Spirit of the Lord doth not dwell in unholy temples;

60 Therefore the Lord did cease to preserve them by his miraculous and matchless power, for they had fallen into a state of unbelief and awful wickedness; and they saw that the Lamanites were more exceeding numerous than they, and except they should cleave unto the Lord their God, they must unavoidably perish.

61 For behold, they saw that the strength of the Lamanites was as great as their strength, even man for man.

62 And thus had they fallen into this great transgression; yea, thus had they become weak, because of their transgression, in the space of not many years.

63 ¶And it came to pass that in this same year, behold, Nephi delivered up the judgment seat, to a man whose name was Cezoram.

64 For as their laws and their governments were established by the voice of the people, and they who chose evil were more numerous than they who chose good, therefore they were ripening for destruction, for the laws had become corrupted;

65 Yea, and this was not all; they were a stiff-necked people, insomuch that they could not be governed by the law nor justice, save it were to their destruction.

66 ¶And it came to pass that Nephi had become weary, be-

cause of their iniquity; and he yielded up the judgment seat, and took it upon him to preach the word of God all the remainder of his days, and his brother Lehi also, all the remainder of his days; for they remembered the words which their father Helaman spake unto them.

67 And these are the words which he spake: Behold, my sons, I desire that ye should remember to keep the commandments of God; and I would that ye should declare unto the people these words;

68 Behold I have given unto you the names of our first parents, who came out of the land of Jerusalem; and this I have done, that when ye remember your names, that ye may remember them; and when ye may remember them, ye may remember their works; and when ye remember their works, ye may know how that it is said, and also written, that they were good:

69 Therefore, my sons, I would that ye should do that which is good, that it may be said of you, and also written, even as it has been said and written of them;

70 And now, my sons, behold, I have somewhat more to desire of you, which desire is, that ye may not do these things that ye may boast, but that ye may do these things to lay up for yourselves a treasure in heaven, yea, which is eternal, and which fadeth not away; yea, that ye may have that precious gift of eternal life, which we have reason to suppose hath been given to our fathers.

71 ¶O remember, remember, my sons, the words which King Benjamin spake unto his people; yea, remember that there is no other way nor means whereby man can be saved, only through the atoning blood of Jesus Christ, who shall come; yea, remember that he cometh to redeem the world.

72 And remember also, the words which Amulek spake unto Zeezrom, in the city of Ammonihah; for he said unto him, that the Lord surely should come to redeem his people; but that he should not come to redeem them in their sins, but to redeem them from their sins.

73 And he hath power given unto him from the Father, to redeem them from their sins, because of repentance; therefore

CHAP. 2.]   BOOK OF HELAMAN.   557

he hath sent his angels to declare the tidings of the conditions of repentance, which bringeth unto the power of the Redeemer, unto the salvation of their souls.

74 And now my sons, remember, remember that it is upon the rock of our Redeemer, who is Christ, the Son of God, that ye must build your foundation, that when the devil shall send forth his mighty winds; yea, his shafts in the whirlwind;

75 Yea, when all his hail and his mighty storm shall beat upon you, it shall have no power over you, to drag you down to the gulf of misery and endless wo, because of the rock upon which ye are built, which is a sure foundation, a foundation whereon if men build, they can not fall.

76 ¶And it came to pass that these were the words which Helaman taught to his sons; yea, he did teach them many things which are not written, and also many things which are written.

77 And they did remember his words; and therefore they went forth, keeping the commandments of God, to teach the word of God among all the people of Nephi, beginning at the city Bountiful; and from thence forth to the city of Gid; and from the city of Gid to the city of Mulek;

78 And even from one city to another, until they had gone forth among all the people of Nephi, who were in the land southward; and from thence into the land of Zarahemla, among the Lamanites.

79 ¶And it came to pass that they did preach with great power, insomuch that they did confound many of those dissenters who had gone over from the Nephites, insomuch that they came forth and did confess their sins, and were baptized unto repentance, and immediately returned to the Nephites, to endeavor to repair unto them the wrongs which they had done.

80 And it came to pass that Nephi and Lehi did preach unto the Lamanites with such great power and authority, for they had power and authority given unto them that they might speak; and they also had what they should speak given unto them;

81 Therefore they did speak unto the great astonishment

of the Lamanites, to the convincing them, insomuch that there were eight thousand of the Lamanites who were in the land of Zarahemla and round about, baptized unto repentance, and were convinced of the wickedness of the traditions of their fathers.

82 ¶And it came to pass that Nephi and Lehi did proceed from thence to go to the land of Nephi.

83 And it came to pass that they were taken by an army of the Lamanites, and cast into prison; yea, even in that same prison in which Ammon and his brethren were cast by the servants of Limhi.

84 And after they had been cast into prison many days without food, behold, they went forth into the prison to take them, that they might slay them.

85 And it came to pass that Nephi and Lehi were encircled about as if by fire, even insomuch that they durst not lay their hands upon them, for fear, lest they should be burned.

86 Nevertheless, Nephi and Lehi were not burned; and they were as standing in the midst of fire, and were not burned.

87 And when they saw that they were encircled about with a pillar of fire and that it burned them not, their hearts did take courage.

88 For they saw that the Lamanites durst not lay their hands upon them; neither durst they come near unto them, but stood as if they were struck dumb with amazement.

89 ¶And it came to pass that Nephi and Lehi did stand forth, and began to speak unto them, saying, Fear not, for behold it is God that has shewn unto you this marvelous thing, in the which is shewn unto you, that ye can not lay your hands on us to slay us.

90 And behold, when they had said these words, the earth shook exceedingly, and the walls of the prison did shake, as if they were about to tumble to the earth; but behold, they did not fall.

91 And behold, they that were in the prison, were Lamanites, and Nephites who were dissenters.

92 And it came to pass that they were overshadowed with a

CHAP. 2.] BOOK OF HELAMAN. 559

cloud of darkness, and an awful, solemn fear came upon them.

93 And it came to pass that there came a voice, as if it were above the cloud of darkness, saying, Repent ye, repent ye, and seek no more to destroy my servants whom I have sent unto you to declare good tidings.

94 ¶And it came to pass when they heard this voice, and beheld that it was not a voice of thunder; neither was it a voice of a great tumultuous noise, but behold, it was a still voice of perfect mildness, as if it had been a whisper, and it did pierce even to the very soul.

95 And notwithstanding the mildness of the voice, behold, the earth shook exceedingly, and the walls of the prison trembled again, as if it were about to tumble to the earth; and behold the cloud of darkness which had overshadowed them, did not disperse.

96 And behold, the voice came again, saying, Repent ye, repent ye, for the kingdom of heaven is at hand; and seek no more to destroy my servants.

97 And it came to pass that the earth shook again, and the walls trembled; and also again the third time the voice came, and did speak unto them marvelous words, which can not be uttered by man; and the walls did tremble again, and the earth shook as if it were about to divide asunder.

98 ¶And it came to pass that the Lamanites could not flee, because of the cloud of darkness which did overshadow them; yea, and also they were immovable, because of the fear which did come upon them.

99 Now there was one among them who was a Nephite by birth, who had once belonged to the church of God, but had dissented from them.

100 And it came to pass that he turned him about, and behold, he saw through the cloud of darkness the faces of Nephi and Lehi; and behold, they did shine exceedingly, even as the faces of angels.

101 And he beheld that they did lift their eyes to heaven; and they were in the attitude as if talking or lifting their voices to some being whom they beheld.

102 ¶And it came to pass that this man did cry unto the multitude, that they might turn and look.

103 And behold, there was power given unto them, that they did turn and look; and they did behold the faces of Nephi and Lehi.

104 And they said unto the man, Behold, what doth all these things mean? and who is it with whom these men do converse?

105 Now the man's name was Aminadab. And Aminadab said unto them, They do converse with the angels of God.

106 And it came to pass that the Lamanites said unto him, What shall we do, that this cloud of darkness may be removed from overshadowing us?

107 And Aminadab said unto them, You must repent, and cry unto the voice, even until ye shall have faith in Christ, who was taught unto you by Alma, and Amulek, and Zeezrom; and when ye shall do this, the cloud of darkness shall be removed from overshadowing you.

108 ¶And it came to pass that they all did begin to cry unto the voice of him who had shook the earth; yea, they did cry even until the cloud of darkness was dispersed.

109 And it came to pass that when they cast their eyes about, and saw that the cloud of darkness was dispersed from overshadowing them, and behold, they saw that they were encircled about, yea, every soul, by a pillar of fire.

110 And Nephi and Lehi were in the midst of them; yea, they were encircled about; yea, they were as if in the midst of a flaming fire, yet it did harm them not, neither did it take hold upon the walls of the prison; and they were filled with that joy which is unspeakable and full of glory.

111 And behold the Holy Spirit of God did come down from heaven, and did enter into their hearts, and they were filled as if with fire; and they could speak forth marvelous words.

112 ¶And it came to pass that there came a voice unto them, yea, a pleasant voice, as if it were a whisper, saying, Peace, peace be unto you, because of your faith in my well beloved, who was from the foundation of the world.

113 And now when they heard this, they cast up their eyes

as if to behold from whence the voice came; and behold, they saw the heavens open: and angels came down out of heaven, and ministered unto them.

114 And there were about three hundred souls who saw and heard these things; and they were bid to go forth and marvel not, neither should they doubt.

115 And it came to pass that they did go forth, and did minister unto the people, declaring throughout all the regions round about, all the things which they had heard and seen, insomuch that the more part of the Lamanites were convinced of them, because of the greatness of the evidences which they had received;

116 And as many as were convinced, did lay down their weapons of war, and also their hatred, and the tradition of their fathers.

117 And it came to pass that they did yield up unto the Nephites, the lands of their possession.

118 ¶And it came to pass that when the sixty and second year of the reign of the Judges had ended, all these things had happened, and the Lamanites had become, the more part of them, a righteous people, insomuch that their righteousness did exceed that of the Nephites, because of their firmness, and their steadiness in the faith.

119 For behold, there were many of the Nephites who had become hardened, and impenitent, and grossly wicked, insomuch that they did reject the word of God, and all the preaching and prophesying which did come among them.

120 Nevertheless the people of the church did have great joy because of the conversion of the Lamanites; yea, because of the church of God, which had been established among them.

121 And they did fellowship one with another, and did rejoice one with another, and did have great joy.

122 And it came to pass that many of the Lamanites did come down into the land of Zarahemla, and did declare unto the people of the Nephites the manner of their conversion, and did exhort them to faith and repentance;

123 Yea, and many did preach with exceeding great power and authority, unto the bringing down many of them into the

depths of humility, to be the humble followers of God and the Lamb.

124 ¶And it came to pass that many of the Lamanites did go into the land northward; and also Nephi and Lehi went into the land northward, to preach unto the people.

125 And thus ended the sixty and third year.

126 And behold, there was peace in all the land, insomuch that the Nephites did go into whatsoever part of the land they would, whether among the Nephites or the Lamanites.

127 And it came to pass that the Lamanites did also go whithersoever they would, whether it were among the Lamanites or among the Nephites; and thus they did have free intercourse one with another, to buy and to sell, and to get gain, according to their desire.

128 ¶And it came to pass that they became exceeding rich, both the Lamanites and the Nephites; and they did have an exceeding plenty of gold, and of silver, and of all manner of precious metals, both in the land south, and in the land north.

129 Now the land south was called Lehi, and the land north was called Mulek, which was after the son of Zedekiah; for the Lord did bring Mulek into the land north, and Lehi into the land south.

130 And behold, there was all manner of gold in both these lands, and of silver, and of precious ore of every kind; and there were also curious workmen, who did work all kinds of ore, and did refine it; and thus they did become rich.

131 They did raise grain in abundance, both in the north and in the south. And they did flourish exceedingly, both in the north and in the south.

132 And they did multiply and wax exceeding strong in the land. And they did raise many flocks and herds, yea, many fatlings.

133 Behold, their women did toil and spin, and did make all manner of cloth, of fine twined linen, and cloth of every kind, to clothe their nakedness.

134 And thus the sixty and fourth year did pass away in peace.

135 And in the sixty and fifth year, they did also have

CHAP. 2.] BOOK OF HELAMAN. 563

great joy and peace; yea, much preaching, and many prophecies concerning that which was to come. And thus passed away the sixty and fifth year.

136 ¶And it came to pass that in the sixty and sixth year of the reign of the Judges, behold, Cezoram was murdered by an unknown hand, as he sat upon the judgment seat.

137 And it came to pass that in the same year that his son, who had been appointed by the people in his stead, was also murdered. And thus ended the sixty and sixth year.

138 And in the commencement of the sixty and seventh year, the people began to grow exceeding wicked again.

139 For behold, the Lord had blessed them so long with the riches of the world, that they had not been stirred up to anger, to wars, nor to bloodsheds; therefore they began to set their hearts upon their riches;

140 Yea, they began to seek to get gain, that they might be lifted up one above another; therefore they began to commit secret murders, and to rob and to plunder that they might get gain.

141 And now behold, those murderers and plunderers were a band who had been formed by Kishkumen and Gadianton.

142 And now it had come to pass that there were many even among the Nephites, of Gadianton's band. But behold, they were more numerous among the more wicked part of the Lamanites.

143 And they were called Gadianton's robbers and murderers; and it was they who did murder the chief judge Cezoram, and his son, while in the judgment seat; and behold they were not found.

144 ¶And now it came to pass that when the Lamanites found that there were robbers among them, they were exceeding sorrowful; and they did use every means in their power, to destroy them off the face of the earth.

145 But behold, Satan did stir up the hearts of the more part of the Nephites, insomuch that they did unite with those bands of robbers, and did enter into their covenants, and their oaths, that they would protect and preserve one another, in whatsoever difficult circumstances they should be placed, that

they should not suffer for their murders, and their plunderings, and their stealings.

146 ¶And it came to pass that they did have their signs, yea, their secret signs, and their secret words; and this that they might distinguish a brother who had entered into the covenant, that whatsoever wickedness his brother should do, he should not be injured by his brother, nor by those who did belong to his band, who had taken this covenant;

147 And thus they might murder, and plunder, and steal, and commit whoredoms, and all manner of wickedness, contrary to the laws of their country and also the laws of their God;

148 And whosoever of those who belonged to their band, should reveal unto the world of their wickedness and their abominations, should be tried, not according to the laws of their country, but according to the laws of their wickedness, which had been given by Gadianton and Kishkumen.

149 Now behold, it is these secret oaths and covenants, which Alma commanded his son should not go forth unto the world, lest they should be a means of bringing down the people unto destruction.

150 Now behold, those secret oaths and covenants did not come forth unto Gadianton from the records which were delivered unto Helaman;

151 But behold, they were put into the heart of Gadianton, by that same being who did entice our first parents to partake of the forbidden fruit; yea, that same being who did plot with Cain, that if he would murder his brother Abel, it should not be known unto the world.

152 And he did plot with Cain and his followers, from that time forth.

153 And also it is that same being who put it into the hearts of the people, to build a tower sufficiently high that they might get to heaven.

154 And it was that same being who led on the people who came from that tower into this land; who spread the works of darkness and abominations over all the face of the land,

until he dragged the people down to an entire destruction, and to an everlasting hell;

155 Yea, it is that same being who put it into the heart of Gadianton, to still carry on the work of darkness, and of secret murder; and he has brought it forth from the beginning of man, even down to this time.

156 And behold, it is he who is the author of all sin. And behold, he doth carry on his works of darkness and secret murder, and doth hand down their plots, and their oaths, and their covenants, and their plans of awful wickedness, from generation to generation, according as he can get hold upon the hearts of the children of men.

157 And now behold, he had got great hold upon the hearts of the Nephites; yea, insomuch that they had become exceeding wicked;

158 Yea, the more part of them had turned out of the way of righteousness, and did trample under their feet the commandments of God, and did turn unto their own ways, and did build up unto themselves idols of their gold and their silver.

159 ¶And it came to pass that all these iniquities did come unto them, in the space of not many years, insomuch that a more part of it had come unto them in the sixty and seventh year of the reign of the Judges over the people of Nephi.

160 And they did grow in their iniquities, in the sixty and eighth year also, to the great sorrow and lamentation of the righteous.

161 And thus we see that the Nephites did begin to dwindle in unbelief, and grow in wickedness and abominations, while the Lamanites began to grow exceedingly in the knowledge of their God; yea, they did begin to keep his statutes and commandments, and to walk in truth and uprightness before him.

162 And thus we see that the Spirit of the Lord began to withdraw from the Nephites, because of the wickedness and the hardness of their hearts.

163 And thus we see that the Lord began to pour out his Spirit upon the Lamanites, because of their easiness and willingness to believe in his word.

164 ¶And it came to pass that the Lamanites did hunt the band of robbers of Gadianton; and they did preach the word of God among the more wicked part of them, insomuch that this band of robbers was utterly destroyed from among the Lamanites.

165 And it came to pass on the other hand, that the Nephites did build them up and support them, beginning at the more wicked part of them, until they had overspread all the land of the Nephites, and had seduced the more part of the righteous until they had come down to believe in their works, and partake of their spoils, and to join with them in their secret murders and combinations.

166 And thus they did obtain the sole management of the government, insomuch that they did trample under their feet, and smite, and rend, and turn their backs upon the poor, and the meek, and the humble followers of God.

167 And thus we see that they were in an awful state, and ripening for an everlasting destruction.

168 And it came to pass that thus ended the sixty and eighth year of the reign of the Judges over the people of Nephi.

CHAPTER 3.

The prophecy of Nephi, the son of Helaman.—God threatens the people of Nephi, that he will visit them in his anger, to their utter destruction, except they repent of their wickedness. God smiteth the people of Nephi with pestilence; they repent and turn unto him. Samuel, a Lamanite, prophesies unto the Nephites.

1 ¶Behold, now it came to pass in the sixty and ninth year of the reign of the Judges over the people of the Nephites, that Nephi, the son of Helaman, returned to the land of Zarahemla, from the land northward: for he had been forth among the people who were in the land northward, and did preach the word of God unto them, and did prophesy many things unto them;

2 And they did reject all his words, insomuch that he could

not stay among them, but returned again unto the land of his nativity;

3 And seeing the people in a state of such awful wickedness, and those Gadianton robbers filling the judgment seats, having usurped the power and authority of the land; laying aside the commandments of God, and not in the least aright before him: doing no justice unto the children of men; condemning the righteous because of their righteousness; letting the guilty and the wicked go unpunished, because of their money;

4 And moreover, to be held in office at the head of government, to rule and do according to their wills, that they might get gain and glory of the world; and moreover that they might the more easy commit adultery, and steal, and kill, and do according to their own wills.

5 Now this great iniquity had come upon the Nephites, in the space of not many years; and when Nephi saw it, his heart was swollen with sorrow within his breast;

6 And he did exclaim in the agony of his soul, O that I could have had my days, in the days when my father Nephi first came out of the land of Jerusalem, that I could have joyed with him in the promised land;

7 Then were his people easy to be entreated, firm to keep the commandments of God, and slow to be led to do iniquity; and they were quick to hearken unto the words of the Lord;

8 Yea, if my days could have been in them days, then would my soul have had joy in the righteousness of my brethren.

9 But behold, I am consigned that these are my days, and that my soul shall be filled with sorrow, because of this the wickedness of my brethren.

10 And behold, now it came to pass that it was upon a tower, which was in the garden of Nephi, which was by the highway which led to the chief market, which was in the city of Zarahemla;

11 Therefore Nephi had bowed himself upon the tower which was in his garden, which tower was also near unto the garden gate which led by the highway.

12 ¶And it came to pass that there were certain men pass-

ing by, and saw Nephi as he was pouring out his soul unto God upon the tower, and they ran and told the people what they had seen, and the people came together in multitudes that they might know the cause of so great mourning for the wickedness of the people.

13 And now when Nephi arose he beheld the multitudes of people who had gathered together.

14 And it came to pass that he opened his mouth and said unto them, Behold, why have ye gathered yourselves together? That I may tell you of your iniquities?

15 Yea, because I have got upon my tower, that I might pour out my soul unto my God, because of the exceeding sorrow of my heart, which is because of your iniquities?

16 And because of my mourning and lamentation, ye have gathered yourselves together, and do marvel; yea, and ye have great need to marvel;

17 Yea, ye had ought to marvel, because ye are given away, that the devil has got so great hold upon your hearts; yea, how could ye have given away to the enticing of him who is seeking to hurl away your souls down to everlasting misery and endless wo?

18 O repent ye, repent ye! why will ye die? Turn ye, turn ye unto the Lord your God. Why has he forsaken you?

19 It is because you have hardened your hearts; yea, ye will not hearken unto the voice of the Good Shepherd; yea, ye have provoked him to anger against you.

20 And behold, instead of gathering you, except ye will repent, behold he shall scatter you forth that ye shall become meat for dogs and wild beasts.

21 O how could you have forgotten your God in the very day that he has delivered you?

22 But behold, it is to get gain, to be praised of men; yea, and that ye might get gold and silver.

23 And ye have set your hearts upon the riches and the vain things of this world, for the which ye do murder, and plunder, and steal, and bear false witness against your neighbor, and do all manner of iniquity; and for this cause wo shall come unto you except ye shall repent.

CHAP. 3.] BOOK OF HELAMAN. 569

24 For if ye will not repent, behold this great city, and also all those great cities which are round about, which are in the land of our possession, shall be taken away, that ye shall have no place in them, for behold, the Lord will not grant unto you strength, as he has hitherto done, to withstand against your enemies.

25 For behold, thus saith the Lord, I will not shew unto the wicked of my strength, to one more than the other, save it be unto those who repent of their sins, and hearken unto my words;

26 Now therefore I would that ye should behold, my brethren, that it shall be better for the Lamanites than for you, except ye shall repent; for behold they are more righteous than you; for they have not sinned against that great knowledge which ye have received;

27 Therefore the Lord will be merciful unto them; yea, he will lengthen out their days and increase their seed, even when thou shalt be utterly destroyed, except thou shalt repent;

28 Yea, wo be unto you because of that great abomination which has come among you; and ye have united yourselves unto it, yea, to that secret band which was established by Gadianton;

29 Yea, wo shall come unto you because of that pride which ye have suffered to enter your hearts, which has lifted you up beyond that which is good because of your exceeding great riches; yea, wo be unto you because of your wickedness and abominations.

30 And except ye repent, ye shall perish; yea, even your lands shall be taken from you, and ye shall be destroyed from off the face of the earth.

31 Behold now I do not say that these things shall be, of myself, because it is not of myself that I know these things; but behold, I know that these things are true, because the Lord God has made them known unto me; therefore I testify that they shall be.

32 ¶And now it came to pass that when Nephi had said these words, behold there were men who were judges, who

also belonged to the secret band of Gadianton, and they were angry,

33 And they cried out against him, saying unto the people, Why do ye not seize upon this man and bring him forth, that he may be condemned according to the crime which he has done?

34 Why seest thou this man, and hearest him revile against this people and against our law?

35 For behold, Nephi had spoken unto them concerning the corruptness of their law; yea, many things did Nephi speak which can not be written; and nothing did he speak which was contrary to the commandments of God.

36 And those judges were angry with him because he spake plain unto them concerning their secret works of darkness; nevertheless they durst not lay their own hands upon him; for they feared the people, lest they should cry out against them; therefore they did cry unto the people, saying, Why do ye suffer this man to revile against us?

37 For behold, he doth condemn all this people, even unto destruction; yea, and also that these our great cities shall be taken from us, that we shall have no place in them.

38 And now we know that this is impossible; for behold we are powerful, and our cities great; therefore our enemies can have no power over us.

39 And it came to pass that thus they did stir up the people to anger against Nephi, and raised contentions among them; for there were some who did cry out, Let this man alone, for he is a good man, and those things which he saith will surely come to pass except we repent;

40 Yea, behold all the judgments will come upon us which he has testified unto us; for we know that he has testified aright unto us concerning our iniquities.

41 And behold they are many; and he knoweth as well all things which shall befall us as he knoweth of our iniquities; yea, and behold if he had not been a prophet he could not have testified concerning those things.

42 And it came to pass that those people who sought to

CHAP. 3.]   BOOK OF HELAMAN.   571

destroy Nephi, were compelled because of their fear, that they did not lay their hands on him.

43 Therefore he began again to speak unto them, seeing that he had gained favor in the eyes of some, insomuch that the remainder of them did fear.

44 Therefore he was constrained to speak more unto them, saying, Behold my brethren, have ye not read that God gave power unto one man, even Moses, to smite upon the waters of the Red Sea, and they parted hither and thither, insomuch that the Israelites, who were our fathers, came through upon dry ground, and the waters closed upon the armies of the Egyptians, and swallowed them up?

45 ¶And now behold, if God gave unto this man such power, then why should ye dispute among yourselves, and say that he hath given unto me no power whereby I may know concerning the judgments that shall come upon you except ye repent?

46 But behold, ye not only deny my words, but ye also deny all the words which hath been spoken by our fathers, and also the words which were spoken by this man, Moses, who had such great power given unto him; yea, the words which he hath spoken concerning the coming of the Messiah.

47 Yea, did he not bear record, that the Son of God should come? And as he lifted up the brazen serpent in the wilderness, even so shall he be lifted up who should come.

48 And as many as should look upon that serpent should live, even so as many as should look upon the Son of God, with faith, having a contrite spirit, might live, even unto that life which is eternal.

49 And now behold, Moses did not only testify of these things, but also all the holy prophets, from his days even to the days of Abraham.

50 Yea, and behold, Abraham saw of his coming, and was filled with gladness, and did rejoice.

51 Yea, and behold I say unto you, that Abraham not only knew of these things, but there were many before the days of Abraham who were called by the order of God; yea, even after the order of his Son;

52 And this that it should be shewn unto the people a great many thousand years before his coming, that even redemption should come unto them.

53 And now I would that ye should know, that even since the days of Abraham, there have been many prophets that have testified these things; yea, behold, the prophet Zenos did testify boldly; for the which he was slain.

54 And behold, also Zenock, and also Ezaias, and also Isaiah, and Jeremiah, (Jeremiah being that same prophet who testified of the destruction of Jerusalem.)

55 And now we know that Jerusalem was destroyed according to the words of Jeremiah. O then why not the Son of God come, according to his prophecy?

56 And now will ye dispute that Jerusalem was destroyed? Will ye say that the sons of Zedekiah were not slain, all except it were Mulek?

57 Yea, and do ye not behold that the seed of Zedekiah are with us, and they were driven out of the land of Jerusalem?

58 But behold, this is not all. Our father Lehi was driven out of Jerusalem, because he testified of these things.

59 Nephi also testified of these things, and also almost all of our fathers, even down to this time; yea, they have testified of the coming of Christ, and have looked forward, and have rejoiced in his day which is to come.

60 And behold, he is God, and he is with them, and he did manifest himself unto them that they were redeemed by him; and they gave unto him glory, because of that which is to come.

61 And now seeing ye know these things and can not deny them, except ye shall lie, therefore in this ye have sinned, for ye have rejected all these things, notwithstanding so many evidences which ye have received;

62 Yea, even ye have received all things, both things in heaven, and all things which are in the earth, as a witness that they are true.

63 But behold, ye have rejected the truth, and rebelled against your holy God; and even at this time, instead of laying up for yourselves treasures in heaven, where nothing

[CHAP. 3.] BOOK OF HELAMAN. 573

doth corrupt, and where nothing can come which is unclean, ye are heaping up for yourselves wrath against the day of judgment;

64 Yea, even at this time ye are ripening, because of your murders, and your fornication and wickedness, for everlasting destruction; yea, and except ye repent, it will come unto you soon;

65 Yea, behold it is now even at your doors; yea, go ye in unto the judgment seat, and search; and behold, your judge is murdered, and he lieth in his blood; and he hath been murdered by his brother, who seeketh to sit in the judgment seat.

66 And behold, they both belong to your secret band, whose author is Gadianton, and the evil one who seeketh to destroy the souls of men.

67 ¶Behold, now it came to pass that when Nephi had spoken these words, certain men who were among them ran to the judgment seat; yea, even there were five who went;

68 And they said among themselves as they went, Behold, now we will know of a surety, whether this man be a prophet, and God hath commanded him to prophesy such marvelous things unto us.

69 Behold, we do not believe that he hath; yea, we do not believe that he is a prophet; nevertheless, if this thing which he has said concerning the chief judge be true, that he be dead, then will we believe that the other words which he has spoken are true.

70 And it came to pass that they ran in their might, and came in unto the judgment seat; and behold the chief judge had fallen to the earth, and did lie in his blood.

71 And now behold, when they saw this, they were astonished exceedingly, insomuch that they fell to the earth; for they had not believed the words which Nephi had spoken concerning the chief judge;

72 But now when they saw, they believed, and fear came upon them, lest all the judgments which Nephi had spoken should come upon the people; therefore they did quake, and had fallen to the earth.

73 Now immediately when the judge had been murdered;

he being stabbed by his brother by a garb of secrecy; and he fled, and the servants ran and told the people, raising the cry of murder among them.

74 And behold the people did gather themselves together unto the place of the judgment seat: and behold, to their astonishment, they saw those five men who had fallen to the earth.

75 And now behold, the people knew nothing concerning the multitude which had gathered together at the garden of Nephi; therefore they said among themselves, These men are they who have murdered the judge, and God has smitten them that they could not flee from us.

76 ¶And it came to pass that they laid hold on them, and bound them, and cast them into prison.

77 And there was a proclamation sent abroad that the judge was slain, and that the murderers had been taken, and were cast into prison.

78 And it came to pass that on the morrow, the people did assemble themselves together to mourn and to fast, at the burial of the great chief judge, who had been slain.

79 And thus were also those judges who were at the garden of Nephi, and heard his words, were also gathered together at the burial.

80 ¶And it came to pass that they inquired among the people, saying, Where are the five who were sent to inquire concerning the chief judge whether he was dead?

81 And they answered and said, Concerning this five whom ye say ye have sent, we know not; but there are five, who are the murderers, whom we have cast into prison.

82 And it came to pass that the judges desired that they should be brought; and they were brought, and behold they were the five who were sent;

83 And behold the judges inquired of them to know concerning the matter, and they told them all that they had done, saying, We ran and came to the place of the judgment seat, and when we saw all things, even as Nephi had testified, we were astonished, insomuch that we fell to the earth; and

CHAP. 3.] BOOK OF HELAMAN. 575

when we were recovered from our astonishment, behold they cast us into prison.

84 Now as for the murder of this man, we know not who has done it, and only this much we know, we ran and came according as ye desired, and behold he was dead according to the words of Nephi.

85 ¶And now it came to pass, that the judges did expound the matter unto the people, and did cry out against Nephi, saying, Behold we know that this Nephi must have agreed with some one to slay the judge, and then he might declare it unto us, that he might convert us unto his faith, that he might raise himself to be a great man, chosen of God, and a prophet;

86 And now behold we will detect this man, and he shall confess his fault and make known unto us the true murderer of this judge.

87 And it came to pass that the five were liberated on the day of the burial.

88 Nevertheless, they did rebuke the judges in the words which they had spoken against Nephi, and did contend with them one by one, insomuch that they did confound them.

89 Nevertheless, they caused that Nephi should be taken and bound and brought before the multitude, and they began to question him in divers ways, that they might cross him, that they might accuse him to death:

90 Saying unto him, Thou art confederate; who is this man that has done this murder? Now tell us, and acknowledge thy fault, saying, Behold here is money; and also we will grant unto thee thy life, if thou wilt tell us and acknowledge the agreement which thou hast made with him.

91 But Nephi said unto them, O ye fools, ye uncircumcised of heart, ye blind, and ye stiff-necked people, do ye know how long the Lord your God will suffer you that ye shall go on in this your way of sin?

92 O ye had ought to begin to howl and mourn, because of the great destruction at this time which doth await you, except ye shall repent.

93 Behold, ye say that I have agreed with a man, that he should murder Seezoram, our chief judge.

94 But behold, I say unto you, that this is because I have testified unto you, that ye might know concerning this thing; yea, even for a witness unto you, that I did know of the wickedness and abominations which are among you.

95 And because I have done this, ye say that I have agreed with a man that he should do this thing; yea, because I shewed unto you this sign, ye are angry with me, and seek to destroy my life.

96 And now behold, I will shew unto you another sign, and see if ye will in this thing seek to destroy me.

97 Behold I say unto you, Go to the house of Seantum, who is the brother of Seezoram, and say unto him, Has Nephi, the pretended prophet, who doth prophesy so much evil concerning this people, agreed with thee, in the which ye have murdered Seezoram, who is your brother? And behold, he shall say unto you, Nay.

98 And ye shall say unto him, Have ye murdered your brother? And he shall stand with fear, and wist not what to say.

99 And behold he shall deny unto you; and he shall make as if he were astonished; nevertheless, he shall declare unto you that he is innocent.

100 But behold, ye shall examine him, and ye shall find blood upon the skirts of his cloak.

101 And when ye have seen this, ye shall say, From whence cometh this blood? Do we not know that it is the blood of your brother? And then shall he tremble, and shall look pale, even as if death had come upon him.

102 And then shall ye say, Because of this fear and this paleness which has come upon your face, behold, we know that thou art guilty.

103 And then shall greater fear come upon him; and then shall he confess unto you, and deny no more that he has done this murder.

104 And then shall he say unto you, that I, Nephi, knew nothing concerning the matter, save it were given unto me by the power of God.

105 And then shall ye know that I am an honest man, and that I am sent unto you from God.

106 ¶And it came to pass that they went and did, even according as Nephi had said unto them.

107 And behold, the words which he had said were true; for according to the words, he did deny; and also according to the words he did confess.

108 And he was brought to prove that he himself was the very murderer, insomuch that the five were set at liberty; and also was Nephi.

109 And there were some of the Nephites who believed on the words of Nephi; and there were some also, who believed, because of the testimony of the five, for they had been converted while they were in prison.

110 And now there were some among the people, who said that Nephi was a prophet; and there were others who said, Behold, he is a god, for except he was a god, he could not know of all things.

111 For behold, he has told us the thoughts of our hearts, and also has told us things; and even he has brought unto our knowledge the true murderer of our chief judge.

112 ¶And it came to pass that there arose a division among the people, insomuch that they divided hither and thither, and went their ways, leaving Nephi alone, as he was standing in the midst of them.

113 And it came to pass that Nephi went his way towards his own house, pondering upon the things which the Lord had shewn unto him.

114 And it came to pass as he was thus pondering, being much cast down because of the wickedness of the people of the Nephites, their secret works of darkness, and their murderings, and their plunderings, and all manner of iniquities—and it came to pass as he was thus pondering in his heart, behold, a voice came unto him, saying,

115 Blessed art thou, Nephi, for those things which thou hast done; for I have beheld how thou hast with unwearyingness declared the word which I have given unto thee, unto this people.

116 And thou hast not feared them, and hast not sought thine own life, but have sought my will, and to keep my commandments.

117 And now because thou hast done this with such unwearyingness, behold, I will bless thee for ever; and I will make thee mighty in word and in deed, in faith and in works; yea, even that all things shall be done unto thee according to thy word, for thou shalt not ask that which is contrary to my will.

118 Behold, thou art Nephi, and I am God.

119 Behold, I declare it unto thee in the presence of mine angels, that ye shall have power over this people, and shall smite the earth with famine, and with pestilence, and destruction, according to the wickedness of this people.

120 Behold, I give unto you power, that whatsoever ye shall seal on earth, shall be sealed in heaven; and whatsoever ye shall loose on earth shall be loosed in heaven; and thus shall ye have power among this people.

121 And thus, if ye shall say unto this temple, It shall be rent in twain, it shall be done.

122 And if ye shall say unto this mountain, Be thou cast down and become smooth, it shall be done.

123 And behold, if ye shall say, that God shall smite this people, it shall come to pass.

124 And now behold, I command you that ye shall go and declare unto this people that, Thus saith the Lord God, who is Almighty, except ye repent, ye shall be smitten, even unto destruction.

125 ¶And behold, now it came to pass that when the Lord had spoken these words unto Nephi, he did stop, and did not go unto his own house, but did return unto the multitudes who were scattered about upon the face of the land, and began to declare unto them the word of the Lord, which had been spoken unto him concerning their destruction, if they did not repent.

126 Now behold, notwithstanding that great miracle which Nephi had done in telling them concerning the death of the

chief judge, they did harden their hearts, and did not hearken unto the words of the Lord;

127 Therefore Nephi did declare unto them the word of the Lord, saying, Except ye repent, thus saith the Lord, Ye shall be smitten, even unto destruction.

128 And it came to pass that when Nephi had declared unto them the word, behold, they did still harden their hearts, and would not hearken unto his words; therefore they did revile against him, and did seek to lay their hands upon him, that they might cast him into prison.

129 But behold, the power of God was with him, and they could not take him to cast him into prison, for he was taken by the Spirit, and conveyed away out of the midst of them.

130 ¶And it came to pass that thus he did go forth in the Spirit, from multitude to multitude, declaring the word of God, even until he had declared it unto them all, or sent it forth among all the people.

131 And it came to pass that they would not hearken unto his words; and there began to be contentions, insomuch that they were divided against themselves, and began to slay one another with the sword.

132 And thus ended the seventy and first year of the reign of the Judges over the people of Nephi.

CHAPTER 4.

1 ¶And now it came to pass in the seventy and second year of the reign of the Judges, that the contentions did increase, insomuch that there were wars throughout all the land among all the people of Nephi.

2 And it was this secret band of robbers who did carry on this work of destruction and wickedness.

3 And this war did last all that year. And in the seventy and third year it did also last.

4 ¶And it came to pass that in this year, Nephi did cry unto the Lord, saying, O Lord do not suffer that this people shall be destroyed by the sword; but O Lord, rather let there be a famine in the land, to stir them up in remembrance of

the Lord their God, and perhaps they will repent and turn unto thee;

5 And so it was done, according to the words of Nephi. And there was a great famine upon the land among all the people of Nephi.

6 And thus, in the seventy and fourth year, the famine did continue, and the work of destruction did cease by the sword, but became sore by famine.

7 And this work of destruction did also continue in the seventy and fifth year.

8 For the earth was smitten, that it was dry, and did not yield forth grain in the season of grain; and the whole earth was smitten, even among the Lamanites as well as among the Nephites, so that they were smitten that they did perish by thousands, in the more wicked parts of the land.

9 ¶And it came to pass that the people saw that they were about to perish by famine, and they began to remember the Lord their God; and they began to remember the words of Nephi.

10 And the people began to plead with their chief judges and their leaders, that they would say unto Nephi, Behold we know that thou art a man of God, and therefore cry unto the Lord our God, that he turn away from us this famine, lest all the words which thou hast spoken concerning our destruction, be fulfilled.

11 And it came to pass that the judges did say unto Nephi, according to the words which had been desired.

12 And it came to pass that when Nephi saw that the people had repented, and did humble themselves in sackcloth, he cried again unto the Lord, saying, O Lord, behold this people repenteth;

13 And they have swept away the band of Gadianton from amongst them, insomuch that they have become extinct, and they have concealed their secret plans in the earth.

14 Now, O Lord, because of this their humility, wilt thou turn away thine anger, and let thine anger be appeased in the destruction of those wicked men whom thou hast already destroyed?

CHAP. 4.]   BOOK OF HELAMAN.   581

15 O Lord, wilt thou turn away thine anger, yea, thy fierce anger, and cause that this famine may cease in this land?

16 O Lord wilt thou hearken unto me, and cause that it may be done according to my words, and send forth rain upon the face of the earth, that she may bring forth her fruit and her grain, in the season of grain?

17 O Lord, thou didst hearken unto my words when I said, Let there be a famine, that the pestilence of the sword might cease; and I know that thou wilt even at this time, hearken unto my words, for thou saidst, that if this people repent, I will spare them;

18 Yea, O Lord, and thou seest that they have repented, because of the famine, and the pestilence and destruction which has come unto them.

19 And now, O Lord, wilt thou turn away thine anger, and try again if they will serve thee? And if so, O Lord, thou canst bless them according to thy words which thou hast said.

20 ¶And it came to pass that in the seventy and sixth year, the Lord did turn away his anger from the people, and caused that rain should fall upon the earth, insomuch that it did bring forth her fruit in the season of her fruit.

21 And it came to pass that it did bring forth her grain, in the season of her grain.

22 And behold, the people did rejoice, and glorify God, and the whole face of the land was filled with rejoicing; and they did no more seek to destroy Nephi, but they did esteem him as a great prophet, and a man of God, having great power and authority given unto him from God.

23 And behold, Lehi, his brother, was not a whit behind him as to things pertaining to righteousness.

24 And thus it did come to pass that the people of Nephi began to prosper again in the land, and began to build up their waste places, and began to multiply and spread, even until they did cover the whole face of the land, both on the northward and on the southward, from the sea west, to the sea east.

25 And it came to pass that the seventy and sixth year did end in peace.

26 And the seventy and seventh year began in peace; and the church did spread throughout the face of all the land; and the more part of the people, both the Nephites and the Lamanites, did belong to the church; and they did have exceeding great peace in the land; and thus ended the seventy and seventh year.

27 And also they had peace in the seventy and eighth year, save it were a few contentions concerning the points of doctrine which had been laid down by the prophets.

28 And in the seventy and ninth year, there began to be much strife.

29 But it came to pass that Nephi and Lehi, and many of their brethren, who knew concerning the true points of doctrine, having many revelations daily, therefore they did preach unto the people, insomuch that they did put an end to their strife in that same year.

30 ¶And it came to pass that in the eightieth year of the reign of the Judges over the people of Nephi, there were a certain number of the dissenters from the people of Nephi, who had some years before gone over unto the Lamanites, and took upon themselves the name of Lamanites;

31 And also, a certain number who were real descendants of the Lamanites, being stirred up to anger by them, or by those dissenters, therefore they commenced a war with their brethren.

32 And they did commit murder and plunder; and then they would retreat back into the mountains, and into the wilderness and secret places, hiding themselves that they could not be discovered, receiving daily an addition to their numbers, inasmuch as there were dissenters that went forth unto them;

33 And thus in time, yea, even in the space of not many years, they became an exceeding great band of robbers; and they did search out all the secret plans of Gadianton; and thus they became robbers of Gadianton.

34 Now behold, these robbers did make great havoc, yea, even great destruction among the people of Nephi, and also among the people of the Lamanites.

35 ¶And it came to pass that it was expedient that there should be a stop put to this work of destruction; therefore they sent an army of strong men into the wilderness, and upon the mountains to search out this band of robbers, and to destroy them.

36 But behold, it came to pass that in that same year, they were driven back even into their own lands.

37 And thus ended the eightieth year of the reign of the Judges over the people of Nephi.

38 ¶And it came to pass in the commencement of the eighty and first year, they did go forth again against this band of robbers, and did destroy many;

39 And they were also visited with much destruction; and they were again obliged to return out of the wilderness and out of the mountains, unto their own lands, because of the exceeding greatness of the numbers of those robbers who infested the mountains and the wilderness.

40 And it came to pass that thus ended this year. And the robbers did still increase and wax strong, insomuch that they did defy the whole armies of the Nephites, and also of the Lamanites; and they did cause great fear to come unto the people, upon all the face of the land;

41 Yea, for they did visit many parts of the land, and did do great destruction unto them; yea, did kill many, and did carry away others captive into the wilderness; yea, and more especially their women and their children.

42 Now this great evil, which came unto the people because of their iniquity did stir them up again in remembrance of the Lord their God.

43 And thus ended the eighty and first year of the reign of the Judges.

44 And in the eighty and second year, they began again to forget the Lord their God.

45 And in the eighty and third year, they began to wax strong in iniquity.

46 And in the eighty and fourth year, they did not mend their ways.

47 And it came to pass in the eighty and fifth year, they

did wax stronger and stronger in their pride, and in their wickedness; and thus they were ripening again for destruction. And thus ended the eighty and fifth year.

48 And thus we can behold how false, and also the unsteadiness of the hearts of the children of men; yea, we can see that the Lord in his great infinite goodness, doth bless and prosper those who put their trust in him;

49 Yea, and we may see at the very time when he doth prosper his people; yea, in the increase of their fields, their flocks, and their herds, and in gold, and in silver, and in all manner of precious things of every kind, and art;

50 Sparing their lives, and delivering them out of the hands of their enemies; softening the hearts of their enemies, that they should not declare wars against them; yea, and in fine, doing all things for the welfare and happiness of his people;

51 Yea, then is the time that they do harden their hearts, and do forget the Lord their God, and do trample under their feet the Holy One; yea, and this because of their ease, and their exceeding great prosperity.

52 And thus we see, that except the Lord doth chasten his people with many afflictions, yea, except he doth visit them with death, and with terror, and with famine, and with all manner of pestilences, they will not remember him.

53 O how foolish, and how vain, and how evil, and devilish, and how quick to do iniquity, and how slow to do good, are the children of men;

54 Yea, how quick to hearken unto the words of the evil one, and to set their hearts upon the vain things of the world; yea, how quick to be lifted up in pride; yea, how quick to boast, and do all manner of that which is iniquity;

55 And how slow are they to remember the Lord their God, and to give ear unto his counsels; yea, how slow to walk in wisdom's paths!

56 Behold, they do not desire that the Lord their God, who hath created them, should rule and reign over them, notwithstanding his great goodness and his mercy towards them; they do set at nought his counsels, and they will not that he should be their guide.

57 O how great is the nothingness of the children of men; yea, even they are less than the dust of the earth.

58 For behold, the dust of the earth moveth hither and thither, to the dividing asunder, at the command of our great and everlasting God;

59 Yea, behold, at his voice doth the hills and the mountains tremble and quake; and by the power of his voice they are broken up, and become smooth, yea, even like unto a valley;

60 Yea, by the power of his voice doth the whole earth shake; yea, by the power of his voice, doth the foundations rock, even to the very center;

61 Yea, and if he say unto the earth, Move, it is moved; yea, if he say unto the earth, Thou shalt go back, that it lengthen out the day for many hours, it is done:

62 And thus according to his word, the earth goeth back, and it appeareth unto man that the sun standeth still: yea, and behold, this is so; for sure it is the earth that moveth, and not the sun.

63 And behold, also, if he say unto the waters of the great deep, Be thou dried up, it is done.

64 Behold, if he say unto this mountain, Be thou raised up, and come over and fall upon that city, that it be buried up, behold it is done.

65 And behold, if a man hide up a treasure in the earth, and the Lord shall say, Let it be accursed, because of the iniquity of him who hath hid it up, behold, it shall be accursed;

66 And if the Lord shall say, Be thou accursed, that no man shall find thee from this time henceforth and for ever, behold, no man getteth it henceforth and for ever.

67 And behold, if the Lord shall say unto a man, Because of thine iniquities thou shalt be accursed for ever, it shall be done.

68 And if the Lord shall say, Because of thine iniquities, thou shalt be cut off from my presence, he will cause that it shall be so.

69 And wo unto him to whom he shall say this, for it shall

be unto him that will do iniquity, and he can not be saved; therefore, for this cause, that men might be saved, hath repentance been declared.

70 Therefore blessed are they who will repent and hearken unto the voice of the Lord their God; for these are they that shall be saved.

71 And may God grant, in his great fullness, that men might be brought unto repentance and good works, that they might be restored unto grace, for grace according to their works.

72 And I would that all men might be saved. But we read that in that great and last day, there are some who shall be cast out; yea, who shall be cast off from the presence of the Lord;

73 Yea, who shall be consigned to a state of endless misery, fulfilling the words which say, They that have done good, shall have everlasting life; and they that have done evil, shall have everlasting damnation. And thus it is. Amen.

CHAPTER 5.

The prophecy of Samuel, the Lamanite, to the Nephites.

1 ¶And now it came to pass in the eighty and sixth year, the Nephites did still remain in wickedness, yea, in great wickedness, while the Lamanites did observe strictly to keep the commandments of God, according to the law of Moses.

2 And it came to pass that in this year, there was one Samuel, a Lamanite, came into the land of Zarahemla, and began to preach unto the people.

3 And it came to pass that he did preach many days, repentance unto the people, and they did cast him out, and he was about to return to his own land.

4 But behold, the voice of the Lord came unto him, that he should return again, and prophesy unto the people whatsoever things should come into his heart.

5 ¶And it came to pass that they would not suffer that he should enter into the city; therefore he went and got upon the wall thereof, and stretched forth his hand and cried with a

loud voice, and prophesied unto the people whatsoever things the Lord put into his heart;

6 And he said unto them, Behold, I, Samuel, a Lamanite, do speak the words of the Lord which he doth put into my heart; and behold he hath put it into my heart to say unto this people, that the sword of justice hangeth over this people; and four hundred years passeth not away save the sword of justice falleth upon this people;

7 Yea, heavy destruction awaiteth this people, and it surely cometh unto this people, and nothing can save this people, save it be repentance and faith on the Lord Jesus Christ, who surely shall come into the world, and shall suffer many things, and shall be slain for his people.

8 And behold, an angel of the Lord hath declared it unto me, and he did bring glad tidings to my soul.

9 And behold, I was sent unto you to declare it unto you also, that ye might have glad tidings; but behold ye would not receive me,

10 Therefore thus saith the Lord, Because of the hardness of the hearts of the people of the Nephites, except they repent I will take away my word from them, and I will withdraw my Spirit from them, and I will suffer them no longer, and I will turn the hearts of their brethren against them;

11 And four hundred years shall not pass away, before I will cause that they shall be smitten; yea, I will visit them with the sword, and with famine, and with pestilence;

12 Yea, I will visit them in my fierce anger, and there shall be those of the fourth generation, who shall live, of your enemies, to behold your utter destruction:

13 And this shall surely come, except ye repent, saith the Lord: and those of the fourth generation shall visit your destruction.

14 But if ye will repent and return unto the Lord your God, I will turn away mine anger, saith the Lord; yea, thus saith the Lord, Blessed are they who will repent and turn unto me, but wo unto him that repenteth not;

15 Yea, wo unto this great city of Zarahemla; for behold it is because of those who are righteous, that it is saved;

16 Yea, wo unto this great city, for I perceive, saith the Lord, that there are many, yea, even the more part of this great city that will harden their hearts against me, saith the Lord. But blessed are they who will repent, for them will I spare.

17 But behold, if it were not for the righteous who are in this great city, behold I would cause that fire should come down out of heaven, and destroy it. But behold, it is for the righteous' sake that it is spared.

18 But behold, the time cometh, saith the Lord, that when ye shall cast out the righteous from among you, then shall ye be ripe for destruction;

19 Yea, wo be unto this great city, because of the wickedness and abominations which are in her;

20 Yea, and wo be unto the city of Gideon, for the wickedness and abominations which are in her;

21 Yea, and wo be unto all the cities which are in the land round about, which are possessed by the Nephites, because of the wickedness and abominations which are in them;

22 And behold, a curse shall come upon the land, saith the Lord of Hosts, because of the people's sake who are upon the land; yea, because of their wickedness and their abominations.

23 ¶And it shall come to pass saith the Lord of Hosts, yea, our great and true God, that whoso shall hide up treasures in the earth, shall find them again no more, because of the great curse of the land, save he be a righteous man, and shall hide it up unto the Lord,

24 For I will, saith the Lord, that they shall hide up their treasures unto me; and cursed be they who hide not up their treasures unto me; for none hideth up their treasures unto me save it be the righteous;

25 And he that hideth not up his treasure unto me, cursed is he, and also the treasure, and none shall redeem it because of the curse of the land.

26 And the day shall come that they shall hide up their treasures, because they have set their hearts upon riches;

27 And because they have set their hearts upon their riches,

and will hide up their treasures when they shall flee before their enemies, because they will not hide them up unto me, cursed be they, and also their treasures; and in that day shall they be smitten, saith the Lord.

28 Behold ye, the people of this great city, and hearken unto my words; yea, hearken unto the words which the Lord saith; for behold, he saith that ye are cursed because of your riches,

29 And also are your riches cursed because ye have set your hearts upon them, and have not hearkened unto the words of him who gave them unto you.

30 Ye do not remember the Lord your God in the things which he hath blessed you, but ye do always remember your riches, not to thank the Lord your God for them;

31 Yea, your heart is not drawn out unto the Lord, but they do swell with great pride, unto boasting, and unto great swelling, envyings, strifes, malice, persecutions, and murders, and all manner of iniquities.

32 For this cause hath the Lord God caused that a curse should come upon the land, and also upon your riches; and this because of your iniquities;

33 Yea, wo unto this people, because of this time which has arrived, that ye do cast out the prophets, and do mock them, and cast stones at them, and do slay them, and do all manner of iniquity unto them, even as they did of old time.

34 And now when ye talk, ye say, If our days had been in the days of our fathers of old, ye would not have slain the prophets; ye would not have stoned them and cast them out.

35 Behold ye are worse than they; for as the Lord liveth, if a prophet come among you, and declareth unto you the word of the Lord, which testifieth of your sins and iniquities, ye are angry with him, and cast him out, and seek all manner of ways to destroy him;

36 Yea, you will say that he is a false prophet, and that he is a sinner, and of the devil, because he testifieth that your deeds are evil.

37 But behold, if a man shall come among you, and shall say, Do this, and there is no iniquity; do that, and ye shall

not suffer; yea, he will say, Walk after the pride of your own hearts; yea, walk after the pride of your eyes, and do whatsoever your heart desireth; and if a man shall come among you and say this, ye will receive him, and ye will say that he is a prophet;

38 Yea, ye will lift him up, and ye will give unto him of your substance; ye will give unto him of your gold, and of your silver, and ye will clothe him with costly apparel;

39 And because he speaketh flattering words unto you, and he saith that all is well, then ye will not find fault with him.

40 O ye wicked and ye perverse generation; ye hardened and ye stiff-necked people, how long will ye suppose that the Lord will suffer you; yea, how long will ye suffer yourselves to be led by foolish and blind guides; yea, how long will ye choose darkness rather than light;

41 Yea, behold the anger of the Lord is already kindled against you; behold, he hath cursed the land, because of your iniquity; and behold, the time cometh that he curseth your riches, that it becometh slippery, that ye can not hold them;

42 And in the days of your poverty, ye can not retain them; and in the days of your poverty, ye shall cry unto the Lord; and in vain shall ye cry, for your desolation is already come upon you, and your destruction is made sure;

43 And then shall ye weep and howl in that day, saith the Lord of Hosts.

44 And then shall ye lament, and say, O that I had repented, and had not killed the prophets, and stoned them, and cast them out;

45 Yea, in that day ye shall say, O that we had remembered the Lord our God, in the day that he gave us our riches, and then they would not have become slippery, that we should lose them; for behold, our riches are gone from us.

46 Behold, we lay a tool here, and on the morrow it is gone; and behold, our swords are taken from us in the day we have sought them for battle.

47 Yea, we have hid up our treasures, and they have slipped away from us, because of the curse of the land.

48 O that we had repented in the day that the word of the

Lord came unto us; for behold the land is cursed, and all things have become slippery, and we can not hold them.

49 Behold we are surrounded by demons, yea, we are encircled about by the angels of him who hath sought to destroy our souls.

50 Behold, our iniquities are great. O Lord, canst thou not turn away thine anger from us? And this shall be your language in those days.

51 But behold, your days of probation are past: ye have procrastinated the day of your salvation, until it is everlastingly too late, and your destruction is made sure;

52 Yea, for ye have sought all the days of your lives for that which ye could not obtain; and ye have sought for happiness in doing iniquity, which thing is contrary to the nature of that righteousness which is in our great and Eternal Head.

53 O ye people of the land, that ye would hear my words. And I pray that the anger of the Lord be turned away from you, and that ye would repent and be saved.

54 ¶And now it came to pass that Samuel, the Lamanite, did prophesy a great many more things which can not be written.

55 And behold, he said unto them, Behold, I give unto you a sign: for five years more cometh, and behold, then cometh the Son of God to redeem all those who shall believe on his name.

56 And behold, this will I give unto you for a sign at the time of his coming; for behold, there shall be great lights in heaven, insomuch that in the night before he cometh, there shall be no darkness, insomuch that it shall appear unto man as if it was day;

57 Therefore there shall be one day and a night, and a day, as if it were one day, and there were no night; and this shall be unto you for a sign; for ye shall know of the rising of the sun, and also of its setting;

58 Therefore they shall know of a surety that there shall be two days and a night; nevertheless the night shall not be darkened; and it shall be the night before he is born.

59 And behold there shall be a new star arise, such an one

as ye never have beheld; and this also shall be a sign unto you.

60 And behold this is not all, there shall be many signs and wonders in heaven.

61 And it shall come to pass that ye shall all be amazed, and wonder, insomuch that ye shall fall to the earth.

62 And it shall come to pass that whosoever shall believe on the Son of God, the same shall have everlasting life.

63 And behold, thus hath the Lord commanded me, by his angel, that I should come and tell this thing unto you; yea, he hath commanded that I should prophesy these things unto you; yea, he hath said unto me, Cry unto this people, Repent and prepare the way of the Lord.

64 And now because I am a Lamanite, and have spoken unto you the words which the Lord hath commanded me, and because it was hard against you, ye are angry with me, and do seek to destroy me, and have cast me out from among you.

65 And ye shall hear my words, for, for this intent I have come up upon the walls of this city, that ye might hear and know of the judgments of God which do await you because of your iniquities, and also that ye might know the conditions of repentance;

66 And also that ye might know of the coming of Jesus Christ, the Son of God, the Father of heaven and of earth, the Creator of all things, from the beginning; and that ye might know of the signs of his coming, to the intent that ye might believe on his name.

67 And if ye believe on his name, ye will repent of all your sins, that thereby ye may have a remission of them through his merits.

68 And behold, again, another sign I give unto you; yea a sign of his death; for behold, he surely must die, that salvation may come;

69 Yea, it behooveth him, and becometh expedient that he dieth, to bring to pass the resurrection of the dead, that thereby men may be brought into the presence of the Lord;

70 Yea, behold this death bringeth to pass the resurrection, and redeemeth all mankind from the first death; that spir-

itual death for all mankind, by the fall of Adam, being cut off from the presence of the Lord, or considered as dead, both as to things temporal and to things spiritual.

71 But behold, the resurrection of Christ redeemeth mankind, yea, even all mankind, and bringeth them back into the presence of the Lord;

72 Yea, and it bringeth to pass the conditions of repentance, that whosoever repenteth, the same is not hewn down and cast into the fire;

73 But whosoever repenteth not, is hewn down and cast into the fire, and there cometh upon them again a spiritual death, yea, a second death, for they are cut off again as to things pertaining to righteousness;

74 Therefore repent ye, repent ye, lest by knowing these things and not doing them, ye shall suffer yourselves to come under condemnation, and ye are brought down unto this second death.

75 But behold, as I said unto you concerning another sign, a sign of his death, behold, in that day that he shall suffer death, the sun shall be darkened and refuse to give his light unto you; and also the moon, and the stars;

76 And there shall be no light upon the face of this land, even from the time that he shall suffer death, for the space of three days, to the time that he shall rise again from the dead;

77 Yea, at the time that he shall yield up the ghost, there shall be thunderings and lightnings for the space of many hours, and the earth shall shake and tremble, and the rocks which are upon the face of the earth, which are both above the earth and beneath, which ye know at this time is solid, or the more part of it is one solid mass, shall be broken up;

78 Yea they shall be rent in twain, and shall ever after be found in seams and in cracks, and in broken fragments upon the face of the whole earth: yea, both above the earth and beneath.

79 And behold there shall be great tempests, and there shall be many mountains laid low, like unto a valley, and there shall be many places, which are now called valleys,

which shall become mountains, whose height thereof is great.

80 And many highways shall be broken up, and many cities shall become desolate, and many graves shall be opened, and shall yield up many of their dead; and many saints shall appear unto many.

81 And behold thus hath the angel spoken unto me; for he said unto me, that there should be thunderings and lightnings for the space of many hours;

82 And he said unto me that while the thunder and the lightning lasted, and the tempest, that these things should be, and that darkness should cover the face of the whole earth, for the space of three days.

83 And the angel said unto me that many shall see greater things than these, to the intent that they might believe that these signs and these wonders should come to pass, upon all the face of this land; to the intent that there should be no cause for unbelief among the children of men;

84 And this to the intent that whosoever will believe, might be saved, and that whosoever will not believe, a righteous judgment might come upon them: and also if they are condemned, they bring upon themselves their own condemnation.

85 And now remember, remember, my brethren, that whosoever perisheth, perisheth unto himself; and whosoever doeth iniquity, doeth it unto himself; for behold ye are free; ye are permitted to act for yourselves; for behold, God hath given unto you a knowledge, and he hath made you free;

86 He hath given unto you that ye might know good from evil, and he hath given unto you that ye might choose life or death, and ye can do good and be restored unto that which is good, or have that which is good restored unto you; or ye can do evil, and have that which is evil restored unto you.

87 And now my beloved brethren, behold, I declare unto you that except ye shall repent, your houses shall be left unto you desolate; yea, except ye repent, your women shall have great cause to mourn in the day that they shall give suck;

88 For ye shall attempt to flee, and there shall be no place for refuge; yea, and wo unto them which are with child, for

they shall be heavy, and can not flee; therefore they shall be trodden down, and shall be left to perish;

89 Yea, wo unto this people who are called the people of Nephi, except they shall repent when they shall see all these signs and wonders which shall be shewed unto them;

90 For behold, they have been a chosen people of the Lord; yea, the people of Nephi hath he loved, and also hath he chastened them; yea, in the days of their iniquities hath he chastened them, because he loveth them.

91 But behold my brethren, the Lamanites hath he hated, because their deeds have been evil continually: and this because of the iniquity of the tradition of their fathers.

92 But behold, salvation hath come unto them, through the preaching of the Nephites; and for this intent hath the Lord prolonged their days.

93 And I would that ye should behold that the more part of them are in the path of their duty, and they do walk circumspectly before God, and they do observe to keep his commandments, and his statutes, and his judgments, according to the law of Moses.

94 Yea, I say unto you, that the more part of them are doing this, and they are striving, with unwearied diligence, that they may bring the remainder of their brethren to the knowledge of the truth; therefore there are many who do add to their numbers daily.

95 And behold ye do know of yourselves, for ye have witnessed it, that as many of them as are brought to the knowledge of the truth, and to know of the wicked and abominable traditions of their fathers, and are led to believe the holy scriptures,

96 Yea, the prophecies of the holy prophets, which are written, which leadeth them to faith on the Lord, and unto repentance, which faith and repentance bringeth a change of heart unto them;

97 Therefore as many as have come to this, ye know of yourselves, are firm and steadfast in the faith, and in the things wherewith they have been made free.

98 And ye know also that they have buried their weapons

of war, and they fear to take them up, lest by any means they should sin; yea, ye can see that they fear to sin;

99 For behold, they will suffer themselves that they be trodden down and slain by their enemies, and will not lift their swords against them; and this because of their faith in Christ.

100 And now because of their steadfastness, when they do believe, in that thing which they do believe; for because of their firmness when they are once enlightened, behold the Lord shall bless them and prolong their days, notwithstanding their iniquity;

101 Yea, even if they should dwindle in unbelief, the Lord shall prolong their days until the time shall come which hath been spoken of by our fathers, and also by the prophet Zenos, and many other prophets, concerning the restoration of our brethren, the Lamanites, again, to the knowledge of the truth;

102 Yea, I say unto you, that in the latter times, the promises of the Lord hath been extended to our brethren, the Lamanites;

103 And notwithstanding the many afflictions which they shall have, and notwithstanding they shall be driven to and fro upon the face of the earth, and be hunted, and shall be smitten and scattered abroad, having no place for refuge, the Lord shall be merciful unto them;

104 And this is according to the prophecy, that they shall again be brought to the true knowledge, which is the knowledge of their Redeemer, and their great and true Shepherd, and be numbered among his sheep.

105 Therefore I say unto you, It shall be better for them than for you, except ye repent.

106 For behold, had the mighty works been shewn unto them which have been shewn unto you; yea, unto them who have dwindled in unbelief because of the traditions of their fathers, ye can see of yourselves, that they never would again have dwindled in unbelief;

107 Therefore, saith the Lord, I will not utterly destroy them, but I will cause that in the day of my wisdom, they shall return again unto me, saith the Lord.

108 And now behold, saith the Lord, concerning the people of the Nephites, If they will not repent, and observe to do my will, I will utterly destroy them saith the Lord, because of their unbelief, notwithstanding the many mighty works which I have done among them; and as surely as the Lord liveth, shall these things be, saith the Lord.

109 ¶And now it came to pass that there were many who heard the words of Samuel, the Lamanite, which he spake upon the walls of the city.

110 And as many as believed on his words, went forth and sought for Nephi; and when they had come forth and found him, they confessed unto him their sins and denied not, desiring that they might be baptized unto the Lord.

111 But as many as there were who did not believe in the words of Samuel, were angry with him; and they cast stones at him upon the wall, and also many shot arrows at him, as he stood upon the wall;

112 But the Spirit of the Lord was with him, insomuch that they could not hit him with their stones, neither with their arrows.

113 Now when they saw that they could not hit him, there were many more who did believe on his words, insomuch that they went away unto Nephi to be baptized.

114 For behold, Nephi was baptizing, and prophesying, and preaching, crying repentance unto the people; shewing signs and wonders; working miracles among the people, that they might know that the Christ must shortly come;

115 Telling them of things which must shortly come, that they might know and remember at the time of their coming that they had been made known unto them beforehand, to the intent that they might believe;

116 Therefore as many as believed on the words of Samuel, went forth unto him to be baptized, for they came repenting and confessing their sins.

117 But the more part of them did not believe in the words of Samuel; therefore, when they saw that they could not hit him with their stones and their arrows, they cried out unto

their captains, saying, Take this fellow and bind him, for behold, he hath a devil;

118 And because of the power of the devil which is in him, we can not hit him with our stones and our arrows; therefore take him and bind him, and away with him.

119 And as they went forth to lay their hands on him, behold, he did cast himself down from the wall, and did flee out of their lands, yea, even unto his own country, and began to preach and to prophesy among his own people.

120 And behold, he was never heard of more among the Nephites; and thus were the affairs of the people.

121 And thus ended the eighty and sixth year of the reign of the Judges over the people of Nephi.

122 And thus ended, also, the eighty and seventh year of the reign of the Judges, the more part of the people remaining in their pride and wickedness, and the lesser part walking more circumspectly before God.

123 And these were the conditions, also, in the eighty and eighth year of the reign of the Judges.

124 And there was but little alteration in the affairs of the people, save it were the people began to be more hardened in iniquity, and do more and more of that which was contrary to the commandments of God, in the eighty and ninth year of the reign of the Judges.

125 ¶But it came to pass in the ninetieth year of the reign of the Judges, there were great signs given unto the people, and wonders; and the words of the prophets began to be fulfilled;

126 And angels did appear unto men, wise men, and did declare unto them glad tidings of great joy; thus in this year the scriptures began to be fulfilled.

127 Nevertheless, the people began to harden their hearts, all save it were the most believing part of them, both of the Nephites, and also of the Lamanites, and began to depend upon their own strength, and upon their own wisdom, saying,

128 Some things they may have guessed right, among so many; but behold, we know that all these great and marvelous works can not come to pass, of which has been spoken.

129 And they began to reason and to contend among themselves, saying, that it is not reasonable that such a being as a Christ shall come;

130 If so, and he be the Son of God, the father of heaven and of earth, as it has been spoken, why will he not shew himself unto us, as well as unto them who shall be at Jerusalem?

131 Yea, why will he not shew himself in this land, as well as in the land at Jerusalem?

132 But behold, we know that this is a wicked tradition, which has been handed down unto us by our fathers, to cause us that we should believe in some great and marvelous thing which should come to pass, but not among us, but in a land which is far distant, a land which we know not;

133 Therefore they can keep us in ignorance, for we can not witness with our own eyes that they are true.

134 And they will, by the cunning and the mysterious arts of the evil one, work some great mystery, which we can not understand, which will keep us down to be servants to their words, and also servants unto them, for we depend upon them to teach us the word;

135 And thus will they keep us in ignorance, if we will yield ourselves unto them all the days of our lives.

136 And many more things did the people imagine up in their hearts, which were foolish and vain;

137 And they were much disturbed, for Satan did stir them up to do iniquity continually; yea, he did go about, spreading rumors and contentions upon all the face of the land, that he might harden the hearts of the people against that which was good, and against that which should come;

138 And notwithstanding the signs and the wonders which were wrought among the people of the Lord, and the many miracles which they did, Satan did get great hold upon the hearts of the people, upon all the face of the land.

139 And thus ended the ninetieth year of the reign of the Judges over the people of Nephi.

140 And thus ended the book of Helaman, according to the record of Helaman and his sons.

THE BOOK OF NEPHI.

THE SON OF NEPHI, WHO WAS THE SON OF HELAMAN.

CHAPTER 1.

And Helaman was the son of Helaman, who was the son of Alma, who was the son of Alma, being a descendant of Nephi who was the son of Lehi, who came out of Jerusalem in the first year of the reign of Zedekiah, the king of Judah.

1 ¶Now it came to pass that the ninety and first year had passed away; and it was six hundred years from the time that Lehi left Jerusalem; and it was in the year that Lachoneus was the chief Judge and the governor over the land.

2 And Nephi, the son of Helaman, had departed out of the land of Zarahemla, giving charge unto his son Nephi, who was his eldest son, concerning the plates of brass, and all the records which had been kept, and all those things which had been kept sacred, from the departure of Lehi out of Jerusalem;

3 Then he departed out of the land, and whither he went, no man knoweth; and his son Nephi did keep the record in his stead, yea, the record of this people.

4 ¶And it came to pass that in the commencement of the ninety and second year, behold the prophecies of the prophets began to be fulfilled more fully; for there began to be greater signs and greater miracles wrought among the people.

5 But there were some who began to say that the time was past for the words to be fulfilled, which were spoken by Samuel, the Lamanite.

6 And they began to rejoice over their brethren, saying, Behold, the time is past, and the words of Samuel are not fulfilled; therefore, your joy and your faith concerning this thing, hath been vain.

7 And it came to pass that they did make a great uproar throughout the land; and the people who believed, began to

be very sorrowful, lest by any means those things which had been spoken, might not come to pass.

8 But behold, they did watch steadfastly for that day, and that night, and that day, which should be as one day, as if there were no night, that they might know that their faith had not been vain.

9 ¶Now it came to pass that there was a day set apart by the unbelievers, that all those who believed in those traditions should be put to death, except the sign should come to pass which had been given by Samuel the prophet.

10 Now it came to pass that when Nephi, the son of Nephi, saw this wickedness of his people, his heart was exceeding sorrowful.

11 And it came to pass that he went out and bowed himself down upon the earth, and cried mightily to his God, in behalf of his people; yea, those who were about to be destroyed because of their faith in the tradition of their fathers.

12 And it came to pass that he cried mightily unto the Lord, all that day; and behold, the voice of the Lord came unto him, saying, Lift up your head and be of good cheer, for behold, the time is at hand, and on this night shall the sign be given,

13 And on the morrow come I into the world, to shew unto the world that I will fulfill all that which I have caused to be spoken by the mouth of my holy prophets.

14 Behold, I come unto my own, to fulfill all things which I have made known unto the children of men, from the foundation of the world, and to do the will, both of the Father, and of the Son of the Father, because of me, and of the Son, because of my flesh.

15 And behold, the time is at hand, and this night shall the sign be given.

16 ¶And it came to pass that the words which came unto Nephi were fulfilled, according as they had been spoken:

17 For behold at the going down of the sun, there was no darkness; and the people began to be astonished, because there was no darkness when the night came.

18 And there were many who had not believed the words

of the prophets, fell to the earth, and became as if they were dead, for they knew that the great plan of destruction which they had laid for those who believed in the words of the prophets, had been frustrated, for the sign which had been given was already at hand; and they began to know that the Son of God must shortly appear;

19 Yea, in fine, all the people upon the face of the whole earth, from the west to the east, both in the land north and in the land south, were so exceedingly astonished, that they fell to the earth;

20 For they knew that the prophets had testified of these things for many years, and that the sign which had been given, was already at hand; and they began to fear because of their iniquity and their unbelief.

21 ¶And it came to pass that there was no darkness in all that night, but it was as light as though it was midday.

22 And it came to pass that the sun did rise in the morning again, according to its proper order; and they knew that it was the day that the Lord should be born, because of the sign which had been given.

23 And it had come to pass, yea, all things, every whit, according to the words of the prophets.

24 And it came to pass also, that a new star did appear, according to the word.

25 And it came to pass that from this time forth, there began to be lyings sent forth among the people by Satan, to harden their hearts, to the intent that they might not believe in those signs and wonders which they had seen;

26 But notwithstanding those lyings and deceivings, the more part of the people did believe, and were converted unto the Lord.

27 And it came to pass that Nephi went forth among the people, and also many others, baptizing unto repentance, in the which, there were a great remission of sins.

28 And thus the people began again to have peace in the land; and there were no contentions, save it were a few that began to preach, endeavoring to prove by the scriptures, that it was no more expedient to observe the law of Moses.

29 Now in this thing they did err, having not understood the scriptures.

30 But it came to pass that they soon became converted, and were convinced of the error which they were in, for it was made known unto them that the law was not yet fulfilled, and that it must be fulfilled in every whit;

31 Yea, the word came unto them that it must be fulfilled; yea, that one jot nor tittle should not pass away, till it should all be fulfilled; therefore in this same year, were they brought to a knowledge of their error, and did confess their faults.

32 And thus the ninety and second year did pass away, bringing glad tidings unto the people because of the signs which did come to pass, according to the words of the prophecy of all the holy prophets.

33 ¶And it came to pass that the ninety and third year did also pass away in peace, save it were for the Gadianton robbers, who dwelt upon the mountains, who did infest the land;

34 For so strong were their holds and their secret places that the people could not overpower them; therefore they did commit many murders, and did do much slaughter among the people.

35 And it came to pass that in the ninety and fourth year, they began to increase in a great degree, because there were many dissenters of the Nephites who did flee unto them, which did cause much sorrow unto those Nephites who did remain in the land;

36 And there was also a cause of much sorrow among the Lamanites, for behold, they had many children who did grow up and began to wax strong in years, that they became for themselves, and were led away by some who were Zoramites, by their lyings and their flattering words, to join those Gadianton robbers;

37 And thus were the Lamanites afflicted also, and began to decrease as to their faith and righteousness, because of the wickedness of the rising generation.

38 ¶And it came to pass that thus passed away the ninety and fifth year also, and the people began to forget those signs

and wonders which they had heard, and began to be less and less astonished at a sign or a wonder from heaven,

39 Insomuch that they began to be hard in their hearts, and blind in their minds, and began to disbelieve all which they had heard and seen, imagining up some vain thing in their hearts, that it was wrought by men, and by the power of the devil, to lead away and deceive the hearts of the people;

40 And thus did Satan get possession of the hearts of the people again, insomuch that he did blind their eyes, and lead them away to believe that the doctrine of Christ was a foolish and a vain thing.

41 ¶And it came to pass that the people began to wax strong in wickedness and abominations; and they did not believe that there should be any more signs or wonders given;

42 And Satan did go about, leading away the hearts of the people, tempting them and causing them that they should do great wickedness in the land.

43 And thus did pass away the ninety and sixth year; and also the ninety and seventh year; and also the ninety and eighth year; and also the ninety and ninth year; and also an hundred years had passed away, since the days of Mosiah, who was king over the people of the Nephites.

44 And six hundred and nine years had passed away, since Lehi left Jerusalem; and nine years had passed away, from the time when the sign was given, which was spoken of by the prophets, that Christ should come into the world.

45 Now the Nephites began to reckon their time from this period when the sign was given or from the coming of Christ;

46 Therefore, nine years had passed away, and Nephi, who was the father of Nephi, who had the charge of the records, did not return to the land of Zarahemla, and could nowhere be found in all the land.

47 ¶And it came to pass that the people did still remain in wickedness, notwithstanding the much preaching and prophesying which was sent among them; and thus passed away the tenth year also; and the eleventh year also passed away in iniquity.

48 And it came to pass in the thirteenth year, there began

CHAP. 1.] BOOK OF NEPHI. 605

to be wars and contentions throughout all the land; for the Gadianton robbers had become so numerous, and did slay so many of the people, and did lay waste so many cities, and did spread so much death and carnage throughout the land, that it became expedient that all the people, both the Nephites, and the Lamanites, should take up arms against them;

49 Therefore all the Lamanites, who had become converted unto the Lord, did unite with their brethren, the Nephites, and were compelled, for the safety of their lives, and their women and their children, to take up arms against those Gadianton robbers;

50 Yea, and also to maintain their rites, and their privileges of their church, and of their worship, and their freedom, and their liberty.

51 And it came to pass that before this thirteenth year had passed away, the Nephites were threatened with utter destruction, because of this war, which had become exceeding sore.

52 And it came to pass that those Lamanites who had united with the Nephites, were numbered among the Nephites: and their curse was taken from them, and their skin became white like unto the Nephites;

53 And their young men and their daughters became exceeding fair, and they were numbered among the Nephites, and were called Nephites. And thus ended the thirteenth year.

54 ¶And it came to pass in the commencement of the fourteenth year, the war between the robbers and the people of Nephi did continue, and did become exceeding sore;

55 Nevertheless, the people of Nephi did gain some advantage of the robbers, insomuch that they did drive them back out of their lands into the mountains, and into their secret places. And thus ended the fourteenth year.

56 And in the fifteenth year they did come forth again against the people of Nephi; and because of the wickedness of the people of Nephi, and their many contentions and dissensions, the Gadianton robbers did gain many advantages over them.

57 And thus ended the fifteenth year, and thus were the people in a state of many afflictions; and the sword of destruction did hang over them, insomuch that they were about to be smitten down by it, and this because of their iniquity.

CHAPTER 2.

1 ¶And now it came to pass that in the sixteenth year from the coming of Christ, Lachoneus, the governor of the land, received an epistle from the leader and the governor of this band of robbers;

2 And these are the words which were written, saying, Lachoneus, most noble and chief governor of the land, behold I write this epistle unto you, and do give unto you exceeding great praise because of your firmness, and also the firmness of your people, in maintaining that which ye suppose to be your right and liberty;

3 Yea, ye do stand well, as if ye were supported by the hand of a God in the defense of your liberty, and your property, and your country, or that which ye do call so.

4 And it seemeth a pity unto me, most noble Lachoneus, that ye should be so foolish and vain as to suppose that ye can stand against so many brave men, who are at my command, who do now at this time stand in their arms, and do await, with great anxiety, for the word, Go down upon the Nephites and destroy them.

5 And I, knowing of their unconquerable spirit, having proved them in the field of battle, and knowing of their everlasting hatred towards you, because of the many wrongs which ye have done unto them, therefore if they should come down against you, they would visit you with utter destruction;

6 Therefore I have wrote this epistle, sealing it with mine own hand, feeling for your welfare, because of your firmness in that which ye believe to be right, and your noble spirit in the field of battle;

7 Therefore I write unto you desiring that ye would yield up unto this my people, your cities, your lands, and your pos-

sessions, rather than that they should visit you with the sword, and that destruction should come upon you;

8 Or in other words, yield yourselves up unto us, and unite with us, and become acquainted with our secret works, and become our brethren, that ye may be like unto us; not our slaves, but our brethren, and partners of all our substance.

9 And behold, I swear unto you, If ye will do this, with an oath, ye shall not be destroyed; but if ye will not do this, I swear unto you, with an oath, that on the morrow month, I will command that my armies shall come down against you,

10 And they shall not stay their hand, and shall spare not, but shall slay you, and shall let fall the sword upon you, yea, even until ye shall become extinct.

11 And behold, I am Giddianhi; and I am the governor of this the secret society of Gadianton; which society, and the works thereof, I know to be good; and they are of ancient date, and they have been handed down unto us.

12 And I write this epistle unto you, Lachoneus, and I hope that ye will deliver up your lands, and your possessions, without the shedding of blood, that this my people may recover their rights and government who have dissented away from you, because of your wickedness in retaining from them their rights of government; and except ye do this, I will avenge their wrongs. I am Giddianhi.

13 ¶And now it came to pass when Lachoneus received this epistle, he was exceedingly astonished, because of the boldness of Giddianhi, in demanding the possession of the land of the Nephites,

14 And also of threatening the people and avenging the wrongs of those that had received no wrong, save it were they had wronged themselves, by dissenting away unto those wicked and abominable robbers.

15 Now behold, this Lachoneus, the governor, was a just man, and could not be frightened by the demands and the threatenings of a robber;

16 Therefore he did not hearken to the epistle of Giddianhi, the governor of the robbers, but he did cause that his people

should cry unto the Lord for strength against the time that the robbers should come down against them;

17 Yea, he sent a proclamation among all the people that they should gather together their women, and their children, their flocks and their herds, and all their substance, save it were their land, unto one place.

18 And he caused that fortifications should be built round about them, and the strength thereof should be exceeding great.

19 And he caused that there should be armies, both of the Nephites and of the Lamanites, or of all them who were numbered among the Nephites, should be placed as guards round about, to watch them, and to guard them from the robbers, day and night;

20 Yea, he said unto them, As the Lord liveth, except ye repent of all your iniquities, and cry unto the Lord, that they could in no wise be delivered out of the hands of those Gadianton robbers.

21 And so great and marvelous were the words and prophecies of Lachoneus, that they did cause fear to come upon all the people, and they did exert themselves in their might, to do according to the words of Lachoneus.

22 ¶And it came to pass that Lachoneus did appoint chief captains over all the armies of the Nephites, to command them at the time that the robbers should come down out of the wilderness against them.

23 Now the chiefest among all the chief captains, and the great commander of all the armies of the Nephites, was appointed, and his name was Gidgiddoni.

24 Now it was the custom among all the Nephites, to appoint for their chief captains, save it were in their times of wickedness, some one that had the spirit of revelation, and also prophecy; therefore this Gidgiddoni was a great prophet among them, and also was the chief judge.

25 Now the people said unto Gidgiddoni, Pray unto the Lord, and let us go up upon the mountains, and into the wilderness, that we may fall upon the robbers and destroy them, in their own lands.

26 But Gidgiddoni saith unto them, The Lord forbid; for if we should go up against them, the Lord would deliver us into their hands;

27 Therefore we will prepare ourselves in the center of our lands, and we will gather all our armies together, and we will not go against them, but we will wait till they shall come against us;

28 Therefore as the Lord liveth, if we do this, he will deliver them into our hands.

29 And it came to pass in the seventeenth year, in the latter end of the year, the proclamation of Lachoneus had gone forth throughout all the face of the land,

30 And they had taken their horses, and their chariots, and their cattle, and all their flocks, and their herds, and their grain, and all their substance,

31 And did march forth by thousands; and by tens of thousands, until they had all gone forth to the place which had been appointed, that they should gather themselves together, to defend themselves against their enemies.

32 And the land which was appointed was the land of Zarahemla and the land which was between the land of Zarahemla and the land Bountiful; yea, to the line which was between the land Bountiful and the land Desolation;

33 And there were a great many thousand people who were called Nephites, who did gather themselves together in this land.

34 Now Lachoneus did cause that they should gather themselves together in the land southward, because of the great curse which was upon the land northward; and they did fortify themselves against their enemies;

35 And they did dwell in one land, and in one body, and they did fear the words which had been spoken by Lachoneus, insomuch that they did repent of all their sins;

36 And they did put up their prayers unto the Lord their God, that he would deliver them in the time that their enemies should come down against them to battle.

37 And they were exceeding sorrowful because of their enemy.

38 And Gidgiddoni did cause that they should make weapons of war, of every kind, that they should be strong with armor, and with shields, and with bucklers, after the manner of his instructions.

39 ¶And it came to pass that in the latter end of the eighteenth year, those armies of robbers had prepared for battle, and began to come down, and to sally forth from the hills, and out of the mountains, and the wilderness, and their strongholds, and their secret places,

40 And began to take possession of the lands both which was in the land south, and which was in the land north, and began to take possession of all the lands which had been deserted by the Nephites, and the cities which had been left desolate.

41 But behold there were no wild beasts nor game in those lands which had been deserted by the Nephites, and there was no game for the robbers save it were in the wilderness.

42 And the robbers could not exist save it were in the wilderness, for the want of food; for the Nephites had left their lands desolate, and had gathered their flocks, and their herds and all their substance, and they were in one body;

43 Therefore there was no chance for the robbers to plunder and to obtain food, save it were to come up in open battle against the Nephites;

44 And the Nephites being in one body, and having so great a number, and having reserved for themselves provisions, and horses, and cattle, and flocks of every kind, that they might subsist for the space of seven years,

45 In the which time they did hope to destroy the robbers from off the face of the land. And thus the eighteenth year did pass away.

46 ¶And it came to pass that in the nineteenth year, Giddianhi found that it was expedient that he should go up to battle against the Nephites, for there was no way that they could subsist, save it were to plunder, and rob, and murder.

47 And they durst not spread themselves upon the face of the land, insomuch that they could raise grain, lest the Nephites should come upon them and slay them;

BOOK OF NEPHI.

48 Therefore Giddianhi gave commandment unto his armies, that in this year they should go up to battle against the Nephites.

49 ¶And it came to pass that they did come up to battle; and it was in the sixth month; and behold, great and terrible was the day that they did come up to battle;

50 And they were girded about after the manner of robbers; and they had a lamb-skin about their loins, and they were dyed in blood; and their heads were shorn; and they had head-plates upon them;

51 And great and terrible was the appearance of the armies of Giddianhi, because of their armor, and because of their being dyed in blood.

52 And it came to pass that the armies of the Nephites, when they saw the appearance of the army of Giddianhi, had all fallen to the earth, and did lift their cries to the Lord their God, that he would spare them, and deliver them out of the hands of their enemies.

53 And it came to pass that when the armies of Giddianhi saw this, they began to shout with a loud voice, because of their joy; for they had supposed that the Nephites had fallen with fear, because of the terror of their armies;

54 But in this thing they were disappointed, for the Nephites did not fear them, but they did fear their God, and did supplicate him for protection;

55 Therefore when the armies of Giddianhi did rush upon them, they were prepared to meet them; yea, in the strength of the Lord they did receive them; and the battle commenced in this the sixth month;

56 And great and terrible was the battle thereof; yea, great and terrible was the slaughter thereof, insomuch that there never was known so great a slaughter among all the people of Lehi since he left Jerusalem.

57 And notwithstanding the threatenings and the oaths which Giddianhi had made, behold, the Nephites did beat them, insomuch that they did fall back from before them.

58 ¶And it came to pass that Gidgiddoni commanded that his armies should pursue them as far as the borders of the

wilderness, and that they should not spare any that should fall into their hands by the way;

59 And thus they did pursue them, and did slay them, to the borders of the wilderness, even until they had fulfilled the commandment of Gidgiddoni.

60 ¶And it came to pass that Giddianhi, who had stood and fought with boldness, was pursued as he fled; and being weary because of his much fighting, he was overtaken and slain. And thus was the end of Giddianhi, the robber.

61 ¶And it came to pass that the armies of the Nephites did return again to their place of security.

62 And it came to pass that this nineteenth year did pass away, and the robbers did not come again to battle; neither did they come in the twentieth year;

63 And in the twenty and first year they did not come up to battle, but they came up on all sides to lay siege round about the people of Nephi;

64 For they did suppose that if they should cut off the people of Nephi from their lands, and should hem them in on every side, and if they should cut them off from all their outward privileges, that they could cause them to yield themselves up according to their wishes.

65 Now they had appointed unto themselves another leader, whose name was Zemnarihah; therefore it was Zemnarihah that did cause that this siege should take place.

66 But behold this was an advantage to the Nephites; for it was impossible for the robbers to lay siege sufficiently long to have any effect upon the Nephites, because of their much provision which they had laid up in store, and because of the scantiness of provisions among the robbers;

67 For behold they had nothing save it were meat for their subsistence, which meat they did obtain in the wilderness.

68 And it came to pass that the wild game became scarce in the wilderness, insomuch that the robbers were about to perish with hunger.

69 And the Nephites were continually marching out by day and by night, and falling upon their armies, and cutting them off by thousands and by tens of thousands.

70 And thus it became the desire of the people of Zemnarihah, to withdraw from their design, because of the great destruction which came upon them by night and by day.

71 ¶And it came to pass that Zemnarihah did give command unto his people, that they should withdraw themselves from the siege, and march into the furthermost parts of the land, northward.

72 And now, Gidgiddoni, being aware of their design, and knowing of their weakness because of the want of food, and the great slaughter which had been made among them, therefore he did send out his armies in the night time, and did cut off the way of their retreat, and did place his armies in the way of their retreat;

73 And this did they do in the night time, and got on their march beyond the robbers, so that on the morrow, when the robbers began their march, they were met by the armies of the Nephites, both in their front and in their rear.

74 And the robbers who were on the south, were also cut off in their places of retreat. And all these things were done by command of Gidgiddoni.

75 And there were many thousands who did yield themselves up prisoners unto the Nephites; and the remainder of them were slain; and their leader, Zemnarihah, was taken, and hanged upon a tree, yea, even upon the top thereof, until he was dead.

76 And when they had hanged him until he was dead, they did fall the tree to the earth, and did cry with a loud voice, saying, May the Lord preserve his people in righteousness and in holiness of heart, that they may cause to be fell to the earth all who shall seek to slay them because of power and secret combinations, even as this man hath been fell to the earth.

77 And they did rejoice and cry again with one voice, saying, May the God of Abraham, and the God of Isaac, and the God of Jacob, protect this people in righteousness, so long as they shall call on the name of their God for protection.

78 And it came to pass that they did break forth, all as one, in singing and praising their God, for the great thing

which he had done for them, in preserving them from falling into the hands of their enemies;

79 Yea, they did cry, Hosanna to the Most High God; and they did cry, Blessed be the name of the Lord God Almighty, the Most High God.

80 And their hearts were swollen with joy, unto the gushing out of many tears, because of the great goodness of God in delivering them out of the hands of their enemies;

81 And they knew it was because of their repentance and their humility that they had been delivered from an everlasting destruction.

82 And now behold there was not a living soul among all the people of the Nephites, who did doubt in the least the words of all the holy prophets who had spoken;

83 For they knew that it must needs be that they must be fulfilled; and they knew that it must be expedient that Christ had come, because of the many signs which had been given, according to the words of the prophets,

84 And because of the things which had come to pass already, they knew that it must needs be that all things should come to pass according to that which had been spoken;

85 Therefore they did forsake all their sins and their abominations, and their whoredoms, and did serve God with all diligence day and night.

86 ¶And now it came to pass that when they had taken all the robbers prisoners, insomuch that none did escape who were not slain, they did cast their prisoners into prison, and did cause the word of God to be preached unto them;

87 And as many as would repent of their sins and enter into a covenant that they would murder no more, were set at liberty;

88 But as many as there were who did not enter into a covenant, and who did still continue to have those secret murders in their hearts; yea, as many as were found breathing out threatenings against their brethren, were condemned and punished according to the law.

89 And thus they did put an end to all those wicked, and

secret, and abominable combinations, in the which there was so much wickedness, and so many murders committed.

90 And thus had the twenty and second year passed away, and the twenty and third year also, and the twenty and fourth, and the twenty and fifth;

91 And thus had twenty and five years passed away, and there had many things transpired which, in the eyes of some, would be great and marvelous;

92 Nevertheless, they can not all be written in this book; yea, this book can not contain even a hundredth part of what was done among so many people, in the space of twenty and five years;

93 But behold there are records which do contain all the proceedings of this people; and a more short but a true account was given by Nephi;

94 Therefore I have made my record of these things according to the record of Nephi, which was engraven on the plates which were called the plates of Nephi.

95 And behold I do make this record on plates which I have made with mine own hands.

96 And behold, I am called Mormon, being called after the land of Mormon, the land in the which Alma did establish the church among this people; yea, the first church which was established among them after their transgression.

97 Behold I am a disciple of Jesus Christ, the Son of God. I have been called of him to declare his word among his people, that they might have everlasting life.

98 And it hath become expedient that I, according to the will of God, that the prayers of those who have gone hence, who were the holy ones, should be fulfilled according to their faith, should make a record of these things, which have been done;

99 Yea, a small record of that which hath taken place from the time that Lehi left Jerusalem, even down until the present time;

100 Therefore I do make my record from the accounts which have been given by those who were before me, until the

commencement of my day; and then do I make a record of the things which I have seen with mine own eyes.

101 And I know the record which I make to be a just and a true record; nevertheless there are many things which, according to our language, we are not able to write.

102 And now I make an end of my saying which is of myself, and proceed to give my account of the things which have been before me. I am Mormon, and a pure descendant of Lehi.

103 I have reason to bless my God and my Savior Jesus Christ, that he brought our fathers out of the land of Jerusalem, (and no one knew it save it were himself and those whom he brought out of that land,) and that he hath given me and my people so much knowledge unto the salvation of our souls.

104 Surely he hath blessed the house of Jacob, and hath been merciful unto the seed of Joseph.

105 And insomuch as the children of Lehi have kept his commandments, he hath blessed them and prospered them according to his word;

106 Yea, and surely shall he again bring a remnant of the seed of Joseph to the knowledge of the Lord their God;

107 And as surely as the Lord liveth will he gather in from the four quarters of the earth, all the remnant of the seed of Jacob, who are scattered abroad upon all the face of the earth;

108 And as he hath covenanted with all the house of Jacob, even so shall the covenant wherewith he hath covenanted with the house of Jacob, be fulfilled in his own due time, unto the restoring all the house of Jacob unto the knowledge of the covenant that he hath covenanted with them;

109 And then shall they know their Redeemer, who is Jesus Christ, the Son of God; and then shall they be gathered in from the four quarters of the earth, unto their own lands, from whence they have been dispersed; yea, as the Lord liveth, so shall it be. Amen.

CHAPTER 3.

1 ¶And now it came to pass that the people of the Nephites did all return to their own lands, in the twenty and sixth year, every man, with his family, his flocks and his herds, his horses and his cattle, and all things whatsoever did belong unto them.

2 And it came to pass that they had not eaten up all their provisions; therefore they did take with them all that they had not devoured, of all their grain of every kind, and their gold, and their silver, and all their precious things,

3 And they did return to their own lands and their possessions, both on the north and on the south, both on the land northward and on the land southward.

4 And they granted unto those robbers who had entered into a covenant to keep the peace of the land, who were desirous to remain Lamanites, lands, according to their numbers, that they might have, with their labors, wherewith to subsist upon; and thus they did establish peace in all the land.

5 And they began again to prosper and to wax great; and the twenty and sixth and seventh years passed away, and there was great order in the land; and they had formed their laws according to equity and justice.

6 And now there was nothing in all the land, to hinder the people from prospering continually, except they should fall into transgressions.

7 And now it was Gidgiddoni, and the judge Lachoneus, and those who had been appointed leaders, who had established this great peace in the land.

8 ¶And it came to pass that there were many cities built anew, and there were many old cities repaired, and there were many highways cast up, and many roads made, which led from city to city, and from land to land, and from place to place.

9 And thus passed away the twenty and eighth year, and the people had continual peace.

10 But it came to pass in the twenty and ninth year, there began to be some disputings among the people;

11 And some were lifted up unto pride and boastings, because of their exceeding great riches, yea, even unto great persecutions: for there were many merchants in the land, and also many lawyers, and many officers.

12 And the people began to be distinguished by ranks, according to their riches, and their chances for learning;

13 Yea, some were ignorant because of their poverty, and others did receive great learning because of their riches;

14 Some were lifted up in pride, and others were exceeding humble; some did return railing for railing, while others would receive railing, and persecution, and all manner of afflictions, and would not turn and revile again, but were humble and penitent before God;

15 And thus there became a great inequality in all the land, insomuch that the church began to be broken up; yea, insomuch that in the thirtieth year the church was broken up in all the land, save it were among a few of the Lamanites, who were converted unto the true faith;

16 And they would not depart from it, for they were firm, and steadfast, and immovable, willing with all diligence to keep the commandments of the Lord.

17 Now the cause of this iniquity of the people, was this: Satan had great power, unto the stirring up of the people to do all manner of iniquity, and to the puffing them up with pride, tempting them to seek for power, and authority, and riches, and the vain things of the world.

18 And thus Satan did lead away the hearts of the people, to do all manner of iniquity; therefore they had not enjoyed peace but a few years.

19 And thus in the commencement of the thirtieth year, the people having been delivered up for the space of a long time, to be carried about by the temptations of the devil whithersoever he desired to carry them, and to do whatsoever iniquity he desired they should; and thus in the commencement of this, the thirtieth year, they were in a state of awful wickedness.

CHAP. 3.] BOOK OF NEPHI. 619

20 Now they did not sin ignorantly, for they knew the will of God concerning them, for it had been taught unto them; therefore they did willfully rebel against God.

21 And now it was in the days of Lachoneus, the son of Lachoneus, for Lachoneus did fill the seat of his father and did govern the people that year.

22 And there began to be men inspired from heaven, and sent forth, standing among the people in all the land, preaching and testifying boldly of the sins and iniquities of the people,

23 And testifying unto them concerning the redemption which the Lord would make for his people; or in other words, the resurrection of Christ; and they did testify boldly of his death and sufferings.

24 Now there were many of the people who were exceeding angry, because of those who testified of these things:

25 And those who were angry, were chiefly the chief judges, and they who had been high priests and lawyers;

26 Yea, all those who were lawyers, were angry with those who testified of these things.

27 Now there was no lawyer, nor judge, nor high priest, that could have power to condemn any one to death, save their condemnation was signed by the governor of the land.

28 Now there were many of those who testified of the things pertaining to Christ, who testified boldly, who were taken and put to death secretly by the judges, that the knowledge of their death came not unto the governor of the land, until after their death.

29 Now behold this was contrary to the laws of the land, that any man should be put to death, except they had power from the governor of the land;

30 Therefore a complaint came unto the land of Zarahemla, to the governor of the land, against these judges who had condemned the prophets of the Lord unto death, not according to the law.

31 ¶Now it came to pass that they were taken and brought up before the judge, to be judged of the crime which they had

done, according to the law which had been given by the people.

32 Now it came to pass that those judges had many friends and kindreds; and the remainder, yea, even almost all the lawyers and the high priests, did gather themselves together, and unite with the kindreds of those judges who were to be tried according to the law;

33 And they did enter into a covenant one with another, yea, even into that covenant which was given by them of old, which covenant was given and administered by the devil, to combine against all righteousness;

34 Therefore they did combine against the people of the Lord, and enter into a covenant to destroy them, and to deliver those who were guilty of murder from the grasp of justice, which was about to be administered according to the law.

35 And they did set at defiance the law and the rights of their country; and they did covenant, one with another, to destroy the governor, and to establish a king over the land, that the land should no more be at liberty, but should be subject unto kings.

36 Now behold, I will shew unto you that they did not establish a king over the land; but in this same year, yea, the thirtieth year, they did destroy upon the judgment seat, yea, did murder the chief judge of the land.

37 And the people were divided one against another; and they did separate one from another, into tribes, every man according to his family, and his kindred and friends; and thus they did destroy the government of the land.

38 And every tribe did appoint a chief, or a leader over them; and thus they became tribes, and leaders of tribes.

39 Now behold, there was no man among them, save he had much family and many kindreds and friends; therefore their tribes became exceeding great.

40 Now all this was done and there were no wars as yet among them; and all this iniquity had come upon the people, because they did yield themselves unto the power of Satan;

41 And the regulations of the government were destroyed,

because of the secret combination of the friends and kindreds of those who murdered the prophets.

42 And they did cause a great contention in the land, insomuch that the more righteous part of the people, although they had nearly all become wicked; yea, there were but few righteous men among them.

43 And thus six years had not passed away, since the more part of the people had turned from their righteousness, like the dog to his vomit, or like the sow to her wallowing in the mire.

44 Now this secret combination which had brought so great iniquity upon the people, did gather themselves together, and did place at their head a man whom they did call Jacob; and they did call him their king;

45 Therefore he became a king over this wicked band; and he was one of the chiefest who had given his voice against the prophets who testified of Jesus.

46 And it came to pass that they were not so strong in number as the tribes of the people who were united together, save it were their leaders did establish their laws, every one according to his tribe;

47 Nevertheless they were enemies, notwithstanding they were not a righteous people; yet they were united in the hatred of those who had entered into a covenant to destroy the government;

48 Therefore Jacob seeing that their enemies were more numerous than they, he being the king of the band, therefore he commanded his people that they should take their flight into the northernmost part of the land,

49 And there build up unto themselves a kingdom, until they were joined by dissenters, (for he flattered them that there would be many dissenters,) and they become sufficiently strong to contend with the tribes of the people.

50 And they did so; and so speedy was their march, that it could not be impeded, until they had gone forth out of the reach of the people.

51 And thus ended the thirtieth year; and thus were the affairs of the people of Nephi.

52 ¶And it came to pass in the thirty and first year, that they were divided into tribes, every man according to his family, kindred and friends;

53 Nevertheless they had come to an agreement that they would not go to war one with another; but they were not united as to their laws, and their manner of government, for they were established according to the minds of those who were their chiefs and their leaders.

54 But they did establish very strict laws that one tribe should not trespass against another, insomuch that in some degree they had peace in the land;

55 Nevertheless, their hearts were turned from the Lord their God, and they did stone the prophets, and did cast them out from among them.

56 ¶And it came to pass that Nephi, having been visited by angels, and also by the voice of the Lord, therefore having seen angels, and being eye witness, and having had power given unto him that he might know concerning the ministry of Christ, and also being eye witness to their quick return from righteousness unto their wickedness and abominations;

57 Therefore, being grieved for the hardness of their hearts, and the blindness of their minds, went forth among them in that same year, and began to testify boldly, repentance and remission of sins through faith on the Lord Jesus Christ.

58 And he did minister many things unto them; and all of them can not be written, and a part of them would not suffice: therefore they are not written in this book. And Nephi did minister with power and with great authority.

59 ¶And it came to pass that they were angry with him, even because he had greater power than they, for it were not possible that they could disbelieve his words, for so great was his faith on the Lord Jesus Christ, that angels did minister unto him daily;

60 And in the name of Jesus did he cast out devils and unclean spirits; and even his brother did he raise from the dead, after he had been stoned and suffered death by the people;

61 And the people saw it, and did witness of it, and were angry with him, because of his power; and he did also do many more miracles, in the sight of the people, in the name of Jesus.

62 ¶And it came to pass that the thirty and first year did pass away, and there were but few who were converted unto the Lord;

63 But as many as were converted, did truly signify unto the people that they had been visited by the power and Spirit of God, which was in Jesus Christ, in whom they believed.

64 And as many as had devils cast out from them, and were healed of their sicknesses and their infirmities, did truly manifest unto the people that they had been wrought upon by the Spirit of God, and had been healed;

65 And they did shew forth signs also, and did do some miracles among the people.

66 ¶Thus passed away the thirty and second year also.

67 And Nephi did cry unto the people in the commencement of the thirty and third year; and he did preach unto them repentance and remission of sins.

68 Now I would have you to remember also, that there were none who were brought unto repentance, who were not baptized with water;

69 Therefore there were ordained of Nephi, men unto this ministry, that all such as should come unto them, should be baptized with water, and this as a witness and a testimony before God, and unto the people, that they had repented and received a remission of their sins.

70 And there were many in the commencement of this year, that were baptized unto repentance: and thus the more part of the year did pass away.

CHAPTER 4.

1 ¶And now it came to pass that according to our record, and we know our record to be true, for behold, it was a just man who did keep the record; for he truly did many miracles in the name of Jesus;

2 And there was not any man who could do a miracle in the name of Jesus, save he were cleansed every whit from his iniquity.

3 And now it came to pass, if there was no mistake made by this man in the reckoning of our time, the thirty and third year had passed away, and the people began to look with great earnestness for the sign which had been given by the prophet Samuel, the Lamanite;

4 Yea, for the time that there should be darkness for the space of three days, over the face of the land.

5 And there began to be great doubtings and disputations among the people, notwithstanding so many signs had been given.

6 ¶And it came to pass in the thirty and fourth year, in the first month, in the fourth day of the month, there arose a great storm, such an one as never had been known in all the land;

7 And there was also a great and terrible tempest; and there was terrible thunder, insomuch that it did shake the whole earth as if it was about to divide asunder; and there were exceeding sharp lightnings, such as never had been known in all the land.

8 And the city of Zarahemla did take fire; and the city of Moroni did sink into the depths of the sea, and the inhabitants thereof were drowned;

9 And the earth was carried up upon the city of Moronihah, that in the place of the city thereof, there became a great mountain; and there was a great and terrible destruction in the land southward.

10 But behold, there was a more great and terrible destruction in the land northward: for behold, the whole face of the land was changed, because of the tempests, and the whirlwinds, and the thunderings, and the lightnings, and the exceeding great quaking of the whole earth;

11 And the highways were broken up, and the level roads were spoiled, and many smooth places became rough, and many great and notable cities were sunk, and many were burned, and many were shook till the buildings thereof had

fallen to the earth, and the inhabitants thereof were slain, and the places were left desolate;

12 And there were some cities which remained; but the damage thereof was exceeding great, and there were many in them who were slain;

13 And there were some who were carried away in the whirlwind; and whither they went, no man knoweth, save they know that they were carried away;

14 And thus the face of the whole earth became deformed, because of the tempests, and the thunderings, and the lightnings, and the quaking of the earth.

15 And behold, the rocks were rent in twain; yea, they were broken up upon the face of the whole earth, insomuch that they were found in broken fragments, and in seams, and in cracks, upon all the face of the land.

16 ¶And it came to pass that when the thunderings, and the lightnings, and the storm, and the tempest, and the quakings of the earth did cease—for behold, they did last for about the space of three hours; and it was said by some that the time was greater;

17 Nevertheless, all these great and terrible things were done in about the space of three hours; and then behold, there was darkness upon the face of the land.

18 ¶And it came to pass that there was thick darkness upon all the face of the land, insomuch that the inhabitants thereof who had not fallen, could feel the vapor of darkness;

19 And there could be no light, because of the darkness; neither candles, neither torches; neither could there be fire kindled with their fine and exceeding dry wood, so that there could not be any light at all;

20 And there was not any light seen, neither fire, nor glimmer, neither the sun, nor the moon, nor the stars, for so great were the mists of darkness which were upon the face of the land.

21 ¶And it came to pass that it did last for the space of three days, that there was no light seen; and there was great mourning, and howling, and weeping among all the people continually;

22 Yea, great were the groanings of the people, because of the darkness and the great destruction which had come upon them.

23 And in one place they were heard to cry, saying, O that we had repented before this great and terrible day, and then would our brethren have been spared, and they would not have been burned in that great city Zarahemla.

24 And in another place they were heard to cry and mourn, saying, O that we had repented before this great and terrible day, and had not killed and stoned the prophets, and cast them out;

25 Then would our mothers, and our fair daughters, and our children have been spared, and not have been buried up in that great city Moronihah; and thus were the howlings of the people great and terrible.

26 ¶And it came to pass that there was a voice heard among all the inhabitants of the earth upon all the face of this land, crying, Wo, wo, wo unto this people; wo unto the inhabitants of the whole earth, except they shall repent,

27 For the devil laugheth, and his angels rejoice, because of the slain of the fair sons and daughters of my people; and it is because of their iniquity and abominations that they are fallen.

28 Behold, that great city Zarahemla have I burned with fire, and the inhabitants thereof.

29 And behold, that great city Moroni have I caused to be sunk in the depths of the sea, and the inhabitants thereof to be drowned.

30 And behold, that great city Moronihah have I covered with earth, and the inhabitants thereof, to hide their iniquities and their abominations from before my face, that the blood of the prophets and of the saints shall not come up any more unto me against them.

31 And behold, the city of Gilgal have I caused to be sunk, and the inhabitants thereof to be buried up in the depths of the earth;

32 Yea, and the city of Onihah, and the inhabitants thereof, and the city of Mocum, and the inhabitants thereof, and the

city of Jerusalem, and the inhabitants thereof, and waters have 1 caused to come up in the stead thereof,

33 To hide their wickedness and abominations from before my face, that the blood of the prophets and the saints shall not come up any more unto me against them.

34 And behold, the city of Gadiandi, and the city of Gadiomnah, and the city of Jacob, and the city Gimgimno, all these have I caused to be sunk, and made hills and valleys in the places thereof,

35 And the inhabitants thereof have I buried up in the depths of the earth, to hide their wickedness and abominations from before my face, that the blood of the prophets and the saints should not come up any more unto me against them.

36 And behold, that great city Jacobugath, which was inhabited by the people of the king of Jacob, have I caused to be burned with fire, because of their sins and their wickedness, which was above all the wickedness of the whole earth, because of their secret murders and combinations;

37 For it was they that did destroy the peace of my people and the government of the land: therefore I did cause them to be burned, to destroy them from before my face, that the blood of the prophets and the saints should not come up unto me any more against them.

38 And behold, the city of Laman, and the city of Josh, and the city of Gad, and the city of Kishkumen, have I caused to be burned with fire, and the inhabitants thereof, because of their wickedness in casting out the prophets, and stoning those whom I did send to declare unto them concerning their wickedness and their abominations;

39 And because they did cast them all out, that there were none righteous among them, I did send down fire and destroy them, that their wickedness and abominations might be hid from before my face, that the blood of the prophets and the saints whom I sent among them, might not cry unto me from the ground against them;

40 And many great destructions have I caused to come upon this land, and upon this people, because of their wickedness and their abominations.

41 ¶ O all ye that are spared, because ye were more righteous than they, will ye not now return unto me, and repent of your sins, and be converted, that I may heal you?

42 Yea, verily I say unto you, If ye will come unto me, ye shall have eternal life.

43 Behold, mine arm of mercy is extended towards you, and whosoever will come, him will I receive; and blessed are those who come unto me.

44 Behold I am Jesus Christ, the Son of God. I created the heavens and the earth, and all things that in them are.

45 I was with the Father from the beginning. I am in the Father, and the Father in me; and in me hath the Father glorified his name.

46 I came unto my own, and my own received me not. And the scriptures, concerning my coming, are fulfilled.

47 And as many as have received me, to them have I given to become the sons of God; and even so will I to as many as shall believe on my name, for behold, by me redemption cometh, and in me is the law of Moses fulfilled.

48 I am the light and the life of the world. I am Alpha and Omega, the beginning and the end.

49 And ye shall offer up unto me no more the shedding of blood; yea, your sacrifices and your burnt offerings shall be done away, for I will accept none of your sacrifices and your burnt offerings; and ye shall offer for a sacrifice unto me a broken heart and a contrite spirit.

50 And whoso cometh unto me with a broken heart and a contrite spirit, him will I baptize with fire and with the Holy Ghost, even as the Lamanites, because of their faith in me, at the time of their conversion, were baptized with fire and with the Holy Ghost, and they knew it not.

51 Behold, I have come unto the world to bring redemption unto the world, to save the world from sin: therefore whoso repenteth and cometh unto me as a little child, him will I receive; for of such is the kingdom of God.

52 Behold, for such I have laid down my life, and have taken it up again; therefore repent, and come unto me ye ends of the earth, and be saved.

53 ¶And now behold, it came to pass that all the people of the land did hear these sayings; and did witness of it.

54 And after these sayings there was silence in the land for the space of many hours; for so great was the astonishment of the people that they did cease lamenting and howling for the loss of their kindred which had been slain; therefore there was silence in all the land for the space of many hours.

55 ¶And it came to pass that there came a voice again unto the people, and all the people did hear, and did witness of it, saying, O ye people of these great cities which have fallen, who are descendants of Jacob; yea, who are of the house of Israel, O, ye people of the house of Israel, how oft have I gathered you as a hen gathereth her chickens under her wings, and have nourished you.

56 And again, how oft would I have gathered you, as a hen gathereth her chickens under her wings; yea, O ye people of the house of Israel, who have fallen;

57 Yea, O ye people of the house of Israel; ye that dwell at Jerusalem, as ye that have fallen; yea, how oft would I have gathered you as a hen gathereth her chickens, and ye would not.

58 O ye house of Israel, whom I have spared, how oft will I gather you as a hen gathereth her chickens under her wings, if ye will repent and return unto me with full purpose of heart.

59 But if not, O house of Israel, the places of your dwellings shall become desolate, until the time of the fulfilling of the covenant to your fathers.

60 ¶And now it came to pass that after the people had heard these words, behold they began to weep and howl again, because of the loss of their kindred and friends.

61 And it came to pass that thus did the three days pass away.

62 And it was in the morning, and the darkness dispersed from off the face of the land, and the earth did cease to tremble, and the rocks did cease to rend, and the dreadful groanings did cease, and all the tumultuous noises did pass away,

63 And the earth did cleave together again, that it stood, and the mourning and the weeping, and the wailing of the people who were spared alive, did cease;

64 And their mourning was turned into joy, and their lamentations into the praise and thanksgiving unto the Lord Jesus Christ, their Redeemer.

65 And thus far were the scriptures fulfilled, which had been spoken by the prophets.

66 And it was the more righteous part of the people who were saved, and it was they who received the prophets, and stoned them not; and it was they who had not shed the blood of the saints, who were spared;

67 And they were spared, and were not sunk and buried up in the earth; and they were not drowned in the depths of the sea; and they were not burned by fire, neither were they fallen upon and crushed to death;

68 And they were not carried away in the whirlwind; neither were they overpowered by the vapor of smoke and of darkness.

69 And now whoso readeth, let him understand; he that hath the scriptures, let him search them, and see and behold if all these deaths and destructions by fire, and by smoke, and by tempests, and by whirlwinds, and by the opening of the earth to receive them, and all these things, are not unto the fulfilling of the prophecies of many of the holy prophets.

70 Behold, I say unto you, Yea, many have testified of these things at the coming of Christ, and were slain because they testified of these things;

71 Yea, the prophet Zenos did testify of these things, and also Zenock spake concerning these things, because they testified particular concerning us, who are the remnant of their seed.

72 Behold our father Jacob also testified concerning a remnant of the seed of Joseph. And behold, are not we a remnant of the seed of Joseph?

73 And these things which testify of us, are they not written upon the plates of brass which our father Lehi brought out of Jerusalem?

74 And it came to pass that in the ending of the thirty and fourth year, behold I will shew unto you that the people of Nephi who were spared, and also those who had been called Lamanites, who had been spared, did have great favors shewn unto them, and great blessings poured out upon their heads, insomuch that soon after the ascension of Christ into heaven, he did truly manifest himself unto them, shewing his body unto them, and ministering unto them;

75 And an account of his ministry shall be given hereafter. Therefore for this time I make an end of my sayings.

CHAPTER 5.

Jesus Christ sheweth himself unto the people of Nephi, as the multitude were gathered together in the land Bountiful, and did minister unto them; and on this wise did he shew himself unto them.

1 ¶And now it came to pass that there were a great multitude gathered together, of the people of Nephi, round about the temple which was in the land Bountiful;

2 And they were marveling and wondering one with another, and were shewing one to another the great and marvelous change which had taken place;

3 And they were also conversing about this Jesus Christ, of whom the sign had been given, concerning his death.

4 ¶And it came to pass that while they were thus conversing one with another, they heard a voice, as if it came out of heaven; and they cast their eyes round about, for they understood not the voice which they heard;

5 And it was not a harsh voice, neither was it a loud voice, nevertheless, and notwithstanding it being a small voice, it did pierce them that did hear, to the center; insomuch that there was no part of their frame that it did not cause to quake; yea, it did pierce them to the very soul, and did cause their hearts to burn.

6 And it came to pass that again they heard the voice, and they understood it not; and again the third time they did hear the voice, and did open their ears to hear it;

7 And their eyes were towards the sound thereof; and they did look steadfastly towards heaven, from whence the sound came; and behold, the third time they did understand the voice which they heard;

8 And it said unto them, Behold, my beloved Son, in whom I am well pleased, in whom I have glorified my name, hear ye him.

9 ¶And it came to pass as they understood, they cast their eyes up again towards heaven; and behold, they saw a man descending out of heaven;

10 And he was clothed in a white robe, and he came down and stood in the midst of them, and the eyes of the whole multitude were turned upon him, and they durst not open their mouths, even one to another, and wist not what it meant, for they thought it was an angel that had appeared unto them.

11 ¶And it came to pass that he stretched forth his hand, and spake unto the people, saying, Behold I am Jesus Christ, of whom the prophets testified should come into the world:

12 And behold I am the light and the life of the world, and I have drunk out of that bitter cup which the Father hath given me, and have glorified the Father in taking upon me the sins of the world, in the which I have suffered the will of the Father in all things, from the beginning.

13 ¶And it came to pass that when Jesus had spoken these words, the whole multitude fell to the earth, for they remembered that it had been prophesied among them that Christ should shew himself unto them after his ascension into heaven.

14 ¶And it came to pass that the Lord spake unto them, saying, Arise and come forth unto me, that ye may thrust your hands into my side, and also that ye may feel the prints of the nails in my hands, and in my feet, that ye may know that I am the God of Israel, and the God of the whole earth, and have been slain for the sins of the world.

15 ¶And it came to pass that the multitude went forth, and thrust their hands into his side, and did feel the prints of the nails in his hands and in his feet;

16 And this they did do, going forth one by one, until they had all gone forth, and did see with their eyes, and did feel with their hands, and did know of a surety, and did bear record, that it was he, of whom it was written by the prophets, should come.

17 ¶And when they had all gone forth, and had witnessed for themselves, they did cry out with one accord, saying, Hosanna! Blessed be the name of the Most High God! And they did fall down at the feet of Jesus, and did worship him.

18 ¶And it came to pass that he spake unto Nephi, (for Nephi was among the multitude,) and he commanded him that he should come forth.

19 And Nephi arose and went forth, and bowed himself before the Lord, and he did kiss his feet.

20 And the Lord commanded him that he should arise. And he arose and stood before him.

21 And the Lord said unto him, I give unto you power that ye shall baptize this people, when I am again ascended into heaven.

22 And again the Lord called others, and said unto them likewise; and he gave unto them power to baptize.

23 And he said unto them, On this wise shall ye baptize; and there shall be no disputations among you.

24 Verily I say unto you, that whoso repenteth of his sins through your words, and desireth to be baptized in my name, on this wise shall ye baptize them: Behold, ye shall go down and stand in the water, and in my name shall ye baptize them.

25 And now behold, these are the words which ye shall say, calling them by name, saying: Having authority given me of Jesus Christ, I baptize you in the name of the Father, and of the Son, and of the Holy Ghost. Amen.

26 And then shall ye immerse them in the water, and come forth again out of the water.

27 And after this manner shall ye baptize in my name, for behold, verily I say unto you, that the Father, and the Son, and the Holy Ghost are one; and I am in the Father, and the Father in me, and the Father and I are one.

28 And according as I have commanded you, thus shall ye baptize.

29 And there shall be no disputations among you, as there hath hitherto been; neither shall there be disputations among you concerning the points of my doctrine, as there hath hitherto been;

30 For verily, verily I say unto you, He that hath the spirit of contention, is not of me, but is of the devil, who is the father of contention, and he stirreth up the hearts of men to contend with anger one with another;

31 Behold, this is not my doctrine, to stir up the hearts of men with anger one against another; but this is my doctrine, that such things should be done away.

32 Behold, verily, verily I say unto you, I will declare unto you my doctrine. And this is my doctrine, and it is the doctrine which the Father hath given unto me;

33 And I bear record of the Father, and the Father beareth record of me, and the Holy Ghost beareth record of the Father and me, and I bear record that the Father commandeth all men, everywhere, to repent and believe in me;

34 And whoso believeth in me, and is baptized, the same shall be saved; and they are they who shall inherit the kingdom of God.

35 And whoso believeth not in me, and is not baptized, shall be damned.

36 Verily, verily I say unto you, that this is my doctrine; and I bear record of it from the Father; and whoso believeth in me, believeth in the Father also;

37 And unto him will the Father bear record of me; for he will visit him with fire and with the Holy Ghost;

38 And thus will the Father bear record of me; and the Holy Ghost will bear record unto him of the Father and me; for the Father, and I, and the Holy Ghost, are one.

39 And again I say unto you, Ye must repent, and become as a little child, and be baptized in my name, or ye can in no wise receive these things.

40 And again I say unto you, Ye must repent, and be bap-

tized in my name, and become as a little child, or ye can in nowise inherit the kingdom of God.

41 Verily, verily I say unto you, that this is my doctrine; and whoso buildeth upon this, buildeth upon my rock; and the gates of hell shall not prevail against them.

42 And whoso shall declare more or less than this, and establish it for my doctrine, the same cometh of evil, and is not built upon my rock, but he buildeth upon a sandy foundation, and the gates of hell standeth open to receive such, when the floods come, and the winds beat upon them.

43 Therefore go forth unto this people, and declare the words which I have spoken, unto the ends of the earth.

44 And it came to pass that when Jesus had spoken these words unto Nephi, and to those who had been called, (now the number of them who had been called and received power and authority to baptize, were twelve,)

45 And behold he stretched forth his hand unto the multitude, and cried unto them, saying, Blessed are ye if ye shall give heed unto the words of these twelve whom I have chosen from among you to minister unto you, and to be your servants;

46 And unto them I have given power, that they may baptize you with water, and after that ye are baptized with water, behold I will baptize you with fire and with the Holy Ghost;

47 Therefore blessed are ye, if ye shall believe in me, and be baptized, after that ye have seen me, and know that I am.

48 And again, more blessed are they who shall believe in your words, because that ye shall testify that ye have seen me, and that ye know that I am.

49 Yea, blessed are they who shall believe in your words, and come down into the depths of humility, and be baptized; for they shall be visited with fire and with the Holy Ghost, and shall receive a remission of their sins.

50 Yea, blessed are the poor in spirit who come unto me, for theirs is the kingdom of heaven.

51 And again, blessed are all they that mourn, for they shall be comforted;

52 And blessed are the meek, for they shall inherit the earth.

53 And blessed are all they who do hunger and thirst after righteousness, for they shall be filled with the Holy Ghost.

54 And blessed are the merciful, for they shall obtain mercy.

55 And blessed are all the pure in heart, for they shall see God.

56 And blessed are all the peacemakers, for they shall be called the children of God.

57 And blessed are all they who are persecuted for my name's sake, for theirs is the kingdom of heaven.

58 And blessed are ye when men shall revile you, and persecute, and shall say all manner of evil against you falsely, for my sake,

59 For ye shall have great joy and be exceeding glad, for great shall be your reward in heaven; for so persecuted they the prophets who were before you.

60 Verily, verily I say unto you, I give unto you to be the salt of the earth; but if the salt shall lose its savor, wherewith shall the earth be salted? The salt shall be thenceforth good for nothing, but to be cast out, and to be trodden under foot of men.

61 Verily, verily I say unto you, I give unto you to be the light of this people. A city that is set on a hill can not be hid.

62 Behold, do men light a candle and put it under a bushel? Nay, but on a candlestick, and it giveth light to all that are in the house;

63 Therefore let your light so shine before this people, that they may see your good works and glorify your Father who is in heaven.

64 Think not that I am come to destroy the law or the prophets. I am not come to destroy but to fulfill;

65 For verily I say unto you, One jot nor one tittle hath not passed away from the law, but in me it hath all been fulfilled.

66 ¶And behold I have given you the law and the commandments of my Father, that ye shall believe in me, and that ye

shall repent of your sins, and come unto me with a broken heart and a contrite spirit.

67 Behold, ye have the commandments before you, and the law is fulfilled; therefore come unto me and be ye saved;

68 For verily I say unto you, that except ye shall keep my commandments, which I have commanded you at this time, ye shall in no case enter into the kingdom of heaven.

69 Ye have heard that it hath been said by them of old time, and it is also written before you, that thou shalt not kill; and whosoever shall kill shall be in danger of the judgment of God.

70 But I say unto you, that whosoever is angry with his brother, shall be in danger of his judgment. And whosoever shall say to his brother, Raca, shall be in danger of the council; and whosoever shall say, Thou fool, shall be in danger of hell fire;

71 Therefore, if ye shall come unto me, or shall desire to come unto me, and rememberest that thy brother hath aught against thee,

72 Go thy way unto thy brother, and first be reconciled to thy brother, and then come unto me with full purpose of heart, and I will receive you.

73 Agree with thine adversary quickly, while thou art in the way with him, lest at any time he shall get thee, and thou shalt be cast into prison.

74 Verily, verily I say unto thee, Thou shalt by no means come out thence, until thou hast paid the uttermost senine.

75 And while ye are in prison, can ye pay even one senine? Verily, verily I say unto you, Nay.

76 Behold, it is written by them of old time, that thou shalt not commit adultery;

77 But I say unto you, that whosoever looketh on a woman to lust after her, hath committed adultery already in his heart.

78 Behold, I give you a commandment, that ye suffer none of these things to enter into your heart; for it is better that ye should deny yourselves of these things, wherein ye will take up your cross, than that ye should be cast into hell.

79 It hath been written, that whosoever shall put away his wife, let him give her a writing of divorcement.

80 Verily, verily I say unto you, that whosoever shall put away his wife, saving for the cause of fornication, causeth her to commit adultery; and whoso shall marry her who is divorced, committeth adultery.

81 And again it is written, Thou shalt not forswear thyself, but shalt perform unto the Lord thine oaths.

82 But verily, verily I say unto you, Swear not at all; neither by heaven, for it is God's throne; nor by the earth, for it is his footstool; neither shalt thou swear by thy head, because thou canst not make one hair black or white;

83 But let your communication be, Yea, yea; Nay, nay; for whatsoever cometh of more than these are evil.

84 And behold, it is written, An eye for an eye, and a tooth for a tooth.

85 But I say unto you, that ye shall not resist evil, but whosoever shall smite thee on thy right cheek, turn to him the other also.

86 And if any man will sue thee at the law, and take away thy coat, let him have thy cloak also.

87 And whosoever shall compel thee to go a mile, go with him twain.

88 Give to him that asketh thee, and to him that would borrow of thee, turn thou not away.

89 And behold, it is written also, that thou shalt love thy neighbor, and hate thine enemy;

90 But behold I say unto you, Love your enemies, bless them that curse you, do good to them that hate you, and pray for them who despitefully use you and persecute you,

91 That ye may be the children of your Father who is in heaven; for he maketh his sun to rise on the evil and on the good; therefore those things which were of old time, which were under the law, in me are all fulfilled.

92 Old things are done away, and all things have become new; therefore I would that ye should be perfect even as I, or your Father who is in heaven is perfect.

93 Verily, verily, I say that I would that ye should do alms

unto the poor; but take heed that ye do not your alms before men to be seen of them; otherwise ye have no reward of your Father who is in heaven.

94 Therefore when ye shall do your alms, do not sound a trumpet before you, as will hypocrites do in the synagogues, and in the streets, that they may have glory of men. Verily, I say unto you, They have their reward.

95 But when thou doest alms, let not thy left hand know what thy right hand doeth;

96 That thine alms may be in secret; and thy Father who seeth in secret, himself shall reward thee openly.

97 ¶And when thou prayest, thou shalt not do as the hypocrites, for they love to pray standing in the synagogues, and in the corners of the streets, that they may be seen of men. Verily, I say unto you, They have their reward.

98 But thou, when thou prayest, enter into thy closet, and when thou hast shut thy door, pray to thy Father who is in secret; and thy Father, who seeth in secret, shall reward thee openly.

99 But when ye pray, use not vain repetitions, as the heathen, for they think that they shall be heard for their much speaking.

100 Be not ye therefore like unto them, for your Father knoweth what things ye have need of before ye ask him.

101 After this manner therefore pray ye,

102 Our Father who art in heaven, hallowed be thy name.

103 Thy will be done on earth as it is in heaven.

104 And forgive us our debts, as we forgive our debtors.

105 And lead us not into temptation, but deliver us from evil.

106 For thine is the kingdom, and the power, and the glory, for ever. Amen.

107 For, if ye forgive men their trespasses, your heavenly Father will also forgive you; but if ye forgive not men their trespasses, neither will your Father forgive your trespasses.

108 Moreover, when ye fast, be not as the hypocrites, of a sad countenance, for they disfigure their faces, that they may

appear unto men to fast. Verily, I say unto you, They have their reward.

109 But thou, when thou fastest, anoint thy head and wash thy face; that thou appear not unto men to fast, but unto thy Father, who is in secret; and thy Father who seeth in secret, shall reward thee openly.

110 ¶Lay not up for yourselves treasures upon earth, where moth and rust doth corrupt, and thieves break through and steal,

111 But lay up for yourselves treasures in heaven, where neither moth nor rust doth corrupt, and where thieves do not break through nor steal.

112 For where your treasure is, there will your heart be also.

113 The light of the body is the eye, if therefore thine eye be single, thy whole body shall be full of light.

114 But if thine eye be evil, thy whole body shall be full of darkness. If therefore the light that is in thee be darkness, how great is that darkness!

115 No man can serve two masters, for either he will hate the one, and love the other: or else he will hold to the one, and despise the other. Ye can not serve God and Mammon.

CHAPTER 6.

1 ¶And now it came to pass that when Jesus had spoken these words, he looked upon the twelve whom he had chosen, and said unto them, Remember the words which I have spoken.

2 For behold, ye are they whom I have chosen to minister unto this people.

3 Therefore I say unto you, Take no thought for your life, what ye shall eat, or what ye shall drink; nor yet for your body, what ye shall put on. Is not the life more than meat, and the body than raiment?

4 Behold the fowls of the air, for they sow not, neither do they reap, nor gather into barns; yet your heavenly Father feedeth them. Are ye not much better than they?

5 Which of you by taking thought can add one cubit unto his stature?

6 And why take ye thought for raiment? Consider the lilies of the field how they grow; they toil not, neither do they spin;

7 And yet I say unto you, that even Solomon, in all his glory, was not arrayed like one of these.

8 Wherefore, if God so clothe the grass of the field, which to-day is, and to-morrow is cast into the oven, even so will he clothe you, if ye are not of little faith.

9 Therefore take no thought, saying, What shall we eat? or, What shall we drink? or, Wherewithal shall we be clothed?

10 For your heavenly Father knoweth that ye have need of all these things.

11 But seek ye first the kingdom of God, and his righteousness, and all these things shall be added unto you.

12 Take therefore no thought for the morrow, for the morrow shall take thought for the things of itself. Sufficient is the day unto the evil thereof.

13 ¶And now it came to pass that when Jesus had spoken these words, he turned again to the multitude, and did open his mouth unto them again, saying, Verily, verily, I say unto you, Judge not, that ye be not judged.

14 For with what judgment ye judge, ye shall be judged; and with what measure ye mete, it shall be measured to you again.

15 And why beholdest thou the mote that is in thy brother's eye, but considerest not the beam that is in thine own eye?

16 Or how wilt thou say to thy brother, Let me pull the mote out of thine eye; and behold, a beam is in thine own eye?

17 Thou hypocrite, first cast the beam out of thine own eye: and then shalt thou see clearly to cast the mote out of thy brother's eye.

18 Give not that which is holy unto the dogs, neither cast ye your pearls before swine, lest they trample them under their feet, and turn again and rend you.

19 ¶Ask, and it shall be given unto you; seek, and ye shall find; knock, and it shall be opened unto you,

20 For every one that asketh, receiveth; and he that seeketh, findeth; and to him that knocketh, it shall be opened.

21 Or what man is there of you, whom, if his son ask bread, will he give him a stone?

22 Or if he ask a fish, will he give him a serpent?

23 If ye then being evil know how to give good gifts unto your children, how much more shall your Father who is in heaven give good things to them that ask him?

24 Therefore all things whatsoever ye would that men should do to you, do ye even so to them, for this is the law and the prophets.

25 ¶Enter ye in at the straight gate; for wide is the gate, and broad is the way, that leadeth to destruction, and many there be who go in thereat:

26 Because straight is the gate, and narrow is the way, which leadeth unto life, and few there be that find it.

27 Beware of false prophets, who come to you in sheep's clothing, but inwardly they are ravening wolves.

28 Ye shall know them by their fruits. Do men gather grapes of thorns, or figs of thistles?

29 Even so every good tree bringeth forth good fruit; but a corrupt tree bringeth forth evil fruit.

30 A good tree can not bring forth evil fruit, neither a corrupt tree bring forth good fruit.

31 Every tree that bringeth not forth good fruit, is hewn down, and cast into the fire.

32 Wherefore, by their fruits ye shall know them.

33 ¶Not every one that saith unto me, Lord, Lord, shall enter into the kingdom of heaven; but he that doeth the will of my Father who is in heaven.

34 Many will say to me in that day, Lord, Lord, have we not prophesied in thy name? and in thy name have cast out devils? and in thy name done many wonderful works?

35 And then will I profess unto them, I never knew you, depart from me, ye that work iniquity.

36 ¶Therefore, whoso heareth these sayings of mine, and

doeth them, I will liken him unto a wise man, who built his house upon a rock, and the rain descended, and the floods came, and the winds blew, and beat upon that house; and it fell not; for it was founded upon a rock.

37 And every one that heareth these sayings of mine, and doeth them not, shall be likened unto a foolish man, who built his house upon the sand, and the rain descended, and the floods came, and the winds blew, and beat upon that house; and it fell, and great was the fall of it.

CHAPTER 7.

1 ¶And now it came to pass that when Jesus had ended these sayings, he cast his eyes round about on the multitude, and said unto them, Behold, ye have heard the things which I have taught before I ascended to my Father;

2 Therefore whoso remembereth these sayings of mine, and doeth them, him will I raise up at the last day.

3 And it came to pass that when Jesus had said these words, he perceived that there were some among them who marveled, and wondered what he would concerning the law of Moses; for they understood not the saying, that old things had passed away, and that all things had become new.

4 And he said unto them, Marvel not that I said unto you, that old things had passed away, and that all things had become new.

5 Behold I say unto you, that the law is fulfilled that was given unto Moses.

6 Behold, I am he that gave the law, and I am he who covenanted with my people Israel; therefore, the law in me is fulfilled, for I have come to fulfill the law; therefore, it hath an end.

7 Behold, I do not destroy the prophets, for as many as have not been fulfilled in me, verily, I say unto you, shall all be fulfilled.

8 And because I said unto you, that old things hath passed away, I do not destroy that which hath been spoken concerning things which are to come.

9 For behold, the covenant which I have made with my people, is not all fulfilled; but the law which was given unto Moses, hath an end in me.

10 Behold, I am the law, and the light; look unto me, and endure to the end, and ye shall live, for unto him that endureth to the end will I give eternal life.

11 Behold, I have given unto you the commandments; therefore keep my commandments.

12 And this is the law and the prophets, for they truly testified of me.

13 ¶And now it came to pass that when Jesus had spoken these words, he said unto those twelve whom he had chosen, Ye are my disciples; and ye are a light unto this people, who are a remnant of the house of Joseph.

14 And behold, this is the land of your inheritance; and the Father hath given it unto you.

15 And not at any time hath the Father given me commandment that I should tell it unto your brethren at Jerusalem; neither at any time hath the Father given me commandment, that I should tell unto them concerning the other tribes of the house of Israel, whom the Father hath led away out of the land.

16 This much did the Father command me, that I should tell unto them, that other sheep I have, which are not of this fold; them also I must bring, and they shall hear my voice; and there shall be one fold, and one shepherd.

17 And now because of stiff-neckedness and unbelief, they understood not my word; therefore I was commanded to say no more of the Father concerning this thing unto them.

18 But, verily, I say unto you, that the Father hath commanded me, and I tell it unto you, that ye were separated from among them because of their iniquity; therefore it is because of their iniquity, that they know not of you.

19 And verily, I say unto you again, that the other tribes hath the Father separated from them; and it is because of their iniquity, that they know not of them.

20 And verily, I say unto you, that ye are they of whom I said, Other sheep I have which are not of this fold; them also

I must bring, and they shall hear my voice, and there shall be one fold, and one shepherd.

21 And they understood me not, for they supposed it had been the Gentiles; for they understood not that the Gentiles should be converted through their preaching;

22 And they understood me not that I said they shall hear my voice; and they understood me not that the Gentiles should not at any time hear my voice; that I should not manifest myself unto them, save it were by the Holy Ghost.

23 But behold, ye have both heard my voice, and seen me, and ye are my sheep, and ye are numbered among those whom the Father hath given me.

24 And verily, verily, I say unto you, that I have other sheep, which are not of this land; neither of the land of Jerusalem; neither in any parts of that land round about, whither I have been to minister.

25 For they of whom I speak, are they who have not as yet heard my voice; neither have I at any time manifested myself unto them.

26 But I have received a commandment of the Father, that I shall go unto them, and that they shall hear my voice, and shall be numbered among my sheep, that there may be one fold, and one shepherd; therefore I go to shew myself unto them.

27 And I command you that ye shall write these sayings, after I am gone, that if it so be that my people at Jerusalem, they who have seen me, and been with me in my ministry, do not ask the Father in my name, that they may receive a knowledge of you by the Holy Ghost, and also of the other tribes whom they know not of,

28 That these sayings which ye shall write, shall be kept, and shall be manifested unto the Gentiles, that through the fullness of the Gentiles, the remnant of their seed who shall be scattered forth upon the face of the earth, because of their unbelief, may be brought in, or may be brought to a knowledge of me, their Redeemer.

29 And then will I gather them in from the four quarters of the earth; and then will I fulfill the covenant which the

Father hath made unto all the people of the house of Israel.

30 And blessed are the Gentiles, because of their belief in me, in and of the Holy Ghost, which witness unto them of me and of the Father.

31 Behold, because of their belief in me, saith the Father, and because of the unbelief of you, O house of Israel, in the latter day shall the truth come unto the Gentiles, that the fullness of these things shall be made known unto them.

32 But wo, saith the Father, unto the unbelieving of the Gentiles, for notwithstanding they have come forth upon the face of this land, and have scattered my people, who are of the house of Israel; and my people who are of the house of Israel, have been cast out from among them, and have been trodden under feet by them;

33 And because of the mercies of the Father unto the Gentiles, and also the judgments of the Father upon my people, who are of the house of Israel, verily, verily, I say unto you, that after all this, and I have caused my people who are of the house of Israel, to be smitten, and to be afflicted, and to be slain, and to be cast out from among them, and to become hated by them, and to become a hiss and a byword among them.

34 And thus commandeth the Father that I should say unto you, At that day when the Gentiles shall sin against my gospel, and shall reject the fullness of my gospel, and shall be lifted up in the pride of their hearts above all nations, and above all the people of the whole earth, and shall be filled with all manner of lyings, and of deceits, and of mischiefs, and all manner of hypocrisy, and murders, and priestcrafts, and whoredoms, and of secret abominations;

35 And if they shall do all these things, and shall reject the fullness of my gospel, behold, saith the Father, I will bring the fullness of my gospel from among them;

36 And then will I remember my covenant which I have made unto my people, O house of Israel, and I will bring my gospel unto them;

37 And I will shew unto thee, O house of Israel, that the Gentiles shall not have power over you, but I will remember

my covenant unto you, O house of Israel, and ye shall come unto the knowledge of the fullness of my gospel.

38 But if the Gentiles will repent, and return unto me, saith the Father, behold, they shall be numbered among my people, O house of Israel;

39 And I will not suffer my people, who are of the house of Israel, to go through among them, and tread them down, saith the Father.

40 But if they will not turn unto me, and hearken unto my voice, I will suffer them, yea, I will suffer my people, O house of Israel, that they shall go through among them, and shall tread them down,

41 And they shall be as salt that hath lost its savor, which is thenceforth good for nothing, but to be cast out, and to be trodden under foot of my people, O house of Israel.

42 Verily, verily, I say unto you, Thus hath the Father commanded me, that I should give unto this people this land for their inheritance.

43 And when the words of the prophet Isaiah shall be fulfilled, which say, Thy watchmen shall lift up the voice; with the voice together shall they sing, for they shall see eye to eye, when the Lord shall bring again Zion.

44 Break forth into joy, sing together, ye waste places of Jerusalem, for the Lord hath comforted his people, he hath redeemed Jerusalem.

45 The Lord hath made bare his holy arm in the eyes of all the nations; and all the ends of the earth shall see the salvation of God.

CHAPTER 8.

1 ¶Behold, now it came to pass that when Jesus had spoken these words, he looked round about again on the multitude, and he said unto them, Behold, my time is at hand.

2 I perceive that ye are weak, that ye can not understand all my words which I am commanded of the Father to speak unto you at this time;

3 Therefore, go ye unto your homes, and ponder upon the

things which I have said, and ask of the Father, in my name, that ye may understand; and prepare your minds for the morrow, and I come unto you again.

4 But now I go unto the Father, and also to shew myself unto the lost tribes of Israel, for they are not lost unto the Father, for he knoweth whither he hath taken them.

5 ¶And it came to pass that when Jesus had thus spoken, he cast his eyes round about again on the multitude, and beheld they were in tears, and did look steadfastly upon him, as if they would ask him to tarry a little longer with them.

6 And he said unto them, Behold, my bowels are filled with compassion towards you: Have ye any that are sick among you, bring them hither.

7 Have ye any that are lame, or blind, or halt, or maimed, or leprous, or that are withered, or that are deaf, or that are afflicted in any manner, bring them hither, and I will heal them, for I have compassion upon you;

8 My bowels are filled with mercy; for I perceive that ye desire that I should shew unto you what I have done unto your brethren at Jerusalem, for I see that your faith is sufficient, that I should heal you.

9 ¶And it came to pass that when he had thus spoken, all the multitude, with one accord, did go forth, with their sick, and their afflicted, and their lame, and with their blind, and with their dumb, and with all they that were afflicted in any manner; and he did heal them every one as they were brought forth unto him;

10 And they did all, both they who had been healed, and they who were whole, bow down at his feet, and did worship him;

11 And as many as could come, for the multitude, did kiss his feet, insomuch that they did bathe his feet with their tears.

12 ¶And it came to pass that he commanded that their little children should be brought.

13 So they brought their little children and sat them down upon the ground round about him, and Jesus stood in the

midst; and the multitude gave way till they had all been brought unto him.

14 And it came to pass that when they had all been brought, and Jesus stood in the midst, he commanded the multitude that they should kneel down upon the ground.

15 And it came to pass that when they had knelt upon the ground, Jesus groaned within himself, and saith, Father, I am troubled because of the wickedness of the people of the house of Israel.

16 And when he had said these words, he himself also knelt upon the earth, and behold he prayed unto the Father, and the things which he prayed, can not be written, and the multitude did bear record who heard him.

17 And after this manner do they bear record; the eye hath never seen, neither hath the ear heard, before, so great and marvelous things as we saw and heard Jesus speak unto the Father;

18 And no tongue can speak, neither can there be written by any man, neither can the hearts of men conceive so great and marvelous things as we both saw and heard Jesus speak;

19 And no one can conceive of the joy which filled our souls at the time we heard him pray for us unto the Father.

20 ¶And it came to pass that when Jesus had made an end of praying unto the Father, he arose; but so great was the joy of the multitude, that they were overcome.

21 And it came to pass that Jesus spake unto them, and bade them arise.

22 And they arose from the earth, and he said unto them, Blessed are ye because of your faith. And now behold my joy is full.

23 And when he had said these words, he wept, and the multitude bear record of it, and he took their little children, one by one, and blessed them, and prayed unto the Father for them.

24 And when he had done this he wept again, and he spake unto the multitude, and saith unto them, Behold your little ones.

25 And as they looked to behold, they cast their eyes to-

wards heaven, and they saw the heavens open, and they saw angels descending out of heaven as it were, in the midst of fire; and they came down and encircled those little ones about;

26 And they were encircled about with fire; and the angels did minister unto them, and the multitude did see and hear, and bear record; and they know that their record is true, for they all of them did see and hear, every man for himself;

27 And they were in number about two thousand and five hundred souls; and they did consist of men, women and children.

28 ¶And it came to pass that Jesus commanded his disciples that they should bring forth some bread and wine unto him.

29 And while they were gone for bread and wine, he commanded the multitude that they should sit themselves down upon the earth.

30 And when the disciples had come with bread and wine, he took of the bread, and break and blessed it; and he gave unto the disciples, and commanded that they should eat.

31 And when they had eat, and were filled, he commanded that they should give unto the multitude.

32 And when the multitude had eaten and were filled, he said unto the disciples, Behold, there shall one be ordained among you, and to him will I give power that he shall break bread, and bless it, and give it unto the people of my church, unto all those who shall believe and be baptized in my name.

33 And this shall ye always observe to do, even as I have done, even as I have broken bread, and blessed it, and gave it unto you.

34 And this shall ye do in remembrance of my body, which I have shewn unto you.

35 And it shall be a testimony unto the Father, that ye do always remember me.

36 And if ye do always remember me, ye shall have my Spirit to be with you.

37 ¶And it came to pass that when he had said these words, he commanded his disciples that they should take of the wine

of the cup, and drink of it, and that they should also give unto the multitude, that they might drink of it.

38 And it came to pass that they did so, and did drink of it, and were filled; and they gave unto the multitude, and they did drink, and they were filled.

39 And when the disciples had done this, Jesus said unto them, Blessed are ye for this thing which ye have done, for this is fulfilling my commandments, and this doth witness unto the Father that ye are willing to do that which I have commanded you.

40 And this shall ye always do unto those who repent and are baptized in my name; and ye shall do it in remembrance of my blood, which I have shed for you, that ye may witness unto the Father that ye do always remember me.

41 And if ye do always remember me, ye shall have my Spirit to be with you.

42 And I give unto you a commandment that ye shall do these things.

43 And if ye shall always do these things, blessed are ye, for ye are built upon my rock.

44 But whoso among you shall do more or less than these, are not built upon my rock, but are built upon a sandy foundation;

45 And when the rain descends, and the floods come, and the winds blow, and beat upon them, they shall fall, and the gates of hell are already open to receive them:

46 Therefore blessed are ye if ye shall keep my commandments, which the Father hath commanded me that I should give unto you.

47 Verily, verily, I say unto you, Ye must watch and pray always, lest ye be tempted by the devil, and ye are led away captive by him.

48 And as I have prayed among you, even so shall ye pray in my church, among my people who do repent and are baptized in my name.

49 Behold I am the light; I have set an example for you.

50 ¶And it came to pass that when Jesus had spoken these words unto his disciples, he turned again unto the multitude,

and said unto them, Behold, verily, verily I say unto you, Ye must watch and pray always, lest ye enter into temptation;

51 For Satan desireth to have you, that he may sift you as wheat; therefore ye must always pray unto the Father in my name; and whatsoever ye shall ask the Father in my name, which is right, believing that ye shall receive, behold it shall be given unto you.

52 Pray in your families unto the Father, always in my name, that your wives and your children may be blessed.

53 And behold, ye shall meet together oft, and ye shall not forbid any man from coming unto you when ye shall meet together, but suffer them that they may come unto you, and forbid them not;

54 But ye shall pray for them, and shall not cast them out; and if it so be that they come unto you oft, ye shall pray for them unto the Father, in my name; therefore hold up your light that it may shine unto the world.

55 Behold I am the light which ye shall hold up—that which ye have seen me do.

56 Behold ye see that I have prayed unto the Father, and ye all have witnessed; and ye see that I have commanded that none of you should go away, but rather have commanded that ye should come unto me, that ye might feel and see;

57 Even so shall ye do unto the world; and whosoever breaketh this commandment, suffereth himself to be led into temptation.

58 ¶And now it came to pass that when Jesus had spoken these words, he turned his eyes again upon the disciples whom he had chosen, and said unto them,

59 Behold, verily, verily I say unto you, I give unto you another commandment, and then I must go unto my Father, that I may fulfill other commandments which he hath given me.

60 And now behold, this is the commandment which I give unto you, that ye shall not suffer any one knowingly, to partake of my flesh and blood unworthily, when ye shall minister it, for whoso eateth and drinketh my flesh and blood unworthily, eateth and drinketh damnation to his soul;

61 Therefore if ye know that a man is unworthy to eat and drink of my flesh and blood, ye shall forbid him; nevertheless ye shall not cast him out from among you, but ye shall minister unto him, and shall pray for him unto the Father, in my name,

62 And if it so be that he repenteth, and is baptized in my name, then shall ye receive him, and shall minister unto him of my flesh and blood;

63 But if he repent not, he shall not be numbered among my people, that he may not destroy my people, for behold I know my sheep, and they are numbered;

64 Nevertheless ye shall not cast him out of your synagogues, or your places of worship, for unto such shall ye continue to minister;

65 For ye know not but what they will return and repent, and come unto me with full purpose of heart, and I shall heal them, and ye shall be the means of bringing salvation unto them.

66 Therefore keep these sayings which I have commanded you, that ye come not under condemnation, for wo unto him whom the Father condemneth.

67 And I give you these commandments, because of the disputations which have been among you.

68 And blessed are ye if ye have no disputations among you.

69 And now I go unto the Father, because it is expedient that I should go unto the Father, for your sakes.

70 ¶And it came to pass that when Jesus had made an end of these sayings, he touched with his hand the disciples whom he had chosen, one by one, even until he had touched them all, and spake unto them as he touched them;

71 And the multitude heard not the words which he spake, therefore they did not bear record; but the disciples bear record that he gave them power to give the Holy Ghost.

72 And I will shew unto you hereafter that this record is true.

73 ¶And it came to pass that when Jesus had touched them

all, there came a cloud and overshadowed the multitude, that they could not see Jesus.

74 And while they were overshadowed, he departed from them, and ascended into heaven.

75 And the disciples saw and did bear record that he ascended again into heaven.

CHAPTER 9.

1 ¶And now it came to pass that when Jesus had ascended into heaven, the multitude did disperse, and every man did take his wife and his children, and did return to his own home.

2 And it was noised abroad among the people immediately, before it was yet dark, that the multitude had seen Jesus, and that he had ministered unto them, and that he would also shew himself on the morrow unto the multitude;

3 Yea, and even all the night it was noised abroad concerning Jesus; and insomuch did they send forth unto the people, that there were many, yea, an exceeding great number did labor exceedingly all that night, that they might be on the morrow in the place where Jesus should shew himself unto the multitude.

4 ¶And it came to pass that on the morrow, when the multitude was gathered together, behold Nephi and his brother whom he had raised from the dead, whose name was Timothy, and also his son, whose name was Jonas, and also Mathoni, and Mathonihah, his brother, and Kumen, and Kumenonhi, and Jeremiah, and Shemnon, and Jonas, and Zedekiah, and Isaiah: now these were the names of the disciples whom Jesus had chosen.

5 And it came to pass that they went forth and stood in the midst of the multitude.

6 And behold, the multitude was so great, that they did cause that they should be separated into twelve bodies.

7 And the twelve did teach the multitude, and behold, they did cause that the multitude should kneel down upon the face of the earth, and should pray unto the Father, in the name of Jesus.

8 And the disciples did pray unto the Father also, in the name of Jesus.

9 And it came to pass that they arose and ministered unto the people.

10 And when they had ministered those same words which Jesus had spoken—nothing varying from the words which Jesus had spoken—behold, they knelt again, and prayed to the Father in the name of Jesus, and they did pray for that which they most desired; and they desired that the Holy Ghost should be given unto them.

11 And when they had thus prayed, they went down unto the water's edge, and the multitude followed them.

12 And it came to pass that Nephi went down into the water, and was baptized.

13 And he came up out of the water, and began to baptize. And he baptized all those whom Jesus had chosen.

14 And it came to pass when they were all baptized, and had come up out of the water, the Holy Ghost did fall upon them, and they were filled with the Holy Ghost, and with fire.

15 And behold, they were encircled about as if it were fire; and it came down from heaven, and the multitude did witness it, and do bear record; and angels did come down out of heaven, and did minister unto them.

16 And it came to pass that while the angels were ministering unto the disciples, behold, Jesus came and stood in the midst, and ministered unto them.

17 And it came to pass that he spake unto the multitude, and commanded them that they should kneel down again upon the earth, and also that his disciples should kneel down upon the earth.

18 And it came to pass that when they had all knelt down upon the earth, he commanded his disciples that they should pray.

19 And behold they began to pray; and they did pray unto Jesus, calling him their Lord and their God.

20 ¶And it came to pass that Jesus departed out of the midst of them, and went a little way off from them and bowed himself to the earth, and he said, Father, I thank thee that

thou hast given the Holy Ghost unto these whom I have chosen; and it is because of their belief in me, that I have chosen them out of the world.

21 Father, I pray thee that thou wilt give the Holy Ghost unto all them that shall believe in their words.

22 Father, thou hast given them the Holy Ghost, because they believe in me, and thou seest that they believe in me, because thou hearest them, and they pray unto me; and they pray unto me because I am with them.

23 And now Father, I pray unto thee for them, and also for all those who shall believe on their words, that they may believe in me, that I may be in them as thou, Father, art in me, that we may be one.

24 ¶And it came to pass, that when Jesus had thus prayed unto the Father, he came unto his disciples, and behold, they did still continue, without ceasing, to pray unto him; and they did not multiply many words, for it was given unto them what they should pray, and they were filled with desire.

25 And it came to pass that Jesus beheld them, as they did pray unto him, and his countenance did smile upon them, and the light of his countenance did shine upon them, and behold they were as white as the countenance, and also the garments of Jesus;

26 And behold the whiteness thereof did exceed all the whiteness, yea, even there could be nothing upon earth so white as the whiteness thereof.

27 And Jesus said unto them, Pray on; nevertheless they did not cease to pray.

28 And he turned from them again, and went a little way off, and bowed himself to the earth; and he prayed again unto the Father, saying, Father, I thank thee that thou hast purified these whom I have chosen, because of their faith,

29 And I pray for them, and also for them who shall believe on their words, that they may be purified in me, through faith on their words, even as they are purified in me.

30 Father I pray not for the world, but for those whom thou hast given me out of the world, because of their faith, that they may be purified in me, that I may be in them as

thou, Father, art in me, that we may be one, that I may be glorified in them.

31 ¶And when Jesus had spoken these words, he came again unto his disciples, and behold they did pray steadfastly, without ceasing, unto him; and he did smile upon them again; and behold they were white, even as Jesus.

32 ¶And it came to pass that he went again a little way off, and prayed unto the Father: and tongue can not speak the words which he prayed, neither can be written by man the words which he prayed.

33 And the multitude did hear, and do bear record, and their hearts were open, and they did understand in their hearts the words which he prayed.

34 Nevertheless, so great and marvelous were the words which he prayed, that they can not be written, neither can they be uttered by man.

35 ¶And it came to pass that when Jesus had made an end of praying, he came again to the disciples, and said unto them, So great faith have I never seen among all the Jews; wherefore I could not shew unto them so great miracles, because of their unbelief.

36 Verily I say unto you, There are none of them that have seen so great things as ye have seen; neither have they heard so great things as ye have heard.

37 ¶And it came to pass that he commanded the multitude that they should cease to pray, and also his disciples.

38 And he commanded them that they should not cease to pray in their hearts.

39 And he commanded them that they should arise and stand upon their feet. And they arose up and stood upon their feet.

40 And it came to pass that he break bread again, and blessed it, and gave to the disciples to eat.

41 And when they had eaten he commanded them that they should break bread, and give it unto the multitude.

42 And when they had given unto the multitude, he also gave them wine to drink, and commanded them that they should give unto the multitude.

43 Now there had been no bread, neither wine, brought by the disciples, neither by the multitude; but he truly gave unto them bread to eat, and also wine to drink;

44 And he said unto them, He that eateth this bread, eateth of my body to his soul, and he that drinketh of this wine, drinketh of my blood to his soul, and his soul shall never hunger nor thirst, but shall be filled.

45 Now when the multitude had all eaten and drunk, behold they were filled with the Spirit, and they did cry out with one voice, and gave glory to Jesus, whom they both saw and heard.

46 And it came to pass that when they had all given glory unto Jesus, he said unto them, Behold now I finish the commandment which the Father hath commanded me concerning this people who are a remnant of the house of Israel.

47 Ye remember that I spake unto you, and said that when the words of Isaiah should be fulfilled, behold they are written, ye have them before you; therefore search them.

48 And verily, verily I say unto you, that when they shall be fulfilled, then is the fulfilling of the covenant which the Father hath made unto his people.

49 O house of Israel, and then shall the remnants which shall be scattered abroad upon the face of the earth, be gathered in from the east, and from the west, and from the south, and from the north; and they shall be brought to the knowledge of the Lord their God, who hath redeemed them.

50 And the Father hath commanded me that I should give unto you this land, for your inheritance.

51 And I say unto you, that if the Gentiles do not repent, after the blessing which they shall receive, after they have scattered my people, then shall ye who are a remnant[1] of the house of Jacob, go forth among them;

52 And ye shall be in the midst of them, who shall be many; and ye shall be among them, as a lion among the beasts of the forest, and as a young lion among the flocks of

[1] Micah 5:7, 8.

sheep, who, if he goeth through, both treadeth down and teareth in pieces, and none can deliver.

53 Thy hand shall be lifted up upon thine adversaries, and all thine enemies shall be cut off.

54 And I will gather my people together, as a man gathereth his sheaves into the floor,² for I will make my people with whom the Father hath covenanted, yea, I will make thy horn iron, and I will make thy hoofs brass.

55 And thou shalt beat in pieces many people; and I will consecrate their gain unto the Lord, and their substance unto the Lord of the whole earth. And behold, I am he who doeth it.

56 And it shall come to pass, saith the Father, that the sword of my justice shall hang over them at that day; and except they repent, it shall fall upon them, saith the Father, yea, even upon all the nations of the Gentiles.

57 And it shall come to pass that I will establish my people, O house of Israel.

58 And behold, this people will I establish in this land, unto the fulfilling of the covenant which I made with your father Jacob; and it shall be a new Jerusalem.

59 And the powers of heaven shall be in the midst of this people; yea, even I will be in the midst of you.

60 Behold, I am he of whom Moses spake, saying, A prophet shall the Lord your God raise up unto you of your brethren, like unto me, him shall ye hear in all things whatsoever he shall say unto you.

61 And it shall come to pass that every soul who will not hear that prophet, shall be cut off from among the people.

62 Verily, I say unto you, Yea; and all the prophets from Samuel, and those that follow after, as many as have spoken, have testified of me.

63 And behold ye are the children of the prophets; and ye are of the house of Israel; and ye are of the covenant which the Father made with your fathers, saying unto Abraham, And in thy seed, shall all the kindreds of the earth be blessed;

---

²Micah 4:13.

64 The Father having raised me up unto you first, and sent me to bless you, in turning away every one of you from his iniquities; and this because ye are the children of the covenant.

65 And after that ye were blessed, then fulfilleth the Father the covenant which he made with Abraham, saying, In thy seed shall all the kindreds of the earth be blessed, unto the pouring out of the Holy Ghost through me upon the Gentiles, which blessing upon the Gentiles, shall make them mighty above all, unto the scattering of my people, O house of Israel: and they shall be a scourge unto the people of this land.

66 Nevertheless, when they shall have received the fullness of my gospel, then if they shall harden their hearts against me, I will return their iniquities upon their own heads, saith the Father.

67 And I will remember the covenant which I have made with my people, and I have covenanted with them, that I would gather them together in mine own due time;

68 That I would give unto them again the land of their fathers, for their inheritance, which is the land of Jerusalem, which is the promised land unto them for ever, saith the Father.

69 ¶And it shall come to pass that the time cometh, when the fullness of my gospel shall be preached unto them, and they shall believe in me, that I am Jesus Christ, the Son of God, and shall pray unto the Father in my name.

70 [3]Then shall their watchmen lift up their voice; and with the voice together shall they sing; for they shall see eye to eye.

71 Then will the Father gather them together again, and give unto them Jerusalem for the land of their inheritance.

72 Then shall they break forth into joy—sing together ye waste places of Jerusalem: for the Father hath comforted his people, he hath redeemed Jerusalem.

73 The Father hath made bare his holy arm in the eyes of

---

[3]Isaiah 52.

all the nations; and all the ends of the earth shall see the salvation of the Father; and the Father and I are one.

74 And then shall be brought to pass that which is written, Awake, awake again, and put on thy strength, O Zion; put on thy beautiful garments, O Jerusalem, the holy city, for henceforth there shall no more come into thee the uncircumcised and the unclean.

75 Shake thyself from the dust; arise, sit down, O Jerusalem; loose thyself from the bands of thy neck, O captive daughter of Zion.

76 For thus saith the Lord, Ye have sold yourselves for naught; and ye shall be redeemed without money.

77 Verily, verily, I say unto you, that my people shall know my name; yea, in that day they shall know that I am he that doth speak.

78 And then shall they say, How beautiful upon the mountains are the feet of him that bringeth good tidings unto them, that publisheth peace: that bringeth good tidings unto them of good, that publisheth salvation; that saith unto Zion, Thy God reigneth!

79 And then shall a cry go forth, Depart ye, depart ye, go ye out from thence, touch not that which is unclean; go ye out of the midst of her; be ye clean, that bear the vessels of the Lord.

80 For ye shall not go out with haste, nor go by flight: for the Lord will go before you; and the God of Israel shall be your rearward.

81 Behold, my servant shall deal prudently, he shall be exalted and extolled, and be very high.

82 As many were astonished at thee; (his visage was so marred more than any man, and his form more than the sons of men,)

83 So shall he sprinkle many nations; the kings shall shut their mouths at him, for that which had been told them shall they see; and that which they had not heard shall they consider.

84 Verily, verily, I say unto you, All these things shall surely come, even as the Father hath commanded me.

85 Then shall this covenant which the Father hath covenanted with his people, be fulfilled; and then shall Jerusalem be inhabited again with my people, and it shall be the land of their inheritance.

86 And verily, I say unto you, I give unto you a sign, that ye may know the time when these things shall be about to take place, that I shall gather in from their long dispersion, my people, O house of Israel, and shall establish again among them my Zion.

87 And behold, this is the thing which I will give unto you for a sign, for verily I say unto you, that when these things which I declare unto you, and which I shall declare unto you hereafter of myself, and by the power of the Holy Ghost, which shall be given unto you of the Father, shall be made known unto the Gentiles,

88 That they may know concerning this people who are a remnant of the house of Jacob, and concerning this my people who shall be scattered by them;

89 Verily, verily, I say unto you, When these things shall be made known unto them of the Father, and shall come forth of the Father, from them unto you, for it is wisdom in the Father that they should be established in this land,

90 And be set up as a free people by the power of the Father, that these things might come forth from them unto a remnant of your seed, that the covenant of the Father may be fulfilled which he hath covenanted with his people, O house of Israel;

91 Therefore, when these works, and the work which shall be wrought among you hereafter, shall come forth from the Gentiles unto your seed, which shall dwindle in unbelief because of iniquity;

92 For thus it behooveth the Father that it should come forth from the Gentiles, that he may shew forth his power unto the Gentiles, for this cause, that the Gentiles, if they will not harden their hearts, that they may repent and come unto me, and be baptized in my name, and know of the true points of my doctrine, that they may be numbered among my people, O house of Israel:

93 And when these things come to pass, that thy seed shall begin to know these things, it shall be a sign unto them, that they may know that the work of the Father hath already commenced unto the fulfilling of the covenant which he hath made unto the people who are of the house of Israel.

94 And when that day shall come, it shall come to pass that kings shall shut their mouths; for that which had not been told them shall they see; and that which they had not heard shall they consider.

95 For in that day, for my sake shall the Father work a work, which shall be a great and a marvelous work among them; and there shall be among them who will not believe it, although a man shall declare it unto them.

96 But behold, the life of my servant shall be in my hand; therefore they shall not hurt him, although he shall be marred because of them.

97 Yet I will heal him, for I will shew unto them that my wisdom is greater than the cunning of the devil.

98 Therefore it shall come to pass, that whosoever will not believe in my words, who am Jesus Christ, whom the Father shall cause him to bring forth unto the Gentiles, and shall give unto him power that he shall bring them forth unto the Gentiles, (it shall be done even as Moses said,) they shall be cut off from among my people who are of the covenant;

99 And my people who are a remnant of Jacob, shall be among the Gentiles, yea, in the midst of them, as a lion among the beasts of the forest, as a young lion among the flocks of sheep, who, if he go through both treadeth down and teareth in pieces, and none can deliver.

100 Their hand shall be lifted up upon their adversaries, and all their enemies shall be cut off.

101 Yea, wo be unto the Gentiles, except they repent, for it shall come to pass in that day, saith the Father, that I will cut off thy horses out of the midst of thee, and I will destroy thy chariots, and I will cut off the cities of thy land, and throw down all thy strongholds;

102 And I will cut off witchcrafts out of thy hand, and thou shalt have no more soothsayers:

103 Thy graven images I will also cut off, and thy standing images out of the midst of thee; and thou shalt no more worship the works of thy hands;

104 And I will pluck up thy groves out of the midst of thee; so will I destroy thy cities.

105 And it shall come to pass that all lyings, and deceivings, and envyings, and strifes, and priestcrafts and whoredoms, shall be done away.

106 For it shall come to pass, saith the Father, that at that day, whosoever will not repent and come unto my beloved Son, them will I cut off from among my people, O house of Israel, and I will execute vengeance and fury upon them, even as upon the heathen, such as they have not heard.

CHAPTER 10.

1 ¶But if they will repent, and hearken unto my words, and harden not their hearts, I will establish my church among them, and they shall come in unto the covenant, and be numbered among this the remnant of Jacob, unto whom I have given this land for their inheritance, and they shall assist my people, the remnant of Jacob;

2 And also, as many of the house of Israel as shall come, that they may build a city, which shall be called the New Jerusalem;

3 And then shall they assist my people that they may be gathered in, who are scattered upon all the face of the land, in unto the New Jerusalem.

4 And then shall the power of heaven come down among them; and I also will be in the midst, and then shall the work of the Father commence, at that day even when this gospel shall be preached among the remnant of this people.

5 Verily, I say unto you, At that day shall the work of the Father commence among all the dispersed of my people; yea, even the tribes which have been lost, which the Father hath led away out of Jerusalem.

6 Yea, the work shall commence among all the dispersed of my people, with the Father, to prepare the way whereby they

may come unto me, that they may call on the Father in my name;

7 Yea, and then shall the work commence, with the Father, among all nations, in preparing the way whereby his people may be gathered home to the land of their inheritance.

8 And they shall go out from all nations; and they shall not go out in haste, nor go by flight; for I will go before them, saith the Father, and I will be their rearward. And then shall that which is written come to pass.

9 ¹Sing, O barren, thou that didst not bear; break forth into singing, and cry aloud, thou that didst not travail with child; for more are the children of the desolate than the children of the married wife, saith the Lord.

10 Enlarge the place of thy tent, and let them stretch forth the curtains of thy habitations; spare not, lengthen thy cords, and strengthen thy stakes;

11 For thou shalt break forth on the right hand and on the left; and thy seed shall inherit the Gentiles, and make the desolate cities to be inhabited.

12 Fear not; for thou shalt not be ashamed; neither be thou confounded; for thou shalt not be put to shame; for thou shalt forget the shame of thy youth, and shalt not remember the reproach of thy widowhood any more.

13 For thy maker, thy husband, the Lord of hosts is his name; and thy Redeemer, the Holy One of Israel; the God of the whole earth shall he be called.

14 For the Lord hath called thee as a woman forsaken and grieved in spirit, and a wife of youth, when thou wast refused, saith thy God.

15 For a small moment have I forsaken thee; but with great mercies will I gather thee.

16 In a little wrath I hid my face from thee for a moment; but with everlasting kindness will I have mercy on thee, saith the Lord thy Redeemer.

17 For this, the waters of Noah unto me, for as I have

---

¹Isaiah 54.

sworn that the waters of Noah should no more go over the earth, so have I sworn that I would not be wroth with thee.

18 For the mountains shall depart and the hills be removed; but my kindness shall not depart from thee, neither shall the covenant of my peace be removed, saith the Lord that hath mercy on thee.

19 ¶O thou afflicted, tossed with tempest, and not comforted! behold, I will lay thy stones with fair colors, and lay thy foundations with sapphires.

20 And I will make thy windows of agates, and thy gates of carbuncles, and all thy borders of pleasant stones.

21 And all thy children shall be taught of the Lord; and great shall be the peace of thy children.

22 In righteousness shalt thou be established; thou shalt be far from oppression, for thou shalt not fear; and from terror, for it shall not come near thee.

23 Behold, they shall surely gather together against thee, not by me; whosoever shall gather together against thee shall fall for thy sake.

24 Behold, I have created the smith that bloweth the coals in the fire; and that bringeth forth an instrument for his work; and I have created the waster to destroy.

25 No weapon that is formed against thee shall prosper; and every tongue that shall revile against thee in judgment thou shalt condemn. This is the heritage of the servants of the Lord, and their righteousness is of me, saith the Lord.

26 And now behold I say unto you, that ye had ought to search these things.

27 Yea, a commandment I give unto you, that ye search these things diligently; for great are the words of Isaiah.

28 For surely he spake as touching all things concerning my people which are of the house of Israel; therefore it must needs be that he must speak also to the Gentiles.

29 And all things that he spake, hath been, and shall be, even according to the words which he spake.

30 Therefore give heed to my words; write the things which I have told you, and according to the time and the will of the Father, they shall go forth unto the Gentiles.

CHAP. 11.] BOOK OF NEPHI. 667

31 And whosoever will hearken unto my words, and repenteth, and is baptized, the same shall be saved.

32 Search the prophets, for many there be that testify of these things.

33 ¶And now it came to pass that when Jesus had said these words, he said unto them again, after he had expounded all the scriptures unto them which they had received, he said unto them, Behold, other scriptures I would that ye should write, that ye have not.

34 And it came to pass that he said unto Nephi, Bring forth the record which ye have kept.

35 And when Nephi had brought forth the records, and laid them before him, he cast his eyes upon them, and said,

36 Verily, I say unto you, I commanded my servant Samuel, the Lamanite, that he should testify unto this people, that at the day that the Father should glorify his name in me, that there were many saints who should arise from the dead, and should appear unto many, and should minister unto them.

37 And he said unto them, Were it not so?

38 And his disciples answered him and said, Yea, Lord, Samuel did prophesy according to thy words, and they were all fulfilled.

39 And Jesus said unto them, How be it that ye have not written this thing, that many saints did arise and appear unto many, and did minister unto them?

40 And it came to pass that Nephi remembered that this thing had not been written.

41 And it came to pass that Jesus commanded that it should be written; therefore it was written according as he commanded.

CHAPTER 11.

1 ¶And now it came to pass that when Jesus had expounded all the scriptures in one, which they had written, he commanded them that they should teach the things which he had expounded unto them.

2 And it came to pass that he commanded them that they

should write the words which the Father had given unto Malachi, which he should tell unto them.

3 And it came to pass that after they were written, he expounded them.

4 And these are the words which he did tell unto them, saying, Thus said the Father unto Malachi,[1] Behold, I will send my messenger, and he shall prepare the way before me, and the Lord, whom ye seek, shall suddenly come to his temple, even the messenger of the covenant, whom ye delight in; behold, he shall come, saith the Lord of hosts.

5 But who may abide the day of his coming? and who shall stand when he appeareth? for he is like a refiner's fire, and like fuller's soap.

6 And he shall sit as a refiner and purifier of silver; and he shall purify the sons of Levi, and purge them as gold and silver, that they may offer unto the Lord an offering in righteousness.

7 Then shall the offering of Judah and Jerusalem be pleasant unto the Lord, as in the days of old, and as in former years.

8 And I will come near to you to judgment; and I will be a swift witness against the sorcerers, and against the adulterers, and against false swearers, and against those that oppress the hireling in his wages, the widow, and the fatherless, and that turn aside the stranger, and fear not me saith the Lord of hosts.

9 For I am the Lord, I change not; therefore ye sons of Jacob are not consumed.

10 ¶Even from the days of your fathers ye are gone away from mine ordinances, and have not kept them. Return unto me, and I will return unto you, saith the Lord of hosts. But ye said, Wherein shall we return?

11 ¶Will a man rob God? Yet ye have robbed me. But ye say, Wherein have we robbed thee? In tithes and offerings.

12 Ye are cursed with a curse, for ye have robbed me, even this whole nation.

---

[1] Malachi 3.

13 Bring ye all the tithes into the storehouse, that there may be meat in my house, and prove me now herewith, saith the Lord of hosts, if I will not open you the windows of heaven, and pour you out a blessing, that there shall not be room enough to receive it.

14 And I will rebuke the devourer for your sakes, and he shall not destroy the fruits of your ground; neither shall your vine cast her fruit before the time in the fields, saith the Lord of hosts.

15 And all nations shall call you blessed, for ye shall be a delightsome land, saith the Lord of hosts.

16 Your words have been stout against me, saith the Lord. Yet ye say, What have we spoken against thee?

17 Ye have said, It is vain to serve God, and what doth it profit that we have kept his ordinances, and that we have walked mournfully before the Lord of hosts?

18 And now we call the proud happy, yea, they that work wickedness are set up; yea, them that tempt God are even delivered.

19 ¶Then they that feared the Lord spake often one to another, and the Lord hearkened, and heard; and a book of remembrance was written before him for them that feared the Lord, and that thought upon his name.

20 And they shall be mine, saith the Lord of hosts, in that day when I make up my jewels; and I will spare them, as a man spareth his own son that serveth him.

21 Then shall ye return and discern between the righteous and the wicked, between him that serveth God, and him that serveth him not.

22 ²For behold, the day cometh, that shall burn as an oven; and all the proud, yea, and all that do wickedly, shall be stubble; and the day that cometh shall burn them up, saith the Lord of hosts, that it shall leave them neither root nor branch.

23 ¶But unto you that fear my name, shall the Son of

---

²Malachi 4.

righteousness arise with healing in his wings; and ye shall go forth and grow up as calves of the stall.

24 And ye shall tread down the wicked; for they shall be ashes under the soles of your feet in the day that I shall do this, saith the Lord of hosts.

25 Remember ye the law of Moses my servant, which I commanded unto him in Horeb for all Israel, with the statutes and judgments.

26 Behold, I will send you Elijah, the prophet, before the coming of the great and dreadful day of the Lord;

27 And he shall turn the heart of the fathers to the children, and the heart of the children to their fathers, lest I come and smite the earth with a curse.

28 ¶And now it came to pass that when Jesus had told these things, he expounded them unto the multitude, and he did expound all things unto them, both great and small.

29 And he saith, These scriptures which ye had not with you, the Father commanded that I should give unto you, for it was wisdom in him that they should be given unto future generations.

30 And he did expound all things, even from the beginning until the time that he should come in his glory;

31 Yea, even all things which should come upon the face of the earth, even until the elements should melt with fervent heat, and the earth should be wrapped together as a scroll, and the heavens and the earth should pass away;

32 And even unto the great and last day, when all people, and all kindreds, and all nations and tongues shall stand before God, to be judged of their works, whether they be good or whether they be evil;

33 If they be good, to the resurrection of everlasting life; and if they be evil, to the resurrection of damnation, being on a parallel, the one on the one hand, and the other on the other hand, according to the mercy, and the justice, and the holiness which is in Christ, who was before the world began.

CHAPTER 12.

1 ¶And now there can not be written in this book, even a hundredth part of the things which Jesus did truly teach unto the people; but behold the plates of Nephi do contain the more part of the things which he taught the people;

2 And these things have I written, which are a lesser part of the things which he taught the people; and I have written them to the intent that they may be brought again unto this people, from the Gentiles, according to the words which Jesus hath spoken.

3 And when they shall have received this, which is expedient that they should have first, to try their faith, and if it shall so be that they shall believe these things, then shall the greater things be made manifest unto them.

4 And if it so be that they will not believe these things, then shall the greater things be withheld from them, unto their condemnation.

5 Behold I were about to write them all which were engraven upon the plates of Nephi, but the Lord forbid it, saying, I will try the faith of my people; therefore I, Mormon, do write the things which have been commanded me of the Lord.

6 And now I, Mormon, make an end of my sayings, and proceed to write the things which have been commanded me; therefore I would that ye should behold that the Lord truly did teach the people, for the space of three days; and after that, he did shew himself unto them oft, and did break bread oft, and bless it, and give it unto them.

7 ¶And it came to pass that he did teach and minister unto the children of the multitude of whom hath been spoken, and he did loose their tongues, and they did speak unto their fathers great and marvelous things, even greater than he had revealed unto the people, and loosed their tongues that they could utter.

8 And it came to pass that after he had ascended into heaven the second time, that he shewed himself unto them, and had gone unto the Father, after having healed all their

sick, and their lame, and opened the eyes of their blind, and unstopped the ears of the deaf, and even had done all manner of cures among them, and raised a man from the dead, and had shewn forth his power unto them, and had ascended unto the Father,

9 Behold, it came to pass on the morrow, that the multitude gathered themselves together, and they both saw and heard these children; yea, even babes did open their mouths, and utter marvelous things; and the things which they did utter were forbidden that there should not any man write them.

10 And it came to pass that the disciples whom Jesus had chosen, began from that time forth to baptize and to teach as many as did come unto them: and as many as were baptized in the name of Jesus were filled with the Holy Ghost.

11 And many of them saw and heard unspeakable things, which are not lawful to be written: and they taught, and did minister one to another; and they had all things common among them, every man dealing justly, one with another.

12 And it came to pass that they did do all things, even as Jesus had commanded them.

13 And they who were baptized in the name of Jesus, were called the church of Christ.

14 ¶And it came to pass that as the disciples of Jesus were journeying and were preaching the things which they had both heard and seen, and were baptizing in the name of Jesus, it came to pass that the disciples were gathered together, and were united in mighty prayer and fasting.

15 And Jesus again shewed himself unto them, for they were praying unto the Father, in his name; and Jesus came and stood in the midst of them, and said unto them, What will ye that I shall give unto you?

16 And they said unto him, Lord, we will that thou wouldst tell us the name whereby we shall call this church; for there are disputations among the people concerning this matter.

17 And the Lord said unto them, Verily, verily I say unto you, Why is it that the people should murmur and dispute because of this thing?

18 Have they not read the scriptures, which say, Ye must

take upon you the name of Christ, which is my name? for by this name shall ye be called at the last day; and whoso taketh upon him my name, and endureth to the end, the same shall be saved at the last day;

19 Therefore, whatsoever ye shall do, ye shall do it in my name; therefore ye shall call the church in my name; and ye shall call upon the Father in my name, that he will bless the church for my sake; and how be it my church, save it be called in my name?

20 For if a church be called in Moses' name, then it be Moses' church; or if it be called in the name of a man, then it be the church of a man; but if it be called in my name, then it is my church, if it so be that they are built upon my gospel.

21 Verily I say unto you, that ye are built upon my gospel; therefore ye shall call whatsoever things ye do call in my name; therefore if ye call upon the Father, for the church, if it be in my name, the Father will hear you;

22 And if it so be that the church is built upon my gospel, then will the Father shew forth his own works in it;

23 But if it be not built upon my gospel, and is built upon the works of men, or upon the works of the devil, verily I say unto you, They have joy in their works for a season, and by and by the end cometh, and they are hewn down and cast into the fire, from whence there is no return;

24 For their works do follow them, for it is because of their works that they are hewn down; therefore remember the things that I have told you.

25 Behold I have given unto you my gospel, and this is the gospel which I have given unto you, that I came into the world to do the will of my Father, because my Father sent me;

26 And my Father sent me that I might be lifted up upon the cross; and after that I had been lifted up upon the cross, I might draw all men unto me:

27 That as I have been lifted up by men, even so should men be lifted up by the Father, to stand before me, to be

judged of their works, whether they be good or whether they be evil;

28 And for this cause have I been lifted up; therefore, according to the power of the Father, I will draw all men unto me, that they may be judged according to their works.

29 And it shall come to pass, that whoso repenteth and is baptized in my name, shall be filled; and if he endureth to the end, behold, him will I hold guiltless before my Father, at that day when I shall stand to judge the world.

30 And he that endureth not unto the end, the same is he that is also hewn down and cast into the fire, from whence they can no more return, because of the justice of the Father: and this is the word which he hath given unto the children of men.

31 And for this cause he fulfilleth the words which he hath given, and he lieth not, but fulfilleth all his words; and no unclean thing can enter into his kingdom;

32 Therefore nothing entereth into his rest, save it be those who have washed their garments in my blood, because of their faith, and the repentance of all their sins, and their faithfulness unto the end.

33 Now this is the commandment, Repent, all ye ends of the earth, and come unto me and be baptized in my name, that ye may be sanctified by the reception of the Holy Ghost, that ye may stand spotless before me at the last day.

34 Verily, verily I say unto you, This is my gospel; and ye know the things that ye must do in my church; for the works which ye have seen me do, that shall ye also do;

35 For that which ye have seen me do, even that shall ye do; therefore if ye do these things, blessed are ye, for ye shall be lifted up at the last day.

CHAPTER 13.

1 ¶Write the things which ye have seen and heard, save it be those which are forbidden; write the works of this people, which shall be even as hath been written of that which hath been;

2 For behold, out of the books which have been written, and which shall be written, shall this people be judged, for by them shall their works be known unto men.

3 And behold, all things are written by the Father; therefore out of the books which shall be written, shall the world be judged.

4 And know ye that ye shall be judges of this people, according to the judgment which I shall give unto you, which shall be just;

5 Therefore what manner of men had ye ought to be? Verily I say unto you, Even as I am. And now I go unto the Father.

6 And verily I say unto you, Whatsoever things ye shall ask the Father, in my name, it shall be given unto you; therefore ask, and ye shall receive; knock, and it shall be opened unto you; for he that asketh, receiveth, and unto him that knocketh, it shall be opened.

7 And now behold, my joy is great, even unto fullness, because of you, and also this generation; yea, and even the Father rejoiceth, and also all the holy angels, because of you and this generation; for none of them are lost.

8 Behold, I would that ye should understand; for I mean them who are now alive, of this generation; and none of them are lost; and in them I have fullness of joy.

9 But behold, it sorroweth me because of the fourth generation from this generation, for they are led away captive by him, even as was the son of perdition; for they will sell me for silver, and for gold, and for that which moth doth corrupt, and which thieves can break through and steal.

10 And in that day will I visit them, even in turning their works upon their own heads.

11 ¶And it came to pass that when Jesus had ended these sayings, he saith unto his disciples, Enter ye in at the straight gate; for straight is the gate and narrow is the way that leads to life, and few there be that find it, but wide is the gate, and broad the way which leads to death, and many there be that travel therein, until the night cometh, wherein no man can work.

12 ¶And it came to pass when Jesus had said these words, he spake unto his disciples, one by one, saying unto them, What is it that ye desire of me after that I am gone to the Father?

13 And they all spake, save it were three, saying, We desire that after we have lived unto the age of man, that our ministry, wherein thou hast called us, may have an end, that we may speedily come unto thee, in thy kingdom.

14 And he said unto them, Blessed are ye, because ye desire this thing of me; therefore after that ye are seventy and two years old, ye shall come unto me in my kingdom, and with me ye shall find rest.

15 And when he had spoken unto them, he turned himself unto the three, and said unto them, What will ye that I should do unto you, when I am gone unto the Father?

16 And they sorrowed in their hearts, for they durst not speak unto him the thing which they desired.

17 And he said unto them, Behold, I know your thoughts, and ye have desired the thing which John, my beloved, who was with me in my ministry, before that I was lifted up by the Jews, desired of me;

18 Therefore more blessed are ye, for ye shall never taste of death, but ye shall live to behold all the doings of the Father, unto the children of men, even until all things shall be fulfilled, according to the will of the Father, when I shall come in my glory, with the powers of heaven;

19 And ye shall never endure the pains of death; but when I shall come in my glory, ye shall be changed in the twinkling of an eye, from mortality to immortality; and then shall ye be blessed in the kingdom of my Father.

20 And again, ye shall not have pain while ye shall dwell in the flesh, neither sorrow, save it be for the sins of the world;

21 And all this will I do because of the thing which ye have desired of me, for ye have desired that ye might bring the souls of men unto me, while the world shall stand; and for this cause ye shall have fullness of joy; and ye shall sit down in the kingdom of my Father;

22 Yea, your joy shall be full, even as the Father hath given me fullness of joy; and ye shall be even as I am, and I am even as the Father; and the Father and I are one;

23 And the Holy Ghost beareth record of the Father and me; and the Father giveth the Holy Ghost unto the children of men, because of me.

24 ¶And it came to pass that when Jesus had spoken these words, he touched every one of them with his finger, save it were the three who were to tarry, and then he departed.

25 And behold, the heavens were opened, and they were caught up into heaven, and saw and heard unspeakable things.

26 And it was forbidden them that they should utter: neither was it given unto them power that they could utter the things which they saw and heard;

27 And whether they were in the body or out of the body, they could not tell; for it did seem unto them like a transfiguration of them, that they were changed from this body of flesh, into an immortal state, that they could behold the things of God.

28 But it came to pass that they did again minister upon the face of the earth; nevertheless they did not minister of the things which they had heard and seen, because of the commandment which was given them in heaven.

29 And now whether they were mortal or immortal, from the day of their transfiguration, I know not; but this much I know, according to the record which hath been given, they did go forth upon the face of the land, and did minister unto all the people, uniting as many to the church as would believe in their preaching; baptizing them;

30 And as many as were baptized, did receive the Holy Ghost; and they were cast into prison by them who did not belong to the church.

31 And the prisons could not hold them, for they were rent in twain, and they were cast down into the earth.

32 But they did smite the earth with the word of God, insomuch that by his power they were delivered out of the

depths of the earth; and therefore they could not dig pits sufficient to hold them.

33 And thrice they were cast into a furnace, and received no harm.

34 And twice they were cast into a den of wild beasts; and behold they did play with the beasts, as a child with a suckling lamb, and received no harm.

35 And it came to pass that thus they did go forth among all the people of Nephi, and did preach the gospel of Christ unto all people upon the face of the land;

36 And they were converted unto the Lord, and were united unto the church of Christ, and thus the people of that generation were blessed, according to the word of Jesus.

37 And now I, Mormon, make an end of speaking concerning these things, for a time.

38 Behold, I was about to write the names of those who were never to taste of death; but the Lord forbade, therefore I write them not for they are hid from the world.

39 But behold I have seen them, and they have ministered unto me; and behold they will be among the Gentiles, and the Gentiles knoweth them not.

40 They will also be among the Jews, and the Jews shall know them not.

41 ¶And it shall come to pass, when the Lord seeth fit in his wisdom, that they shall minister unto all the scattered tribes of Israel, and unto all nations, kindreds, tongues and people, and shall bring out of them unto Jesus many souls, that their desire may be fulfilled, and also because of the convincing power of God which is in them;

42 And they are as the angels of God, and if they shall pray unto the Father in the name of Jesus, they can shew themselves unto whatsoever man it seemeth them good;

43 Therefore great and marvelous works shall be wrought by them, before the great and coming day, when all people must surely stand before the judgment seat of Christ;

44 Yea, even among the Gentiles shall there be a great and marvelous work wrought by them, before that judgment day.

45 And if ye had all the scriptures which give an account

of all the marvelous works of Christ, ye would, according to the words of Christ, know that these things must surely come.

46 And wo be unto him that will not hearken unto the words of Jesus, and also to them whom he hath chosen and sent among them,

47 For whoso receiveth not the words of Jesus, and the words of those whom he hath sent, receiveth not him; and therefore he will not receive them at the last day; and it would be better for them if they had not been born.

48 For do ye suppose that ye can get rid of the justice of an offended God, who hath been trampled under feet of men, that thereby salvation might come?

49 And now behold, as I spake concerning those whom the Lord had chosen, yea, even three who were caught up into the heavens, that I knew not whether they were cleansed from mortality to immortality.

50 But behold, since I wrote, I have inquired of the Lord, and he hath made it manifest unto me, that there must needs be a change wrought upon their bodies, or else it needs be that they must taste of death;

51 Therefore that they might not taste of death, there was a change wrought upon their bodies, that they might not suffer pain nor sorrow, save it were for the sins of the world.

52 Now this change was not equal to that which should take place at the last day; but there was a change wrought upon them, insomuch that Satan could have no power over them, that he could not tempt them, and they were sanctified in the flesh, that they were holy, and that the powers of the earth could not hold them;

53 And in this state they were to remain until the judgment day of Christ; and at that day they were to receive a greater change, and to be received into the kingdom of the Father to go no more out, but to dwell with God eternally in the heavens.

54 And now behold, I say unto you, that when the Lord shall see fit, in his wisdom, that these sayings shall come unto the Gentiles, according to his word, then ye may know that the covenant which the Father hath made with the children

of Israel, concerning their restoration to the lands of their inheritance, is already beginning to be fulfilled;

55 And ye may know that the words of the Lord, which have been spoken by the holy prophets, shall all be fulfilled; and ye need not say that the Lord delays his coming unto the children of Israel;

56 And ye need not imagine in your hearts that the words which have been spoken are vain, for behold, the Lord will remember his covenant which he hath made unto his people of the house of Israel.

57 And when ye shall see these sayings coming forth among you, then ye need not any longer spurn at the doings of the Lord, for the sword of his justice is in his right hand, and behold at that day, if ye shall spurn at his doings, he will cause that it shall soon overtake you.

58 Wo unto him that spurneth at the doings of the Lord; yea, wo unto him that shall deny the Christ and his works;

59 Yea, wo unto him that shall deny the revelations of the Lord, and that shall say, The Lord no longer worketh by revelation, or by prophecy, or by gifts, or by tongues, or by healings, or by the power of the Holy Ghost;

60 Yea, and wo unto him that shall say at that day, that there can be no miracle wrought by Jesus Christ, to get gain; for he that doeth this, shall become like unto the son of perdition, for whom there was no mercy, according to the word of Christ.

61 Yea, and ye need not any longer hiss, nor spurn, nor make game of the Jews, nor any of the remnant of the house of Israel, for behold the Lord remembereth his covenant unto them, and he will do unto them according to that which he hath sworn;

62 Therefore ye need not suppose that ye can turn the right hand of the Lord unto the left, that he may not execute judgment unto the fulfilling of the covenant which he hath made unto the house of Israel.

CHAPTER 14.

1 ¶Hearken, O, ye Gentiles, and hear the words of Jesus Christ, the Son of the living God, which he hath commanded me that I should speak concerning you, for, behold he commandeth me that I should write, saying,

2 Turn all ye Gentiles, from your wicked ways, and repent of your evil doings, of your lyings and deceivings, and of your whoredoms, and of your secret abominations, and your idolatries, and of your murders, and your priestcrafts, and your envyings, and your strifes, and from all your wickedness and abominations,

3 And come unto me, and be baptized in my name, that ye may receive a remission of your sins, and be filled with the Holy Ghost, that ye may be numbered with my people, who are of the house of Israel.

THE BOOK OF NEPHI

WHO IS THE SON OF NEPHI, ONE OF THE DISCIPLES OF JESUS CHRIST.

CHAPTER 1.

An account of the people of Nephi, according to his record.

1 ¶And it came to pass that the thirty and fourth year passed away, and also the thirty and fifth, and behold the disciples of Jesus had formed a church of Christ in all the lands round about.

2 And as many as did come unto them, and did truly repent of their sins, were baptized in the name of Jesus; and they did also receive the Holy Ghost.

3 ¶And it came to pass in the thirty and sixth year, the people were all converted unto the Lord, upon all the face of the land, both Nephites and Lamanites, and there were no contentions and disputations among them, and every man did deal justly one with another;

4 And they had all things common among them, therefore there were not rich and poor, bond and free, but they were all made free, and partakers of the heavenly gift.

5 ¶And it came to pass that the thirty and seventh year passed away also, and there still continued to be peace in the land.

6 And there were great and marvelous works wrought by the disciples of Jesus, insomuch that they did heal the sick, and raise the dead, and cause the lame to walk, and the blind to receive their sight, and the deaf to hear;

7 And all manner of miracles did they work among the children of men; and in nothing did they work miracles save it were in the name of Jesus.

8 And thus did the thirty and eighth year pass away, and also the thirty and ninth, and the forty and first, and the forty and second; yea, even until forty and nine years had passed away, and also the fifty and first, and the fifty and second; yea, and even until fifty and nine years had passed away;

9 And the Lord did prosper them exceedingly, in the land: yea, insomuch that they did build cities again where there had been cities burned; yea, even that great city Zarahemla did they cause to be built again.

10 But there were many cities which had been sunk, and waters came up in the stead thereof; therefore these cities could not be renewed.

11 ¶And now behold it came to pass that the people of Nephi did wax strong, and did multiply exceeding fast, and became an exceeding fair and delightsome people.

12 And they were married, and given in marriage, and were blessed according to the multitude of the promises which the Lord had made unto them.

13 And they did not walk any more after the performances and ordinances of the law of Moses, but they did walk after the commandments which they had received from their Lord and their God, continuing in fasting and prayer, and in meeting together oft, both to pray and to hear the word of the Lord.

14 And it came to pass that there was no contention among all the people, in all the land, but there were mighty miracles wrought among the disciples of Jesus.

15 ¶And it came to pass that the seventy and first year passed away, and also the seventy and second year; yea, and in fine, until the seventy and ninth year had passed away; yea, even an hundred years had passed away, and the disciples of Jesus, whom he had chosen, had all gone to the paradise of God, save it were the three who should tarry;

16 And there were other disciples ordained in their stead; and also many of that generation which had passed away.

17 And it came to pass that there was no contention in the land, because of the love of God which did dwell in the hearts of the people.

18 And there were no envyings, nor strifes, nor tumults, nor whoredoms, nor lyings, nor murders, nor any manner of lasciviousness;

19 And surely there could not be a happier people among all the people who had been created by the hand of God:

20 There were no robbers, nor murderers, neither were there Lamanites, nor any manner of ites; but they were in one, the children of Christ, and heirs to the kingdom of God;

21 And how blessed were they, for the Lord did bless them in all their doings; yea, even they were blessed and prospered, until an hundred and ten years had passed away; and the first generation from Christ had passed away, and there was no contention in all the land.

22 ¶And it came to pass that Nephi, he that kept the last record, (and he kept it upon the plates of Nephi,) died, and his son Amos kept it in his stead; and he kept it upon the plates of Nephi also;

23 And he kept it eighty and four years, and there was still peace in the land, save it were a small part of the people who had revolted from the church, and took upon them the name of Lamanites; therefore there began to be Lamanites again in the land.

24 ¶And it came to pass that Amos died also, (and it was an hundred and ninety and four years from the coming of

Christ,) and his son Amos kept the record in his stead; and he also kept it upon the plates of Nephi; and it was also written in the book of Nephi, which is this book.

25 And it came to pass that two hundred years had passed away, and the second generation had all passed away save it were a few.

26 And now I, Mormon, would that ye should know that the people had multiplied, insomuch that they were spread upon all the face of the land, and that they had become exceeding rich, because of their prosperity in Christ.

27 And now in this two hundred and first year, there began to be among them those who were lifted up in pride, such as the wearing of costly apparel, and all manner of fine pearls, and of the fine things of the world.

28 And from that time forth they did have their goods and their substance no more common among them, and they began to be divided into classes, and they began to build up churches unto themselves, to get gain, and began to deny the true church of Christ.

29 ¶And it came to pass that when two hundred and ten years had passed away, there were many churches in the land; yea, there were many churches which professed to know the Christ, and yet they did deny the more part of his gospel, insomuch that they did receive all manner of wickedness, and did administer that which was sacred unto him to whom it had been forbidden, because of unworthiness.

30 And this church did multiply exceedingly, because of iniquity, and because of the power of Satan who did get hold upon their hearts.

31 And again, there was another church which denied the Christ; and they did persecute the true church of Christ; because of their humility, and their belief in Christ, and they did despise them, because of the many miracles which were wrought among them;

32 Therefore they did exercise power and authority over the disciples of Jesus who did tarry with them, and they did cast them into prison;

33 But by the power of the word of God, which was in

them, the prisons were rent in twain, and they went forth doing mighty miracles among them.

34 Nevertheless, and notwithstanding all these miracles, the people did harden their hearts, and did seek to kill them, even as the Jews at Jerusalem sought to kill Jesus, according to his word,

35 And they did cast them into furnaces of fire, and they came forth receiving no harm; and they also cast them into dens of wild beasts, and they did play with the wild beasts even as a child with a lamb; and they did come forth from among them, receiving no harm.

36 Nevertheless, the people did harden their hearts, for they were led by many priests and false prophets to build up many churches, and to do all manner of iniquity.

37 And they did smite upon the people of Jesus; but the people of Jesus did not smite again.

38 And thus they did dwindle in unbelief and wickedness, from year to year, even until two hundred and thirty years had passed away.

39 And now it came to pass in this year, yea, in the two hundred and thirty and first year, there was a great division among the people.

40 And it came to pass that in this year there arose a people who were called the Nephites, and they were true believers in Christ; and among them there were those who were called by the Lamanites, Jacobites, and Josephites, and Zoramites;

41 Therefore the true believers in Christ, and the true worshipers of Christ, (among whom were the three disciples of Jesus who should tarry,) were called Nephites, and Jacobites, and Josephites, and Zoramites.

42 And it came to pass that they who rejected the gospel, were called Lamanites, and Lemuelites, and Ishmaelites; and they did not dwindle in unbelief, but they did willfully rebel against the gospel of Christ;

43 And they did teach their children that they should not believe, even as their fathers, from the beginning, did dwindle.

44 And it was because of the wickedness and abominations of their fathers, even as it was in the beginning.

45 And they were taught to hate the children of God, even as the Lamanites were taught to hate the children of Nephi, from the beginning.

46 ¶And it came to pass that two hundred and forty and four years had passed away, and thus were the affairs of the people.

47 And the more wicked part of the people did wax strong, and became exceeding more numerous than were the people of God.

48 And they did still continue to build up churches unto themselves, and adorn them with all manner of precious things.

49 And thus did two hundred and fifty years pass away, and also two hundred and sixty years.

50 And it came to pass that the wicked part of the people began again to build up the secret oaths and combinations of Gadianton.

51 And also the people who were called the people of Nephi, began to be proud in their hearts, because of their exceeding riches, and became vain, like unto their brethren, the Lamanites.

52 And from this time, the disciples began to sorrow for the sins of the world.

53 ¶And it came to pass that when three hundred years had passed away, both the people of Nephi and the Lamanites had become exceeding wicked one like unto another.

54 And it came to pass that the robbers of Gadianton did spread over all the face of the land; and there were none that were righteous, save it were the disciples of Jesus.

55 And gold and silver did they lay up in store in abundance, and did traffic in all manner of traffic.

56 ¶And it came to pass that after three hundred and five years had passed away, (and the people did still remain in wickedness,) Amos died, and his brother Ammoron did keep the record in his stead.

57 And it came to pass that when three hundred and

twenty years had passed away, Ammoron, being constrained by the Holy Ghost, did hide up the records which were sacred;

58 Yea, even all the sacred records which had been handed down from generation to generation, which were sacred, even until the three hundred and twentieth year from the coming of Christ.

59 And he did hide them up unto the Lord, that they might come again unto the remnant of the house of Jacob, according to the prophecies and the promises of the Lord. And thus is the end of the record of Ammoron.

THE BOOK OF MORMON.

CHAPTER 1.

1 ¶And now I, Mormon, make a record of the things which I have both seen and heard, and call it the book of Mormon.

2 And about the time that Ammoron hid up the records unto the Lord, he came unto me, (I being about ten years of age; and I began to be learned somewhat after the manner of the learning of my people,) and Ammoron said unto me, I perceive that thou art a sober child, and art quick to observe;

3 Therefore when ye are about twenty and four years old, I would that ye should remember the things that ye have observed concerning this people;

4 And when ye are of that age, go to the land of Antum, unto a hill, which shall be called Shim; and there have I deposited unto the Lord, all the sacred engravings concerning this people.

5 And behold, ye shall take the plates of Nephi unto yourself, and the remainder shall ye leave in the place where they are: and ye shall engrave upon the plates of Nephi, all the things that ye have observed concerning this people.

6 And I, Mormon, being a descendant of Nephi, (and my father's name was Mormon,) I remembered the things which Ammoron commanded me.

7 And it came to pass that I, being eleven years old, was carried by my father into the land southward, even to the land of Zarahemla; the whole face of the land having become covered with buildings, and the people were as numerous almost, as it were the sand of the sea.

8 And it came to pass in this year, there began to be a war between the Nephites, who consisted of the Nephites and the Jacobites, and the Josephites, and the Zoramites; and this war was between the Nephites and the Lamanites, and the Lemuelites, and the Ishmaelites.

9 Now the Lamanites, and the Lemuelites, and the Ishmaelites were called Lamanites, and the two parties were Nephites and Lamanites.

10 And it came to pass that the war began to be among them in the borders of Zarahemla, by the waters of Sidon.

11 And it came to pass that the Nephites had gathered together a great number of men, even to exceed the number of thirty thousand.

12 And it came to pass that they did have in this same year a number of battles, in the which the Nephites did beat the Lamanites, and did slay many of them.

13 And it came to pass that the Lamanites withdrew their design, and there was peace settled in the land, and peace did remain for the space of about four years, that there was no blood shed.

14 But wickedness did prevail upon the face of the whole land, insomuch that the Lord did take away his beloved disciples, and the work of miracles and of healing did cease, because of the iniquity of the people.

15 And there were no gifts from the Lord, and the Holy Ghost did not come upon any, because of their wickedness and unbelief.

16 And I, being fifteen years of age, and being somewhat of a sober mind, therefore I was visited of the Lord, and tasted, and knew of the goodness of Jesus.

17 And I did endeavor to preach unto this people, but my mouth was shut, and I was forbidden that I should preach unto them; for behold they had willfully rebelled against

their God, and the beloved disciples were taken away out of the land, because of their iniquity.

18 But I did remain among them, but I was forbidden to preach unto them, because of the hardness of their hearts; and because of the hardness of their hearts, the land was cursed for their sake.

19 And these Gadianton robbers, who were among the Lamanites, did infest the land, insomuch that the inhabitants thereof began to hide up their treasures in the earth; and they became slippery, because the Lord had cursed the land, that they could not hold them nor retain them again.

20 And it came to pass that there were sorceries, and witchcrafts, and magics; and the power of the evil one was wrought upon all the face of the land, even unto the fulfilling of all the words of Abinadi, and also Samuel the Lamanite.

21 And it came to pass that in that same year, there began to be a war again between the Nephites and the Lamanites.

22 And notwithstanding I being young, was large in stature, therefore the people of Nephi appointed me that I should be their leader, or the leader of their armies.

23 Therefore it came to pass that in my sixteenth year I did go forth at the head of an army of the Nephites, against the Lamanites; therefore three hundred and twenty and six years had passed away.

24 And it came to pass that in the three hundred and twenty and seventh year, the Lamanites did come upon us with exceeding great power, insomuch that they did frighten my armies; therefore they would not fight, and they began to retreat towards the north countries.

25 And it came to pass that we did come to the city of Angola, and we did take possession of the city, and make preparations to defend ourselves against the Lamanites.

26 And it came to pass that we did fortify the city with our mights; but notwithstanding all our fortifications, the Lamanites did come upon us, and did drive us out of the city.

27 And they did also drive us forth out of the land of David. And we marched forth and came to the land of Joshua, which was in the borders west, by the sea-shore.

28 And it came to pass that we did gather in our people as fast as it were possible, that we might get them together in one body.

29 But behold, the land was filled with robbers and with Lamanites; and notwithstanding the great destruction which hung over my people, they did not repent of their evil doings;

30 Therefore there was blood and carnage spread throughout all the face of the land, both on the part of the Nephites, and also on the part of the Lamanites: and it was one complete revolution throughout all the face of the land.

31 And now the Lamanites had a king, and his name was Aaron; and he came against us with an army of forty and four thousand.

32 And behold, I withstood him with forty and two thousand. And it came to pass that I beat him with my army, that he fled before me.

33 And behold, all this was done and three hundred and thirty years had passed away.

34 And it came to pass that the Nephites began to repent of their iniquity, and began to cry even as had been prophesied by Samuel the prophet; for behold no man could keep that which was his own, for the thieves, and the robbers, and the murderers, and the magic art, and the witchcraft which was in the land.

35 Thus there began to be a mourning and a lamentation in all the land, because of these things; and more especially among the people of Nephi.

36 And it came to pass that when I, Mormon, saw their lamentations, and their mourning, and their sorrowing before the Lord, my heart did begin to rejoice within me, knowing the mercies and the long suffering of the Lord, therefore supposing that he would be merciful unto them, that they would again become a righteous people.

37 But behold this my joy was vain, for their sorrowing was not unto repentance, because of the goodness of God, but it was rather the sorrowing of the damned, because the Lord would not always suffer them to take happiness in sin.

38 And they did not come unto Jesus with broken hearts

and contrite spirits, but they did curse God, and wish to die.

39 Nevertheless they would struggle with the sword for their lives.

40 And it came to pass that my sorrow did return unto me again, and I saw that the day of grace was past with them, both temporally and spiritually, for I saw thousands of them hewn down in open rebellion against their God, and heaped up as dung upon the face of the land.

41 And thus three hundred and forty and four years had passed away.

42 ¶And it came to pass that in the three hundred and forty and fifth year, the Nephites did begin to flee before the Lamanites, and they were pursued until they came even to the land of Jashon, before it was possible to stop them in their retreat.

43 And now the city of Jashon was near the land where Ammoron had deposited the records unto the Lord, that they might not be destroyed.

44 And behold, I had gone according to the word of Ammoron, and taken the plates of Nephi, and did make a record according to the words of Ammoron.

45 And upon the plates of Nephi I did make a full account of all the wickedness and abominations; but upon these plates I did forbear to make a full account of their wickedness and abominations, for behold, a continual scene of wickedness and abominations has been before mine eyes ever since I have been sufficient to behold the ways of man.

46 And wo is me, because of their wickedness, for my heart has been filled with sorrow because of their wickedness, all my days; nevertheless, I know that I shall be lifted up at the last day.

47 ¶And it came to pass that in this year the people of Nephi again were hunted and driven.

48 And it came to pass that we were driven forth until we had come northward to the land which was called Shem.

49 And it came to pass that we did fortify the city of Shem, and we did gather in our people as much as it were possible, that perhaps we might save them from destruction.

50 And it came to pass in the three hundred and forty and sixth year, they began to come upon us again.

51 And it came to pass that I did speak unto my people, and did urge them with great energy, that they would stand boldly before the Lamanites, and fight for their wives, and their children, and their houses and their homes.

52 And my words did arouse them somewhat to vigor, insomuch that they did not flee from before the Lamanites, but did stand with boldness against them.

53 And it came to pass that we did contend with an army of thirty thousand, against an army of fifty thousand.

54 And it came to pass that we did stand before them with such firmness, that they did flee from before us.

55 And it came to pass that when they had fled, we did pursue them with our armies, and did meet them again, and did beat them;

56 Nevertheless the strength of the Lord was not with us; yea, we were left to ourselves, that the Spirit of the Lord did not abide in us; therefore we had become weak, like unto our brethren.

57 And my heart did sorrow because of this the great calamity of my people; because of their wickedness and their abominations.

58 But behold we did go forth against the Lamanites, and the robbers of Gadianton, until we had again taken possession of the lands of our inheritance.

59 And the three hundred and forty and ninth year had passed away.

60 And in the three hundred and fiftieth year, we made a treaty with the Lamanites and the robbers of Gadianton, in which we did get the lands of our inheritance divided.

61 And the Lamanites did give unto us the land northward; yea, even to the narrow passage which led into the land southward.

62 And we did give unto the Lamanites all the land southward.

63 ¶And it came to pass that the Lamanites did not come to battle again until ten years more had passed away.

64 And behold, I had employed my people, the Nephites, in preparing their lands and their arms against the time of battle.

65 And it came to pass that the Lord did say unto me, Cry unto this people, Repent ye, and come unto me and be ye baptized, and build up again my church, and ye shall be spared.

66 And I did cry unto this people, but it was in vain, and they did not realize that it was the Lord that had spared them and granted unto them a chance for repentance.

67 And behold they did harden their hearts against the Lord their God.

68 And it came to pass that after this tenth year had passed away, making, in the whole, three hundred and sixty years from the coming of Christ, the king of the Lamanites sent an epistle unto me, which gave unto me to know that they were preparing to come again to battle against us.

69 And it came to pass that I did cause my people that they should gather themselves together at the land Desolation, to a city which was in the borders, by the narrow pass which led into the land southward.

70 And there we did place our armies, that we might stop the armies of the Lamanites, that they might not get possession of any of our lands; therefore we did fortify against them with all our force.

71 ¶And it came to pass that in the three hundred and sixty and first year, the Lamanites did come down to the city of Desolation to battle against us; and it came to pass that in that year, we did beat them, insomuch that they did return to their own lands again.

72 And in the three hundred and sixty and second year, they did come down again to battle.

73 And we did beat them again, and did slay a great number of them, and their dead were cast into the sea.

74 And now because of this great thing which my people, the Nephites, had done, they began to boast in their own strength, and began to swear before the heavens, that they would avenge themselves of the blood of their brethren who had been slain by their enemies.

75 And they did swear by the heavens, and also by the throne of God, that they would go up to battle against their enemies, and would cut them off from the face of the land.

76 ¶And it came to pass that I, Mormon, did utterly refuse from this time forth, to be a commander and a leader of this people, because of their wickedness and abomination.

77 Behold, I had led them, notwithstanding their wickedness, I had led them many times to battle, and had loved them, according to the love of God which was in me, with all my heart;

78 And my soul had been poured out in prayer unto my God all the day long, for them; nevertheless, it was without faith, because of the hardness of their hearts.

79 And thrice have I delivered them out of the hands of their enemies, and they have repented not of their sins.

80 And when they had sworn by all that had been forbidden them, by our Lord and Savior Jesus Christ, that they would go up unto their enemies to battle, and avenge themselves of the blood of their brethren, behold, the voice of the Lord came unto me, saying, Vengeance is mine, and I will repay; and because this people repented not after I had delivered them, behold, they shall be cut off from the face of the earth.

81 And it came to pass that I utterly refused to go up against mine enemies; and I did even as the Lord had commanded me; and I did stand as an idle witness to manifest unto the world the things which I saw and heard, according to the manifestations of the Spirit which had testified of things to come.

82 Therefore I write unto you, Gentiles, and also unto you, house of Israel, when the work shall commence, that ye shall be about to prepare to return to the land of your inheritance;

83 Yea, behold, I write unto all the ends of the earth; yea, unto you, twelve tribes of Israel, who shall be judged according to your works, by the twelve whom Jesus chose to be his disciples in the land of Jerusalem.

84 And I write also unto the remnant of this people, who shall also be judged by the twelve whom Jesus chose in this

land; and they shall be judged by the other twelve whom Jesus chose in the land of Jerusalem.

85 And these things do the Spirit manifest unto me; therefore I write unto you all.

86 And for this cause I write unto you, that ye may know that ye must all stand before the judgment seat of Christ; yea, every soul who belongs to the whole human family of Adam;

87 And ye must stand to be judged of your works, whether they be good or evil; and also that ye may believe the gospel of Jesus Christ, which ye shall have among you;

88 And also that the Jews, the covenant people of the Lord, shall have other witness besides him whom they saw and heard, that Jesus whom they slew, was the very Christ, and the very God;

89 And I would that I could persuade all ye ends of the earth to repent and prepare to stand before the judgment seat of Christ.

CHAPTER 2.

1 ¶And now it came to pass that in the three hundred and sixty and third year, the Nephites did go up with their armies to battle against the Lamanites, out of the land of Desolation.

2 And it came to pass that the armies of the Nephites were driven back again to the land of Desolation.

3 And while they were yet weary, a fresh army of the Lamanites did come upon them; and they had a sore battle, insomuch that the Lamanites did take possession of the city Desolation, and did slay many of the Nephites, and did take many prisoners; and the remainder did flee and join the inhabitants of the city Teancum.

4 Now the city Teancum lay in the borders by the seashore; and it was also near the city Desolation.

5 And it was because the armies of the Nephites went up unto the Lamanites, that they began to be smitten; for were

it not for that, the Lamanites could have had no power over them.

6 But behold, the judgments of God will overtake the wicked; and it is by the wicked, that the wicked are punished; for it is the wicked that stir up the hearts of the children of men unto bloodshed.

7 And it came to pass that the Lamanites did make preparation to come against the city Teancum.

8 ¶And it came to pass in the three hundred and sixty and fourth year, the Lamanites did come against the city Teancum, that they might take possession of the city Teancum also.

9 And it came to pass that they were repulsed and driven back by the Nephites.

10 And when the Nephites saw that they had driven the Lamanites, they did again boast of their own strength: and they went forth in their own might, and took possession again of the city Desolation.

11 And now all these things had been done, and there had been thousands slain on both sides, both the Nephites and the Lamanites.

12 And it came to pass that the three hundred and sixty and sixth year had passed away, and the Lamanites came again upon the Nephites to battle; and yet the Nephites repented not of the evil they had done, but persisted in their wickedness continually.

13 And it is impossible for the tongue to describe, or for man to write a perfect description of the horrible scene of the blood and carnage which was among the people; both of the Nephites and of the Lamanites; and every heart was hardened, so that they delighted in the shedding of blood continually.

14 And there never had been so great wickedness among all the children of Lehi, nor even among all the house of Israel, according to the words of the Lord, as were among this people.

15 ¶And it came to pass that the Lamanites did take pos-

session of the city Desolation, and this because their number did exceed the number of the Nephites.

16 And they did also march forward against the city Teancum, and did drive the inhabitants forth out of her, and did take many prisoners, both women and children, and did offer them up as sacrifices unto their idol gods.

17 And it came to pass that in the three hundred and sixty and seventh year, the Nephites, being angry because the Lamanites had sacrificed their women and their children, that they did go against the Lamanites with exceeding great anger, insomuch that they did beat again the Lamanites, and drive them out of their lands;

18 And the Lamanites did not come again against the Nephites until the three hundred and seventy and fifth year.

19 And in this year they did come down against the Nephites with all their powers; and they were not numbered because of the greatness of their number.

20 And from this time forth did the Nephites gain no power over the Lamanites, but began to be swept off by them even as a dew before the sun.

21 And it came to pass that the Lamanites did come down against the city Desolation; and there was an exceeding sore battle fought in the land Desolation, in the which they did beat the Nephites.

22 And they fled again from before them, and they came to the city Boaz; and there they did stand against the Lamanites with exceeding boldness, insomuch that the Lamanites did not beat them until they had come again the second time.

23 And when they had come the second time, the Nephites were driven and slaughtered with an exceeding great slaughter; their women and their children were again sacrificed unto idols.

24 And it came to pass that the Nephites did again flee from before them, taking all the inhabitants with them, both in towns and villages.

25 And now I, Mormon, seeing that the Lamanites were about to overthrow the land, therefore I did go to the hill

Shim, and did take up all the records which Ammoron had hid up unto the Lord.

26 ¶And it came to pass that I did go forth among the Nephites, and did repent of the oath which I had made, that I would no more assist them; and they gave me command again of their armies; for they looked upon me as though I could deliver them from their afflictions.

27 But behold, I was without hopes, for I knew the judgments of the Lord which should come upon them; for they repented not of their iniquities, but did struggle for their lives, without calling upon that being who created them.

28 And it came to pass that the Lamanites did come against us as we had fled to the city of Jordan; but behold, they were driven back that they did not take the city at that time.

29 And it came to pass that they came against us again, and we did maintain the city.

30 And there were also other cities which were maintained by the Nephites, which strongholds did cut them off that they could not get into the country which lay before us to destroy the inhabitants of our land.

31 But it came to pass that whatsoever lands we had passed by, and the inhabitants thereof were not gathered in, were destroyed by the Lamanites, and their towns, and villages, and cities were burned with fire; and thus the three hundred and seventy and nine years passed away.

32 ¶And it came to pass that in the three hundred and eightieth year, the Lamanites did come again against us to battle, and we did stand against them boldly; but it was all in vain; for so great were their numbers that they did tread the people of the Nephites under their feet.

33 And it came to pass that we did again take to flight, and those whose flight was swifter than the Lamanites did escape, and those whose flight did not exceed the Lamanites were swept down and destroyed.

34 And now behold, I, Mormon, do not desire to harrow up the souls of men in casting before them such an awful scene of blood and carnage as was laid before mine eyes,

35 But I, knowing that these things must surely be made

known, and that all things which are hid must be revealed upon the house tops, and also that a knowledge of these things must come unto the remnant of these people, and also unto the Gentiles, which the Lord hath said should scatter this people, and this people should be counted as nought among them,

36 Therefore I write a small abridgment, daring not to give a full account of the things which I have seen, because of the commandment which I have received, and also that ye might not have too great sorrow because of the wickedness of this people.

37 And now behold, this I speak unto their seed, and also to the Gentiles, who have care for the house of Israel, that realize and know from whence their blessings come.

38 For I know that such will sorrow for the calamity of the house of Israel; yea, they will sorrow for the destruction of this people; they will sorrow that this people had not repented, that they might have been clasped in the arms of Jesus.

39 Now these things are written unto the remnant of the house of Jacob; and they are written after this manner, because it is known of God that wickedness will not bring them forth unto them; and they are to be hid up unto the Lord, that they may come forth in his own due time.

40 And this is the commandment which I have received; and behold they shall come forth according to the commandment of the Lord, when he shall see fit, in his wisdom.

41 And behold they shall go unto the unbelieving of the Jews; and for this intent shall they go; that they may be persuaded that Jesus is the Christ, the Son of the living God;

42 That the Father may bring about, through his most beloved, his great and eternal purpose, in restoring the Jews, or all the house of Israel, to the land of their inheritance, which the Lord their God hath given them, unto the fulfilling of his covenant,

43 And also that the seed of this people may more fully believe his gospel, which shall go forth unto them from the Gentiles;

44 For this people shall be scattered, and shall become a dark, a filthy, and a loathsome people, beyond the description of that which ever hath been amongst us; yea, even that which hath been among the Lamanites; and this because of their unbelief and idolatry.

45 For behold, the Spirit of the Lord hath already ceased to strive with their fathers, and they are without Christ and God in the world, and they are driven about as chaff before the wind.

46 They were once a delightsome people, and they had Christ for their Shepherd; yea, they were led even by God, the Father.

47 But now, behold they are led about by Satan, even as chaff is driven before the wind, or as a vessel is tossed about upon the waves, without sail or anchor, or without anything wherewith to steer her; and even as she is, so are they.

48 And behold, the Lord hath reserved their blessings, which they might have received in the land, for the Gentiles who shall possess the land.

49 But behold, it shall come to pass that they shall be driven and scattered by the Gentiles; and after they have been driven and scattered by the Gentiles, behold, then will the Lord remember the covenant which he made unto Abraham, and unto all the house of Israel.

50 And also the Lord will remember the prayers of the righteous, which have been put up unto him for them.

51 And then, O ye Gentiles, how can ye stand before the power of God, except ye shall repent and turn from your evil ways!

52 Know ye not that ye are in the hands of God?

53 Know ye not that he hath all power, and at his great command the earth shall be rolled together as a scroll?

54 Therefore repent ye, and humble yourselves before him, lest he shall come out in justice against you; lest a remnant of the seed of Jacob shall go forth among you as a lion, and tear you in pieces, and there is none to deliver.

CHAPTER 3.

1 ¶And now I finish my record concerning the destruction of my people, the Nephites.

2 And it came to pass that we did march forth before the Lamanites.

3 And I, Mormon, wrote an epistle unto the king of the Lamanites, and desired of him that he would grant unto us that we might gather together our people unto the land of Cumorah, by a hill which was called Cumorah, and there we would give them battle.

4 And it came to pass that the king of the Lamanites did grant unto me the thing which I desired.

5 And it came to pass that we did march forth to the land of Cumorah, and we did pitch our tents round about the hill Cumorah; and it was in a land of many waters, rivers and fountains; and here we had hope to gain advantage over the Lamanites.

6 And when three hundred and eighty and four years had passed away, we had gathered in all the remainder of our people unto the land Cumorah.

7 ¶And it came to pass that when we had gathered in all our people in one to the land of Cumorah, behold I, Mormon, began to be old; and knowing it to be the last struggle of my people, and having been commanded of the Lord that I should not suffer that the records which had been handed down by our fathers, which were sacred, to fall into the hands of the Lamanites, (for the Lamanites would destroy them,)

8 Therefore I made this record out of the plates of Nephi, and hid up in the hill Cumorah, all the records which had been entrusted to me by the hand of the Lord, save it were these few plates which I gave unto my son Moroni.

9 And it came to pass that my people, with their wives and their children, did now behold the armies of the Lamanites marching towards them; and with that awful fear of death which fills the breasts of all the wicked, did they wait to receive them.

10 And it came to pass that they came to battle against us,

and every soul was filled with terror, because of the greatness of their numbers.

11 And it came to pass that they did fall upon my people with the sword, and with the bow, and with the arrow, and with the ax, and with all manner of weapons of war.

12 And it came to pass that my men were hewn down, yea, even my ten thousand who were with me; and I fell wounded in the midst; and they passed by me that they did not put an end to my life.

13 And when they had gone through and hewn down all my people save it were twenty and four of us, (among whom was my son Moroni,)

14 And we having survived the dead of our people, did behold on the morrow, when the Lamanites had returned unto their camps, from the top of the hill Cumorah, the ten thousand of my people who were hewn down, being led in the front by me; and we also beheld the ten thousand of my people who were led by my son Moroni.

15 And behold, the ten thousand of Gidgiddonah had fallen, and he also in the midst; and Lama had fallen with his ten thousand; and Gilgal had fallen with his ten thousand; and Limhah had fallen with his ten thousand; and Jeneum had fallen with his ten thousand; and Cumenihah, and Moronihah, and Antionum, and Shiblom, and Shem, and Josh, had fallen with their ten thousand each.

16 ¶And it came to pass that there were ten more who did fall by the sword, with their ten thousand each; yea, even all my people, save it were those twenty and four who were with me, and also a few who had escaped into the south countries, and a few who had deserted over unto the Lamanites, had fallen,

17 And their flesh, and bones, and blood lay upon the face of the earth, being left by the hands of those who slew them, to moulder upon the land, and to crumble and to return to their mother earth.

18 And my soul was rent with anguish, because of the slain of my people, and I cried, O ye fair ones, how could ye have departed from the ways of the Lord! O ye fair ones,

how could ye have rejected that Jesus, who stood with open arms to receive you!

19 Behold, if ye had not done this, ye would not have fallen. But behold, ye are fallen, and I mourn your loss.

20 O ye fair sons and daughters, ye fathers and mothers, ye husbands and wives, ye fair ones, how is it that ye could have fallen!

21 But behold, ye are gone, and my sorrows can not bring your return; and the day soon cometh that your mortal must put on immortality, and these bodies which are now mouldering in corruption, must soon become incorruptible bodies;

22 And then ye must stand before the judgment seat of Christ, to be judged according to your works; and if it so be that ye are righteous, then are ye blessed with your fathers who have gone before you.

23 O that ye had repented before this great destruction had come upon you. But behold, ye are gone, and the Father, yea, the eternal Father of heaven knoweth your state; and he doeth with you according to his justice and mercy.

24 ¶And now behold, I would speak somewhat unto the remnant of this people who are spared, if it so be that God may give unto them my words, that they may know of the things of their fathers; yea, I speak unto you, ye remnant of the house of Israel; and these are the words which I speak, Know ye that ye are of the house of Israel.

25 Know ye that ye must come unto repentance, or ye can not be saved.

26 Know ye that ye must lay down your weapons of war, and delight no more in the shedding of blood, and take them not again, save it be that God shall command you.

27 Know ye that ye must come to the knowledge of your fathers, and repent of all your sins and iniquities, and believe in Jesus Christ, that he is the Son of God, and that he was slain by the Jews, and by the power of the Father he hath risen again, whereby he hath gained the victory over the grave; and also in him is the sting of death swallowed up.

28 And he bringeth to pass the resurrection of the dead,

whereby man must be raised to stand before his judgment seat.

29 And he hath brought to pass the redemption of the world, whereby he that is found guiltless before him at the judgment day, hath it given unto him to dwell in the presence of God in his kingdom, to sing ceaseless praises with the choirs above, unto the Father, and unto the Son, and unto the Holy Ghost, which are one God, in a state of happiness which hath no end.

30 Therefore repent, and be baptized in the name of Jesus, and lay hold upon the gospel of Christ, which shall be set before you, not only in this record, but also in the record which shall come unto the Gentiles from the Jews, which record shall come from the Gentiles unto you.

31 For behold, this is written for the intent that ye may believe that; and if ye may believe that, ye will believe this also; and if ye believe this, ye will know concerning your fathers, and also the marvelous works which were wrought by the power of God among them;

32 And ye will also know that ye are a remnant of the seed of Jacob; therefore ye are numbered among the people of the first covenant;

33 And if it so be that ye believe in Christ, and are baptized, first with water, then with fire and with the Holy Ghost, following the example of our Savior according to that which he hath commanded us, it shall be well with you in the day of judgment. Amen.

CHAPTER 4.

1 ¶Behold I, Moroni, do finish the record of my father Mormon. Behold, I have but few things to write, which things I have been commanded of my father.

2 And now it came to pass that after the great and tremendous battle at Cumorah, behold, the Nephites who had escaped into the country southward, were hunted by the Lamanites, until they were all destroyed; and my father also

was killed by them; and I, even remain alone to write the sad tale of the destruction of my people.

3 But behold, they are gone, and I fulfill the commandment of my father.

4 And whether they will slay me, I know not; therefore I will write and hide up the records in the earth, and whither I go it mattereth not.

5 Behold, my father hath made this record, and he hath written the intent thereof.

6 And behold, I would write it also, if I had room upon the plates; but I have not; and ore I have none, for I am alone; my father hath been slain in battle, and all my kinsfolks, and I have not friends, nor whither to go; and how long the Lord will suffer that I may live, I know not.

7 Behold, four hundred years have passed since the coming of our Lord and Savior.

8 And behold, the Lamanites have hunted my people, the Nephites, down from city to city, and from place to place, even until they are no more, and great has been their fall; yea, great and marvelous is the destruction of my people, the Nephites.

9 And behold, it is the hand of the Lord which hath done it.

10 And behold also, the Lamanites are at war one with another; and the whole face of this land is one continual round of murder and bloodshed; and no one knoweth the end of the war.

11 And now behold, I say no more concerning them, for there are none, save it be the Lamanites and robbers, that do exist upon the face of the land;

12 And there are none that do know the true God, save it be the disciples of Jesus, who did tarry in the land until the wickedness of the people was so great that the Lord would not suffer them to remain with the people; and whether they be upon the face of the land, no man knoweth.

13 But behold, my father and I have seen them, and they have ministered unto us.

14 And whoso receiveth this record, and shall not con-

demn it because of the imperfections which are in it, the same shall know of greater things than these.

15 Behold, I am Moroni; and were it possible, I would make all things known unto you.

16 Behold, I make an end of speaking concerning this people.

17 I am the son of Mormon, and my father was a descendant of Nephi; and I am the same who hideth up this record unto the Lord; the plates thereof are of no worth, because of the commandment of the Lord.

18 For he truly saith, that no one shall have them to get gain; but the record thereof is of great worth; and whoso shall bring it to light, him will the Lord bless.

19 For no one can have power to bring it to light, save it be given him of God; for God will that it shall be done with an eye single to his glory, or the welfare of the ancient and long dispersed covenant people of the Lord.

20 And blessed be him that shall bring this thing to light; for it shall be brought out of darkness unto light, according to the word of God;

21 Yea, it shall be brought out of the earth, and it shall shine forth out of darkness, and come unto the knowledge of the people: and it shall be done by the power of God; and if there be faults, they be faults of a man.

22 But behold, we know no fault; nevertheless, God knoweth all things; therefore he that condemneth, let him beware lest he shall be in danger of hell fire.

23 And he that saith, Shew unto me, or ye shall be smitten, let him beware lest he commandeth that which is forbidden of the Lord.

24 For behold, the same that judgeth rashly, shall be judged rashly again; for according to his works shall his wages be; therefore, he that smiteth, shall be smitten again of the Lord.

25 Behold what the scripture says: Man shall not smite, neither shall he judge; for judgment is mine, saith the Lord; and vengeance is mine also, and I will repay.

26 And he that shall breathe out wrath and strifes against

the work of the Lord, and against the covenant people of the Lord, who are the house of Israel, and shall say, We will destroy the work of the Lord, and the Lord will not remember his covenant which he hath made unto the house of Israel, the same is in danger to be hewn down and cast into the fire; for the eternal purposes of the Lord shall roll on, until all his promises shall be fulfilled.

27 Search the prophecies of Isaiah. Behold, I can not write them.

28 Yea, behold I say unto you, that those saints who have gone before me, who have possessed this land, shall cry; yea, even from the dust will they cry unto the Lord; and as the Lord liveth, he will remember the covenant which he hath made with them.

29 And he knoweth their prayers that they were in behalf of their brethren.

30 And he knoweth their faith; for in his name could they remove mountains; and in his name could they cause the earth to shake; and by the power of his word did they cause prisons to tumble to the earth;

31 Yea, even the fiery furnace could not harm them; neither wild beasts, nor poisonous serpents, because of the power of his word.

32 And behold, their prayers were also in behalf of him that the Lord should suffer to bring these things forth.

33 And no one need say, They shall not come, for they surely shall, for the Lord hath spoken it; for out of the earth shall they come, by the hand of the Lord, and none can stay it;

34 And it shall come in a day when it shall be said that miracles are done away; and it shall come even as if one should speak from the dead.

35 And it shall come in a day when the blood of the saints shall cry unto the Lord, because of secret combinations and the works of darkness;

36 Yea, it shall come in a day when the power of God shall be denied, and churches become defiled, and shall be lifted up in the pride of their hearts; yea, even in a day when leaders

of churches, and teachers, in the pride of their hearts, even to the envying of them who belong to their churches;

37 Yea, it shall come in a day when there shall be heard of fires, and tempests, and vapors of smoke in foreign lands; and there shall also be heard of wars and rumors of wars, and earthquakes in divers places;

38 Yea, it shall come in a day when there shall be great pollutions upon the face of the earth;

39 There shall be murders and robbing, and lying, and deceivings, and whoredoms, and all manner of abominations, when there shall be many who will say, Do this, or do that, and it mattereth not, for the Lord will uphold such at the last day.

40 But wo unto such, for they are in the gall of bitterness, and in the bonds of iniquity.

41 Yea, it shall come in a day when there shall be churches built up that shall say, Come unto me, and for your money you shall be forgiven of your sins.

42 O ye wicked and perverse, and stiff-necked people, why have ye built up churches unto yourselves to get gain?

43 Why have ye transfigured the holy word of God, that ye might bring damnation upon your souls?

44 Behold, look ye unto the revelations of God. For behold, the time cometh at that day when all these things must be fulfilled.

45 Behold, the Lord hath shewn unto me great and marvelous things concerning that which must shortly come at that day when these things shall come forth among you.

46 Behold, I speak unto you as if ye were present, and yet ye are not.

47 But behold, Jesus Christ hath shewn you unto me, and I know your doing; and I know that ye do walk in the pride of your hearts;

48 And there are none, save a few only, who do not lift themselves up in the pride of their hearts, unto the wearing of very fine apparel, unto envying, and strifes, and malice, and persecutions, and all manner of iniquity;

49 And your churches, yea, even every one, have become polluted because of the pride of your hearts.

50 For behold, ye do love money, and your substance, and your fine apparel, and the adorning of your churches, more than ye love the poor and the needy, the sick and the afflicted.

51 O ye pollutions, ye hypocrites, ye teachers, who sell yourselves for that which will canker, why have ye polluted the holy church of God?

52 Why are ye ashamed to take upon you the name of Christ?

53 Why do you not think that greater is the value of an endless happiness, than that misery which never dies, because of the praise of the world?

54 Why do ye adorn yourselves with that which hath no life, and yet suffer the hungry, and the needy, and the naked, and the sick, and the afflicted to pass by you, and notice them not?

55 Yea, why do ye build up your secret abominations to get gain, and cause that widows should mourn before the Lord, and also orphans to mourn before the Lord; and also the blood of their fathers and their husbands to cry unto the Lord from the ground, for vengeance upon your heads?

56 Behold the sword of vengeance hangeth over you; and the time soon cometh that he avengeth the blood of the saints upon you, for he will not suffer their cries any longer.

57 And now, I speak also concerning those who do not believe in Christ.

58 Behold, will ye believe in the day of your visitation; behold, when the Lord shall come; yea, even that great day when the earth shall be rolled together as a scroll, and the elements shall melt with fervent heat;

59 Yea, in that great day when ye shall be brought to stand before the Lamb of God, then will ye say that there is no God?

60 Then will ye longer deny the Christ, or can ye behold the Lamb of God?

61 Do ye suppose that ye shall dwell with him under a consciousness of your guilt?

62 Do ye suppose that ye could be happy to dwell with that holy being, when your souls are racked with a consciousness of your guilt that ye have ever abused his laws?

63 Behold I say unto you, that ye would be more miserable to dwell with a holy and just God, under a consciousness of your filthiness before him, than ye would to dwell with the damned souls in hell.

64 For behold, when ye shall be brought to see your nakedness before God, and also the glory of God, and the holiness of Jesus Christ, it will kindle a flame of unquenchable fire upon you.

65 O then ye unbelieving, turn ye unto the Lord; cry mightily unto the Father in the name of Jesus, that perhaps ye may be found spotless, pure, fair and white, having been cleansed by the blood of the Lamb, at that great and last day.

66 And again I speak unto you, who deny the revelations of God, and say that they are done away, that there are no revelations, nor prophecies, nor gifts, nor healing, nor speaking with tongues, and the interpretation of tongues.

67 Behold I say unto you, He that denieth these things, knoweth not the gospel of Christ; yea, he has not read the scriptures; if so, he does not understand them.

68 For do we not read that God is the same yesterday, today, and for ever; and in him there is no variableness neither shadow of changing.

69 And now, if ye have imagined up unto yourselves a god who doth vary, and in him there is shadow of changing, then have ye imagined up unto yourselves a god who is not a god of miracles.

70 But behold, I will shew unto you a God of miracles, even the God of Abraham, and the God of Isaac, and the God of Jacob; and it is that same God who created the heavens and the earth, and all things that in them are.

71 Behold, he created Adam; and by Adam came the fall of man. And because of the fall of man, came Jesus Christ, even the Father and the Son; and because of Jesus Christ came the redemption of man.

72 And because of the redemption of man, which came by

Jesus Christ, they are brought back into the presence of the Lord; yea, this is wherein all men are redeemed, because the death of Christ bringeth to pass the resurrection, which bringeth to pass a redemption from an endless sleep, from which sleep all men shall be awoke by the power of God, when the trump shall sound;

73 And they shall come forth, both small and great, and all shall stand before his bar, being redeemed and loosed from this eternal band of death, which death is a temporal death;

74 And then cometh the judgment of the Holy One upon them; and then cometh the time that he that is filthy, shall be filthy still, and he that is righteous, shall be righteous still; he that is happy, shall be happy still; and he that is unhappy, shall be unhappy still.

75 And now, O all ye that have imagined up unto yourselves a god who can do no miracles, I would ask of you, Have all these things past, of which I have spoken? Has the end come yet?

76 Behold I say unto you, Nay; and God has not ceased to be a God of miracles.

77 Behold, are not the things that God hath wrought marvelous in our eyes? Yea, and who can comprehend the marvelous works of God?

78 Who shall say that it was not a miracle, that by his word the heaven and the earth should be; and by the power of his word, man was created of the dust of the earth; and by the power of his word, hath miracles been wrought?

79 And who shall say that Jesus Christ did not do many mighty miracles?

80 And there were many mighty miracles wrought by the hands of the apostles.

81 And if there were miracles wrought, then why has God ceased to be a God of miracles, and yet be an unchangeable being.

82 And behold I say unto you, He changeth not; if so, he would cease to be God; and he ceaseth not to be God, and is a God of miracles.

83 And the reason why he ceaseth to do miracles among

the children of men, is because that they dwindle in unbelief, and depart from the right way, and know not the God in whom they should trust.

84 Behold I say unto you, that whoso believeth in Christ, doubting nothing, whatsoever he shall ask the Father in the name of Christ, it shall be granted him; and this promise is unto all, even unto the ends of the earth.

85 For behold, thus saith Jesus Christ, the Son of God, unto his disciples who should tarry; yea, and also to all his disciples, in the hearing of the multitude,

86 Go ye into all the world, and preach the gospel to every creature; and he that believeth and is baptized, shall be saved, but he that believeth not, shall be damned.

87 And these signs shall follow them that believe: in my name shall they cast out devils; they shall speak with new tongues; they shall take up serpents; and if they drink any deadly thing, it shall not hurt them; they shall lay hands on the sick, and they shall recover;

88 And whosoever shall believe in my name, doubting nothing, unto him will I confirm all my words, even unto the ends of the earth.

89 And now behold, who can stand against the works of the Lord? Who can deny his sayings?

90 Who will rise up against the almighty power of the Lord? Who will despise the works of the Lord? Who will despise the children of Christ?

91 Behold, all ye who are despisers of the works of the Lord, for ye shall wonder and perish.

92 O then despise not, and wonder not, but hearken unto the words of the Lord, and ask the Father in the name of Jesus for what things soever ye shall stand in need.

93 Doubt not, but be believing, and begin as in times of old, and come unto the Lord with all your heart, and work out your own salvation with fear and trembling before him.

94 Be wise in the days of your probation; strip yourselves of all uncleanness; ask not, that ye may consume it on your lusts, but ask with a firmness unshaken, that ye will yield to no temptation, but that ye will serve the true and living God.

95 See that ye are not baptized unworthily; see that ye partake not of the sacrament of Christ unworthily; but see that ye do all things in worthiness, and do it in the name of Jesus Christ, the Son of the living God: and if ye do this, and endure to the end, ye will in no wise be cast out.

96 Behold, I speak unto you as though I spake from the dead; for I know that ye shall have my words.

97 Condemn me not because of mine imperfection; neither my father, because of his imperfection; neither them who have written before him, but rather give thanks unto God that he hath made manifest unto you our imperfections, that ye may learn to be more wise than we have been.

98 ¶And now behold, we have written this record according to our knowledge in the characters, which are called among us the reformed Egyptian, being handed down and altered by us, according to our manner of speech.

99 And if our plates had been sufficiently large, we should have written in the Hebrew; but the Hebrew hath been altered by us also; and if we could have written in the Hebrew, behold, ye would have had no imperfection in our record.

100 But the Lord knoweth the things which we have written, and also that none other people knoweth our language, and because that none other people knoweth our language, therefore he hath prepared means for the interpretation thereof.

101 And these things are written, that we may rid our garments of the blood of our brethren who have dwindled in unbelief.

102 And behold, these things which we have desired concerning our brethren, yea, even their restoration to the knowledge of Christ, is according to the prayers of all the saints who have dwelt in the land.

103 And may the Lord Jesus Christ grant that their prayers may be answered according to their faith; and may God the Father remember the covenant which he hath made with the house of Israel; and may he bless them for ever, through faith on the name of Jesus Christ. Amen.

BOOK OF ETHER.

CHAPTER 1.

1 ¶And now I, Moroni, proceed to give an account of those ancient inhabitants who were destroyed by the hand of the Lord upon the face of this north country.

2 And I take mine account from the twenty and four plates which were found by the people of Limhi, which is called the book of Ether.

3 And as I suppose that the first part of this record, which speaks concerning the creation of the world, and also of Adam, and an account from that time even to the great tower, and whatsoever things transpired among the children of men until that time, is had among the Jews,

4 Therefore I do not write those things which transpired from the days of Adam until that time; but they are had upon the plates; and whoso findeth them, the same will have power that he may get the full account.

5 But behold, I give not the full account, but a part of the account I give, from the tower down until they were destroyed. And on this wise do I give the account.

6 He that wrote this record was Ether, and he was a descendant of Coriantor; and Coriantor was the son of Moron; and Moron was the son of Ethem; and Ethem was the son of Ahah; and Ahah was the son of Seth; and Seth was the son of Shiblon; and Shiblon was the son of Com; and Com was the son of Coriantum; and Coriantum was the son of Amnigaddah; and Amnigaddah was the son of Aaron; and Aaron was a descendant of Heth, who was the son of Hearthom; and Hearthom was the son of Lib; and Lib was the son of Kish; and Kish was the son of Corum; and Corum was the son of Levi; and Levi was the son of Kim; and Kim was the son of Morianton; and Morianton was a descendant of Riplakish; and Riplakish was the son of Shez; and Shez was the son of Heth; and Heth was the son of Com; and Com was

the son of Coriantum; and Coriantum was the son of Emer; and Emer was the son of Omer; and Omer was the son of Shule; and Shule was the son of Kib; and Kib was the son of Orihah, who was the son of Jared;

7 Which Jared came forth with his brother and their families, with some others and their families, from the great tower, at the time the Lord confounded the language of the people, and swear in his wrath that they should be scattered upon all the face of the earth; and according to the word of the Lord the people were scattered.

8 And the brother of Jared being a large and a mighty man, and being a man highly favored of the Lord, for Jared his brother said unto him, Cry unto the Lord, that he will not confound us that we may not understand our words.

9 And it came to pass that the brother of Jared did cry unto the Lord, and the Lord had compassion upon Jared; therefore he did not confound the language of Jared; and Jared and his brother were not confounded.

10 Then Jared said unto his brother, Cry again unto the Lord, and it may be that he will turn away his anger from them who are our friends, that he confound not their language.

11 And it came to pass that the brother of Jared did cry unto the Lord, and the Lord had compassion upon their friends, and their families also, that they were not confounded.

12 And it came to pass that Jared spake again unto his brother, saying, Go and inquire of the Lord whether he will drive us out of the land, and if he will drive us out of the land, cry unto him whither we shall go.

13 And who knoweth but the Lord will carry us forth into a land which is choice above all the earth.

14 And if it so be, let us be faithful unto the Lord, that we may receive it for our inheritance.

15 ¶And it came to pass that the brother of Jared did cry unto the Lord according to that which had been spoken by the mouth of Jared.

16 And it came to pass that the Lord did hear the brother

of Jared, and had compassion upon him, and said unto him, Go to and gather together thy flocks, both male and female, of every kind; and also of the seed of the earth of every kind, and thy family; and also Jared thy brother and his family; and also thy friends and their families, and the friends of Jared and their families.

17 And when thou hast done this, thou shalt go at the head of them down into the valley, which is northward.

18 And there will I meet thee, and I will go before thee into a land which is choice above all the land of the earth.

19 And there will I bless thee and thy seed, and raise up unto me of thy seed, and of the seed of thy brother, and they who shall go with thee, a great nation.

20 And there shall be none greater than the nation which I will raise up unto me of thy seed, upon all the face of the earth.

21 And this I will do unto thee because this long time ye have cried unto me.

22 ¶And it came to pass that Jared, and his brother, and their families, and also the friends of Jared and his brother, and their families, went down into the valley which was northward, (and the name of the valley was Nimrod, being called after the mighty hunter,) with their flocks which they had gathered together, male and female, of every kind.

23 And they did also lay snares and catch fowls of the air, and they did also prepare a vessel, in which they did carry with them the fish of the waters;

24 And they did also carry with them deseret, which, by interpretation is a honey bee; and thus they did carry with them swarms of bees, and all manner of that which was upon the face of the land, seeds of every kind.

25 And it came to pass that when they had come down into the valley of Nimrod, the Lord came down and talked with the brother of Jared; and he was in a cloud, and the brother of Jared saw him not.

26 And it came to pass that the Lord commanded them that they should go forth into the wilderness, yea, into that quarter where there never had man been.

27 And it came to pass that the Lord did go before them, and did talk with them as he stood in a cloud, and gave directions whither they should travel.

28 And it came to pass that they did travel in the wilderness, and did build barges, in which they did cross many waters, being directed continually by the hand of the Lord.

29 And the Lord would not suffer that they should stop beyond the sea in the wilderness, but he would that they should come forth even unto the land of promise, which was choice above all other lands, which the Lord God had preserved for a righteous people;

30 And he had sworn in his wrath unto the brother of Jared, that whoso should possess this land of promise, from that time henceforth and for ever, should serve him, the true and only God, or they should be swept off when the fullness of his wrath should come upon them.

31 And now we can behold the decrees of God concerning this land, that it is a land of promise, and whatsoever nation shall possess it, shall serve God, or they shall be swept off when the fullness of his wrath shall come upon them.

32 And the fullness of his wrath cometh upon them when they are ripened in iniquity; for behold, this is a land which is choice above all other lands; wherefore he that doth possess it shall serve God, or shall be swept off; for it is the everlasting decree of God.

33 And it is not until the fullness of iniquity among the children of the land, that they are swept off.

34 And this cometh unto you, O ye Gentiles, that ye may know the decrees of God, that ye may repent, and not continue in your iniquities until the fullness come, that ye may not bring down the fullness of the wrath of God upon you, as the inhabitants of the land have hitherto done.

35 Behold, this is a choice land, and whatsoever nation shall possess it, shall be free from bondage, and from captivity, and from all other nations under heaven, if they will but serve the God of the land, who is Jesus Christ who hath been manifested by the things which we have written.

36 And now I proceed with my record; for behold it came

to pass that the Lord did bring Jared and his brethren forth even to that great sea which divideth the lands.

37 And as they came to the sea, they pitched their tents; and they called the name of the place Moriancumer; and they dwelt in tents; and dwelt in tents upon the sea-shore for the space of four years.

38 And it came to pass at the end of four years, that the Lord came again unto the brother of Jared, and stood in a cloud and talked with him.

39 And for the space of three hours did the Lord talk with the brother of Jared, and chastened him because he remembered not to call upon the name of the Lord.

40 And the brother of Jared repented of the evil which he had done, and did call upon the name of the Lord for his brethren who were with him.

41 And the Lord said unto him, I will forgive thee and thy brethren of their sins; but thou shalt not sin any more, for ye shall remember that my Spirit will not always strive with man; wherefore if ye will sin until ye are fully ripe, ye shall be cut off from the presence of the Lord.

42 And these are my thoughts upon the land which I shall give you for your inheritance; for it shall be a land choice above all other lands.

43 And the Lord said, Go to work and build, after the manner of barges which ye have hitherto built.

44 And it came to pass that the brother of Jared did go to work, and also his brethren, and built barges after the manner which they had built, according to the instructions of the Lord.

45 And they were small, and they were light upon the water, even like unto the lightness of a fowl upon the water; and they were built after a manner that they were exceeding tight, even that they would hold water like unto a dish;

46 And the bottom thereof was tight like unto a dish; and the sides thereof were tight like unto a dish; and the ends thereof were peaked; and the top thereof was tight like unto a dish; and the length thereof was the length of a tree; and the door thereof, when it was shut, was tight like unto a dish.

CHAP. 1.]   BOOK OF ETHER.   719

47 And it came to pass that the brother of Jared cried unto the Lord, saying, O Lord I have performed the work which thou hast commanded me, and I have made the barges according as thou hast directed me.

48 And behold, O Lord, in them there is no light, whither shall we steer?

49 And also we shall perish, for in them we can not breathe, save it is the air which is in them; therefore we shall perish.

50 And the Lord said unto the brother of Jared, Behold, thou shalt make a hole in the top thereof, and also in the bottom thereof; and when thou shalt suffer for air, thou shalt unstop the hole thereof, and receive air.

51 And if it so be that the water come in upon thee, behold, ye shall stop the hole thereof, that ye may not perish in the flood.

52 And it came to pass that the brother of Jared did so, according as the Lord had commanded.

53 And he cried again unto the Lord, saying, O Lord, behold, I have done even as thou hast commanded me; and I have prepared the vessels for my people, and behold, there is no light in them.

54 Behold, O Lord, wilt thou suffer that we shall cross this great water in darkness?

55 And the Lord said unto the brother of Jared, What will ye that I should do that ye may have light in your vessels?

56 For behold, ye can not have windows, for they will be dashed in pieces; neither shall ye take fire with you, for ye shall not go by the light of fire; for behold, ye shall be as a whale in the midst of the sea; for the mountain waves shall dash upon you.

57 Nevertheless, I will bring you up again out of the depths of the sea; for the winds have gone forth out of my mouth, and also the rains and the floods have I sent forth.

58 And behold, I prepare you against these things; for howbeit, ye can not cross this great deep, save I prepare you against the waves of the sea, and the winds which have gone forth, and the floods which shall come.

59 Therefore what will ye that I should prepare for you, that ye may have light when ye are swallowed up in the depths of the sea?

60 ¶And it came to pass that the brother of Jared, (now the number of the vessels which had been prepared, was eight,) went forth unto the mount, which they called the mount Shelem, because of its exceeding height, and did moulten out of a rock sixteen small stones;

61 And they were white and clear, even as transparent glass, and he did carry them in his hands upon the top of the mount, and cried again unto the Lord, saying, O Lord, thou hast said that we must be encompassed about by the floods.

62 Now behold, O Lord, and do not be angry with thy servant because of his weakness before thee; for we know that thou art holy, and dwellest in the heavens, and that we are unworthy before thee;

63 Because of the fall, our natures have become evil continually; nevertheless, O Lord, thou hast given us a commandment that we must call upon thee, that from thee we may receive according to our desires.

64 Behold, O Lord, thou hast smitten us because of our iniquity, and hath driven us forth, and for this many years we have been in the wilderness; nevertheless, thou hast been merciful unto us.

65 O Lord, look upon me in pity, and turn away thine anger from this thy people, and suffer not that they shall go forth across this raging deep in darkness, but behold these things which I have moulten out of the rock.

66 And I know, O Lord, that thou hast all power, and can do whatsoever thou wilt for the benefit of man; therefore touch these stones, O Lord, with thy finger, and prepare them that they may shine forth in darkness: and they shall shine forth unto us in the vessels which we have prepared, that we may have light while we shall cross the sea.

67 Behold, O Lord, thou canst do this. We know that thou art able to shew forth great power, which looks small unto the understanding of men.

68 And it came to pass that when the brother of Jared had said these words, behold, the Lord stretched forth his hand and touched the stones, one by one, with his finger;

69 And the vail was taken from off the eyes of the brother of Jared, and he saw the finger of the Lord; and it was as the finger of a man, like unto flesh and blood; and the brother of Jared fell down before the Lord, for he was struck with fear.

70 And the Lord saw that the brother of Jared had fallen to the earth; and the Lord said unto him, Arise, why hast thou fallen?

71 And he saith unto the Lord, I saw the finger of the Lord, and I feared lest he should smite me; for I knew not that the Lord had flesh and blood.

72 And the Lord said unto him, Because of thy faith thou hast seen that I shall take upon me flesh and blood; and never has man come before me with such exceeding faith as thou hast; for were it not so, ye could not have seen my finger. Sawest thou more than this?

73 And he answered, Nay, Lord, shew thyself unto me.

74 And the Lord said unto him, Believest thou the words which I shall speak?

75 And he answered, Yea, Lord, I know that thou speakest the truth, for thou art a God of truth, and canst not lie.

76 And when he had said these words, behold the Lord shewed himself unto him, and said, Because thou knowest these things, ye are redeemed from the fall; therefore ye are brought back into my presence; therefore I shew myself unto you.

77 Behold, I am he who was prepared from the foundation of the world to redeem my people. Behold, I am Jesus Christ. I am the Father and the Son.

78 In me shall all mankind have life, and that eternally, even they who shall believe on my name; and they shall become my sons and my daughters.

79 And never have I shewed myself unto man whom I have created, for never has man believed in me as thou hast.

80 Seest thou that ye are created after mine own image?

Yea, even all men were created in the beginning, after mine own image?

81 Behold this body, which ye now behold, is the body of my spirit; and man have I created after the body of my spirit; and even as I appear unto thee to be in the spirit, will I appear unto my people in the flesh.

82 ¶And now, as I, Moroni, said I could not make a full account of these things which are written, therefore it sufficeth me to say, that Jesus shewed himself unto this man in the spirit, even after the manner and in the likeness of the same body, even as he shewed himself unto the Nephites;

83 And he ministered unto him, even as he ministered unto the Nephites; and all this, that this man knew that he was God, because of the many great works which the Lord had shewed unto him.

84 And because of the knowledge of this man, he could not be kept from beholding within the vail; and he saw the finger of Jesus, which, when he saw, he fell with fear; for he knew that it was the finger of the Lord;

85 And he had faith no longer, for he knew, nothing doubting; wherefore, having this perfect knowledge of God, he could not be kept from within the vail; therefore he saw Jesus, and he did minister unto him.

86 ¶And it came to pass that the Lord said unto the brother of Jared, Behold, thou shalt not suffer these things which ye have seen and heard, to go forth unto the world, until the time cometh that I shall glorify my name in the flesh; wherefore, ye shall treasure up the things which ye have seen and heard, and shew it to no man.

87 And behold, when ye shall come unto me, ye shall write them and shall seal them up, that no one can interpret them; for ye shall write them in a language that they can not be read.

88 And behold, these two stones will I give unto thee, and ye shall seal them up also, with the things which ye shall write.

89 For behold, the language which ye shall write, I have confounded; wherefore I will cause in mine own due time that

these stones shall magnify to the eyes of men, these things which ye shall write.

90 And when the Lord had said these words, he shewed unto the brother of Jared all the inhabitants of the earth which had been, and also all that would be; and the Lord withheld them not from his sight, even unto the ends of the earth;

91 For the Lord had said unto him in times before, that if he would believe in him, that he could shew unto him all things—it should be shewn unto him; therefore the Lord could not withhold anything from him; for he knew that the Lord could shew him all things.

92 And the Lord said unto him, Write these things and seal them up, and I will shew them in mine own due time unto the children of men.

93 ¶And it came to pass that the Lord commanded him that he should seal up the two stones which he had received, and shew them not, until the Lord should shew them unto the children of men.

94 And the Lord commanded the brother of Jared to go down out of the mount from the presence of the Lord, and write the things which he had seen; and they were forbidden to come unto the children of men, until after that he should be lifted up upon the cross;

95 And for this cause did King Benjamin [Mosiah?] keep them, that they should not come unto the world until after Christ should shew himself unto his people.

96 And after Christ truly had shewed himself unto his people, he commanded that they should be made manifest.

97 And now, after that, they have all dwindled in unbelief, and there is none, save it be the Lamanites, and they have rejected the gospel of Christ; therefore I am commanded that I should hide them up again in the earth.

98 Behold, I have written upon these plates the very things which the brother of Jared saw; and there never was greater things made manifest, than that which was made manifest unto the brother of Jared; wherefore, the Lord hath commanded me to write them; and I have written them.

99 And he commanded me that I should seal them up; and he also hath commanded that I should seal up the interpretation thereof; wherefore I have sealed up the interpreters, according to the commandment of the Lord.

100 For the Lord said unto me, They shall not go forth unto the Gentiles until the day that they shall repent of their iniquity, and become clean before the Lord;

101 And in that day that they shall exercise faith in me, saith the Lord, even as the brother of Jared did, that they may become sanctified in me, then will I manifest unto them the things which the brother of Jared saw, even to the unfolding unto them all my revelations, saith Jesus Christ, the Son of God, the Father of the heavens and of the earth, and all things that in them are.

102 And he that will contend against the word of the Lord, let him be accursed; and he that shall deny these things, let him be accursed; for unto them will I shew no greater things, saith Jesus Christ, for I am he who speaketh;

103 And at my command the heavens are opened and are shut; and at my word, the earth shall shake; and at my command the inhabitants thereof shall pass away, even so as by fire;

104 And he that believeth not my words, believeth not my disciples; and if it so be that I do not speak, judge ye; for ye shall know that it is I that speaketh, at the last day.

105 But he that believeth these things which I have spoken, him will I visit with the manifestations of my Spirit; and he shall know and bear record.

106 For because of my Spirit, he shall know that these things are true; for it persuadeth men to do good; and whatsoever thing persuadeth men to do good, is of me; for good cometh of none, save it be of me.

107 I am the same that leadeth men to all good; he that will not believe my words, will not believe me, that I am; and he that will not believe me, will not believe the Father who sent me.

108 For behold, I am the Father, I am the light, and the life, and the truth of the world.

109 Come unto me, O ye Gentiles, and I will shew unto you the greater things, the knowledge which is hid up because of unbelief.

110 Come unto me, O ye house of Israel, and it shall be made manifest unto you how great things the Father hath laid up for you, from the foundation of the world; and it hath not come unto you, because of unbelief.

111 Behold, when ye shall rend that vail of unbelief which doth cause you to remain in your awful state of wickedness and hardness of heart, and blindness of mind, then shall the great and marvelous things which have been hid up from the foundation of the world from you;

112 Yea, when ye shall call upon the Father in my name, with a broken heart and a contrite spirit, then shall ye know that the Father hath remembered the covenant which he made unto your fathers, O house of Israel;

113 And then shall my revelations which I have caused to be written by my servant John, be unfolded in the eyes of all the people.

114 Remember, when ye see these things, ye shall know that the time is at hand that they shall be made manifest in very deed; therefore, when ye shall receive this record, ye may know that the work of the Father has commenced upon all the face of the land.

115 Therefore, repent all ye ends of the earth, and come unto me, and believe in my gospel, and be baptized in my name; for he that believeth, and is baptized, shall be saved; but he that believeth not, shall be damned; and signs shall follow them that believe in my name.

116 And blessed is he that is found faithful unto my name, at the last day, for he shall be lifted up to dwell in the kingdom prepared for him from the foundation of the world.

117 And behold, it is I that hath spoken it. Amen.

CHAPTER 2.

1 ¶And now I, Moroni, have written the words which were commanded me, according to my memory; and I have told you the things which I have sealed up; therefore touch them

not, in order that ye may translate; for that thing is forbidden you, except by and by it shall be wisdom in God.

2 And behold, ye may be privileged that ye may shew the plates unto those who shall assist to bring forth this work; and unto three shall they be shewn by the power of God: wherefore they shall know of a surety that these things are true.

3 And in the mouth of three witnesses shall these things be established; and the testimony of three, and this work, in the which shall be shewn forth the power of God, and also his word, of which the Father, and the Son, and the Holy Ghost beareth record; and all this shall stand as a testimony against the world, at the last day.

4 And if it so be that they repent and come unto the Father in the name of Jesus, they shall be received into the kingdom of God.

5 And now, if I have no authority for these things, judge ye, for ye shall know that I have authority when ye shall see me, and we shall stand before God at the last day. Amen.

CHAPTER 3.

1 ¶And now I, Moroni, proceed to give the record of Jared and his brother.

2 For it came to pass after the Lord had prepared the stones which the brother of Jared had carried up into the mount, the brother of Jared came down out of the mount, and he did put forth the stones into the vessels which were prepared, one in each end thereof; and behold, they did give light unto the vessels thereof.

3 And thus the Lord caused stones to shine in darkness, to give light unto men, women and children, that they might not cross the great waters in darkness.

4 ¶And it came to pass that when they had prepared all manner of food, that thereby they might subsist upon the water, and also food for their flocks and herds, and whatsoever beast, or animal, or fowl that they should carry with them.

5 And it came to pass that when they had done all these things, they got aboard of their vessels or barges, and set forth into the sea, commending themselves unto the Lord their God.

6 And it came to pass that the Lord God caused that there should a furious wind blow upon the face of the waters, towards the promised land: and thus they were tossed upon the waves of the sea before the wind.

7 And it came to pass that they were many times buried in the depths of the sea, because of the mountain waves which broke upon them, and also the great and terrible tempests which were caused by the fierceness of the wind.

8 ¶And it came to pass that when they were buried in the deep, there was no water that could hurt them, their vessels being tight like unto a dish, and also they were tight like unto the ark of Noah;

9 Therefore when they were encompassed about by many waters, they did cry unto the Lord, and he did bring them forth again upon the top of the waters.

10 And it came to pass that the wind did never cease to blow towards the promised land, while they were upon the waters: and thus they were driven forth before the wind;

11 And they did sing praises unto the Lord; yea, the brother of Jared did sing praises unto the Lord, and he did thank and praise the Lord all the day long; and when the night came, they did not cease to praise the Lord.

12 And thus they were driven forth; and no monster of the sea could break them, neither whale that could mar them; and they did have light continually, whether it was above the water or under the water.

13 And thus they were driven forth, three hundred and forty and four days upon the water; and they did land upon the shore of the promised land.

14 And when they had set their feet upon the shores of the promised land, they bowed themselves down upon the face of the land, and did humble themselves before the Lord, and did shed tears of joy before the Lord, because of the multitude of his tender mercies over them.

15 ¶And it came to pass that they went forth upon the face of the land, and began to till the earth.

16 And Jared had four sons; and they were called Jacom, and Gilgah, and Mahah, and Orihah.

17 And the brother of Jared also begat sons and daughters.

18 And the friends of Jared and his brother, were in number about twenty and two souls; and they also begat sons and daughters, before they came to the promised land; and therefore they began to be many.

19 And they were taught to walk humbly before the Lord; and they were also taught from on high.

20 ¶And it came to pass that they began to spread upon the face of the land, and to multiply and to till the earth; and they did wax strong in the land.

21 And the brother of Jared began to be old, and saw that he must soon go down to the grave; wherefore he said unto Jared, Let us gather together our people that we may number them, that we may know of them what they will desire of us before we go down to our graves.

22 And accordingly the people were gathered together.

23 Now the number of the sons and the daughters of the brother of Jared were twenty and two souls; and the number of the sons and daughters of Jared were twelve, he having four sons.

24 And it came to pass that they did number their people; and after that they had numbered them, they did desire of them the things which they would that they should do before they went down to their graves.

25 And it came to pass that the people desired of them that they should anoint one of their sons to be a king over them.

26 And now behold, this was grievous unto them.

27 But the brother of Jared said unto them, Surely, this thing leadeth into captivity.

28 But Jared said unto his brother, Suffer them that they may have a king; and therefore he said unto them, Choose ye out from among our sons a king, even whom ye will.

29 ¶And it came to pass that they chose even the first-born of the brother of Jared; and his name was Pagag.

30 And it came to pass that he refused and would not be their king.

31 And the people would that his father should constrain him; but his father would not; and he commanded them that they should constrain no man to be their king.

32 And it came to pass that they chose all the brothers of Pagag, and they would not.

33 And it came to pass that neither would the sons of Jared, even all, save it were one; and Orihah was anointed to be king over the people.

34 And he began to reign, and the people began to prosper; and they became exceeding rich.

35 And it came to pass that Jared died, and his brother also.

36 And it came to pass that Orihah did walk humbly before the Lord, and did remember how great things the Lord had done for his father, and also taught his people how great things the Lord had done for their fathers.

37 ¶And it came to pass that Orihah did execute judgment upon the land in righteousness all his days, whose days were exceeding many.

38 And he begat sons and daughters; yea, he begat thirty and one, among whom were twenty and three sons.

39 And it came to pass that he also begat Kib in his old age.

40 And it came to pass that Kib reigned in his stead; and Kib begat Corihor.

41 And when Corihor was thirty and two years old, he rebelled against his father, and went over and dwelt in the land of Nehor; and he begat sons and daughters; and they became exceeding fair; wherefore Corihor drew away many people after him.

42 And when he had gathered together an army, he came up unto the land of Moron where the king dwelt, and took him captive, which brought to pass the saying of the brother of Jared, that they would be brought into captivity.

43 Now the land of Moron where the king dwelt, was near the land which is called Desolation by the Nephites.

44 And it came to pass that Kib dwelt in captivity, and his people under Corihor his son, until he became exceeding old; nevertheless Kib begat Shule in his old age, while he was yet in captivity.

45 ¶And it came to pass that Shule was angry with his brother; and Shule waxed strong, and became mighty, as to the strength of a man; and he was also mighty in judgment.

46 Wherefore he came to the hill Ephraim, and he did moulten out of the hill, and made swords out of steel for those whom he had drawn away with him; and after he had armed them with swords, he returned to the city Nehor and gave battle unto his brother Corihor, by which means he obtained the kingdom, and restored it unto his father Kib.

47 And now because of the thing which Shule had done, his father bestowed upon him the kingdom; therefore he began to reign in the stead of his father.

48 And it came to pass that he did execute judgment in righteousness; and he did spread his kingdom upon all the face of the land, for the people had become exceeding numerous.

49 And it came to pass that Shule also begat many sons and daughters.

50 And Corihor repented of the many evils which he had done; wherefore Shule gave him power in his kingdom.

51 And it came to pass that Corihor had many sons and daughters.

52 And among the sons of Corihor there was one whose name was Noah.

53 ¶And it came to pass that Noah rebelled against Shule, the king, and also his father Corihor, and drew away Cohor his brother, and also all his brethren and many of the people.

54 And he gave battle unto Shule, the king, in which he did obtain the land of their first inheritance; and he became a king over that part of the land.

55 And it came to pass that he gave battle again unto Shule the king; and he took Shule the king, and carried him away captive into Moron.

56 And it came to pass as he was about to put him to

death, the sons of Shule crept into the house of Noah by night and slew him, and broke down the door of the prison and brought out their father, and placed him upon his throne in his own kingdom; wherefore the son of Noah did build up his kingdom in his stead;

57 Nevertheless they did not gain power any more over Shule the king; and the people who were under the reign of Shule the king, did prosper exceedingly and wax great.

58 And the country was divided; and there were two kingdoms, the kingdom of Shule and the kingdom of Cohor, the son of Noah.

59 And Cohor, the son of Noah, caused that his people should give battle unto Shule, in which Shule did beat them, and did slay Cohor.

60 And now Cohor had a son who was called Nimrod; and Nimrod gave up the kingdom of Cohor unto Shule, and he did gain favor in the eyes of Shule: wherefore Shule did bestow great favors upon him, and he did do in the kingdom of Shule according to his desires;

61 And also in the reign of Shule there came prophets among the people, who were sent from the Lord, prophesying that the wickedness and idolatry of the people was bringing a curse upon the land, and they should be destroyed, if they did not repent.

62 ¶And it came to pass that the people did revile against the prophets, and did mock them.

63 And it came to pass that King Shule did execute judgment against all those who did revile against the prophets; and he did execute a law throughout all the land, which gave power unto the prophets that they should go whithersoever they would; and by this cause the people were brought unto repentance.

64 And because the people did repent of their iniquities and idolatries, the Lord did spare them, and they began to prosper again in the land.

65 And it came to pass that Shule begat sons and daughters in his old age.

66 And there were no more wars in the days of Shule; and

he remembered the great things that the Lord had done for his fathers in bringing them across the great deep into the promised land; wherefore he did execute judgment in righteousness all his days.

67 ¶And it came to pass that he begat Omer, and Omer reigned in his stead.

68 And Omer begat Jared; and Jared begat sons and daughters.

69 And Jared rebelled against his father, and came and dwelt in the land of Heth.

70 And it came to pass that he did flatter many people, because of his cunning words, until he had gained the half of the kingdom.

71 And when he had gained the half of the kingdom, he gave battle unto his father, and he did carry away his father into captivity, and did make him serve in captivity.

72 And now in the days of the reign of Omer, he was in captivity the half of his days.

73 And it came to pass that he begat sons and daughters, among whom were Esrom and Coriantumr; and they were exceeding angry because of the doings of Jared their brother, insomuch that they did raise an army, and gave battle unto Jared.

74 And it came to pass that they did give battle unto him by night.

75 And it came to pass that when they had slain the army of Jared, they were about to slay him also; and he plead with them that they would not slay him, and he would give up the kingdom unto his father.

76 And it came to pass that they did grant unto him his life.

77 And now Jared became exceeding sorrowful because of the loss of the kingdom, for he had set his heart upon the kingdom, and upon the glory of the world.

78 Now the daughter of Jared being exceeding expert, and seeing the sorrow of her father, thought to devise a plan whereby she could redeem the kingdom unto her father.

79 Now the daughter of Jared was exceeding fair. And

it came to pass that she did talk with her father, and said unto him, Whereby hath my father so much sorrow?

80 Hath he not read the record which our fathers brought across the great deep?

81 Behold, is there not an account concerning them of old, that they by their secret plans did obtain kingdoms and great glory?

82 And now therefore, let my father send for Akish, the son of Kimnor; and behold, I am fair, and I will dance before him, and I will please him, that he will desire me to wife; wherefore if he shall desire of thee that ye shall give unto him me to wife, then shall ye say, I will give her if ye will bring unto me the head of my father, the king.

83 And now Omer was a friend to Akish, wherefore when Jared had sent for Akish, the daughter of Jared danced before him, that she pleased him, insomuch that he desired her to wife.

84 And it came to pass that he said unto Jared, Give her unto me to wife.

85 And Jared said unto him, I will give her unto you, if ye will bring unto me the head of my father, the king.

86 And it came to pass that Akish gathered in unto the house of Jared all his kinsfolks, and said unto them, Will ye swear unto me that ye will be faithful unto me in the thing which I shall desire of you.

87 And it came to pass that they all swear unto him by the God of heaven, and also by the heavens, and also by the earth, and by their heads, that whoso should vary from the assistance which Akish desired, should lose his head;

88 And whoso should divulge whatsoever thing Akish made known unto them, the same should lose his life. And it came to pass that thus they did agree with Akish.

89 And Akish did administer unto them the oaths which were given by them of old, who also sought power, which had been handed down even from Cain, who was a murderer from the beginning.

90 And they were kept up by the power of the devil to administer these oaths unto the people, to keep them in dark-

ness, to help such as sought power, to gain power, and to murder, and to plunder, and to lie, and to commit all manner of wickedness and whoredoms.

91 And it was the daughter of Jared who put it into his heart to search up these things of old; and Jared put it into the heart of Akish; wherefore Akish administered it unto his kindreds and friends, leading them away by fair promises to do whatsoever thing he desired.

92 And it came to pass that they formed a secret combination, even as they of old; which combination is most abominable and wicked above all, in the sight of God;

93 For the Lord worketh not in secret combinations, neither doth he will that man should shed blood, but in all things hath forbidden it, from the beginning of man.

94 And now I, Moroni, do not write the manner of their oaths and combinations, for it hath been made known unto me that they are had among all people, and they are had among the Lamanites, and they have caused the destruction of this people of whom I am now speaking, and also the destruction of the people of Nephi;

95 And whatsoever nation shall uphold such secret combinations, to get power and gain, until they shall spread over the nation, behold, they shall be destroyed, for the Lord will not suffer that the blood of his saints, which shall be shed by them, shall always cry unto him from the ground for vengeance upon them, and yet he avenge them not;

96 Wherefore, O ye Gentiles, it is wisdom in God that these things should be shewn unto you, that thereby ye may repent of your sins, and suffer not that these murderous combinations shall get above you, which are built up to get power and gain, and the work, yea, even the work of destruction come upon you;

97 Yea, even the sword of the justice of the eternal God, shall fall upon you, to your overthrow and destruction, if ye shall suffer these things to be;

98 Wherefore the Lord commandeth you, when ye shall see these things come among you, that ye shall awake to a sense of your awful situation, because of this secret combination

which shall be among you, or wo be unto it, because of the blood of them who have been slain; for they cry from the dust for vengeance upon it, and also upon those who build it up.

99 For it cometh to pass that whoso buildeth it up, seeketh to overthrow the freedom of all lands, nations and countries:

100 And it bringeth to pass the destruction of all people, for it is built up by the devil, who is the father of all lies; even that same liar who beguiled our first parents;

101 Yea, even that same liar who hath caused man to commit murder from the beginning; who hath hardened the hearts of men, that they have murdered the prophets, and stoned them, and cast them out from the beginning.

102 Wherefore I, Moroni, am commanded to write these things, that evil may be done away, and that the time may come that Satan may have no power upon the hearts of the children of men, but that they may be persuaded to do good continually, that they may come unto the fountain of all righteousness and be saved.

CHAPTER 4.

1 ¶And now I, Moroni, proceed with my record.

2 Therefore behold, it came to pass that because of the secret combinations of Akish and his friends, behold they did overthrow the kingdom of Omer; nevertheless the Lord was merciful unto Omer, and also to his sons and to his daughters, who did not seek his destruction.

3 And the Lord warned Omer in a dream that he should depart out of the land; wherefore Omer departed out of the land with his family, and traveled many days, and came over and passed by the hill of Shim,

4 And came over by the place where the Nephites were destroyed, and from thence eastward, and came to a place which was called Ablom, by the sea-shore, and there he pitched his tent, and also his sons and his daughters, and all his household, save it were Jared and his family.

5 ¶And it came to pass that Jared was anointed king over

the people, by the hand of wickedness; and he gave unto Akish his daughter to wife.

6 And it came to pass that Akish sought the life of his father-in-law; and he applied unto those whom he had sworn by the oath of the ancients, and they obtained the head of his father-in-law, as he sat upon his throne, giving audience to his people;

7 For so great had been the spreading of this wicked and secret society, that it had corrupted the hearts of all the people; therefore Jared was murdered upon his throne, and Akish reigned in his stead.

8 And it came to pass that Akish began to be jealous of his son, therefore he shut him up in prison, and kept him upon little or no food, until he had suffered death.

9 And now the brother of him that suffered death, (and his name was Nimrah,) was angry with his father, because of that which his father had done unto his brother.

10 And it came to pass that Nimrah gathered together a small number of men, and fled out of the land, and came over and dwelt with Omer.

11 And it came to pass that Akish begat other sons, and they won the hearts of the people, notwithstanding they had sworn unto him to do all manner of iniquity, according to that which he desired.

12 Now the people of Akish were desirous for gain, even as Akish was desirous for power; wherefore the sons of Akish did offer them money, by which means they drew away the more part of the people after them;

13 And there began to be a war between the sons of Akish and Akish, which lasted for the space of many years; yea, unto the destruction of nearly all the people of the kingdom;

14 Yea, even all, save it were thirty souls, and they who fled with the house of Omer; wherefore Omer was restored again to the land of his inheritance.

15 And it came to pass that Omer began to be old, nevertheless, in his old age he begat Emer; and he anointed Emer to be king to reign in his stead.

16 And after that he had anointed Emer to be king, he

saw peace in the land for the space of two years, and he died, having seen exceeding many days, which were full of sorrow.

17 And it came to pass that Emer did reign in his stead, and did fill the steps of his father.

18 And the Lord began again to take the curse from off the land, and the house of Emer did prosper exceedingly under the reign of Emer;

19 And in the space of sixty and two years, they had become exceeding strong, insomuch that they became exceeding rich, having all manner of fruit, and of grain, and of silks, and of fine linen, and of gold, and of silver, and of precious things,

20 And also all manner of cattle, of oxen, and cows, and of sheep, and of swine, and of goats, and also many other kind of animals which were useful for the food of man;

21 And they also had horses, and asses, and there were elephants, and cureloms, and cumoms: all of which were useful unto man, and more especially the elephants, and cureloms, and cumoms.

22 And thus the Lord did pour out his blessings upon this land, which was choice above all other lands; and he commanded that whoso should possess the land, should possess it unto the Lord, or they should be destroyed when they were ripened in iniquity; for upon such, saith the Lord, I will pour out the fullness of my wrath.

23 And Emer did execute judgment in righteousness, all his days, and he begat many sons and daughters; and he begat Coriantum, and he anointed Coriantum to reign in his stead.

24 And after he had anointed Coriantum to reign in his stead, he lived four years, and he saw peace in the land; yea, and he even saw the Son of righteousness, and did rejoice and glory in his day; and he died in peace.

25 And it came to pass that Coriantum did walk in the steps of his father, and did build many mighty cities, and did administer that which was good unto his people, in all his days.

26 And it came to pass that he had no children, even until he was exceeding old.

27 And it came to pass that his wife died, being an hundred and two years old.

28 And it came to pass that Coriantum took to wife, in his old age, a young maid, and begat sons and daughters; wherefore he lived until he was an hundred and forty and two years old.

29 And it came to pass that he begat Com, and Com reigned in his stead; and he reigned forty and nine years, and he begat Heth; and he also begat other sons and daughters.

30 And the people had spread again over all the face of the land, and there began again to be an exceeding great wickedness upon the face of the land, and Heth began to embrace the secret plans again of old, to destroy his father.

31 And it came to pass that he did dethrone his father: for he slew him with his own sword: and he did reign in his stead.

32 And there came prophets in the land again, crying repentance unto them; that they must prepare the way of the Lord, or there should come a curse upon the face of the land; yea, even there should be a great famine, in which they should be destroyed, if they did not repent.

33 But the people believed not the words of the prophets, but they cast them out; and some of them they cast into pits, and left them to perish.

34 And it came to pass that they done all these things according to the commandment of the King Heth.

35 And it came to pass that there began to be a great dearth upon the land, and the inhabitants began to be destroyed exceeding fast, because of the dearth, for there was no rain upon the face of the earth; and there came forth poisonous serpents also upon the face of the land, and did poison many people.

36 And it came to pass that their flocks began to flee before the poisonous serpents, towards the land southward, which was called by the Nephites, Zarahemla.

37 And it came to pass that there were many of them which did perish by the way: nevertheless there were some which fled into the land southward.

38 And it came to pass that the Lord did cause the serpents that they should pursue them no more, but that they should hedge up the way, that the people could not pass; that whoso should attempt to pass, might fall by the poisonous serpents.

39 And it came to pass that the people did follow the course of the beasts, and did devour the carcasses of them which fell by the way, until they had devoured them all.

40 Now when the people saw that they must perish, they began to repent of their iniquities, and cry unto the Lord.

41 And it came to pass that when they had humbled themselves sufficiently before the Lord, he did send rain upon the face of the earth, and the people began to revive again, and there began to be fruit in the north countries, and in all the countries round about.

42 And the Lord did shew forth his power unto them in preserving them from famine.

43 And it came to pass that Shez, who was a descendant of Heth, for Heth had perished by the famine, and all his household, save it were Shez; wherefore Shez began to build up again a broken people.

44 And it came to pass that Shez did remember the destruction of his fathers, and he did build up a righteous kingdom, for he remembered what the Lord had done in bringing Jared and his brother across the deep; and he did walk in the ways of the Lord, and he begat sons and daughters.

45 And his eldest son, whose name was Shez, did rebel against him; nevertheless, Shez was smitten by the hand of a robber, because of his exceeding riches, which brought peace again unto his father.

46 And it came to pass that his father did build up many cities upon the face of the land, and the people began again to spread over all the face of the land.

47 And Shez did live to an exceeding old age; and he be-

gat Riplakish, and he died. And Riplakish reigned in his stead.

48 And it came to pass that Riplakish did not do that which was right in the sight of the Lord, for he did have many wives and concubines, and did lay that upon men's shoulders which was grievous to be borne; yea, he did tax them with heavy taxes; and with the taxes he did build many spacious buildings.

49 And he did erect him an exceeding beautiful throne; and he did build many prisons, and whoso would not be subject unto taxes, he did cast into prison; and whoso was not able to pay taxes, he did cast into prison;

50 And he did cause that they should labor continually for their support; and whoso refused to labor, he did cause to be put to death; wherefore he did obtain all his fine work; yea, even his fine gold he did cause to be refined in prison, and all manner of fine workmanship he did cause to be wrought in prison.

51 And it came to pass that he did afflict the people with his whoredoms and abominations; and when he had reigned for the space of forty and two years, the people did raise up in rebellion against him, and there began to be war again in the land, insomuch that Riplakish was killed, and his descendants were driven out of the land.

52 ¶And it came to pass after the space of many years, Morianton, (he being a descendant of Riplakish,) gathered together an army of outcasts, and went forth and gave battle unto the people; and he gained power over many cities;

53 And the war became exceeding sore, and did last for the space of many years, and he did gain power over all the land, and did establish himself king over all the land.

54 And after that he had established himself king, he did ease the burden of the people, by which he did gain favor in the eyes of the people, and they did anoint him to be their king.

55 And he did do justice unto the people, but not unto himself, because of his many whoredoms; wherefore he was cut off from the presence of the Lord.

56 And it came to pass that Morianton built up many cities, and the people became exceeding rich under his reign, both in buildings, and in gold, and in silver, and in raising grain, and in flocks, and herds, and such things which had been restored unto them.

57 And Morianton did live to an exceeding great age, and then he begat Kim; and Kim did reign in the stead of his father; and he did reign eight years, and his father died.

58 And it came to pass that Kim did not reign in righteousness, wherefore he was not favored of the Lord.

59 And his brother did raise up in rebellion against him, by which he did bring him into captivity; and he did remain in captivity all his days; and he begat sons and daughters in captivity; and in his old age he begat Levi, and he died.

60 ¶And it came to pass that Levi did serve in captivity after the death of his father, for the space of forty and two years.

61 And he did make war against the king of the land, by which he did obtain unto himself the kingdom.

62 And after he had obtained unto himself the kingdom, he did that which was right in the sight of the Lord; and the people did prosper in the land, and he did live to a good old age, and begat sons and daughters; and he also begat Corom, whom he anointed king in his stead.

63 And it came to pass that Corom did that which was good in the sight of the Lord, all his days; and he begat many sons and daughters; and after he had seen many days, he did pass away, even like unto the rest of the earth; and Kish reigned in his stead.

64 And it came to pass that Kish passed away also, and Lib reigned in his stead.

65 And it came to pass that Lib also did that which was good in the sight of the Lord.

66 And in the days of Lib the poisonous serpents were destroyed; wherefore they did go into the land southward, to hunt food for the people of the land; for the land was covered with animals of the forest.

67 And Lib also himself became a great hunter.

68 And they built a great city by the narrow neck of land, by the place where the sea divides the land.

69 And they did preserve the land southward for a wilderness, to get game.

70 And the whole face of the land northward was covered with inhabitants; and they were exceeding industrious, and they did buy and sell, and traffic one with another, that they might get gain.

71 And they did work in all manner of ore, and they did make gold, and silver, and iron, and brass, and all manner of metals; and they did dig it out of the earth; wherefore they did cast up mighty heaps of earth to get ore, of gold, and of silver, and of iron, and of copper.

72 And they did work all manner of fine work.

73 And they did have silks, and fine twined linen; and they did work all manner of cloth, that they might clothe themselves from their nakedness.

74 And they did make all manner of tools to till the earth, both to plow and to sow, to reap and to hoe, and also to thrash.

75 And they did make all manner of tools with which they did work their beasts.

76 And they did make all manner of weapons of war.

77 And they did work all manner of work of exceeding curious workmanship.

78 And never could be a people more blessed than were they, and more prospered by the hand of the Lord.

79 And they were in a land that was choice above all lands, for the Lord had spoken it.

80 And it came to pass that Lib did live many years, and begat sons and daughters; and he also begat Hearthom.

81 And it came to pass that Hearthom reigned in the stead of his father.

82 And when Hearthom had reigned twenty and four years, behold the kingdom was taken away from him.

83 And he served many years in captivity; yea, even all the remainder of his days.

84 And he begat Heth, and Heth lived in captivity all his days.

85 And Heth begat Aaron, and Aaron dwelt in captivity all his days; and he begat Amnigaddah, and Amnigaddah also dwelt in captivity all his days; and he begat Coriantum, and Coriantum dwelt in captivity all his days; and he begat Com.

86 And it came to pass that Com drew away the half of the kingdom.

87 And he reigned over the half of the kingdom forty and two years: and he went to battle against the king Amgid, and they fought for the space of many years, during which time Com gained power over Amgid, and obtained power over the remainder of the kingdom.

88 And in the days of Com there began to be robbers in the land; and they adopted the old plans, and administered oaths after the manner of the ancients, and sought again to destroy the kingdom.

89 Now Com did fight against them much; nevertheless he did not prevail against them.

90 And there came also in the days of Com many prophets, and prophesied of the destruction of that great people, except they should repent and turn unto the Lord, and forsake their murders and wickedness.

91 ¶And it came to pass that the prophets were rejected by the people, and they fled unto Com for protection, for the people sought to destroy them; and they prophesied unto Com many things; and he was blessed in all the remainder of his days.

92 And he lived to a good old age, and begat Shiblom; and Shiblom reigned in his stead.

93 And the brother of Shiblom rebelled against him; and there began to be an exceeding great war in all the land.

94 ¶And it came to pass that the brother of Shiblom caused that all the prophets who prophesied of the destruction of the people, should be put to death;

95 And there was great calamity in all the land, for they had testified that a greater curse should come upon the land,

and also upon the people, and that there should be a great destruction among them, such an one as never had been upon the face of the earth;

96 And their bones should become as heaps of earth upon the face of the land, except they should repent of their wickedness.

97 And they hearkened not unto the voice of the Lord, because of their wicked combinations; wherefore there began to be wars and contentions in all the land, and also many famines and pestilences, insomuch that there was a great destruction, such an one as never had been known upon the face of the earth, and all this came to pass in the days of Shiblom.

98 And the people began to repent of their iniquity; and inasmuch as they did, the Lord did have mercy on them.

99 ¶And it came to pass that Shiblom was slain, and Seth was brought into captivity; and did dwell in captivity all his days.

100 And it came to pass that Ahah, his son, did obtain the kingdom; and he did reign over the people all his days.

101 And he did do all manner of iniquity in his days, by which he did cause the shedding of much blood; and few were his days.

102 And Ethem, being a descendant of Ahah, did obtain the kingdom; and he also did do that which was wicked in his days.

103 And it came to pass in the days of Ethem, there came many prophets and prophesied again unto the people; yea, they did prophesy that the Lord would utterly destroy them from off the face of the earth, except they repented of their iniquities.

104 And it came to pass that the people hardened their hearts, and would not hearken unto their words; and the prophets mourned and withdrew from among the people.

105 ¶And it came to pass that Ethem did execute judgment in wickedness all his days; and he begat Moron.

106 And it came to pass that Moron did reign in his stead; and Moron did that which was wicked before the Lord.

107 And it came to pass that there arose a rebellion among the people, because of that secret combination which was built up to get power and gain; and there arose a mighty man among them in iniquity, and gave battle unto Moron, in which he did overthrow the half of the kingdom; and he did maintain the half of the kingdom for many years.

108 And it came to pass that Moron did overthrow him, and did obtain the kingdom again.

109 And it came to pass that there arose another mighty man; and he was a descendant of the brother of Jared.

110 And it came to pass that he did overthrow Moron and obtain the kingdom; wherefore Moron dwelt in captivity all the remainder of his days; and he begat Coriantor.

111 ¶And it came to pass that Coriantor dwelt in captivity all his days.

112 And in the days of Coriantor there also came many prophets, and prophesied of great and marvelous things, and cried repentance unto the people, and except they should repent, the Lord God would execute judgment against them to their utter destruction;

113 And that the Lord God would send or bring forth another people to possess the land, by his power, after the manner which he brought their fathers.

114 And they did reject all the words of the prophets, because of their secret society and wicked abominations.

115 And it came to pass that Coriantor begat Ether, and he died, having dwelt in captivity all his days.

CHAPTER 5.

1 ¶And it came to pass that the days of Ether were in the days of Coriantumr; and Coriantumr was king over all the land.

2 And Ether was a prophet of the Lord; wherefore Ether came forth in the days of Coriantumr, and began to prophesy unto the people, for he could not be restrained because of the Spirit of the Lord which was in him;

3 For he did cry from the morning, even until the going

down of the sun, exhorting the people to believe in God unto repentance, lest they should be destroyed, saying unto them, that by faith all things are fulfilled;

4 Wherefore, whoso believeth in God, might with surety hope for a better world, yea, even a place at the right hand of God, which hope cometh of faith, maketh an anchor to the souls of men, which would make them sure and steadfast, always abounding in good works, being led to glorify God.

5 And it came to pass that Ether did prophesy great and marvelous things unto the people, which they did not believe, because they saw them not.

6 And now I, Moroni, would speak somewhat concerning these things; I would shew unto the world that faith is things which are hoped for and not seen;

7 Wherefore, dispute not because ye see not, for ye receive no witness until after the trial of your faith, for it was by faith that Christ shewed himself unto our fathers, after he had risen from the dead;

8 And he shewed not himself unto them, until after they had faith in him; wherefore, it must needs be that some had faith in him, for he shewed himself not unto the world.

9 But because of the faith of men, he has shewn himself unto the world, and glorified the name of the Father, and prepared a way that thereby others might be partakers of the heavenly gift, that they might hope for those things which they have not seen;

10 Wherefore ye may also have hope, and be partakers of the gift, if ye will but have faith.

11 Behold, it was by faith that they of old were called after the holy order of God; wherefore, by faith was the law of Moses given.

12 But in the gift of his Son, hath God prepared a more excellent way, and it is by faith that it hath been fulfilled;

13 For if there be no faith among the children of men, God can do no miracle among them; wherefore he shewed not himself until after their faith.

14 Behold, it was the faith of Alma and Amulek that caused the prison to tumble to the earth.

15 Behold, it was the faith of Nephi and Lehi, that wrought the change upon the Lamanites, that they were baptized with fire and with the Holy Ghost.

16 Behold, it was the faith of Ammon and his brethren, which wrought so great a miracle among the Lamanites; yea, and even all they who wrought miracles, wrought them by faith, even those who were before Christ, and also them who were after.

17 And it was by faith that the three disciples obtained a promise that they should not taste of death; and they obtained not the promise until after their faith.

18 And neither at any time hath any wrought miracles until after their faith; wherefore they first believed in the Son of God.

19 And there were many whose faith was so exceeding strong even before Christ came, who could not be kept from within the vail, but truly saw with their eyes the things which they had beheld with an eye of faith, and they were glad.

20 And behold we have seen in this record, that one of these was the brother of Jared; for so great was his faith in God, that when God put forth his finger, he could not hide it from the sight of the brother of Jared, because of his word which he had spoken unto him, which word he had obtained by faith.

21 And after the brother of Jared had beheld the finger of the Lord, because of the promise which the brother of Jared had obtained by faith, the Lord could not withhold anything from his sight; wherefore he shewed him all things, for he could no longer be kept without the vail.

22 And it is by faith that my fathers have obtained the promise that these things should come unto their brethren through the Gentiles; therefore the Lord hath commanded me, yea, even Jesus Christ.

23 And I said unto him, Lord, the Gentiles will mock at these things, because of our weakness in writing; for Lord thou hast made us mighty in word by faith, but thou hast not made us mighty in writing;

24 For thou hast made all this people that they could speak

much, because of the Holy Ghost which thou hast given them; and thou hast made us that we could write but little, because of the awkwardness of our hands.

25 Behold, thou hast not made us mighty in writing like unto the brother of Jared, for thou madest him that the things which he wrote, were mighty even as thou art, unto the overpowering of man to read them.

26 Thou hast also made our words powerful and great, even that we can not write them; wherefore, when we write, we behold our weakness, and stumble because of the placing of our words; and I fear lest the Gentiles shall mock at our words.

27 And when I had said this, the Lord spake unto me, saying, Fools mock, but they shall mourn; and my grace is sufficient for the meek, that they shall take no advantage of your weakness; and if men come unto me, I will shew unto them their weakness.

28 I give unto men weakness, that they may be humble; and my grace is sufficient for all men that humble themselves before me; for if they humble themselves before me, and have faith in me, then will I make weak things become strong unto them.

29 Behold, I will shew unto the Gentiles their weakness, and I will shew unto them that faith, hope, and charity, bringeth unto me the fountain of all righteousness.

30 And I, Moroni, having heard these words, was comforted, and said, O Lord, thy righteous will be done, for I know that thou workest unto the children of men according to their faith; for the brother of Jared said unto the mountain Zerin, Remove, and it was removed.

31 And if he had not had faith, it would not have moved; wherefore thou workest after men have faith; for thus did thou manifest thyself unto thy disciples.

32 For after they had faith and did speak in thy name, thou didst shew thyself unto them in great power; and I also remember that thou hast said that thou hast prepared a house for man; yea, even among the mansions of thy Father, in which man might have a more excellent hope; wherefore

man must hope, or he can not receive an inheritance in the place which thou hast prepared.

33 And again I remember that thou hast said that thou hast loved the world, even unto the laying down of thy life for the world, that thou mightest take it again to prepare a place for the children of men.

34 And now I know that this love which thou hast had for the children of men, is charity; wherefore, except men shall have charity, they can not inherit that place which thou hast prepared in the mansions of thy Father.

35 Wherefore, I know by this thing which thou hast said, that if the Gentiles have not charity, because of our weakness, that thou wilt prove them, and take away their talent, yea, even that which they have received, and give unto them who shall have more abundantly.

36 ¶And it came to pass that I prayed unto the Lord that he would give unto the Gentiles grace, that they might have charity.

37 And it came to pass that the Lord said unto me, If they have not charity, it mattereth not unto thee, thou hast been faithful; wherefore thy garments shall be made clean.

38 And because thou hast seen thy weakness, thou shalt be made strong, even unto the sitting down in the place which I have prepared in the mansions of my Father.

39 And now I, Moroni, bid farewell unto the Gentiles, yea, and also unto my brethren whom I love, until we shall meet before the judgment seat of Christ, where all men shall know that my garments are not spotted with your blood;

40 And then shall ye know that I have seen Jesus, and that he hath talked with me face to face, and that he told me in plain humility, even as a man telleth another in mine own language, concerning these things; and only a few have I written, because of my weakness in writing.

41 And now I would commend you to seek this Jesus of whom the prophets and apostles have written, that the grace of God the Father, and also the Lord Jesus Christ, and the Holy Ghost, which beareth record of them, may be, and abide in you for ever. Amen.

CHAPTER 6.

1 ¶And now I, Moroni, proceed to finish my record concerning the destruction of the people of whom I have been writing.

2 For behold, they rejected all the words of Ether; for he truly told them of all things, from the beginning of man; and that after the waters had receded from off the face of this land, it became a choice land above all other lands, a chosen land of the Lord;

3 Wherefore the Lord would have that all men should serve him, who dwell upon the face thereof; and that it was the place of the New Jerusalem, which should come down out of heaven, and the holy sanctuary of the Lord.

4 Behold, Ether saw the days of Christ, and he spake concerning a New Jerusalem upon this land; and he spake also concerning the house of Israel, and the Jerusalem from whence Lehi should come; after it should be destroyed, it should be built up again a holy city unto the Lord;

5 Wherefore it could not be a New Jerusalem, for it had been in a time of old, but it should be built up again, and become a holy city of the Lord: and it should be built up unto the house of Israel;

6 And that a New Jerusalem should be built up upon this land, unto the remnant of the seed of Joseph, for which things there has been a type; for as Joseph brought his father down into the land of Egypt, even so he died there;

7 Wherefore the Lord brought a remnant of the seed of Joseph out of the land of Jerusalem, that he might be merciful unto the seed of Joseph, that they should perish not, even as he was merciful unto the father of Joseph, that he should perish not;

8 Wherefore the remnant of the house of Joseph shall be built up upon this land; and it shall be a land of their inheritance; and they shall build up a holy city unto the Lord, like unto the Jerusalem of old; and they shall no more be confounded, until the end come, when the earth shall pass away.

9 And there shall be a new heaven and a new earth; and

they shall be like unto the old, save the old have passed away, and all things have become new.

10 And then cometh the New Jerusalem; and blessed are they who dwell therein, for it is they whose garments are white through the blood of the Lamb; and they are they who are numbered among the remnant of the seed of Joseph, who were of the house of Israel.

11 And then also cometh the Jerusalem of old; and the inhabitants thereof, blessed are they, for they have been washed in the blood of the Lamb;

12 And they are they who were scattered and gathered in from the four quarters of the earth, and from the north countries, and are partakers of the fulfilling of the covenant which God made with their father Abraham.

13 And when these things come, bringeth to pass the scripture which saith, There are they who were first, who shall be last; and there are they who were last, who shall be first.

14 ¶And I was about to write more, but I am forbidden; but great and marvelous were the prophecies of Ether, but they esteemed him as nought, and cast him out, and he hid himself in the cavity of a rock by day, and by night he went forth viewing the things which should come upon the people.

15 And as he dwelt in the cavity of a rock, he made the remainder of this record, viewing the destructions which came upon the people by night.

16 And it came to pass that in that same year which he was cast out from among the people, there began to be a great war among the people, for there were many who rose up who were mighty men, and sought to destroy Coriantumr, by their secret plans of wickedness, of which hath been spoken.

17 And now Coriantumr, having studied himself in all the arts of war, and all the cunning of the world, wherefore he gave battle unto them who sought to destroy him;

18 But he repented not, neither his fair sons nor daughters; neither the fair sons and daughters of Cohor; neither the fair sons and daughters of Corihor; and in fine, there was

none of the fair sons and daughters upon the face of the whole earth, who repented of their sins;

19 Wherefore it came to pass that in the first year that Ether dwelt in the cavity of a rock, there was many people who were slain by the sword of those secret combinations fighting against Coriantumr, that they might obtain the kingdom.

20 And it came to pass that the sons of Coriantumr fought much and bled much.

21 And in the second year, the word of the Lord came to Ether, that he should go and prophesy unto Coriantumr, that if he would repent, and all his household, the Lord would give unto him his kingdom, and spare the people,

22 Otherwise they should be destroyed, and all his household, save it were himself, and he should only live to see the fulfilling of the prophecies which had been spoken concerning another people receiving the land for their inheritance;

23 And Coriantumr should receive a burial by them; and every soul should be destroyed save it were Coriantumr.

24 And it came to pass that Coriantumr repented not, neither his household, neither the people; and the wars ceased not; and they sought to kill Ether, but he fled from before them, and hid again in the cavity of the rock.

25 And it came to pass that there arose up Shared, and he also gave battle unto Coriantumr; and he did beat him, insomuch that in the third year he did bring him unto captivity.

26 And the sons of Coriantumr, in the fourth year, did beat Shared, and did obtain the kingdom again unto their father.

27 Now there began to be a war upon all the face of the land, every man with his band, fighting for that which he desired.

28 And there were robbers, and in fine, all manner of wickedness upon all the face of the land.

29 And it came to pass that Coriantumr was exceeding angry with Shared, and he went against him with his armies to battle; and they did meet in great anger; and they did

meet in the valley of Gilgal; and the battle became exceeding sore.

30 And it came to pass that Shared fought against him for the space of three days.

31 And it came to pass that Coriantumr beat him, and did pursue him until he came to the plains of Heshlon.

32 And it came to pass that Shared gave him battle again upon the plains; and behold he did beat Coriantumr, and drove him back again to the valley of Gilgal.

33 And Coriantumr gave Shared battle again in the valley of Gilgal, in which he beat Shared, and slew him.

34 And Shared wounded Coriantumr in his thigh, that he did not go to battle again for the space of two years, in which time all the people upon all the face of the land were shedding blood, and there was none to restrain them.

35 And now there began to be a great curse upon the land, because of the iniquity of the people, in which, if a man should lay his tool or his sword upon the shelf, or upon the place whither he would keep it, and behold, upon the morrow, he could not find it, so great was the curse upon the land.

36 Wherefore every man did cleave unto that which was his own, with his hands, and would not borrow, neither would he lend; and every man kept the hilt of his sword thereof in his right hand, in the defense of his property and his own life, and of his wives and children.

37 And now after the space of two years, and after the death of Shared, behold, there arose the brother of Shared, and he gave battle unto Coriantumr, in which Coriantumr did beat him, and did pursue him to the wilderness of Akish.

38 And it came to pass that the brother of Shared did give battle unto him in the wilderness of Akish; and the battle became exceeding sore, and many thousands fell by the sword.

39 And it came to pass that Coriantumr did lay siege to the wilderness, and the brother of Shared did march forth out of the wilderness by night, and slew a part of the army of Coriantumr, as they were drunken.

40 And he came forth to the land of Moron, and placed himself upon the throne of Coriantumr.

41 And it came to pass that Coriantumr dwelt with his army in the wilderness, for the space of two years, in which he did receive great strength to his army.

42 Now the brother of Shared, whose name was Gilead, also received great strength to his army because of secret combinations.

43 And it came to pass that his high priest murdered him as he sat upon his throne.

44 And it came to pass that one of the secret combinations murdered him in a secret pass, and obtained unto himself the kingdom; and his name was Lib; and Lib was a man of great stature, more than any other man among all the people.

45 And it came to pass that in the first year of Lib, Coriantumr came up unto the land of Moron, and gave battle unto Lib.

46 And it came to pass that he fought with Lib, in which Lib did smite upon his arm that he was wounded; nevertheless, the army of Coriantumr did press forward upon Lib, that he fled to the borders upon the sea-shore.

47 And it came to pass that Coriantumr pursued him; and Lib gave battle unto him upon the sea-shore.

48 And it came to pass that Lib did smite the army of Coriantumr, that they fled again to the wilderness of Akish.

49 And it came to pass that Lib did pursue him until he came to the plains of Agosh.

50 And Coriantumr had taken all the people with him, as he fled before Lib, in that quarter of the land whither he fled.

51 And when he had come to the plains of Agosh, he gave battle unto Lib, and he smote upon him until he died; nevertheless the brother of Lib did come against Coriantumr in the stead thereof, and the battle became exceeding sore, in the which Coriantumr fled again before the army of the brother of Lib.

52 Now the name of the brother of Lib was called Shiz.

53 And it came to pass that Shiz pursued after Coriantumr, and he did overthrow many cities, and he did slay both women and children, and he did burn the cities thereof;

54 And there went a fear of Shiz throughout all the land;

yea, a cry went forth throughout the land, Who can stand before the army of Shiz? Behold, he sweepeth the earth before him!

55 And it came to pass that the people began to flock together in armies, throughout all the face of the land.

56 And they were divided, and a part of them fled to the army of Shiz, and a part of them fled to the army of Coriantumr.

57 And so great and lasting had been the war, and so long had been the scene of bloodshed and carnage, that the whole face of the land was covered with the bodies of the dead;

58 And so swift and speedy was the war, that there was none left to bury the dead, but they did march forth from the shedding of blood, to the shedding of blood, leaving the bodies of both men, women and children, strewed upon the face of the land, to become a prey to the worms of the flesh;

59 And the scent thereof went forth upon the face of the land, even upon all the face of the land; wherefore the people became troubled by day and by night, because of the scent thereof;

60 Nevertheless, Shiz did not cease to pursue Coriantumr, for he had sworn to avenge himself upon Coriantumr of the blood of his brother, who had been slain, and the word of the Lord came to Ether, that Coriantumr should not fall by the sword.

61 And thus we see that the Lord did visit them in the fullness of his wrath, and their wickedness and abominations, had prepared a way for their everlasting destruction.

62 And it came to pass that Shiz did pursue Coriantumr eastward, even to the borders of the sea-shore, and there he gave battle unto Shiz for the space of three days;

63 And so terrible was the destruction among the armies of Shiz, that the people began to be frightened, and began to flee before the armies of Coriantumr;

64 And they fled to the land of Corihor, and swept off the inhabitants before them, all they that would not join them; and they pitched their tents in the valley of Corihor.

65 And Coriantumr pitched his tents in the valley of Shurr.

66 Now the valley of Shurr was near the hill Comnor; wherefore Coriantumr did gather his armies together, upon the hill Comnor, and did sound a trumpet unto the armies of Shiz, to invite them forth to battle.

67 And it came to pass that they came forth, but were driven again; and they came the second time; and they were driven again the second time.

68 And it came to pass that they came again the third time, and the battle became exceeding sore.

69 And it came to pass that Shiz smote upon Coriantumr, that he gave him many deep wounds.

70 And Coriantumr having lost his blood, fainted, and was carried away as though he were dead.

71 Now the loss of men, women and children, on both sides, was so great that Shiz commanded his people that they should not pursue the armies of Coriantumr; wherefore they returned to their camp.

72 ¶And it came to pass when Coriantumr had recovered of his wounds, he began to remember the words which Ether had spoken unto him;

73 He saw that there had been slain by the sword already nearly two millions of his people, and he began to sorrow in his heart; yea, there had been slain two millions of mighty men, and also their wives and their children.

74 He began to repent of the evil which he had done; he began to remember the words which had been spoken by the mouth of all the prophets, and he saw them that they were fulfilled, thus far, every whit, and his soul mourned, and refused to be comforted.

75 And it came to pass that he wrote an epistle unto Shiz, desiring him that he would spare the people, and he would give up the kingdom for the sake of the lives of the people.

76 And it came to pass that when Shiz had received his epistle, he wrote an epistle unto Coriantumr, that if he would give himself up, that he might slay him with his own sword, that he would spare the lives of the people.

77 And it came to pass that the people repented not of their iniquity; and the people of Coriantumr were stirred up to anger against the people of Shiz;

78 And the people of Shiz were stirred up to anger against the people of Coriantumr; wherefore the people of Shiz did give battle unto the people of Coriantumr.

79 And when Coriantumr saw that he was about to fall, he fled again before the people of Shiz.

80 And it came to pass that he came to the waters of Ripliancum, which, by interpretation, is large, or to exceed all; wherefore, when they came to these waters, they pitched their tents; and Shiz also pitched his tents near unto them; and therefore on the morrow, they did come to battle.

81 And it came to pass that they fought an exceeding sore battle, in which Coriantumr was wounded again, and he fainted with the loss of blood.

82 And it came to pass that the armies of Coriantumr did press upon the armies of Shiz, that they beat them, that they caused them to flee before them; and they did flee southward, and did pitch their tents in a place which was called Ogath.

83 And it came to pass that the army of Coriantumr did pitch their tents by the hill Ramah; and it was that same hill where my father Mormon did hide up the records unto the Lord which were sacred.

84 And it came to pass that they did gather together all the people, upon all the face of the land, who had not been slain, save it was Ether.

85 And it came to pass that Ether did behold all the doings of the people; and he beheld that the people who were for Coriantumr, were gathered together to the army of Coriantumr; and the people who were for Shiz, were gathered together to the army of Shiz;

86 Wherefore they were for the space of four years, gathering together the people, that they might get all who were upon the face of the land, and that they might receive all the strength which it was possible that they could receive.

87 And it came to pass that when they were all gathered together, every one to the army which he would, with their

wives, and their children; both men, women and children being armed with weapons of war, having shields, and breastplates, and head-plates, and being clothed after the manner of war, they did march forth one against another, to battle; and they fought all that day, and conquered not.

88 And it came to pass that when it was night they were weary, and retired to their camps; and after they had retired to their camps, they took up a howling and a lamentation for the loss of the slain of their people; and so great were their cries, their howlings and lamentations, that it did rend the air exceedingly.

89 And it came to pass that on the morrow they did go again to battle, and great and terrible was that day;

90 Nevertheless they conquered not, and when the night came again, they did rend the air with their cries, and their howlings, and their mournings, for the loss of the slain of their people.

91 ¶And it came to pass that Coriantumr wrote again an epistle unto Shiz, desiring that he would not come again to battle, but that he would take the kingdom, and spare the lives of the people.

92 But behold, the Spirit of the Lord had ceased striving with them, and Satan had full power over the hearts of the people, for they were given up unto the hardness of their hearts, and the blindness of their minds, that they might be destroyed; wherefore they went again to battle.

93 And it came to pass that they fought all that day, and when the night came they slept upon their swords; and on the morrow they fought even until the night came;

94 And when the night came they were drunken with anger, even as a man who is drunken with wine; and they slept again upon their swords; and on the morrow they fought again;

95 And when the night came they had all fallen by the sword, save it were fifty and two of the people of Coriantumr, and sixty and nine of the people of Shiz.

96 And it came to pass that they slept upon their swords that night, and on the morrow they fought again, and they

contended in their mights with their swords, and with their shields, all that day;

97 And when the night came there were thirty and two of the people of Shiz, and twenty and seven of the people of Coriantumr.

98 And it came to pass that they ate and slept, and prepared for death on the morrow.

99 And they were large and mighty men, as to the strength of men.

100 And it came to pass that they fought for the space of three hours, and they fainted with the loss of blood.

101 And it came to pass that when the men of Coriantumr had received sufficient strength, that they could walk, they were about to flee for their lives, but behold, Shiz arose, and also his men, and he swore in his wrath that he would slay Coriantumr, or he would perish by the sword;

102 Wherefore he did pursue them, and on the morrow he did overtake them; and they fought again with the sword.

103 And it came to pass that when they had all fallen by the sword, save it were Coriantumr and Shiz, behold, Shiz had fainted with the loss of blood.

104 And it came to pass that when Coriantumr had leaned upon his sword, that he rested a little, he smote off the head of Shiz.

105 And it came to pass that after he had smote off the head of Shiz, that Shiz raised upon his hands and fell; and after that he had struggled for breath, he died.

106 And it came to pass that Coriantumr fell to the earth, and became as if he had no life.

107 And the Lord spake unto Ether, and said unto him, Go forth.

108 And he went forth, and beheld that the words of the Lord had all been fulfilled; and he finished his record; (and the hundredth part I have not written;) and he hid them in a manner that the people of Limhi did find them.

109 Now the last words which are written by Ether, are

these: Whether the Lord will that I be translated, or that I suffer the will of the Lord in the flesh, it mattereth not, if it so be that I am saved in the kingdom of God. Amen.

THE BOOK OF MORONI.

CHAPTER 1.

1 ¶Now I, Moroni, after having made an end of abridging the account of the people of Jared, I had supposed not to have written more, but I have not as yet perished; and I make not myself known to the Lamanites, lest they should destroy me.

2 For behold, their wars are exceeding fierce among themselves; and because of their hatred, they put to death every Nephite that will not deny the Christ.

3 And I, Moroni, will not deny the Christ; wherefore, I wander whithersoever I can, for the safety of mine own life.

4 Wherefore I write a few more things, contrary to that which I had supposed; for I had supposed not to have written any more; but I write a few more things, that perhaps they may be of worth unto my brethren, the Lamanites, in some future day, according to the will of the Lord.

CHAPTER 2.

1 ¶The words of Christ, which he spake unto his disciples, the twelve whom he had chosen, as he laid his hands upon them.

2 And he called them by name, saying, Ye shall call on the Father in my name, in mighty prayer; and after ye have done this, ye shall have power that on him whom ye shall lay your hands, ye shall give the Holy Ghost; and in my name shall ye give it, for thus do mine apostles.

3 Now Christ spake these words unto them at the time of his first appearing; and the multitude heard it not, but the

disciples heard it, and on as many as they laid their hands, fell the Holy Ghost.

CHAPTER 3.

1 ¶The manner which the disciples, who were called the elders of the church, ordained priests and teachers.

2 After they had prayed unto the Father in the name of Christ, they laid their hands upon them, and said, In the name of Jesus Christ I ordain you to be a priest; (or if he be a teacher;) I ordain you to be a teacher, to preach repentance and remission of sins through Jesus Christ, by the endurance of faith on his name to the end. Amen.

3 And after this manner did they ordain priests and teachers, according to the gifts and callings of God unto men; and they ordained them by the power of the Holy Ghost, which was in them.

CHAPTER 4.

1 ¶The manner of their elders and priests administering the flesh and blood of Christ unto the church.

2 And they administered it according to the commandments of Christ; wherefore we know the manner to be true; and the elder or priest did minister it.

3 And they did kneel down with the church, and pray to the Father in the name of Christ, saying,

4 O God, the eternal Father, we ask thee in the name of thy Son Jesus Christ, to bless and sanctify this bread to the souls of all those who partake of it, that they may eat in remembrance of the body of thy Son, and witness unto thee, O God the eternal Father, that they are willing to take upon them the name of thy Son, and always remember him, and keep his commandments which he hath given them, that they may always have his Spirit to be with them. Amen.

CHAPTER 5.

1 ¶The manner of administering the wine.

2 Behold, they took the cup, and said,

3 O God, the eternal Father, we ask thee, in the name of thy Son Jesus Christ, to bless and sanctify this wine to the souls of all those who drink of it, that they may do it in remembrance of the blood of thy Son which was shed for them, that they may witness unto thee, O God, the eternal Father, that they do always remember him, that they may have his Spirit to be with them. Amen.

CHAPTER 6.

1 ¶And now I speak concerning baptism.

2 Behold, elders, priests, and teachers were baptized; and they were not baptized, save they brought forth fruit meet that they were worthy of it; neither did they receive any unto baptism, save they came forth with a broken heart and a contrite spirit, and witnessed unto the church that they truly repented of all their sins.

3 And none were received unto baptism, save they took upon them the name of Christ, having a determination to serve him to the end.

4 And after they had been received unto baptism, and were wrought upon and cleansed by the power of the Holy Ghost, they were numbered among the people of the church of Christ,

5 And their names were taken, that they might be remembered and nourished by the good word of God, to keep them in the right way, to keep them continually watchful unto prayer, relying alone upon the merits of Christ, who was the author and the finisher of their faith.

6 And the church did meet together oft, to fast and to pray, and to speak one with another concerning the welfare of their souls: and they did meet together oft to partake of bread and wine, in remembrance of the Lord Jesus;

7 And they were strict to observe that there should be no

iniquity among them; and whoso was found to commit iniquity, and three witnesses of the church did condemn them before the elders;

8 And if they repented not, and confessed not, their names were blotted out, and they were not numbered among the people of Christ; but as oft as they repented, and sought forgiveness, with real intent, they were forgiven.

9 And their meetings were conducted by the church, after the manner of the workings of the Spirit, and by the power of the Holy Ghost; for as the power of the Holy Ghost led them whether to preach or exhort, or to pray, or to supplicate, or to sing, even so it was done.

CHAPTER 7.

1 ¶And now I, Moroni, write a few of the words of my father Mormon, which he spake concerning faith, hope and charity; for after this manner did he speak unto the people, as he taught them in the synagogue which they had built for the place of worship.

2 And now I, Mormon, speak unto you, my beloved brethren; and it is by the grace of God, the Father, and our Lord Jesus Christ, and his holy will, because of the gift of his calling unto me, that I am permitted to speak unto you at this time;

3 Wherefore I would speak unto you that are of the church, that are the peaceable followers of Christ, and that have obtained a sufficient hope, by which ye can enter into the rest of the Lord, from this time henceforth, until ye shall rest with him in heaven.

4 And now my brethren, I judge these things of you because of your peaceable walk with the children of men; for I remember the word of God, which saith, By their works ye shall know them; for if their works be good, then they are good also.

5 For behold, God hath said, A man being evil, can not do that which is good; for if he offereth a gift, or prayeth unto

God, except he shall do it with real intent, it profiteth him nothing.

6 For behold, it is not counted unto him for righteousness.

7 For behold, if a man being evil, giveth a gift, he doeth it grudgingly; wherefore it is counted unto him the same as if he had retained the gift; wherefore he is counted evil before God.

8 And likewise also is it counted evil unto a man, if he shall pray, and not with real intent of heart; yea, and it profiteth him nothing; for God receiveth none such; wherefore, a man being evil, can not do that which is good; neither will he give a good gift.

9 For behold, a bitter fountain can not bring forth good water; neither can a good fountain bring forth bitter water; wherefore a man being a servant of the devil, can not follow Christ; and if he follow Christ, he can not be a servant of the devil.

10 Wherefore, all things which are good, cometh of God; and that which is evil, cometh of the devil; for the devil is an enemy unto God, and fighteth against him continually, and inviteth and enticeth to sin, and to do that which is evil continually.

11 But behold, that which is of God, inviteth and enticeth to do good continually; wherefore, everything which inviteth and enticeth to do good, and to love God, and to serve him, is inspired of God.

12 Wherefore take heed, my beloved brethren, that ye do not judge that which is evil to be of God, or that which is good and of God, to be of the devil.

13 For behold, my brethren, it is given unto you to judge, that ye may know good from evil; and the way to judge is as plain, that ye may know with a perfect knowledge, as the daylight is from the dark night.

14 For behold, the Spirit of Christ is given to every man, that they may know good from evil; wherefore I shew unto you the way to judge: for everything which inviteth to do good, and to persuade to believe in Christ, is sent forth by the power and gift of Christ;

15 Wherefore ye may know with a perfect knowledge, it is of God; but whatsoever thing persuadeth men to do evil, and believe not in Christ, and deny him, and serve not God, then ye may know with a perfect knowledge it is of the devil,

16 For after this manner doth the devil work, for he persuadeth no man to do good, no not one; neither doth his angels; neither do they who subject themselves unto him.

17 ¶And now, my brethren, seeing that ye know the light by which ye may judge, which light is the light of Christ, see that ye do not judge wrongfully; for with that same judgment which ye judge, ye shall also be judged.

18 Wherefore I beseech of you, brethren, that ye should search diligently in the light of Christ, that ye may know good from evil; and if ye will lay hold upon every good thing, and condemn it not, ye certainly will be a child of Christ.

19 And now, my brethren, how is it possible that ye can lay hold upon every good thing?

20 And now I come to that faith, of which I said I would speak; and I will tell you the way whereby ye may lay hold on every good thing.

21 For behold, God knowing all things, being from everlasting to everlasting, behold he sent angels to minister unto the children of men, to make manifest concerning the coming of Christ; and in Christ there should come every good thing.

22 And God also declared unto prophets by his own mouth, that Christ should come.

23 And behold, there were divers ways that he did manifest things unto the children of men, which were good; and all things which are good, cometh of Christ, otherwise men were fallen, and there could no good thing come unto them.

24 Wherefore, by the ministering of angels, and by every word which proceedeth forth out of the mouth of God, men began to exercise faith in Christ; and thus by faith, they did lay hold upon every good thing; and thus it was until the coming of Christ.

25 And after that he came, men also were saved by faith in his name; and by faith, they become the sons of God.

26 And as sure as Christ liveth, he spake these words unto our fathers, saying, Whatsoever thing ye shall ask the Father in my name, which is good, in faith believing that ye shall receive, behold it shall be done unto you.

27 Wherefore, my beloved brethren, hath miracles ceased, because Christ hath ascended into heaven, and hath set down on the right hand of God, to claim of the Father his rights of mercy which he hath upon the children of men;

28 For he hath answered the ends of the law, and he claimeth all those who have faith in him; and they who have faith in him, will cleave unto every good thing; wherefore he advocateth the cause of the children of men; and he dwelleth eternally in the heavens?

29 And because he hath done this, my beloved brethren, hath miracles ceased?

30 Behold, I say unto you, Nay; neither have angels ceased to minister unto the children of men.

31 For behold, they are subject unto him, to minister according to the word of his command, shewing themselves unto them of strong faith and a firm mind, in every form of godliness.

32 And the office of their ministry is, to call men unto repentance, and to fulfill and to do the work of the covenants of the Father which he hath made unto the children of men, to prepare the way among the children of men, by declaring the word of Christ unto the chosen vessels of the Lord, that they may bear testimony of him;

33 And by so doing, the Lord God prepareth the way that the residue of men may have faith in Christ, that the Holy Ghost may have place in their hearts, according to the power thereof;

34 And after this manner bringeth to pass the Father the covenants which he hath made unto the children of men.

35 And Christ hath said, If ye will have faith in me, ye shall have power to do whatsoever thing is expedient in me.

36 And he hath said, Repent all ye ends of the earth, and come unto me and be baptized in my name, and have faith in me, that ye may be saved.

37 ¶And now my beloved brethren, if this be the case that these things are true which I have spoken unto you, and God will shew unto you with power and great glory at the last day, that they are true; and if they are true, has the day of miracles ceased?

38 Or have angels ceased to appear unto the children of men?

39 Or has he withheld the power of the Holy Ghost from them?

40 Or will he, so long as time shall last, or the earth shall stand, or there shall be one man upon the face thereof to be saved?

41 Behold I say unto you, Nay, for it is by faith that miracles are wrought; and it is by faith that angels appear and minister unto men;

42 Wherefore if these things have ceased, wo be unto the children of men, for it is because of unbelief, and all is vain; for no man can be saved, according to the words of Christ, save they shall have faith in his name;

43 Wherefore, if these things have ceased, then has faith ceased also; and awful is the state of man: for they are as though there had been no redemption made.

44 But behold, my beloved brethren, I judge better things of you, for I judge that ye have faith in Christ because of your meekness; for if ye have not faith in him, then ye are not fit to be numbered among the people of his church.

45 And again my beloved brethren, I would speak unto you concerning hope.

46 How is it that ye can attain unto faith, save ye shall have hope? And what is it that ye shall hope for?

47 Behold I say unto you, that ye shall have hope through the atonement of Christ and the power of his resurrection, to be raised unto life eternal; and this because of your faith in him according to the promise;

48 Wherefore, if a man have faith, he must needs have hope; for without faith there can not be any hope.

49 And again, behold I say unto you, that he can not have faith and hope, save he shall be meek and lowly of heart; if

so, his faith and hope is vain, for none is acceptable before God, save the meek and lowly of heart;

50 And if a man be meek and lowly in heart, and confesses by the power of the Holy Ghost, that Jesus is the Christ, he must needs have charity; for if he have not charity, he is nothing; wherefore he must needs have charity.

51 And charity suffereth long, and is kind, and envieth not, and is not puffed up, seeketh not her own, is not easily provoked, thinketh no evil, and rejoiceth not in iniquity, but rejoiceth in the truth, beareth all things, believeth all things, hopeth all things; endureth all things; wherefore, my beloved brethren, if ye have not charity, ye are nothing, for charity never faileth.

52 Wherefore, cleave unto charity, which is the greatest of all, for all things must fail; but charity is the pure love of Christ, and it endureth for ever; and whoso is found possessed of it at the last day, it shall be well with them.

53 Wherefore, my beloved brethren, pray unto the Father with all the energy of heart, that ye may be filled with this love which he hath bestowed upon all who are true followers of his Son Jesus Christ, that ye may become the sons of God, that when he shall appear, we shall be like him; for we shall see him as he is, that we may have this hope, that we may be purified even as he is pure. Amen.

CHAPTER 8.

1 ¶An epistle of my father Mormon, written to me, Moroni: and it was written unto me soon after my calling to the ministry.

2 And on this wise did he write unto me, saying, My beloved son, Moroni, I rejoice exceedingly that your Lord Jesus Christ hath been mindful of you, and hath called you to his ministry, and to his holy work.

3 I am mindful of you always in my prayers, continually praying unto God the Father, in the name of his holy child, Jesus, that he, through his infinite goodness and grace, will

keep you through the endurance of faith on his name to the end.

4 ¶And now my son I speak unto you concerning that which grieveth me exceedingly; for it grieveth me that there should disputations rise among you.

5 For if I have learned the truth, there has been disputations among you concerning the baptism of your little children.

6 And now my son, I desire that ye should labor diligently, that this gross error should be removed from among you; for, for this intent I have written this epistle.

7 For immediately after I had learned these things of you, I inquired of the Lord concerning the matter.

8 And the word of the Lord came to me by the power of the Holy Ghost, saying, Listen to the words of Christ, your Redeemer, your Lord, and your God.

9 Behold, I came into the world not to call the righteous, but sinners to repentance; the whole need no physician, but they that are sick; wherefore little children are whole, for they are not capable of committing sin; wherefore the curse of Adam is taken from them in me, that it hath no power over them; and the law of circumcision is done away in me.

10 And after this manner did the Holy Ghost manifest the word of God unto me; wherefore my beloved son, I know that it is solemn mockery before God, that ye should baptize little children.

11 Behold I say unto you, that this thing shall ye teach, repentance and baptism unto those who are accountable and capable of committing sin; yea, teach parents that they must repent and be baptized, and humble themselves as their little children, and they shall all be saved with their little children: and their little children need no repentance, neither baptism.

12 Behold, baptism is unto repentance to the fulfilling the commandments unto the remission of sins.

13 But little children are alive in Christ, even from the foundation of the world; if not so, God is a partial God, and also a changeable God, and a respecter to persons; for how many little children have died without baptism.

14 Wherefore, if little children could not be saved without baptism, these must have gone to an endless hell.

15 Behold I say unto you, that he that supposeth that little children need baptism, is in the gall of bitterness, and in the bonds of iniquity; for he hath neither faith, hope, nor charity; wherefore, should he be cut off while in the thought, he must go down to hell.

16 For awful is the wickedness to suppose that God saveth one child because of baptism, and the other must perish because he hath no baptism.

17 Wo be unto him that shall pervert the ways of the Lord after this manner, for they shall perish, except they repent.

18 Behold, I speak with boldness, having authority from God; and I fear not what man can do; for perfect love casteth out all fear; and I am filled with charity, which is everlasting love; wherefore all children are alike unto me; wherefore I love little children with a perfect love; and they are all alike, and partakers of salvation.

19 For I know that God is not a partial God, neither a changeable being; but he is unchangeable from all eternity to all eternity.

20 Little children can not repent; wherefore it is awful wickedness to deny the pure mercies of God unto them, for they are all alive in him because of his mercy.

21 And he that saith that little children need baptism, denieth the mercies of Christ, and setteth at naught the atonement of him and the power of his redemption.

22 Wo unto such, for they are in danger of death, hell, and an endless torment.

23 I speak it boldly, God hath commanded me.

24 Listen unto them and give heed, or they stand against you at the judgment seat of Christ.

25 For behold that all little children are alive in Christ, and also all they that are without the law.

26 For the power of redemption cometh on all they that have no law; wherefore, he that is not condemned, or he that is under no condemnation, can not repent; and unto such baptism availeth nothing.

27 But it is mockery before God, denying the mercies of Christ, and the power of his Holy Spirit, and putting trust in dead works.

28 Behold, my son, this thing ought not to be; for repentance is unto them that are under condemnation, and under the curse of a broken law.

29 And the first-fruits of repentance is baptism; and baptism cometh by faith, unto the fulfilling the commandments; and the fulfilling the commandments bringeth remission of sins; and the remission of sins bringeth meekness, and lowliness of heart; and because of meekness and lowliness of heart, cometh the visitation of the Holy Ghost, which Comforter filleth with hope and perfect love, which love endureth by diligence unto prayer, until the end shall come, when all the saints shall dwell with God.

30 Behold, my son, I will write unto you again if I go not out soon against the Lamanites.

31 Behold, the pride of this nation, or the people of the Nephites, hath proven their destruction, except they should repent.

32 Pray for them, my son, that repentance may come unto them.

33 But behold, I fear lest the Spirit hath ceased striving with them; and in this part of the land they are also seeking to put down all power and authority, which cometh from God; and they are denying the Holy Ghost.

34 And after rejecting so great a knowledge, my son, they must perish soon, unto the fulfilling of the prophecies which were spoken by the prophets, as well as the words of our Savior himself.

35 Farewell, my son, until I shall write unto you, or shall meet you again. Amen.

CHAPTER 9.

The Second Epistle of Mormon to his son Moroni.

1 ¶My beloved son, I write unto you again, that ye may know that I am yet alive, but I write somewhat that which is grievous.

2 For behold, I have had a sore battle with the Lamanites, in which we did not conquer; and Archeantus has fallen by the sword, and also Luram and Emron; yea, and we have lost a great number of our choice men.

3 And now behold, my son, I fear lest the Lamanites shall destroy this people, for they do not repent, and Satan stirreth them up continually to anger, one with another.

4 Behold, I am laboring with them continually; and when I speak the word of God with sharpness, they tremble and anger against me; and when I use no sharpness, they harden their hearts against it; wherefore I fear lest the Spirit of the Lord hath ceased striving with them.

5 For so exceedingly do they anger, that it seemeth me that they have no fear of death; and they have lost their love, one towards another; and they thirst after blood and revenge continually.

6 And now my beloved son, notwithstanding their hardness, let us labor diligently; for if we should cease to labor, we should be brought under condemnation; for we have a labor to perform whilst in this tabernacle of clay, that we may conquer the enemy of all righteousness, and rest our souls in the kingdom of God.

7 ¶And now I write somewhat concerning the sufferings of this people.

8 For according to the knowledge which I have received from Amoron, behold, the Lamanites have many prisoners, which they took from the tower of Sherrizah; and there were men, women and children.

9 And the husbands and fathers of those women and children they have slain; and they feed the women upon the flesh of their husbands, and the children upon the flesh of their fathers; and no water, save a little, do they give unto them.

10 And notwithstanding this great abomination of the Lamanites, it doth not exceed that of our people in Moriantum.

11 For behold, many of the daughters of the Lamanites have they taken prisoners: and after depriving them of that which was most dear and precious above all things, which is

chastity and virtue; and after they had done this thing, they did murder them in a most cruel manner, torturing their bodies even unto death; and after they have done this, they devour their flesh like unto wild beasts, because of the hardness of their hearts; and they do it for a token of bravery.

12 O my beloved son, how can a people like this, that are without civilization; (and only a few years have passed away, and they were a civil and a delightsome people;) but O my son, how can a people like this, whose delight is in so much abomination, how can we expect that God will stay his hand in judgment against us?

13 Behold, my heart cries, Wo unto this people.

14 Come out in judgment, O God, and hide their sins, and wickedness, and abominations from before thy face.

15 And again, my son, there are many widows and their daughters who remain in Sherrizah; and that part of the provisions which the Lamanites did not carry away, behold, the army of Zenephi has carried away, and left them to wander whithersoever they can for food; and many old women do faint by the way and die.

16 And the army which is with me, is weak; and the armies of the Lamanites are betwixt Sherrizah and me; and as many as have fled to the army of Aaron, have fallen victims to their awful brutality.

17 O the depravity of my people! they are without order and without mercy.

18 Behold, I am but a man, and I have but the strength of a man, and I can not any longer enforce my commands; and they have become strong in their perversion;

19 And they are alike brutal, sparing none, neither old nor young; and they delight in everything save that which is good; and the sufferings of our women and our children upon all the face of this land, doth exceed everything; yea, tongue can not tell, neither can it be written.

20 And now my son, I dwell no longer upon this horrible scene.

21 Behold, thou knowest the wickedness of this people; thou knowest that they are without principle, and past feel-

ing; and their wickedness doth exceed that of the Lamanites.

22 Behold, my son, I can not recommend them unto God lest he should smite me.

23 But behold, my son, I recommend thee unto God, and I trust in Christ that thou wilt be saved; and I pray unto God that he would spare thy life, to witness the return of his people unto him, or their utter destruction;

24 For I know that they must perish, except they repent and return unto him; and if they perish it will be like unto the Jaredites, because of the willfulness of their hearts, seeking for blood and revenge.

25 And if it so be that they perish, we know that many of our brethren have dissented over unto the Lamanites, and many more will also dissent over unto them;

26 Wherefore, write somewhat a few things, if thou art spared; and I should perish and not see thee; but I trust that I may see thee soon; for I have sacred records that I would deliver up unto thee.

27 My son, be faithful in Christ; and may not the things which I have written, grieve thee, to weigh thee down unto death, but may Christ lift thee up, and may his sufferings and death, and the shewing his body unto our fathers, and his mercy and long suffering, and the hope of his glory, and of eternal life, rest in your mind for ever.

28 And may the grace of God the Father, whose throne is high in the heavens, and our Lord Jesus Christ, who sitteth on the right hand of his power, until all things shall become subject unto him, be, and abide with you for ever. Amen.

CHAPTER 10.

1 ¶Now I, Moroni, write somewhat as seemeth me good; and I write unto my brethren the Lamanites, and I would that they should know that more than four hundred and twenty years have passed away, since the sign was given of the coming of Christ.

2 And I seal up these records, after I have spoken a few words by way of exhortation unto you.

3 Behold, I would exhort you that when ye shall read these things, if it be wisdom in God that ye should read them, that ye would remember how merciful the Lord hath been unto the children of men, from the creation of Adam, even down until the time that ye shall receive these things, and ponder it in your hearts.

4 And when ye shall receive these things, I would exhort you that ye would ask God, the eternal Father, in the name of Christ, if these things are not true;

5 And if ye shall ask with a sincere heart, with real intent, having faith in Christ, he will manifest the truth of it unto you, by the power of the Holy Ghost; and by the power of the Holy Ghost, ye may know the truth of all things.

6 And whatsoever thing is good, is just and true; wherefore, nothing that is good denieth the Christ, but acknowledgeth that he is.

7 And ye may know that he is, by the power of the Holy Ghost; wherefore I would exhort you, that ye deny not the power of God; for he worketh by power, according to the faith of the children of men, the same to-day and to-morrow, and for ever.

8 And again I exhort you, my brethren, that ye deny not the gifts of God, for they are many; and they come from the same God.

9 And there are different ways that these gifts are administered; but it is the same God who worketh all in all; and they are given by the manifestations of the Spirit of God unto men, to profit them.

10 For behold, to one is given by the Spirit of God, that he may teach the word of wisdom; and to another, that he may teach the word of knowledge by the same Spirit; and to another exceeding great faith; and to another, the gifts of healing by the same Spirit.

11 And again, to another, that he may work mighty miracles; and again, to another, that he may prophesy concerning all things; and again, to another, the beholding of angels and ministering spirits; and again, to another, all kinds of

tongues; and again, to another, the interpretation of languages and of divers kinds of tongues.

12 And all these gifts come by the Spirit of Christ; and they come unto every man severally, according as he will.

13 And I would exhort you my beloved brethren, that ye remember that every good gift cometh of Christ.

14 And I would exhort you, my beloved brethren, that ye remember that he is the same yesterday, to-day, and for ever, and that all these gifts of which I have spoken, which are spiritual, never will be done away, even as long as the world shall stand, only according to the unbelief of the children of men.

15 Wherefore, there must be faith; and if there must be faith, there must also be hope; and if there must be hope, there must also be charity; and except ye have charity, ye can in no wise be saved in the kingdom of God;

16 Neither can ye be saved in the kingdom of God, if ye have not faith; neither can ye if ye have no hope; and if ye have no hope, ye must needs be in despair; and despair cometh because of iniquity.

17 And Christ truly said unto our fathers, If ye have faith, ye can do all things which is expedient unto me.

18 And now I speak unto all the ends of the earth, that if the day cometh that the power and gifts of God shall be done away among you, it shall be because of unbelief.

19 And wo be unto the children of men, if this be the case; for there shall be none that doeth good among you, no not one.

20 For if there be one among you that doeth good, he shall work by the power and gifts of God.

21 And wo unto them who shall do these things away and die, for they die in their sins, and they can not be saved in the kingdom of God; and I speak it according to the words of Christ, and I lie not.

22 And I exhort you to remember these things; for the time speedily cometh that ye shall know that I lie not, for ye shall see me at the bar of God, and the Lord God will say unto you, Did I not declare my words unto you, which were written by this man, like as one crying from the dead?

CHAP. 10.] BOOK OF MORONI. 777

23 Yea, even as one speaking out of the dust?

24 I declare these things unto the fulfilling of the prophecies.

25 And behold, they shall proceed forth out of the mouth of the everlasting God; and his word shall hiss forth from generation to generation.

26 And God shall shew unto you, that that which I have written is true.

27 And again I would exhort you, that ye would come unto Christ, and lay hold upon every good gift and touch not the evil gift, nor the unclean thing.

28 And awake, and arise from the dust, O Jerusalem; yea, and put on thy beautiful garments, O daughter of Zion, and strengthen thy stakes, and enlarge thy borders for ever, that thou mayest no more be confounded, that the covenants of the eternal Father which he hath made unto thee, O house of Israel, may be fulfilled.

29 Yea, come unto Christ, and be perfected in him, and deny yourselves of all ungodliness, and if ye shall deny yourselves of all ungodliness, and love God with all your might, mind and strength, then is his grace sufficient for you, that by his grace ye may be perfect in Christ; and if by the grace of God ye are perfect in Christ, ye can in no wise deny the power of God.

30 And again, if ye, by the grace of God, are perfect in Christ, and deny not his power, then are ye sanctified in Christ by the grace of God, through the shedding of the blood of Christ, which is in the covenant of the Father, unto the remission of your sins, that ye become holy without spot.

31 And now I bid unto all, farewell. I soon go to rest in the paradise of God, until my spirit and body shall again reunite, and I am brought forth triumphant through the air, to meet you before the pleasing bar of the great Jehovah, the eternal Judge of both quick and dead. Amen.

THE END.

Index.

Aaron, city of, 327, 486.
Aaron, descendant of Heth, 714; dwells in captivity, 743.
Aaron, king of Lamanites, 690; defeated by army of Moroni, 690; brutality of army of, 773.
Aaron, son of Mosiah, 289; teaches people of Zarahemla, 289; refuses kingdom, 292; in prison at Middoni, 377, 382; released from prison, 380, 382; goes to Jerusalem, 381; teaches atonement, 381, 385; goes to Ani-Anti, 382; goes to Middoni, 382; goes to land of Nephi, 383; account of, 388; and brethren establish churches, 389; rejoices, 397; rebukes Ammon, 398; rejoices in meeting Alma, 403; goes with Alma to Zoramites, 417; goes to Jershon, 432; returns to Zarahemla, 433.
Abinadi, prophesies to people of Noah, 241, 243, 254, 257; brought bound before Noah, 244; cast into prison, 244, 256; ten commandments quoted by, 247; Isaiah quoted by, 245, 254; prophesies of Christ, 251; condemned to death by Noah, 256; suffers death by fire, 257; words of, Alma blessed because of faith in, 283; words of fulfilled, 396, 689.
Abinadom, 200.
Abish, conversion of, 374; raises queen, 376.
Ablom, Omer pitches tent at, 735.
Abomination, of Lamanites and Nephites, 772.
Abraham, kindreds of earth blessed through, 45; seed of to rejoice in Lord, 152; covenant with, 158; counted to be obedient, 175; tithes paid by, 350.
Abridgment of record of Mormon, 699.
Account of Nephi, 3.
Adam and Eve, plates of brass contain account of, 15.
Adam, and tree of life, 452; cut off from presence of God, 452; fall of man through, 710.
Agosh, Lib pursues Coriantumr to plains of, 754; gives battle to Lib, slays Lib, 754.
Aha, son of Zoram, 359.
Ahah, son of Seth, 714; becomes king, 744.
Akish, son of Kimnor, 733; daughter of Jared dances before, 733; swears kinsfolks of Jared, 733; oaths administered by, 733; overthrows kingdom of Omer, 735; marries daughter of Jared, 736; seeks life of Jared, 736; obtains kingdom, 736; causes death of son, 736; war between and sons, 736.
Akish, wilderness of, Coriantumr pursues brother of Shared to, 753; army of Coriantumr flees to, 754.
All things common, among disciples of Christ, 672, 682.
Alma, believes words of Abinadi, 256; cast out, life sought by Noah, 256; teaches words of Abinadi, 258; flees to place of Mormon, 258; baptizes, 259; ordains priests, 260; teachings, 260; discovered by King Noah, 261; departs into wilderness, 261, 273; declines to be king, 273; teachings of, 274; high priest, 274; consecrates priests

and teachers, 274; people of surrender to Lamanites, 275; and people oppressed by Amulon and people, 277; and people gather flocks, 278; depart into wilderness, 278; valley of, 279; and people arrive at Zarahemla, 279; records of read by Mosiah, 279; preaches to people of Nephi, 280; baptizes people of Limhi, 281; permitted to establish churches, 281; dissenters brought before, 282; given authority over church by Mosiah, 282, 283; receives direction from the Lord, 283; regulates all affairs of church, 285; church complains to, 285; son of, an unbeliever, 286; appoints son high priest, 297; dies, 297; age of, 298; founder of church, 298.

Alma, son of Alma, 286; seeks to destroy church, 286; angel appears to, 286; becomes dumb, 287; explains his conversion, 288; teaches people, 289; receives plates, records, and interpreters, from Mosiah, 292; to keep records, 292; appointed chief judge, 297; appointed high priest by his father, 297; Nehor sentenced by, 300; head of armies of Nephites, 304; slays Amlici, 306; contends with king of Lamanites, 306; sends army to repulse Lamanites, 309; baptizes in Sidon, 310; consecrates elders, priests, and teachers, 311; appoints man to enact laws by voice of people, 312; surrenders chief judgeship, retains office of high priest, 312; delivers word of Lord in land of Zarahemla, 313; recites history of people of Zarahemla, 313; ordains priests and elders, 321; regulates church in Zarahemla, 321; goes to valley of Gideon, 322; address to people of Gideon, 322; teaches baptism, 324; teaches faith, 326; establishes order of church in Gideon, 326; returns to Zarahemla, 326; teaches people of Melek, 326; baptizes at Melek, 327; preaches at Ammonihah, 327, 330; angel commands return of to Ammonihah, 328; meets Amulek, 328; people of Ammonihah angry with, 334; speaks to Zeezrom and people, 343; questioned by Antionah, 345; teaches repentance, 351; bound, 352; smitten by chief judge, 354; breaks cords which bind, 356; departs from Ammonihah, goes to Sidom, 356; heals Zeezrom, 357; baptizes Zeezrom, 358; establishes church, consecrates priests and teachers at Sidom, 358; returns to Zarahemla, 358; preaches repentance, 360; journeys from Gideon toward Manti, meets sons of Mosiah, 362; meets Ammon, 403; joy is great, 403; conducts sons of Mosiah to Zarahemla, 404; visits Anti-Nephi-Lehies, 404; relates his conversion, 404; Korihor brought before, 412; testifies of Christ, 413; preaches to Zoramites, 417; takes sons Shiblon and Corianton to Zoramites, 417; prayer of, 419; and brethren separate, 420; teaches upon hill Onidah, 421; preaches to poor of Onidah, 421; goes to Jershon, 432; and sons and brethren return to Zarahemla, 433; commandment of to son Helaman, 434, 443; commandments to son Shiblon, 443; commits plates to Helaman, 437, 489; angel appears to, 444; commandments to son Corianton, 445; explanations concerning future state of man, 448; teaches concerning fall and restoration of man, 452; and sons go forth to preach, 455; word of Lord through to Moroni, 458; end of record of, 465; visits Helaman, 466; prophesies sin and destruction of Nephites, 466; blesses sons, and the earth for the righteous' sake, 467; blesses the church,

INDEX. 781

467; departs from Zarahemla, and is heard of no more, 467; saying of church concerning, 467.
Altar, built by Lehi, 5.
Amaleki, speaks concerning Mosiah, 20; born in days of Mosiah, 202; completes writing on plates, 203; delivers plates to King Benjamin, 202, 205; accompanies Ammon to land of Nephi, 227.
Amalekites, and others build city of Jerusalem, 381; become harder than Lamanites, 381; Aaron preaches to, 381; after order of Nehors, 381; but one converted, 390; rebel against king of Anti-Nephi-Lehies, 394, 402; appointed chief captains of Lamanites, 456; inspire Lamanites to fight, 460.
Amalickiah, leader of opposition to Helaman, 468; seeks to be king, 468; supported by lower judges, 468; seeks to destroy church and liberty, 469; departs into land of Nephi, 472; headed off by Moroni, 472; people of put to death by Moroni, 472; stirs up Lamanites against Nephites, 473; given command of army of Lamanites, 473; seeks to dethrone king of Lamanites, 474; confers with Lehonti, 475; army of surrounded by Lehonti, 475; causes death of Lehonti, 475; appointed chief commander of Lamanites, 475; marches army to city of Nephi, 475; servant of slays king of Lamanites, 476; takes possession of city of Nephi, 476; summoned by queen of Lamanites, 477; marries queen of Lamanites, and becomes king, 477; inspires Lamanites against Nephites, 478; appoints chief captains of Zoramites, 478; army of moves toward Zarahemla, 478; curses God and Moroni, 484; again stirs up Lamanites, 491; takes command of Lamanite army, 491; takes city of Moroni, 493; takes cities of Nephihah, Lehi, Morianton, Omner, Gid, Mulek, 493; headed and defeated by Teancum, 493; slain by Teancum, 494; brother of appointed king of Lamanites, 495.
Amalickiahites, depart for land of Nephi, 472; headed by armies of Moroni, 472; put to death by Moroni, 472; army of surrendered to Lehonti, 475; astonished at preparations of Nephites, 482; march to land of Noah, 482.
Amaron, Omni confers plates upon, 200; writes in book of his father, 200; delivers plates to Chemish, 200.
Amgid, subdued by Com, 743.
Aminadab, teaches Lamanites to repent, 560.
Aminadi, descendant of Nephi, 334.
Amlici, seeks to be king, 303; rejected by people, 303; consecrated king, 303; slain by Alma, 306.
Amlicites, 304; war against Nephites, 304; join with Lamanites, 305; marked in foreheads, 307, 308.
Ammah, in prison at Middoni, 377, 382; released from prison, 380, 382; preaching at Ani-Anti, 382; goes to Middoni, 382.
Ammon, descendant of Zarahemla, 227; speaks to King Limhi, 228; speaks to people of Limhi, 231; reads record of people of Limhi, 231; taken by King Limhi, 269; leads people of Limhi, 272.
Ammon, son of Mosiah, 289; teaches people of Zarahemla, 289; goes to land of Ishmael, 364; bound by Lamanites, 364; becomes servant of Lamoni, 365; protects flocks of king, 366; teaches King Lamoni, 370; rehearses history of Laman and Lemuel, 371; falls

to earth, 374; Lamanite attempts to slay, 375; arises, 376; forbidden to go to land of Nephi, 377; and Lamoni start for Middoni, 377; meets father of Lamoni, 377; smites king of Lamanites, 379; secures release of brethren, 380, 382; returns to land of Ishmael, 382; teaches people of Lamoni, 383; account of, 388; and brethren go to land of Ishmael, 391; rejoices, 397; addresses brethren, 397; rebuked by Aaron, 398; inquires of Lord, 403; goes to Zarahemla, 403; meets Alma, 403; falls because of joy, 403; returns to Anti-Nephi-Lehies, 404; people of numbered with church of God, 405; high priest over people of, 411; Korihor brought before, 411; goes with Alma to Zoramites, 417; goes to Jershon, 432; Zoramites angry with people of, 432; people of depart from Jershon for Melek, 433; returns to Zarahemla, 433; people of defended by Nephites, 457; gave of substance to Nephites, 457; people of joined by servants of king of Lamanites, 476; Moroni like unto, 480; declares word of God, 484; people of persuaded not to take oath, 501; sons of people of take name of Nephites and covenant to fight for Nephites, 502; sons of people of choose Helaman to be leader, 502, 509; sons of people of defeat Lamanites, 514; none of slain, 515; all wounded, none slain, 518; Lamanite prisoners sent to dwell with people of, 535; Lamanite prisoners join people of, 537; people of go into land northward, 549.

Ammonihah, Alma preaches word of God at, 327, 330; people of cast wives, children, and records into fire, 353; people of flee from Alma and Amulek, 356; Alma and Amulek depart from, 356; people of repent not, 358; people of destroyed by Lamanites, 359, 360, 395; called Desolation of Nehors, 360; city of rebuilt and fortified by Moroni, 481; Lamanites march against, 481.

Ammoron, appointed king of Lamanites, 495; attacks Nephites in borders of west sea, 496; proposes exchange of prisoners with Moroni, 503; epistle of Moroni to, 503; epistle of to Moroni, 504; orders Lamanites not to attack Judea, 511; refuses epistle of Helaman, 515; with army of Lamanites in land of Moroni, 537; slain by Teancum, 538; Tubaloth, son of, 544.

Ammoron, brother of Amos, keeps records, 686; hides up records, 687, 691; end of record of, 687; speaks to Mormon concerning records, 687; records hid up by taken by Mormon, 697.

Amnigaddah, son of Aaron, 714; dwells in captivity, 743.

Amnihu, hill of, 304.

Amnor, spy of Nephites, 305.

Amnor, of silver, 339.

Amos, son of Amos, keeps record, 684; record of written in Book of Nephi, 684; dies, 686.

Amos, son of Nephi, keeps record, 683; death of, 683.

Amoron, Mormon receives knowledge from, 772.

Amulek, receives Alma, 328; preaches to people of Ammonihah, 334; son of Giddonah, 334; angel appears to, 336; questioned by Zeezrom, 340; teaches restoration and resurrection, 342; bound, 352; smitten by chief judge, 354; breaks cords with which bound, 356; departs from Ammonihah, goes to Sidom, 356; rejected by kindred, 358; goes to Zarahemla, 358; preaches repentance, 360;

INDEX. 783

goes to Zoramites, 417; preaches at Onidah, 428; testifies of Christ, 428; goes to Jershon, 432; returns to Zarahemla, 433.

Amulon, land of, 276; leader of priests of King Noah, 276; and brethren join Lamanites, 276; made king over people of Helam, 276; and brethren appointed teachers by king of Lamanites, 276; oppresses Alma and people, 277; descendants of take name of Nephites, 280; people of and others build city of Jerusalem, 381; seed of, 395; slain by Lamanites, 396.

Amulonites, harder than Lamanites, 381; after order of Nehors, 381; those not converted take up arms, 391; rebel against king of Anti-Nephi-Lehies, 391; seed of Amulon, 395; slain by Lamanites, 396.

Ancient inhabitants, Moroni gives account of, 714.

Angel, speaks to Laman and Lemuel, 9; to Nephi, 9, 38-42; appears to Nephi, 28, 29, 30, 33; makes things known to Nephi, 42; words of concerning coming of Messiah, 65; appears to Jacob, 99; speaks to Benjamin, 215; appears to Alma and sons of Mosiah, 286; appears to Alma, 328, 434, 444; appears to Amulek, 335; appears to Samuel, 587.

Angels, in Lehi's vision, 2; minister to Nephi, 93; speak with tongues of, 162, 163; to the devil, 174; minister to Jacob, 190; declaring word to many, 351; appear to Lamanites, 376; visit people of Anti-Nephi-Lehi, 392; declare tidings of repentance, 557; faces of Nephi and Lehi shine as, 559; minister to Nephites and Lamanites, 561; appear to wise men, 598; visit Nephi, 622; of devil rejoice in calamities of people, 626; minister to little children, 650; minister to twelve disciples, 655; three Nephite disciples as, 678; office and ministry of, 766.

Anger, people drunken with, 758; of Nephites, 772.

Angola, Nephites fortify city of, Lamanites drive Nephites from, 689.

Ani-Anti, Aaron goes to, 382; Muloki at, 382.

Animals, found in land of promise, 63; raised by people of Nephi, 95; to dwell in peace, 159; possessed by Jaredites, 737.

Anti-christ, in Zarahemla, 409; in Gideon, 411.

Antionah, ruler of people of Ammonihah, questions Alma, 345.

Antion, of gold, 339.

Anti-Nephi-Lehi, made king, 391; Ammon and brethren counsel with Lamoni and, 391; forbids people to go to war, 391.

Anti-Nephi-Lehies, name of Lamanites converted, 390; friendly with Nephites, 391; Amulonites, Amalekites, and Lamanites rebel against king of, 391; Anti-Nephi-Lehi made king of, 391; would not go to war, 391, 402; bury swords and other weapons, 392; prostrate themselves before Lamanites, 394; slain by Lamanites, 394; joined by Lamanites, 396; observe law of Moses, 396; Amalekites slay, 402; depart out of land, 403; commanded to depart into wilderness, 403; proclamation concerning, 404; land of Jershon given to, 404; protected by Nephites, 404; Alma visits, 404; take possession of Jershon, 405; hatred of Lamanites towards, 457; would not take up arms, 457.

Antiomno, king of Middoni, 377.

Antionum, settled by Zoramites, 416, 456; east of Zarahemla, 416; Lamanites come into land of, 456; Lamanites gathered in land of,

BOOK OF MORMON.

457; Lamanites depart from, 458; leader of ten thousand slain, 702.

Antiparah, city of taken by Lamanites, 510; Lamanites march from to attack Helaman, 512; Nephites regain city of, 515.

Antipas, Lamanites gather at mount of, 474; place of arms, 474.

Antipus, Helaman goes to assistance of at Judea, 509, 510; pursues Lamanites, 512; overtakes Lamanites, 514; and leaders fall by sword, 514; Helaman and army rescue, 514.

Antum, land of, sacred records deposited in, by Ammoron, 687.

Apostles, Israel fights against, 30; all nations fight against, 30; judge tribes of Israel, 31; book goes forth by hand of, 35; record of true, 38; one of seen by Nephi, 41; writes of end of world, 41; things written just and true, 41; Apostle of Lamb to write, name John, 42; have power to give Holy Ghost, 760.

Archeantus, fallen by sword, 772.

Atonement, infinite, 106; claims of, 109; satisfies demands of justice, 109; all men lost without, 191; law of Moses avails nothing except through, 217, 249; prepared from foundation of world, 220; without men shall perish, 249; preached by Amulek, 334, 342; taught by Aaron, 381, 385; taught by king of Anti-Nephi-Lehies, 392; Korihor preaches against, 410; God atones for sins of world, 453; bringeth mercy and resurrection, 454; no salvation outside of, 556.

Babylon, captives carried to, 3; to be destroyed, 141.

Ball of Brass, found by Lehi, 48; directions of followed, 49, 50; pointers of work according to faith, 50; compass ceased to work, 61; delivered to Mosiah by Benjamin, 209.

Baptism, prophet to administer, 24, 29; Holy Spirit follows, 29; all men must be obedient to, 108; of Lamb of God, 29, 161; commanded, 161; of fire and Holy Ghost, 162; gate by which to enter is repentance and, 162; taught and administered by Alma, 259; 281, 283, 285; administered in Sidon, 310, 321; Alma teaches, 324; Alma baptizes at Melek, 327, at Sidom, 358; Alma baptizes Zeezrom, 358; baptism administered to Lamanites, 376; Helaman and brethren preach, 539; thousands enter church by, 551; Nephites baptized, 557; eight thousand Lamanites baptized, 558; Nephi baptizing, 597; Nephi and others baptize, 602; all who repented baptized, 623; of fire and Holy Ghost promised by Christ, 628; Christ commands disciples to administer, 633; is immersion, 635; twelve given power to administer, 635; those baptized to receive bread and wine, 651; twelve disciples baptized, 655; those baptized promised salvation, 667; disciples of Christ baptize, 672; those baptized called church of Christ, 672; commanded, 674; disciples of Christ baptize, 677; Gentiles commanded to be, 681; baptized in name of Jesus, 681; not to be administered to those unworthy, 713; commanded of Christ, 725; teaching concerning, 762; of little children gross error, 769; first-fruits of repentance, 771.

Barges, built by Jared and brother, 717, 718; description of, 718, 719; number of, 720; people embark in, 727; driven before wind, 727; voyage of, 727.

Barley, 339.

INDEX.   785

Beggar, not to petition in vain, 221.
Beggars, all are, 222.
Benjamin, reigns instead of Mosiah, 202; war in days of, 202; receives plates from Amaleki, 202; reign of, 204; plates handed down from reign of, 205; contentions among people of, 205; fights with sword of Laban, 206; drives out Lamanites, 206; establishes peace in land, 206; peace remainder of days, 207; sons of, 207; teaches sons language of fathers, 207; teaches sons, 207; words of to Mosiah, 208; confers kingdom upon Mosiah, 209; gives Mosiah charge of records, plates, sword of Laban, and ball or director, 209; addresses his people, 210, 219; declares Mosiah king, 214; takes names of those entering into covenant, 226; consecrates son Mosiah to be king, 226; appoints priests to teach people, 226; death of, 226; words of not understood by some, 281.
Benjamin, King, kept records written by brother of Jared, 723.
Bethabara, prophet to baptize at, 24.
Bible, Gentiles say there can not be any more, 156; to proceed from Jews, 156; not to contain all the words of God, 157.
Boaz, Nephites flee to city of, 697; Nephites driven from, 697.
Book, given to Lehi, 2, 3; Nephi writes in, 25; carried forth among Gentiles, 35, 36; contains covenants of Lord, 35; of Lamb of God, 37; proceeding out of mouth of Jew, 41; Joseph's seed to hearken to words of, 90; words of righteous sealed up in, 146; to be sealed, 149; words of to be brought forth, 149; to contain revelation from beginning to end of world, 149; words of to be read upon housetops, 149; three witnesses of, 150; words of delivered to learned, 150; learned unable to read it, 150; unlearned to read words of, 150; sealed up again unto the Lord, 151; deaf to hear words of, 152; many to believe words of, 158.
Books, other, 38; sealed, 42; to come forth in their purity to house of Israel, 42; world to be judged out of, 157; world to be judged by words written in, 675.
Bountiful, land of, 52, 53, 387; inhabited by Nephites, 388; appearance of Christ in, 632.
Bountiful, Nephites possess land north of, 486; Moroni and people in, 488; Lamanites drive Nephites to borders of, 493; Teancum's army at borders of, 493; Moroni orders Teancum to fortify, 495; Moroni marches to to assist Teancum, 496; returns to city of, 497; Moroni and army arrive at, 497; Lehi meets Lamanites near, 498; Lamanite prisoners marched to, 499; Lamanites erect fortifications about city of by order of Moroni, 500; prisoners of Lamanites caused to labor in, 500; Hagoth builds ship on borders of, 540; Coriantumr marches toward, 545; Lamanites obtain possession of lands near, 553; Nephi and Lehi begin preaching at, 557.
Breastplates found by people of Limhi, 232.
Brother of Jared, man highly favored of the Lord, 715; language of not confounded, 715; promised choice land, 716, 717; seed of and of brother to become great nation, 716; and brother go into Valley of Nimrod, 716; the Lord talks with, 716, 718; commanded to

depart into wilderness, 716; chastened and repents, 718; molts stones from Shelem, 720; sees finger of Lord, 721; sees the Lord, 721; could not be kept from within the vail, 722; given two stones or interpreters, 722, 723; commanded to write and seal up records, 722, 723; commanded to write in a language confounded, 722; shown all inhabitants of earth, 723; to seal up two stones, 723; puts stones into vessels, 726; embarks for promised land, 727; and people reach promised land, 727; begets sons and daughters, 728; number of sons and daughters, 728; Pagag, son of, chosen to be king, refuses, 728, 729; sons of refuse to be king, 728; death of, 729; descendant of subdues Moron, 745; commands mountain to be moved, 748.

Burnt offerings, offered by Lehi, 14, 19.

Cain, 733.

Cement, expert in use of, 549.

Cezoram, Nephi delivers judgment seat to, 555; murdered, 563; son of, appointed judge and murdered, 563.

Charity, all men should have, 147; Nephi has, 165; defined, 768; can not be saved without, 776.

Chastity, God delights in, 172.

Chemish, receives plates from Amaron, 200; writes in book of his brother, 200.

Chief, of tribe, 620.

Children, born in wilderness, 52; confidence of lost, 172; husbands and wives love, 174; speak marvelous things to fathers, 671, 672; baptism of little, a gross error, 769; little, alive in Christ, 769.

Christ, people believe in, 143; made alive in, 143; preach, talk, and write of, 143; life in, 143; law fulfilled in, 143; to show himself to children of Lehi, 144; Jews and Gentiles must be convinced of, 145; doctrine of, 160; name of taken upon by baptism, 161; feasting upon word of, 163; no other name whereby man can be saved, 163; words of, 163, 166; prophets had hope of glory of, 175; coming of foretold, 216; atonement and salvation through only, 217; to be called by name of, 225; resurrection through, 253, 312; death swallowed up in, 255; life and light of world, 255; church of, 260; Alma's prophecy concerning, 323; Amulek teaches concerning coming of, 342; Alma teaches concerning coming of, 351; to appear after his resurrection, 361; Ammon teaches Lamoni of, 371; testifies of, 373; queen of Lamanites testifies of, 376; atonement of taught by Aaron, 381; Anti-christ speaks against, 409, 410; Alma testifies of, 413, 446; denied by Zoramites, 418; spoken of by Moses, 427; Amulek testifies of, 428; only means of salvation, 444; bringeth to pass resurrection of dead, 447; atonement of, 453; believers in called Christians by Moroni, 470; many died in faith of, 473; Moroni firm in faith of, 479; gate of heaven open to those who believe on, 551; atonement of, 556; to redeem from sins, 556; faith in taught by Aminadab, 560; Holy Spirit bears witness of, 560; death of redeems mankind, 592; signs of coming of, 591, 593, 601; doctrine of called foolish and vain, 604; nine years from birth of, 604; tenth, eleventh, thirteenth years from, 604, 605;

INDEX. 787

fourteenth year, 605; fifteenth year, 605, 606; sixteenth year from coming of, 606; seventeenth year, 609; eighteenth year, 610; nineteenth year, 610, 612; twentieth and twenty-first years, 612; twenty-second, twenty-third, twenty-fourth, and twenty-fifth years, 615; twenty-sixth, twenty-seventh years, 617; twenty-eighth year, 617; twenty-ninth, 618; thirtieth, 618; death and resurrection of testified of, 619; thirtieth year, 620; thirty-first year, 622, 623; Nephi testifies of remission of sins through, 622; thirty-second year, 623; thirty-third year, 623, 624; thirty-fourth year, 624; speaks to people after destruction of cities, 626 and 628; law of Moses fulfilled in, 628; thirty-fourth year, 631; manifests himself unto Nephites and Lamanites, 631; appearance and words of, 632; speaks to Nephi, 633; doctrine of, 634; calls twelve apostles, 633, 635; instructs twelve disciples, 640, 644, 650, 651; teaching to the multitude, 641, 647, 651; law of Moses fulfilled in, 643; speaks concerning all nations of Gentiles, 646, 647, 658; to go to lost tribes of Israel, 648; heals the afflicted, 648; blesses little children, 649; teaching to disciples, 650, 652; administers bread and wine, 650, 657; ordains one to administer bread and wine, 650; a light and an example, 651; forbids partaking of flesh and blood unworthily, 652; sheep of known and numbered, 653; disciples given power to give Holy Ghost, 653; ascension of, 654; appears again to multitude, 655; commands multitude and disciples to pray, 655; prays to Father, 655, 657; speaks to multitude, 657; speaks to disciples, 658; spoken of by Moses, 659; commands twelve to write scriptures, 667; commands words of Samuel to be recorded, 667; expounds words of Malachi, 667; teachings of contained on plates of Nephi, 671; shows himself often and breaks bread and administers, 671; administers to children, 671; heals afflicted, 671; raises man from dead, 672; disciples of baptize, 672; all things common among disciples of, 672; those baptized called church of, 672; appears again, 672; church to be called in name of, 673; all things to be done in name of, 673; admonishes disciples, 675; speaks to disciples, 675; desires of disciples, 676; promise to, 676; three of disciples of not to taste of death, 676, 678; touches all disciples save three, 677; ascension of, 677; disciples of caught up into heaven, 677; disciples of cast into furnace and den of wild beasts, 678; three disciples of, change wrought upon, 679; Lamanites and Nephites all converted unto, 681; children of, 683; first generation from passed away, 683; second generation after, 684; churches deny more part of gospel of, 684; a church denies, 684; Nephites once had for Shepherd, 700; Mormon exhorts house of Israel to believe in, 703; shows Gentile nations to Moroni, 708; results of faith in, 712; commission of, 712; words of to twelve, 760; manner of administering flesh and blood of, 761, 762; effects of faith in, 766; circumcision done away in, 769; little children alive in, 769; that which is good denieth not, 775. (See under Jesus Christ, and Messiah.)

Christians, believers in Christ called, 470; cause of, 470.

Church, great and abominable, 33; destroys saints of God, 34; takes from book plain and precious things, 36; founded by devil, etc., 39; utter destruction of, 39, 40, 154; whore of all the earth, 40; dominion over all the earth, 40; gathered together to fight, 40; of Lamb of God, 40; numbers of few, 40, 100; wrath of God upon, 41; wars among nations of, 41; of Christ, 260; people of to impart of substance, 261; Alma high priest of, 274; of God, those baptized belong to, 281; Alma regulates affairs of, 285; prosperity and persecution of, 285; murmurs, 285; nothing to overthrow it but transgression of people, 287; became rich, 302; wealthy and prosperous, 302; thirty-five hundred additions to, 310; people wax proud, 310; elders, priests, teachers consecrated unto, 311; evils of, 311; in city of Zarahemla, 313; received into after baptism, 321; transgressors cast out of, 321; established in city of Zarahemla, 321; commanded to fast and pray, 321; regulations of made by Alma, 321; Alma establishes order of in Gideon, 326; established at Sidom, 358; establishment of general among Nephites, 361; established among Lamanites, 376, 561; of God, people of Ammon numbered with, 405; performances of, 417; Alma and brethren sought to destroy, 434; Alma blesses, 467; saying of concerning Alma, 467; established by Helaman and brethren, 468; priests and teachers appointed over, 468; dissenters from church under Amalickiah, 469; established by Helaman and brethren, 539; pride and contention in, 548, 552; great prosperity in, 551; brethren of persecuted, 552; fasting and praying of, 552; dissension in, 552; abominations among, 553; began to dwindle and disbelieve, 555; spread throughout face of land, 582; contention among, 582; broken up in all land, 618; to be established among Gentiles, 662, 664, 666; those baptized called church of Christ, 672; to be called by name of Christ, 673; to be built upon gospel of Christ, 673; disciples of Christ unite people to, 677; all converted united with, 678; disciples form, in all lands round about, 681; all people converted unto, 681; began to deny true, 684; another, which denied the Christ, 684; of Christ, those baptized into, 762; meet together often, 762.

Churches, two only, 40; not unto the Lord, 152; to contend, to deny the Holy Ghost, 153; become corrupted, 153; rob the poor, persecute meek, 154; pride and wickedness of, 154; taught by precepts of men, 154; Alma permitted to establish, 281; seven in land of Zarahemla, 281; established by Aaron and brethren, 389; built up to themselves to get gain, 684, many churches, 684, 685; built up to themselves—richly adorned, 686; to become defiled, 707; to forgive sins to get gain, 708; every one polluted by pride, 709.

Circumcision, done away in Christ, 769.

Cities, built in Zarahemla, 286; many built, 486; many built and repaired, 617; destroyed, 624; built where formerly burned, 682.

Classes, among people, 684.

Cloth, woven by people of Zeniff, 237, 302, 562; made by Jaredites, 742.

Cohor, brother of Noah, drawn away by Noah, 730.

Cohor, son of Noah, kingdom of, 731; gives battle to Shule, slain by,

731; kingdom of given to Shule by Nimrod, 731; sons and daughters repent not, 751.
Com, son of Coriantum, 714, 715; reigns as king, 738; dethroned by Heth, 738; reigns over half of kingdom, 743; subdues Amgid, 743; prophets flee to for protection, 743.
Combinations, secret, plans to be kept from people, 440, 441; judgments of God upon, 441, 543, 547, 548, 563; signs and words of, 564; wickedness of, 564; origin of, 564; plots handed down by devil—among all nations, 565; destroyed among Lamanites, 566; Nephites build up, 566, 577; control government, 567; judges included in, 570; chief judge slain because of, 573; war caused by, 579; war and destruction caused by, 582, 583, 603; leader of slain, 613; Nephites make end of, 614; judges enter into against government, 620; destroy government, 620; gathered together and appoint king, 621; people of migrate northward to establish kingdom, 621; people again build up, 686; work to come forth in a day of, 707; built up to get gain, 709; secret, 733; swearing of people into, 733; oaths of handed down by Cain, 733; abominable and wicked above all in sight of God, 734; Lord worketh not in, 734; cause destruction of Nephites and Jaredites, 734; Gentiles warned against, 734; built up by devil to destroy all nations, 735; Jared murdered by, 736; Heth embraces, 738; Com fights against, 743; people rebel because of, 745; reject words of prophets because of, 745; many of people of slain, 752; Gilead receives strength from, 754; cause murder of Gilead, 754. (See under Gadianton.)
Commandments, Lord prepares a way for accomplishment of, 7, 23, 52.
Comnor, hill, 756.
Compass, ceases working, 61; again works, 63, 441. (See Director, and Ball.)
Concubines, prohibited, 172, 173; and wives of King Noah, 239.
Contention forbidden, 260, 274; appears through Amlici, 303; among church, 311; among Lamanites because of Ammon, 375; cause of wars and destructions of Nephites, 487; concerning lands of Lehi and Morianton, 487; concerning law, 490, 491; among Nephites, 539; in church, 548; among people, 549, 550, 552; Gadiantons stir up among Nephites, 570; people divided by, 579; slay because of, 579; concerning doctrine, 582; ended by preaching of Nephi and Lehi, 582; concerning law of Moses, 602; caused by secret combinations, 621; not of Christ, 634; none in all the land, 681, 683.
Corianton, son of Alma, goes to Zoramites, 417; commandments of Alma to, 445; called to preach, 455; declares word of God, 484; sails with provisions to people of land northward, 541.
Corinator, Ether descendant from, 714; son of Moron, 714, 745; dwells in captivity, 745; begets Ether, 745; death of, 745.
Coriantum, son of Amnigaddah, 714; dwells in captivity, 743.
Coriantum, son of Emer, 715; anointed king by Emer, 737.
Coriantumr, account of people of, 202; discovered by people of Zarahemla, 202; son of Omer, 732; and Esrom defeat Jared, 732; king of Jaredites, 745; destruction sought, 751; fought against by secret combinations, 752; taken captive by Shared, 752; sons of regain kingdom from Shared, 752; defeats Shared in battle,

753; defeated by Shared, 753; slays Shared in battle, wounded by Shared, 753; defeats brother of Shared, 753; brother of Shared places himself upon throne of, 753; gives battle to Lib, 754; wounded, 754; defeated by Lib, 754; flees to Agosh, 754; gives battle to Shiz, 755; flees before Lib, 754; not to fall by sword, 755; gives battle to Shiz, 755; gathers armies at hill Comnor, 756; wounded by Shiz, 756; repentance of, 756; writes epistle to Shiz, 756; flees before Shiz, 757; comes to waters of Ripliancum, 757; wounded at Ripliancum, 757; defeats Shiz, 757; encamps at hill Ramah, 757; final battle with Shiz, 757; epistle of to Shiz, 758; slays Shiz, 759.

Coriantumr, led army of Lamanites, 544; takes city of Zarahemla, 544; slays Pacumeni, 545; marches toward Bountiful, 545; slain, 546.

Corihor, land of, Shiz flees to, 755.

Corihor, son of Kib, 729; rebels against father, 729; dwells in land of Nehor, 729; takes father captive in Moron, 729; given battle by Shule, 730; kingdom taken from by Shule, 730; repents, given power by Shule, 730; Noah rebels against, 730; sons and daughters repent not, 751.

Corom, made king, 741; death of, 741.

Corum, son of Levi, 714.

Covenant, made to Abraham, 45; people enter into, 224; names of those entering into, 226; secret, of Kishkumen, 543.

Crime, Jacob speaks of grosser, 171.

Cross, Lamb of God lifted upon, 30.

Cumeni city of taken by Lamanites, 510; surrendered to Helaman, 516.

Cumenihah, leader of ten thousand slain, 702.

Cumorah, land and hill of, 701, 704; Nephites march to and defeated by Lamanites at, 701; Mormon hides records in hill of, 701.

Damnation, to be subject to devil is, 255.

Darkness, over face of land, 625; vapor of felt, 625; three days of, 625; passed away, 629.

Daughters, sorrow and mourning of, 172; not to be led away captive, 172.

David, desired wives and concubines, 168; had wives and concubines, 171; having of wives and concubines abominable, 171.

David, Nephites driven from land of, 689.

Death, passed upon all men, 106; and hell, 106; spiritual, 106; is the grave, 107; and hell deliver up dead, 107; swallowed up in Christ, 255, 405; chains of, 436; murder punished by, 410; temporal, 711.

Deseret, meaning honey-bee, 716.

Desolation, land of, 387; place of first landing, 387; people of Morianton headed at, 488; Hagoth launches ship near, 540; Mormon gathers Nephites to, 693; Nephites defeat Lamanites in, 693; Nephites go out of to attack Lamanites, 695; Lamanites take city of, 695; city of Teancum near city of, 695; Nephites retake, 696; Lamanites take city of, 696; Lamanites defeat Nephites in land of, 697; Moron near, 729.

Desolation of Nehors, 360.

INDEX. 791

Devil, captivity of, 39, 106; founder of abominable church, 39, 40; beguiled first parents, 106; transforms himself, 106; and angels the filthy ones, 108; go into everlasting fire, 108; of all devils, 110; foundation of secret combinations, 147; kingdom of must shake, 154; to rage in hearts of men, to stir men to anger against good, 154; leadeth men to hell, 155; master of sin, 221; has power over wicked, 254, 255; takes possession of wicked, 448; father of secret combinations, 735.

Directors, ball of brass, 48; Alma directs Helaman to preserve, 439; prepared that word of God might be fulfilled, 440; called Liahona, 441. (See Ball.)

Disciples, all die except three, others ordained in their stead, 683; of Jesus cast into prison, prisons rent in twain, miracles wrought by, 684; cast into furnaces of fire, 685; taken away because of wickedness, 688; three, minister to Mormon and Moroni, 705.

Diseases, removed by plants and roots, 473.

Dissenters, more hardened than Lamanites, 477; to Lamanites, 552; with Lamanites obtain land southward from Nephites, 553; confess sins and are baptized, 557; endeavor to repair wrongs, 557, 558; commence war, 582.

Division, caused among the people, 159; great among people, 685.

Doctrine, points of to be made known, 44; false, to be confounded, 88; of Christ, 160, 163, 164, 634; Sherem tries to overthrow, 189; false taught by Nehor and others, 300.

Dream of Lehi, 4, 7, 19.

Earth, knowledge of Lord to cover, 160; created by power of word, 176; moves, not the sun, 585; destructions upon at crucifixion, 624.

Earthquake, Alma and Amulek delivered by, 356; Nephi and Lehi delivered by, 558.

Earthquakes, 624, 625.

Eden, man cast out of, 452.

Egypt, Moses to deliver Israel from, 88.

Egyptian, reformed, records written in, 713.

Egyptians, language of, 2.

Elders, consecrated by Alma 311; ordained by Alma, 321; manner of ordaining priests and teachers by, 761; ministering flesh and blood of Christ, 761, 762.

Emer, son of Omer, 715; anointed king by Omer, 736; dies, 737.

Emron, slain by sword, 772.

Enos, plates given to by Jacob, 193; conversion of, 193, 194; prophesies to people of Nephi, 195.

Ephraim, hill of, 720.

Equality, enjoined, 285; practiced, 301, 302.

Esrom, son of Omer, 732; and Coriantumr defeat Jared, 732.

Eternal torment, 435.

Ethem, son of Ahah, 714; becomes king, 744.

Ether, account of ancient inhabitants taken from book of, 714; descendant of Coriantor, 714, 745; lived in days of Coriantumr, 745; prophesies to people, 745; words of rejected, 750; sees days of Christ, 750; prophecies of, great and marvelous, 751; hides in cavity of rock, 751, 752; makes record, 751; prophesies to Coriantumr, 752; prophesies of Coriantumr, 755; all gathered to armies except, 757; beholds destruction of people, 759; finishes and hides record, 759; record of found by people of Limhi, 759, 270; last words written by, 759.

Ezrom, of silver, 339.

Faith, effects of, 4, 6, 176; God worketh by, 151; manifestation by, 167; to pray with, 173; of Enos unshaken, 194; Holy Spirit manifesteth according to, 197; remission of sins through, 219; brings joy, 224; hearts changed through, 224; miracles wrought by, 233; Alma blessed because of, 283; Alma teaches, 326, 357; of wife of Lamoni, 373; knowledge greater than, 422; compass works by, 442; lives of some of people of Ammon preserved by, 518; power manifested through, 707; brings knowledge, 712; Ether and Moroni concerning, 746; Moroni on and charity, 748; brings power to do whatever is expedient, 766; effects of, 766; God worketh among men according to their, 775; can not be saved without, 776.

Fall, came by transgression, 106, 453.

Family of Lehi, 4.

Famine, people of Zeniff smitten with, 234; upon Nephites and Lamanites, 580; people repent because of, 580; removed, 581; among Jaredites, 738, 739, 744.

Father, work of to commence, 41.

Fire, as fire and brimstone, 108, 189; endless torment, 108.

Fornication, warnings against, 174.

Foundation, only sure, 177, 557.

Free men, to maintain free government, 490; voice of people favor, 490.

Gad, city of burned, 627.

Gadiandi, city sunk, 627.

Gadianton, leader of band of Kishkumen, 547; band of flee into wilderness, 548; secret combinations of, 551; band of murderers formed by, 563; more numerous among Lamanites, 563; band of murdered Cezoram and his sons, 563; more numerous part of Nephites join band of, 563; signs and words of, 564; laws given by, 564; origin of system of, 564; band of destroyed among Lamanites, 566; band of built up by Nephites, 566; band of obtain possession of government, 566; robbers of filling judgment seats, 567; at head of government, 567; judges belong to band of, 570; band of slay chief judge, 573; secret band of cause war, 579; band of swept away, 580; secret plans of concealed, 580; robbers of, 582; driven back, 583; defy armies of Nephites and Lamanites, 583; robbers of infest land and increase, 603; robbers of joined by Nephites and Lamanites, 603; robbers of become numerous, Nephites and Lamanites arm against, 605; war between robbers of and Nephites, 605; robbers of gain over Nephites, 605; leader of robbers of writes to Lachoneus, 606; Giddianhi, governor of society of, 607; works of of ancient date, 607; Nephites prepare against robbers of, 608; Nephites gather together against robbers of, 609; robbers of go against Nephites, 611; Nephites defeat robbers of, 611, 613; robbers of besiege Nephites, 612; leader of robbers of

INDEX. 793

hanged, 613; band of destroyed, 614; robbers of given lands, 617; people again begin to build up secret oaths and combinations of. 686; robbers of spread over face of land, 686; robbers of infest land, 689; Nephites go against robbers of, 692; Nephites make treaty with robbers of, 692.

Gadiomnah, city of, sunk, 627.

Gazelem, stone prepared for, 440.

Genealogy, of forefathers, 7; of father of Nephi, 8.

Gentiles, Messiah to be made manifest to, 25; Lehi compares with olive tree, 25; to receive fullness of gospel, 25; foundation of great and abominable church among, 33; waters divide from seed of Nephi's brethren, 34; upon land of promise, 34; smite seed of Nephi's brethren, 34; described, 34; delivered from other nations, 35; prospered, 35; book carried amo 35; not to remain in blindness, 36; not to destroy seed of brethren, 36; to stumble, 37; plain and precious things to be restored to, 37; books from Gentiles to Jews, 38; Shepherd to manifest himself unto, 38; to be numbered among seed of Israel, 39; promises to, 39; woe unto, 39; fullness of gospel to come unto, 44; seed of Lehi scattered by, 45; power of God manifested through, 45; promises to, 100; must be convinced that Jesus is the Christ, 145; smite seed of Lehi, 146; pride, greatness, and stumbling-block of, 146; build up many churches, 146; put down power and miracles of God, preach their own learning, 146; grind upon face of poor, 146; secret combinations of, 147; and Jew alike unto God, 148; shall be drunken with iniquity, 148; to be visited with destructions from the Lord, 148; will deny God, 156; shall say can not be any more Bible, 156; who repent are covenant people, 158; Nephi prophesieth concerning, 158; book written unto, 158; blessed because of belief in Christ, 646; abominations among, 646; promises and warnings to, 647; scourge to people of this land, 660; work to be brought forth among, 663; work of Christ to come forth among, 662, 666; to be a free people on this land, 662; promises to, 662; warnings concerning, 663; remnant of Jacob to tread down, 663; church to be established among, 664; three Nephites disciples to be among, 678; commanded to be baptized, 681; Mormon writes to, 694; written unto by Mormon, 699; to receive blessing reserved for Nephites, 700; admonished to repent, 700; remnant Jacob to tear in pieces, 663, 700; warned by Mormon concerning decrees of God, 717; sealed records not to come forth in days of wickedness of, 724; warned against secret combinations, 734; weakness of to be shown unto, 748; Moroni bids farewell to, 749.

Gid, chief captain among Nephites, 519; and Teomner take city of Manti, 522.

Gid, city of, taken by Amalickiah, 493; Nephites guarded by Lamanites in, 506; Moroni arms prisoners in, 507; surrendered to Moroni, 508; Moroni causes Lamanites to erect fortifications about, 508; Nephi and Lehi preach at, 557.

Giddianhi, governor of society of Gadianton, 607; robbers of take possession of lands vacated by Nephites, 610; orders robbers against Nephites, 611; slain by Nephites, 612.

794 BOOK OF MORMON.

Giddonah, Amulek son of, 334.
Giddonah, high priest of Gideon, 411.
Gideon, attacks King Noah, 262; searches for King Noah, 263; advises King Limhi, 271; a teacher, 299; withstands teaching of Nehor, 299; slain by Nehor, 299; valley of, 305; Alma declares word to church in valley of, 322; Alma establishes order of church in, 326; Korihor goes to land of, 411; Giddonah, high priest of, 411; people of send Korihor to Zarahemla, 412; Pahoran flees to land of, 532; Moroni joins Pahoran in, 534.
Gidgiddoni, chief captain of Nephites, 608; great prophet and chief judge, 608; arms Nephites, 610; orders Nephites to pursue Gadianton robbers, 611; robbers of besiege Nephites, 612; surrounds army of Gadianton robbers, 613; army of destroy army of Gadianton robbers, 613; and Lachoneus establish peace, 617; leader of ten thousand slain, 702.
Gifts, different administrations of, 775; every good gift of Christ, 776; not to be done away except because of sins, 776.
Gilead, brother of Shared, fights Coriantumr and is driven to Akish, 753; assumes throne of Coriantumr, 753; receives strength because of secret combinations, 754; murdered by his high priest, 754.
Gilgah, son of Jared, 728.
Gilgal, battle in valley of, 753; Coriantumr defeated by Shared at, 753; Coriantumr slays Shared in, 753.
Gilgal, city of sunk, inhabitants buried, 626.
Gilgal, leader of ten thousand slain, 702.
Gimgimno, city of sunk, 627.
God, justice of, 39, 46; wrath of poured out, 41; worketh not in darkness, 147; lays down life, 147; inviteth all men to partake of goodness of, 148; commandeth that there be no priestcrafts, 147; commandeth all to have charity, 147; commands against all iniquities, 148; denieth none that come to him, 148; all alike unto, 148.
Gold, senine of, 339; seon of, 339; shum of, 339; limnah of, 339; antion of, 339; abundant among Nephites and Lamanites, 562.
Gospel, to be preached among Jews, 25; Gentiles to receive fullness of, 25; parts taken away, 36; to be with Nephites, 37, 38; to be declared to seed of Nephi, 159; church to be built upon, 673; taught by Christ, 674; those who reject, called Ishmaelites, etc., 685; those who deny miracles know not, 710.
Grave, must deliver up its captive bodies, 106, 107.
Great Spirit, Ammon called, 367, 368, 370, 375, 384.
Hagoth, launches ship near Bountiful and Desolation, 540; builds other ships, 541.
Healing of sick, 30.
Hearthom, son of Lib, 714; succeeds Lib as king, 742; kingdom taken from, 742.
Hebrew, language, altered by Nephites, 713.
Helam, baptized by Alma, 259; land of, 274; city of, 275; land of taken by Lamanites, 275; guards set round about, 276; Alma and people depart from, 279; captivity of people in, 287.
Helaman, son of Benjamin, 207.

INDEX.

Helaman, son of Alma, 417; commandment of Alma to, 434; Alma commits plates to, commanded to keep records, 437, 489; commanded to preserve directors, 439; to take care of sacred things, 443; account of Nephites in days of, 465; visited by Alma, 466; foretold destruction of Nephites by Alma, 466; declares word among people, 468; and brethren establish the church, 468; and brethren appoint priests and teachers over church, 468; and brethren opposed by Amalickiah, 468; and brethren high priests, 469; and high priests maintain order in church, 473, 484; preaches and baptizes, 480; persuades people of Ammon not to break oath, 501; chosen leader of sons of people of Ammon, 502; epistle of to Moroni, 509; marches to city of Judea, 510; and army pursued by Lamanites, 512; and army defeat and capture Lamanites, 514; and army return to Judea, 515; sends epistle to king of Lamanites, 515; takes city of Cumeni, 516; sends embassy to governor at Zarahemla, 520; takes city of Manti, 523; Moroni reinforces, 535; returns to land of Zarahemla, 539; resumes preaching of word, 539; death of, 540.

Helaman, son of Helaman, receives sacred things, 541; appointed chief judge, 546; servant of kills Kishkumen, 547; filled judgment seat with judgment and equity, 550; Nephi and Lehi sons of, 550; death of, 552; words of to sons, 556; gives son Nephi charge of records, 600; departs and no more heard of, 600.

Helem, accompanies Ammon to land of Nephi, 227.

Hell, must deliver up dead, 107; chains of, 352; pains of, 353, 435; powers of, 480; gates of not to prevail, 635.

Helorum, son of Benjamin, 207.

Hem, accompanies Ammon to land of Nephi, 227.

Hermounts, wilderness of, 307.

Heshlon, Shared flees to plains of, 753.

Heth, son of Com, 715, 738; embraces secret plans, 738; dethrones Com, 738; perishes by famine, 739.

Heth, son of Hearthom, 714; land of, 732; born in captivity, 743.

High priests, Alma, 274, 297; Alma retains office of, 312; Ammon high priest over people of, 411; and lawyers angry because of testimony concerning Christ, 619; could not condemn to death, 619.

High priests, of King Noah, 240; Abinadi examined by, 244; teach law of Moses, 245; flee into wilderness, 263, 264; seize daughters of Lamanites, 264; seed of high priests of King Noah, 395; Helaman and brethren high priests, 468; Helaman and maintain order in church, 473.

Highways, and roads from city to city, 617; broken up, 624.

Himni, son of Mosiah, 289; teaches people of Zarahemla, 289; account of, 388; rejoices, 397; rejoices in meeting Alma, 403; remains at Zarahemla, 417.

History, of Nephites on other plates, 98, 167.

Holy Ghost, denial of, unpardonable sin, 445; to bear record, 634; twelve disciples given power to give, 653; fell upon disciples, 655; to be sanctified by, 674; beareth record of Father and Son, 677; did not come upon any because of wickedness and unbelief, 688; power given twelve to bestow, 760; gifts administered by, 775.

BOOK OF MORMON.

Holy One of Israel, 99; they who believe in, 108, 109; keeper of gate, 110; is Son of God, 158.
Holy Order of God, men ordained to, 484; Moroni speaks of, 746.

Holy stand of Zoramites, 417.
Husbands, wickedness and abominations of, 172; love wives, 173.
Idol gods, Lamanites offer Nephites as sacrifices to, 697.
Idolatry, among Nephites, 700.
Inequality, of church, 311; none among church, 361; because of sin, 407; among Nephites, 618.
Interpreters, Ammon speaks of, 233; sealed up by Mormon, 724.
Irreantum, sea called, 53.
Isaac, offering of a similitude of Only Begotten Son, 175.
Isabel, harlot of Siron, 445.
Isaiah, words of, 45, 647, 660, 661, 665; taught by Nephi, 67; taught by Jacob, 98; words of written by Nephi, 115, 116, 139; Nephi speaks concerning words of, 139; quoted by Abinadi, 245, 254; prophecies of to be searched, 707.
Isaiah, one of twelve, 654.
Ishmael, and family brought into wilderness, 17; daughters of rebel against, 17; mother and children plead for Nephi, 19; and family join Lehi, 19; daughters of marry, 48; sons of murmur, 49; daughters of mourn, 51; dies, 51; sons of chastened, 52; sons of spoken to by Lehi, 91; sons of angry with Nephi, 92.
Ishmael, Giddonah son of, 334; descendant of Aminadi, 334.
Ishmael, land of visited by Ammon, 364; Ammon and Lamoni return to, 382; synagogues built in, 383; people of converted, 390; Ammon and brethren go to land of, 391.
Ishmaelites, those who reject gospel called, etc., 685; war with Nephites, 688; called Lamanites, 688.
Israel, compared to olive tree, 25, 44; to be scattered and gathered, 25; fights against apostles, 30; Gentiles to be numbered among seed of, 39; covenants of the Lord unto, 39; covenants to, 40; work of the Father to commence among, 41; sealed books to come unto, 42; righteous branch raised up unto, 87; Messiah to be made manifest to in latter days, 87; house of to be restored, 88, 156; tribes of to write words of Lord, 158; to be gathered home, 158; likened to tame olive tree, 177; to be restored to land of, 100, 140, 645, 660; to be gathered to own lands, 616, 645, 660; Christ speaks to, 629; other tribes of, 645; Lord to remember covenant to, 646; Christ to go to lost tribes of, 648; covenant with, 659; Mormon writes to, 694; to be restored to land of inheritance, 699; Mormon speaks to remnant of house of, 703.
Jacob, born in wilderness, 61; Lehi speaks to, 82; flees with Nephi into wilderness, 95; consecration of, 97, 168; speaks to people of Nephi, 98; not to be ashamed, 152; Nephi commands concerning small plates, 167; distinguishes the people, 168; teaches in temple, 168, 169; magnifies office, 168; words of, 169; speaks concerning grosser crimes, 171; plates of made by hand of Nephi, 175; ministers much, 175; prophecies, 177; exhortation of, 188; Sherem comes to, 190; confounds Sherem, 190; prayer of answered, 192; begins

INDEX. 797

to be old, 193; people of tried, 193; delivers plates to son Enos, 193; makes end of writing upon plates, 193.

Jacob, called king of secret band, 621; and people go north to establish kingdom, 621.

Jacob, city of, sunk, 627.

Jacob, Lamanite leader of Mulek, 497; marches against Teancum, 497; surrounded by Moroni and Levi, 498; killed, 499; army of, surrenders to Moroni, 499.

Jacob, remnant of, 471.

Jacobites, among those who believed, 685; war with Lamanites, 688; called Nephites, 688.

Jacobugath, city of, burned, 627.

Jacom, son of Jared, 728.

Jared, came from great tower, 715; language of, not confounded, 715; promised choice land, 716; seed of, and of brethren to become a great nation, 716; and brother go into valley of Nimrod, 716; and brethren brought to great sea, 718; embark for promised land, 727; reach promised land, 727; number of sons and daughters of, 728; all of sons but Orihah refuse to be king, 729; death of, 729.

Jared, son of Omer, 732; rebels against father, 732; dwells in land of Heth, 732; carries father into captivity, 732; defeated by Esrom and Coriantumr, 732; daughter of, 733; anointed king, 735; murdered, 736.

Jaredites, perish because of willfulness, 774.

Jarom writes according to command of Enos, 197.

Jashon, Nephites flee to land of, 691; city of, near land where records were deposited, 691.

Jeneum, leader of ten thousand Nephites, 702.

Jeremiah, one of the twelve, 654.

Jeremiah, plates of brass contain prophecies of, 15.

Jershon, land of, given to Anti-Nephi-Lehies, 404; they take possession of, 405; Korihor goes to land of, 411; people of, banish Korihor, 411; Alma and Amulek and brethren go to, 432; believers from among Zoramites come to, 432; people of Ammon depart from, 433; Nephites prepare for war in land of, 456; Moroni meets Lamanites in borders of, 457.

Jerusalem, destruction of, prophesied, 2, 3, 24, 77; abominations of, 3; Nephi and brethren return to, 7, 10, 17; Lord brought people out of, 54; people of, to be scourged, 66; thirty years after leaving, 97; people of, slain and made captives, 99; people of, to return again, 99, 140; Lord to show himself to people of, 105, 140; Nephi declares had been destroyed, 140; wars and rumors of wars among, 140; to crucify Messiah, 141; to be destroyed again, 141; kings reign five hundred nine years after leaving, 298; Son of God to be born at, 323; six hundred years, 600; six hundred nine years, 604; city of, water comes instead thereof, 627; new, 659; to be inhabited again, 662; twelve in land of, to judge tribes of Israel, 694; twelve in land of, to judge twelve chosen on Western Continent, 695; to be rebuilt, 750; inhabitants to be blessed, 751.

Jerusalem, on borders of Mormon, 380; city of, 381.

Jesus Christ, to be Messiah, 142; no other name whereby man can be saved, 142; gospel to be declared, 159; God of promised land, 717; shows himself to brother of Jared, 721, 722; shows brother of Jared all inhabitants of earth, 723; statement concerning Gentiles, 724; promises and admonitions of, 724; commands baptism, 725; Emer sees coming of, 737. (See under Christ.)

Jews, learning of, 1; Lehi mocked by, 3; angry at Lehi, 4; record of, 7; plates of brass contain record of, 15; gospel to be preached among, 25; dwindle in unbelief, 25; book received from mouth of, 35; Shepherd to manifest himself unto, 38; book proceedeth out of the mouth of, 41, 42; restoration of, in latter days, 45; not confounded nor scattered again, 45; to be scattered among all nations, 141; to be restored again, 141; words of Lord to be brought unto, 141; must be convinced that Jesus is the Christ, 145; and Gentiles alike unto God, 148; shall be drunken with iniquity, 148; to be visited with destructions from the Lord, 148; Bible to proceed from, 156; diligence of, 156; to write words of the Lord, 158; who do not repent cast off, 158; Nephi prophesies concerning, 158; to begin to believe in Christ, 159; to gather, 159; to become a delightsome people, 159; stiff-necked, 177; looked beyond mark, 177; reject the stone, 177; three Nephite disciples to be among, 678; records to go to unbelieving of, 699.

John, name of the apostle of the Lamb, 42; revelations of, to be unfolded to all people, 725.

Jonas, son of Timothy, one of the twelve, 654.

Jordan, Nephites repulse Lamanites at city of, 698.

Joseph, son of Lehi, born in wilderness, 61; spoken to by Lehi, 87; seed not to be utterly destroyed, 87; seed of, to hearken to words of book, 90; one mighty to be raised from seed of, 90; to hearken to words of Nephi, 90; flees with Nephi into wilderness, 95; consecration of, 97, 168; labors of, 168.

Joseph of Egypt, Lehi descendant of, 15, 87, 335; covenants made unto, 87; seer raised up unto, 87; fruit of loins to write, 87; spokesman for choice seer, 89; seer to write, 89; fruit of loins of, to cry from dust, 89; Nephi speaks concerning prophecies of, 90; promise to, 142; righteous branch from loins of, 172; remnant of seed of, 471, 630; part of coat of, preserved, 471.

Josephites, among those who believed, 685; war with Lamanites, 688; called Nephites, 688.

Josh, city of, burned, 627.

Josh, leader of ten thousand Nephites, slain, 702.

Joshua, Nephites come to land of, 689.

Judea, Helaman marches to city of, 510; Helaman returns to, 515.

Judge, Nephihah made chief, 312; chief j. of Ammonihah, 354; after order of Nehor, 354; smites Alma and Ammonihah, 355; of Ammonihah slain by fall of prison walls, 356; chief j. sends proclamation concerning people of Anti-Nephi-Lehi, 404; Nephihah, chief j. dies, 489; Pahoran appointed chief, 489; death of told by Nephi, 573; slain, 573, 574; Seezoram name of, who was slain, 575; chief j. Lachoneus, 600; Lachoneus murdered, 620.

INDEX.

Judges, appointment of, recommended by Mosiah, 293; to be judged by voice of people, 295; people make choice of, 297; reign of, commences in Zarahemla, 297; first year, 298; laws established by Mosiah recognized under, 298; second year, 301; fifth year, 303, 309, 310; voice of people laid before, 303; sixth year, 310; seventh year, 310; eighth year, 310, 311; ninth year, 311, 312, 326; tenth year, 326, 335, 355, 358; eleventh year, 359, 360; fourteenth year, 360, 362; fifteenth year, 406; sixteenth year, 409; seventeenth year, 409, 433; eighteenth year, 433, 456, 465; nineteenth year 466, 468, 473, 478, 481, 484; lower, among the Nephites, 486; twentieth year, 485, 486; twenty-first year, 486, 487; twenty-second and twenty-third years, 487; twenty-fourth year, 489; twenty-fifth year, 490, 491, 494; twenty-sixth year, 494, 496; twenty-seventh year, 496, 497; twenty-eighth year, 497, 503; twenty-ninth year, 503, 509; thirtieth year, 509, 525, 535; thirty-first year, 535, 538; chief, chosen, 539; thirty-fourth year, 681; thirty-fifth year, 540, 681; thirty-sixth year, 540, 681; thirty-seventh year, 540, 541, 682; thirty-eighth year, 541, 682; thirty-ninth year, 541, 542, 682; fortieth year, 542, 544; forty-first year, 544, 546, 682; forty-second year, 546, 548, 682; forty-third year, 548; forty-fourth year, 548; forty-fifth year, 548; forty-sixth year, 548, 550; forty-seventh, forty-eighth, and forty-ninth years, 550; forty-ninth year, 551, 682; fiftieth year, 551; fifty-first year, 552, 682; fifty-second year, 552, 682; fifty-third year, 552; fifty-fourth year, 552; fifty-sixth year, 552; fifty-seventh year, 553; fifty-eighth year, 553; fifty-ninth year, 553, 682; sixtieth year, 553; sixty-first year, 554; sixty-second year, 554, 561; sixty-third year, 562; sixty-fourth year, 562; sixty-fifth year, 562, 563; sixty-sixth year, 563; sixty-seventh year, 563, 565; sixty-eighth year, 565, 566; sixty-ninth year, 566; belong to secret band of Gadianton, 570; seventy-first and seventy-second years, 579, 683; seventy-third year, 579; seventy-fourth year, 580; seventy-fifth year, 580; seventy-sixth year, 581; seventy-seventh year, 582; seventy-eighth year, 582; seventy-ninth year, 582, 683; eightieth year, 582, 583; eighty-first year, 583; eighty-second year, 583; eighty-third year, 583; eighty-fourth year, 583; eighty-fifth year, 583, 584; eighty-sixth year, 586, 598; eighty-seventh, eighty-eighth, and eighty-ninth years, 598; ninetieth year, 598, 599; ninety-first year, 600; ninety-second year, 600, 603; ninety-third, ninety-fourth, and ninety-fifth years, 603; ninety-sixth to one hundredth year, 604; one hundredth and one hundredth and tenth years, 683; one hundred and ninety-fourth year, 683; two hundredth year, 684; two hundred and first year, 684; put to death secretly, 619; complaint against, 619; judged by chief judge according to law, 619; enter into secret combination to destroy government and establish king, 620.

Judgment, all men appear before, 107, 108; spotless at judgment seat, 165.

Justice could not be destroyed, 453; no j. without law, 454.

Kib, son of Orihah, 715, 729; taken captive by Corihor, 729; and people dwell in captivity, 730; begets Shule, 730; kingdom restored to, 730; bestows kingdom on Shule, 730.

Kimnor, Akish son of, 733.

Kim, son of Morianton, 714; made king, 741; brought into captivity, 741; death of, 741.

King, Nephi refuses to be, 96; Nephi anoints a man to be, 167; to be known by the name of Nephi, 168; reign of second, 168; Alma refuses to be, 273; people make choice of, 292; Mosiah commands that there be no k., 295; appointed in Zarahemla, makes alliance with Lamanites, 532; Pachus, k. of dissenters, executed, 534; judges seek to establish, 619; Jacob appointed k. of secret band, 621; sons of Jared refuse to be, 729; Orihah chosen, 729.

Kings, reigns of, 274; incidents of righteous and unrighteous, 295.

Kishkumen, city of, burned, 627.

Kishkumen, murders Pahoran, 543; secret covenant of, 543, 547; seeks to destroy Helaman, 547; Gadianton leader of band of, 547; slain by servant of Helaman, 547; band of murderers formed by, 563; signs and secret words of band of; laws given by, 564.

Kish, son of Corom, 714; is made king, 741; death of, 741.

Korihor, preaches shall be no Christ, 410; preaches against the atonement, 410; goes to land of Jershon, 411; banished by people of Jershon, 411; goes to Gideon, 411; addresses Giddonah, 411; banished by people of Gideon, 412; brought before Alma, 412; asks Alma for a sign, 414; struck dumb, 414; begs for support, 416; dies, 416.

Kumen, one of the twelve, 654.

Kumenonhi, one of the twelve, 654.

Laban, has record of Jews, 7; Laman asks records of, 7; refuses records, 8; records demanded of, 9; Lehi's sons flee from, 9; angel speaks to, 9; slain by Nephi, 11; descendant of Joseph, 15; he and fathers kept records, 15.

Labor, all commanded to, 285; priest and others do, 301.

Laborer, in Zion, to labor for Zion, 148; to perish if labor for money, 148.

Lachoneus, chief judge and governor, 600; receives epistle from leader of robbers, 606; sends proclamation to people to gather, 608; guards from robbers, 608; words and prophecy of, 608; appoints chief captains, 608; helps to bring peace in land, 617.

Lachoneus, son of Lachoneus, fills seat of father, 619; murdered, 620.

Lama, leader of ten thousand Nephites, 702.

Laman, king enters into treaty with Zeniff, 229; craftiness of, brings people of Zeniff into bondage, 235; stirs people to war with people of Zeniff, 235; death of. 237; son reigns, 237.

Laman, murmuring of, 5, 49, 54; hardness and cursing of, 6; lot falls to, 7; angel speaks to, 9; and Lemuel angry with Sam and Nephi, 9; returns to Jerusalem, 9, 17; rebellion of, 17, 58, 61; repentance of, 19; seed become dark and loathsome, 33; proposes to slay Lehi and Nephi, 51; chastened of the Lord, 52; shaken, 59; about to worship Nephi, 59; binds Nephi, 61; sons and daughters spoken to by Lehi, 90; seed not to perish, 91; sons of, angry with Nephi, 92.

Laman, river of, 5, 48.

Laman, servant of king of Lamanites, goes to city of Gid, 506.

Laman, son of Laman, repulses people of Limhi, 268; son of, appoints Amulon and brethren teachers, 277.

Laman, city of, burned with fire, 627.

Lamanites, people called, 96; hatred of, 96; Nephi ruler and teacher of, 97; seed of, cursed with blackness, 97; those mixing seed with, to be cursed; idle and evil people, 97; to become white and delightsome people, 159; distinguished from Nephites, 168; greater iniquity than, 172; to scourge Nephites, 173; more righteous than Nephites, 173; observe command to have but one wife, 173; to become blessed people, 173; love their wives, 173; efforts to re·tore, 192; records of Nephites to come unto, 195; become wild, bloodthirsty, and ferocious, 195; war with Nephites, 196, 198, 205; love murder, 198; driven out, 206; people depart from Lehi-Nephi, 235; war with people of Zeniff, 237; ferocity of, 238; driven from land of Zeniff, 239; attack people of Noah, 241, 262; exact tribute of King Noah, 262; oath of king of, 264; daughters of seized by priests of Noah, 264; attack people of Limhi, 265; king of, wounded, 265; pursue people of Limhi, 273; take possession of land of Helam, 275; find priests of King Noah, 276; discover land of Helam, 276; break covenant with Alma, 276; king of, appoints Amulon king of land of Helam, 276; taught language of Nephi, 277; taught to keep records, 277; grow in civilization, 277; more numerous than people of Zarahemla and of Nephi, 279; sons of Mosiah go to preach to, 291; joined by Amlicites, 305; king of, attacked by Alma, 306; defeated by Nephites, 306; skins dark, naked, and heads shorn, 307; army of, attacks Nephites, 309; destroy people of Ammonihah, 359; invade borders of Noah, 359; defeated by Zoram, 360; sons of Mosiah teach among, 362; condition of, 364; bind Ammon, 364; converted to the Lord, 376; see angels, 376; king of, smites Ammon, 379; king of, smitten by Ammon, 379; and others build city of Jerusalem, 381; many converted by sons of Mosiah, 382; king of, preached to by Aaron, 384; stricken, 385; raised by Aaron, 386; king of, and household converted, 386; king of, sends proclamation, 387, 388; divided from Nephites, 387; territory of, 387; fortified against by Nephites, 388; king of, protects sons of Mosiah, 388; people in lands of Ishmael, Middoni, Shilom, Shemlon, and cities of Nephi, Lemuel, and Shimnilom, converted, 390; Amulonites, Amalekites, and Lamanites rebel against king of Anti-Nephi-Lehies, 391; king of dies, 391; slay people of Anti-Nephi-Lehi, 394; throw down weapons, 394; join people of God, 394; swear vengeance against the Nephites, 395; converted, 395; slay seed of Amulon, 396; some join people of Anti-Nephi-Lehi, 396; follow people of Ammon into wilderness, 405; great number of, slain, 405; driven and slain, 405; with Zoramites make preparations for war, 433; war with Nephites, 433, 456; Zoramites become, 456; come into land of Antionum, 456; Zoramites and

BOOK OF MORMON.

Amalekites made chief captains over, 456; compound of different races, 457; army naked, except Zoramites and Amalekites, 458; march by head of river Sidon, 458; are attacked by Nephites under Lehi at Sidon, 460; flee toward Sidon, 460; met by Moroni, 460; flee toward Manti, 460; fight desperately, 460; flee before Moroni, 461; surrounded at Sidon, 462; many surrender, and depart into wilderness, 464; slaughter great among, 465; entire army disarmed and allowed to depart, 465; Amalickiah stirs up to anger, 473; king of, issues proclamation to his people, 473; Amalickiah given command of, 473; portion of, flee to Onidah, 474; Amalickiah seeks kingdom, 474; king of, slain by servant of Amalickiah, 476; servants of king of, join people of Ammon, 476; queen of, summons Amalickiah, 477; Amalickiah made king of, 477; stirred up against Nephites, 478; approach city of Ammonihah, 481; astonished at preparation of Nephites, 482; attack Noah, 483; many slain among, 484; flee to wilderness, 484; driven out of east wilderness by Moroni, 485; Amalickiah preparing for war against Nephites, 491; Amalickiah heads army of, 491; take cities under Amalickiah, 493; met by Teancum, 493; retreat to Mulek, 495; Ammoron made king of, 495; armies of, march against Teancum, 497; chief captains flee from Lehi, 498; surrounded by Moroni and Lehi, 498; surrender to Moroni, 499; prisoners of, taken to Bountiful, 500; surrender to Moroni, 508; prisoners of set to work to fortify Gid, 508; take Manti, Zeezrom, Cumeni, Antiparah, 510; overtaken by Antipus, 514; Helaman turned upon by, 514; captured by Helaman, 514, 515; prisoners of, sent to Zarahemla, 515; Helaman sends epistle to, 515; leave city of Antiparah, 515; lose city of Manti, 522; attack city of Nephihah, 525; capture Nephihah, 525; join people of Ammon, 537; flee from land of Moroni, 538; war on people of Moronihah, 542; wage war on Nephites, 544; surrounded and defeated by Moronihah and Lehi, 546; Nephites become, 550; go against Nephites in battle, 553; obtain possession of Zarahemla, 553; Nephi and Lehi preach to, 557; eight thousand of, baptized, 558; cast Nephi and Lehi into prison, 558; yield possession of land to Nephites, 561; become righteous people, 561; go to land northward, 562; grow in belief of God, 565; preach word of God, 566; destroy Gadiantons by preaching, 566; Samuel a prophet of, 586; join Gadianton robbers, 603; fight against Gadiantons, 605; unite with Nephites, 605; curse taken from, 605; Christ appears to, 632; all converted to Christ, 681; a people called, 685; rejected gospel, 685; become exceeding wicked, 686; war with Nephites, 688; beaten by Nephites, 688; war with Nephites, 689; drive Nephites out of Angola and land of David, 689; Aaron king of, 690; pursue Nephites to land of Jashon, 691; come against Nephites again, 692; flee before Nephites, 692; Nephites make treaty with, 692; king of, sends epistle to Mormon, 693; Nephites beat, 693; drive Nephites out of Desolation, 695; come against Teancum, 696; repulsed by Nephites at Teancum, 696; come again to battle with Nephites, 696; regain Desolation, 696; offer women and children as sacrifices, 697; are driven from land

INDEX. 803

by Nephites, 697; beat Nephites at Desolation, 697; come against Nephites at Jordan, are driven back, 698; beat Nephites again, 698; Moroni sends epistle to king of, 701; destroy Nephites at Cumorah, 702; at war among themseves, 705; put to death those who will not deny Christ, 760; take prisoners from tower of Sherrizah and feed women on flesh of husbands, children upon flesh of fathers, 772; Moroni writes unto, 774.

Lamb of God, Son of eternal Father, 28, 32; among men, 29; lifted upon cross, 30; multitudes fight against, 30; plainness in, 36; to be manifest to seed of Nephi, 37; book of, proceedeth from Jew, 38; records to witness of, 38; all men must come unto, 38; words of, 38; church of, 40; numbers few, 40; baptism of, 161; Holy Ghost descends upon, 161.

Lamoni, descendant of Ishmael, king of Lamanites, 365; Ammon becomes servant of, 365; traditions of, 367, 370; father of, king over all land, 368; taught by Ammon, 369; spoken to by Ammon, 371; falls to earth, 372, 374; arises, 373, 376; teaches people, 376; and Ammon go to Middoni, 377; meets father of Lamoni, 377; commanded to slay Ammon, 378; secures release of brethren of Ammon, 380, 382; returns to land of Ishmael, 382; builds synagogues, 383; and Anti-Nephi-Lehi counseled with Ammon and brethren, 391.

Land northward, people depart into, 540; second migration into, 541; emigration to, from Zarahemla, 548; Nephi and Lehi and Lamanites go to, 562; whole face of changed, 624; Lamanites give to Nephites, 692.

Land of promise, 6, 11; plates carried to, 16; seed to be raised up in, 17; led unto 25, 30; mist of darkness upon, 31; visitations upon, 31; discovered, 34; to be led toward, 54; driven before wind unto, 61; Lehi and company arrive at, 63; beasts of every kind, 63; ores found, 63; Lehi speaks of, 77; decrees of God concerning, 717, 718; people who possess, will be free, 717; barges driven toward, 727; people of Jared land upon, 727.

Language of Lehi, 2; of Egyptians, 2; of people of Zarahemla corrupted, 201; people of Zarahemla taught l. of Mosiah, 202; Benjamin teaches sons l. of fathers, 207; of Egyptians, 207; of Nephites, 234; of Nephi taught among Lamanites, 277; confounded by the Lord, means of interpretation of, 291, 292; no other people knew l. of Moroni, 713; of Jaredites not confounded, 715; brother of Jared confounded, writes in, 722; interpretation of, by Holy Spirit, 775.

Land southward, Nephites give, to Lamanites, 692.

Lasciviousness warned against, 174.

Law, preserved and executed, 302; of Moses, 15, 143, 338; fulfilled in Christ, 143; words of Christ to be, 144; of Moses kept by Nephites, 175, 198, 210, 396, 409; of land exceeding strict, 197; of Moses effective through atonement, 217; no l. of God governing belief, 409, 410; punishing men according to crimes, 410; Zoramites do not observe the l. of Moses, 417; no l. without punishment, 454.

Laws, to be enacted by voice of people, 312; Pahoran refuses to alter, 490.
Lawyers skilled in their profession, 336; Zeezrom, one of the l., accuses Alma, 338; many, 354.
Leah of silver, 339.
Lebanon to become a fruitful field, 152.
Lehi, attacks army of Lamanites, 460; pursues Lamanites, 460; army of, east of Sidon, 462; appointed chief captain over city of Noah, 482; meets Lamanites at Bountiful, 498; and Moroni surrounded Lamanites, 498; given command of Mulek, 500; and Teancum given command of army, 534; forces sent to, 535; encamps around land of Moroni, 537; heads Coriantumr, 546.
Lehi, city of, 486; land of, source of contention, 487; people of, flee to Moroni, 488; peace with Morianton, 490; taken by Amalickiah, 493; Moroni goes to land of, 537; Lamanites flee from, to land of Moroni, 537; land south called, 562.
Lehi, language of, 2; prays for his people, 2; vision of, 2; receives book, 2; prophesies, 3; mocked by Jews, 3; Jews angry at, 4; dream of, 4; commanded to depart into wilderness, 4; arrives at borders of Red Sea, 4; family of, 5; builds an altar, 5; speaks to Laman and Lemuel, 5; dwells in tent, 6; sons of, flee from Laban, 9; comforts Sariah, 14; and Sariah offer sacrifices and burnt offerings, 14, 19; receives plates of brass, 14; plates contain genealogy of, 15, 16; descendant of Joseph, 15, 16, 87; prophecies, 15; record of, 16; sons of to take wives, 16; gathers seeds, 19; dream of, 19; vision of tree, 20; prophecies concerning coming of the Messiah, 24; speaks concerning Gentiles, 25; dwells in valley of Lemuel, 25; Gentiles to be numbered among seed of, 39; words of, hard to be understood, 43; sons dispute with, 43; seed of, to come to knowledge of Redeemer, 44; commanded to take journey, 48; finds ball of brass, 48; inquires of the Lord, 50; chastened, 50; looks upon ball, 50; and family go into ship, 60; begets two sons in wilderness, 61; pleads for Nephi, 61; and company arrive at promised land, 63; till the earth, 63; speaks to sons, 77; prophesies that his seed shall reject Messiah, 79; speaks to Zoram, 81; to Jacob, 82; to Joseph, 87; descendant of Joseph of Egypt, 87, 335; speaks to Laman's sons and daughters, 90; speaks to Lemuel's sons and daughters, 91; speaks to sons of Ishmael, 91; speaks to Sam, 91; dies, 91; commandments to, 172; words of, verified, 487.
Lehi, son of Helaman, 550; preaches many things to people, 554; preaches remainder of his days, 556; preaches in Bountiful, Gid, Mulek, 557; preaches to Lamanites, 557; goes to land of Nephi, 558; cast into prison, 558; protected, 558; faces of and Nephi shine as angels, 559; goes into land northward, 562; preaches to people, 582.
Lehi, son of Zoram, 359.
Lehi-Nephi, land or city of, 227; Mosiah sends men to, 227; Zeniff and people possess, 235; walls of city of repaired, 235.
Lehonti, invited by Amalickiah to counsel, 474; and men surround

INDEX. 805

Amalickiah, 475; Amalickiah surrenders to, 475; death of, 475.
Lemuel, Levi speaks to, 5; murmuring of, 5, 49, 54; valley of, 5, 48; hardness and cursing of, 6; and Laman angry with Sam and Nephi, 9; angel speaks to, 9; returns to Jerusalem, 9, 17; rebellion of, 17, 58; repentance of, 19; Lehi dwells in valley of, 25; chastened of Lord, 52; shaken, 59; about to worship Nephi, 59; binds Nephi, 61; sons and daughters spoken to by Lehi, 91; seed of, not to be destroyed, 91; sons of, angry with Nephi, 92; spoken of by Ammon, 371; people converted, 390.
Lemuelites, a people called, who rejected the gospel, 685.
Levi, son of Kim, 714, 741; served in captivity, but wars and is made king, 741; is just and people prosper, 741; begets Corom, 741.
Liahona, directors called, 441.
Lib, son of Kish, 714; reigns in stead of Kish, 741; serpents destroyed in reign of, 741; people prosper, till the earth, 742; begets Hearthom, 742; made king of Jaredites, of great stature, 745; fights with Coriantumr, 754; wounds Coriantumr, but flees to seashore, 754; drives Coriantumr back to Akish and Agosh, is killed, 754; brother of, drives army of Coriantumr, 754.
Liberty, title of, 469; land of l. south of land Desolation, 470; to be preserved, 471; Moroni plants standard of l. among Nephites, 473; Nephites prepare to preserve, 478; king-men compelled to hoist standard of, 492; Moroni raises standard of, 534.
Limhi, son of Noah, 227; people of, in bondage to Lamanites, 228; issues proclamation, 229; people of, pay tribute to Lamanites, 230; plates containing record of people of, 231; people of, search for land of Zarahemla, 232, 270; people of, discover ruins and records of earlier inhabitants, 232, 270; taken captive by Lamanites, 263; made king, 264; defends against Lamanites, 265; people of, repulsed by Lamanites, 268; and people make covenant with God, 270; desire baptism, 271; takes voice of people, 271; hearkens to Gideon, 272; people of, depart into wilderness, 272; reach land of Zarahemla, 272; record of people of, received by Mosiah, 273; people of, baptized by Alma, 281; delivers plates to Mosiah, 291; twenty-four plates found by, 714, 759.
Limnah of gold, 339.
Limnah, leader of ten thousand Nephites, 702.
Limher, spy of Nephites, 305.
Luram, slain by sword, 772.
Lyings and deceivings sent forth by Satan, 602.
Mahah, son of Jared, 728.
Malachi, words of, 668.
Manasseh, Lehi descendant of, 335.
Man, cursed is he who trusteth in, 155.
Manti, Nehor executed on hill of, 300; Alma journeys to, 362; Lamanites march to take possession of, 458; Moroni takes part of army to, 459; Lamanites flee toward, 460; taken by Lamanites, 510; retaken by Gid and Teomner, 522; Helaman enters city, 523.
Manti, sent by Alma to spy on Amlicites, 305.
Marriage among the Nephites, 682.

BOOK OF MORMON.

Marvelous work and a wonder among children of men, 39, 141; to be done, 151; shall proceed to do, 156.

Mary, mother of Christ, 216; Son of God to be born of, 323.

Mathonihah, one of twelve, 654.

Mathoni, one of twelve, 654.

Melchisedec, priesthood of, 350; king of Salem, 350.

Men, all commanded to write words of God, 157; Lord speaks to, according to their language, 160.

Messiah, coming of, 4, 24, 65; to be baptized, 24; to be slain, to rise, 25; to be manifest among Gentiles, 25; Gentiles to come to knowledge of, 25; Son of God, 26; Lamb of God, 32; to be manifest unto children of men, 44; to be made manifest in latter days, 87; people wait for coming of, 100; Jews to be convinced of the true, 141; but one true, 142; name of, Jesus Christ, 142; signs of birth to be given, 144.

Metals, Nephi teaches people to work in, 96; Nephites become rich in, 198; mentioned in taxing, 239; used by Noah, 240; gold and silver values, 338, 339; among Jaredites, 742.

Micah, words of, 658, 659.

Middoni, Aaron, Muloki, and Ammah in prison at, 377; Antiomno, king of, 377; Lamoni and Ammon start to, 377; meet father of Lamoni, 377; arrive at, 380; brethren of Ammon released from prison at, 380; Aaron, Muloki, and Ammah preach at, 382; they are cast into prison at, 382; Ammon and Lamoni return from, to land of Ishmael, 382; people converted in, 390.

Midian, land of, 391.

Minon, land of, 305.

Miracles, among disciples of Jesus, 683; ceased because of wickedness, 688.

Mocum, water comes instead of city of, 626.

Moriancumer, place called, 718.

Morianton, descendant of Riplakish, 714, 740; gains power over land and made king, 740; does justice, 740; builds cities and people prosper, 741; begets Kim, 741; death of, 741.

Morianton, land of, source of contention, 487; people of, take arms against people of Lehi, 488; people of, restored to land, 489, 490; taken by Amalickiah, 493.

Morianton, leader of people of Morianton, 488; beats maid-servant, 488; slain by Teancum, 489.

Moriantum, abominations of Nephites at, 772.

Mormon, about to deliver record to Moroni, 204; makes abridgment of plates, 204; finds small set of plates, 204; finishes record on plates of Nephi, 205; makes plates with own hands, 615, calling of, 615; record of, 616; pure descendant of Lehi, 616; words of, 616, 684; writes things commanded, 671; makes record, 687; spoken to by Ammoron, 687; told to take plates of Nephi, 687; visited by Lord, 688; endeavors to preach, 688; leader of Nephites, 689; withstands Aaron, 690; gets plates of Nephi, 691; flees to Shem, 691; teaches people, 693; gets epistle from king of Lamanites, 693; refuses command of Nephites, 694; writes to Gentiles and house of Israel, 694; gets all records hid by Ammoron, 698; again takes command, 698; defends Jordan and other cities against Lamanites, 698; abridgment of record of, 699; to house of Jacob, also to Gentiles, 699; finishes record, 701; writes epistle to king of Lamanites, 701; hides records in hill Cumorah, 701; wounded, 702; lamentation of, 702; speaks to remnant, 703; slain in battle, 704, 705; descendant of Nephi, 706; words of, 763; epistle of, to Moroni, 768; second epistle of to Moroni, 771; has sacred records to deliver to Moroni, 774.

Mormon, Alma and followers flee to, 258; waters of, 258, 259, 261; place of, 258, 261; Jerusalem on the borders of, 380.

Moroni, son of Mormon, receives record from Mormon, 204, 701; leader of ten thousand Nephites, 702; finishes record of his father, 704; lone survivor of Nephites, 704; hides record, 706; instructs to search prophecy of Isaiah, 707; prophesies concerning coming forth of record, 707; teaches concerning resurrection, 711; writes of language, 713; gives account of ancient inhabitants, 714; commanded to seal up records of brother of Jared, 724; writes according to memory, 725; teaches concerning faith, 746; on faith and charity, 748; bids farewell to Gentiles, 749; ends abridgment of record of people of Jared, 760; resumes writing, 760; writes words of Mormon, 763; epistle of Mormon to, 768; second epistle of Mormon to, 771; Mormon has sacred records to deliver to, 774; writes to Lamanites, 774; seals up records, 774.

Moroni, chief captain of Nephites, 457; meets Lamanites in Jershon, 457; sends men to Alma, 458; takes part of army to near Manti, 459; takes part of army to hill Riplah, part to river Sidon, and Manti, 459; meets Lamanites near Sidon, 460; addresses Zerahemnah, 462; receives surrender of Zerahemnah, 463; addressed by Zerahemnah, 463; swords and weapons of Zerahemnah, 463; many Lamanites surrender to, 464; renews battle against Lamanites, 464; disarms and paroles Lamanites, 465; returns with army to land of Nephites, 465; writes on piece of garment, 469; prays for cause of Christians, 470; intercepts army of Amalickiah, 472; puts to death some of the Amalickiahites, 472; plants standard of liberty among Nephites, 473; fortifies land, 478; description of, 479; like unto Alma and Ammon, 480; appoints Lehi chief captain of city of Noah, 482; continues preparation for defense, 485; drives Lamanites from east wilderness, 485; maid-servant tells about people of Morianton, 488; sends army to head Morianton, 488; heads them at Desolation, 488; wroth with king men, 491; marches against king men, 492; puts end to king men, 492; sends orders to Teancum to fortify land Bountiful, 495; arrives at city of Bountiful, 497; holds counsel with Teancum and others, 497; takes possession of Mulek, 498; and Lehi surround Lamanites, 498; wounded, 499; Lamanites surrender to, 499; gives Lehi command of Mulek, 500; causes Lamanite prisoners to fortify Bountiful, 500; sends epistle to Ammoron, 503; Ammoron writes to, 504; appoints Laman to go to Gid, 506; arms prisoners, 507; Lamanites surrender to, 508; receives epistle from Helaman, 509; writes to

Pahoran, 526, 531; gives Lehi and Teancum command of part of army, 534; raises standard of liberty, 534; sends forces to Lehi and Teancum, 535; goes with Pahoran towards Nephihah, 535; makes night attack on Nephihah, 536; regains Nephihah, 536; goes to land of Lehi, 537; camps around land of Moroni, 537; returns to Zarahemla, 539; gives command of army to Moronihah, 539; death of, 540.

Moroni, city of, 486; Lamanites come into, 493; taken by Amalickiah, 493; sinks in sea, 624.

Moronihah, Moroni appoints as commander of army, 539; Lamanites war against people of, 542; sends Lehi to head Coriantumr, 546; takes Zarahemla, 546; succeeds in obtaining many cities from Lamanites, 554; preaches many things to people, 554; regains half of possessions, 554.

Moronihah, city of, earth carried upon, 624, 626.

Moronihah, leader of ten thousand Nephites, 702.

Moron, Coriantor son of, 714; son of Ethem, 714; reigns instead of Ethem, 744; wicked man battles with and gets half of kingdom, 745; regains kingdom, 745; descendant of brother of Jared takes Moron captive, 745; begets Coriantor, 745.

Moron, land of, where king dwelt, 729; near land of Desolation, 729; Noah takes Shule captive into land of, 730.

Moses, plates of brass contain five books of, 15; Nephi reads words of, 67; to deliver people from Egypt, 88; to have power in rod, 89; spokesman for, 89; law of, kept by Nephites, 95, 143, 175, 197, 210; law of, taught, 198; law of, availeth nothing except through atonement, 217; law of, 338; law of, taught to people of Noah, 245; not always to be taught, 249; kept, 396, 409; Zoramites would not observe law of, 417; speaks of Son of God, 427; words of, 428; law of, Lamanites observe, 586, 595; contention concerning law of, 602; law of, fulfilled in Christ, 628, 643; no longer observed, 682; law of, given by faith, 746.

Mosiah, Amaleki speaks concerning, 201; warned to flee from land of Nephi, 201; language of, taught to people of Zarahemla, 202; unites with people of Zarahemla and is appointed king, 202; interprets engraving on stone, 202; death of, 202.

Mosiah, son of Benjamin, is given charge of sword of Laban, ball, or directors, plates of Nephi, 209; makes proclamation, 209; declared king, 214; consecrated king, 226; walks in way of Lord, 226; causes people to till the earth, 226; no contention, 226; sends men to land of Lehi-Nephi, 227; receives records of and people of Limhi, 273, 291; receives people of Alma, 279; reads records of Zeniff and of Alma, 279; permits Alma to establish churches, 281; gives Alma authority over church, 282, 283; sends proclamation, 285; sons of, unbelievers, 286; angel appears to sons of, 286; Ammon, Aaron, Omner, Himni, sons of, teach people of Zarahemla, 289; sons of, desire to preach to Lamanites, 290; sons of, refuse the kingdom, 291; translates records, 291; confers plates, record, interpreters on Alma, son of Alma, 292; asks will of people regarding king, 292; message of Mosiah to people concerning a king, 292;

INDEX.

recommends judges, 293; loved by the people, 297; death of, 298; laws of, acknowledged by people of Nephi, 298, 337; sons of, met by Alma, 362; sons of, have spirit of, 362; sons of, preach to Lamanites fourteen years, 362; laws of, altered, 555.

Melek, land of, Alma teaches people of, 326; people baptized, 327; people of Ammon come into, 433; taken by Amalickiah, 493.

Mulek, Lamanites retreat to, 495; Teancum ordered to attack, 496; Jacob leader of Lamanites at, 497; taken by Moroni, 498; Moroni gives command of, to Lehi, 500; Nephi and Lehi preach at, 557; land north called, 562.

Mulok, descendants of, 279.

Muloki, in prison, 377, 382; released, 380, 382; at Ani-Anti, 382.

Murmur, brothers of Nephi do, 7.

Murmuring of Laman and Lemuel, 5; of brothers of Nephi, 7; of Nephites, 267, 386; of the church, 285.

Nahom, Ishmael buried in, 51.

Narrow neck of land, Moroni orders Teancum to secure, 495.

Nations, all to write words of Lord, 158; all to be taught by men of own race, 408.

Nehor, teaches among people, 299; slays Gideon, 299; pleads before Alma, 300; condemned to death, 300; executed on Manti, 300; judge after order of, 354, 358; Desolation of, 360; Amalickites and Amulonites after order of, 381; after order of, 394.

Nehor, land of, Corihor rebels and goes to, 729.

Nephi, birth of, 1; taught in learning of fathers, 1; afflictions of, 1; favored of the Lord, 1, 2, 6; record of, 2, 3; account of, 3; plates of, 3; description of, 6; obedience of, 6; speaks to Sam, 6; to be ruler and teacher, 6; seed of, to be scourged, 6; and brethren to return to Jerusalem, 7; brothers of, murmur, 7; obedience of, 7; statement of, 7, 23, 26; genealogy of father of, 8; exhorts brethren, 8, 10, 17, 43, 45, 50, 55, 61, 72, 92; and brethren return to land of inheritance, 9; offer to purchase records of Laban, 9; and brethren flee from Laban, 9; angel speaks to, 9; slays Laban, 11; obtains plates, 12; returns to father in wilderness, 13; record of, 16; descendant of Joseph, 16; returns to Jerusalem, 17; brethren rebel against, 17; bound with cords, 18; plates of, contain full account of people, 23; two sets of plates, 23; reign and ministry of, 24; writes in book, 25; vision of, 26; angel appears to, 28; seed of, and of brethren, 30; angel speaks to, 39, 41; forbidden to write, 42; grieved by hardness of their hearts, 43; overcome, 43; sees fall of people, 43; takes daughter of Ishmael to wife, 48; breaks bow, 49; commanded to build ship, 53; makes tools, 54; stretches forth hand and brethren shaken by the Lord, 59; brethren offer to worship, 59; completes ship, 60; goes into ship, 60; bound with cords by brethren, 61; Lehi pleads for, 62; makes plates of ore, 63; makes records on plates, 64; reads words of Moses, 67; reads from plates of brass, 72; Joseph to hearken to, 90; speaks concerning Joseph of Egypt, 90; Laman and Lemuel and sons of Ishmael angry with, 92; ministered to by angels, 93; life sought by brethren, 94; Nephi and others depart in wilderness,

95; place and people named after, 95; teaches people in metals and wood, 96; builds temple, 96; refuses to be king, 96; consecrates Jacob and Joseph, 97; keeps records upon plates, 97; makes other plates, 97; Jacob speaks unto people of, 98; writes words of Isaiah, 115; soul delighteth in plainness, 139; speaks concerning words of Isaiah, 139; declares Jerusalem had been destroyed, 140; prophesies destruction of his people, 145; promises to, to be remembered, 156; seed of, to be remembered, 156; prophesies concerning Jews and Gentiles, 158; mourns because of wickedness, 164; has charity, 165; commands Jacob to write on small plates, 166; anoints man to be king, 167; loved by people, 167; wields sword of Laban, 167; to be name of kings, 168; dies, 168; consecrates priests and teachers, 168; makes plates called plates of Jacob, 175; other plates of, 199; plates of, conferred on Mosiah, 209; language of, taught to Lamanites, 277; words of God, to first, 308; Abinadi, son of, 334; son of Lehi, 335.

Nephi, people of, to fortify against Lamanites, 192; people of till ground and raise animals, 196; Ammon and brethren go to land of, 227; Zeniff has knowledge of, 234; children of the daughters of Lamanites and priests take name of, 280; Alma speaks to people of, 280; land of, 287; Aaron goes to land of, 383; people converted, 390; armies of, set around Jershon, 405; great slaughter among, 405; account of people of, in days of Helaman, 465; people of, rejoice in peace, 466; Amalickiah goes to land of, 472; returns to land of, 475; Amalickiah possesses the city of, 476; Lamanites flee to land of, 484; peace among, because of diligence to word of God, 484; land of, in straight course from east to west sea, 485; Gadiantons gain many advantages over land of, 605; prosper, 682; people of, proud in hearts, become exceeding wicked, 686.

Nephihah, appointed chief judge, 312; dies, 489.

Nephihah, city or land of, 486; taken by Amalickiah, 493; people of, attacked by Lamanites, 525; city of, captured, 525; Moroni and Pahoran go to city of, 535; plains of, 536; Moroni enters at night, 536; Moroni regains city of, 536.

Nephites, to write words of the Lord, 158; not Lamanites, 168; friendly toward Nephi, 168; grow hard in hearts, 168; desire many wives and concubines, 168; pride of, 170; excuse themselves in committing whoredoms, 171; to be scourged by Lamanites, 173; Lamanites more righteous than, 173; Jacob warns against sins, 174; records of, to be preserved, 195; war with Lamanites, 198; culture of, 198; weapons of, 198; more wicked part destroyed, righteous spared, 200; drive out Lamanites, 203; people of, not so numerous as people of Zarahemla, 279; prepared to meet Amlicites, 304; war with Amlicites, 304; defeat Amlicites, 304; defeat Lamanites and Amlicites at Sidon, 306; Lamanite army attacks, 309; Zoram leads army of, against the Lamanites, 360; church established generally among people of, 361; murmuring of, 386; nearly surrounded by Lamanites, 387; surrounded, 388; Lamanites swear vengeance against, 395; separation from Zoramites, 416; war with

INDEX. 811

Lamanites, 433, 456; give lands to people of Ammon, 457; obliged to contend with brethren, 457; Moroni, leader of, 457; meet Lamanites in Jershon, 458; part of, attack Lamanites under Lehi, 460; inspired by rights of worship, 461; Alma prophesies concerning, 466; Helaman and brethren established church among, 468; forgetfulness of, 469; standard of liberty planted among by Moroni, 473; Lamanites come against, 478; faith and belief of, 479; fortify Ammonihah, 481; none slain among, 484; possess all land northward of land Bountiful, 486; waxed strong, 486; driven at city of Moroni, 493; harassed by Ammoron, 496; people of Ammon take name of, 502; prisoners among Lamanites rescued, 508; regain Antiparah, 515; many go northward, 541; contention among, 542; Lamanites wage war on, 544; flee from Zarahemla, 545; become Lamanites, 550; disaster among, due to pride, 554; under Moronihah regain half of cities, 554; obtain their land from Lamanites, 561; rejoice for church established among, 561; go to land northward, 562; many in Gadianton band, and secret combinations, 563; dwindle in unbelief, 565; encourage Gadiantons, 566; begin to slay each other, 579; great famine among, 580; people repent, 580; prosper, 581; join Gadianton robbers, 603; fight Gadiantons, 605; unite with Lamanites, 605; war with robbers 605; gather in Zarahemla, 609; make weapons of war, 610; battle with Gadianton robbers, 611; beat the robbers, 611, 613; hang Zemnariah, 613; return to own land, 617; conditions of rank and wickedness among, 618; separate into tribes, 620; Christ appears to, 632; all converted to Christ, 681; marriage among, 682; miracles among, 683; great prosperity, 683; a people again called, 685; war with and beat Lamanites, 688; war with Lamanites, 689; retreat to north country, 689; take possession of Angola and fortify, driven out, 689; go to land of Joshua, 689; repent of iniquity, 690; lamentation of, 690; curse God, 691; flee before Lamanites to land of Jashon, 691; flee to Shem, 691; Lamanites come upon, 692; pursue and beat Lamanites, 692; regain land of inheritance, 692; make treaty with Lamanites, 692; beat Lamanites, 693; Mormon refuses command of, 694; go to battle with Lamanites in Desolation, 695; are driven back, 695; some flee to city Teancum, 695; repulse Lamanites, 696; driven by Lamanites from Teancum, 697; beat Lamanites and drive them from land, 697; driven with slaughter from Desolation to Boaz, 697; again give Mormon command, 698; defend Jordan against Lamanites, 698; beaten, 698; to become a dark people, 700; march to land of Cumorah, 701; all slain but twenty-four at Cumorah, 702; those escaping were killed, 705; those who deny not Christ put to death by Lamanites, 760; denying Holy Ghost, 771; anger of, 772; sufferings of, 772; abominations of, 772; devour flesh of Lamanites, 772.

Nephi, son of Helaman, 550; made judge, 552; preaches many things to people, 554; delivers judgment seat to Cezoram, 555; to preach remainder of days, 556; preaches in Bountiful, Gid, Mulek, 557; preaches to Lamanites, 557; Nephi and Lehi preach to all people of Nephi, 557; goes to land of Nephi, 558; cast into prison, 558;

protected, 558; faces of Nephi and Lehi shine as faces of angels, 559; returns to Zarahemla, 566; prays upon tower, 567; speaks to people, 568, 571, 575, 578, 582; tells of death of judges, 573; bound, 575; set at liberty, 577; voice speaks to, 577; conveyed away by Spirit, 579; prays for people, 580; esteemed as a prophet, 581; people baptized by, 597; teaches people, 597; given records by Helaman, 600; nowhere to be found, 604.

Nephi, son of Nephi, prays for people, 601; hears a voice, 601; goes forth preaching and baptizing, 602; plates of, made with hands, 615; visited by angels daily, 622; raises brother from the dead, 622; preaches repentance, ordains men to ministry, 623; Christ speaks to, is given authority to baptize, 633; one of twelve, 654; baptized 655; Christ commands to bring forth record, 667; plates of, contain Christ's teachings, 671; death of, 683; Mormon gets plates of, 691.

Neum, words of, 65.

New Jerusalem, 659, 664; location of, 750; inhabitants to be blessed, 751.

Nimrah, son of Akish, angry with father, 736; joins Omer, 736.

Nimrod, Jared and brother go into valley of, 716.

Nimrod, son of Cohor, 731; gives up kingdom to Shule, 731.

Noah, land of, Lamanites come into borders of, 359; Lamanites depart from land of, 482; become strong as Ammonihah, 482; Lehi appointed captain over, 482; Lamanites attack, 483.

Noah, son of Corihor, rebels against Shule and Corihor, 730; draws away Cohor, 730; gives battle against, 730; takes Shule captive into Moron, 730; slain by sons of Shule, 731; sons of, build up kingdom, 731; Cohor, son of, 731.

Noah, Zeniff confers kingdom on, 239; had many wives and concubines, 239; tax levied by, 239; puts down priests consecrated by his father, 240; builds spacious buildings, palace, towers, 240; sets apart high priests, 240; plants vineyards, 241; Lamanites slay people of, 241; Abinadi prophesies to, 241; seeks life of Abinadi, 242; Abinadi brought before, and cast into prison, 244; condemns Abinadi to death, 256; seeks to slay Alma, 256; causes death of Abinadi, 257; discovers Alma and people, 261; sends army to destroy Alma and people, 261; contentions among people of, 261; attacked by Gideon, 262; and people flee from Lamanites, 262; people of, pay tribute to Lamanites, 263; Gideon searches for, 263; put to death by fire, 263; people of, return to land of Nephi, 264; Alma and people depart into wilderness from people of, 273; priests of, found by Lamanites, 276; priests of, 395.

Northward, land, 388.

Ogath, Shiz flees to, 757.

Olive tree, Gentiles and Israel compared to, 25; natural branches of, 43; house of Israel compared to, 44; seed of Lehi to be grafted into, 44; house of Israel like unto a tame, 177.

Omer, son of Shule, 715; reigns instead of Shule, 732; Jared rebels against, 732; in captivity, 732; friend of Akish, 733; kingdom of, overthrown, 735; warned in dream and departs to hill Shim, 735;

at Ablon, 735; restored to kingdom, 736; gives kingdom to Emer, his son, 736; death of, 737.

Omner, city of, Amalickiah takes, 493.

Omner, son of Mosiah, teaches people of Zarahemla, 289; account of, 388; rejoices, 397; rejoices on meeting Alma, 403; Alma takes him to preach to Zoramites, 417.

Omni, Jarom delivers plates to, 199; a wicked man, 199; confers plates on Amaron, 200.

Onidah, sermon of Alma upon hill, 421; Amulek preaches at hill, 428; portion of Lamanites flee to, 474; place of arms, 474.

Onihah, water comes instead thereof, 626.

Only Begotten, to show himself to the people of Jerusalem, 140; to be crucified by them, 141; to rise from the dead, 141.

Onti of silver, 339.

Ordaining, manner of, 761.

Ores, found in land of promise, 63; plates of ore made by Nephi, 63.

Orihah, son of Jared, 715, 728; appointed king of people, 729; walked humbly before the Lord, 729.

Paanchi, son of Pahoran, claims judgment seat, 543; rebels against and is condemned by voice of people, 543.

Pachus, king of dissenters at Zarahemla, slain, 534.

Pacumeni, son of Pahoran, claims judgment seat, 542; made chief judge, 544; flees from Coriantumr and is slain, 545.

Pagag, son of brother of Jared, chosen to be king, refuses, 728.

Pahoran, appointed chief judge, 489; refuses to alter laws, 490; retains judgment seat by voice of people, 490; Moroni writes to, 526; writes epistle to Moroni, 531; flees to land of Gideon, 532; restored to judgment seat, 534; and Moroni go toward Nephihah, 535; regains city of Nephihah, 536; returns to judgment seat, 539; death of, 542.

Pahoran, son of Pahoran, claims judgment seat, 542; appointed chief judge and governor, 543; slain by Kishkumen, 543.

Palace built by Noah, 240.

Paradise, delivers spirits of righteous, 107; spirits of righteous received into, 448.

People not to be succored in transgression, 230.

Pillar of fire before Lehi, 2.

Plates, of Nephi, 3; of brass, 7; asked of Laban, 7; obtained by Nephi, 12; taken into wilderness, 13; of brass received by Lehi, 14; of brass contain five books of Moses and account of Adam and Eve and record of Jews and prophecies of Jeremiah, 15; record of, 193; delivered to Enos, 193; of brass contain genealogy of Lehi, 15; prediction concerning, 15; to be carried towards land of promise, 16; of Nephi contain full account of his people, 23; two sets of, 23; of ore made by Nephi, 63; to be handed down from generation to generation, 64; of brass, things written on, 67; Nephi reads from p. of brass, 72; of brass, prophecies of Joseph written upon, 90; other plates, 92; of brass, 92; of brass, records on, 95; Nephi keeps records upon, 97; Nephi makes other, 97; history of Nephites on other, 98; Jacob commanded to write on small,

166; history of Nephi's people on other plates, 167; a hundredth part not written on, 174; many proceedings written on larger, 174; of Jacob, made by hand of Nephi, 175; things written on p. must remain, 175; Jacob makes end of writing upon, 193; Jarom writes upon, 197; small, 199; other p. of Nephi, 199; Omni confers p. on Amoron, 200; delivered to Chemish, 200; of brass, Zarahemla rejoices concerning, 201; filled by Amaleki, 203; Mormon makes abridgment of, 204; Mormon finds small set of, 204; of Nephi, Mormon finishes record of, 205; handed down from Benjamin, 205; record of, taught to sons of Benjamin, 207; containing record kept by Limhi, 231; found by people of Limhi, 232, 270; of brass, of Nephi, of Lehi, translated by Mosiah, 291; conferred on Alma, son of Alma, 292; Helaman commanded to keep record on p. of Nephi, 437; to retain their brightness, 437; given Nephi by Helaman, 600; of Nephi, 615; things written on p. of brass, 630; of Nephi, contain Christ's teachings, 671; Amos keeps p. of Nephi, 683; son of Amos keeps p. of Nephi, 684; of Nephi, Mormon told to take, 687; Mormon makes record on p. of Nephi, 691; if p. were larger would have written in Hebrew, 713; twenty-four p. found by Limhi, 714; to be shown, 725.

Poor, substance to be imparted to, 223.

Prayer, Spirit teaches, 164; Nephi prays continually, 165; of Jacob answered, 182.

Precepts, blessed are those who hearken unto, 155.

Priestcraft seeks not the welfare of Zion, 147; taught by Nehor, 299.

Priests, Jacob and Joseph to be teachers and, 97; appointed by King Benjamin, 226; ordained by Alma, 260; to labor with their own hands, 260, 285; of Noah flee, 263; and teachers consecrated by Alma, 274, 282; consecrated by Alma, 311; ordained by Alma, 321; after profession of Nehor, 354; visit Alma and Amulek in prison, 355; Alma consecrates and teachers p. in land of Sidon, 358; teachings of, 361; consecrated by Aaron, 389; of Noah, 395; Helaman and brethren appointed priests and teachers, 468; false p. and teachers, 685; and teachers, manner of ordaining, 761; ministering flesh and blood of Christ, 761, 762.

Probation, day of, 109, 165.

Prophecy, of Enos to people of Nephi, 195; Abinadi makes p. to people of Noah, 241, 243, 251, 254, 257; sons of Mosiah have spirit of, 362; of Alma concerning Nephites, 466; of Samuel, 587; of Lachoneus, 608; of Mormon, 700; of Isaiah, 707; of Moroni concerning coming forth of record, 707; of Ether, 746, 755.

Prophet, to prepare the way of the Lord, 24; Nephi sees in vision, 29; Lamb of God baptized by, 29; to baptize Lamb of God, 161.

Prophets, predict destruction of Jerusalem, 2, 3, 4, 8, 24; record of p. true, 38; those who stone and slay p. shall perish, 144; false p. punished, 206; holy, 206; Benjamin establishes peace with aid of, 206; come among people of Shule, 731; come into land in reign of Heth, 738; come in days of Com, 743; put to death by brother of Shiblon, 743; come in days of Ethem, 744; come in days of Coriantor, 745.

INDEX. 815

Rabbanah, "power and great king," 369.
Ramah, Coriantumr camps at, 757.
Rameumpton, holy stand of Zoramites, 418.
Records, of Nephi, 2; of plates of brass, 3; of the Jews, 7; of Laban, 7; offer to purchase of Laban, 9; last to establish truth of the first, 38; to witness of Lamb of God, 38; on plates of brass, 95; Nephi keeps r. upon plates, 97; Nephi makes other, 97; of Nephites to be preserved, 195; Mormon about to deliver up r. to Moroni, 204; Mormon delivers to Moroni, 204; on plates kept by Limhi, 231; of people of Limhi, 273; Lamanites taught to keep, 277; Mosiah reads r. of Zeniff and Alma, 279; Mosiah translates, 291; conferred on Alma, son of Alma, 292; cast into fire by people of Ammonihah, 353; Ammon rehearsed r. of people, 371; Helaman is given r. of Nephi, 437, 489; Ammon reads things on r. to convert, 438; of Alma, end of, 465; many kept particular and large, 549; kept chiefly by Nephites, 550; given to Nephi by Helaman, 600; which contain all proceedings of the people, 615; of Mormon, 616; known to be true, 623; kept by Nephi, brought forth, 667; Amos keeps, 683; son of Amos keeps, 684; hid by Ammoron, 687; end of r. of Ammoron, 687; made by Mormon, 687; Mormon takes all r. hid by Ammoron, 698; Mormon hides r. in hill Cumorah, 701; Mormon gives to Moroni, 701; imperfections in, 706; to shine forth out of darkness, 706; Moroni prophesies concerning coming forth of, 707; Moroni told to hide r. of brother of Jared, 724; made by Ether in cavity of rock, 751; Moroni makes end of r. of people of Jared, 760; Mormon has sacred r. to deliver to Moroni, 774; Moroni seals up, 774.
Redeemer of world, Nephi sees in vision, 29; ministers to people, 29; Lamoni testifies to, 373.
Redemption, none save through atonement of Christ, 382.
Red Sea, Lehi arrives at borders of, 4; river Laman empties into, 5; travel in borders near, 49.
Reign of Zedekiah, 2.
Remnant of house of Israel to come to knowledge of true Messiah, 25, 44.
Repentance, commanded of the Lord, 161; gate which ye should enter, 162, 189; brings forgiveness, 284; Alma teaches, 351; Alma and Amulek preach, 360; Alma speaks of, 452; none without punishment, 454; Nephi baptizes to, 623; and baptism commanded, 674.
Restoration, to begin among all nations, 159; taught by Amulek, 342; explained by Alma, 450, 451.
Resurrection, fall and r. by transgression, 106; power of, 107; spirit and body restored to itself, 107; passes upon all men, 108; signs of Christ's r. to be given, 144; knowledge of, 176; in Christ, 189; first and second, 253, 255; Amulek teaches, 342; taught by priests, 361; people of Ammon hope in, 405; to be after coming of Christ, 447; of dead, 447; condition of souls between death and, 448, 449; of Christ, 449; of dead, atonement brings, 454; Lord dieth to bring about, 592; of Christ, testified of, 619; Moroni teaches, 711.
Revelations, many had, 167; of God not to be despised, 176.

Righteous, words of the, to be written, 146; branch, to be raised from loins of Joseph of Egypt, 172.

Riplakish, son of Shez, 714; reigns in stead of Shez, had many wives and concubines, oppression of, killed, 740.

Riplah, Moroni conceals a part of army near, 459.

Ripliancum, Coriantumr flees to waters of, 757.

Roads, built from city to city, 617; spoiled, 624.

Rock, he that buildeth upon, 155; to found church upon, 635.

Rod of iron, seen in Lehi's vision, 21; is word of God, 28, 29.

Sabbath, Alma commands keeping of the, 260.

Sacrament, not to be taken unworthily, 713.

Saints, power of God descends upon, 41; delivered from Devil, 108; those who slay shall perish, 144; blood of s. to cry from ground, 153.

Sam, Nephi speaks to, 6; brothers angry with, 9; Lehi speaks to, 91; seed of to be blessed, 91; flees with Nephi into wilderness, 95.

Samuel, Lamanite prophet, comes to Zarahemla, 586; prophecy of, 587; shot at, 597; flees to own country and preaches, 598; sign given by, fulfilled, 601; Christ commands words of to be recorded, 667; words of, fulfilled, 689, 690.

Sariah, wife of Lehi, 4, 12; complains against Lehi and is comforted, 14.

Satan, to have power over hearts of men, 160.

Savior, knowledge of, to spread to every nation, 218.

Sealed book, to come forth, 149; words of, to be read upon housetops, 149; words of, to be delivered to learned, 150; learned can read not, 150; things to be brought forth, 151; many shall believe, 158.

Seantum, brother of Seezoram, 576; confesses murder of chief judge, 577.

Sebus, waters of, 366, 368, 375.

Secret, combinations, devil stirreth up children to, 106; founded by devil, 147; things shall be revealed, 160; works, 440; combinations, judgments of God upon, 441; plans to be kept from people, 441; plans of wickedness, seek to destroy Coriantumr, 751.

Seed, of Nephi and brethren, 30, 44; to become dark and loathsome people, 33; of Nephi to write many plain and precious things, 37; of Joseph not to be destroyed, 87; of Laman not to perish, 91; of Lemuel not to be destroyed, 91; of Sam blessed, 91; of Lamanites to be cursed, 97; of Nephi to be remembered, 156; remnant of, shall know, 159; of Nephi to be restored to knowledge of Jesus Christ, 159; of Lehi shall become white and delightsome people, 159; commandment concerning raising up of, 172; of Christ, 252; of Lamanites distinguished, 308; of Jared and his brother to be a great nation, 716.

Seeds, gathered, 19; taken into wilderness, 48; taken into ship, 60; sown in land of promise, 63; reaped in abundance, 95; people of Zeniff plant all kinds of, 235.

Seer, choice, raised up of the fruit of the loins of Joseph, 87; Ammon speaks of, 233; possessor of stones called, 291.

Seezoram, chief judge, who was slain, 575.

INDEX. 817

Senine of gold, 339.

Senum of silver, 339.

Seon of gold, 339.

Seth, Ahah son of, 714; son of Shiblon, 714; dwells in captivity, 744.

Shared, gives battle to Coriantumr, 752; beaten by sons of Coriantumr, 752; fights with Coriantumr, flees to plains of Heshlon, driven back, beaten and slain, wounds Coriantumr, 753; brother of, fights Coriantumr and is driven to Akish, 753; brother of, goes to Moron on throne of Coriantumr, 753.

Shazer, Lehi pitches tents at, 49.

Sheep, other sheep not of this fold, 644, 645; are known and numbered, 653.

Shelum, stones molten out of, 720.

Shemlon, spies sent around about, 237; tower of Noah overlooks, 240; daughter of, Lamanites gather at, 264; Amulon appointed teacher over his people in, 276; people converted in land of, 390.

Shem, leader of ten thousand Nephites, 702.

Shem, Noah flees to city of, and fortifies, 691.

Shemnon, one of twelve, 654.

Shepherd, to manifest himself unto Jews and Gentiles over all the earth, 38.

Sherem, comes among Nephites, preaches there shall be no Christ, 189; comes to Jacob, teaches law of Moses, smitten of God, 191; confesses the truth, dies, 192.

Sherrizah, Lamanites take prisoners from tower of, 772; people carried away from, 772.

Shez, son of Heth, 714; builds up a broken people, a righteous kingdom, 739; Shez, son of, rebels against, 739; begets Riplakish and dies, 740.

Shez, son of Shez, smitten by robbers, 739.

Shiblom, leader of ten thousand Nephites, 702.

Shiblom, son of Com, 714, 743; brother rebels against, 743; brother of puts prophets to death, 743; reigns, 743; famine and pestilence in days of, 744; slain, 744.

Shiblon of silver, 339.

Shiblon, son of Alma, 417; commandment of Alma to son, 443; faithful among Zoramites, 443; declares word of God, 484; takes possession of sacred things, 540; death of, 541; confers sacred things upon Helaman, son of Helaman, 541.

Shiblum of silver, 339.

Shilom, Ammon and party at, 227, 228; city of, 229; land of, possessed by Zeniff, 235; walls of, repaired, 235; spies come to, 237; tower of Noah overlooks, 240; many buildings in, 240; tower on hill north of, 240; people of Limhi depart in wilderness of, 272; Amulon teacher over people in, 276; people converted in, 390.

Shim, Ammoron deposits sacred engravings in hill called, 687.

Shim, Omer passed by hill, 735.

Shimnilom, people converted in city of, 390.

Ship, constructed of, commanded, 53; completion of, 60; put forth in sea and driven before wind, 61; arrives at promised land, 63.

BOOK OF MORMON.

Shiz, brother of Lib, pursues Coriantumr, 754; three-day battle, 755; repulsed three times, wounds Coriantumr, 756; Coriantumr writes epistle to, 756; people of Coriantumr flee from, to waters of Ripliancum, 757; beaten by Coriantumr, 757; final battle with Coriantumr, 757; gets epistle from Coriantumr, 758; killed by Coriantumr, 759.

Shule, son of Kib, 715, 730; becomes mighty in judgment, 730; makes steel swords, 730; battles with Corihor, 730; restores kingdom to Kib, 730; made king by Kib, 730; righteous, 730; gives Corihor power, 730; given battle and taken captive by Noah, 730; replaced on throne by sons, 731; people of prosperous, 731; given kingdom by Nimrod, 731; prophets come among people of, 731; righteous, 731; Omer son of, reigns, 732.

Shum, of gold, 339.

Shurr, Coriantumr in valley of, 756.

Sidom, Alma and Amulek depart from Ammonihah to land of, 356; Zeezrom and those cast out from Ammonihah found at, 357; Alma establishes church at, 358.

Sidon river, Amlicites slain at, 304; Nephites defeat allies at, 305; dead cast into, 307; many baptized at, by Alma, 310; valley of Gideon east of river of, 322; Melek west of, 326; Lamanites march by head of, 458; army of Moroni secreted near, 459; Lamanites attacked at, 460; Lamanites surrounded, 462; Lamanite dead cast into, 465; war by waters of, 688.

Sign sought by Sherem, 191.

Silver, senum, amnor, ezrom, onti, shiblon, shiblum, 339.

Siron, Corianton goes to, 445.

Solomon, Nephi builds temple after manner of temple of, 96; and David, 168; and David had many wives and concubines, which is an abomination, 171.

Son of righteousness shall heal, 145.

Souls, condition of, between death and resurrection, 448; of wicked, state of, 448.

Southward land, 388.

Spirit of body, restored, 107; speaketh truth, 177.

Spirits of all men taken home to God, 448.

Spokesman for Moses, 89; for choice seer, 89.

Star, new, appears, 602.

Stone, brought to Mosiah, 202; prepared for Gazelem, 440.

Stones, two given to brother of Jared, 722; sealed, 723.

Stones, used by Mosiah in translating, 291; molten by brother of Jared, 720; description of, 720; touched by finger of Lord, 721, 726; put into vessels, give light, 726.

Storm, great, arises, 624.

Substance, people of church to impart of, 261, 301.

Sword of Laban, Nephi slays Laban with, 11; Nephi makes many swords after manner of, 95; Nephi wields, 167; Benjamin fights with, 206; Benjamin confers on Mosiah, 209.

Teachers, Jacob and Joseph to be priests and, 97; to labor with own hands, 260, 285; consecrated by Alma, 311, 358; consecrated by

INDEX. 819

Aaron, 389; appointed by Helaman and brother, 468; manner of ordaining, 761. (See under Priests.)

Teancum, city of, Nephites flee to, 695; near Desolation, 695; Lamanites come against, 696; drive Nephites from, 697.

Teancum, leader of army which heads people of Morianton, 489; slays Morianton, 489; meets Lamanites, 493; and defeats them, 494; kills Amalickiah, 494; ordered to secure narrow neck of land, 495; ordered to attack Mulek, 497; returns to city Bountiful, 497; holds council with Moroni and others, 497; Lamanites marched against, 497; and Lehi given command of part of army, 534; forces sent to, 535; encamps around land of Moroni, 537; slain, 538.

Temple, built by Nephi, 96; Jacob teaches in, 168, 169; people of Zarahemla gather to, 209; at land of Nephi, 240; in Bountiful, Christ appears at, 631.

Ten commandments quoted by Abinadi, 247.

Teomner secretes himself in the wilderness, 522.

Three disciples, not to taste of death, 676; Moroni and father administered to by, 705.

Timber, land desolate of, 549; shipped from land southward to land northward, 549.

Time measured only to men, 448.

Timothy, brother of Nephi, one of twelve, 654.

Tithes paid by Abraham, 350.

Tower, Noah builds, 240; Jared came from, 715.

Treasure hidden up, 689.

Tree, Lehi's vision of, 20; Nephi's vision of, 27; is love of God, 28, 29; of life, 46, 47, 452.

Tribes, Nephites divided into, 620; not to fight among themselves, 622; Christ to go to lost, 648; twelve t. of Israel to be judged, 694.

Tubaloth, son of Ammoron, king of Lamanites, 544.

Twelve, follow Redeemer, 29; apostles of the Lamb fought against, 30; all nations fight against t. apostles, 30; ordained of God, 31; apostles to judge tribes of Israel, 31; twelve ministers to be judged by, 31; book goes forth from t. apostles, 35; one of t. apostles seen by Nephi, 41; chosen, 635; given power to baptize, 635; instructions to, 640, 644, 650, 652, 658; given power to give Holy Ghost, 653; names of, 654; teach multitude, 654; baptized by Nephi, 655; Holy Ghost falls upon, 655; angels minister unto, 655; pray, 655; told to write scriptures, 667; Christ shows himself often to, 671; commanded to judge, 675; Christ speaks to, 675; desires of, 676; promises to, 676; three of t. not to taste of death, 676, 678; Christ touches all save three, 677; three (?) caught up into heaven, 677; preach and baptize, 677; cast into and delivered from prisons, 677; cast into furnaces and dens of beasts, 678; the three as angels of God, 678; three caught up into heaven and changed, 679; all die except three, and others ordained in their stead, 683; cast into fire, 685; to judge people in this land, 694; in Jerusalem to judge twelve in this land, 695; words of Christ to, 760; power given to give Holy Ghost, 760.

Vineyards, Noah plants, 241.

Virgin, Nephi sees in vision, 28; mother of Son of God, 28; bears child in arms, 28.
Vision, of Lehi, 2, 3; of Nephi, 26.
Voice of the people, 271; Aaron chosen king by, 292; judges to be judged by, 295; supreme, 303; against Amlici, 303; to enact laws by, 312, 337; obtain concerning Anti-Nephi-Lehies, 404; contention concerning law settled by, 490; authorized Moroni to go against king men, 492; Pacumeni unites with, 543; condemns Paanchi to death, 543; laws and government established by, 555; laws given by, 620.
Voice, heard by all people, 626, 629; people hear v. as out of heaven, 631.
War, multitudes gather to, 30, 32; among all nations, 41; and contentions with Lamanites, 98; and rumors at Jerusalem, 140; and contentions to be, 144; written upon larger plates, 174; Lamanites delight in, 192; caused by hatred of Lamanites, 193; between Nephites and Lamanites, 196, 198, 199; equipment of Nephites for, 198; among people of Zarahemla, 201; in days of Benjamin, 202; in land of Nephi, 235, 236; between Nephites and Amlicites, 304; and contentions, 309; cry of w. in the land, 359; between Nephites and Lamanites, 360; weapons of w. laid down, 390; weapons of w. buried, 393; of Lamanites against Anti-Nephi-Lehies, 394; Lamanites throw down weapons of, 394; weapons of w. buried, 396; account of, 405, 406; Lamanites and Zoramites prepare for, 433. (See under Lamanites, Nephites, and Jaredites.)
Waters, divide Gentiles from seed of Nephi, 34; large bodies of, 488; land of many rivers, 548.
Whoredoms an abomination, 172.
Wicked to perish, 144, 154, 159.
Wife, more than one forbidden, 172, 173.
Wilderness, Nephi and brothers hide in cavity of rock in, 9; Lamanites and Amlicites driven into, 306; of Hermounts, 307.
Witnesses, of book, three, 150; testimony of two nations, 157; testimony of three w. concerning these things, 726.
Wives, hearts of, broken, 172; Lamanites love their, 173; Noah had many w. and concubines, many prohibited, 172, 173; and concubines of King Noah, 239.
Women, God delights in chastity of, 172.
Wood, Nephi teaches to work in, 96.
Words of them that have slumbered, 149.
Workmanship of Nephites, 198.
World, redemption of, 4.
Years, after leaving Jerusalem, thirty, 97; forty, 98; fifty-five, 166; one hundred seventy-nine, 196; two hundred, 197; two hundred thirty-eight, 199; two hundred seventy-six, 199; two hundred eighty-two, 200; three hundred twenty, 200; four hundred seventy-six, 226; five hundred nine years to end of reign of kings, 298.
    five hundred nine years to end of reign of kings, 298; six hundred, 600; pages 600, 603, 604; six hundred and nine, 604.
Years of reign of judges, pages 301, 303, 309, 310, 311, 312, 326, 335,

INDEX. 821

355, 358, 359, 360, 362, 406, 409, 433, 456, 465, 466, 468, 473, 478, 481, 484, 485, 486, 487, 489, 490, 491, 494, 496, 497, 503, 509, 525, 535, 538, 540, 541, 542, 544, 546, 548, 550, 551, 552, 553, 554, 561, 562, 563, 565, 566, 579, 580, 581, 582, 583, 584, 586, 598, 599, 600; Years, after sign, nine, 604; pages 605, 606, 609, 610, 612, 615, 617, 618, 621, 622, 623, 624, 681, 682, 683, 684, 685, 686, 687, 689, 690, 691, 692, 693, 695, 696, 697, 698, 701, 705, 774.

Years Jaredite history, pages 718, 737, 740, 743.

Zarahemla, peace in land of, 207; people of, come to temple, 210; Benjamin addresses people of, 210; Mosiah declared king over people of, 214; land of, 227; Ammon descendant of, 227; people of Limhi search for land, 232, 270; people of Limhi join people of, 272; Alma and people arrive in land of, 279; land and people of, 201; rejoices concerning plates of brass, 201; people of, come from Jerusalem, 201; language of people of, corrupted, 201; gives genealogy of his fathers, 202; people of, unite with Mosiah, 202; Mosiah made king over land of, 202; people discover Coriantumr, 202; descendant of Mulock, 279; people of, more numerous than Nephites, people of numbered with Nephites, 280; seven churches in, 281; people of, taught by sons of Mosiah, 289; reign of the judges commences in, 297; River Sidon runs by, 304; city of, 305; Alma delivers word of Lord in land and city of, 313; church established in city of, 321; Alma returns to, 326; Alma and Amulek arrive at, 358; sons of Mosiah leave, 363; divided from land of Nephi, 387; land of Desolation discovered by people of, 387; Lamanites go into land of, 395; sons of Mosiah return to, 404; Anti-christ preaches in, 409; Korihor brought to Alma at, 412; Antionum, east of land of, 416; Alma and Ammon and brethren return to land of, 433; Alma departs from, and is heard from no more, 467; prisoners from Amalickiah taken to land of, 472; servants of king Lamanites flee to, 476; Moroni causes people of to possess east wilderness by seashore, 485; prisoners of Lamanites sent to, 515; Helaman sends message to, 520; people of appoint king at, 532; Helaman and Moroni return to, 539; Coriantumr goes against Nephites at, 544; Coriantumr takes city of, 545; Nephites flee from, 545; Moronihah retakes, 546; many depart from, into land northward, 548; Lamanites obtain possession of land of, 553; Lamanites exhort Nephites at, 561; Nephi returns to, 566; Nephites gather in for safety, 609; city of, takes fire, 624, 626; rebuilt, 682; Mormon carried to land of, 688; war in borders of, near waters of Sidon, 688; a land southward called by Nephites, 738.

Zedekiah, one of the twelve, 654.

Zedekiah, reign of, 2; king of Judah, 15.

Zeezrom, accuses Alma and Amulek, 338; questions Amulek, 340; confounded by words of Amulek, 343; pleads for Alma and Amulek, 353; cast out by people, 353; sick with fever at Sidon, 357; healed by faith through administration of Alma, 357; baptized by Alma and begins to preach, 357; goes with Alma to Zoramites, 417.

Zeezrom, city of, taken by Lamanites, 510.

Zemnariah, leader of Gadiantons, 612; attempts to withdraw from siege, surrounded by Nephites, hanged, 613.

Zenephi, army of, 773.

Zeniff, who came from Zarahemla, 227; Laman enters into treaty with, 229; taught in language of Nephites, 234; account of people of, 234; posesses land of Lehi-Nephi and Shilom, 235; people of, till the ground, 235; people of, in war with Lamanites, 236; goes up to battle against Lamanites, 237; people of, slay Lamanites, 239; confers kingdom on son Noah, 239; records of, read by Mosiah, 279.

Zenock, words of, 65, 427, 428; prophecies of, 630.

Zenos, words of, 65, 66, 177, 426, 428; prophecies of, 66, 630; prophecies of, to come to pass, 188.

Zerahemnah, leader of Lamanites, appoints Amalekites and Zoramites chief captains, 456; army of, not prepared as Nephites, 458; inspires army, 461; addressed by and surrenders to Moroni, 463; addressed Moroni, receives weapons from Moroni, 463; attacks Moroni, smitten by soldier, renews battle, 464.

Zeram, sent by Alma to spy on Amlicites, 305.

Zerin, brother of Jared commands to remove, 748.

Zion, seek to bring forth, 37; they that fight against, 100; welfare not sought by priestcraft, 147; laborer in, shall labor for, 148; nations that fight against her shall be as a dream, 148; woe unto him that is at ease in, 155; to be established, 662.

Zoram, captain of Nephites, 359; Lehi and Aha, sons of, 359; march over river Sidon, 360; drive Lamanites, 360; rescues prisoners, 360.

Zoram, leader of Zoramites, 416; Alma and brethren separate in land of, 420.

Zoram, servant of Laban, 12; accompanies Nephi, 13; takes daughter of Ishmael to wife, 48; Lehi speaks to, 81; flees with Nephi into wilderness, 95.

Zoramites, led by Zoram, 416; separation from Nephites, 416; word of God preached to, 417; prayer of, 418; will not hearken to Alma and Amulek, 432; cast out those who believe Alma and Amulek, 432; mix with Lamanites, 433, 456; those converted driven from land, 433; Shiblon faithful among, 443; Antionum, land of, 456; appointed chief captains of Lamanites, 456, 478; a people called, 685.

Zoramite, Jacob a, 497.

www.ingramcontent.com/pod-product-compliance
Lightning Source LLC
Chambersburg PA
CBHW052004070526
44584CB00016B/1620

THIS BOOK BELONGS TO

_____

CONGRATS!

MR. & MRS.